OXFORD WORLD'S CLASSICS

GREEK LIVES

PLUTARCH was born about AD 45, and lived most of his life in the small town of Chaeronea in central Greece, dying some time after 120. In the first decades of the second century AD, when he did much of his writing, the Roman Empire was in its most prosperous and peaceful period. Plutarch wrote a large number of dialogues, treatises, and essays covering diverse subjects, such as the oracle at Delphi, vegetarianism, and the nature of love, which are loosely classified as his *Moralia* or *Moral Essays*. Alongside these essays, Plutarch created a collection of 46 biographies of ancient Greek and Roman statesmen, arranged in pairs ('parallel'), a Roman matching a Greek. These *Parallel Lives* were written when he was at the height of his powers, and are his major and enduring achievement. Drawing upon earlier histories, anecdotes, inscriptions, and his own researches and broad acquaintance, he shaped masterful portraits of the most famous figures of the classical world. The value of the *Lives* as a historical source, questioned in the nineteenth century, has been reaffirmed by recent scholarship.

ROBIN WATERFIELD was born in 1952. After graduating from Manchester University, he went on to research ancient Greek philosophy at King's College, Cambridge. He has been a university lecturer (at Newcastle upon Tyne and St Andrews), and an editor and publisher. Currently, however, he is a self-employed consultant editor and writer, whose books range from philosophy to children's fiction. He has previously translated, for Oxford World's Classics, Plato's *Republic*, *Symposium*, and *Gorgias*, Aristotle's *Physics*, and Herodotus' *Histories*.

PHILIP A. STADTER, Falk Professor in the Humanities at the University of North Carolina at Chapel Hill, is the author of *A Commentary on Plutarch's Pericles* (Chapel Hill, 1989) and editor of *Plutarch and the Historical Tradition* (London, 1992). He has written *The Public Library of Renaissance Florence: Niccolò Niccoli, Cosimo de' Medici and the Library of San Marco* (Padua, 1972, with B. L. Ullman) and *Arrian of Nicomedia* (Chapel Hill, 1980), as well as numerous articles and reviews on Plutarch and other ancient historians, including Herodotus, Thucydides, Xenophon, and Arrian.

OXFORD WORLD'S CLASSICS

*For over 100 years Oxford World's Classics have brought
readers closer to the world's great literature. Now with over 700
titles—from the 4,000-year-old myths of Mesopotamia to the
twentieth century's greatest novels—the series makes available
lesser-known as well as celebrated writing.*

*The pocket-sized hardbacks of the early years contained
introductions by Virginia Woolf, T. S. Eliot, Graham Greene,
and other literary figures which enriched the experience of reading.
Today the series is recognized for its fine scholarship and
reliability in texts that span world literature, drama and poetry,
religion, philosophy and politics. Each edition includes perceptive
commentary and essential background information to meet the
changing needs of readers.*

OXFORD WORLD'S CLASSICS

PLUTARCH

Greek Lives
A selection of nine Greek Lives

Translated by
ROBIN WATERFIELD

With Introductions and Notes by
PHILIP A. STADTER

OXFORD
UNIVERSITY PRESS

OXFORD

UNIVERSITY PRESS

Great Clarendon Street, Oxford OX2 6DP

Oxford University Press is a department of the University of Oxford.
It furthers the University's objective of excellence in research, scholarship,
and education by publishing worldwide in

Oxford New York

Athens Auckland Bangkok Bogotá Buenos Aires Calcutta
Cape Town Chennai Dar es Salaam Delhi Florence Hong Kong Istanbul
Karachi Kuala Lumpur Madrid Melbourne Mexico City Mumbai
Nairobi Paris São Paulo Singapore Taipei Tokyo Toronto Warsaw

with associated companies in Berlin Ibadan

Oxford is a registered trade mark of Oxford University Press
in the UK and in certain other countries

Published in the United States
by Oxford University Press Inc., New York

British Library Cataloguing in Publication Data

Data available

Library of Congress Cataloging in Publication Data

Plutarch.
[Lives. English. Selections]
Greek lives / Plutarch; translated by Robin Waterfield; with
introduction and notes by Philip Stadter.
Oxford world's classics (Oxford University Press)
Includes bibliographical references and indexes.
1. Greece—Biography.   I. Waterfield, Robin, 1952–
II. Stadter, Philip A.   III. Title.   IV. Series.
DE7.P7213   1988   920.0495—dc21   98–17490

ISBN 978-0-19-954005-1

4

Typeset by Graphicraft Limited, Hong Kong
Printed in Great Britain by
Clays Ltd, St Ives plc

To the people and village of Theologos

GENERAL INTRODUCTION

Of all the ancient writers, Plutarch is in many ways the most accessible. Readers as diverse as Beethoven, Rousseau, and Harry Truman
have admired the vividness of his narrative and the immediacy of his
anecdotes in the *Parallel Lives*. When he wrote in the first decades
of the second century AD, the Roman empire was in its most prosperous and peaceful period. While the emperor Trajan drove back the
barbarian tribes of eastern Europe and the Parthians in Asia, expand-
ing the empire to its greatest extent, Plutarch and his friends in Athens,
Corinth, and his home town of Chaeronea met, dined, discussed philosophy, and considered the lessons of history. Yet the edge of chaos
was not far off. Plutarch was about 23 in 68, when insurrection and
civil war ended the reign of Nero: three emperors whirled on and off
stage in one year before Vespasian established himself upon the throne.
Plutarch later toured the battlefield of Bedriacum in northern Italy
with a Roman friend who had fought there, and was told of piles of
corpses higher than the tops of the eagle standards: in civil wars no
prisoners are taken (*Otho* 14). Some twenty years later, the emperor
Domitian became afraid that philosophers teaching in Rome might
encourage tyrannicides, and expelled them all from the city. Plutarch
may well have been among their number. Domitian raged against
senators, authors, and others who might oppose him, until he was
assassinated in 96. The short reign of Nerva which followed prepared
for the twenty-year rule of Trajan (98–118).

In this time of recently acquired and still insecure serenity Plutarch lived in Chaeronea and Athens (of which he was also a citizen),
teaching philosophy to a small group of young men and writing an
enormous volume of work, of which we possess perhaps half. His
family wealth and education set him among the élite of Greece, and
he regularly entertained powerful and cultured friends, both Greeks
and Romans. Since his youth he had served on commissions to meet
with the Roman governor, and he was on good terms with Romans
of the highest rank. His culture and heritage was fully and proudly
Greek, but he like other members of his class accepted the Roman
imperial system and worked within it. The nearby sanctuary of Apollo
at Delphi, of which he was priest for many years, gave him another

occasion to meet important visitors, as well as to investigate both historical and theological questions tied to this venerable site. His cosmopolitan interests did not stop him from serving even in small ways at Chaeronea: he mentions supervising stones and mortar being transported. Living in a small town, which lacked the books and learned discussion which could be found in a large city, he chose 'to cling to his town, lest it become smaller' (*Dem.* 2).

The Parallel Lives: *Scope and Purpose*

His major work, a series of parallel biographies which gradually grew to 48, of which we possess 46,[1] probably was begun early in the reign of Trajan, and continued until Plutarch's death *c*.120–5.[2] Prior to the biographies, and continuing alongside them, Plutarch wrote a large number of short essays and some larger collections, which we now subsume under the title of *Moralia*, or *Moral Essays*. The title is indeed appropriate to some, such as *Control of Anger*, *Quiet of Mind*, *Brotherly Love*, and *Talkativeness*, which present philosophical and ethical truths in a charming and thoughtful format.[3] Others explore religious and theological topics dear to the author: several 'Pythian' dialogues on the sanctuary at Delphi and its oracles, and others on *Superstition*, *Isis and Osiris*, the *Face in the Moon*, and *Socrates' Sign*. A third category encompasses contemporary politics and the role of the philosopher in them. Most interesting of these is the *Advice on Public Life*, addressed to a young aristocrat of Sardis who wished to play a major role in the life of his city, and perhaps beyond. The nine books of *Table Talk* show the philosopher chatting with his friends at dinner, on topics ranging from the effect of old age on sight to the proper time for sex, with special attention to the best customs for a dinner party. Such a list is only a sampling of the riches to be found

---

[1] The first two Lives, *Scipio* and *Epaminondas*, have been lost. Four other extant Lives do not belong to the *Parallel Lives*: *Galba* and *Otho*, part of a series of Lives of the emperors, and *Aratus* and *Artaxerxes*, were written independently, as were other lost Lives.

[2] Cf. C. P. Jones, 'Towards a Chronology of Plutarch's Works', *Journal of Roman Studies*, 56 (1966), 61–74, repr. in B. Scardigli, *Essays on Plutarch's Lives* (Oxford: Clarendon Press, 1995), 95–123.

[3] I use the English titles given by D. A. Russell in his listing of the *Moralia* in *Plutarch* (London: Duckworth, 1973), 164–72 and *Plutarch: Selected Essays and Dialogues* (Oxford: Oxford University Press, 1973), pp. xxiii–xxix. The titles vary slightly among translators. Russell's *Plutarch* provides an excellent general introduction to Plutarch.

in this marvellously varied collection, a delight and inspiration for
Montaigne and Emerson.[4]

The *Parallel Lives* represent a new initiative, which nevertheless
grows naturally out of the earlier essays. A major feature of the essays
had been Plutarch's effort to encourage his readers to allow the effect
of philosophy to penetrate their daily lives and their way of thinking about the world, whether in shaping their own character and
behaviour, or in considering the workings of the gods and the after-
life. Over time, however, he seems to have become dissatisfied with
this format, and decided to turn to biography. In the series of Lives
of the Roman emperors from Augustus to Vitellius, written perhaps
shortly after Domitian's death, of which only *Galba* and *Otho* survive, he seems to have tested his skill at writing historical narrative
from a philosophical perspective.[5] With the *Parallel Lives* he undertakes a grand project to explore, in the lives of famous statesmen and
commanders, all major historical figures, the interplay of character and
political action. In the proem to his Life of Nicias, whose defeat in
Sicily had been the focus of some of the most memorable pages of
Thucydides' history, Plutarch writes,

I have touched briefly on the essentials [from Thucydides and Philistus,
another historian]—enough to avoid gaining a reputation for carelessness
and indolence—while trying to collect the facts which may have been
mentioned here and there by other writers or which can be found recorded
on ancient votive offerings or in decrees, but are unnoticed by most people.
My purpose was not to gather meaningless historical data, but to record data
which promote the understanding of character and personality. (*Nic.* 1)

In *Alexander*, in a frequently quoted passage, he asserts,

I am not writing history but biography, and the most outstanding exploits
do not always have the property of revealing the goodness or badness of
the agent; often in fact, a casual action, the odd phrase, or a jest reveals
character better than battles involving the loss of thousands upon thousands of lives, huge troop movements, and whole cities besieged. . . . I must
be allowed to devote more time to those aspects which indicate a person's
mind and to use these to portray the life of each of my subjects. (*Alex.* 1)

Exactly this focus on character sets the *Lives* apart from military and
political histories and gives them their interest, charm, and usefulness.

    [4] See the essays translated in the World's Classics by Russell, *Plutarch: Selected Essays
and Dialogues* and by Robin Waterfield, *Plutarch: Essays* (Harmondsworth: Penguin, 1992).
    [5] Cf. A. Georgiadou, 'The Lives of the Caesars and Plutarch's Other Lives', *Illinois
Classical Studies*, 13 (1988), 349–56.

Nevertheless, a tension exists between Plutarch's professed aim—to treat character—and the subjects he chose for his biographies, all of whom are statesmen, and most are generals who commanded large armies and won or lost great battles. Earlier authors interested in ethics had written the lives of philosophers or lawgivers. By turning to lives of statesmen, Plutarch changes the nature of the inquiry, which becomes not what is the best way to live, but how have real men of influence, acting in real situations, brought their lives to a successful conclusion, or failed to do so. Once it was believed that Plutarch regularly depended on earlier biographies for his *Lives*: now it has been established that his major sources for most if not all of the *Lives* were histories. Plutarch's project thus involved a massive rethinking of this historical material in terms of his philosophical understanding of character and moral behaviour.

The *Parallel Lives* set a Greek and a Roman biography side by side, each pair making a single unit. The modern practice of dividing the *Lives* into two series, one Greek and one Roman—followed also in the present collection—is based on our historical interests, a natural result of our distance from the ancient world. Since the *Lives* are such an important source for our knowledge of leaders and of events, it is useful, clearer, and more accessible to treat the course of Greek and Roman history separately. Plutarch, who presumed that his readers would be familiar with their own history and would have access to full histories of both countries, found several advantages in a parallel presentation. First of all, the comparison between Greek and Roman statesmen, at a time when Greece itself was under Roman rule, asserted the dignity and long tradition of Greece, and suggested the idea of a close collaboration in government based on that tradition. Second, Plutarch knew from his rhetorical training that comparison was a powerful means of analysis and instruction. Comparison of the lives of two men would reveal the underlying qualities of each, and highlight their similarities and differences.[6] One of the most important results of the scholarship of the last twenty-five years has been the

---

[6] Cf. *Virtues in Women* 243b–d: 'There is no way of understanding the similarities and differences between virtue in women and virtue in men, other than by comparing life with life, action with action, as works of a great craft . . . Virtues do, of course, acquire differences—peculiar colours, as it were—because of the nature of the persons, and are assimilated to their underlying habits, physical temperaments, diet, and way of life. Achilles was brave in a different way from Ajax. Odysseus' wisdom was not like Nestor's. Cato and Agesilaus were not just in the same way.' (Trans. Russell, *Plutarch: Selected Essays and Dialogues*, 307.)

recognition that Plutarch thought of each pair as a single work, developing a single overall impression, and linking the two lives not only in external features or accidents, but in many small ways regarding both events and traits of character. Thus, while the modern reader will usually approach each life individually, it is useful to keep the other member of the pair constantly in mind, as an aid to recognizing the features which Plutarch finds significant in the life. For this reason, in the introductions to the individual Lives in this book, special attention is given to the relation of each to its pair.

The individual books of the *Parallel Lives* (i.e. each pair of biographies) follow a standard pattern. Most often there is a proem, which serves as introduction to the pair. This may discuss the reasons for coupling these two men, or Plutarch's sentiments behind writing these biographies, or other features of interest. Where a clearly defined proem is lacking, the function of the proem is served by the opening chapters of the first life (e.g. in *Lycurgus* or *Solon*, where Plutarch's discussion of problems of chronology and sources leads into the pair).[7] The two biographies follow, first the Greek, then the Roman, with three exceptions.[8] Finally, most of the pairs add on a *synkrisis* or 'Comparison' which reviews certain major elements of the two lives in an overtly comparative form, often drawing conclusions or expressing opinions different from the narratives themselves.[9] Since the two lives form one book, there is often a development of thought and analysis not only within each life, but from one life to another, so that the first life regularly serves as a kind of introduction to the second.[10] As a result, the Greek lives sometimes present in a simpler fashion character traits which appear more complex or extreme in the Roman lives, many of which are significantly longer than their Greek counterparts. In *Agesilaus*, for example, we see a leader both friendly and able to relate well with others, yet aggressive in pursuing his own

[7] See in general P. A. Stadter, 'The Proems of Plutarch's Lives', *Illinois Classical Studies*, 13 (1988), 275–95; for a different approach, T. G. Rosenmeyer, 'Beginnings in Plutarch's Lives', *Yale Classical Studies*, 29 (1992), 205–30.

[8] *Coriolanus–Alcibiades, Aemilius Paulus–Timoleon, Sertorius–Eumenes*. Some editions reverse these to make the Romans follow.

[9] There are no comparisons for four pairs, *Themistocles–Camillus, Pyrrhus–Marius, Phocion–Cato Minor*, and *Alexander–Caesar*.

[10] Cf. C. Pelling, 'Syncrisis in Plutarch's Lives', in F. Brenk and I. Gallo (eds.), *Miscellanea Plutarchea* (*Quaderni del giornale filologico ferrarese* 8; Ferrara, 1986), 83–96. This feature seems to explain why in certain pairs Plutarch has the Roman Life precede the Greek.

honour and military success, to the extent that he creates enemies for Sparta and ultimately presides over its collapse as a major power. The corresponding life, *Pompey*, is almost twice as long, and shows a man of similar characteristics, whose pursuit of his honour and susceptibility to his friends leads to civil war at Rome, and finally to his own death and the end of the Roman republic.

Plutarch expected both his readers and himself to benefit from the *Parallel Lives*. In the proem of *Aemilius*, he writes:

Although I originally took up the writing of Lives for others, I find that the task has grown on me and I continue with it for my own sake too, in the sense that I treat the narrative as a kind of mirror and try to find a way to arrange my life and assimilate it to the virtues of my subjects. The experience is like nothing so much as spending time in their company and living with them: I receive and welcome each of them in turn as my guest, so to speak, observe 'his stature and his qualities', and choose from his achievements those which it is particularly important and valuable for me to know. 'And oh, what greater delight could one find than this?' And could one find a more effective means of moral improvement either?   (*Aem.* 1. 1–3)

It is worth exploring more exactly how Plutarch expected this 'moral improvement' to occur. Plutarch's readership most likely was that same circle of Greek and Roman friends to whom he dedicated his other works and whom we meet in the conversations of *Table Talk* and other dialogues. Comments in Plutarch's works and inscriptional and literary evidence allow us to identify many of these people as members of the ruling class in Greece and in the Roman empire.[11] The Greeks were among the wealthiest in the province, and held major offices in Athens, Sparta, and elsewhere. Among the Romans, no less than nine had held the consulship, a mark of special honour even at this time. Q. Sosius Senecio, the close friend to whom he dedicated the *Parallel Lives*, *Table Talk*, and *Progress in Virtue*, was a lead consul (*consul ordinarius*) in 99, the first full year of Trajan's reign, and again in 107, and held a high command during Trajan's wars in Dacia (modern Romania), for which he was awarded special honours and a public statue by Trajan. He clearly was a close associate of the emperor. Other friends held the important posts of proconsul in Asia or Africa. One friend, Antiochus Philopappus, grandson of the last king of

---

[11] See B. Puech, 'Prosopographie des amis de Plutarque', *ANRW* II.33.6 (1992), 4831–93 and C. P. Jones, *Plutarch and Rome* (Oxford: Clarendon Press, 1971), 39–64.

Commagene, was consul in 109 (the first Athenian to become consul) as well as a fellow citizen of Athens: his grandiose monument stands opposite the Acropolis on the hill of the Muses. Plutarch's friends and readers, then, were not apolitical provincials, dabbling in philosophy or history to while away their time, but men with responsibilities and obligations, active in imperial and provincial politics, some of them in close contact with the emperor.

Plutarch's biography project needs to be seen in the context of this audience. The conversations which Plutarch reports show that these men were trained in basic philosophy and history. The *Moral Essays* of Plutarch were written to give them more specific guidance on particular points, often in response to a request of a friend. But the *Parallel Lives* reveal that Plutarch found these works unsatisfactory in responding to the ethical needs of men active in public life, and sought a different solution. A century and a half before, Cicero had complained that philosophers did not provide clear guidelines on making choices in business or political contexts. When the stakes were high, many respectable men chose something advantageous to themselves over a higher good. He cites as examples the actions of Pompey and Caesar, each fighting for his own honour rather than the good of Rome.[12] Plutarch's *Parallel Lives* are an attempt to fill that gap, and to provide the material which will allow men in power, statesmen and commanders themselves, to become aware of results of personal choices, and the moral decisions—and often ambiguities—inherent in political action.

In aiming at this audience of politically involved readers, Plutarch follows his own advice in such works as *Philosophers and Princes* and *Old Men in Politics*, that a philosopher should not hold back from attempting to influence public affairs. Throughout the *Parallel Lives*, Plutarch is fascinated by the figure of the wise adviser in politics, of which the model might be Solon, advising successively the Athenian people, Croesus and other foreign kings, and the tyrant Pisistratus. Legislators, such as Lycurgus and Numa, fit this role, and the very limited number of philosopher-statesmen who are protagonists of Lives: Dion, Phocion, Cato the Younger, Brutus. More often the adviser is an important influence on the protagonist: Anaxagoras for Pericles, Socrates for Alcibiades, Aristotle for Alexander. Romans tend

[12] See Cicero, *On Duties*, book 3, esp. 3. 73–88.

to be influenced by Greek culture and philosophy in general, not a particular adviser, as in the case of Aemilius Paulus, Cicero, or Caesar. Plutarch undoubtedly saw himself in the role of adviser to his political friends and readers, helping them take a philosophical view of their situations and actions.[13]

In perusing one of Plutarch's *Lives*, the reader encounters a major statesman, one well known in history and admired for his achievements, seen not through a single witty anecdote, or a short speech in a history book, but through the whole course of his life. In the beginning the reader is introduced to the subject's family, major personality traits, and intellectual influences, as far as they are known. Then he or she is led through the statesman's life, with a focus on major turning points and crises, until his death. Along the way Plutarch offers comments, interpretations, and especially anecdotes which can suggest the character (*ēthos*) which underlies the statesman's actions.

Plutarch, although generally a Platonist, took his basic philosophy of ethics from Aristotle. He believed that it was possible by constant practice to progress step by step in virtue. In *Control of Anger*, he presents one of his friends, Minucius Fundanus, explaining how he learned to control his temper. Fundanus describes himself as actively taking command of his temper, first by making himself sensitive to its effects, then by conscious, well-prepared effort to subject it more and more to his rational control. Little is said about rules or precepts: rather the emphasis is on sensitizing oneself to the nature of anger, its effects, and the circumstances which produce it, then working carefully to strengthen oneself in these areas. Of major importance is the observation in others of the fault you are trying to correct, noting especially the effects of the fault on their friends, wives, and families, and the subsequent realization that the same thing is happening to you. Such observation, Fundanus affirms, is like having someone hold up a mirror to you during your moments of rage.[14] Observation also allows us to understand the general nature of vice and virtue, and of the emotions and passions which lead to vice—knowledge learned only

---

[13] Cf. A. Wardman, *Plutarch's Lives* (London: Elek, 1974), 211–20; S. Swain, 'Hellenic Culture and the Roman Heroes of Plutarch', *Journal of Hellenic Studies*, 110 (1990), 126–45 (= Scardigli, *Essays on Plutarch's Lives*, 229–64); and C. Pelling, 'Plutarch: Roman Heroes and Greek Culture', in M. Griffith and J. Barnes (eds.), *Philosophia Togata: Essays on Philosophy and Roman Society* (Oxford, 1989), 199–232.

[14] *Control of Anger* 455e–456b.

abstractly in philosophy lessons. The same is true of good qualities as of bad, of virtue as of vice. We can learn by observing in others not only given qualities, but the effects that they have on the men involved, their families, and their states.

When in *Aemilius* Plutarch speaks of meeting the men whose biographies he writes, of inviting them into his house, and considering them at close range, he describes exactly this process of observation. Like Fundanus, he compares such inspection to holding up a mirror before oneself. A mirror enables us to see ourselves as others see us, and to approve or correct our appearance as needed. Plutarch wished his *Parallel Lives* to serve this function, not in some abstract forum, but for men who wished and were able, like his statesmen and commanders, to have some effect in the larger affairs of Greece and of the Roman empire. The statesmen of the *Lives*, then, are not simply models to be imitated, or paradigms of virtue—many in fact are unsavoury types, or at the best unsatisfactory models—but case studies in political behaviour, set out to be considered and evaluated by the reader. Although Plutarch often points the way to the interpretation of an action which he considers preferable, the reader is encouraged to work actively in evaluating the behaviour and choices of the heroes, forming his own judgement as to their value and effect. Plutarch invites his readers to observe, then fashion their own lives based on what they have learned.

Furthermore, as Plutarch notes elsewhere, observation of behaviour in one area can be applied in other contexts. In the last book of the *Iliad*, Achilles receives Priam in his tent, has pity on him, and determines to give back Hector's body to his father. But he wisely decides not to bring the mutilated and disfigured body into Priam's sight before carefully washing and preparing it, lest Priam become angry, and Achilles end up killing him. Plutarch approves of Achilles' foresight concerning his own emotions, and the use of reason to guard against his irrational passion. But Plutarch goes on to assert that this lesson can be generalized, and be applied in different contexts: in the same way, one who is given to drink should be wary of drunkenness, or one given to love be wary of love, as was Agesilaus with the kiss of the beautiful boy.[15]

---

[15] *On Reading the Poets* 31bc, referring to Homer, *Iliad* 24. 560–86. The story of Agesilaus and the kiss is found in *Ages.* 11.

Each individual Life, while presenting a vivid portrait of an ancient statesman in action, invites moral reflection. As has been noted, this process is enriched by the technique of presenting the Lives in pairs: the reader is induced to shift focus back and forth between the two, comparing, changing perspective, re-evaluating. The formal syncrisis repeats this process, again shifting perspective, refocusing the elements of comparison. Both techniques prepare readers to use the pair as a double mirror for their own lives. The *Lives* acts as a powerful imaginative tool, recreating with extraordinary vividness the characteristics of statesmen of the past, and bringing them alive in the readers' minds.

The understanding of the human self implied in Plutarch's biographies differs from that of many modern thinkers. Although he treats major historical figures, his general rule is not to glorify them as independent spirits, breaking away from their social world by an act of will to create an autonomous self. Nor does he see them as unique personalities, unparalleled in the particular conglomeration of environmental influences and personal drives at the basis of their personality, which create strong tensions pulling them in different directions. Greek thinkers thought of the human person first of all as a rational animal, able to act on the basis of reasoning which was generally available to other humans as well. This thinking, as developed by Plato, Aristotle, and the Stoics in different ways, argued that it was theoretically possible for a person, in active co-operation with other persons, to arrive at '(*a*) objective knowledge of what constitutes the best in human life and (*b*) a corresponding character and way of life'.[16] In addition, an individual who was acting like a human being (i.e. reasonably) would attempt to shape his life according to that knowledge. In this conception, the individual could and would want to form his own life according to objective criteria of behaviour, rather than follow spontaneous responses to the situation of the moment, or a set of moral principles established solely by oneself, and subject to change based on new experience. This is the basis for the moral thinking which pervades the *Lives*, and which modern readers sometimes find intrusive or gratuitous. Plutarch as a Platonist accepts that there are moral truths which, at least in theory, can be established by reason, to which any

---

[16] The formulation is that of C. Gill, *Personality in Greek Epic, Tragedy, and Philosophy: The Self in Dialogue* (Oxford: Clarendon Press, 1996), 12.

sensible person would wish to subscribe, and according to which he would shape his behaviour. From this standpoint Plutarch is able to evaluate the behaviour of his heroes, offer judgements and criticisms, and suggest alternative behaviour. Moreover, this is precisely the perspective from which Plutarch is able to use his heroes as mirrors for himself and his readers, presuming that they, like him, wish to shape their lives by reason in the most suitable way.

However, Plutarch's Platonism was strongly tinged with scepticism, the philosophical notion that many truths were in fact not knowable, so that one may have to hold back from a final decision in individual cases. This awareness of the difficulty of certitude allows Plutarch to be unusually flexible and even tolerant in his judgements, or to leave questions in abeyance. To take an example: Pericles' refusal to back down from a confrontation with Sparta precipitated the Peloponnesian War, a war between Greeks of which Plutarch could not approve. The decision could be a major black mark against Pericles, and Plutarch initially treats it that way. As his discussion proceeds, however, and he examines various reasons Pericles may have had, he ends up withholding judgement: 'So these are the reasons given by my sources to explain why he did not allow the people to yield to the Spartans; the truth is, however, uncertain.'[17] For this reason also the formal comparison often presents a different evaluation of an action from the narrative, or there are different evaluations in different Lives. While moralist in theory, Plutarch's sensitivity to human motives and circumstances creates a vivid picture of the dynamics of moral decision, and in the last resort transfers to the reader the final judgement on his hero's behaviour.

Another aspect of the ancient view of character was that a number of traits tend to cluster in one type of character: an early philosophical example is Plato's descriptions of the different kinds of lives associated with different regimes in *Republic* books 8 and 9. Whereas moderns tend to emphasize the complexity of character, looking for those unexpected traits or quirks which make each individual unique, Plutarch tends to search for unifying factors. This results in what have been called 'integrated' characters:

a man's qualities are brought into some sort of relation with one another, and every trait goes closely with the next. We are unsurprised if Antony

---

[17] *Per.* 32. The whole discussion is at 30–2.

is simple, passive, ingenuous, susceptible, soldierly, boisterous, yet also noble and often brilliant; or the younger Cato is high-principled and determined, rigid in his philosophy, scruffy (as philosophical beings often are), strange but bizarrely logical in the way he treats his women, and disablingly inflexible and insensitive in public life.[18]

In this kind of integrated character-portrayal, the different traits of character are seen as naturally cohering facets of a given combination of inborn qualities, education, and mind-set. Antony's or Cato's characters are unique, yet in a certain sense expected, because the different elements which might seem contradictory in fact complement each other so well. Thus the deceptive simplicity of Plutarchan character-drawing hides an exceptional sensitivity to the variety and complexity of human behaviour. The reader is not shocked by startling quirks or unexplained outbursts of genius, but gradually led to see, in the course of the biography, the complex and often surprising results of traits already visible in childhood or at the beginning of a political career.

Biographical Method

Plutarch's method is generally to set out at the beginning basic features of his subject's nature and the influences which affected it: thus we learn in the first chapters of the respective Lives of Agesilaus' training in the Spartan educational system and his ambitious competitiveness, and of Antony's tendency to let others set his agenda and susceptibility to women. Physical appearance, when it is reported, often provides a clue to character: Sulla's blotched face and intimidating eyes point to the harshness of the later tyrant. This preliminary sketch prepares for the statesman's political career, which usually proceeds in a series of stages, with one or two major peaks. The Life ends with the subject's death, though often Plutarch chooses to follow out some narrative thread—the fate of his children, or of his murderers, or his successors—to reach an effective closure.

This basic outline, which implies that the structure is straightforwardly chronological, is deceptive. Writing in an age when rhetoric

---

[18] C. Pelling, 'Aspects of Plutarch's Characterization', *Illinois Classical Studies*, 13 (1988), 256–74 at 262; cf. also his 'Childhood and Personality in Greek Biography', in Pelling (ed.), *Characterization and Individuality in Greek Literature* (Oxford: Clarendon Press, 1990), 213–44.

formed the basis of education, Plutarch carefully shapes his presentation for maximum effectiveness. Each Life is thought out in terms of the problems which it presents, the features which Plutarch wishes to highlight, and the material available. The resulting organization therefore combines chronological, thematic, and rhetorical principles. While maintaining for clarity a basic chronological scheme, Plutarch uses flashbacks and future references to call attention to continuing traits or explain particular incidents. Moreover, he regularly introduces anecdotal material from all periods of the life to exemplify traits which he treats in connection with a given event.

Anecdotes are frequently clustered at major points in the subject's life, e.g. in *Themistocles* 18, just after the victory at Salamis; in *Alexander* 21–3, after the victory at Issus. The first sixteen chapters of *Alcibiades* are almost continuous anecdotes, which gradually lead from Alcibiades' youth to his relations with his lovers and with Socrates to the beginnings of his political career.[19] The anecdotes may be taken from every sort of source, historical, philosophical, or rhetorical, and can be combined in different lengths and degree of elaboration. 'They need not be correctly placed in date in relation to their neighbours,'[20] so that extreme caution is needed in trying to fit them into a chronological sequence. While all anecdotes assist in portraying *ēthos*, Plutarch's method of employment can be extremely flexible. *Alexander* provides numerous examples. Alexander's taming of Bucephelas (*Alex.* 6) seems to be especially significant, raising the question of mastery and training of genius. The sequence which forms the account of naphtha in *Alex.* 35 falls immediately after the battle of Gaugamela and is often considered a digression, but in fact comments on *ēthos*, exploring Alexander's own dangerous fieriness. Sequences of anecdotes build up a larger picture: after Alexander wins the battle of Issus, three chapters of anecdotes show his idea of kingship and his self-restraint (*Alex.* 21–3). They can also create a sense of false continuity, when a series of anecdotes serves in place of historical narrative, as at *Alex.* 25–6 and 45–56. Finally, Plutarch can use a sequence of anecdotes as a technique to comment on and interpret his subject's behaviour, as he does in *Alex.* 45–56. In presenting the most scandalous actions of Alexander's career, anecdotes are able

---

[19] See D. A. Russell, 'Plutarch Alcibiades 1–16', *Proceedings of the Cambridge Philological Society* (1966), 37–47 (= Scardigli, *Essays on Plutarch's Lives*, 191–207).

[20] Russell in Scardigli (above n. 19), 206.

to suggest that Alexander was not completely guilty and that the Macedonians also had some responsibility in the events.[21]

The whole is united by a remarkably facile style: 'learned and allusive, imaginative and metaphorical, exuberant and abundant.'[22] Strongly influenced by classical models, he fashioned a literary language for his own day, a varied and rich instrument to express his thinking on everything from philosophy and medicine to vegetarianism and astronomy. His style tends to be generous rather than spare: he regularly doubles synonyms, and employs amplification, in the form of examples, general thoughts, and anecdotes, to enlarge on a topic. Frequent poetic quotations give authoritative support to an argument as well as a cultured flavour. When he wishes a higher style, the sentences can become quite long, built up carefully from subordinate clauses, creating luxuriant accumulation of words and ideas. Throughout, the range and aptness of examples and metaphors delights and instructs, while the vividness of the narrative charms the imagination.

Historical Value

The *Parallel Lives*, however, are most often read as historical sources for the periods which he treats. They are in fact extraordinarily valuable as sources, both because they give us Plutarch's insight into the men he treats and because they preserve a vast spectrum of evidence which otherwise would have been lost, collected in the course of Plutarch's omnivorous reading and his special research for the *Lives*. His historical contribution came under severe scrutiny from positivist historians in the nineteenth century, but in the latter half of the twentieth century, as we have learned more of his method and his purpose, a clearer picture has emerged of his value to the historian.

Although he famously protests that he is a biographer, not a historian (*Alex.* 1), historical narratives provide the base for his biographies. Political biography before Plutarch was not a common genre. The only example we possess is a Latin writer and contemporary of Cicero,

---

[21] Cf. P. A. Stadter, 'Anecdotes and the Thematic Structure of Plutarchean Biography', in J. A. Fernández Delgado and F. Pordomingo Pardo (eds.), *Estudios sobre Plutarco: Aspectos formales* (Madrid: Ediciones Clásicas, 1996), 291–303.

[22] Russell, *Plutarch*, 20. The whole chapter, 18–41, is an excellent study of his style, to which this paragraph is indebted.

Cornelius Nepos, and his biographies, though they treat many of the same Greek figures as Plutarch, have a much more limited scope.[23] There do not seem to have been biographies in any way similar to Plutarch's before he wrote the *Lives*.

Plutarch was one of the most educated men of antiquity. His reading from childhood on provided him a comfortable background in the history of Greece. Latin, however, he admits to learning late and imperfectly (*Dem.* 2). He cites many fewer Latin authors than Greek, and does not cite passages from Latin poets, though he frequently quotes from Greek poets. He knows and quotes all the major Greek historians—Herodotus, Thucydides, Xenophon, Polybius—and many historians and antiquarians now lost to us. But these historical narratives are supplemented with information from contemporary letters and poetry, inscriptions and public documents, philosophical authors, and his own autopsy and conversations with knowledgeable friends.[24]

A clearer idea of Plutarch's method of using these sources emerges when we compare his account against an extant source, as we can in many Lives, or when we compare two accounts of the same events in two Lives. Particularly instructive are the Lives of the late republic at Rome, six of which apparently were written at about the same time and used many of the same sources (*Crassus, Pompey, Caesar, Cato, Brutus, Antony*).[25] For these lives he used first-hand sources, probably Pollio for the Civil Wars and Dellius for the Parthian War of Antony, memoirs, Cicero's *Second Philippic*, Livy, Sallust, and other writers. In addition he used oral tradition, both Greek and Roman. We can identify two stages of composition, an initial reading of sources (undoubtedly less necessary for the Greek lives than for the Roman) and preparation of detailed notes, before the final draft or drafts.

[23] Cf. J. Geiger, *Cornelius Nepos and Ancient Political Biography* (*Historia* Einzelschriften 47; Stuttgart, 1985).

[24] Cf. e.g. B. X. de Wet, 'Plutarch's Use of the Poets', *Antiquité Classique*, 31 (1988), 13–25; F. Frost, 'Some documents in Plutarch's Lives', *Classica et mediaevalia*, 22 (1961), 182–94; P. Desideri, 'I documenti di Plutarco', *ANRW* II.33.6 (1992), 4536–67; J. Buckler, 'Plutarch and Autopsy', *ANRW* II.33.6 (1992), 4788–830.

[25] Cf. C. Pelling, 'Plutarch's Method of Work in the Roman Lives', *Journal of Hellenic Studies*, 99 (1979), 74–96 and 'Plutarch's Adaptation of his Source Material', *Journal of Hellenic Studies*, 100 (1980), 127–40 (= Scardigli, *Essays on Plutarch's Lives*, 265–318 (with postscript) and 125–54 respectively), to which the following paragraph is indebted. *Cicero* and *Lucullus* were written earlier.

In adapting the historical material, Plutarch took several steps to focus attention on his protagonist. Thus he may abridge his source by simplifying it, either conflating several similar incidents into one (e.g. meetings of the senate), by chronological compression (making two items seem to follow closely which in fact were separated by a period of time), or reorganizing events in non-chronological order, especially to bring out causal or logical connections. Occasionally he may even transfer an item from one character to another, whether consciously or not. More commonly, he may attribute to his protagonist an action which might be generally ascribed to a group (the senate, the city) in his source, personalizing an impersonal action. On the other hand, he will expand inadequate material, not by free invention but by a visualization of what must have been the case, what antecedents would naturally precede an action, or what context seems to be implied by a historical notice.[26]

His interpretations of his characters' motives are not fixed, but can vary depending on the biography in which they are given. Naturally, more complex motives are likely to appear when the actor is protagonist of a Life. Moreover, generally Plutarch tends to view his protagonist more favourably than other characters in a Life, and to adopt the protagonist's perspective on the events of which he takes part. This focalization via the protagonist of a Life, and therefore on multiple protagonists in several Lives dealing with the same events, is a significant aspect of Plutarch's metamorphosis of history into biography, and supported his philosophical purpose by permitting his readers to identify individually with each protagonist, moving, for instance, from Pompey to Cato to Caesar in different pairs of Lives. Again, different Lives will emphasize different aspects of the protagonist: some will concentrate on historical incident (e.g. *Caesar*), others will be more philosophical or personal, such as *Cato the Younger* or *Pompey*.

Of course, the effort to bring out parallel aspects of Lives which form a pair has a significant effect on choice of detail and overall presentation, and sometimes on the interpretation of particular incidents. Plutarch might have passed over as insignificant Pericles' offer to give his land to the city if it were not ravaged in the war, though it is

---

[26] Cf. C. Pelling, 'Truth and Fiction in Plutarch's Lives', in D. A. Russell (ed.), *Antonine Literature* (Oxford: Clarendon Press, 1990), 19–52.

recorded in Thucydides, if he had not known that Hannibal caused difficulties at Rome to Pericles' parallel figure, Fabius, by sparing Fabius' land.[27]

Viewed from a historical perspective, Plutarch's work has a number of limitations, many tied to his biographical purpose, others reflecting the views of his class and his society, others still his Platonism. Although more familiar than most men of his time with the society of classical Greece, he is not always able to abandon a somewhat idealized picture of the great age of Greece. His basic political scheme, seen again and again in both Greek and Roman lives, is set in terms of a conflict between élite and populace, where the élite may be land-owning Athenians, leading Spartans, or the Roman senate. Within the élite struggles will occur, and some men will appeal to the emotions of the crowd. This scheme glides over the marked differences between different systems of government, and the nature of practical politics at different times. Plutarch rarely takes a larger view of his protagonist's actions, and generally refrains from commenting on their effect in the history of their city or of world affairs: he clearly expects his readers already to have some idea of the importance of these figures on the stage of history. Finally, given the fact that our historical sources are often so meagre, the potential misunderstandings and distortions introduced by Plutarch's biographical technique can offer frustrating barriers to modern efforts at historical reconstruction and interpretation. Nevertheless, it is hard for the historian to imagine ancient history without him: his contribution to our understanding is invaluable.

Plutarch encapsulates the greatness of Greece and Rome, and brings alive the great moments of history as lived by their protagonists. The range of his sources is immense, and he regularly uses contemporary materials otherwise not available to us. To these he adds his own narrative gift and insight into the dynamics of character,[28] which bring

---

[27] *Per.* 33, cf. *Fab.* 7. On such parallels, see e.g. P. Stadter, 'Plutarch's Comparison of Pericles and Fabius Maximus', *Greek, Roman and Byzantine Studies*, 16 (1975), 77–85 (= Scardigli, *Essays on Plutarch's Lives*, 155–64), and id., 'Paradoxical Paradigms: Lysander and Sulla' and A. B. Bosworth, 'History and Artifice in Plutarch's Eumenes', in P. Stadter (ed.), *Plutarch and the Historical Tradition* (London: Routledge, 1992), 41–55 and 56–89.

[28] Cf. e.g. C. Pelling, 'Plutarch and Thucydides', in *Plutarch and the Historical Tradition* (London: Routledge, 1992), 10–40, noting that Plutarch's comments on character can be more perceptive than Thucydides'.

alive in a uniquely vivid presentation scores of figures from classical antiquity. It was this drama of living which Shakespeare recognized in Plutarch, from whom he drew not just the plot, but many of the scenes and the dynamics of action for *Coriolanus*, *Julius Caesar*, and *Antony and Cleopatra*. The liveliness, intimacy, and imagination of Plutarch's vision of his heroes has moulded our modern understanding of classical antiquity.

This Selection of Greek Lives

The nine Lives in this collection have been selected to allow a synoptic view of the major figures and periods of classical Greece. They are the most fascinating from the point of view of the modern reader, and the most useful for gaining an understanding of Athenian democracy, the Spartan military state, and the excitement of Alexander's conquests. The legislators responsible for the political and social structure of the major states, Athens and Sparta, lead the parade. The two Lives take strikingly different views of the lawgiver's work: *Lycurgus* presents an idealized picture of an ordered society, a living model of the Platonic *Republic*, one which certainly never existed at Sparta. *Solon* shows the sage trying to create a constitution which his city will accept, working through compromise, and only partially successful. *Themistocles* shows us the brilliant Athenian general in the Persian Wars, taking us through his rise, outstanding naval victory at Salamis, and rejection by Athens. The next four follow the history of Athens after the Persian wars, down to their defeat by the Spartans in 404. Cimon and Pericles were political opponents, one appealing to aristocratic sentiment, the other able to win more popular support. *Cimon* supplies historical information on the middle of the fifth century which helps fill the gap between the narratives of Herodotus and Thucydides; *Pericles* fleshes out Thucydides' brief account with Pericles' decrees and especially with the attacks made on him by the comic poets. The two are invaluable for understanding Athenian politics under the democracy. *Nicias* and *Alcibiades* again present a pair of opponents, Nicias the more conservative and sensible, Alcibiades an outrageous aristocrat who played to the crowd. Once more Plutarch supplements Thucydides, describing Nicias' magnificent religious mission to Delos, or including the indictment made against Alcibiades which drove him into exile. The lives also show us unattractive sides of democracy: Nicias' fear of an arbitrary and irrational popular assembly; Alcibiades' ability, thanks to his brillance and rhetorical skill, to change tack with the shifting winds of popular feeling, but ultimate failure to avoid the storms which he himself had stirred up. *Agesilaus* takes us to the Spartan dominance of the fourth century, in which the lame king played a major role for over forty years. At its height in the years immediately following its defeat of Athens, Sparta saw its power rapidly decline, in part because of Agesilaus' policies. Finally *Alexander* traces the world-shaking career of the conqueror who brought into the Greek sphere lands from the Danube to the Indus and Nile. Plutarch, however, prefers to focus on Alexander's character, and especially the question whether he was able to master himself as he could master his enemies.

TRANSLATOR'S NOTE

The Greek text used as the basis for this translation is the Teubner edition. Any places where I have adopted a text different from that of the Teubner have been marked in the translation with an obelus, which refers the interested reader to a note in the Textual Notes section at the back of the book. The Teubner editions of Plutarch's Lives are currently (1997) in the process of being updated, but this process is not complete. To be precise, therefore, I have used the following editions:

For Solon, Themistocles, and Cimon: *Plutarchus, Vitae Parallelae*, I.1, ed. K. Ziegler (1969).

For Pericles, Nicias, and Alcibiades: *Plutarchus, Vitae Parallelae*, I.2, ed. K. Ziegler, addenda by H. Gärtner (1994).

For Alexander; *Plutarchus, Vitae Parallelae*, II.2, ed. K. Ziegler, addenda by H. Gärtner (1994).

For Lycurgus and Agesilaus: *Plutarchus, Vitae Parallelae*, III.2, ed. K. Ziegler (1973).

SELECT BIBLIOGRAPHY

(Further reading on the individual lives will be found after the introductions to each life.)

Background and Criticism

Brenk, F. E., Hershbell, J. P., and Stadter, P. A. (eds.), *Illinois Classical Studies*, 13: 2 (1988), special volume devoted to Plutarch.

Haase, W. and Temporini, H. (eds.), *Aufstieg und Niedergang der Römischen Welt (ANRW)* Pt. II, vol. 33.6 (Berlin and New York, 1992) has many articles on Plutarch in English and other languages.

Jones, C. P., *Plutarch and Rome* (Oxford: Clarendon Press, 1971).

Mossman, J. (ed.), *Plutarch and his Intellectual World: Essays on Plutarch* (London: Duckworth, 1997).

Russell, D. A., *Plutarch* (London: Duckworth, 1973).

Scardigli, B. (ed.), *Essays on Plutarch's Lives* (Oxford: Clarendon Press, 1995).

Stadter, P. A. (ed.), *Plutarch and the Historical Tradition* (London: Rout-ledge, 1992).

Wardman, A., *Plutarch's Lives* (London: Elek, 1974).

Articles

Bosworth, A. B., 'History and Artifice in Plutarch's Eumenes', in Stadter, *Plutarch and the Historical Tradition*, 56–89.

Buckler, J., 'Plutarch and Autopsy', *ANRW* II.33.6 (1992), 4788–830.

Desideri, P., 'I documenti di Plutarco', *ANRW* II.33.6 (1992), 4536–67.

Frost, F., 'Some Documents in Plutarch's Lives', *Classica et mediaevalia*, 22 (1961), 182–94.

Geiger, J., 'Plutarch's Parallel Lives: The Choice of Heroes', *Hermes*, 109 (1981), 85–104.

Georgiadou, A., 'The Lives of the Caesars and Plutarch's Other Lives', *Illinois Classical Studies*, 13 (1988), 349–56.

Jones, C. P., 'Towards a Chronology of Plutarch's Works', *Journal of Roman Studies*, 56 (1966), 61–74 (repr. in Scardigli, *Essays*, 95–123).

Pelling, C., 'Plutarch's Method of Work in the Roman Lives', *Journal of Hellenic Studies*, 99 (1979), 74–96 (repr. in Scardigli, *Essays*, 265–318, with postscript).

—— 'Plutarch's Adaptation of his Source Material', *Journal of Hellenic Studies*, 100 (1980), 127–40 (reprinted in Scardigli, *Essays*, 125–54).

—— 'Syncrisis in Plutarch's Lives', in F. Brenk and I. Gallo (eds.), *Miscellanea Plutarchea* (*Quaderni del giornale filologico ferrarese* 8; Ferrara, 1986), 83–96.

—— 'Aspects of Plutarch's Characterization', *Illinois Classical Studies*, 13 (1988), 256–74.

—— 'Plutarch: Roman Heroes and Greek Culture', in M. Griffith and J. Barnes (eds.), *Philosophia Togata: Essays on Philosophy and Roman Society* (Oxford, 1989), 199–232.

—— 'Childhood and Personality in Greek Biography', in C. Pelling (ed.), *Characterization and Individuality in Greek Literature* (Oxford: Clarendon Press, 1990), 213–44.

—— 'Plutarch and Thucydides', in Stadter, *Plutarch and the Historical Tradition*, 10–40.

Puech, B., 'Prosopographie des amis de Plutarque', *ANRW* II.33.6 (1992), 4831–93.

Russell, D. A., 'On reading Plutarch's Lives', *Greece and Rome*, 13 (1966*a*), 139–54.

—— 'Plutarch Alcibiades 1–16', *Proceedings of the Cambridge Philological Society* (1966*b*), 37–47 (repr. in Scardigli, *Essays*, 191–207).

Stadter, P. A., 'Plutarch's Comparison of Pericles and Fabius Maximus', *Greek, Roman and Byzantine Studies*, 16 (1975), 77–85 (repr. in Scardigli, *Essays*, 155–64).

—— 'The Proems of Plutarch's Lives', *Illinois Classical Studies*, 13 (1988), 275–95.

—— 'Paradoxical Paradigms: Lysander and Sulla', in Stadter, *Plutarch and the Historical Tradition*, 41–55.

—— 'Anecdotes and the Thematic Structure of Plutarchean Biography', in J. A. Fernández Delgado and F. Pordomingo Pardo (eds.), *Estudios sobre Plutarco: Aspectos formales* (Madrid: Ediciones Clásicas, 1997), 291–303.

Swain, S., 'Hellenic Culture and the Roman Heroes of Plutarch', *Journal of Hellenic Studies*, 110 (1990), 126–45 (repr. in Scardigli, *Essays*, 229–64).

—— 'Plutarch, Plato, Athens, and Rome', in J. Barnes and M. Griffin (eds.), *Philosophia Togata II: Plato and Aristotle at Rome* (Oxford: Clarendon Press, 1997), 165–87.

Wet, B. X. de, 'Plutarch's Use of the Poets', *Antiquité Classique*, 31 (1988), 13–25.

Select Bibliography

Translations

Lives:

A companion volume to this will contain translations of *Cato the Elder*,
  Aemilius Paullus, *Gracchi*, *Marius*, *Sulla*, *Pompey*, *Caesar*, and *Antony*.
Selected lives have been translated in the following volumes:
Scott-Kilvert, I., *Plutarch. The Fall of the Roman Republic* (Harmondsworth,
  Penguin, 1958).
—— *Plutarch. The Rise and Fall of Athens* (Harmondsworth, Penguin, 1960).
—— *Plutarch. Makers of Rome* (Harmondsworth, Penguin, 1965).
—— *Plutarch. The Age of Alexander* (Harmondsworth, Penguin, 1973).
Talbert, R., *Plutarch on Sparta* (Harmondsworth, Penguin, 1988).

Moralia:

The complete *Moralia* are translated in the Loeb Classical Library,
  Plutarch Moralia (Cambridge, Mass., and London, 1927–76, 14 vols. (with
  facing Greek)) and W. W. Goodwin, a revision of an 18th-cent. version
  'by many hands' (Boston, 1874–8). There are three recent translations
  of selected essays:
Russell, D. A., *Plutarch: Selected Essays and Dialogues* (Oxford: Oxford
  University Press, Oxford World's Classics, 1993).
Warner, R., *Plutarch: Moral Essays* (Harmondsworth: Penguin, 1971).
Waterfield, R., *Plutarch: Essays* (Harmondsworth: Penguin, 1992).

CHRONOLOGY

Dates with ? are approximate.

776	Traditional foundation date of the Olympic games
8th cent.	Spartan conquest of Messenia
594/3	Traditional date of Solon's archonship and constitutional reform
561/0	Pisistratus' first attempt at tyranny at Athens
544 ?	Croesus of Lydia defeated by Cyrus the Great of Persia
528/7	Death of Pisistratus at Athens
510	Expulsion of tyrants from Athens
490	Athenians defeat Persian army at Marathon
480	Persian victories at Thermopylae and Artemisium
	Persian defeat in naval battle at Salamis
479	Greek victory over Persians at Plataea
478	Athens establishes Delian league in the Aegean
471?	Ostracism of Themistocles
468?	Cimon's victory at Eurymedon
462	Ephialtes' and Pericles' reform of the Areopagus court
461	Ostracism of Cimon
458?	Battle of Tanagra
450?	Death of Cimon at Cyprus
446	Spartan invasion of Attica; thirty-year peace treaty
443?	Ostracism of Thucydides son of Melesias
431	Spring: outbreak of Peloponnesian War
430	Spring: plague strikes Athens
429	Autumn: death of Pericles
425	Athenians under Cleon capture Spartans at Sphacteria
421	April: peace of Nicias between Athens and Sparta
416?	Ostracism of Hyperbolus
415–413	Athenian expedition to Sicily
415	Alcibiades called back for trial, flees to Sparta
413	Death of Nicias
407	Alcibiades returns to Athens
404	Athens surrenders to Sparta, end of Peloponnesian War
400	Agesilaus becomes one of Spartan kings

399	Death of Socrates
396–395	Agesilaus in Asia Minor
395–386	Corinthian War
394	Agesilaus recalled, battle of Coronea
386	Peace of Antalcidas, dictated by Persia
371	Thebes and its allies defeat Spartans at Leuctra
369	Creation of an independent Messenian state
362	Theban victory at Mantinea, Epaminondas dies
360	Agesilaus' expedition to Egypt and death
356	Alexander the Great born
347	Death of Plato
338	Philip II and Alexander defeat Greeks at Chaeronea
336	Philip II assassinated, Alexander takes throne
334	Spring: Alexander crosses to Asia, battle of Granicus
333	November: battle of Issus
331	1 Oct. (?): battle of Gaugamela
330	Death of Philotas
326	Battle against Porus at the Hydaspes
325	Alexander at the mouth of the Indus
323	13 June: death of Alexander in Babylon

MAP I. SICILY AND SOUTH ITALY

MAP 2. GREECE AND THE AEGEAN

Altitude in metres
over 1000
200–1000
0–200

0   20   40   60   80   100 miles
0   40   80   120   160 km

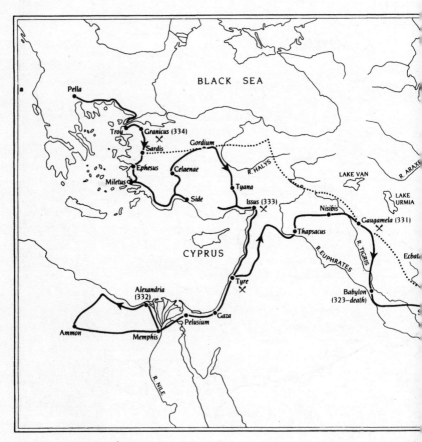

MAP 3. ALEXANDER'S ROUTE

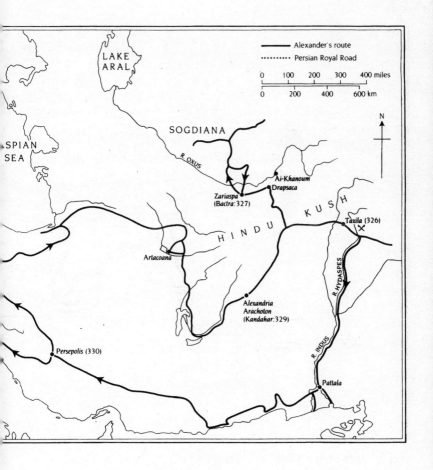

LAKE
ARAL

Alexander's route
Persian Royal Road

0   100   200   300   400 miles
0   200   400   600 km

N

SPIAN
SEA

SOGDIANA

R. OXUS

Ai-Khanoum
Drapsaca

Zariaspa
(Bactra:327)

H I N D U
K U S H

Taxila (326)

Artacoana

R. HYDASPES

Alexandria
Arachoton
(Kandahar:329)

R. INDUS

Persepolis (330)

Pattala

GREEK LIVES

LYCURGUS

INTRODUCTION

> ... the point of all his arrangements and institutions had been to enable
> the Spartans to be free, autonomous, and self-disciplined for as long
> as possible. This political scheme has been taken over by everyone
> who has come to be admired for attempting to address these issues,
> including Plato, Diogenes, and Zeno, even though they left to poster-
> ity nothing but words and ideas. Lycurgus, however, left no mere
> words and ideas, but created an actual and unrivalled system of
> government.
>
> (*Lyc.* 31)

Lycurgus is not so much a biography as the account of a way of life, the
Spartan regime and social system (*agōgē*) which was ascribed to Lycurgus
and which set Sparta apart from the other cities of classical Greece. As in
Numa (with which it is paired) and *Solon*, the protagonist is thought of as
a legislator whose fundamental purpose is education, a man who has tried,
in Plato's phrase, 'to make his fellow citizens better'. Solon, however, is
clearly a historical figure as well as a major poet, and Numa, while semi-
legendary, is firmly anchored in the list of the early Roman kings, immediately after Romulus. Lycurgus, on the other hand, is a legendary figure
about whom Plutarch admits, 'there is nothing indisputable to be said' (1).
We are no better off. The Life is of necessity different from the others in
this collection. Plutarch nevertheless undertakes to 'follow those accounts
which have attracted the least controversy and have the most distinguished
witnesses on their side' (1).

Sparta was an amalgam of four villages in the fertile Eurotas valley of
the south-eastern Peloponnese. At some time, probably in the late eighth
century, the Spartans had extended their control west across the Taygetus
mountains, doubling their territory by conquering Messenia, and establishing
their dominion over the whole of the southern Peloponnese, from the Aegean
on the east coast to the Ionian Sea on the west. During the sixth century
the immense effort of holding this land against revolts from the subject
Messenians or attacks from outside, especially from Argos, forced a re-
structuring of Spartan society which gave it the severe and military character, unique in Greece, by which it was known in classical Greece and
ever since. This was the social framework which in the fifth century made
the Spartans the leaders of the Greeks in the Persian Wars and permitted
them to defeat the Athenians in the Peloponnesian War (cf. Plutarch's

Themistocles, *Pericles*, *Nicias*, and *Alcibiades*). Even after the loss of
Messenia following the Theban victory at Leuctra in 371 (cf. *Agesilaus*),
the Spartan state kept something of its basic structure, and was spoken of
with admiration by Plato and Aristotle.

Substantial reforms were made by the kings Agis and Cleomenes in the
late third century (Plutarch wrote Lives of these men as well), and more
were made under Roman rule. Under Agis and Cleomenes especially, an
effort was made to restore the original Lycurgan constitution, so that some
features ascribed to Lycurgus may in fact belong to that period. The Stoic
philosopher Sphaerus, author of a book on the Lycurgan constitution,
was instrumental in helping Cleomenes restore the traditional system
(cf. *Cleomenes* 11, and N. M. Kennell, *The Gymnasium of Virtue* (Chapel
Hill, 1995), 11–12, 98–101). In Plutarch's day, the current version of the
Lycurgan system attracted young men from all over Greece who wished
to participate in the revived training regime. Sparta became also an important tourist city, putting on regular shows and festivals for large crowds
(cf. P. Cartledge and A. Spawforth, *Hellenistic and Roman Sparta* (London
and New York, 1989), 197–211). Thus when Plutarch mentions being present at a ritual, when many young men were 'dying under the lash at the
altar of Artemis Orthia' (18) this does not represent a tradition continuously preserved, but a revival created in a later period.

Although modern scholars usually place the 'Lycurgan' reforms (though
usually not Lycurgus) in the sixth century BC, there were strong traditions
which place him and his reforms much earlier. Herodotus does not give
specific dates, but seems to set Lycurgus' reforms several generations before
Croesus, that is at the end of the seventh century (Hdt. 1. 65–6), and other
authors place him even earlier. Plutarch vacillates (cf. 1, 23, 29) between
assigning him to the time of the founding of the Olympic Games (traditionally dated to 776 BC) and to 500 years before King Agis, the son of
Archidamus (427–400), that is, to *c*.925–900. Unfortunately, we are not able
to give a historical account for these centuries. We must remain in doubt
whether a single major legislator existed, or whether in later times a pattern of unwritten traditions was ascribed to this semi-legendary figure. It
is unlikely that the whole body of Spartan social and educational practices
described by Plutarch goes back to one legislator, however influential. More
important is that Plutarch gives us our best synthesis of the developed
Spartan social system as it was understood in ancient times. He tries to
give the original political and training system of Lycurgus, although, as
has been said, he may in fact be including some features of the system as
it was later reconstituted.

The treatment of the actual life of Lycurgus is confined chiefly to
the first part of the Life, cc. 1–5. Here Plutarch discusses his date, the

various accounts of his family which place him at different points in the Spartan king lists, his accession to the throne after his brother's death and his surrender of the throne to his posthumously born nephew, his extended stay abroad in Crete, Ionia, and Egypt until his nephew came of age, and his return, seizure of power, and implementation of his reforms. The body of the Life describes those reforms (5–28). The final section (29–31) describes the oath of the elders to maintain the laws, Lycurgus' trip to Delphi, his death, and the honours he was given.

Lycurgus' reforms as discussed by Plutarch can be gathered under the following headings:

The Fundamental Institutions

1. The Council of Elders, the *gerousia* (5–17). (The Great Rhetra mentions this council, and refers also to divisions of the people. The Board of Ephors is a later development.)
2. Redistribution of land (8; this was accompanied by monetary reform and the expulsion of crafts, 9).
3. Institution of a common mess (10–12).
4. Three rhetras (unwritten laws): (*a*) there is to be no written law, (*b*) only axes and saws are to be used in constructing a house, (*c*) there is a ban on frequent campaigns against the same foes (13).

The System of Training (agōgē)

1. Marriage and infant regulations (including raising of girls, female nudity, and children, 14–16).
2. Training of boys from age 7 to 20 (16–18), followed by comments on this training: the use of laconic speech (19–20), the use of poetry (21), practices in warfare (22), and Lycurgus' own peaceful disposition (23).
3. Adult life at Sparta (24–5).
4. The election of the elders (26).
5. Funerals and treatment of foreigners (27).
6. Treatment of helots (28).

In this central section, each item is accompanied by Plutarch's own interpretation and evaluation of the practice. Plutarch reflects earlier Greek tradition in treating the 'Lycurgan constitution' more as a philosophical than a historical problem. The ancient legislator was thought to be responsible for the entire life of the city. Thus the rules which govern a city, its 'constitution' (*politeia*), form a statement on the good life and how to achieve it in a community. Philosophers, most notably Plato in his *Republic* and *Laws*, wrote books outlining the principles and laws of the ideal state. The Spartan model, attributed to Lycurgus, became central to this discussion (cf. on Plato, E. N. Tigerstedt, *The Legend of Sparta in Classical Antiquity* (Stockholm and Uppsala, 1965–78), i. 244–76).

Here, as in his *Solon*, Plutarch places himself in this tradition, showing himself more interested in the ideas behind the customs than in their historicity. In particular, he examines how Lycurgus aimed at the best education for a citizen, training the passions and giving command to the noblest parts of the soul. Plutarch evaluates the Spartan traditional system according to his own Platonic psychology, which divided the soul into three parts, the rational intellect, an irrational but potentially noble 'spirited' part, and the irrational and potentially destructive passions. Throughout he stresses the formative nature of the Lycurgan system, with its holistic approach, appreciation of intelligence and music, and communitarian values. The moral aspect of this training is noted by Plutarch especially in the chapters on physical training of both males and females (14–17). His rather paradoxical conclusion (31, quoted above) is that Lycurgus had been able to construct the ideal 'philosophic' city, better even than the one envisioned in Plato's *Republic*, because it existed in reality and not in theory.

Numa Pompilius, the Roman king and lawgiver, and the legislator paired with Lycurgus, makes a good foil to him. There were a number of obvious parallels between Rome and Sparta: the two consuls and the two kings, the senate and the council of elders, the military success of both cities. Although both Rome and Sparta were famous for their achievements in war, Plutarch presents both lawgivers as peaceful men with philosophical goals. Numa in the ancient tradition was regularly seen as a religious man, author of laws regulating cult and ritual, and one dedicated to peace in contrast to the two kings who preceded and followed him, Romulus and Hostilius Tullus, both very active in war. Plutarch describes at length his religious institutions and the peace which endured throughout the forty-three years of his reign, comparing him to Plato's ideal philosopher-king (*Numa* 20). However, Plutarch notes that he established no rules for raising children, so that the peace of his reign died with him, whereas Lycurgus was able by his system of training, which changed the inner disposition of the people, to maintain his reforms for many generations.

Our information on Lycurgus begins with Herodotus, who gives the earliest extant account (1. 65). He speaks of the favour of Apollo at Delphi and notes that Sparta became well governed and militarily successful after Lycurgus' reforms, among which he mentions the establishment of military units, the council of elders, and the ephors. In the early fourth century Xenophon's *Constitution of the Lacedaemonians* glorified the ancient system of Sparta, while noting how far the Spartans fell short of its moral code in his own day. This work is the only extant example of the many accounts of the Spartan system written in antiquity.

Plutarch cites Xenophon in c. 1; and clearly uses him in other sections. He also mentions the lost *Constitution of the Lacedaemonians* by Aristotle in cc. 1, 5, 6, 28, and 31. He found the *Constitution of the Athenians* extremely useful in his *Solon*, and he undoubtedly used Aristotle heavily for *Lycurgus* as well. Although Aristotle's *Constitution* is lost, it probably served as a basis for Aristotle's observations on Sparta in his *Politics* ($1269^a29–1271^b19$), and a brief summary is preserved by Heraclides Lembos. Plutarch cites other ancient accounts of the Spartan constitution as well: Sphaerus (5), Critias (9), and Dioscurides (11). Historians who spoke of Lycurgus, such as Ephorus and Polybius, probably were used as well. Frequent poetic citations and references to historians, both well known (Thucydides, Timaeus) and obscure, enrich the discussion.

A difficult source problem is raised by several collections found in the Plutarchan corpus, gathered under the title *Spartan Sayings*, 208b–242d. This contains first, a collection of sayings attributed to different named Spartans, including 31 of Lycurgus, and arranged in alphabetical order by speakers, with anonymous sayings at the end (208b–236e); second, a series of short notices on Spartan institutions (236f–240b); and third, a collection of sayings of Spartan women, also in alphabetical order (240c–242d). Both the sayings and the institutions have a close connection with *Lycurgus*: those found also in *Lycurgus* are in much the same order as in the life. This has led scholars to argue that these works are a major source for the life, especially the section on institutions. Recently, moreover, Kennell has argued that the institutions section reflects very closely the work of Sphaerus on the Spartan constitution in the third century BC. However, our current knowledge of Plutarch's process of selection and rethinking in creating a Life make it most improbable that he would simply follow the order of a pre-existing collection in arranging his own account. Therefore it is more likely that the *Spartan Sayings*, including the section on institutions, represents an earlier stage of Plutarch's own literary activity, which in turn used earlier accounts. Combining as it does so many sources now lost to us, *Lycurgus* is a precious source for the structure and training programme of the early Spartan state, despite the fact that many details may reflect later reshaping of the tradition.

Plutarch in this Life does not simply reflect tradition, but builds his own philosophical account of Lycurgus' laws, and selects only those elements which fit his purpose. Xenophon's account, for example, has more to say on the military organization of the Spartans. Plutarch, living under the Roman empire, contrasts Spartan simplicity to luxuries (9) and to expensive furniture, hot baths, and gluttonous eating (10), which while present at all times, were especially accessible to the super-rich élite of his own day. In the end, Plutarch's conception of the Lycurgan constitution must be treated on its own terms. *Lycurgus* is not just history, but a statement of the value of the simple, disciplined, communitarian life against the individualist pursuit of pleasure.

Cartledge, P., *Sparta and Lakonia: A Regional History, 1300–362 BC* (London: Routledge and Kegan Paul, 1979). A regional study of early and classical Sparta.

—— 'Spartan Wives: Liberation or License?', *Classical Quarterly*, 31 (1981), 84–105.

Cartledge, P., and A. Spawforth, *Hellenistic and Roman Sparta: A Tale of Two Cities* (London and New York: Routledge, 1989). A description of post-classical Sparta, 362 BC to late Roman times.

Finley, M. I., *Economy and Society in Ancient Greece* (London: Chatto and Windus, 1981). Chapter 2 is on Sparta.

Forrest, W. G., *A History of Sparta 950–192 BC*, 2nd edn. (London: Duckworth, 1980). A general history.

Hodkinson, S., ' "Blind Ploutos?": Contemporary Images of the Role of Wealth in Classical Sparta', in A. Powell and S. Hodkinson (eds.), *The Shadow of Sparta* (London: Routledge, 1994), 183–222.

Kennell, N. M., *The Gymnasium of Virtue: Education and Culture in Ancient Sparta* (Chapel Hill: University of North Carolina Press, 1995). A study of the changes in the Spartan educational system over the centuries, beginning from Roman times and working back.

Michell, H., *Sparta* (Cambridge: Cambridge University Press, 1952). A general history.

Rawson, E., *The Spartan Tradition in European Thought* (Oxford: Oxford University Press, 1969). European ideas of the Lycurgan system.

Schneeweiss, G., 'History and Philosophy in Plutarch. Observations on Plutarch's Lycurgus', in G. W. Bowersock, W. Burkert, and M. C. J. Putnam (eds.), *Arktouros, Hellenic Studies presented to B. M. W. Knox* (Berlin and New York, 1979), 376–82. An analysis of important themes in *Lycurgus*.

Szegedy-Maszak, A., 'Legends of the Greek Lawgivers', *Greek, Roman and Byzantine Studies*, 19 (1978), 199–209. The standard pattern found in Greek accounts of lawgivers.

Talbert, R., *Plutarch on Sparta* (Harmondsworth: Penguin, 1988). Translations of various ancient works on Sparta.

Tigerstedt, E. N., *The Legend of Sparta in Classical Antiquity*, 3 vols. (Stockholm and Uppsala: 1965–78). A scholarly study, with massive footnotes.

LYCURGUS

[1] Even allowing for the fact that there is nothing indisputable to be said about Lycurgus the legislator, since there are divergent accounts of his family, his travels abroad, his death, and above all precisely what he achieved with regard to the laws and the constitution, there is particularly little agreement about when the man lived. Some people, including the philosopher Aristotle, say that he was contemporary with Iphitus and helped him arrange the Olympic truce;* to corroborate this, Aristotle adduces the discus preserved at Olympia which has Lycurgus' name inscribed on it.* Others, however, such as Eratosthenes and Apollodorus, use the list of successive Spartan kings to work out when he lived, and demonstrate that he preceded the first Olympiad by quite a few years. Then again, Timaeus suggests that there might have been two Lycurguses in Sparta at different times, one of whom became so famous that both of their achievements came to be attributed to him; he conjectures that the elder Lycurgus lived close to Homer's time, and others claim that he actually met Homer face to face. Xenophon too gives an impression of antiquity in the passage where he says that the man lived at the time of the Heraclidae,* since although the latest Spartan kings were of course Heraclidae, Xenophon was apparently meaning to use the name 'Heraclidae' of the original ones, the immediate descendants of Heracles. Nevertheless, in spite of such a confused record, I shall try, in the course of my narrative of the man, to follow those accounts which have attracted the least controversy and have the most distinguished witnesses on their side.*

<...>† After all, even the poet Simonides does not make Lycurgus' father Eunomus, but has both Lycurgus and Eunomus as sons of Prytanis, whereas almost no one else gives this account of his lineage. They say, on the contrary, that his lineage runs as follows: Procles the son of Aristodamus, then Soüs, then Eurypon, then Prytanis, then Eunomus, whose sons were Polydectes by his first wife and—the younger son—Lycurgus by Dionassa. This is the account given by Dieutychidas, which makes Lycurgus a sixth-generation descendant of Procles and an eleventh-generation descendant of Heracles.*

[2] Among these ancestors of his, Soüs was particularly admired. It was during his reign that the Spartiates* enslaved the helots,* took over a great deal of Arcadian territory, and made it their own. There is a story that once Soüs was trapped by the Cleitorians in a harsh, waterless spot, and he agreed to surrender the land he had captured if he and all his men could drink from the nearby spring. Once the two sides had pledged themselves to honour these terms, he gathered his men together and offered his kingdom to anyone who would not take a drink. None of them could resist, however: they all drank from the spring. He was the last to go down, and when he did so, he splashed water on to himself in front of the enemy, who were still there, and then left—and kept the land, on the grounds that not all of them had taken a drink. However, although he was respected for his achievements, his family—the Eurypontidae—was named after his son rather than him, because Eurypon, in his pursuit of popularity and favour with the common people, was apparently the first to relax the excessively autocratic nature of the kingship. But this led to the people becoming presumptuous, and later kings either became hated for trying to put pressure on the masses, or won tolerance at the price of flattery or weakness. Lawlessness and disorder prevailed in Sparta for a long time, and it was as a result of this that Lycurgus' father came to lose his life while he was king. He was trying to prevent a brawl when he was fatally struck with a meat-cleaver, leaving the kingdom to his eldest son, Polydectes.

[3] Not long afterwards, however, Polydectes died as well, and the kingdom devolved by right on to Lycurgus—or so everyone thought. In fact, he did rule, but only until it was obvious that his brother's wife was pregnant. As soon as he noticed this, he declared that the kingdom belonged to the child, if it was male, and that he was looking after the kingdom merely as guardian, or 'representative', as the Lacedaemonians calls the guardians of royal orphans. The woman, however, entered into secret communication with him, saying that she was willing to kill the baby provided that he would marry her when he was king of Sparta. Although he found her immorality abhorrent, he raised no objection to the actual proposal, but pretended to approve of it and welcome it. He said that there was no need for her to abuse her body and endanger her life by taking drugs to abort the foetus, because he would see to it that the baby was got rid of as soon as it was born. With this argument he succeeded in tricking the woman

for the whole period of her pregnancy. When he saw that her time had come, he sent some of his men to sit beside her and watch over her during her labour, with instructions to hand the child over to the womenfolk if it was a girl, but if it was a boy to bring it to him, no matter what he was doing. As a matter of fact he was dining with the magistrates when his servants arrived, bringing him the baby boy that had been born. The story goes that he took the child in his arms and said to the assembled company, 'Spartiates, a king has been born for you.' Then he laid him in the king's place and named him Charilaus because all the people there were delighted,* as well as being very impressed by his high-mindedness and justice. He had reigned for eight months altogether.

This was not the only thing that made his fellow citizens admire him, and those who stood by him and were ready to carry out his commands because of his excellent qualities outnumbered those who obeyed him because he was the king's guardian and had a king's power. However, there was also some disaffection and an attempt to impede the rise to power of one who was so young, especially from the relatives and friends of the king's mother, who felt that she had been treated with disrespect. On one occasion, in fact, her brother Leonidas was quite outspokenly rude to Lycurgus, and added that he knew perfectly well that Lycurgus intended to be king. This lie made Lycurgus an object of suspicion and ensured in advance that if anything did happen to the king, he would be accused of having plotted against him. Similar slanderous rumours were also spread around by the king's mother. All this made Lycurgus angry and afraid of what might happen, so he decided to avoid suspicion by leaving the country and travelling abroad until his nephew was grown up and had fathered an heir apparent for the throne.

[4] After leaving Sparta, the first place he visited was Crete, where he studied the various types of government and spent time with the most distinguished men of the island.* He admired some of their customs, but did not think much of the rest; the ones he admired he appropriated, with the intention of taking them back home and putting them into practice. Moreover, he got on close and friendly enough terms with one of the men there who had a name for wisdom and statesmanship to send him to Sparta. This was Thales,* who had a reputation as a composer of lyric verse and used this art to cloak his true activities, which were those of any powerful legislator, in the sense

that his songs were actually arguments in favour of obedience and political concord. This aspect of his songs was enhanced by the music and
rhythm, which were so orderly and soothing that anyone listening
to them became, without being aware of it, a more even-tempered
person and learnt to replace the mutual hostility which prevailed
there at the time with an admiration for noble qualities. And so in a
sense Thales was a forerunner for Lycurgus' famous programme for
educating his people.

From Crete Lycurgus sailed over to Asia because, we are told, like
a doctor who compares unsound and sickly bodies with healthy ones,
he wanted to compare the frugality and severity of the Cretan way of
life with Ionian extravagance and luxury, and observe the differences
between their lives and political systems. It was while he was in Asia
that he first came across the Homeric poems, which were apparently
preserved by the descendants of Creophylus.* When he noticed that
the poems contained, interspersed among the passages designed to
promote pleasure and self-indulgence, a political and educational element which called for at least as much serious attention, he became
very excited by them, and had them written down and collected so
that he could bring them here to Greece. Homer's epics already had
a vague reputation among the Greeks, and a few people had managed
to get hold of certain parts of them thanks to the chance distribution
of the poetry here and there, but their fame is due above all to
Lycurgus, who was the first to make them known here.

The Egyptians think that Lycurgus visited them as well, and was
so highly impressed with their separation of the warrior castes from
all the others* that he transferred the system to Sparta and made the
constitution there one of genuine refinement and purity by allowing
the artisans and craftsmen no part in it.* This claim by the Egyptians is in fact supported by some Greek writers, but the story that
Lycurgus also went to Libya and Iberia, and even travelled to India
and spent time with the Gymnosophists, has to my knowledge the
authority of no one except the Spartiate Aristocrates the son of
Hipparchus.*

[5] The Lacedaemonians missed Lycurgus while he was away and
often asked him to return, because for them it was only the title and
the prestige that distinguished their kings from the masses, whereas
Lycurgus, they could see, was a natural leader with the power to get
people to follow him. In fact, however, even the kings wanted him

back, in the hope of receiving less disrespectful treatment from the masses when he was there. As soon as Lycurgus returned, then, to find them in this frame of mind, he set in motion a plan to effect a revolution and bring about constitutional change, because he could see no point or benefit in piecemeal legislation rather than a fresh start, just as in dealing with a body which was in a terrible state, riddled with all kinds of diseases, one would first eliminate and alter the current blend of the humours by means of drugs and purgatives and then begin on a new regimen. Once he had made up his mind that this was the way to proceed, he first made a trip to Delphi. After sacrificing and consulting the god, he returned to Sparta with the famous oracle in which the Pythia called him 'beloved of the gods' and 'a god rather than a man'.* He claimed that when he had asked for lawfulness the god had granted and promised him a political system of such quality that it would leave all the rest far behind.

Encouraged by this, he set about winning over the best Spartiates and inviting them to help him do what had to be done. He began by entering into secret negotiations with his friends, and then he gradually approached more and more people in the same way until he had formed a group of conspirators. At the opportune moment he ordered the thirty leaders of his party to advance at dawn under arms into the city square, so as to terrify and intimidate his opponents. Hermippus has provided us with a list of the twenty most distinguished men on Lycurgus' side, and Arthmiadas is generally named as Lycurgus' main associate in all his enterprises and as the one who particularly supported his constitutional reforms.

At the beginning of the disturbance, King Charilaus became frightened, imagining that the whole business was a plot directed against him, and took refuge in the Bronze House.* Later, when he became convinced of the truth and had received pledges guaranteeing his safety, he emerged from there and played a part in the proceedings, since he was an even-tempered person—which is the context of the story that his fellow king Archelaus once remarked to those who were praising the young man, 'Of course Charilaus isn't a good man: he doesn't even get cross with bad people.'

Among Lycurgus' many reforms, the first and most important was the institution of the elders, who were, as Plato says, a source of security and restraint since they tempered the 'feverish' rule of the kings and had 'an equal voice in affairs of moment'.* The political system had previously been unstable, with a tendency to come down at one time on the side of the kings and to veer towards tyranny, and at another on the side of the masses and democracy; but the ballast provided by the government of the elders restored the ship of state to an even keel and enabled the constitution to find the safest possible arrangement and condition for itself, as the twenty-eight elders periodically sided with the kings when it was a matter of resisting democracy, but then supported the people to prevent the occurrence of tyranny. Aristotle says that the reason for there being this number of elders was that two of the thirty leaders of Lycurgus' party abandoned the enterprise out of cowardice, but Sphaerus* says that there had been twenty-eight conspirators in on the plot from the start. It may also be relevant that 28 is the product of 4 and 7, and that since it is equal to the sum of its parts, it is a perfect number (the next in the sequence after 6), but I think that the main reason Lycurgus instituted this number of elders was to reach a total of thirty when the two kings were added to the twenty-eight elders.*

[6] Lycurgus took the government of the elders so seriously that he brought an oracle back from Delphi about it, which they call a 'rhetra'. It runs as follows: 'Found a sanctuary of Zeus Scyllanius and Athena Scyllania, form tribes and septs, establish a Council of Elders consisting of thirty men including the leaders, and then from time to time hold an apella between Babyca and Cnacium, and so make your proposals and vetos. But power and authority is to rest with the people.'*† In these words 'form tribes and septs' refers to the division and distribution of the population into groups, which he calls 'tribes' and 'septs', 'leaders' refers to the kings, and to 'hold an apella' is to hold a general assembly, because he took Apollo to be the origin and instigator of the constitution. The modern name for Babyca is <. . .>† and for Cnacium is Oenous. Aristotle says that Cnacium is a river and Babyca a bridge. They used to hold their assemblies between these two places, even though there were no halls or structures of any kind there, because he thought that these things made no contribution at all towards the process of sound deliberation, and even hindered it by making the minds of the people gathered there for the assembly foolish and vacuous with inane thoughts brought on by gazing at statues and inscriptions, or at the stage in a theatre, or at the over-ornate roof of a council-hall.* Once the general populace had gathered there, on Lycurgus' system no one was allowed to express an opinion

except the elders and the kings, but the people did have the authority to decide about the measures proposed by the elders and the kings. Later, however, when the masses had started distorting and warping proposals by their additions and subtractions, the kings Polydorus and Theopompus* added a rider to the rhetra, as follows: 'However, if the people vote in favour of a deformed motion, the elders and leaders are to wield a veto'—which is to say that they were not to ratify it, but to veto it altogether and to dismiss the people on the grounds that the amendments and alterations they were making to the proposal were not for the best. What is more, Polydorus and Theopompus convinced their fellow citizens that it was the god who had ordained this rider, as Tyrtaeus seems to imply in the following lines:

> They heard the voice of Phoebus and brought home from Pytho
> Oracles of the god and words of sure fulfilment:
> Authority in council belongs to the god-favoured kings
> Who are responsible for the lovely city of Sparta,
> And to the elders, and then to the common people
> As they respond with straight rhetras.*

[7] So Lycurgus fashioned a mixed constitution.* His successors, however, were still faced with an oligarchy that was undiluted and strong. When they saw it 'chafing and spirited', as Plato puts it, 'as a bridle they imposed on it the office of the ephorate'.* The first ephors, Elatus and his colleagues, were appointed about 130 years after Lycurgus, during the reign of Theopompus. Another thing that is said about Theopompus is that when his wife scolded him and said that the kingship he would pass on to his sons would be inferior to the one he had received, he replied, 'No, greater, because it will last longer.' And in fact, once it had shed its extreme aspects, the kingship stopped attracting envy and made itself secure enough to avoid what the Messenians and Argives did to their kings when they refused to give up or release any of their power to the people. Nothing made Lycurgus' wisdom and foresight more obvious than a survey of the misgovernment and feuding between the people and the kings that afflicted Messenia and Argos, the kinsmen and neighbours of the Lacedaemonians. They had started with the same opportunities, and in fact were held to have done better than the Lacedaemonians out of the allocation of land,* but their prosperity did not last long. Thanks to the arrogance of the kings and the unruliness of the masses their

institutions were thrown into chaos—thus proving what a truly divine piece of good fortune it was for the Spartiates to have had someone to construct a mixed constitution. But I have got ahead of my story.

[8] The second, and the most revolutionary of Lycurgus' constitutional reforms was the redistribution of the land. There was terrible inequality, crowds of paupers without property and without any means of support were accumulating in the city, and wealth was entirely concentrated in the hands of a few people. In order to banish arrogance, envy, crime, luxury, and those more chronic and serious political afflictions, wealth and poverty, Lycurgus persuaded them to pool all the land and then redistribute it all over again, so that everyone would live on equal terms and with the same amount of property to provide an income. In the future the only ascendancy they would seek would be assessed by the criterion of excellence, on the basis that there was to be no difference or inequality between any one of them and another except as determined by criticism of shameful deeds and praise of noble ones.

Putting his ideas into practice, he divided most of Laconia into 30,000 plots of land which were distributed among the perioeci,* and the part of Laconia which was assessed as belonging to the city of Sparta into 9,000 plots.* This was the number of plots in the hands of Spartiates, but some writers say that Lycurgus distributed 6,000 of them and then later Polydorus added another 3,000, while others say that Polydorus and Lycurgus were responsible for allocating 4,500 each. Each person's allotment was large enough to produce a yield of seventy medimni of barley for a man, plus twelve for his wife, and a proportionate amount of fruit,* since in Lycurgus' opinion that amount of food was enough to guarantee an adequate degree of health and fitness without them needing anything else. There is a story from later in his life that once on his return from a trip abroad he was passing through the countryside just after harvest-time, and when he saw all the equal stacks of grain, one after another, he smiled and commented to the people who were with him that the whole of Laconia looked like an estate which had recently been divided between a large number of brothers.

[9] He next tried to divide up their furniture too, so as to get rid of every last trace of inequality and discrepancy, but when he saw that people were not prepared to tolerate the direct confiscation of their goods, he took a circuitous route to the same end and attacked their

greed by political means. First he revoked all gold and silver coinage and made iron the only legal tender; then he gave even a considerable weight and amount of iron such a low value that ten minas' worth needed a large storeroom in one's house and a team of cattle to transport it.* Once this decree was in force, many types of crime disappeared from Lacedaemon. Who would set out to embezzle, or accept as a bribe, or rob, or steal something which was impossible to conceal, which no one particularly wanted to have, and which could not even be profitably cut up? For it is said that Lycurgus had the hammered iron cooled when red hot in vinegar, which made it too brittle and unworkable to have any other use or function.

He next set about ridding the state of useless, superfluous professions.* In fact, most of them would have left along with internationally acceptable coinage, without anyone having to banish them, since there was no longer any market for their products. The iron money could not be taken elsewhere in Greece, where it had no value and was held in contempt, and this meant that no one could buy any foreign trash, no cargo was imported into their harbours, no verbal casuist set foot on Laconian territory, no vagabond diviner, no keeper of prostitutes, no maker of gold or silver ornaments, because there was no money to pay them with. Once luxury was deprived of the things that enliven it and nourish it, it gradually wasted away of its own accord, and there was no advantage in owning a great deal of property because wealth had no means of displaying itself in public, but had to stay shut up in idleness at home. And so essential daily utensils such as beds, chairs and tables began to be made to a high degree of excellence there, and the Laconian drinking-cup, according to Critias, was especially famous for its utility during military expeditions. For the unpleasant appearance of the kinds of water the soldiers were inevitably drinking was disguised by the colour of the cup, and the muddy sediment caught against the inside of the lip of the cup and went no further, so that the liquid that actually reached their mouths and was drunk was cleaner than it might otherwise have been. The legislator was responsible for even this, in the sense that once craftsmen were released from non-essential work, they began to display their skill on essential items.

[10] Now, Lycurgus intended to eradicate admiration of wealth altogether, so he increased his assault on luxury with his third and finest reform, which was to introduce the system of common messes,

by which people came together to eat along with others the same specified savouries and foods. This stopped them spending time at home reclining at table on expensive couches, fattening themselves up in the dark like insatiable animals on the produce of craftsmen and cooks, and ruining themselves morally as well as physically by indulging every whim and gorging themselves until they needed long sleeps, hot baths, a great deal of quiet, and, so to speak, daily nursing. This was a considerable achievement, but the fact that he made riches undesirable, as Theophrastus says, and by means of shared meals and simplicity of diet made wealth no wealth is even more important. For when rich and poor went to the same meal, the rich could not even use or enjoy, let alone gaze upon or display, all their paraphernalia. The upshot was—and this was how everybody put it—that Sparta was the only city in the world where Wealth could be seen truly blind,* lying as lifeless and inert as a picture. It was not even possible for a rich man to eat at home first and then go to the common mess with a full stomach, because everyone else was alert to the possibility, and they used to watch out for people who would not drink or eat with them and taunt them for their lack of self-control and for being too delicate to take the common diet.

[11] It was apparently this reform above all which made the rich members of Spartan society angry with Lycurgus. They formed themselves into a party to oppose him and used to band together to shout him down and express their irritation. Eventually the time came when he had to run out of the city square under a hail of missiles from them. He managed to reach a sanctuary ahead of most of them, and take refuge there, but a young man called Alcander (who, apart from his impatience and quick temper, was a fairly decent man) was hot on his heels, and when Lycurgus turned round Alcander hit him with his stick and knocked out his eye. This injury did not make Lycurgus give in, however. He stood and confronted his fellow citizens, showing them his bloody face and ruined eye. They were so overcome by remorse and horror at the sight that they handed Alcander over to him and escorted him home, unanimous in their outrage at what Alcander had done. Lycurgus thanked them and sent them all away with the exception of Alcander, whom he took inside. He did him no harm, however, and did not even tell him off, but dismissed his usual servants and attendants and told Alcander to attend to him instead. And because Alcander was a man of honour, he

carried out his orders in silence. As he lived with Lycurgus and shared
his life, he came to observe his self-possession and high-mindedness,
his ascetic lifestyle, and his inexhaustible capacity for hard work, and
he became extremely attached to him. He used to tell his friends and
acquaintances that Lycurgus was not dour or surly, but was uniquely
gentle and even-tempered with others. So this was Alcander's punishment, and the penalty he had to undergo was to change from being
an insubordinate, badly behaved young man to a very well-mannered
and responsible adult.

In memory of his injury Lycurgus had a sanctuary of Athena built,
under the name Athena Optilletis, because the local Dorian word for
eyes is *optilloi*. But some writers (including Dioscorides, who wrote
a monograph on the Laconian constitution) say that although Lycurgus
was struck in the eye, he did not lose his sight in that eye, and had
the sanctuary built for Athena in gratitude for his recovery. Be that
as it may, after this accident the Spartiates abandoned the practice of
carrying sticks when attending the assembly.

[12] The Cretan word for these common messes is *andreia* or men's
quarters, but the Lacedaemonians call them *phiditia*, either because
they promote friendship (*philia*) and loyalty, with a 'd' in place of
the 'l', or because they train men in frugality and thrift (*pheidō*).
However, it is also possible, as some claim, that the first letter has
been added from elsewhere, and that they were originally named *editia*
after the words for 'diet' (*diaita*) and 'eating' (*edōdē*).*

They used to meet in groups of fifteen, give or take a little either
way. Each member of the group would bring per month a medimnus of ground barley, eight choes of wine, five minas of cheese, two
and a half minas of figs, and also a very small sum of money for the
purchase of savouries.* Apart from this, if anyone had made a
sacrifice of first fruits or had been out hunting, he sent a portion to
his mess; for eating at home was permitted if one had made a
sacrifice or got back late from hunting, even though everyone else had
to be at the mess. This custom of eating together was strictly
observed for a long time. At any rate, when King Agis returned from
his campaigns after his defeat of the Athenians, he wanted to eat with
his wife and he asked for his portions to be sent to him at home, but
the polemarchs refused to do so. He was so angry that the next day
he refused to carry out the obligatory sacrifices, and the polemarchs
fined him.*

Male children also used to go to these common messes: it was as if they were attending schools of discipline. They used to listen to political discussions and watch entertainments suitable for free men, and they themselves were taught to entertain others and tell jokes without descending to vulgarity, and to be teased without getting annoyed. (This is another thing that is generally held to be a particular feature of Laconian character: the ability to take a joke.) If someone found a joke intolerable, he was allowed to protest to the person making it, who then stopped.

As any of its members entered the mess, the oldest member indicated the doors and said, 'Not a word is to reach the outside world through these.' Apparently, anyone who wanted to join a mess was assessed in the following way. Each member of the mess would take a piece of bread in his hand and without saying a word would toss it, like a voting pebble, into a basket carried by a slave on his head. Anyone supporting the candidate's entry threw the bread in just as it was, while anyone who wanted to exclude the candidate would first squeeze the bread hard in his hand. A squashed piece of bread means the same as a holed ballot.* If they find even one squashed piece of bread in the basket, the candidate is refused entry, since they want everyone to be happy with everyone else's company. In their terms, a rejected candidate has been *kaddished*—a word deriving from the name of the basket into which the pieces of bread are thrown, which is *kaddikhos*.

The savoury dish they rate most highly is their famous black broth.* In fact, the older men refuse even a morsel of meat, and leave it all for the younger men, while for them a bowlful of the broth is a feast. There is a story that one of the kings of Pontus actually bought a Laconian cook because he wanted to try the broth, and when he found that he did not like the taste of it the cook said, 'My lord, it's only people who have washed in the Eurotas who should drink this broth.'* They drink only a moderate amount of wine and then leave without carrying a torch. They are not allowed to use a light on this or any other journey, so that they get used to making their way boldly and fearlessly in darkness and at night. So much for their system of common messes.

[13] Lycurgus did not commit his laws to writing; in fact, one of the so-called rhetras expressly forbids it. He was of the opinion that the principles which make the most substantial and important

contribution towards the prosperity and excellence of a state remain stable if they are implanted in the characters and training of the citizens, and thereby form a stronger bond than compulsion (which is what young men normally get out of their education) by including a steady inclination which recreates the intention of the legislator in each and every person. At the same time, minor business contracts, where the details change from occasion to occasion according to the requirements of the particular case, were best left unrestricted by written constraints and unchangeable conventions, so that they could have clauses added or deleted as the occasion would demand and as educated men would decide. In short, from start to finish he made all his legislation depend on education, and that is why, as I have already mentioned, one of his rhetras prohibited the use of written laws.

Then again, there was another rhetra against extravagance, stating that in house-building only an axe should be used to make the roof, and that a saw and no other tool was to be used in making the doors. The point later expressed by Epaminondas* who, on taking his place at his own table, is supposed to have said, 'A meal like this does not promote treachery,' was first appreciated by Lycurgus: a house like that does not promote luxury and extravagance, and there is no one vulgar or stupid enough to bring into a simple, everyday house silver-footed couches, purple-dyed covers, golden cups, and all the extravagance that goes with such things. His couch is bound to be consistent and compatible with his house, his clothing with his couch, and all the rest of his provisions and furniture with his clothing. Once the elder Leotychidas* was dining in Corinth, and when he saw the expensively panelled ceiling of the house he asked his host, because of what he had become accustomed to at home, whether trees grew square in Corinth.

There are accounts of a third rhetra issued by Lycurgus which forbade repeated campaigns against the same enemy, in order to avoid them getting used to defending themselves and so becoming expert fighters. Later, this became a particular complaint they brought against King Agesilaus: they said his constant invasions and frequent campaigns against Boeotia had made them a match for the Lacedaemonians. This is why when Antalcidas saw him wounded he said, 'What an excellent way the Thebans have found to pay you for the lessons you gave them when they had neither the inclination nor the expertise to fight!'*

Anyway, they called these decrees of his 'rhetras' because they regarded them as oracular utterances brought to Sparta from the god.*

[14] He thought that there was no field more important or worth-while for the legislator than education, so he began to tackle the topic from a remote point, with a review, right at the start of his legisla-tion, of the regulations concerning marriage and childbirth. Aristotle was wrong to say that Lycurgus gave up on his attempt to restrain women when he found that he was unable to control the consider-able freedom and influence they had gained as a result of their hus-bands' frequent periods of military service, when the men had no choice but to leave the women in charge, with the result that they used to defer to them to an unsuitable extent and gave them the title of Mistress.* In actual fact, Lycurgus made all the provisions he could for women. He instigated a tough regime of physical exercise for unmarried women, involving running, wrestling, discus, and javelin, so that when the time came for embryos to take root in their wombs they would gain a healthy start in healthy bodies and develop well, while the women themselves would have the strength to endure child-birth and would cope well and easily with the trials of labour. He removed their physical frailty, stopped them spending all their time indoors, and in general got rid of their femininity; he made girls just as used as boys to parading naked,* and to dancing and singing at certain festivals, with young men present as spectators. There was even an opportunity for the girls to taunt the young men one by one and helpfully criticize their errors, or alternatively to list in songs they had composed the praiseworthy achievements of those who deserved such eulogies. All this used to fill the young men with ambition and rivalry, because anyone who was praised for his manly qualities and acquired a favourable reputation among the young women left feel-ing proud that he had won their praise, while their light-hearted taunts stung just as much as serious rebukes, since the kings and the elders came to attend the spectacle along with all their fellow citizens.

There was nothing shameful in the young women's nakedness— never a trace of lewdness, but only modesty. On the contrary, nudity accustomed them to simplicity and made them admire physical fitness. It also gave women a taste for a positive kind of pride, since excellence and ambition were just as much for them as for men. As a result women learnt to speak and think as we are told Gorgo the wife of Leonidas did.* When some woman—a foreigner, apparently

—said to her, 'You Laconian women are the only ones who control your men', she replied, 'That's because we're the only ones who give birth to men.'

[15] These practices—I mean having young women join in the parades, shed their clothes, and take part in athletic competitions, all with young men looking on—also encouraged marriage, because the young men were drawn by, as Plato* puts it, sexual rather than logical necessity. Moreover, Lycurgus also imposed a certain loss of privilege on unmarried men, who were not allowed to watch the Festival of Unarmed Dancing,* and who by governmental edict had to walk naked around the perimeter of the city square in winter, while singing a song composed to fit their circumstances, about how this punishment of theirs was fair because they had disobeyed the laws. They were also not to be shown the respectful attention which their elders usually received from young men, which explains why no one found fault with the remark made to Dercyllidas:* despite his distinguished career as a military commander, once when he came into the theatre a younger man refused to give up his seat for him, and said, 'No, because you have no son to give up his seat for me one day.'

Their marriage ceremony involved the forcible abduction of the woman, who would not be a child, too young for marriage, but a woman in her prime, ripe and ready for it. The abducted woman was then handed over to the so-called bridesmaid, who would cut her hair very short, dress her in a man's clothes and shoes, and leave her lying alone on a straw mattress without any light to see by. The groom, who was not drunk or otherwise rendered impotent, but was as sober as usual, first dined in his *phidition* and then slipped into the room, undid the woman's belt, picked her up, and carried her over to the bed. He spent only a short time with her before leaving quietly, and going to the same sleeping-quarters he had been sharing before with the other young men. This pattern continued in the future: he would spend the day with the men of his age-group, and take his rest with them as well, but he would visit his wife secretly, taking every precaution out of embarrassment and fear of being seen by anyone in the house. Meanwhile his wife would be devising plans and helping to find opportunities for them to meet without anyone else knowing about it. They went on behaving like this for quite a long while; in fact, in some cases there were children born before the men saw their own wives by the light of day. In the first place, this manner of meeting provided training in self-control and restraint; secondly, it brought the couple together for sex when they were physically fertile and always fresh and ready for love, rather than being sated and jaded from unrestricted sexual intercourse, so that every time they parted a feeling remained in each of them which would act as a stimulus for desire and affection.

Despite making marriage such a chaste and decorous affair, Lycurgus also banished the vain, womanish feeling of jealousy by making it acceptable to share the business of procreating children with others of sufficient excellence, provided there remained no place for any kind of outrageous or disorderly behaviour within the marriage. In other words, the idea that this is something that cannot be shared and held in common, and the use of murder and warfare to back up such an idea, struck Lycurgus as absurd. Suppose an older man with a young wife liked and approved of a young man of nobility and virtue: he could introduce him to her and then, once the younger man had impregnated his wife with his noble seed, he could adopt the child as his own. Or again, suppose a man of high principles admired a woman who was married to someone else for her modesty and fine children: he could prevail upon her husband to let him sleep with her, so that he could sow his seed in rich and fertile soil, so to speak, and produce excellent children who would be blood relatives of others just as fine.*

The point is, first, that to Lycurgus' way of thinking children did not belong to their fathers, but to the state in common; and so he wanted the citizens of the state to come from the best stock, not just any random parents. In the second place, he thought there was a great deal of stupidity and hypocrisy contained in others' legislation on these matters, when people arranged for their bitches and mares to be mounted by the best males by prevailing upon their owners in the name of friendship or by paying them, but kept their wives guarded under lock and key, claiming that they and they alone had the right to have children by them, whether they, the husbands, were idiots or dotards or invalids. This, as far as Lycurgus was concerned, was to ignore the fact that children born from bad parents are bad above all for those who have them and bring them up, and that on the contrary it is children who are lucky enough to have good parents who are good for those who have them and bring them up. This conduct of theirs was originally both natural and in the best interests of the state, and was so far removed from the promiscuity which was later attributed to their womenfolk that adultery was completely unknown there. In fact, something said by Geradas, a Spartiate from the very distant past, has been preserved. He was once asked by a visitor how they punished adulterers in Sparta. 'My friend,' he said, 'we don't have adulterers.' 'But suppose there were one,' the visitor persisted. Geradas said, 'His fine would be a bull large enough to bend over Mount Taygetus and drink from the Eurotas.' The man was astonished and said, 'How could there ever be a bull that big?' Geradas laughed and said, 'How could there ever be an adulterer in Sparta?'* So much for what has been recorded about Lycurgus' provisions for marriage.

[16] It was not up to the father whether or not the child was to be brought up. Instead, the child was taken to a place called a *leskhē*, or 'assembly place', where a session of the eldest men of his tribe was convened.* They examined the baby and if it was sturdy and strong they told the father to bring it up, and assigned it one of the 9,000 plots of land; if it was flawed and deformed, however, they sent it to the place called *Apothetai*, the 'place of exposure', a rugged spot near Mount Taygetus, on the assumption that death was preferable for both the child and the state given that from the moment of its birth it had been inadequately endowed with health and strength. The reason, then, why in Sparta the women used to wash babies in wine rather than water was as a kind of test of their constitution. For washing a baby which is liable to seizures and illness in undiluted wine apparently induces a fit and putrefaction of the flesh, whereas the condition of a healthy child is toughened and improved.

Nurses there had special responsibilities and skills. They trained the babies to use their limbs and bodies freely by dispensing with swaddling clothes, and also not to be fussy and fastidious about their food, not to be scared of the dark or frightened of being left alone, and never to demean themselves with tantrums or tears. This is why people from abroad sometimes used to buy Laconian nurses for their children; in fact, Amycla, the nurse of Alcibiades of Athens, is said to have been a Laconian woman.*

However, as Plato records,* Pericles put Alcibiades in the care of a tutor called Zopyrus, who was no more than an ordinary slave, whereas Lycurgus refused to put the sons of Spartiates under tutors who were slaves bought and owned, or at best hired assistants. At the same time, however, he did not allow people to decide on their own how to bring up and educate their sons: as soon as the children were seven years old, Lycurgus personally took them all in hand and enrolled them in various 'herds',* so that they became used to playing together and learning together under the same rules and régime. The boy who showed the greatest intelligence and the most fighting spirit was put in charge of his herd, and the rest kept their eyes on him, listened to his orders, and endured his punishments, so that their education was a training in obedience. They were watched at play by older men who, as the occasion arose, often used to get them to fight and compete with one another, which was no idle activity, but enabled them to assess how courageous each boy was and whether or not he was likely to avoid confrontation.

The boys learnt to read and write as much as they would need to get by, while all the rest of their education was geared towards inculcating ready obedience, the capacity to endure hard work, and the ability to win in battle. That is why, as they grew older, their training was stepped up: their hair was cut short and they became accustomed to go about barefoot and usually to play without any clothes on. At the age of twelve they stopped wearing tunics and were given one cloak a year. Their skin was weathered, their bodies unfamiliar with bathing and oiling, which were comforts they experienced only a few times a year. They slept along with others from their unit or herd on straw mattresses they packed themselves with the tips of reeds growing alongside the Eurotas which they broke off with their bare hands, not with knives. In winter they used to add some wolfshape, as it is called, to the make-up of the straw mattresses they lay on, since this plant is supposed to be have warming properties.*

[17] By the time they were this old the boys used to be accompanied as they went about by lovers from among the young men of good families. The older men also used to pay them more attention, visiting the wrestling-grounds and hanging around while they fought and teased one another. Nor was it the case that the older men had nothing to do there: in a sense they all regarded all the boys as their sons, pupils, and wards, which meant that there was never a time or a place when the boys would be without someone to criticize and correct their mistakes.

Moreover, there was also a post of 'boy-herder'* which was filled by one of the outstanding men of the city, and the boys of each herd themselves appointed the most sensible and warlike of the eirens, as they are known, to be in charge of them—an 'eiren' being someone in the year after childhood, while the oldest of the boys are called 'near-eirens'.* So this eiren, aged twenty, takes command of those assigned to serve under him in their battles, and has them attend to him indoors at mealtimes. He tells the sturdy boys to fetch wood and the smaller ones vegetables—and they go and get the things by stealing them. Some of them go to people's gardens, while others show a fine turn of cunning and caution and sneak into the men's common messes. Any boy who is caught is given a thorough thrashing for turning out to be a careless and incompetent thief. They also steal any food they can, and so learn the art of getting past sleeping people and careless guards. A boy goes hungry, as well as being beaten, if he is caught, because their meals are never generous, so that they learn to rely on themselves to ward off hunger by their own bravery and cunning.*

While this is the main purpose of their scanty rations, a secondary one, according to the Lacedaemonians, is to help the boys' physical development. For when the vital breath is unimpeded and unhindered—that is, when it is not forced down into the depths and sides of the body by the bulk of a large quantity of food, but rather follows the upward course dictated by its lightness—it contributes towards height, because the body can then develop straightforwardly and easily. A light diet is also held to make people good-looking, since spare, lean frames allow the features to be distinct, whereas the weight of fat, over-fed bodies tells against any such definition. This no doubt also explains why women who purge themselves during pregnancy produce babies which are lean, but well formed and nicely shaped, since the material the women provide is light enough to be dominated by the shaping agent.* But the cause which produces this result still needs further investigation.

[18] How seriously the boys go about their thieving is shown by the story that when one of them had a fox cub he had stolen hidden under his cloak, rather than be found out he put up with it fatally lacerating his guts with its claws and teeth.* Even this story seems perfectly plausible, given that we have seen large numbers of the Lacedaemonian youths of today dying under the lash at the altar of Artemis Orthia.*

Once the eiren had eaten, he would lie back on his couch and get one of the boys to sing songs, while he asked another one a question which needed a careful reply. He might ask him, for instance, which man was outstanding, or what he made of something a particular person had done. This got the boys from a very early age in the habit of assessing excellence and concerning themselves with their fellow citizens' affairs, since the inability to answer when asked who in Sparta was a good man, or who had a poor reputation, was taken to be the sign of a dull mind which lacked the desire to win recognition. The answer also had to be accompanied by a demonstration of its validity—a demonstration reduced to a brief and succinct argument. The punishment for a wrong answer was a bite on the thumb from the eiren, who would also often punish the boys under the supervision of some elders and magistrates, so that they could see whether or not his punishments were reasonable and appropriate. Not that he was stopped while he was actually taking disciplinary action, but after the boys had left he would be reprimanded if his punishments were unnecessarily severe or, on the other hand, too lenient and indulgent.

Whatever reputation the boys acquired, for good or ill, was shared by their lovers. In fact we hear that once when a boy degraded himself by crying out during a battle his lover was fined by the magistrates. Although passionate love was so highly thought of in Sparta that even noble and respectable women used to have love-affairs with unmarried girls, yet rivalry in love was unknown; instead, if two men were in love with the same boy, they would let this forge a bond of friendship between them and from then on would share their efforts to improve their beloved.*

[19] The boys were also taught how to speak in a way which was brusque but elegant, and which contained a great deal of food for thought in a few words. Lycurgus may have made large amounts of the iron coinage worth little, as I have already explained, but he did the opposite with the coinage of speech: a simple short sentence had to convey a great deal of subtle meaning. He turned out boys with the ability, trained by long periods of silence, of giving pointed, honed responses. The seed of a man who exercises no self-restraint in his sexual life is usually sterile and unproductive; by the same token, lack of self-restraint in talking makes what one says vain and pointless. Once, when some Athenian or other was joking about how short Laconian swords were and remarked how easily stage conjurers swallowed them, King Agis replied, 'But we certainly reach our enemies with them.'* And I add that in my opinion the Laconian style may seem terse, but it certainly gets to the point and touches the minds of the listeners.

In fact, as far as we can tell from his recorded sayings, Lycurgus himself seems to have been a man of few but pointed words. For example, there is his *bon mot* about government, spoken in response to someone who was wanting to make the state a democracy: 'Only after you've made your home a democracy,' he said. Then again, when someone asked him why the sacrifices he arranged were so small and inexpensive, he said, 'So that we never have to stop paying our respects to the gods.' Or again, we hear that he allowed his fellow citizens to take part only in those sports which did not involve them raising a hand.*† Similar responses also occur in extant letters of his to his fellow citizens: 'How should we repel a hostile invasion?' 'By staying poor and by each man among you having no desire to be greater than anyone else.' And on the subject of defensive walls he said, 'Brave men, not bricks, constitute a city's fortifications.' However, it is not easy to know whether to believe or disbelieve in the authenticity of these letters and others like them.*

[20] Here are some apophthegms which illustrate Spartan aversion to longwindedness. When someone chose a bad moment to raise a not unimportant matter with King Leonidas* he said, 'You're right, my friend, but the time is wrong.' When Charilaus, Lycurgus' nephew, was asked about the small number of laws Lycurgus had made, he said that people of few words need few laws. When some people were criticizing the sophist Hecataeus for having kept silent at the mess to which he had been invited, Archidamidas said, 'People who know how to speak also know when to speak.'*

Here are some examples of the kinds of sayings I described earlier as brusque but not without elegance. Once an objectionable fellow hammered Demaratus* with a whole lot of inopportune questions, including 'Who is the best of the Spartiates?'—to which Demaratus replied, 'The one who is least like you.' When some people were praising the Eleans for their excellent and fair conduct of the Olympian Games, Agis* said, 'What's so great about the Eleans behaving fairly for one day every four years?' When a visitor from abroad was letting Theopompus* see how much he liked Laconia, and was saying that in his home town he was known for his loyalty to Laconia, Theopompus said, 'It would be better if you were known for your loyalty to your own state, my friend.' On hearing an Athenian orator describe the Lacedaemonians as men of no learning, Pleistonax* the son of Pausanias said, 'You're right: we're the only Greeks who've learnt nothing bad from you.' When someone asked Archidamidas how many Spartiates there were, he replied, 'Enough to keep us safe from bad men, my friend.'

Lacedaemonian ways can even be judged by their light-hearted quips, since it was never their way to waste words or to say anything which did not somehow contain a thought that would repay further reflection. So when one of them was invited to listen to a man imitating a nightingale he said, 'I've heard the real thing.' Then again, once a Spartan read the following epitaph:

Bronze-clad Ares* took these men while they were involved in an attempt
To extinguish the flames of tyranny. They died by the gates of Selinous.

'They deserved to die,' he commented. 'They should have let tyranny burn itself out completely.' A young man was once promised some cocks that would give their lives fighting: 'No, thank you,' he said. 'Give me some that will *take* lives fighting.' At the sight of some men sitting on stools to relieve themselves, another Spartan remarked, 'I hope I never find myself sitting where I can't get up and offer my place to someone older than me.'

These apophthegms are so typical that it is not odd for people to claim, as they sometimes do, that devotion to the intellect is more definitive of Laconian character than devotion to exercise.*

[21] They were just as interested in studying poetry and song as they were in achieving purity and perfection in the spoken word. In fact, their songs were designed as stimulants to arouse their spirits and motivate them to wholehearted, effective action. They were plain and unpretentious in style, and sung of impressive, morally sound achievements. The usual themes were praise of those who had died for Sparta, who were counted happy; condemnation of cowards,* dwelling on the wretched, miserable lives they lived; and either promises of future bravery or the proud recounting of past bravery, whichever was appropriate to the singers' ages. It is quite instructive to give an example of a song belonging to this latter category, by way of illustration. At their festivals, three choruses were formed, one from each age-group, and first the chorus of old men would sing, 'We once were valiant young men.' Next the chorus of men in their prime would take up the theme with 'But it's our turn now: please try us out.' And finally the chorus of boys would sing, 'But we shall prove mightier by far.'

Anyone who has made a study of Laconian poetry, some examples of which have survived down to the present day, and has familiarized himself with the marching rhythms they used, to the accompaniment of the pipes, as they advanced on the enemy,* will agree with Terpander and Pindar when they associate music and courage. One of Terpander's poems about the Lacedaemonians contains the following lines:

> Where thrives the young men's warlike spirit and the clear-voiced
>   Muse;
> Where thrives Justice on the spacious streets of the city.

And Pindar says:

> Where flourish unsurpassed the councils of elders,
> The warlike endeavours of young men,
> Choruses, the Muse and celebration.

As far as these two poets were concerned, the Lacedaemonians were the most cultured* as well as the most warlike people. As the Laconian poet said:

> Good playing of the lyre counterbalances iron weaponry.

Before engaging an enemy, in fact, the king used to sacrifice to the Muses, presumably to remind his men of their upbringing and the choices they had made, in order to get them ready to risk their lives and to perform memorable deeds of valour in battle.

[22] Another thing they used to do in wartime is relax the most rigid aspects of the young men's training: they used to let them make their hair attractive and decorate their weaponry and clothing, and they enjoyed the sight of these horses, so to speak, prancing and whinnying in eagerness for the fray. That is why as soon as they came of age they let their hair grow long, and they used to look after it especially in times of danger, making sure that they kept it sleek and well combed,* because they remembered something Lycurgus had said about long hair—that it increases the attractiveness of handsome men and the fearsomeness of ugly men. They also took less arduous exercise while out on campaign, and in general the way of life the young men were required to follow was not as curtailed by rules and regulations as usual, which meant that they were the only people in the world for whom warfare was more restful than their preparations for it.

When they were actually drawn up in their phalanx* within sight of the enemy the king would sacrifice the traditional she-goat, give the command for everyone to put on their garlands, and tell the pipe-players to play the Ode to Castor,* while he would strike up a march-ing paean. The resulting spectacle was both impressive and terrifying, as the men advanced in time with the pipes in a solid, unbroken phalanx, suffering from no inner perturbation, but marching up to face danger in a composed and cheerful manner to the sound of the music. It is reasonable to expect that men in this frame of mind will feel neither fear nor excessive rage, but rather a steady self-assurance sustained by hope, courage and the belief that the gods are on their side.

The king's escort, as he advanced against the enemy, consisted of men who had been victorious in athletic competitions where the prize was a garland.* There is a story that once a Spartan was offered a great deal of money in the Olympic Games, but turned it down; he overcame his opponent in the wrestling, but it was an extremely tough contest, and afterwards he was asked what he had gained from his victory. He smiled and said, 'The right to a place in the unit defend-ing the king in battles against our enemies.'

If they succeeded in defeating and routing enemy troops, they chased them until their victory had been made secure by their opponents' flight, but then turned back, because as far as they were concerned hacking and slaughtering men who had given up and withdrawn was degrading and inappropriate for any Greek. As well as being honourable and noble behaviour, this also had a practical side: once their oppon-ents realized that Lacedaemonians killed people who resisted them, but spared those who surrendered, they began to regard flight as more expedient than standing their ground.*

[23] The sophist Hippias says that Lycurgus himself was a par-ticularly fine strategist and a veteran of many campaigns, and Philo-stephanus also attributes to him the division of the cavalry into *oulamoi*. On Lycurgus' system, an *oulamos* was a body of fifty horsemen drawn up in a square formation. But according to Demetrius of Phalerum Lycurgus undertook no military activities at all, since it was a time of peace when he established his constitution. And the idea of an Olympic truce also seems to indicate a man of even temper and a peaceful disposition. However, there is also the story, recorded by Hermippus on the authority of some writers, that at first Lycurgus had no interest in Iphitus and was not his partner in the scheme

from the start, but happened to be there on a visit from Sparta on some other business and went to watch the games. He heard what sounded like a man's voice behind him, telling him off and expressing surprise at his failure to encourage his fellow citizens to join in the festival. He turned around, but could see no one there who could have spoken to him, and so came to the conclusion that the voice was divine. He therefore teamed up with Iphitus and helped him organize the festival on a more magnificent scale and establish it on a securer basis.

[24] Spartan education did not end when they reached adulthood, in the sense that no one was allowed to live just as he pleased. Life in the city was like life in a military camp: people lived in a prescribed way and spent their time on communal concerns, because it never occurred to them to regard themselves as autonomous rather than as subject to their country. And so, unless they had been given some other job to do, they would always be found supervising the boys and teaching them something useful, or learning themselves from their elders. The point is that one particular benefit and blessing which Lycurgus arranged for the citizens of Sparta was an enormous amount of leisure; he did not allow them to become involved in any manual work at all, and there was not the slightest need for them to engage in business and undertake the laborious and troublesome task of accumulating money, because wealth was no longer something to be admired and respected. The helots worked the land for them and paid them in tribute the amounts mentioned earlier.* Once a Spartan was abroad in Athens when the lawcourts were in session there, and he heard that someone who had been fined for not working* was going around in a state of depression with a retinue of sympathetic friends sharing his sorrow and grief—but the Spartan asked his companions to point out to him the man who had been found guilty of freedom. This shows how servile they considered artisanship and money-making to be. Lawsuits, of course, vanished along with coinage, since greed and want had been banished from their midst, and were replaced by equality in sufficiency and the comforts of a simple lifestyle. Normally, all their time was spent on choral festivals, celebrations, feasts, hunting expeditions, exercises, and assemblies, unless they happened to be out on campaign.*

[25] Men under the age of thirty never went to the city square, but had all their domestic needs met by their relatives and lovers.

Moreover, it was considered demeaning for older men to be seen constantly engaged in these matters, rather than spending most of the
day exercising and at their 'assembly places', as they called them.*
For when they came together at these assembly places they passed
the time together in a respectable fashion. No mention was made
of anything concerned with money-making or commercial matters;
instead, the main business of the time they spent there was to praise
what was honourable and condemn what was disgraceful, but to do
so in an easy and jocular manner which lightly bore the person under
scrutiny to a point of castigation and reproof.* In fact, not even
Lycurgus himself was unremittingly serious: it was he, according to
Sosibius, who set up the statuette of Laughter and made the telling
of appropriate jokes a feature of Spartan recreations such as symposia,
as a way of sweetening the rigours of their lifestyle.

In short, as a result of Lycurgus' reforms, his fellow citizens lost
both the will and the ability to live as individuals. Instead, they became
accustomed, bee-like, to always being organic parts of the life of the
community, to swarm around their leader in a state of near ecstasy
induced by their eager desire for recognition, and to commit themselves wholly to their country. This intention can be seen in some of
their remarks too. For instance, when Pedaritus failed to be chosen
to join the ranks of the Three Hundred,* he left with a broad grin
on his face, as if to show how glad he was that the state had three
hundred men better than him. When Polystratidas* and the other
members of a diplomatic delegation to the Persian king's commanders were asked whether they were there on a private or public mission, he replied: 'A public one if we succeed; a private one if we fail.'
Once some people from Amphipolis came to Lacedaemon and paid
Argileonis, the mother of Brasidas, a visit. She asked whether Brasidas
had died well, without letting Sparta down. They began to lavish
praises on the man, and said that there was no one to compare
with him in Sparta. 'Don't say that, my friends,' she said. 'For all
Brasidas' admirable qualities, there are many men better than him
in Sparta.'*

[26] At first, as already mentioned,* Lycurgus personally appointed
the elders from among those who had been his co-conspirators, but
later he arranged things so that the place of someone who died would
be filled by whichever man over the age of sixty was judged to be
of outstanding quality. No contest in the world was held to be as

important as this one, and none was as highly prized. This was not a test to find who could outrun or outwrestle his peers: the person chosen had to surpass his peers in virtue and sound sense, and his excellence would be rewarded by the possession, for the rest of his life, of what it is hardly any exaggeration to describe as absolute political power, since he would have the right to decide about all the most important aspects of his fellow citizens' lives, such as death and dishonour.

The selection was made as follows. The assembly met, and chosen men were shut up in a room near by, where they could neither see what was going on nor be seen, but could only hear the shouts of the assembled people, since as usual the contest would be decided by acclamation. The candidates were not introduced all at once; they came in one by one, in an order decided by lot, and walked in silence through the assembly. Now, the men shut up in the room had writing-tablets, and in each case they noted down the volume of the shouting without knowing the identity of the candidate, only that he was the first or second or third or whatever to be brought in front of the assembly. So they proclaimed whoever received the longest and loudest shouting the winner.* Crowned with a garland, the winner visited the sanctuaries of the gods one after another, followed by a crowd of young men applauding and praising him, and by a large number of women too, who would recount in song his excellent qualities and the blessings attending his life. On the way, each of his closest friends would serve him something to eat and say, 'With this table the state honours you.' Once he had completed his rounds, he went off to his mess, where everything was as usual except that he was served an extra portion of food, which he accepted and kept safe. His female relatives gathered by the doors of the *phidition* and after the meal he called for the one he regarded most highly and gave her the extra portion of food, saying that he was giving her the prize he had been given for his excellence. She was then congratulated and escorted home by the rest of the women.

[27] Lycurgus also made excellent arrangements for their funerals. In the first place, he banished all the superstitious beliefs surrounding death by lifting the prohibition on burying the dead within the city limits and on locating tombs near sanctuaries. This meant that young people grew up seeing things of this kind and became so familiar with them that they were not upset by the sights and did not fear

death or believe that it polluted those who touched a dead body or walked through a graveyard. In the second place, he made it illegal to bury anything with the corpse; all they used to do when they laid out the body was cover it with a red cloak and olive leaves. He also made it illegal to inscribe the name of the dead person on the tomb, unless it was a man who had died in war or a woman who had died in childbirth.* He limited the amount of time spent in mourning to eleven days; on the twelfth day they were to sacrifice to Demeter and give up their grief. In fact, Lycurgus left nothing unemployed, but put everything to work: he found a way to include in every essential task some feature that would lead people to strive for goodness or dislike badness. He created so many educational examples that no aspect of life in the city remained uncovered. As a result, since they were all† constantly coming across them and were surrounded by them in their formative years, they were inevitably shaped and moulded by the ideal of excellence.

This also explains why he did not let them leave Sparta and travel abroad freely, to acquire foreign habits and copy the ways of people who lacked culture and lived under different political systems. In fact, he even expelled the crowds of people who streamed into Sparta from abroad for no particular reason. Thucydides is wrong to suggest that he did this because he was afraid that they would copy his political system and learn some valuable moral lessons;* no, he was more afraid of the corrupting influence these foreigners might exert. Foreigners inevitably bring with them into a country foreign notions, novel ideas lead to novel choices, and these in turn are bound to cause the development of a number of feelings and inclinations which clash with the euphony, as it were, of the existing political system. So to Lycurgus' mind it was more important to protect the state from infection by pestilential customs than it was to keep people from abroad bringing disease in with them.

[28] Now, there is no trace in all this of the injustice or rapacity which some people have found in Lycurgus' laws. They accuse him of framing laws which were good at promoting courage, but defective when it came to justice. Conceivably, it was the existence in Lacedaemon of the so-called *krypteia*, or secret service—assuming that Aristotle* is right in saying that it was Lycurgus who set it up—that gave Plato* this opinion of the man and his constitution.

Here is how the *krypteia* worked. From time to time the young men's commanders would send those who gave them the impression of being the most intelligent out into the countryside—to different districts at different times—with nothing more than a dagger each and a bare minimum of supplies. By day the young men spread out and found remote spots where they could hide and rest, but at night they came down to the roads and murdered any helots they caught. They also often used to walk through the fields and kill the helots who were in the best shape and condition. Also in this context, Thucydides records in his *History of the Peloponnesian War* how once some helots who had distinguished themselves by their bravery were crowned by the Spartiates in token of their freedom and visited each of the sanctuaries of the gods in turn, but then a short while later every single one of them—more than 2,000 men—vanished, and neither straight away nor subsequently could anyone say precisely how they had met their deaths.* There is also the point Aristotle makes, that the first thing the ephors did on taking office was declare war on the helots, so that killing them would not pollute the killer.

There were other ways in which their treatment of the helots was harsh and brutal. For instance, they used to force them to drink large quantities of undiluted wine and then bring them into the common messes, to show the young men what it was like to be drunk. They also used to get them to make fools of themselves by performing degrading songs and dances, while denying them the right to perform any which were suited to free men. This puts in context the later story that during their invasion of Laconia the Thebans wanted the helots they captured to sing some compositions by Terpander, Alcman, and Spendon of Laconia, but the helots refused, on the grounds that their masters would not approve.* So the claim that there is no one more free than a free man in Lacedaemon, and no one more of a slave than a slave there, rests on sound observation of the difference between the two.

It is my view that this kind of harsh treatment of the helots was a later development among the Spartiates, starting particularly after the great earthquake, when, we hear, the helots and the Messenians seized the opportunity to attack, wrought terrible havoc throughout the countryside, and brought the city to the very brink of destruction.* I myself would be reluctant to attribute to Lycurgus a disgusting institution like the *krypteia*. I base this judgement of his character on his equability and fairness in other respects—an assessment which the god supported as well.*

[29] The time came when his most important measures had become ingrained in the Lacedaemonians' customs and he had nurtured his constitution enough, so that it was capable of supporting itself and seeing to its own preservation. Just as the god, according to Plato,* was enchanted by the birth of the world and its first movements, so now that his legislation was in operation and proceeding on its way Lycurgus found its elegance and grandeur deeply satisfying, and he wanted to leave it to posterity as immortal and unchanging, in so far as a mere human being could look ahead and achieve this. So he convened a general assembly and told the people that although basically things were running adequately enough to guarantee the material and moral welfare of the state, there was still something of critical importance to be done, but he would not tell them about it until he had consulted the god. He went on to say that they therefore had to abide by the existing laws, without making any changes or alterations, until he returned in person from Delphi, because then he would carry out the god's recommendations. They all agreed to this and told him to be on his way. Once he had exacted an oath from the kings and the elders, and then subsequently the rest of the citizen body, to the effect that they would abide by and keep to the existing constitution until his return, he left for Delphi.

On his arrival at the oracular shrine, he sacrificed to the god, and then asked whether the laws he had made were in fact good enough to guarantee the material and moral welfare of the state. The god replied that the legislative measures he had taken were good, and that by keeping to Lycurgus' constitution the state would continue to be held in the highest honour. Lycurgus had the oracle written down and sent to Sparta, but he himself sacrificed once more to the god and embraced his friends and his son. He had decided never to release his fellow citizens from their oath, but to kill himself there and then. He had reached an age when the choice between further life and putting an end to it may fairly be made, and his dependants seemed to be sufficiently prosperous and happy, so he starved himself to death.

He was of the opinion that even in death a statesman should benefit his state, that even the end of a statesman's life should not be vain, but should be classed as an effective act of virtue. After all the wonderful things he had achieved, he felt that for him personally his death would truly constitute the perfection of his happiness, and that for his fellow citizens he would bequeath his death to protect all the admirable benefits he had provided them with during his lifetime, since they had sworn to keep to his constitution until his return. Nor were his calculations misguided, because there was no state in Greece to match Sparta for lawfulness and fame for a very long time, since it adhered to Lycurgus' laws for five hundred years; for fourteen generations after him not one of the kings made any constitutional changes, until the time of Agis the son of Archidamus.* For the existence of the ephorate strengthened rather than weakened the constitution, and although it seemed to favour the common people, it actually increased the power of the aristocracy.

[30] It was during Agis' reign that money first poured into Sparta, and along with money greed and admiration of wealth assaulted the land. This was Lysander's fault: even though he was impervious to money himself, it was because he brought back gold and silver from the war, flouting Lycurgus' laws, that the country became infected with love of wealth and with luxury.* Previously, under Lycurgus' laws, Sparta had not so much a political constitution as the lifestyle of a trained and intelligent man. Or a better analogy might be how the poets describe Heracles in their stories as traversing the world with his lion skin and club, punishing lawless and savage tyrants. So, one might say, with no more than a single *skytale** and a thin cloak Sparta ruled Greece with the willing consent of its inhabitants, dissolving unjust power blocks and overthrowing tyrannies in various states, mediating in wars, putting an end to civil strife—and managing to do all this often without any military intervention at all, but by sending a solitary envoy. Just as on the appearance of their leader bees cluster round him in a neat and orderly array,* so everyone concerned would immediately carry out the commands of the Spartan envoy. All this shows that Sparta had lawfulness and justice to spare.

I fail to understand, then, how some people can say that Lacedaemonians made good subjects but bad rulers, and can cite with approval the remark of King Theopompus, who replied, when someone was claiming that that the security of Sparta was due to the leadership of its kings, 'No, it's due to the obedience of its citizens.' After all, people refuse to obey those who are incapable of command; obedience is a lesson taught by a commander, because it takes the right sort of leader to inculcate the right sort of compliance. Just as the object of horsemanship is to produce an even-tempered, tractable horse, so the function of kingship is to instil obedience in men. In fact, what the Lacedaemonians instilled in other Greeks was not so much obedience as a positive desire to be commanded and ruled by them. People tended not to ask the Lacedaemonians to send them ships or money or hoplites, but a single Spartiate leader, and when they got him they treated him with the kind of respect and awe that Gylippus received from the Sicilians, Brasidas from the Chalcidians, and Lysander, Callicratidas, and Agesilaus from all the Greeks living in Asia.* They called them 'harmosts' or imposers of order and discipline on people and rulers everywhere, and they regarded the Spartiate city as a whole as a tutor or teacher of respectable living and stable government. This seems to be the point of Stratonicus' joke,* when he proposed a mock law to the effect that the Athenians should conduct mysteries and processions, the Eleans should be responsible for athletic contests, because that is what they do best, and the Lacedaemonians should be flogged for any mistakes the Athenians and Eleans might make! This may have been no more than a piece of fun, but all the same, when faced with Theban pride after the battle of Leuctra, Antisthenes the Socratic remarked that they were behaving just like children prancing about in delight at having beaten up their tutor.*

[31] However, Lycurgus' main purpose at the time was not to leave his city in command of a huge numbers of places. He thought that happiness in the life of a whole city was due to the same factors as in the life of a single individual, namely virtue and internal unanimity,* and so the point of all his arrangements and institutions had been to enable the Lacedaemonians to be free, autonomous, and self-disciplined for as long as possible. This political scheme has been taken over by everyone who has come to be admired for attempting to address these issues, including Plato, Diogenes, and Zeno, even though they left to posterity nothing but words and ideas.* Lycurgus, however, left no mere words and ideas, but created an actual and unrivalled system of government. To those who doubt the existence of the condition said to be attained by the wise man, he showed that a whole state could be devoted to wisdom, and so it is not surprising that he is the best known Greek statesman there has ever been. That is why Aristotle says that in Lacedaemon Lycurgus has received less recognition than he should, despite the fact that he has had the highest honours conferred upon him, since he has a sanctuary there, and they

offer him sacrifices once a year as if he were a god. There is even a story that after his body had been brought home a thunderbolt struck his tomb, and this is something which happened to hardly any other eminent person later except Euripides, who died and was buried near Arethusa in Macedonia. So Euripides' admirers count it as an important piece of evidence supporting their opinion of the man that what happened to him after his death had previously happened only to a person who was dearly loved by the gods and lived a life of unsurpassed piety.

Some say that Lycurgus died in Cirrha, but Apollothemis says that he was taken to Elis and died there, while Timaeus and Aristoxenus claim that he ended his days in Crete.* Aristoxenus adds that the Cretans show people his tomb beside the Foreigners' Road in Pergamia. We hear that he left a single son, Antiorus,* who died childless, at which point Lycurgus' family became extinct. His friends and relatives, however, instituted a kind of school which met for many years, and called the days when they met 'Lycurgan days'. Aristocrates the son of Hipparchus says that after Lycurgus had died in Crete his guest-friends there burnt his body and, in accordance with his own wishes, scattered the ashes on the sea, to ensure that his remains were never taken back to Lacedaemon, and prevent the Lacedaemonians altering his constitution on the grounds that he had returned and therefore their oaths were null and void. This is all I have to say about Lycurgus.*

SOLON

INTRODUCTION

Lawgiver, sage, poet: at the beginning of Athenian history Solon combines in one person intelligence, practicality, and persuasion. Solon held the office of archon and enacted his reform of the Athenian constitution in 594 BC. Despite the absence of contemporary historical accounts, Plutarch is able to blend four disparate sources into an imaginative and thought-provoking Life.

Plutarch's (and our) only contemporary written sources were Solon's poems, collected by scholars long after his death, and the preserved text of his laws. Though the poems are known to us only in fragments, some found only in this Life,[1] Plutarch had access to many complete poems—he notes, for example (8), that the Salamis poem ran to one hundred lines, although he only quotes the first two—and incorporates passages from them into his portrait. In his poems, Solon presented the moral justification for his reforms and describes the tension between aristocratic landowners and impoverished farmers: 'I stood protecting rich and poor with my stout shield | And saw that neither side prevailed unjustly'(18). But the poems contain little specific on his reform: for this Plutarch went to the inscribed law code of Solon, still partially preserved in his own day at Athens, and the subject of learned commentaries. This code was officially revised at the end of the fifth century, and there is the possibility that some provisions ascribed to Solon in fact reflect later changes. Nevertheless, Plutarch cites a number of laws known from no other source, and overall gives us the most complete surviving account of Solon's legislation (15–25).[2]

After the recovery in 1890 from the sands of Egypt of the *Constitution of the Athenians*, written by Aristotle or close associates in his school, it became apparent that Plutarch had also relied heavily on the account of

---

[1] Collected in M. L. West (ed.), *Iambi et Elegi Graeci ante Alexandrum cantati*, 2nd edn. (Oxford: Clarendon Press, 1992), 139–65. In the notes, quotations are identified by the number in this edition. All Solon's poems are translated in *Elegy and Iambus*, ed. J. M. Edmonds (Cambridge, Mass.: Harvard University Press, and London: Heinemann, 1931); selected poems are translated in Andrew M. Miller, *Greek Lyric: An Anthology in Translation* (Indianapolis and Cambridge: Hackett, 1996), 64–76.

[2] The fragments of Solon's laws are collected by E. Ruschenbusch, *Solonos nomoi. Die Fragmente des solonischen Gesetzeswerkes mit einer Text- und Überlieferungsgeschichte*, *Historia* Einzelschrift 9, 2nd edn. (Wiesbaden: Steiner, 1983).

Solon's reforms given there.[3] This work, one of a series treating some 150 Greek city-states, offered a brief history of the stages of constitutional development at Athens: Solon's reforms occupy cc. 5–12, with sections before and after treating the political situation preceding and following the reforms. Like Plutarch, Aristotle incorporated citations of Solon's poems, and it is of some interest to observe the different ways in which the two writers exploit this common source. The other major source for Plutarch was the fifth-century historian Herodotus, whose famous (and largely fictional) account of the meeting of Solon with Croesus of Lydia lies behind his own account of their meeting in cc. 27–8.

For the modern historian, Solon's reforms addressed several problems which came to a head at the end of the seventh century. First, control of the land was in the hands of a restricted aristocracy. Whatever the nature of the *hektēmoros* system of tenant farming, from the poems it appears that large numbers of farmers were deeply in debt and liable even to being enslaved: Solon's *seisachtheia* (relief of debts) in large part resolved this problem. Second, by making eligibilty to office dependent on wealth and not birth, Solon broke the political control of the landed aristocracy, although they would still dominate politics for the next 150 years. The military importance of hoplite warriors and the economic power of the new wealth held by non-aristocratic landowners and merchants now could find political expression. Finally, by establishing an elected council alongside the Areopagus council and by giving the right of appeal to citizen courts, Solon laid the foundations for the Cleisthenic and Periclean democracies which would follow.

This 'historian's view' is fleshed out in the life with Plutarch's imaginative reconstruction of events in Solon's life from the poems and other material: Solon's early erotic relation with Pisistratus, his travels as a merchant, his contact with other sages, his role in annexing (or recovering) Salamis. An ardent admirer of Plato, Plutarch includes Plato's story that Solon brought back from Egypt the account of the ancient war between Athens and Atlantis (26, 31–2). In addition, he cited occasionally other authors for details or interpretations. These include Heraclides of Pontus and Phanias of Eresus, two students of Plato; the commentary of the grammarian Didymus on Solon's laws; and Hermippus, author of works on the seven sages and on lawgivers. For a variant account of Solon's *seisachtheia*, he refers to Androtion, a fourth-century author of a chronicle of Athens

---

[3] For all questions relating to matter treated in this important text, see the excellent *Commentary on the Aristotelian Athenaion Politeia* by P. J. Rhodes (Oxford: Clarendon Press, 1981). Cf. also Aristotle, *The Athenian Constitution*, translated and with notes by P. J. Rhodes (Harmondsworth: Penguin, 1984).

(15), and he may have used him for other items as well. Plutarch can enlarge on his sources in imagining what must have taken place, putting before the reader Solon's thinking before reciting his Salamis poem, or the pressures upon him to make himself tyrant (8, 14). These passages must be taken for what they are, historical reconstruction, and not as actual records of the time.

Plutarch's personal preference was for aristocratic government, so Solon's reputation as founder of the democracy was not a recommendation. In the biography, he notes the foolishness of popular thinking (e.g. 5, Anacharsis' words, and 29). Instead he enhances Solon's image of fairness to both rich and poor. Other special touches include his approval of child-rearing despite the risks of pain that children bring (6). The general statement on living with risk which follows can be interpreted as a justification for risking one-self in the political arena. The encounter with Thespis, the founder of Attic tragedy, raises serious questions about the role of spectacle and performance in public life. Solon's strictures seem to reflect both Plato's rejection of tragedy and Plutarch's aversion to the confusion of play-acting and real life which Nero's reign had raised to an art form.

The portrait that Plutarch shapes from these sources is original. Solon is coupled with the Roman Publicola, a leader who helped expel the Tarquins and set up the new republic, won great popular favour, and took decisive action against attempts to reinstitute tyranny. The two lives compare the two founders of the Athenian democracy and the Roman republic, with special emphasis on their handling of tyranny and their relation to the pop-ulace. But while throughout Publicola is characterized as a man of action, Solon is presented as a philosopher, one of the Seven Sages of ancient Greece, whose role is more that of adviser and counsellor than actor. Solon advises the people on Salamis, he advises them through his poems and his legislation, he warns them against the tyrannical designs of Pisistratus, but when offered absolute power himself, he refuses to take it. Once he has completed his legislation, he leaves Athens for ten years, and he withdraws from public life rather than fight Pisistratus. While travelling, he gives advice to king Philocyprus, and most famously to Croesus (and through him to Cyrus, 28); on his return, once Pisistratus has become tyrant, he advises him as well (31). Solon thus emerges as first of all the wise counsellor, bring-ing to populace and ruler the light of reason and proportion; Publicola as the doer, putting this wisdom into practice. It is perhaps not hazardous to speculate that Plutarch may have seen something of himself in Solon, of Publicola in Sosius Senecio and other prominent Romans who were his readers. Having lived under Nero and Domitian, both philosopher and imperial official had had experience of tyrants.

Andrewes, A., *Cambridge Ancient History*, iii. 3, 2nd edn. (Cambridge: Cambridge University Press, 1982), 368–98. A basic narrative.

Anhalt, E. K., *Solon the Singer: Politics and Poetics* (Lanham, Md.: Rowman and Littlefield, 1993). A study of the interrelation of Solon's poetry and political ethics.

Bowra, C. M., *Early Greek Elegists* (Cambridge, Mass.: Harvard University Press, 1938). A basic introduction and appreciation.

Miller, A. M., *Greek Lyric: An Anthology in Translation* (Indianapolis and Cambridge: Hackett, 1996), 64–76. A modern translation of the major fragments of Solon's poems.

Murray, O., *Early Greece*, 2nd edn. (London: Fontana Press, 1993). A recent general narrative.

Snodgrass, A., *Archaic Greece: The Age of Experiment* (Berkeley and Los Angeles: University of California Press, 1980). A history with special emphasis on the contribution of archaeology.

Wallace, R. W., 'The Date of Solon's Reforms', *American Journal of Ancient History*, 8 (1983), 81–95. Defends the traditional date of 594.

SOLON

[1] In his *Response to Asclepiades on Solon's Tables of Law* Didymus the Grammarian* quotes the remark of a certain Philocles to the effect that Solon's father was Euphorion.* However, this contradicts the view of everyone else who has ever written about Solon, because they all without exception say that his father was Execestides, who was, according to them, a man of moderate wealth and political influence, but a member of the most distinguished family in the state, since he was descended from Codrus.* As for Solon's mother, Heraclides of Pontus records that she was the cousin of Pisistratus' mother. At first, the fact that they were related made Pisistratus and Solon very close to each other, and another factor was Pisistratus' good looks and youthful charms, because Solon was, on some accounts, in love with him. If so, this would probably explain why later, when they had become political opponents, the hostilities between them were carried out in a spirit free of brutality and ruthlessness; their earlier pacts remained in their minds and, 'smouldering with the lingering flame of Zeus' fire',* preserved the memory of their love and a sense of gratitude. That Solon was not immune to good-looking young men, and did not boldly challenge love 'like a boxer to a fist-fight',* can also be inferred from his poems. Then again, he proposed to make it illegal for a slave to give himself a rub-down in the gymnasium or to have a boy as a lover, because he thought it was a fine, honourable practice and was therefore, in a sense, encouraging men of superior quality to take up the practices he was proscribing for men of inferior quality. Pisistratus is said in turn to have been in love with Charmus, and apparently it was he who dedicated the statue of Love in the part of the Academy where the runners in the sacred torch-race light their torches.*

[2] Now, despite the fact that his father had reduced the estate by what Hermippus describes as certain acts of humane kindness, Solon would have had no difficulty in finding people who were willing to help him out, but coming from a family which had traditionally been the benefactor of others, he was too proud to accept help and so he started out, while he was still a young man, as a trader. Some people, however, say that his travels were undertaken to increase his

experience and to acquire information, rather than for business reasons, and it is undoubtedly true that he had a passionate desire for knowledge,* since even at quite an advanced age he used to say that he 'never stopped learning—and learning a lot—as he grew old'. Moreover, he was not impressed by wealth, but in fact goes so far as to say that two people are equally well off when one

> has much silver
> And gold, and wide wheat-bearing fields,
> And horses and mules, while the other has only enough
> To keep belly, body and feet in comfort,
> And to enjoy the youthful bloom of woman and boy
> When they too arrive, and become agreeable in their season.

But elsewhere he says:

> Money I would like to have, but not unjustly gained;
> For in the end justice always comes.

There is indeed no reason why a man of integrity who is involved in state business should either value the possession of superfluous wealth or despise the use of an adequate income on necessary expenses. In those days, as Hesiod puts it, 'work was no disgrace';* it was not considered demeaning to have a profession, and trading was actually highly regarded, since it familiarized people with foreign lands and customs, gained them the friendship of kings, and provided them with extensive practical experience. Some traders even became the founders of important cities; one thinks, for example, of how Protis won the friendship of the Celts living on the banks of the Rhône and founded Massalia.* Even Thales is said to have engaged in trade, and so is Hippocrates the mathematician; and Plato is supposed to have disposed of some olive oil in Egypt to help cover the cost of his trip there.*

[3] So the extravagance and luxury of Solon's lifestyle, and the fact that in his poems he addresses the subject of pleasure more like a common man than a philosopher, are generally attributed to his life as a trader, in the sense that in return for all the considerable risks he ran he demanded a degree of comfort and indulgence. However, he classified himself as poor rather than rich, as is clear from the following lines:

> While good men are often poor, many bad men are rich;
> Still, I would not exchange with them
> My goodness for their wealth; for goodness endures,
> While different men have money at different times.

He also seems to have approached the composition of poetry lightly at first, as a minor matter and as a pleasant way of spending his spare time. Later, however, he began to put philosophical maxims into verse as well, and he wove into his poems a great deal of political material, not as a way of investigating and preserving information, but in order to justify his actions and sometimes to advise, rebuke, and scold the people of Athens. According to some writers, he also tried to promulgate his laws in the form of epic verse; they quote the following opening lines:

> Let us begin with a prayer to Lord Zeus, the son of Cronus,
> That he may grant these laws good fortune and acclaim.

In the sphere of ethics, he was particularly attracted to political philosophy, which was the norm for thoughtful men at the time; in the realm of physics his ideas are extremely simplistic and old-fashioned, as the following lines show:

> Clouds give rise to the force of snow and hail,
> And thunder comes from bright lightning.
> The sea is churned up by the winds, but if no wind
> Disturbs it, there is nothing more equable.

By and large, it seems that in those days Thales was the only one whose mind could speculate beyond the bounds of functional necessity, while the rest of the sages* gained their reputation for wisdom as a result of applying their skills in the political arena.

[4] There is a story that they all met together in Delphi and then again in Corinth, where it was Periander who organized a kind of communal meeting-cum-symposium for them. But their renown and reputation were even more firmly established by the circulation among them of the famous tripod, which made a complete round of them all, with each of them deferring to the next person and endeavouring to outdo the one before in courtesy. What happened—so the story goes—was that Coan fishermen were hauling in a net and some visitors from Miletus bought the catch off them sight unseen, but when the haul reached dry land it turned out to include a golden tripod

which is supposed to have been dropped there by Helen during her voyage from Troy, when she called to mind the injunction of a certain ancient oracle. At first a dispute arose between the Milesian visitors and the fishermen about who should keep the tripod, and then their respective states took up the quarrel which escalated into warfare. At that point the Pythia delivered an oracle meant for both sides which stated that the tripod should be given 'to the wisest'. It was first sent to Thales in Miletus, since the Coans had no qualms about presenting him, a single individual, with the object which had been the cause of their going to war with the whole population of Miletus *en masse*. Thales, however, declared that Bias was wiser than him, and passed the tripod on to Bias—who in turn sent it on to someone else, on the grounds that *he* was wiser. And so it carried on around, one person sending it on to another, until it came back to Thales again! Eventually it was taken from Miletus to Thebes and dedicated to Ismenian Apollo there.

Theophrastus, however, says that Bias was the first recipient of the tripod in Priene, and that he then sent it on to Thales in Miletus; on this version, then, after it had made a complete circuit of them all it came back to Bias and was eventually sent to Delphi. These are the most common versions of the story, but there are others to the effect that the gift was not this tripod but either a bowl sent by Croesus or a cup left behind by Bathycles.*

[5] Here is an account, as reported by my sources, of two private meetings and conversations Solon had, the first with Anacharsis and the second with Thales. Once, on a visit to Athens, Anacharsis went to Solon's house, knocked on the door, and said, 'I'm not from here, but I've come to forge ties of friendship and hospitality with you.' Solon replied that this was something better done at home, but Anacharsis said, 'Well, you're the one at home, so why don't *you* forge ties of friendship and hospitality with *me*.' Impressed by the man's wit, Solon made Anacharsis welcome and had him to stay for quite a while.

Now, this was at a time when Solon was involved in state affairs and was drafting his laws, and when Anacharsis found out what Solon was up to, he mocked his belief that he could use mere decrees to curb his fellow citizens' injustice and rapacity. 'These decrees of yours are no different from spiders' webs,' he said. 'They'll restrain anyone weak and insignificant who gets caught in them, but they'll be torn to shreds by people with power and wealth.' Solon is supposed to have replied that people do in fact abide by their agreements when neither party gains by infringing them, and that he was tailoring his laws to his fellow citizens so as to prove to everyone that honesty is always better than criminality. In actual fact, though, the results justified Anacharsis' conjecture rather than Solon's expectations. Anacharsis also expressed astonishment, after a visit to the Assembly, that in Greece the proposals are made by clever people, but the decisions are made by fools.

[6] When Solon visited Thales in Miletus, the story goes that he expressed surprise at Thales' complete disinterest in marriage and parenthood. Thales said nothing at the time, but a few days later he got a visitor from abroad to say that he had just arrived from Athens where he had been ten days earlier. Solon asked what news there was of Athens, whereupon the man followed his instructions and said, 'Nothing—oh, except for the funeral procession of a certain young man, which was attended by the whole population. I was told that his father was someone distinguished, whose excellence made him the foremost man in Athens. The father wasn't there, however; they said he was abroad and had been for a long time.' 'What was the poor man's name?' asked Solon. 'I was told it,' the visitor said, 'but I've forgotten it. All I can remember is that people went on about his wisdom and justice.'

Everything the man said made Solon more and more afraid, until eventually he became so distraught that he blurted out his name to the visitor and asked whether the dead man had been called the son of Solon. 'Yes,' said the visitor. Solon began to beat his head with his hands and generally to behave and speak as people do when crushed by grief—and then Thales took him by the hand and said with a smile, '*This* is what makes me steer clear of marriage and parenthood, Solon. It overwhelms even you, and there is no one stronger than you. But don't be alarmed at this tale, because it isn't true.' Anyway, that, according to Hermippus, is the story told by Pataecus—the person who claimed to have Aesop's soul.

[7] However, it is strange and churlish behaviour to be so afraid of losing things that one forgoes what one ought to have; this attitude would make one dissatisfied with having wealth, prestige, or intelligence, for fear of losing it. After all, we can see that even virtue, the most important and enjoyable possession in the world, can be displaced

by illness and medicines,* and Thales' refusal to marry could not make his life any freer of fear, unless he also avoided having friends, family, and country. Besides, he actually adopted his sister's son Cybisthus, we are told. The point is that the mind inherently possesses a faculty of affection; it is in its constitution to love, just as it is to perceive, think, and remember. When the mind takes on this faculty, it attaches itself to external objects which are completely alien to it; as if it were a house or a piece of land abandoned by its legitimate heirs, this capacity for affection is occupied and taken over by other people's children, illegitimate children—even slaves—who make it not only love them, but fret and worry about them too. As a result you can see men who rather hard-heartedly resist marriage and parenthood later racked with sorrow and making ignoble noises over the illness or death of a slave's or concubine's child. Grief affects some of them so much that they go so far as to behave in a shocking and intolerable manner at the death of a dog or a horse.* Others, by contrast, do not suffer torments or behave disgracefully even when they have lost a valued child, but continue to follow the dictates of reason for the rest of their lives.*

For it is not affection but emotional weakness which burdens men with endless troubles and anxieties if they have not been trained by reason in how to cope with fortune. Such people cannot enjoy the possession even of something they really want, because it only makes them suffer pangs of anxiety and apprehension about the future, in case they lose it. Rather than using poverty as a shield against loss of wealth, or avoiding friendship in order to guard against the loss of friends, or refusing to have children in order to protect oneself against their death, one should make reason one's defence against every eventuality. But I have gone on too long about this in the present context.

[8] After a protracted and difficult war with Megara over the island of Salamis, the exhausted Athenian population passed a law making it illegal and punishable by death for anyone ever again to propose, in writing or in speech, that the city should lay claim to Salamis.* Solon found the humiliation hard to bear, and he also noticed that a considerable proportion of the younger generation wanted to see the initial moves that would lead to war, but did not dare to make these moves themselves because of the law. He therefore pretended to have taken leave of his senses, and his family spread the word around the

city that he was insane. He secretly composed some elegiac couplets, practised them until he had learnt them by heart, and then made a sudden, unexpected appearance in the city square, wearing a felt cap on his head.* A large crowd quickly gathered—whereupon Solon mounted the herald's block and recited the elegiac poem which begins:

> I have come as a herald from fair Salamis
> With no speech but a composition in ordered verse.

The poem—which is called 'Salamis'—is 100 lines long, and very elegant. Anyway, at the time in question, after he had recited it, his friends began to applaud, and Pisistratus in particular proceeded to exhort and urge the people of Athens to follow the speaker's recommendations. And eventually they repealed the law and resumed the war, with Solon appointed as their commander.

The commonly cited version of the story of the campaign is as follows. Solon, along with Pisistratus, took the fleet to Cape Colias,* where he found all the women performing the traditional sacrifical rites to Demeter. He therefore sent a fake deserter—someone he could trust—to Salamis to tell the Megarians that they could capture all the leading women of Athens if they sailed with him to Cape Colias without delay. The Megarians fell for it and detailed a contingent of heavy-armed troops for the mission. When Solon saw the ship making its way from the island, he ordered the women to make themselves scarce and had those of his men who were still too young to have beards dress up in the women's costumes, head-dresses and sandals. Then he sent them to play and dance by the sea-shore—armed with short swords concealed in their clothing—and to wait for the enemy troops to land, when they could seize the ship. So this plan was put into effect. The Megarians were lured on by the sight, beached their ship near by, and leapt out to get the 'women', competing with one another to reach them first.† The upshot was that none of them escaped; as soon as they were all dead, the Athenian fleet set out for the island and took possession of it.

[9] However, there is an alternative account of the way the island fell. According to this version. Solon first received the following oracle from the god at Delphi:

> Sacrifice to the local heroes who founded the land
> And win their favour. The vales of Asopia conceal them now,
> Where they lie in death facing the setting sun.

So Solon sailed to the island under cover of darkness and sacrificed to the heroes Periphemus and Cychreus.* Then he chose 500 Athenian volunteers to take with him (who had been promised by official decree political control of the island, if they took it), set sail in a large number of fishing-boats, with a triaconter as an escort, and anchored off Salamis by a breakwater which projects towards Euboea.† A vague rumour reached the Megarians in the town of Salamis; they armed themselves in some confusion and set out. They also dispatched a ship to reconnoitre for the enemy, but Solon captured it as soon as it came close to his position. He captured the Megarian crew and then put the best of his Athenian troops on board with instructions to sail to the town, doing all they could not to alert anyone to their presence. Meanwhile, he took the remaining Athenians and joined battle with the Megarians on land, and while they were still fighting, the Athenians on the ship reached the town and occupied it.

There is also a dramatic enactment of events which seems to corroborate this version. An Athenian ship used to sail up to the island, with the crew initially keeping quiet, but then charging into the attack yelling and screaming, while one man in full armour used to run to Cape Sciradium and fetch the men on land.† Also, near by there is a temple to Enyalius founded by Solon to commemorate his defeat of the Megarians. After his victory, he released under a truce all the Megarians who had survived the battle.

[10] Even so, the Megarians remained belligerent, and the war continued with each side giving as good as it got. Casualties and damage were heavy, and eventually they arranged for the Lacedaemonians to act as mediators and arbiters of the conflict. Now, most writers claim that Solon enlisted the support of Homer, with all his authority, in the sense that he inserted a line into the 'Catalogue of Ships' and then read it out during the trial:

> Ajax brought twelve ships from Salamis
> *And posted them where the Athenian troops were stationed.**

However, the Athenians themselves think that this story is nonsense; according to them, Solon proved to the judges that Ajax's sons Philaeus and Eurysaces took Athenian citizenship, donated the island to the people of Athens, and settled in Attica—one of them in Brauron, the other in Melite. (In fact, there is a village in Attica called Philaïdae after Philaeus; this is the village where Pisistratus was born.)

The Athenians add that in order to make his refutation of the
Megarians even more convincing, Solon used the dead heroes buried
there to build a strong case, pointing out that they had not been buried
in the Megarian fashion—that is, facing east—but in the Athenian
fashion, facing west. But Hereas of Megara counters this with the claim
that the Megarians too position their corpses facing west and, even
more importantly, that the Athenians give their dead individual
graves, whereas it is the Megarians who use a single grave for up to
three or four corpses.* Be that as it may, the Athenians also say that
Solon had the support of a number of oracles from Delphi, in which
the god described Salamis as 'Ionian'. The judges of this case were
five Spartiates—Critolaïdas, Amompharetus, Hypsichidas, Anaxilas,
and Cleomenes.*

[11] By now, and especially because of all this, Solon had become
a well-known and important public figure. But his celebrity and fame
rose throughout Greece with the speech he made on the temple at
Delphi, to the effect that the Greeks should not stand idle while the
Cirrhaeans violated the oracle, but should come to its assistance and
help the people of Delphi defend the god.* In fact it was because
they were won over by his arguments that the member-states of the
Amphictyonic League went to war. Aristotle is far from being the only
person to vouch for this when in the course of his list of victors at
the Pythian Games he credits Solon with the plan. However, Solon
was not given a military command for this war (according to Hermippus, citing Euanthes of Samos), and in fact Aeschines the orator
does not mention him in this context, and the records at Delphi have
Alcmaeon, not Solon, down as the Athenian commander.*

[12] The pollution originating with the famous Cylonian affair
had been a source of turmoil to Athens for a long time, ever since
Megacles, who was an archon at the time, persuaded Cylon and his
gang to come down from Athena's temple, where they had sought
sanctuary, and stand trial. They tied a length of spun wool to the
goddess's statue and held on to it, but on their way down, when they
reached the shrine of the August Goddesses, the thread broke of its
own accord, whereupon Megacles and his fellow archons leapt in to
arrest them, because Athena, as the archons saw it, was refusing to
give them sanctuary. Megacles and the others stoned to death those
who were caught in the open and murdered those who had taken refuge
at some altar or other; the only ones they spared were those who had

sought sanctuary with the archons' own wives.* As a result of this
the archons were called 'the Accursed', and they became unpopular,
while the survivors from Cylon's party regained their position of
strength. There followed a period of constant political feuding between
them and Megacles' party. At the time in question the dispute had
reached a particular peak, with the general population of Athens
taking sides, but Solon, who by then was held in high regard, joined
forces with the most distinguished men in Athens and acted as intermediary between the two sides. His appeals and arguments had the
effect of persuading the Accursed to submit to a trial and to allow
themselves to be judged, provided that the jury of 300 was selected
from the top of the social scale. Myron of Phlya brought the prosecution and the defendants were found guilty.* Those of the Accursed
who were living were banished, and the corpses of those who had died
were dug up and cast out beyond the borders of Attica.

As if all this were not turmoil enough, the Megarians attacked at
the same time, and as a result the Athenians lost Nisaea and were driven
once again off Salamis.* Also, the city was overrun by superstitious
fears and apparitions, and the word from the diviners was that their
sacrifices pointed to the existence of acts of evil, causing pollution which
required purification.

Under these circumstances they sent to Crete for Epimenides
of Phaestus, who duly arrived. Some of those who do not count
Periander as one of the Seven Sages include Epimenides instead. He
was held to be a favourite of the gods and to have an inspired and
mystical insight into matters pertaining to the gods; accordingly, his
contemporaries called him the son of a nymph named Blaste, and a
'New Coures'.* During his time in Athens he befriended Solon and
helped him a great deal, in the sense that he paved the way for his
legislation.* What he did was organize the way people went about their
religious observances and get them to express grief in a less frenzied
manner by the immediate introduction of certain sacrificial rites
into their funerary practices, and by abolishing the savage, barbaric
customs which had usually been followed by female mourners up
to that time.

The most important thing he did, however, was institute certain
propitiatory and purificatory rituals, and found places of worship,
because this enabled him to make Athens a reverent and religious city,
observant of justice and more inclined to heed the call of unity. It is

also said that when he saw Munychia, he studied it for a long time and then remarked to those who were with him, 'How blind man is to the future! If the Athenians could look ahead and see how much suffering this place is going to cause them, they would chew it up with their very own teeth!'*

Another person who is supposed to have made a similar conjecture about the future is Thales. The story goes that he gave instructions to the effect that after his death he was to be buried in an insignificant and obscure part of Miletus, with the prediction that this spot would one day be the Milesians' city square. Anyway, Epimenides made a huge impression on the Athenians, but refused their offer of large sums of money and of important privileges; he wanted nothing more than a sprig from the sacred olive tree,* and once he had been given it, he returned home.

[13] When the turmoil surrounding the Cylonian affair had died down, and after the banishment of the Accursed, which I have already described, Athens returned to a long-standing political dispute, with people forming as many different political parties as there were different kinds of terrain in the country. There were the Men of the Hills, who were the most democratic party, the Men of the Plain, who were the most oligarchic, and thirdly the Men of the Coast, who favoured an intermediate, mixed kind of system and who opposed the other two parties and made it hard for them to gain power.*

Moreover, at that time the disparity between rich and poor had, as it were, reached a peak. The city was in an extremely precarious state, and it looked as though the only way it could settle down and put an end to all the turmoil was by the establishment of a tyranny.* All the common people were in debt to the wealthy members of society, because either they paid them a sixth of the produce they gained from working the land (which earned them the name of sixth-parters or hired hands*), or else they put up their own persons as collateral for their debts and were forfeit to their creditors, in which case they might become slaves right there in Attica or be sold into slavery abroad. The creditors were so ruthless that people were often force to sell even their own children—there was no law prohibiting this—or to go into exile. However, a great many of them (the most resolute of them, in fact) banded together and began to urge one another to do something about the situation—to choose a reliable man as a champion for their cause and then to remove the debtors from the grasp of their creditors, redistribute the land, and form an entirely new system of government.

[14] At this point the most sensible Athenians began to look to Solon. They could see that he was possibly unique in keeping his distance from all the problems—that he had no part in the wrongdoing of the rich, and was not caught up in the afflictions of the poor either. So they asked him to become involved in public life and to resolve their disputes. However, Phanias of Lesbos writes that Solon's desire to save the city led him to deal in an underhand fashion with both parties, without his involvement being solicited; he reports that he secretly promised those who were badly off that he would redistribute the land, while at the same time promising the plutocrats that he would reaffirm their existing contracts. Solon himself, however, says that his engagement in politics was hesitant at first, because he was worried about the consequences of one side's greed and the other side's presumption.

In any case, he was elected archon, following Philombrotus' term of office, with the power to resolve disputes and make laws.* The rich found him acceptable because of his wealth, and the poor because of his integrity. Besides, we hear that there was a remark of his, made before the election, going around the city, to the effect that equality does not cause war, which pleased both the well-to-do and the disadvantaged—the former because they expected the forthcoming equality to be based on merit and calibre, the latter because they assumed it would be assessed arithmetically and numerically.

Both sides, then, had high hopes, and their leaders kept on at Solon, constantly recommending tyranny to him and arguing that he could seize control of the city with all the more confidence now that he was in a position of authority. Even many Athenians who did not belong to either of the political extremes saw that it would be a hard and laborious task to effect change by means of reasoned argument and legal measures, and so did not dislike the idea of having a single person in charge, given that he was a man of such honesty and intelligence. And on some accounts Solon also received the following oracle from Pytho:

> Take your place amidships, accept the pilot's job,
> And steer the ship; you will find many allies in Athens.

His friends and supporters remonstrated with him particularly vehemently for turning his back on absolute power merely because it had a bad name, as if the calibre of the person with the power would not immediately make it become lawful sovereignty, or as if there were not precedents for this in the case of Tynnondas in Euboea, and just recently in the fact that the people of Mytilene had made Pittacus tyrant over them.*

However, none of this deflected Solon from his purpose. To his friends he is supposed to have said that while tyranny may be a delightful spot, there is no way back from it; and to Phocus, in his poems, he wrote:

> And did I spare the land of my birth?
> Did I refrain from tyranny and brutality,
> Preferring to keep my name unblemished by disgrace?
> There is no shame for me in this. In fact, I think
> It will set me above all other men.

All this makes it clear that he was held in very high regard even before his legislation. However, his refusal of the tyranny earned him a great deal of scorn, which he wrote about as follows:

> 'A man of shallow intellect was Solon, of no good sense;
> He spurned the bounty offered by the gods. The fool:
> His net was fat and full of fish—he did not pull it in!
> He lacked the courage, and sanity as well.
> Else, if he† had taken power, accepted boundless wealth,
> And ruled as tyrant over Athens for just one day,
> He'd gladly then have been flayed into a wineskin
> And let his family be wiped off the face of the earth.'

[15] This is what, in his poem, he has the base majority say about him. However, his rejection of tyranny did not mean that his handling of affairs was particularly gentle, or that he meekly deferred to influential people or enacted the kind of legislation he thought would please those who had elected him. But where the present situation seemed acceptable, he did not apply remedies or open new wounds, because he was afraid that 'If he made a complete mess and muddle of the state, it would be beyond his abilities to restore order', and arrange things for the best. The guiding principle of his actions was, as he himself says, 'to harmonize force and justice'; that is, he acted where he expected to find people receptive to his proposals and submissive to the application of pressure. And that is why, when he was subsequently asked whether the laws he had introduced were the best

possible ones for the Athenians, he replied, 'They were the best they would accept.'

Now, recent writers have pointed out that the Athenians had the slick habit of glossing over the distasteful aspects of their affairs by using inoffensive and charitable terms to disguise them. For instance, they used to call prostitutes 'escorts', taxes 'contributions', garrisons in cities 'protectors', and prison 'quarters'. However, it looks as though this trick originated with Solon's description of the cancellation of debts as an 'alleviation'—the first of his measures being the enactment of a law whereby all existing debts were rescinded, and whereby in the future it would be illegal for any lender to require the borrower's own person as collateral.* Some writers, though, including Androtion,* have claimed that the measure taken for the relief of the poor was a moderation of the rate of interest, not a cancellation of debts—a charitable act which pleased them so much that they called it an 'alleviation', a term which also covered the upward rescaling of the weights and measures and of the value of the currency. This was part of the same piece of legislation, according to Androtion and the others, because whereas a mina had previously been valued at 73 drachmas, Solon made it 100 drachmas, the upshot of which was that although the amount they paid was the same on paper, it was worth less, which benefited the debtors a great deal, without harming the creditors in the slightest.* However, most writers agree that the 'alleviation' was the abolishment of all due debts, and that makes better sense of what Solon wrote in his poems, because he prides himself there on having 'removed' from the mortgaged land

> The frequent markers planted here and there;
> A land enslaved once now is free.*

As for those of his fellow citizens whose persons had become forfeit through debt, he either brought them back from abroad

> With Attic Greek no longer on their tongues,
> Forgotten in their wide and long wanderings;
> While the others, held in sorry servitude here,
> In their native land,

he claims to have freed.

This business is said to have got him into more trouble than anything else in his life. What happened was that once he had resolved to do away with the debts, he reached the stage of casting around for suitable arguments and for a good opportunity to introduce the measure, and he divulged to his most trusted and intimate friends—Conon, Cleinias, Hipponicus, and their circle—that he was going to leave the land as it was, but had decided to cancel the debts. These friends of his immediately pre-empted the legislation and stole a march by borrowing large sums of money from wealthy people and combining to purchase huge tracts of land. Then, after the decree had become law, they reaped the profits from these estates, while refusing to repay their debts. These actions of theirs earned Solon a great deal of hostile criticism, on the serious charge that he had not so much been one of the victims of the crime as party to it. However, he lost no time in repudiating this charge by means of the famous five talents— or fifteen talents, according to some, including Polyzelus of Rhodes —which was the amount of money it emerged that he had lent, and he was the first to obey the new law and write off what was owed to him. But for the rest of their lives those friends of his were known as 'the debt-cheats'.*

[16] This measure of his did not meet with the approval of either party. His cancellation of the debts annoyed the rich, and the poor were even more aggrieved at his failure to redistribute the land as they had expected, and because he had not completely removed the disparities and inequalities between men's lives and incomes, as Lycurgus had done.* Lycurgus, however, was eleventh in descent from Heracles, and had been on the throne of Lacedaemon for a number of years; he was therefore well equipped with prestige, supporters, and power to help see his constitutional reforms through, and in any case—and this actually cost him an eye—he relied on force rather than persuasion to achieve the goal of enormously enhancing the stability and unity of the state by arranging things so that no citizen was either rich or poor. This kind of equality was not the outcome of Solon's policies: he was an ordinary citizen, with moderate resources. Nevertheless, considering that he was acting solely on the basis of his fellow citizens' acceptance of his proposals as sound and trustworthy, he made full use of the power available to him.

We have his own words on the fact that he offended most of the people of Athens by failing to fulfil their expectations. He says:

> Once their minds were filled with vain hopes, but now
> In anger all look askance at me, as if I were their foe.*

But in fact, he says, anyone else with that much power

> Would not have curbed the people or stopped
> Until he had extracted the butter from the churned milk.

Before long, however, they saw the advantages of his reforms, laid aside their purely personal complaints, and established a public sacrificial ritual, which they called the 'Alleviation'. They also gave Solon the power to reform the constitution and institute legislation, and not in a piecemeal fashion either: they entrusted everything to him without hesitation—offices, assemblies, lawcourts, and councils. In every case it was up to him to decide what property qualification would be required, how many of each of them there should be, and when the appointments and meetings should be held. He could discontinue or preserve elements of the existing system as he saw fit.

[17] The first thing he did was repeal all of Draco's laws, except the ones on homicide, on the grounds that they were too harsh and prescribed penalties that were too severe. For a single penalty—the death penalty—had been fixed for almost all crimes, which meant that even people convicted of not working were to be put to death, and that the theft of vegetables or fruit carried the same penalty as temple-robbery and homicide.* This explains why Demades later became famous for commenting that Draco had written his laws in blood rather than ink. The story goes that Draco himself was once asked why he had made most crimes carry the death penalty; he replied that petty crimes deserved it, in his opinion, and he could not find a heavier penalty to impose on serious crimes.

[18] The second thing Solon did was assess the property qualifications of the Athenian citizens, because he wanted to leave all the political offices in the hands of the well-to-do, as before, but to diversify the rest of the political apparatus, from which the common people had previously been excluded. In his system, the top class consisted of those whose annual income was at least 500 units of dry and wet goods together, who were known as the 'Men of 500 Medimni'. The second class consisted of those who could afford to keep a horse or whose income was 300 units, who were known as the 'Payers of the Knight's Tax'. The third property qualification was fixed at an income of 200 units of dry and wet goods, and its members were called the 'Men with a Team of Oxen'. The rest of the population were called 'Hired Hands'; they were excluded from holding office, and were

involved in the political apparatus only to the extent that they could attend the Assembly and act as jurors.* The fact that they could act as jurors was at first taken to be unimportant, but it later turned out to be absolutely critical, since most disputes fell within their jurisdiction, because Solon granted the right of appeal to a popular court even in cases which were to be tried, in his system, by office-holders. It is also said that the reason why his laws were phrased somewhat obscurely and ambiguously was to increase the power of the courts, in the sense that since people could not resolve their differences simply by reference to the law, in the end they turned to the juries of the courts for help and brought every dispute before them, so that they were in a way the masters of the laws.* He congratulates himself on this in the following lines:

> For I granted the people an adequate amount of power
> And sufficient prestige—not more nor less.
> But I found a way also to maintain the status
> Of the old wielders of power with their fantastic riches.
> I stood protecting rich and poor with my stout shield,
> And saw that neither side prevailed unjustly.

Nevertheless, he felt he should make still further provisions for the weakness of the common people, so he gave every citizen the right to institute a lawsuit on behalf of someone who had suffered wrong. So if someone had been the victim of an assault, for instance, and had been beaten up or injured, it was possible for anyone who had the resources and the will to bring a lawsuit against the offender and prosecute him.* This was a sound move on the part of the legislator: he was conditioning the people of Athens to regard themselves as so many parts of a single body, and so to share one another's feelings and suffering. There is a saying of Solon's that has come down to us which is consistent with this piece of legislation: apparently he was once asked which was the best city to live in, and he replied, 'The one where there is no difference between the victims of a crime and anyone else in terms of how vigorously they charge and punish the criminal.'

[19] After he had constituted the Council of the Areopagus out of each year's former archons (he himself being, as an ex-archon, one of the members), he noticed that the common people were still full of themselves and that the cancellation of their debts had made them more assertive, so he instituted another Council as well, consisting of

100 men selected from each of the four tribes. He gave this second Council the job of debating issues before they reached the people, and of ensuring that the Assembly was not presented with any motions that had not previously been through this process of deliberation, and at the same time established the upper Council as a general over-seer of the state and guardian of the constitution. His thinking was that if the state was moored, so to speak, with two anchors—the two Councils—it would be better equipped to ride out any swell and to contain the restlessness of the general population.*

Most writers report that the Council of the Areopagus was con-stituted by Solon, as I have said, and this view seems to be strongly supported by the fact that Draco nowhere mentions the Areopagites by name, but always refers to the ephetae* in cases of homicide. However, Solon's thirteenth table contains the eighth of his laws, phrased exactly as follows:

Of the disenfranchised all those who were disenfranchised prior to the archonship of Solon are to regain their rights except those who were con-victed by the Areopagus, the Ephetae, or the city hall (that is, the king-archons) of homicide, murder or tyrannical ambition and were already in exile when this law was published.

So this proves that, on the contrary, the Council of the Areopagus existed before Solon's archonship and legislation. After all, if Solon had been the first to give the Council of the Areopagus its judicial powers, how could anyone have been convicted of anything in the Areopagus before Solon's time? Of course, the wording of the law may possibly be ambiguous or incomplete, so that what it really means is that those found guilty on charges which are *currently* tried by the Areopagites, the Ephetae, and the officers of the city hall are to remain disenfranchised, while all the others are to regain their rights and fran-chises. But the reader must make up his own mind about this.

[20] One of his other laws is extremely idiosyncratic and odd. It ordains that anyone who takes neither side in a political dispute is to be disenfranchised.* Presumably he means that no one should be so indifferent and insensitive to the common good that he just sees to the safety of his own private affairs and congratulates himself on his distance from the pain and suffering afflicting his country, rather than immediately joining whichever side is acting with a higher degree of integrity and justice—that he should offer them his support and

co-operation in the dangers they face, rather than waiting safely on the sidelines to see which side gains the upper hand.

Another strange, even ridiculous law of his is the one stating that if the husband of an heiress (who under the law has control and authority over her) is impotent, she has the right to have sex with close relatives of his.* There are, however, people who claim that this was a good move to make, to prevent an impotent man from marrying an heiress for her money and using the protection of the law to abuse nature, because when the heiress's promiscuity comes to his attention, he will be faced with the choice of either divorcing her or persisting in a marriage that only brings him shame, as a punishment for his avarice and abuse. It is also a good idea to restrict the heiress's choice of partner to her husband's relatives, so that any child that is born belongs to the same family and lineage. This is also helped by the stipulation that the woman is shut away in a room with her new husband after eating a quince,* and that he is to have sex with her three times a month without fail. The point is that, leaving aside the issue of procreation, the husband is thereby indicating that he respects his wife for her self-restraint, and feels fond of her, which always removes a great deal of any accumulated resentment and stops any quarrels becoming a cause of complete estrangement.*

Where other marriages were concerned, Solon abolished dowries and stipulated that a bride was to bring with her at the most three items of clothing and some inexpensive household items, but nothing else. He did this because he wanted to take the mercenary and commercial aspect out of marriage and make child-bearing, mutual gratitude and affection the point of a husband and wife living together. After all, when Dionysius' mother wanted to become the wife of one of his subjects, he remarked that although he had broken the laws of the state by becoming tyrant, he could not abuse the laws of nature by arranging marriages which the prospective partners' ages made out of the question.* Indeed, states should not connive at this aberration or allow inappropriate and unloving unions to take place when there is nothing about them remotely connected to the function or purpose of marriage. No, any true archon or legislator who found an old man marrying a young woman would quote the words spoken to Philoctetes: 'You poor devil! What a fine state you're in for marriage!'* And if he discovered in the rooms of a rich old woman a young man growing partridge-plump in her company, he would

remove him from there and give him instead to a young unmarried
woman who needed a husband. But that is enough about this.

[21] Another law of Solon's which has met with approval is the one
making it illegal to slander a dead person. This is a good idea because
piety requires us to regard the dead as sacred, decency requires us to
refrain from attacking people in their absence, and political expediency requires us not to let a conflict go on for ever. He also made it
an offence to slander a living person in or near temples, lawcourts,
and government offices, and during publicly attended games and
competitions—an offence punishable by a fine of three drachmas to
the individual involved and two more drachmas to the state treasury.
For there are certain places where it is uncouth and undisciplined to
fail to keep one's temper, but it is also hard (and for some people
impossible) to succeed in doing so everywhere; at the same time, a
legislator has to take feasibility into consideration when framing his
laws, otherwise he will end up punishing large numbers of people
ineffectively, rather than achieving his goal of punishing a few people
effectively.

He also became famous for his legislation on wills. It had not previously been possible to make a will: a person's money and land had
to stay within his family. Solon, however, left it up to a man to dispose of his estate as he wished, provided that he had no children; in
other words, he valued friendship over kinship and gratitude over duty,
and made money the property of those who had it. At the same time,
however, he did not allow bequests to be made without some limits
and qualifications: the person making the bequest had to be free of
the influence of illness, drugs, imprisonment, coercion, or the persuasive powers of a woman.* He included the latter stipulation because
he thought—and the idea is perfectly correct and unassailable—that
persuading someone to go against his best interests is no different
from forcing him to do so; in fact, he held that trickery and coercion,
and pleasure and pain, belong in the same category in the sense that
they are all equally capable of undermining a person's powers of
reason.

Other laws of his imposed certain conditions of neatness and
orderliness on women when they were outdoors, and also on the way
mourners expressed their grief and on the conduct of festivals. When
a woman was outdoors, she was not to wear more than three items
of clothing, nor to carry more than an obol's worth of food or drink,

or a basket more than a cubit in length, nor was she to travel at night except on a cart with a lamp on the front. He banned mourners from lacerating themselves and using set dirges, and outsiders from lamenting at others' funerals. He made it illegal to sacrifice a cow, to lay out more than three sets of clothing for the corpse, and to visit the tombs of people outside one's own family except during the actual funeral procession. Most of these practices are also banned under our laws, but ours also state that offenders are to be punished by the Superintendents of Women,* on the grounds that they are indulging in unmanly and effeminate feelings and faults.

[22] People were constantly pouring into Attica from everywhere else because it was a safe place to live, and the city was becoming crowded, while at the same time the land was largely infertile and poor, and seafarers were not in the habit of importing goods for those who had nothing to give them in return. His awareness of all these factors prompted Solon to encourage his fellow citizens to take up manufacturing, and he made a law to the effect that a son who had not been taught one of the manufacturing arts by his father was under no obligation to support him. Now, Lycurgus lived in a city which was untainted by hordes of foreigners, and had land which, as Euripides puts it, 'was capacious enough for many, and was even more capacious for twice the number',* and most importantly had masses of helots spread out all over Lacedaemon, whom it was in the national interest not to leave with nothing to do, but to grind down with toil and labour; so it was all very well for *him* to release his fellow citizens from laborious manual pursuits so that they could concentrate on the arts of war and master and practise just this one area of expertise.* Solon, however, was adapting his laws to the situation rather than the situation to his laws; he could see that the land could barely supply the needs of those who worked it and was incapable of feeding a mass of idle, unemployed people, so he covered artisanship in a cloak of respectability and got the Council of the Areopagus to look into how every single person made a living and to punish those who were unemployed.

An even stricter regulation of his was the one exempting sons born out of wedlock from supporting their fathers, which Heraclides of Pontus records. The thinking behind this was that anyone who disregards the honourable state of marriage is plainly looking only for a woman to give him pleasure, not to give him children; so now he is paid back in full, and he has no comeback against his children, because he has made their very birth a source of shame.

[23] By and large it is Solon's laws about women that seem the most strange. In his code, for instance, although an adulterer caught in the act could be killed, the crime of raping a free woman was punishable by a fine of 100 drachmas, and the seduction of a free woman by a fine of twenty drachmas. He excluded from this provision those who openly sell their bodies, or in other words prostitutes, since they do not disguise the fact that they have sex with anyone who pays their price. He also made it illegal for anyone to offer his daughters or sisters for sale, unless that person found that one of them, though unmarried, had slept with a man. But it makes no sense to punish one and the same offence with ruthless severity in some circumstances, and then with lenient mildness in others, fixing the penalty as some slight fine or other; perhaps there was a shortage of money in circulation in the city at the time, in which case the difficulty of raising it would have made these monetary penalties severe.

At any rate, when it came to estimating the value of sacrificial offerings, he reckoned a sheep and a medimnus of wheat to be worth a drachma, and he set the reward for victory in the Isthmian Games at 100 drachmas, for victory in the Olympic Games at 500 drachmas, and for bringing in a wolf five drachmas, or one drachma for a wolf cub, which were respectively, according to Demetrius of Phalerum, the value of an ox and a sheep.* Although the prices he fixes in his sixteenth table are presumably considerably higher than usual, since they are for choice sacrificial victims, they are still low compared to today's prices. The Athenians have been battling wolves ever since ancient times, because their land is better for livestock farming than for arable farming. And there are people who claim that the names of the Athenian tribes are not derived from Ion's sons, but from the various ways of making a living originally followed there. So people were called Hopletes if they were members of the warrior class, Argadians if they were artisans, and, of the remaining two classes, the arable farmers were called Geleontes, while those who spent their time grazing and farming sheep and goats were called Aegicorians.*

Water is a scarce commodity in Attica, with its lack of constant rivers, any lakes, or prolific springs; instead most of the population used to rely on artificial wells. Solon therefore made a law to the effect that people were to make use of any public wells that were a *hippikon* or less away from their land—a *hippikon* being a unit of distance measuring four stades*—but that where the distance was greater, people should try to find their own water; however, if they had not struck water on their land after digging to a depth of ten fathoms, they could then get it from a neighbour, by filling a six-choes jar twice a day.* The idea behind this rule was to help the needy while at the same time not encouraging idleness.

He showed a great deal of expert knowledge in prescribing the distances to be followed when planting trees as well. He stated that no one was to plant a tree in a field within five feet of his neighbour's land, or nine feet in the case of fig trees and olive trees, whose roots extend further, and which damage some plants by their proximity, in the sense that they might even deny them nourishment, and they emit a secretion which can be harmful. He also fixed the minimum gap between a pit or a ditch and someone else's land as equal to the depth of excavation, and a bee-hive was to be set at least 300 feet away from the site of hives previously established by someone else.

[24] The only natural product he allowed to be disposed of abroad was olive oil; the export of everything else was banned. He decreed that the archon was to curse anyone who tried to export any forbidden product, or otherwise to pay into the public treasury himself a fine of 100 drachmas. Now, this law is actually inscribed on the first of his tables, so there are grounds for not finding entirely untrustworthy the tradition that in the old days the export of figs was forbidden and that a person who exposed and informed on exporters of figs was known as a 'fig-informer'.*

He also passed a law about injuries caused by animals, which included the provision that a dog which had the habit of biting was to have a clog three cubits long tied on to it—a nice safety-measure.

Another puzzling law of his is the one about naturalized citizens. The only classes of people he allowed to become citizens were those who had been permanently banished from their own country or who had moved their whole household to Athens in order to practise a profession. It is said that his reason for making this law was not so much to drive other categories of people away as to invite these ones to Athens with a guaranteed prospect of citizenship, and that he also thought that people who had been expelled from their own countries against their wills and those who had deliberately decided to leave were the kinds of people whose loyalty one could rely on.*

Another typical piece of legislation by Solon governed the privilege of being fed at the publicly funded table, which he called 'table-sharing'.* He made it illegal for a single person to be fed there over and over again, because he thought this showed greed, and at the same time he made refusal to take up one's right to do so a punishable offence, because he thought this showed contempt for the state.

[25] He decreed that all his laws were to remain in force for 100 years.* They were inscribed on revolving wooden tables enclosed in frames; fragments of these tables have survived right up to modern times in the City Hall. According to Aristotle, they were called 'tablets', and the comic poet Cratinus says somewhere:

> I swear it by Solon and Draco, whose tablets
> Nowadays are used to cook barley.

However, some people say that the word 'tablets' applies properly only to the means of displaying the legislation concerning religious rituals and sacrifices, while all the rest were called 'tables'.* In any case, the Council collectively took an oath that they would uphold Solon's laws, and each member of the legislative committee swore a separate oath at the stone in the city square in which he declared that if he failed to abide by any of the laws he would set up as a dedicatory offering at Delphi a life-sized golden statue.*

He was aware of the irregularity of the month—that is, that the movement of the moon is not quite synchronized with the setting or the rising of the sun, but that the moon often catches up with and passes the sun in the course of a single day. He therefore decreed that when this happened the day was to be called the Day of the Old and the New, on the grounds that the portion of it which occurs before the conjunction between the sun and moon belongs to the month that is coming to an end, while the remainder of it belongs to the month that is now beginning (which apparently makes him the first to have understood Homer's words 'While the one month was waning, the other was drawing in'), and it was the next day that was the first day of the month. From the twentieth to the thirtieth he did not count the days forwards but backwards, in reverse order, following the visible behaviour of the moon.*

Once his laws were in force, not a day passed without several people coming up to him to express approval or disapproval, or to recommend the insertion of some point or other into the statutes, or the removal of something from them. Moreover, a great many people had queries about the legislation; they would question him about it and ask him to explain in detail the meaning and purpose of every single point, and it was clear to him that it would be odd not to answer these questions and invidious to do so. He wanted to extricate himself completely from this predicament and to avoid his fellow citizens' peevish quibbling (as he himself says, 'On important issues, it's hard to please everyone'), so he claimed that as a ship-owner he had business to attend to and used this as an excuse to set off on his travels.* He sought and was granted permission by the Athenians to live abroad for ten years, by which time he expected them to have become used even to his laws.

[26] The first place he visited was Egypt, where he stayed, in his own words, 'by that mouth of the Nile which adjoins the Canobic shore'. He also spent some time studying philosophy as a member of the groups surrounding Psenopis of Heliopolis and Sonchis of Saïs, who were the most learned of the Egyptian priests. It was from them, as Plato says, that he heard the story of Atlantis, which he tried to introduce to Greece in the form of a poem.*

He sailed next to Cyprus, where he made great friends with one of the kings, Philocyprus. Now, Philocyprus' domain consisted of a smallish town (founded by Demophon the son of Theseus), which was situated on the banks of the River Clarius, in territory that was easy to defend, but too rugged and infertile to have anything else to recommend it. So Solon persuaded him to move down to the beautiful plain below and to build there a larger and more attractive town. Moreover, since he was there, he took charge of the resettlement and arranged things so that the new town was not only an excellent place to live, but also very secure. As a result, settlers applied to Philocyprus in large numbers, and all the other local kings looked up to him. And that is why Philocyprus paid Solon the honour of renaming the town Soli after him, whereas it had previously been called Aepeia.*

Solon mentions the foundation of this town himself in the elegiac poem in which he addresses Philocyprus as follows:

> For you, I pray that you may long dwell here as lord
> Of this town of Soli, and your descendants after you;
> As for me, may violet-crowned Cypris keep me unharmed
> On my journey from this famous isle in my swift ship,
> And, with this town here founded, may she grant me favour,
> Fame, and a safe journey home to my fatherland.

[27] Some people think they can prove, on chronological grounds, that the famous meeting between Solon and Croesus is a fiction.* However, when a story is so famous and well attested and, more importantly, so much in keeping with Solon's character and worthy of his self-assurance, I for one do not feel inclined to reject it on the basis of some so-called chronological tables, which have so far proved incapable of making the slightest progress towards resolving all the inconsistencies, despite the revisions undertaken by countless writers. In any case, the story goes that Solon went to Sardis at Croesus' invitation and behaved much like a landlubber on his way down to the sea for the first time, who imagines that every successive river he sees is the sea. As he walked through the courtyard he saw plenty of courtiers swaggering around in their expensive robes, surrounded by retainers and personal guards, and he took each of them to be Croesus, until he was brought into the presence of the man himself, whose outfit lacked nothing that men regard as remarkable or extraordinary or desirable in the way of precious stones, dyed clothing, and wrought gold jewellery—nothing that might help him present a thoroughly impressive and gorgeous spectacle. Contrary to Croesus' expectations, however, Solon stood there opposite him unmoved by the spectacle and without passing any comment on it; in fact, anyone with any sense could see that he actually despised the vulgarity and tawdriness of it all. So Croesus gave his men instructions to open up for Solon the treasure-chambers where he stored his money and to take him on a tour to show him how magnificently appointed everything was—an unnecessary tour, since his very person was sufficient evidence of his character.

Anyway, after Solon had seen everything and been brought back into his presence, Croesus asked whether there was anyone on earth, to his knowledge, who was happier than him. Solon replied that he did know of someone—Tellus, an Athenian like himself. He explained that Tellus had been a man of integrity, with distinguished sons to succeed him, who had lacked for none of life's essentials while he was alive and had died a glorious death winning the prize for valour in defence of his homeland. This reply showed Solon, to Croesus' mind, to be eccentric and naive, since he did not take abundant silver and gold to be the measure of happiness, but preferred the life and death of an ordinary private citizen to his own vast power and dominion. Nevertheless, he put the same question to him again and asked whether, apart from Tellus, he knew of anyone else who was happier than him. Solon again said that he did, and this time he named Cleobis and Biton, brothers whose devotion to each other and to their mother was unrivalled; once, he explained, when their mother's oxen were delayed, they harnessed themselves to the yoke of her cart and took her to the temple of Hera. Her fellow citizens called her a happy woman, and she was glad. Later, after her sons had performed their sacrifices and drunk their wine, they went to sleep and never got up in the morning, but were found to have capped their great glory with an easy, painless death.*

By now Croesus had lost his temper, and he cried, 'Do I come nowhere in your list of happy men?' Now, Solon refused to flatter Croesus, but he also did not want to make him any more angry than he already was, so he said, 'My lord, we Greeks have basically been only moderately endowed by the gods, and this limitation explains why our understanding is apparently so cautious and ordinary, rather than being splendid and fit for a king. Because this average intelligence of ours sees that life is constantly liable to vicissitudes of all kinds, it stops us getting overexcited when things are going well for us, or being impressed by a person's good fortune when there is still time for things to change. The future that bears down on each of us is variable and determined by unknowable factors, and so we consider a man happy only when the gods have granted him success right up to the end of his life. However, to count anyone happy while he is still alive and still faced with all the uncertainties of life is as unsound and invalid as proclaiming an athlete the winner and crowning him while the contest is still in progress.' With these words Solon left the room, leaving Croesus in some distress, but without having shown him the error of his ways.

[28] Now, the storyteller Aesop (who happened to be in Sardis as an honoured guest of Croesus) was annoyed that Solon was never treated with any kindness and offered him some advice. 'Solon,' he said, 'there are only two ways to deal with a king—with the utmost brevity or the utmost flattery.' 'No, no,' Solon replied. 'With the utmost brevity or the utmost honesty.'*

At that time, then, Croesus had a low opinion of Solon, but later, after defeat by Cyrus and the loss of his city, when he had been taken prisoner and was due to be burnt alive, and he had climbed in chains, with all the Persians watching and in Cyrus' presence, up on to the pyre, he called out Solon's name three times at the top of his voice.

Cyrus was puzzled and he sent men to ask who in heaven or on earth this Solon was, and why he was the only one Croesus called on in his desperate situation. Croesus' reply was frank: 'He was one of the sages of Greece,' he said. 'He was a guest of mine, but not because I had any desire to hear what he had to say or to learn what I needed to know. No, I wanted him to observe, and then to testify after he left to my happiness—a happiness where the advantage of possession is, as I now see, outweighed by the disadvantage of loss. For the only advantage to having it lay in what others would say and think of me, whereas the torment and unbearable hardship brought on by its loss are real. So inferring what the future held for me from the way things were then he told me to look to the end of life and not to puff myself up with insolent pride on the basis of precarious fancies.'

Now, Cyrus was blessed with more intelligence than Croesus, so when his men told him what Croesus had said, the present instance showed him the force of Solon's argument. He therefore not only released Croesus, but treated him with honour for the rest of his life; and Solon gained the reputation of having with a single saying saved one king and educated another.*

[29] While Solon was abroad, the citizens of Athens resumed their political feuding. The Men of the Plain were championed by Lycurgus, the Men of the Coast by Megacles the son of Alcmaeon, and the Men of the Hills (who included the common rabble of hired hands, with their bitter enmity towards the rich) by Pisistratus.* The upshot of the feuding was that although the city was still governed constitutionally, everyone was anticipating an imminent revolution and looking forward to a new system of government, not because they expected a state of equality, but because they hoped to gain the upper hand during the upheaval and to trounce their adversaries.

This was the situation facing Solon on his return to Athens. However, although he was universally admired and respected, he was now too old to have either the energy or the inclination to speak in public and take part in politics. But he held private meetings with the leaders of the parties, in which he tried to get them to reconcile and resolve their differences, and Pisistratus seemed particularly receptive to the attempt. There was, after all, something subtly charming about the way he spoke; he was quick to come to the help of the poor, and he approached his political conflicts in a reasonable fashion and with moderation. He was so good at simulating faculties with which he was not naturally endowed that he was credited with them more than those who really did have them, and was therefore taken to be a cautious, restrained man, a staunch democrat, and an enemy of anyone with subversive and revolutionary designs. He deceived most people in these respects, but Solon soon grasped what he was really like and was the first to recognize his schemes for what they were. This did not make him dislike him, however; instead he tried to calm him down and show him the error of his ways. In fact he told him, and others too, that all it would take to bring out his unrivalled natural tendency towards virtue and to make him a model citizen would be the excision from his mind of his overweening ambition and the purging of his desire to be tyrant.

Now, the first tragedies were being performed then, under the direction of Thespis* and his fellow poets, and the novelty of the enterprise was attracting crowds of people, even though it had not yet been developed as a competitive contest. Since Solon was naturally fond of a recital and eager to learn, and even more because in his old age he was giving himself over to relaxation and fun—yes, and even to drinking and music—he went to watch Thespis personally acting in one of his own plays, as was the custom in the old days. After the performance he had a question for Thespis: 'Aren't you ashamed to tell such enormous lies in front of so many people?' he asked. Thespis replied that there was nothing wrong with saying and doing this kind of thing for fun, whereupon Solon gave the ground a mighty blow with his stick and said, 'But if we accept this "fun" and think highly of it, before long we'll start to find it cropping up in important areas of life.'

[30] After Pisistratus' self-inflicted wound and the return from exile which had him carried into the city square on a cart,* he began to stir up the general populace by claiming that his enemies had conspired against him because of his political views. He was starting to win over large numbers of people, united by their loudly voiced grievances, when Solon came up to him, stood by his side and said, 'Pisistratus, you're not playing the part of Homer's Odysseus correctly. You've disfigured yourself just as he did, but in his case it was to trick his enemies, not to mislead his fellow citizens.'*

Later, when the people of Athens were ready to take up arms for Pisistratus, they convened a general assembly at which Ariston proposed that Pisistratus should be allowed a bodyguard of fifty club-bearers. Solon stood up and delivered a speech against the motion, in which he went on at length in a similar vein to some lines in one of his poems:

> For you pay heed to the tongue and words of a subtle man.
> Individually, each one of you walks with the steps of a fox,
> But when you come together your thinking is vain.*

However, when he saw that the poor were clamorously determined to gratify Pisistratus, while the rich were slinking away to avoid conflict, he walked out of the assembly, remarking that he had more intelligence than the one party and more courage than the other. He meant that he had more intelligence than those who failed to understand what was going on, and more courage than those who could see what was going on, but who were still too cowardly to offer any resistance to tyranny. So the people of Athens endorsed Ariston's motion, but then stopped worrying Pisistratus about the precise number of body-guards he had and let him get away with blatantly maintaining and recruiting as many men as he felt like, until in the end he seized the Acropolis.

After this, with the city in chaos, Megacles and the rest of the Alcmaeonidae lost no time in fleeing into exile; Solon, however, despite his extreme old age and his political isolation, appeared in the city square and addressed his fellow citizens. He had two objectives: to berate them for their ill-advised timidity, and to try to rouse them to further action and to urge them not to throw their freedom away. This was also the occasion when he famously said that though it would have been easier for them to have stopped the tyranny early, while it was still fledgling, it was more important and more glorious to eradicate it and destroy it now that it had already grown to maturity. People were too afraid to pay any attention to him, however, so he went back home, took his arms and armour, and put them in the lane in front of his door. 'I have played my part,' he said. 'I have done all I could to help my homeland and the laws.' And from then on he kept himself to himself. He ignored the advice of his friends to go into exile, and wrote poems in which he rebuked the Athenians:

> Your own cowardice is to blame for your wretched lives;
> Bear no ill will against the gods for them.
> It was you who gave these men guards and made them great,
> And that is why base servitude holds you now.

[31] Because of these poems people often used to try to set him straight and warn him that he would be put to death by the tyrant. When they asked him what gave him the confidence to be so reckless, he said, 'My old age.' Once Pisistratus had gained power, however, he set about winning Solon over; he expressed such admiration for him, showed him such kindness, and sent for him so often, that Solon actually became his adviser and approved of many of his measures. After all, most of Solon's legislation remained intact under Pisistratus, who not only led the way in abiding by the laws, but also insisted on his associates doing so as well. Once, for instance, when he was already tyrant, he was summoned to the Areopagus on a charge of homicide, and he duly appeared to defend himself (even though the prosecutor failed to turn up). He also made some laws of his own, one of which decrees that people disabled in war are to be maintained at public expense. Heraclides, however, says that Solon had made a law to this effect even earlier, to cover the case of a disabled man called Thersippus, and that Pisistratus merely copied this law of Solon's. And Theophrastus reports that it was Pisistratus, not Solon, who enacted the law against not working, which enabled him to increase the productivity of the countryside and the peacefulness of the city.*

Solon made a start on his *magnum opus* covering the history or legend of Atlantis,* which was peculiarly relevant to Athens, according to the learned priests of Saïs who were his informants, but he abandoned it. His reason for doing so was because he was afraid that he was too old to complete such a lengthy poem—not, as Plato says, because he was too busy. After all, the following words show that he had plenty of free time:

> I never stop learning—and learning a lot—as I grow old.

And again:

> Dear to me now are the works of the Cyprus-born goddess,
> Of Dionysus, and of the Muses; for they give men comfort.

[32] Plato treats the subject of Atlantis as if it were an abandoned plot of fine land (and it was in a sense his by right of kinship*). He was eager to work it up and embellish it, and he started by endowing it with huge porches, enclosures and courtyards, of a kind never before seen in any history, legend, or poem. He turned to the task too late, however, and his life came to an end before the writing did,

which means that the more we enjoy what he wrote, the more we regret what he left undone. As the temple of Olympian Zeus is to the city of Athens, so the story of Atlantis is to Plato's skill as a writer: a single incomplete work standing among plenty of fine products.*

Anyway, Solon survived into the period of Pisistratus' tyranny—a long time, as Heraclides of Pontus reports, but less than two years, according to Phanias of Eresus. Pisistratus' rule began in the archonship of Comias, and according to Phanias Solon died during the archonship of Hegestratus, which immediately followed that of Comias.* The story that he was cremated and his ashes were scattered on the island of Salamis is so odd that one would regard it as a completely untrustworthy fable, if it were not for the fact that it is written down by a number of reputable authors, including Aristotle the philosopher.*

THEMISTOCLES

INTRODUCTION

In 490 BC the Persian king sent an army across the Aegean Sea against Athens. It landed in Athenian territory, at Marathon, and was driven off in a great battle. Ten years later, Darius's successor Xerxes launched another, much larger, expedition against Greece as a whole. They advanced as far as Athens, sacked the city and burnt buildings and temples, but then suffered a major naval defeat at Salamis, off the coast of Attica. The Persian army retreated northward, only to return in spring 479 to occupy Attica once again. It finally fled from Europe after its defeat by the united Greeks at the battle of Plataea.

Themistocles emerged as the greatest Athenian leader of this period, for three reasons: he urged the Athenians to make their fleet the most power-ful in Greece, he led the Athenian naval forces and won a brilliant victory at Salamis, and he advised the rapid rebuilding of Athens' walls and stalled the Spartans until it could be accomplished. These three actions established the basis for the Athenian dominance of the Aegean Sea in the fifth cen-tury. Nevertheless, less than a decade later, Themistocles was driven into exile and pursued by the angry Athenians. He finally fled to Persia, where he was honoured by King Xerxes and established in luxury in Asia Minor.

The story of the Persian Wars was recorded incomparably by Herodotus: Themistocles is the hero of his eighth book, which focuses on Salamis. In addition, Thucydides preserves the story of his deception of the Spartans after the war, the rebuilding of the walls, and his flight from Athens to Persia (1. 90–3, 135–8).

The *Life of Themistocles* might easily have featured a retelling of the great battles against the Persians. Instead, Plutarch focuses on two aspects of Themistocles' character, his ambition and his intelligence. Relying on his audience's familiarity with the Persian Wars, he touches upon military events only as they illuminate Themistocles' character. The companion *Life of Camillus* shows that this was a conscious decision by Plutarch. Camillus saved Rome after it was sacked by the Gauls in 397 BC: the Life describes at length the attack of the Gauls on Rome, even though Camillus himself was in exile at the time. There is no introduction or final comparison to this pair, to explain Plutarch's thinking: the abrupt beginning of *Themistocles* may mean that the introduction was lost, and perhaps the comparison as well.

Both men came from relatively poor beginnings to exceptional honour, thanks to their military victories, but both also fell out of favour and were exiled. Both recovered their cities after they were sacked by their enemies, and supervised their rebuilding. Both were good generals, but Themistocles especially shines for his intelligence. As Thucydides put it, 'Themistocles, by his own wit, and without special study or experience, understood the present circumstances with the least planning, and anticipated the future course of events with the greatest success. Whatever he had in hand, he was able to explain clearly, and what he had little experience of, he could judge sufficiently. In particular, he foresaw in an unclear situation what was better and what was worse: to say it in a word, by his natural ability and with little practice he always divined what was necessary' (1. 138. 3). Plutarch shapes *Themistocles* by the continuing tension between this brilliance and the statesman's other distinguishing quality, his ambition. In this Life, despite the major events which Themistocles helped determine, much of the portrait is conveyed by the anecdotes which he reports in clusters at the turning points of his life.

The first two chapters indicate his less privileged background and native intelligence; the next three the wellsprings of his ambition, his rivalry with two other Athenian statesmen, Aristides and Miltiades.[1] This section culminates in a series of anecdotes illustrating Themistocles' ambition, and a sentence noting the ostracism of Aristides, his chief rival. The major section (6–17) is devoted to Themistocles' role in the battle of Salamis. Here also anecdotes dominate, and the military and political events are left in the background. For military events, one should read Herodotus book 8; for the sense of a brilliant and rather unscrupulous popular leader in a crisis, Plutarch. Realizing the need for Greek unity, Themistocles helps end the wars between the different states (6), accepts the Spartan Eurybiades as a commander of the fleet (7), and moves the recall of his opponent Aristides from exile (11). He 'introduced supernatural portents and oracles' to persuade the Athenians to trust their lives to their fleet (10). More riskily, he sends his agent Sicinnus to Xerxes, to urge him to attack the Greeks while they were in the straits of Salamis: the one manoeuvre which would both force the Greeks to fight there and exploit the narrow straits to gain an advantage against the Persians' superior force. The double effect of this trick is typical of Themistocles' brilliance, and is repeated when he sends Arnaces to urge Xerxes to flee back across the Hellespont to Asia. After the victory, Plutarch's narrative pauses to provide more anecdotes of Themistocles' ambition (18). These set the stage for the reversal (19–24), told not chronologically but by categories: the growing hostility of the

---

[1] The latter was credited with the victory at Marathon, the former led the Athenian contingent at Plataea, and is the subject of a life by Plutarch, in which Aristides' honesty and disinterest in money contrasts sharply with Themistocles' ambition and greedy self-interest.

Spartans (19–20) and the other Greeks (21) and finally the envy at home
(22) which led to his ostracism, exile, and flight across Greece. The journey to the Persian king (25–9) continues the adventure: as at Salamis,
Themistocles appears equal to every challenge, and can make his tricks
against the king during the war seem evidence of his pro-Persian feelings.
Once more, his success attracts enemies, this time among the Persian nobles
in Asia Minor (30–1). The honours he receives from the king do not induce
him to fight Greece, however, and he dies honoured not only by the king
and by the citizens of Magnesia, his new home, but even perhaps in Athens,
where there is a tomb overlooking the harbour of the Piraeus, the home of
the great fleet he convinced the Athenians to build, inscribed with the name
Themistocles (32). In an elegant concluding touch, Plutarch refers to the
continuation of the family over the centuries, down to a contemporary and
friend of Plutarch's, also named Themistocles.

The basis of Plutarch's account had to be Herodotus, the chief source
in antiquity for the Persian Wars. But he picks and chooses what he will
report, and provides his own interpretations. In addition, he pillages more
than twenty other authors, from Themistocles' contemporaries (Simonides,
author of lyric and narrative poems on the battle of Salamis, and Timocreon of Rhodes) to Hellenistic authors, to give his reader interesting
sidelights and alternate interpretations of events. To take one example:
Themistocles' flight from Athens to Persia (23–9) is based on Thucydides
1. 135–8, which tells of his flight to Epirus in north-west Greece, his journey
across the peninsula and across the Aegean Sea to Ephesus, his letter to
Artaxerxes, and finally the meeting with the king and the honours he
received.

In addition to Thucydides, however, Plutarch cites many items from other
sources. He reports Leobotes' indictment against Themistocles (23), perhaps from a documentary source; the notice of Stesimbrotus of Thasos that
Themistocles also travelled to Sicily (24); and items from the philosopher
Theophrastus and from Thucydides which tell against Stesimbrotus (25).
He contrasts the historian Theopompus' report of the money Themistocles left in Athens with that of Theophrastus (25). Later, on the disputed
question whether Themistocles had met with King Xerxes or his son
Artaxerxes, Plutarch cites Charon of Lampsacus, a fifth-century historian,
contemporary of Herodotus, and Thucydides on one side, and a group of
later historians, Ephorus, Dinon, Cleitarchus, and Heraclides, on the other
(27). The meeting with Artabanus he reports from Phanias, with an added
detail from Eratosthenes (27). He again cites Phanias, along with Neanthes
of Cyzicus for two cities given to Themistocles not mentioned in other
sources (29). Other anecdotes from this section are not found in Thucydides, and must come from unnamed sources: his letter back to Athens from

Argos (23), the dinner, prophecy, and dream at Nicogenes' house and his travel as a woman in a cart (26), Xerxes' rejoicing that he had Themistocles (28). Some of these stories we know from other sources, many we do not. A legend built up around Themistocles quite early, as is evident already in Herodotus and Thucydides: later writers embroidered his story in novelistic fashion.

We cannot say whether Plutarch consulted all these writers while preparing this Life: he would have read and heard accounts of Themistocles since childhood, and his adventures were a popular theme in the rhetorical schools. The various authorities on the Xerxes/Artaxerxes question he may have found collected in one of his sources. But Stesimbrotus he knew directly and cited frequently in *Cimon* and *Pericles*; Charon is cited in his work *On the Malice of Herodotus* and elsewhere, and Phanias appears frequently in this Life (1, 7, 13, 27, 29). Finally, Plutarch drew on personal knowledge: he or one of his friends had seen the temple to Artemis 'the Best Adviser' (22), and he was a friend of a descendant of Themistocles (32).[2]

What then is the value of *Themistocles*? As a historical source it preserves precious bits of information which supplement Herodotus and Thucydides, though it is not easy to separate fact from artful invention. It provides a window on to the legend which grew up around the statesman over the centuries. Finally, it provides a moral portrait of a great man with significant weaknesses, a saviour of his country yet rejected by it, who ended his life in exile, honoured by his former enemies. The Life incites to political involvement, while warning of the instability of public favour.

Burn, A. R., *Persia and the Greeks*, 2nd edn. (London: Duckworth, 1984), with postscript by D. M. Lewis. An account of the Persian Wars.

Frost, F. J., 'Themistocles' Place in Athenian Politics', *California Studies in Classical Antiquity*, 1 (1968), 105–24.

—— *Plutarch's Themistocles: A Historical Commentary* (Princeton: Princeton University Press, 1980). Valuable introduction and discussion of historical issues.

Larmour, D. H. J., 'Making Parallels: Synkrisis and Plutarch's "Themistocles and Camillus",' *ANRW* II.33.6 (1992), 4154–200. On the significance of the parallel with Camillus.

Lenardon, R. J., *The Saga of Themistocles* (London: Thames and Hudson, 1978). Explores the Themistocles legend.

---

[2] Although he cites the Roman Cornelius Nepos in other lives, there would have been no reason for Plutarch to use Nepos' *Themistocles*.

THEMISTOCLES

[1]<. . .>† As for Themistocles, however, the circumstances of his birth were initially too humble to promise future distinction.* His father Neocles (who was of the deme Phrearrhii and the tribe Leontis*) was not a particularly eminent man in Athens, and on his mother's side he was of mixed descent. This is vouched for by the following inscription:

> Habrotonon am I, a woman of Thrace; and yet I gave birth
> To an illustrious Greek—I mean, of course, Themistocles.

Phanias, however, reports that Themistocles' mother was not from Thrace, but Caria, and was called Euterpe rather than Habrotonon; and Neanthes adds the name of her native city in Caria as well—Halicarnassus.*

Now, Athenians considered illegitimate used to be enrolled in Cynosarges, a gymnasium outside the city gates which is dedicated to Heracles because he was not fully legitimate either, compared to his fellow deities, but had the taint of mixed descent thanks to his mother, who was mortal. But Themistocles set about persuading some well-born youths to go out to Cynosarges and exercise there with him, which they did—thereby earning him the reputation of having used his cunning to abolish the distinction between the illegitimate and legitimate members of Athenian society. However, there can be no doubt that he was connected to the Lycomidae family, because, as Simonides records, he personally paid for the restoration and decoration with paintings of the initiatory shrine at Phlya, which was owned collectively by the Lycomidae and had been burned down by the Persians.

[2] It is generally agreed that even as a child he was full of restless energy, and combined natural intelligence with an inclination towards involvement in activities and public life. For instance, in his spare time, when he was not busy with lessons, he tended not to play games or lounge around as most other boys did, but could be found rehearsing or composing speeches to himself—speeches designed to prosecute or defend one of the other children. This habit of his caused his teacher to say to him, 'You're not destined for obscurity, child: you'll certainly be something outstanding—for good or for ill.'

Also, he was a slow and reluctant student of subjects which were moral in tone, or which were designed to promote a cultured sense of pleasure and delight, and he showed an unchildlike contempt† for a merely theoretical approach to intelligence and practical activity, preferring to rely on his natural abilities. This led in later years, when men of reputed culture would tease him in refined and polite society, to his being forced to respond, in a rather meretricious fashion, by saying that although he did not know how to tune a lyre or handle a harp, he had taken a small and insignificant state and made it a place of distinction and importance. Stesimbrotus, it is true, says that Themistocles attended Anaxagoras' lectures and studied with Melissus, the natural scientist, but this is an anachronism: Melissus commanded the forces which resisted Pericles during his blockade of Samos, and Anaxagoras was a close associate of Pericles, and Pericles was much younger than Themistocles. More trustworthy is the view that Themistocles was an admirer of Mnesiphilus of Phrearrhii, a man who was not an orator or one of the so-called natural scientists, but who cultivated what passed in those days for wisdom—that is, political ingenuity and practical intelligence—and preserved it as if it were the teaching of a philosophical sect, passed down from one generation to another from Solon onwards. Mnesiphilus' successors, who combined this 'teaching' with forensic skills and diverted its application away from practical activities and towards oratory, were the so-called sophists.

It was Mnesiphilus, then, with whom Themistocles associated when he was just beginning his public career. However, his early adolescent impulses made him erratic and unstable, because he followed only his natural inclinations, which, if left unchecked by reason and education, cause dramatic shifts in a person's activities from one extreme to another, and often make him degenerate. Themistocles himself admitted as much in later life, by declaring that the best horses come from the most recalcitrant foals, as long as they receive the appropriate training and schooling. Some writers, however, have invented fictional consequences of Themistocles' instability: they say that he was disinherited by his father and that his mother was so upset by her son's bad reputation that she committed suicide. But this is surely false. Moreover, there are also those who say, to the contrary, that his father tried to discourage him from engaging in politics by showing him the wrecks of old, neglected triremes on the seashore—the implication being that the common people treated their leaders in the same way too, once they had outlived their usefulness.

[3] It looks as though politics became a prevalent and vigorous influence on Themistocles early in his life, and as though the desire for public recognition gained a thorough hold over him. It was this desire that led to his ambition, from the very start, to be the leading citizen of Athens, and therefore to his willing acceptance of the clashes between himself and the city's power-possessors and leaders. In particular, Aristides the son of Lysimachus was a constant opponent. But the origin of the hostility between the two men was apparently rather juvenile: according to Ariston the philosopher, they were both in love with the good-looking Stesilaus, who came from Ceos, and afterwards they continued to be rivals in the public arena too.* Nevertheless, it seems likely that the dissimilarities between their lifestyles and characters exacerbated their enmity. Aristides' character was moderate and conservative, and his political career was motivated not by a desire for gratification or reputation, but by the goal of maximizing the city's advantage to the fullest extent that was consistent with both safety and justice. He was therefore forced time and again to resist Themistocles' attempts to arouse the people of Athens and introduce major innovations, and to impede the growth of his power.

For instance, Themistocles was so carried away by his desire for recognition and so passionately longed to achieve something important—that is, he was so ambitious—that while he was still young, when the generalship of Miltiades was the talk of the town after the battle of Marathon against the Persians,* he could very often be found wrapped up in his own thoughts, and he lay awake at night and turned down opportunities for carousing as usual. When people expressed surprise at this change in his life and asked him about it, he told them that Miltiades' trophy would not let him sleep. For while everyone else thought that the Persian defeat at Marathon was the end of the war, Themistocles saw it as the start of a greater contest, and he therefore set about oiling himself and training his city to champion all Greece, since he looked far into the future and saw what was to come.

[4] The first consequence of this was that although the Athenians were accustomed to distribute among themselves the revenue from the silver mines at Laurium, Themistocles was the only one who dared to come forward in the Assembly and argue that they had to stop the distribution. He proposed that they should use the money from the

mines to build a fleet for the war against the Aeginetans, which was the most intense war being fought in Greece at the time and in which the Aeginetans had control of the sea, thanks to the size of their fleet. This made it even simpler for Themistocles to win the Athenian people over to his point of view. He did not have to wave Darius or the Persians at them: their distance from Athens made their coming seem a remote prospect and not one to cause people any particularly constant anxiety. Instead he opportunistically made use of the bitterness of his fellow citizens' rivalry with Aegina as a way of getting the fleet built. The money from Laurium went towards the construction of a hundred triremes, which were also used in the war at sea against Xerxes.*

After this, he gradually enticed the city down to the sea. He argued that on land they were no match even for their neighbours, whereas with naval power they could go so far as to keep the Persians at bay and make themselves the masters of Greece. And so he made them mariners and seafarers rather than 'steady infantrymen', to quote Plato.* In the process, he brought down on himself the following charge: 'Themistocles has robbed his fellow citizens of the spear and the shield and reduced the Athenian people to the rowing-bench and the oar.' In order to achieve this, he had, as Stesimbrotus reports, to overcome Miltiades' objections.

Whether or not this achievement of his compromised the perfection and purity of the Athenian constitution is a matter I prefer to leave the philosophers to consider. However, Xerxes' own actions prove more effectively than anything else that at the time the sea was the means of Greece's salvation and that these triremes of Themistocles' were responsible for restoring the Athenians' city after it had been burned to the ground. For after his defeat at sea Xerxes turned tail; even though his land forces remained undamaged, he considered himself outclassed. And it seems to me that Xerxes' reasons for leaving Mardonius behind had more to do with stopping the Greeks pursuing him than with subduing them.*

[5] Some writers claim that Themistocles had a keen eye for opportunities to make money and that this should be understood in the context of his generosity: he was fond of inviting people round to sacrificial feasts and lavished money grandly on his guests, with the result that he needed a copious income. Others, however, accuse him of considerable stinginess and meanness, and maintain that he used

to sell even the donated food.* When Diphilides the horse-breeder refused to give him a colt he had asked for, Themistocles threatened to turn his house, before long, into a wooden horse, which was a hint that he would stir up recriminations within his family and provoke lawsuits between the man and his own relatives.

There was no one more ambitious than him. While he was still young, before he had come to public notice, he prevailed upon Epicles of Hermione, a popular lyre-player in Athens, to play at his house, because he wanted large numbers of people to find out where he lived and to beat a path to his door.* Once, on a visit to Olympia, he offended the Greeks by trying to outdo Cimon with the grandeur of his dinners, pavilions, paraphernalia and so on; the same behaviour which was found excusable in Cimon's case, because he was young and came from an important family, was taken to be excessive and presumptuous self-aggrandizement on Themistocles' part, with the result that he gained a reputation for pretentiousness.* Again, as an impresario he was victorious with the tragedies he staged, although the competition was fiercely contested even at that early date. He set up a tablet commemorating his victory with the following inscription: 'Produced by Themistocles of Phrearrhii and directed by Phrynichus, in the archonship of Adeimantus.'*

At the same time, however, he made himself popular with the general populace, in the first place because he could readily call every one of his fellow citizens by name, and in the second place because he made himself available as a reliable arbiter of business deals. It was in this context that when Simonides of Ceos asked him to use his position as a military commander to do him an unfair favour, he replied, 'You would be a poor poet if you contravened harmonic law when composing your songs, and I would be a poor archon if I contravened constitutional law when doing people favours.'* On another occasion he teased Simonides by saying that it was stupid of him to put the Corinthians down when they had a great city to live in, while having statues made of himself when he was so ugly to look at. His power grew, thanks to his popularity with the common people, until he eventually won his fight against Aristides and succeeded in getting him banished by ostracism.*

[6] Later, when the Persian king was descending on Greece and the Athenians were trying to choose a commander, they say that everyone else was so terrified at the danger facing them that they

withdrew, of their own accord, from the running for the position, leaving Epicydes the son of Euphemides (a popular leader who was a skilful orator, but who had an irresolute character and was open to bribes) to go for it, with a good chance of being successful in the voting. Themistocles, they say, was afraid that with the leadership in Epicydes' hands everything would be completely ruined, so he bribed his ambition out of him.*

Another action of his which meets with approval in my sources is his treatment of the bilingual man who was in the delegation sent by the Persian king to demand earth and water.* He arrested this man, who was acting as an interpreter, and then procured a decree to have him put to death, for his shameless use of the Greek language to transmit foreigners' demands. Similar approval is given to his treatment of Arthmius of Zelea as well; again, at Themistocles' suggestion, this man's name was entered in the lists of the disenfranchised, along with those of his sons and his whole family. The grounds were that he had brought Persian gold to give to the Greeks.* His greatest achievement, however, was to end all the inter-Greek fighting and get the various states to come to terms with one another, by persuading them that their hostilities should take second place to the war with Persia. It is said that Cheileos of Arcadia was particularly helpful to Themistocles in this regard.*

[7] As soon as he had taken up his command, he set about getting his fellow citizens to board their triremes, and he tried to persuade them to abandon their city and meet the Persians at sea as far away as possible from Greece. These ideas met with a great deal of opposition, however, so he joined forces with the Lacedaemonians and led a sizeable army into the field at Tempe, where they intended to meet the invasion and defend Thessaly, because at that time it was not yet known that Thessaly was collaborating with the enemy.* Later, however, after the army pulled back from there without having achieved its purpose, and once the Thessalians had joined the Persian king and everywhere up to and including Boeotia was supporting the Persian cause, the Athenians were more inclined to listen to what Themistocles was saying about the sea, and he was sent with a fleet to Artemisium to guard the strait.*

At this juncture the Greeks asked Eurybiades and the Lacedaemonians to take command, but the Athenians refused to be subordinate to anyone, because they had more ships than almost everyone else put together. Themistocles appreciated the danger of this situation and not only waived the command in favour of Eurybiades, but also set about calming the Athenians down by guaranteeing to get the Greeks to submit willingly to them after the war, provided that they proved their courage during it. This is why Themistocles is held to be responsible, more than anyone else, for the preservation of Greece, and to have played a particularly important part in bringing about the general recognition of the Athenians' superiority to their enemies in courage and to their allies in diplomacy.

Eurybiades was terrified by the size of the fleet facing him, once the Persian force reached Aphetae, and when he found out that there were 200 more ships sailing around the northern side of Sciathos,* he wanted to take the shortest route back to the interior of Greece, where he could remain in communication with the Peloponnese and use the fleet as additional protection for the land army. It was his view that the Persian king was too strong to be overcome at sea. The Euboeans became afraid that the Greeks were going to abandon them, so they entered into secret negotiations with Themistocles and sent Pelagon to him with substantial amounts of money. According to Herodotus, Themistocles accepted this bribe and gave it to Eurybiades.*

Among his fellow citizens, it was Architeles, the commander of the sacred vessel, who most strongly resisted Themistocles' plans.* The reason he wanted to sail back home was because he did not have the money to pay his crew. Themistocles inflamed the crew's resentment against Architeles even more, until they rushed at him and stole his meal. Architeles was depressed and dismayed by this turn of events—but then Themistocles sent him a meal of bread and meat in a basket, at the bottom of which he had placed a talent's weight of silver coin, with the suggestion that he should eat his meal right away and then take care of his crew the next day; otherwise, he said, he would denounce him in front of his fellow citizens for having accepted a bribe from the enemy. Anyway, this is what Phanias of Lesbos says Themistocles did.

[8] Despite all this, although the battles that took place on that occasion against the Persian fleet in and around the strait did not crucially influence the outcome of the whole war, the experience the Greeks gained was of inestimable value to them, in the sense that their actual achievements in the face of danger taught them that men who know

how to fight at close quarters and have the courage to engage the enemy have nothing to fear from huge numbers of ships, brightly decorated figureheads, boastful cries, or barbaric war-chants. It is rather the case, they learnt, that they should disregard everything like that and just make for their actual physical enemies, come to grips with them and fight on to the bitter end. It looks as though Pindar too appreciated this point well enough when he said of the battle of Artemisium that it was 'where Athens' sons laid the gleaming foundation of freedom', because courage is the true origin of victory.

Artemisium is a north-facing beach in Euboea, past Hestiaea; it lies more or less opposite Olizon, which is in the land once ruled by Philoctetes. There is at Artemisium a small temple of 'East-looking' Artemis, as she is known there, which stands in a grove of trees, surrounded by blocks of white marble fixed in the ground. Rubbing this marble with one's hand yields a saffron-like colour and smell. One of the blocks of stone has been inscribed with the following elegiac poem:

> There was a time when on this stretch of sea the sons of Athens
> In battle overcame a varied host of men of Asian stock;
> To mark their destruction of the army of the Medes,
> They erected these tokens in honour of the maiden Artemis.

One is shown a part of the beach where in the middle of all the surrounding sand the depths throw up a dark, ash-like dust which looks as though it is the result of fire; it is believed that the wrecked ships and bodies of the dead were burnt on this spot.

[9] However, when news of events at Thermopylae reached Artemisium—when they learnt that Leonidas had fallen and that Xerxes was in control of the land routes*—they proceeded to pull back into the interior of Greece. In this manoeuvre the Athenians, who were elated at their achievements, were posted as rearguard because of the courage they had displayed. Whenever Themistocles spotted, as he sailed along the coast, places where the enemy would inevitably land and shelter, he inscribed in plain view a message on the rocks—perhaps rocks he found by chance or perhaps ones he set up himself at the anchorages and watering-places. In this message he urged the Ionians to come over, if they could, to the side of the Athenians, who were, after all, their forefathers and who were bearing the brunt of the danger in the fight for their liberation; or, failing that, to obstruct and disrupt the foreign army during any fighting that took

place. He hoped that this might have one of two consequences: it would either get the Ionians to desert or it would sow confusion in the Persian army by increasing their suspicion of the Ionians.*

Although Xerxes had marched up through Doris and invaded Phocis, and was putting the Phocian settlements to the torch, the Greeks did not go to their relief, despite the fact that the Athenians were begging them to take to the field in Boeotia and make a stand against the enemy there in defence of Attica, to match the way they— the Athenians—had sailed to Artemisium to help the Greek cause. These Athenian pleas fell on deaf ears, however, since everyone else refused to leave the Peloponnese; they wanted to collect all the Greek forces together within the Isthmus and to build a defensive wall right across the Isthmus from sea to sea. The Athenians were angry at this betrayal, and also dismayed and distressed at being deserted by their allies. They were not about to take on an army consisting of so many thousands of men, and the situation left them with no choice but to evacuate the city and take to their ships. This plan was causing widespread discontent, however: people argued that they did not want that kind of victory† and that they could not understand what 'safety' might mean if it involved abandoning the temples of the gods and their ancestral tombs.*

[10] At this point Themistocles was stuck: there was no way for him to win the general populace over to his point of view by human arguments. Instead, then, he acted like a tragic poet hoisting up his stage machinery, and introduced supernatural portents and oracles.* As a portent, he availed himself of the business with the snake, which is supposed to have vanished from the sacred precinct at about this time; when the priests found that the daily offerings made to it were untouched, they told the people (acting as mouthpieces for Themistocles) that the goddess had left the city and was showing them the way to the sea. He also made use of the famous oracle to try to sway the populace again, this time with the argument that the 'wooden wall' could only refer to their fleet, and that the reason the god had called Salamis 'divine', rather than 'dreadful' or 'cruel', was because it was destined to become synonymous with a piece of great good fortune for Greece. Once he had won them over to his point of view, he proposed a decree whereby the city was to be entrusted for safe keeping to 'Athena, protectress of Athens', all the men of military age were to board their triremes, and each man was to make the best

provisions for the safety of his children, wives and slaves that he could.*
After the decree had been ratified, most of the Athenians sent their
families as refugees to Troezen, where the Troezenians did their best
to outdo one another in making them welcome; they passed a decree
that the state was to pay for their maintenance with a daily allowance
of two obols per person, that children could pick fruit from anywhere,
and that the state was to pay for the children's schooling. This decree
was proposed by Nicagoras.*

Since the Athenians had no public funds, the Council of the
Areopagus took on the main burden of responsibility for the man-
ning of the triremes by advancing eight drachmas to each man serving in the armed forces. This is what Aristotle says,* anyway, but
Cleidemus portrays it as another expedient by Themistocles. He says
that while the Athenians were making their way down to the Piraeus
the Gorgon's-head device was lost from the statue of the goddess.
Themistocles therefore searched everything, on the pretext of looking for the device, and kept finding large amounts of money hidden
in people's luggage, which† was confiscated for public use and meant
that the ships' crews had easily enough money and provisions.

The sight of the city taking to the sea provoked sorrow in some
spectators, but others were amazed at the courage involved, since
the Athenians were sending their families off elsewhere, while they
themselves were crossing over to the island, unmoved by the cries and
tears and embraces of their parents. In fact, however, the large num-
bers† of their fellow citizens who were being left behind because they
were too old to make the journey did excite pity, and there was also
a certain sensitive softening of the heart occasioned by the domestic
animals and pets running alongside their masters emitting cries of
longing. There is a story that one of these animals, a dog belonging
to Xanthippus, the father of Pericles, was so upset at being abandoned
by him that it leapt into the sea, swam beside the trireme and was
washed ashore on Salamis, only to collapse and die straight away. Even
today one is shown a place called 'Dog's Tomb', which is said to be
where it is buried.

[11] Apart from these undoubtedly important achievements of his,
Themistocles also noticed that his fellow citizens were missing
Aristides, and were afraid that he might be disgruntled enough to join
the Persian side and cause the downfall of Greece. (Aristides had lost
his feud against Themistocles before the start of the war and been

banished by ostracism.*) He therefore introduced a decree to the effect that, provided an exile was not under a lifelong sentence, he could return and put all his actions and words in the service of the best interests of Greece alongside his fellow citizens.

Now, the high regard in which Sparta was held meant that Eurybiades was in command of the fleet, but he tended to be irresolute in times of danger. He was in favour of setting sail for the Isthmus, where the Peloponnesian land army had also been assembled, but Themistocles argued against this plan. This was the occasion, they say, of certain *bons mots* by Themistocles.* So, when Eurybiades said to him, 'Themistocles, at the games they flog those who are too quick off the mark', Themistocles replied, 'Yes, but they award no prizes to those who get left behind.' When Eurybiades raised his stick and it looked as though he was going to hit him with it, Themistocles said, 'All right, hit me—but hear what I have to say.'

Eurybiades, impressed with his self-possession, gave him permission to speak, and Themistocles started to try to bring him back to the main issues. When someone queried the propriety of a stateless person telling those who still had homelands to abandon them and give them up, Themistocles turned to him and retorted, 'Yes, you wretch, it's true that we have abandoned our homes and our city walls: we choose not to suffer slavery for the sake of lifeless objects. In actual fact, though, we have a city greater than any in Greece—our 200 triremes—which are standing by ready to help you if you want to be saved by them. And if you treacherously forsake us a second time, it will soon become common knowledge throughout Greece that the Athenians have found themselves a free city and a country that is no worse than the one they lost.' These words of Themistocles' made Eurybiades think, and he began to be afraid that the Athenians might abandon the Greeks and leave. Then, when the Eretrian commander tried to make a point against him, he said, 'You're a fine lot to be talking about war, when like cuttlefish you have swords, but no hearts.'

[12] There is a story to be found in some sources that while Themistocles was discussing these matters on the top deck of the ship,† an owl was spotted flying from left to right over the ships, until it perched in his rigging. This was in fact the main reason why the Greeks fell in with Themistocles' plans and got ready to meet the enemy at sea. However, when the arrival of the enemy fleet in the Phaleric Gulf* blotted out the surrounding shoreline, and when the Persian

king came down to the coast in person along with the land army, and was seen with all his troops assembled, this combination of forces made Themistocles' words fade from the Greeks' memories; the Peloponnesians again began to turn their eyes longingly towards the Isthmus and to become angry whenever an alternative course of action was mentioned. In fact, they decided to withdraw under cover of darkness and the helmsmen were given the order to prepare for sailing.

At this point Themistocles stepped in. The thought that the Greeks were going to throw away the topographical advantages afforded them by the narrow waters there and disperse to their various cities upset him so much that after some reflection he devised the famous business with Sicinnus.* This was a man who, despite being a Persian prisoner-of-war, was loyal to Themistocles, and was in fact his children's tutor. Themistocles sent Sicinnus on a secret mission to Xerxes, with instructions to deliver the following message: 'Themistocles, the commander of the Athenian forces, who is a supporter of the Persian cause, is letting you know by this message what you will not yet have heard from anyone else—that the Greeks are intending to slip away. He urges you not to let them escape, but to attack while they are in disarray and separated from their land forces, and to wipe out their navy.' Xerxes, believing that the message was an act of friendship, delightedly accepted the information at face value. He lost no time in issuing his naval commanders with their instructions: they were to make the bulk of the fleet ready for battle at their leisure, but 200 ships were to put to sea immediately, encircle the entire strait, and link the islands, to prevent any break-out by the enemy.

The first person to notice what Xerxes was up to was Aristides the son of Lysimachus. He immediately went to Themistocles' tent, even though he did not like the man, and Themistocles had been responsible for getting him ostracized, as I mentioned earlier.* When Themistocles emerged from his tent, Aristides told him that they were surrounded. Themistocles was aware of the nobility of Aristides' character and was impressed that he had come to him, so he told him about the business with Sicinnus. Then he asked him to help him restrain the Greeks and, since the Greeks trusted him more, to join him in trying to ensure that they would engage the enemy at sea in the straits. After telling Themistocles that he approved of his actions, Aristides visited the rest of the general staff and the trierarchs, and tried to motivate them for the forthcoming battle. In spite of everything, they were still unsure whether or not to believe him, but just then there appeared a Tenian trireme, which had deserted from the enemy. This trireme, captained by Panaetius, brought the news that they were surrounded, and so in the end it was a combination of anger and necessity that made the Greeks set out to face the danger.

[13] At dawn the next day Xerxes seated himself on high ground, from where he could survey the fleet and its deployment. Phanodemus says that this vantage-point overlooked the sanctuary of Heracles, where Salamis is separated from Attica by a narrow channel; according to Acestodorus, however, it was on the border between Attica and the Megarid, on top of the peaks known as the Horns. He had a golden stool set down, and was attended by plenty of scribes, whose job it was to write down what happened in the course of the battle.

While Themistocles was performing the sacrificial rites alongside the flagship, three extremely handsome prisoners-of-war were brought to him, arrayed in magnificent clothing and golden jewellery. Their parents were said to be Sandace, who was the king's sister, and Artayctes. Just as the diviner, Euphrantides, caught sight of them, a brilliant flame shot up high into the air from the entrails and, significantly, a sneeze was heard on the right. Euphrantides therefore took Themistocles by the hand and told him to consecrate the young men and then sacrifice them, with a prayer, to Dionysus the Eater of Raw Flesh, because then the Greeks would not be destroyed and would win the day. Themistocles was shocked at such gross and obscene instructions from the diviner, but the general populace (who in times of crisis, when important issues are at stake, typically expect their salvation to be won by irrational rather than rational means) with a single voice took up the cry of 'Dionysus!'. They dragged the prisoners to the altar and compelled the sacrifice to be carried out as the diviner had demanded. Anyway, this is what Phanias of Lesbos says happened, and he was a philosopher with considerable experience of historical writings as well.*

[14] As regards the number of ships on the Persian side, in *The Persians* the poet Aeschylus, speaking from a position of expert knowledge, confidently asserts:

As I well know, Xerxes had one thousand ships
At his command, then twice one hundred
And seven ships of surpassing speed. So stands the count.*

The Athenians, on the other hand, had 180 ships, each with an eighteen-strong contingent of marines to fight from the decks, consisting of four archers and fourteen hoplites.

Themistocles is generally held to have discerned the right time for fighting with the same degree of skill as he picked the location, in the sense that he did not deploy his triremes prow-on towards the Persian fleet until it was that time of day when, as usual, the fresh breeze blows in from the open sea and a swell gets up in the straits. This did not create any problems for the Greek ships, because they were light and lay low in the water, but when it caught the Persian ships, with their high sterns and raised decks and weight, it slewed them round and made them present their broadsides to the Greeks, who were bearing down on them eagerly, keeping their eyes on Themistocles, because they thought he saw best what was to be done. And this was why Xerxes' naval commander Ariamenes—a brave man and by far the best and most honest of Xerxes' brothers, who was ranged opposite Themistocles—kept firing arrows and hurling javelins from his huge ship, as though he were on the wall of a city. This was the man encountered by Ameinias of Decelea and Socles of Piraeus,*† who were both on board the same ship. What happened was that the two ships collided prow to prow and their bronze beaks became firmly entangled together; so Ariamenes tried to board their ship, but Ameinias and Socles made a stand against him and hit him so hard with their spears that he fell into the sea. As his body was drifting here and there among the wreckage, Artemisia recognized it and recovered it for Xerxes.*

[15] It was at this point in the battle, they say, that a bright light blazed out from the direction of Eleusis, and a noise—a cry—echoed over the Thriasian Plain and down to the sea. It sounded as though a large crowd of people was escorting the mystic Iacchus in the procession. Then a cloud appeared to rise gradually up into the sky from the shouting throng before sinking down again and setting on the triremes.* Others seemed to see apparitions, the ghosts of armed men coming from Aegina with their hands held out to protect the Greek warships; they took these armed men to be the Aeacidae, to whom prayers for help had been offered before the start of the battle.

The first man to capture a ship was Lycomedes, an Athenian trierarch, who was later to cut the figurehead off the ship and dedicate it to Laurel-bearing Apollo at Phlya.* The narrowness of the straits cancelled out the numerical advantage of the Persian fleet and meant that they could only attack squadron by squadron and that they got in one another's way, and so, although the Persians 'held out till night-fall', to quote Simonides,* the Greeks drove them back and won that fine and famous victory—a victory more splendid than any other that has been achieved at sea by either Greeks or non-Greeks—thanks not only to the courage and concerted commitment of the combatants, but also to the soundness of Themistocles' judgement and to his ingenuity.

[16] After the battle, with his failure still rankling, Xerxes set about building a causeway over to Salamis, by means of which he could lead his land army against the Greeks there, once he had dammed up the intervening sound. Themistocles, however, wanting to see how Aristides would respond, proposed that the Greeks should take the fleet to the Hellespont and break up the pontoon bridge, 'in order to trap Asia within Europe,' as he put it.

The idea did not meet with Aristides' approval, though. 'At the moment,' he said, 'the invader we have fought is taking life easy. However, if we shut him up in Greece and leave a man with such powerful resources at his command no choice but to act out of fear, he'll no longer watch battles while taking his ease on a seat beneath a golden canopy. Instead, he'll run every risk there is; he'll person-ally be present at every engagement, he'll make amends for his ear-lier negligence, and he'll listen to better advice about his affairs in general. No, Themistocles,' he concluded, 'we should not be destroy-ing the present bridge: it would be better for us to build another one alongside it, if we could, so as to throw the man out of Europe with as little delay as possible.'

'In that case,' said Themistocles, 'if this strikes you as the best course of action, now is the time for all of us to put our minds to it and come up with ways to get him out of Greece as quickly as possible.'

Once this plan had been adopted, he dispatched one of the royal eunuchs—a man called Arnaces, whom he discovered among the prisoners-of-war—with instructions to deliver the following message to the king: 'Now that they have mastery of the sea, the Greeks have decided to sail up to the Hellespont and dismantle the bridge of boats. However, I have your best interests at heart. I would advise you to waste no time in crossing back over to your own territory, while I will find ways to slow my allies down and delay their pursuit of you.'

The Persian king was terrified by this message and began pulling back without delay. The wisdom of Themistocles' and Aristides' policy was proved later in the campaign against Mardonius, in the sense that although at Plataea the Greeks fought against only the merest fraction of Xerxes' forces, they stood in danger of losing everything.*

[17] According to Herodotus, collective battle honours went to Aegina, but the individual first place was unanimously awarded to Themistocles, even though people's envy made them reluctant to do so. What happened was that when the military commanders withdrew to the Isthmus and picked up their voting pebbles from the altar, each of them declared himself the winner, but gave the second place to Themistocles. Moreover, the Lacedaemonians brought him down to Sparta, and while they awarded Eurybiades an olive-branch garland as the prize for valour, they gave Themistocles one as a prize for wisdom; they also presented him with the finest chariot the city could provide and gave him an honorary escort of 300 young men as far as the border.* And it is said that in the course of the next Olympic Games,* when Themistocles entered the stadium, the spectators ignored the contestants and spent the whole day watching him instead and pointing him out to visitors from abroad with admiring applause. Themistocles, the story goes on, was well pleased; he acknowledged to his friends that he was now reaping the reward for all his labours in the service of Greece.

[18] He was in fact extremely ambitious for prestige, to judge by the recorded stories about him. For instance, during his time as Athens' elected fleet commander, he used to refuse to do his jobs one at a time, whether they were private or public business, but would delay every task that came his way until the day when he was due to sail, so that, as a result of doing a lot of things at once and dealing with a wide variety of people, he would give the impression of being an important person with a great deal of power. Once, looking at some enemy corpses washed ashore along the coastline, he noticed that they were wearing golden bracelets and torques. He himself walked on by, but he pointed them out to a friend who was with him and said, 'You can help yourself; you are not Themistocles.' To Antiphates, who as a good-looking boy had treated him dismissively, but who later fawned on him because of his standing in society, he said, 'Young man, we may have left it late, but now we have both come to our senses.'

He used to say that the Athenians did not really appreciate or admire him, but treated him like a plane-tree: in bad weather they would run for shelter under him, but when the prevailing weather was good they pruned him and curbed his growth. When the man from Seriphos told him that he owed his fame to his city rather than his own merits, he replied, 'You're right; but just as fame wouldn't have come my way if I were from Seriphos, so it wouldn't come your way even if you were from Athens.'*

When one of his fellow military commanders, who imagined that he had been of service to Athens, behaved brashly in Themistocles' presence and compared his own accomplishments with his, he said: 'In the course of an argument between Day-after and Holiday, Day-after pointed out that whereas Holiday was all hustle and bustle, *she* provided the opportunity for everyone to enjoy at their leisure every-thing that had gone into Holiday. "That's true," Holiday replied, "but *you* would not exist without *me*." By the same token,' Themistocles added, 'if I had not been around then, where would all of you be now?' When his son was wilfully bossing his mother about, and so indirectly bossing Themistocles himself, he jokingly described him as the most powerful person in Greece, since everyone else in Greece took orders from the Athenians, while they took orders from him, he did from the boy's mother, and the boy's mother did from the lad himself!

His desire always to be original once led him, when he was selling one of his estates, to have the auctioneer announce that the estate also had an excellent neighbour. When two men wanted to marry his daughter, he chose the good one in preference to the rich one, because, he said, he was looking for a man without money rather than money without a man. This was the kind of person his sayings reveal him to be.

[19] With these great exploits over, he immediately set about rebuild-ing and fortifying the city. Theopompus records that he did so by bribing the ephors not to raise any objections, but the majority of the sources say that he merely tricked them.* What happened was that during a visit of his to Sparta, when his name was down on the register as an envoy, the Spartiates brought up the complaint that the Athenians were fortifying the city, and Polyarchus was sent over from Aegina to make a formal accusation to that effect. Themistocles denied the charge and suggested that they send a delegation to Athens to look the place over, first because this delay would give the process

of fortifying the city more time, and, second, because he wanted the Athenians to have the delegation in their power, to match his position in Sparta. This is in fact what happened. When the Lacedaemonians became aware of what was actually going on, they concealed their resentment and sent him back home without doing him any harm.

Afterwards, he began to work on the Piraeus, since he had noticed the quality of its harbours and wanted to join the city as a whole to the sea. In a sense, then, the policy he was pursuing ran counter to that of the old kings of Athens, because it had been their concern, we are told, to tear their subjects away from the sea and get them used to cultivating the land rather than living a seafaring life. It was in pursuit of this aim that they disseminated the story about how when Poseidon was disputing Athena's claim to the land she produced for the judges the sacred olive and so won the contest. Themistocles, however, while he fell short of 'cementing the Piraeus' on to the city, as the comic poet Aristophanes puts it,* did nevertheless make Athens depend on the Piraeus and the land on the sea. This also enabled him to increase the power of the common people, to the detriment of the aristocratic party, until they became filled with presumptuousness, since power now rested with the crews of the ships, those who called the time for the rowers, and the helmsmen. And this also explains why the platform in the Pnyx, which had been built so as to face towards the sea, was later turned inland by the Thirty: to their minds, the origins of democracy lay with Athens' maritime empire, while oligarchy was more to the liking of those who worked the land.*

[20] Themistocles, however, had even more grandiose schemes in mind for confirming Athens' power at sea. After Xerxes' departure, when the Greek fleet had put in at Pagasae for the winter, he delivered a speech in front of the Athenians in which he said that there was something they could do which would bring them many advantages, including their security, but which could not be widely discussed. The Athenians told him to confide his plan to Aristides alone, and to proceed with it if it met with *his* approval. So Themistocles told Aristides that his plan was to burn the other Greeks' ships where they lay beached. Aristides stood up before the Athenian people and told them that the operation Themistocles had in mind was undoubtedly highly advantageous—and highly criminal. The Athenians therefore ordered Themistocles to take the matter no further.

When at sessions of the Amphictyonic League the Lacedaemonians introduced a motion to the effect that any states which had failed to join the alliance against the Persians should be excluded from the League, Themistocles became worried. He was afraid that the exclusion from the sessions not just of the Thessalians and Argives, but of the Thebans too, would mean that the Lacedaemonians would completely dominate the voting, and would be able to get their way in everything. He therefore spoke up on behalf of the threatened states and changed the mood of the meeting. He pointed out that only thirty-one states, most of which were very small indeed, had played an active part in the war, and that therefore the proscription of the rest of Greece would create an intolerable situation whereby the sessions would be controlled by two or three powerful states.* It was this episode, more than any other, which opened up the breach between the Lacedaemonians and Themistocles and which led to their trying to advance Cimon's standing in Athens and to turn him into someone who could rival Themistocles in politics.

[21] He also incurred the hatred of the allies by sailing around the Aegean islands and trying to extort money from them. When, for instance, he tried to demand money from the people of Andros, the interchange between them went as follows, according to Herodotus. He said that he had come with two gods in his train, namely Persuasion and Compulsion; they replied that they too had a pair of powerful gods, Poverty and Insufficiency, who made it impossible for them to give him any money.*

The lyric poet Timocreon of Rhodes launched a fairly bitter attack on Themistocles in one of his songs, claiming that he had, for a fee, arranged for other exiles to be restored to their native countries, but took a bribe to leave him in the lurch, despite the fact that they were acquaintances, and that he was a guest-friend of Themistocles. This is what he says:

> You may sing the praises of Pausanias or Xanthippus
> Or Leotychidas, but I praise Aristides,
> The one honest man to come from holy Athens.
> Leto loathes Themistocles—that liar, cheat, and traitor—
> Who allowed himself to be swayed by base money
> And refused to bring back home to Ialysus
> Timocreon, for all that he was his guest-friend.
> No, he took his three talents and sailed off to perdition.

> Some he brought back home who never deserved it,
> Others he sent packing into exile, still others he killed;
> Stuffed with money, at the Isthmus he played mine host,
> Making a fool of himself by serving up cold meat—
> They ate, while praying for Themistocles' death.*

After Themistocles had been condemned and banished Timocreon resorted to considerably more immoderate and unrestrained abuse in the poem which begins:

> O Muse, grant to this song of mine
> Fame throughout Greece,
> As is only fair and just.

Timocreon is said to have been exiled for collaborating with the Persians, with Themistocles as one of those who voted to condemn him. So when Themistocles was accused of being a Persian sympathizer, Timocreon railed against him in the following poem:

> So Timocreon was not the only one
> To make a deal with the Persians:
> There are other wicked men around, it seems.
> I'm not the only one with a stump for a tail—
> There are other foxes to be found.

[22] Finally, when envy led even his fellow citizens to be happy to entertain slanderous tales about him, he was forced into the position, offensive as it was, of frequently alluding in the Assembly to his own achievements. When people expressed annoyance at this, he said, 'Do you find it boring to have favours frequently done you by the same men?' He also irritated the general populace by constructing the shrine of Artemis, giving her the name Aristoboule, the Best Adviser, and so intimating that he was the best adviser Athens and the Greeks had. He built the shrine in Melite, near his house, on the site where nowadays the public executioners cast out the bodies of executed criminals and take the clothes and nooses of those who are strangled to death. There was also a small bust of Themistocles, which was still standing in the shrine of Artemis Aristoboule in my day; he appears to have been a man of heroic features, as well as heroic temperament.*

So they sentenced him to banishment by ostracism, as a way of curbing his prestige and pre-eminence; this was their usual practice in the case of anyone whose power struck them as oppressive and as incompatible with democratic equality. The point is that ostracism was not a means of punishing a crime, but a way of relieving and assuaging envy—an emotion which finds its pleasure in humbling outstanding men and vents its resentment by imposing this loss of status.*

[23] After his expulsion from Athens, and during his stay in Argos, the business with Pausanias gave his enemies a handle against him.* It was Leobotes the son of Alcmaeon of the deme Agryle who brought the indictment, with the Spartiates supporting his case. What happened was that although Pausanias started off by concealing from Themistocles, despite their friendship, the notorious double-dealing he was engaged in, when he saw that Themistocles had been banished and was bitter about it, he felt confident enough to invite him to join him in his treachery; he showed him a letter written by the Persian king and roused his anger against the Greeks by describing them as worthless and ungrateful people. Now, while Themistocles rejected Pausanias' approaches and refused point blank to join him, he told no one else about their conversations and did not denounce Pausanias' activities, perhaps because he expected him to stop, or perhaps because he expected him to be found out anyway, since his motivation was so irrational and his objectives so wild and reckless. Consequently, after Pausanias had been put to death, certain letters and documents relating to these matters came to light which threw suspicion on Themistocles. The Lacedaemonians vociferously denounced him, and those of his fellow citizens who were envious of his power brought charges against him. Although he was not there to defend himself, he did so in writing, relying above all on the earlier accusations he had faced. He wrote in this letter that his adversaries were slanderously trying to convince his fellow citizens that he never stopped wanting to rule, and had neither the capacity nor the will to be ruled; but in that case, he argued, he would be the last person to sell himself, along with Greece, to the Persians or to his country's enemies. However, the Athenian people found his accusers' arguments persuasive, and they sent men with orders to arrest him and bring him back to stand trial before a panhellenic tribunal.

[24] Themistocles received advance warning of what was happening, however, so he crossed over to Corcyra, where he was registered as a public benefactor of the state. (This came about as a result of his actions as mediator in a dispute between Corcyra and Corinth: he ended the hostilities by deciding that Corinth should pay Corcyra twenty

talents and that Leucas should be administered as a joint colony of
both states.) From Corcyra he fled to Epirus, but the Athenians and
Lacedaemonians continued to follow him, so he took a terrible risk
and sought refuge with Admetus, the king of the Molossians. Now,
Admetus had once approached the Athenians with a request and had
been rudely turned down by Themistocles, who was at the height of
his power at the time, so he had a permanent grudge against him and
had made it clear that he would take his revenge if Themistocles ever
fell into his hands. Under the circumstances, however, Themistocles
felt he had more to fear from recent, personal hostility than from some
old, regal grudge, so he went and threw himself on the king's mercy.
The way in which he presented himself as a suppliant of Admetus
was quite striking, and is peculiar to that country: he took hold of the
king's young son and prostrated himself at the hearth. This is held
by the Molossians to be the most powerful form of supplication and,
uniquely, more or less unrefusable. Some say that it was Phthia, the
king's wife, who suggested this form of supplication to Themistocles
and had the boy take a seat at the hearth with him, others that it was
Admetus himself who set up the supplication and joined in the performance, so that when faced with the posse of pursuers he could give
religious grounds for the necessity of not giving Themistocles up.*

   Stesimbrotus reports that Themistocles' wife and children were
smuggled out of Athens and sent to him in Molossis by Epicrates of
the deme Acharnae (an action for which Cimon later took Epicrates
to court and had him put to death); later, however, Stesimbrotus seems
mysteriously to have forgotten them—or perhaps he has Themistocles
forget them!—because he claims that Themistocles sailed to Sicily and
asked the tyrant Hiero for his daughter's hand in marriage, in return
for guaranteeing to make the Greeks his subjects. Hiero rejected him,
however, and it was then, according to Stesimbrotus, that Themistocles
set sail for Asia.

   [25] This is unlikely to have happened, however. After all, in *On
Kingship* Theophrastus records how, when Hiero sent horses to compete at Olympia and set up an expensively ornamented tent for them,
Themistocles made a speech before the Greeks, in which he said that
they should tear down the tyrant's tent and bar his horses from the
competition.* Moreover, Thucydides says that Themistocles made
his way down to the Aegean coast and set sail from Pydna, without
anyone on board knowing who he was until adverse winds carried

the boat to Naxos. At the time Naxos was being blockaded by an Athenian force, and Themistocles was scared enough to reveal his identity to the ship's owner and the helmsman. Partly by pleading with them, and partly by threatening to denounce them to the Athenians with the lie that they knew all along who he was and had been bribed to take him on board, he compelled them to sail by the island and reach the Asian coastline.* A lot of his money was smuggled across to Asia by friends, but even so 100 talents (according to Theopompus, but Theophrastus says eighty talents) were discovered and sequestered for the public treasury, when Themistocles had not had even three talents' worth of property before entering public life.

[26] After landing at Cyme, he discovered that a great many people up and down the coast (chiefly Ergoteles, Pythodorus and their men) were watching out for an opportunity to capture him. For people who did not mind how they made money, the hunt promised to be lucrative, since the king had put a price of 200 talents on his head.* Themistocles therefore fled to an Aeolian town called Aegae, where no one knew him except his guest-friend Nicogenes (the wealthiest man in Aeolis and a familiar face to the influential men from up country), at whose house Themistocles spent several days hiding.* Then one evening, after the dinner following some sacrifice or other, Olbius, the tutor of Nicogenes' sons, went into an inspired trance and chanted the following verse: 'Let night speak, let night advise you, let night give you victory.'

When Themistocles went to sleep later that night he dreamt that a snake wound its way over his stomach and crept up to his neck; as soon as it touched his face, it turned into an eagle, which wrapped its wings around him, lifted him up, and bore him away on a long journey. Then a golden staff, of the kind used by heralds, appeared; the eagle set him safely down on the staff, and his feeling of helpless fear and confusion passed away.

So Nicogenes found a way to allow Themistocles to continue his journey. Non-Greek races in general, and the Persians in particular, are fiercely—even savagely—protective of their womenfolk. They keep a strict watch over not only their wives, but even their slaves and concubines, who are consequently never seen by strangers, but live their lives in seclusion at home, and when they go outside travel on wagons under awnings with curtains drawn all around them. So what Nicogenes did was have this kind of wagon made up for

Themistocles, who climbed inside and went on his way, while the members of his retinue responded to any enquiries from people they met by saying that they were taking a Greek woman from Ionia to one of the king's courtiers.

[27] According to Thucydides and Charon of Lampsacus, Xerxes had died, and it was his son Artaxerxes with whom Themistocles had his audience.* However, a number of other writers (including Ephorus, Dinon, Cleitarchus, and Heraclides) say that it was Xerxes he went to. Thucydides' version seems to fit the chronological data better, even though they have hardly been securely established. Anyway, the dreaded moment arrived, and Themistocles first met with Artabanus, one of the king's chamberlains; he explained that he was a Greek, and that he wanted an audience with the king to discuss with him important matters which were of particular interest to him.

'Stranger,' Artabanus replied, 'men's customs vary. What is proper in one place is improper elsewhere, but everyone considers it right and proper to value and perpetuate their own customs. We hear that you Greeks admire freedom and equality above all, but in our case the finest of our many fine customs is that we regard the king as the image of the god who is responsible for the perpetuation of the universe, and therefore revere him and prostrate ourselves before him. If you approve of this custom of ours and are prepared to prostrate yourself before him, you can see the king and talk to him. But if you think otherwise, you will have to communicate with him through intermediaries. For in our tradition the king does not give an audience to anyone unless he prostrates himself before him.'

Themistocles listened to what Artabanus had to say, and then said: 'My reason for coming here, Artabanus, is to enhance the king's reputation and power. Not only will I comply with your customs myself, since that is the will of the god who exalts the Persians, but I will also be instrumental in increasing the numbers of people who prostrate themselves before the king. So let this issue not be the slightest hindrance to the discussion I want to have with him.'

'And who shall we announce?' Artabanus asked. 'A Greek, to be sure, but which one? You seem to be a man of exceptional intelligence.'

'Artabanus,' Themistocles replied, 'the king must be the first to hear the answer to this question of yours.'

This is Phanias' version of events, and in his treatise *On Wealth* Eratosthenes adds the detail that it was through the agency of an

Eretrian woman of the chamberlain's that Themistocles gained his introduction to him and had this meeting.

[28] Be that as it may, once he was taken in to the king, he prostrated himself and then stood in silence, until the king told his translator to ask who he was. The translator asked him, and Themistocles said, 'I am Themistocles of Athens, my lord. I have come to you as an exile, with the Greeks on my trail. It is true that I have been responsible for doing you Persians a great deal of harm, but this is outweighed by the good I did you when, as soon as Greece had been brought into a state of security and the safety of my personal affairs gave me the chance to do you a favour too, I put a stop to the Greeks' pursuit. As for myself, whatever happens will be consistent with my present misfortunes, so I have come prepared either to receive thanks from one who is merciful enough to forgive, or to avert the anger of one who holds a grudge. As far as you are concerned, you may take the existence of my enemies as proof of the service I have done Persia, and you can now use my misfortunes as an opportunity for a display of benevolence rather than for the satisfaction of a grudge. For if you keep me alive, you will be saving a suppliant of yours, but if you put me to death, you will be killing an enemy of Greece.'

Themistocles went on to enlist the supernatural to support his case, by describing the dream he had in Nicogenes' house and the oracle he had received from Zeus at Dodona; he explained that after he had been told to go to the god's namesake, he had come to the conclusion that he was being directed to him—to the king—since both he and Zeus were and were called 'great kings'. The king listened to Themistocles' speech, but said not a word in reply, although he was impressed by his pride and his courage. In front of his friends, however, he gloated over what he regarded as a huge piece of good fortune and prayed that Ahriman would never stop influencing his enemies' thinking in this way, so that they banished their best men.* And it is said that he began drinking straight after sacrificing to the gods, and that during the night he shouted out in joy three times in his sleep: 'I have Themistocles the Athenian!'

[29] Early the next morning he called his favourites together and had Themistocles summoned. Themistocles was inclined to think the worst, because when the guards outside the doors learnt his name as he went in they showed their hostility and were rude to him. Also, when on his way forward he came up to Rhoxanes, the chamberlain

gently exhaled—the king was seated and everyone else was silent—
and said, 'You wily Greek snake, you have the king's guardian spirit
to thank for your presence here.' However, once he had come into
Xerxes' presence and prostrated himself again, the king welcomed
him and spoke to him with kindness. In fact, he said that he already
owed him 200 talents, because he was entitled to the reward offered
for bringing him in, since it was he who brought himself in! He
promised him a great deal more besides, told him that he had no cause
for alarm, and gave him permission freely to speak his mind about
the state of affairs in Greece.

In reply Themistocles compared human speech to an embroidered
tapestry; he said that like a tapestry human speech had to be extended
to show its design, but when rolled up tight it concealed and distorted
it, and that he would therefore like more time. The king appreciated
his simile and gave him all the time he wanted. Themistocles asked
for a year and in that time learnt to speak Persian well enough to con-
verse with the king directly rather than through a translator. People
who were not involved supposed that these conversations were concerned solely with matters pertaining to Greece, but they coincided
with the introduction by the king of a large number of innovations
affecting life at court and his favourites, and the result was that
Themistocles incurred the resentment of the influential men at court,
who imagined that he had presumed to use his freedom of speech with
the king to do them down. And in fact he did receive more privileges
than other foreigners: he went hunting with the king and joined in
his indoor activities as well, even to the extent of being allowed into
the presence of the queen mother, whose friend he became, and also,
at the king's suggestion, becoming a student of the Magi.

Once, Demaratus of Sparta was told that he could ask for a favour,
and he asked to be allowed to drive into and through Sardis wearing
his *tiara* upright in the royal fashion. Mithropaustes, the king's
cousin, tapped Demaratus' *tiara* and said, 'This *tiara* has no brains
to cover. The possession of a thunderbolt still won't make you Zeus.'
In anger at Demaratus' request, the king banned him from his presence and it looked as though he was never going to forgive him, until
Themistocles put in a plea on Demaratus' behalf, won the king over
and patched things up between the two men.*

It is also said that whenever later Persian kings (during whose reigns
there was an increase in Persian involvement in Greek affairs)

wanted to get a man from Greece, they would state in their letters to whoever it was that he would be more important at court than Themistocles had been. And, to return to the man himself, the story goes that once, when a splendid banquet had been put on for Themistocles, who was by this stage an important man at court and whose patronage was in great demand, he told his sons: 'Children, our success is due to our ruin.' The majority of my sources agree that he was given three towns to keep him in bread, wine and savouries (respectively, Magnesia, Lampsacus and Myous), but Neanthes of Cyzicus and Phanias add two others, Percote and Palaescepsis, for his bedding and clothing.*

[30] Once, when he was on his way down to the coast on Greek business, a Persian called Epixyes, who was the satrap of upper Phrygia, triggered a plot against him; the plot involved some Pisidians, whom Epixyes had commissioned a long time before to kill Themistocles if he ever came and sought shelter in a village called Lionhead. But, the story goes on, while Themistocles was having a midday nap the Mother of the Gods* came to him in a dream and said, 'Themistocles, don't be in a hurry to reach a lion's head, in case you encounter a lion. In return for this favour I require from you Mnesiptolema to be my servant.'

Themistocles, shaken by the dream, offered up prayers to the goddess. He then left the main road, found another route which enabled him to bypass the place in question, and finally, at nightfall, he pitched camp. Now, one of the pack-animals—the one which was carrying his tent—had fallen into the river, so Themistocles' slaves had hung out the awnings, which were soaking wet, to dry them off. At that moment the Pisidians, swords drawn, approached the camp. In the light of the moon they could not clearly make out what these drying objects were, and they mistook them for Themistocles' tent, inside which they expected to find the man himself asleep. They drew near and were just raising one of the awnings when the guards fell on them and captured them. Because he had escaped danger in this way, and because he was impressed with the way in which the goddess had manifested herself, he built a temple to Dindymene in Magnesia and made his daughter Mnesiptolema a priestess.

[31] On another occasion he was visiting Sardis.* Finding himself with some spare time, he went on a sightseeing tour of the temples, to see their design and the huge numbers of dedicatory offerings they

contained. In the temple of the Mother he spotted the two-cubit tall bronze statue of a girl which is known as 'The Water-carrier'. Now, this was a statue which he himself had set up as a dedicatory offering during his period as Superintendent of Water Supplies at Athens; he had paid for it out of the fines exacted from those who were steal-ing public water and diverting it to their own use. When he saw this offering, he was moved, perhaps, by its captive state, or perhaps he just wanted to show the Athenians how high his standing was with the king and how much power he had in Persia; in any case, he approached the satrap of Lydia and asked if the statue of the girl could be sent back to Athens. The Persian responded angrily and threatened to write a letter to the king, which scared Themistocles. He turned to the women's quarters for help, bribed his way into the favour of the satrap's concubines, and so managed to placate him. After this incident, Themistocles always behaved more cautiously, because he was now afraid of getting on bad terms with the Persians. As Theopompus says, he stopped travelling around Asia and settled in Magnesia instead, living off the harvest of generous gifts he received, and with the equivalent status of a high-ranking Persian. And so for a long time he lived a trouble-free life, while the king was too busy with events in the interior to be particularly concerned with Greece.

Later, however, Egypt revolted with Athenian help, Greek triremes could be found at sea as far east as Cyprus and Cilicia, and Cimon was in control of the sea.* All this forced the king's attention back on to the Greeks, since he had to resist them and stop them expand-ing into his territory. At last, then, while the king's forces were being mobilized and his military commanders deployed, messages began to reach Themistocles in Magnesia, conveying the king's demand that he should keep his promises and get to grips with the Greek prob-lem. What moved Themistocles to act as he did? He was not at all angry and bitter at his former fellow citizens, nor was he elated by the enormous prestige and power he was to receive in the war. Perhaps he thought the job was just plain impossible, what with the incredible military successes Cimon was enjoying at the time, let alone all the other great commanders Greece had; but above all he was motivated by a refusal to sully the glory of his own exploits and the trophies they had brought in their train. At any rate, he decided that his best course of action was to end his life in an appropriate manner. He sacrificed to the gods, summoned his friends and made them welcome, and then either drank bull's blood (which is the usual version) or took a quick-acting poison (as some writers say*). And so he died in Magnesia aged sixty-five, after spending most of his life as a political and military leader. The story goes that when the king heard about his reasons for taking his life, and the manner in which he did so, his admiration for the man grew, and he continued to treat his friends and family with kindness.

[32] Themistocles was survived by three sons by Archippe, the daughter of Lysander of the deme Alopece: they were Archeptolis, Polyeuctus, and Cleophantus, whom the philosopher Plato says was redeemed from insignificance only by his excellence as a horseman. There were two older sons, but one of them, Neocles, died young from the effects of a horse-bite, and Diocles was adopted by his grandfather, Lysander. He had more daughters than sons, of whom Mnesiptolema, the daughter of his second wife, married her half-brother Archeptolis, Italia married Panthoedes of Chios, and Sybaris married Nicodemus of Athens; Nicomache was given in marriage after Themistocles' death by her brothers to Themistocles' nephew Phrasicles, who took a boat over to Magnesia, and also became responsible for the upbringing of Asia, the youngest of Themistocles' children.*

Themistocles' magnificent tomb stands in the city square of Magnesia. Where his remains are concerned, there is no reason to believe what Andocides says in his *To My Companions*—that the Athenians stole his remains and scattered them here and there—because these lies of his are motivated by a desire to inflame the oligarchs against the people of Athens. Also, when Phylarchus behaves like the composer of a tragedy and all but hoists up stage machinery for his account, and introduces characters called Neocles and Demopolis, the sons of Themistocles, he is only wanting to stir up conflicting emotions in his audience, and it must be obvious to everyone that he has made the story up.*

In *On Tombs* Diodorus the geographer says—while admitting that it is a conjecture rather than something he knows—that near the great harbour of the Piraeus there is a kind of elbow-like promontory opposite Alcimus, and that as you round this elbow, coming from the open sea in to where there is still water, there is a fair-sized plinth with an altar-shaped tomb on it which is the tomb of Themistocles. He thinks the comic poet Plato supports his view in the following lines:

The mound of your tomb, in such a good location,
Will serve as a landmark for all seafaring traders:
Whether sailing in or sailing out, it will watch them,
And every boat-race will have it as a spectator.

Certain perquisites, which have been kept up in Magnesia for Themistocles' descendants right down to modern times, were still being enjoyed by Themistocles of Athens, who became my good friend at the school of Ammonius the philosopher.*

CIMON

INTRODUCTION

The extraordinary opening story of Damon and the citizens of Chaeronea establishes a climate of sex and violence which will occasionally resurface in *Cimon* and its pair *Lucullus*, but the principal theme which will be developed in the following lives is found in the calming influence which the Roman commander Lucullus brings to the strife within and between communities (first at Chaeronea, and then between the cities of Chaeronea and Orchomenus). A secondary theme is the relation of Greeks and non-Greeks. Peripoltas, the ancient seer, led his people into Boeotia, expelling the pre-Greek peoples there; centuries later his descendant Damon, also called Peripoltas, killed a Roman officer whose advances he resented. Yet the Roman Lucullus and the unnamed Roman governor of Macedonia preserve the city.

In Plutarch's interpretation, calmness (*praotēs*) when passions are high distinguish both Cimon and Lucullus: they are 'even-tempered statesmen who gained for their homelands, in particular, a respite from civil strife' (3). Lucullus avoided the civil war between Marius and Sulla, and generally held himself aloof from political rivalry at Rome. Cimon laboured actively to reduce conflicts in his own city and with other Greek states, both Athens' constant rival Sparta and the Greek cities of the Aegean who became, thanks to his diplomacy, subject allies of Athens. Cimon's first political act (5) reduced the potential tension between aristocratic cavalry and democratic rowers at the time of the Persian invasion of 480 BC. Himself an aristocrat and of great wealth, he dedicated his horse's bridle to Athena as a sign of his recognition that Athens must take to the sea and of his willingness to join the common effort in the fleet, rather than oppose Themistocles and insist on his traditional élite role as cavalryman. His very calmness and simplicity made him a favourite of the people (*dēmos*), a welcome contrast to the cleverness of Themistocles (5).

His relaxed and affable ways won him the support of the Greek allies as well, who were repulsed by the Spartan commander Pausanias' harshness, suspicion, and tyrannical behaviour. By gentleness he won power over the allies for Athens (6). Later his easy-going remission of the allies' obligations towards the alliance allowed Athens to consolidate its hold on its power, and make the allies its subjects (11, cf. 16, 18).[1] In the fifth

---

[1] Both passages are adaptations of Thucydides' observations on the origin and strengthening of Athenian rule in the Aegean at 1. 94–5, 99. But Thucydides does not mention Cimon in this connection.

century, Athens was attempting to assert its role as an independent and powerful state against the hegemony of Sparta. Plutarch sees Cimon's policy as one of respect and support for Sparta as a partner in Greece rather than as an inveterate enemy, and he emphasizes Cimon's 'Laconian' attitudes (typical of many aristocrats at Athens) and efforts to calm tensions between the two states. At the time of the earthquake at Sparta and the revolt of the helots Cimon urged Athens to help Sparta, 'its yoke-fellow', (16–17), and later, when he is recalled from ostracism after Tanagra (18), he arranged a peace between the two states.

Cimon's conduct of the war against the Persians was a major source of his influence, as of his wealth. His successes won him unprecedented acclaim, such as the three herms with epigrams set up after the conquest of Eïon (7–8). Plutarch emphasizes this honour by comparing it to the treatment the Athenians gave Miltiades and Themistocles, the victors of Marathon and Salamis. Cimon's greatest victory came at the Eurymedon river in southern Asia Minor, a sea and land battle which forced the Persian king to renounce any effort to control the Aegean Sea or the cities along its coast (12–13). Plutarch connects this with the Peace of Callias, a formal treaty between Athens and Persia mentioned by fourth-century authors and later sources. In modern times this Peace has often been disassociated from Cimon, either by placing it in 449 or 448, after Cimon's death and some twenty years later than Eurymedon, or by denying its existence completely.[2] For Plutarch, however, the treaty confirms Cimon's exceptional victory and is a sign of the excellence of Cimon's policy of peace at home coupled with conquest or booty-rich victories abroad. His death at Cyprus occurred when he was on campaign once more against the Persians, preferring to win victories for Athens rather than remain at home to contest with Pericles the leadership of the city.

The booty won from the Persians permitted Cimon to exercise the liberality proper to a true aristocrat. Plutarch refers to his benefactions early on (3), and repeatedly calls instances to his readers' attention. The victory at Eïon won for Athens a rich country, ready for colonization (7), and other booty permitted Cimon's unprecedented largesse towards his fellow citizens. Plutarch tells us, following Theopompus and Aristotle, that Cimon opened his fields to those who needed food, provided meals to the poor, and clothes and money to the needy (10). The Eurymedon campaign permitted more grandiose public works: the rebuilding of the south wall of the Acropolis, above which the Parthenon soon would stand, the foundations for the long walls to the Piraeus, the plane trees in the *agora* or marketplace, and the grove of the Academy (13). Thus Cimon's Persian booty provided both

[2] See below, p. 116.

for the power of the city by strengthening its walls, and the pleasure of its citizens by creating pleasant and shady areas from dry and sun-baked earth. Plutarch notes in his *Rules for Politicians* that Cimon by thus beautifying the agora of Athens showed a generous and benevolent ambition and won favour from the people, so that he was able to restrain their less controlled and more irrational desires.[3]

Plutarch's praise of Cimon's generosity (and in the second Life, of Lucullus') reflects not only the aristocratic concept of *noblesse oblige* and the philosophical notion of the magnanimous man already found in Aristotle, but sentiments which flourished in the Roman empire of Plutarch's day. The emperor, of course, was the source of the greatest largesse, reaching into his treasury to beautify cities, reconstruct buildings after earthquakes or other natural disasters, and make donations of food or materials. But local magnates also vied for the honour which accompanied civic generosity, building temples, baths, porticoes, and gardens which would enhance the life of their citizens and glorify the city. They were rewarded by titles, honorary inscriptions, and crowns. Time and again the same words used by Plutarch of Cimon occur in the inscriptions: generosity (*megalophrosynē*), kindness (*philanthropia*), ambition (*philotimia*, here in a good sense), brilliance (*lamprotēs*), self-possession (*praotēs*).[4] Plutarch sets Cimon into this world, and thus makes his behaviour a model for his contemporaries.

External wars as a mode to gain wealth and distract citizens from internal quarrels, on the other hand, were in the second century only available to the emperor, or such few commanders as he trusted with the glory and influence they might win. Trajan, who came to power in AD 98, fought two wars against barbarian tribes in Dacia, the territory north of the Danube roughly corresponding to modern Romania, and in 107 created the province of Dacia. After a few years of quiet, in 114 he undertook a new war against the Parthians, marching from Armenia to the capital Ctesiphon (near modern Baghdad) and to the Persian Gulf, annexing all of Mesopotamia as a new province. Did Plutarch really wish to influence Trajan, either by recommending or seeming to support these wars against the external enemy? Certainly they were much preferable to the civil wars among the various contenders for power after the fall of Nero which he had seen in his twenties.

As in other Athenian Lives, Plutarch defends his hero from Plato's criticism that the great Athenian leaders had pandered to the populace with

[3] *Rules for Politicians* 818d.
[4] Cf. for an overview of the ancient attitude toward such philanthropy P. Veyne, *Le Pain et le cirque: sociologie historique d'un pluralisme politique* (Paris, 1976) or the abridged Eng. trans., *Bread and Circuses: Historical Sociology and Political Pluralism* (London: Allen Lane, The Penguin Press, 1990).

public munificence. A contemporary of Plato, the historian Theopompus (now lost) had attacked Cimon even more fiercely, denouncing his dishonesty, as one writer reports: 'Theopompus writes about him [Cimon] that he was an extraordinary thief and more than once was accused of being overcome by shameful grasping, and [in fact] the lesson of bribery which fell on the generals at Athens began first with him.'[5] Plutarch's account of Cimon's openhandedness towards his citizens (10) is derived from Theopompus, who apparently cited it as an example of how Cimon used his wealth to seduce the Athenian populace—pure demagoguery. Theopompus' overall view, however, is emphatically rejected by the biographer: 'Those muckrakers who describe this as pandering to the rabble and as demagoguery are refuted by the man's general principles, which are those of a pro–Lacedaemonian aristocrat' (10).

On the contrary, Plutarch uses every device of rhetorical augmentation to heighten the importance of Cimon's generosity. First, he cites a variety of authors, from Aristotle to the comic poet Cratinus. Then he contrasts Cimon with the wealthy Spartan Lichas, who used to host foreign visitors to the Spartan Festival of Unarmed Dancing. (Xenophon had made a similar comparison, arguing that Socrates was more generous than Lichas in almost the same words.) Finally Cimon is likened to the Athenian Triptolemus, who in mythical times had brought the knowledge of wheat cultivation to the Greek world: his open fields recall the Golden Age of Cronus. This effusive rhetoric recalls Pliny the Younger's praise of the emperor Trajan's system of grain distribution, the *congiaria* and *annona*.[6] Plutarch sees in Cimon the model for the statesman's generosity towards the populace, but the model is imperial rather than democratic. Cimon's immense wealth derives from his conquests at the head of the Athenian navy; his generosity distributes to the Athenians what they had won. In Cimon's 'aristocratic' behaviour there is a lesson for Plutarch's contemporaries. At other points in the Life, comparisons with previous victors magnify Cimon's unparalleled successes (8, to Themistocles and Miltiades; 13, the two battles of Eurymedon compared to Salamis and Plataea). Themistocles' decision to commit suicide rather than undertake a war against Cimon (18) glorifies the latter's generalship as well as continuing the theme of peace among Greeks. The final comparison with the demagogues who later ran Athenian politics and with the campaigns of King Agesilaus of Sparta in Asia in the 390s completes Plutarch's portrait of a statesman who was a peacemaker among Greeks and a conqueror of Persians.

There was no ancient historian who provided a firm narrative framework for the events of the middle of the fifth century. Plutarch had to piece

---

[5] Theopompus *FGrHist* 115 F 90 (= Cyril, *Contra Julianum* VI, p. 188a Spanh.).
[6] *Panegyricus* 28–31.

his biography together from a variety of sources. His best touches come from the contemporary sources which he is able to uncover: the memoirs of Ion of Chios, the tract of Stesimbrotus, the elegies of the contemporary poets Melanthius and Archelaus, the comedies of Cratinus and Eupolis. These give glimpses of Cimon's private life, his relations with his sister Elpinice, his astute handling of the allies. Plutarch derives much information from commentaries on literary works, especially comedy. Other material comes from fourth-century or later writers. The account of the herms set up after the victory of Eïon (7) is probably derived from the orator Aeschines (3. 183–5); the historian Theopompus, as we have seen, is important for c. 10. Ephorus provided the best continuous narrative of this period, and probably lies at the base of the account of the Eurymedon battles and the final expedition to Cyprus, supplemented by Phanodemus, a historian of Athens. The biography ties these brief notices together into a portrait.

Although full of gaps and uncertainties, *Cimon* is invaluable for the understanding of this part of the fifth century. Without it we would know little about a major figure in Athenian politics of the period 475–450. The three-page biography by Nepos is extremely general and full of errors (confusing e.g. the battle of Mycale, 479, with that of Eurymedon), although it does include other items of Cimon's generosity, such as providing burial for indigents (Nepos, *Cim.* 4). Excavations have now revealed some 500 ostraca with Cimon's name, including one confirming Plutarch's account of Elpinice's position in the public mind: 'Let him get out and take his sister with him!'[7]

Plutarch's account of Eurymedon is our most detailed; and he is our chief source for the Peace of Callias, although his text has created endless controversy. For some years Plutarch's testimony was rejected and the Peace (if it was accepted at all) was set after Cimon's expedition on Cyprus, *c*.448 BC, following Diodorus (12. 3–4). Recently, however, some historians have revived the idea of connecting the peace with the Eurymedon victory, as Plutarch does.[8]

This Life also provides a number of unique details: Cimon dedicating his bridle on the Acropolis (5), the award of the prize to Sophocles by a special jury of the ten generals (8), Ion's anecdote of tricking the allies (9), the bribe of Rhoesaces (10), the refitting of triremes to carry infantry and the capture of Phaselis (12), the plane trees in the agora and the grove in the Academy (13, cf. also *Rules for Politicians* 818d), Cimon's Chersonesan campaign (14), Periclidas' request for help (16), the confrontation with the

---

[7] H. Mattingly, 'Facts and Artifacts: the Researcher and his Tools', *Univ. of Leeds Review*, 14 (1971–2), 277–97, at 284.

[8] e.g. E. Badian, *From Plataea to Potidaea: Studies in the History and Historiography of the Pentecontaetia* (Baltimore: Johns Hopkins University Press, 1993).

Corinthian Lachartus (17), the bad omens before the Cyprian expedition (18), and his cenotaph at Citium (19). Other passages connect Cimon with events known from other historians but not connected by them with Cimon: e.g. the seduction of the allies from the command of Pausanias (6, in Diodorus ascribed to Aristides alone), encouraging the allies to support the Athenian league with tribute rather than ships (11), and the repression of Thasos' revolt (14).

Badian, E., 'The Peace of Callias', in *From Plataea to Potidaea: Studies in the History and Historiography of the Pentecontaetia* (Baltimore: Johns Hopkins University Press, 1993), 1–72. Reviews the discussion and presents a theory which tries to reconcile our conflicting evidence.

Blamire, A., *Life of Kimon* (London, Bulletin of Classical Studies Suppl. 56, 1989). A careful historical commentary.

Ma, J., 'Black Hunter Variations', *Proceedings of the Cambridge Philological Society*, 40 (1994), 49–80. Presents several interpretations of *Cimon* 1–2.

CIMON

[I] Peripoltas the diviner, who led King Opheltas and his people down from Thessaly into Boeotia, founded a family which achieved fame and prominence for a good many years. Most of them lived in Chaeronea, which was the first city taken when they expelled the non-Greek inhabitants.* Now, since most members of this family were of a warlike and courageous temperament, they gave freely of their lives and were killed during the Persian invasions and the wars against the Galatians.* However, one survivor was an orphaned boy who was called Damon, but was known as Peripoltas. Despite being the outstanding young man of his generation in terms of both physical good looks and nobility of spirit, in other respects he had an uncultured and harsh temperament.

The Roman commander of a cohort which had taken up winter quarters in Chaeronea fell in love with Damon, who was then just past childhood, and when he failed to win him over by his advances and gifts, it became clear that he was going to resort to force (in those days our country was in an abject state, and was condemned to obscurity by its insignificance and poverty*). This prospect made Damon afraid, and he was already enraged just by the Roman's advances, so he decided to take revenge and enlisted the help of some others, young men like himself, until there were sixteen of them; they kept the number small for fear of discovery. One night the conspirators smeared their faces with soot, and then at daybreak, after swallowing some neat wine, they fell on the Roman while he was performing a sacrifice in the town square. They succeeded in killing him and several of his companions, and then they escaped from the town.

During the ensuing uproar, the council of Chaeronea met and condemned the conspirators to death (which was the basis of the defence later offered to the Romans on the town's behalf). But in the evening, when the officers of the council were dining together as usual, Damon burst into their offices and slaughtered them, before once again fleeing the town.

Now, it so happened that these events coincided with the presence in the region of Lucius Lucullus with a body of troops on some mission or other. He broke off his journey to investigate the events while they were still fresh, and he not only acquitted the town of any guilt, but in fact found that it had been one of the victims, rather than the perpetrator of any crime. So he retrieved his troops and left along with them. Damon, however, turned to pillaging and raiding the countryside. He even threatened the town itself, but the townspeople enticed him back by sending him delegations and by passing conciliatory decrees, and on his return they made him gymnasiarch.* Later, they murdered him in the vapour-bath, as he was anointing himself there. For a long time afterwards—or so our local tradition has it—ghosts used to appear in the place and groans could be heard, which led our ancestors to wall up† the vapour-bath; and even now people who live next to the place imagine that it is the source of certain disturbing sights and sounds. As for his descendants (because some members of his family survive, particularly near Steiris in Phocis, and speak the Aeolic dialect†), they are known by people as 'the Besooted', after Damon's smearing himself with soot before going out to commit murder.

[2] Relations between Chaeronea and its neighbour, Orchomenus, were strained, and the Orchomenians hired a Roman informer who denounced the town as if it were a single individual, and initiated proceedings against it for the murder of those who had been killed by Damon. At that time the Romans had not started sending governors to the various regions of Greece, so the case was heard before the governor of Macedonia. In their speeches, the people defending the town appealed for Lucullus' evidence. When the governor wrote to him, he gave a true account of events, and so the town was acquitted in its hour of supreme peril.

The Chaeroneans who were saved then erected a marble statue of Lucullus in the town square, next to Dionysus. As for me, despite being many generations distant, I think the debt of gratitude extends all the way down to those of us who are alive today. Since I regard a portrait which displays a person's character and personality as far superior to one which reproduces his body and features, in my sketch—that is, in these *Parallel Lives*—I shall include and give a true account of the man's actions. With this record my debt of gratitude is adequately discharged; he would have refused to accept a false and fictional account of himself as payment for his true testimony. When painters are faced with a slight blemish of some kind on the beautiful and pleasing figures they portray, we do not expect them either to omit it altogether (which would stop their portraits being true likenesses) or to stress it (which would make them ugly to look at). By the same token, since it is difficult—or, more probably, impossible—to represent a man's life as entirely free from shortcomings and blemishes, we should supply the truth, confident in its verisimilitude, when dealing with the good aspects of our subject's life. However, the flaws and defects which, prompted by emotion or by political necessity, taint his actions we should regard as lapses from a virtue rather than as manifestations of vice. We should not, then, be particularly eager to overemphasize these flaws in our account, but should write instead as if we felt ashamed of the fact that human nature fails to produce any character which is absolutely good or unequivocally virtuous.

[3] After thinking it over, I decided to pair Lucullus with Cimon. Both were men of war, and both were outstandingly successful against foreigners.* They were also even-tempered statesmen who gained for their homelands, in particular, a respite from civil strife, while abroad they set up trophies and won famous victories. The fame of these victories is due to the fact that no Greek before Cimon and no Roman before Lucullus had taken the theatre of war so far from home, if we exclude the exploits of Heracles and Dionysus, and Perseus' achievements against the Ethiopians or Medes, not to mention Jason's against the Armenians, assuming that any element of the stories that have come down to us from those ancient times is trustworthy. In a sense Cimon and Lucullus also share the fact that neither of them brought his campaigns to a conclusion: each of them crushed his adversary, but neither of them finished him off. Above all, however, their closeness shows up in the extravagant prodigality with which they put on parties and dispensed favours, and in their youthful and relaxed lifestyles. There may also be other similarities which I have failed to mention here, but which can easily be gleaned from the actual narrative.

[4] Cimon's father was Miltiades, but his mother, Hegesipyle, was a Thracian by birth, the daughter of King Olorus, as we read in the poems by Archelaus and Melanthius addressed to Cimon himself.* This also explains why the father of Thucydides the historian, who was related by birth to Cimon's family, was called Olorus, since the father took the name from his ancestor, and owned gold mines in Thrace. He is said to have died there too, murdered in a place called Scapte Hyle; but his remains were brought back to Attica and one is shown his tombstone in the Cimoneia* alongside the grave of

Cimon's sister Elpinice. Thucydides, however, was from the deme Halimous, while Miltiades was from Laciadae.

Miltiades died in prison, where he had been committed pending payment of a fine of fifty talents, and the young Cimon was left completely alone, along with his sister, who was still a young, unmarried girl. At first he had a poor reputation in Athens and was known, to his discredit, for his lack of self-control, for his heavy drinking, and for taking after his grandfather, Cimon, who was so stupid, apparently, that he was called 'the Dunce'. In fact Stesimbrotus of Thasos, who was more or less contemporary with Cimon, says that he was never taught any of the subjects usually studied by free men in Greece, such as music, that he completely lacked typical Attic ingenuity and fluency, and that his most prominent qualities were nobility and honesty. The cast of his mind was, according to Stesimbrotus, more Peloponnesian than Attic—'a plain, no-nonsense man, good in a crisis': this Euripidean description of Heracles may serve to sum up what Stesimbrotus has written.*

He was accused, while still a young man, of committing incest with his sister. As a matter of fact, they say that Elpinice had no self-restraint, and included Polygnotus the painter among her lovers, and that this is why, when he painted the Trojan women in what was in those days called the Pisianactean Stoa (the Painted Stoa nowadays), he used Elpinice as his model for Laodice's features. Polygnotus was no artisan: he did not paint the stoa for money, but for free, because he was anxious to win the favour of the Athenians. This is vouched for not only by historians, but also by the poet Melanthius, in the following lines:

> For at his own expense he adorned with the mighty deeds
> Of heroes the temples of the gods and Cecrops' square.

Some say that the affair between Elpinice and Cimon was no secret, but that they lived together after being openly married, because thanks to her poverty she was unable to find a husband worthy of her station. They also say, however, that once Callias, who was one of the richest men in Athens, had fallen in love with her and approached her, expressing his willingness to pay into the state treasury the fine incurred by her father, he won her over and Cimon gave her in marriage to Callias. Despite this, it seems clear that Cimon was of a fundamentally amorous disposition where women were concerned.

For instance, in an elegiac poem the poet Melanthius teases Cimon by mentioning his devotion to a woman from Salamis called Asteria, and also to a certain Mnestra. However, Cimon evidently also felt very strongly about Isodice, the daughter of Euryptolemus and grand-daughter of Megacles, who was his legal wife. He took her death very hard, to judge by a consolatory elegiac poem addressed to him, whose author, in the opinion of the philosopher Panaetius, was the natural scientist Archelaus, which from a chronological point of view is a reasonable guess.

[5] Otherwise, Cimon's character presented nothing but admirable and noble qualities. It is generally agreed that he was as brave as Miltiades and as intelligent as Themistocles, and more honest than either of them. Moreover, where the qualities required in a soldier were concerned, there was nothing at all to tell between him and them, and as for those required in a statesman, even as a young man, before he had gained any experience of actual warfare, he outshone them to an incredible degree. Take, for instance, the time when the Persians were approaching and Themistocles was trying to persuade the Athenian people to evacuate the city, abandon the countryside, concentrate their forces on the fleet in defence of Salamis, and fight it out at sea. Most people were terrified by such a radical proposal, but Cimon could be seen leading a group of his companions up to the Acropolis with a smile on his face and a horse's bridle in his hands to dedicate to the goddess, realizing that in the present crisis the city needed men to fight at sea rather than from horseback. He dedicated the bridle, took down one of the shields which was hanging on the walls of the temple, and, after a prayer to the goddess, made his way down to the coast—all of which put heart into quite a large number of people.

No one could find fault with his appearance either: the poet Ion tells us that he was a tall man, with thick, curly hair. His glorious and courageous exploits in the actual battle led before long to his being well and highly thought of in Athens, and crowds of people began to flock to him, insisting that now was the time for him to contemplate and perform deeds worthy of Marathon.* His entry into public life was welcomed by the common people, who were fed up with Themistocles. They found his even temper and straightforwardness accommodating and congenial, so they set about promoting him to the highest political offices and positions. No one furthered his political career more than Aristides the son of Lysimachus, who recognized

Cimon's fine qualities and set him up to counterbalance, so to speak, Themistocles' ingenuity and adventurousness.*

[6] Following the Persian retreat from Greece Cimon was sent out on missions as Athens' military commander (this was before the Athenians gained their maritime empire; they were still subordinate to Pausanias and the Lacedaemonians*). During these campaigns he first caused the Athenian troops under his command to be wonderfully well disciplined and far more highly motivated than any of the other contingents. Secondly, at the time when Pausanias began to communicate with the Persians and to write letters to the Persian king with a view to betraying Greece, he also began to treat the allied forces with wilful cruelty; he abused his power and acted with such unthinking authoritarianism that time and again he committed acts of violence against them. Cimon listened sympathetically to the grievances of Pausanias' victims and dealt with them in a kindly fashion, and as a result, by the strength of his reasoning and his character rather than by force of arms, he gradually assumed the command of Greece, in the sense that most of the allies sided with him and Aristides, since they found Pausanias' cruelty and arrogance unbearable. As well as winning this following, Cimon and Aristides also sent a message to the ephors, suggesting that they recall Pausanias, since Sparta was earning itself a bad name and Greece was in confusion.

There is a story that once Pausanias sent for a young Byzantine woman called Cleonice—a woman from a distinguished family—with a view to disgracing her, and her parents were too frightened to do anything but let their daughter go to him. She asked the guards outside his room to remove the torches, but as she made her way silently through the darkness to the bed, where Pausanias was already asleep, she accidentally stumbled against the lampstand and knocked it over. Disturbed by the noise, Pausanias drew the dagger which he kept near by and, assuming that some enemy was creeping up on him, he struck the girl and killed her. After her death from this stab wound, she gave Pausanias no peace. She haunted him at night as an apparition in his dreams, repeating this epic line in an angry tone of voice: 'Draw closer to justice: violence spells certain doom for men.'*

The allies found this affair especially hard to take, and they joined Cimon in blockading the city until Pausanias surrendered. After his expulsion from Byzantium, the story goes on, he continued to be harassed by the apparition, until eventually he resorted to the oracle of the dead at Heraclea, where he summoned up Cleonice's ghost and begged her forgiveness. When she appeared, she told him that his misery would end soon after he reached Sparta—which was apparently an enigmatic reference to his impending death. This story can be found in a large number of writers.

[7] Now that he had the support of the allies, Cimon took command and sailed to Thrace. He had found out that high-ranking Persians, who were related to the king and had control of the town of Eïon, which is situated on the banks of the Strymon, were harassing the Greek settlers in that region. First he defeated the Persians in battle and pinned them inside the town, and then he eliminated their source of provisions by dispossessing the Thracians who lived east of the Strymon and securing the whole area. As a result, he made life so difficult for the people trapped inside the town that Boges, the Persian king's military governor, realizing that his position was hopeless, set fire to the town and perished in the conflagration along with all his friends and property. This meant that Cimon's capture of the town failed to net him any significant profit, since nearly everything had been burnt up along with the Persians, but he did present the Athenians with the very fertile and attractive land around the town, for them to colonize. The Athenian people gave him permission to set up the famous stone herms,* the first of which bears the following inscription:

> They too proved their brave hearts, those men who once
> At Eïon, by Strymon's streams, brought burning hunger
> And chilling war to the sons of Persia;
> Never before had foes found no way out.

The inscription on the second herm reads:

> This is a token, given by Athens to her leaders
> In payment for their service and great favours.
> Seeing this, men of the future will more incline
> To go to war in their country's cause.

And on the third:

> Once Menestheus led his men from this city of ours
> To the sacred plain of Troy with Atreus' sons.
> Of all the Greeks in their fine cuirasses it was he
> Whose skills at warcraft Homer called the best.
> 'Tis no surprise, then, that the Athenians are known
> For their warcraft and their disciplined prowess.*

[8] Although the name of Cimon is nowhere to be seen on these herms, they were regarded by the people of the time as an unparalleled honour, since neither Themistocles nor Miltiades had ever been granted anything like it. In fact, when Miltiades asked for a garland of olive, Sophanes of Decelea stood up in the middle of the Assembly and objected to the proposal, in terms which were blunt, but which met with the approval of the Athenian people of the time. 'Miltiades,' he said, 'when you have fought and conquered the Persians by yourself, then you can also expect to be honoured by yourself.' Why, then, were they so delighted with Cimon's achievement? Presumably because during Themistocles' and Miltiades' periods of command the point of their resistance to the Persians had been to avoid disaster, whereas under Cimon the tables were turned: now they made *enemy* territory the theatre of war and were in a position to wreak havoc there, and in addition they acquired extra land and colonized both Eïon and Amphipolis.

They also colonized Scyros, which fell into Cimon's hands in the following way. The Dolopian inhabitants of the island were poor farmers, and had since ancient times been sea-pirates. In the end things got so bad that even friends who put in at their harbours and did business with them were not safe—they robbed and imprisoned some Thessalian traders who had anchored off Ctesium. The Thessalians escaped from prison, however, and managed to get the Amphictyonic League to condemn the citizens of Scyros, who, however, refused to make public restitution and ordered the actual robbers, who had the stolen property, to give it back.* The terrified thieves wrote a letter to Cimon in which they invited him to come with his fleet and capture the town, which they said they would betray to him. But after Cimon had secured the island in this way, he expelled the Dolopians and made the Aegean safe for sailors.

He subsequently found out that the legendary hero Theseus the son of Aegeus had come to Scyros after being banished from Athens and had been treacherously killed there by King Lycomedes, who was afraid of him. Cimon took a lot of trouble over trying to find Theseus' burial-place, especially since the Athenians had been commanded by an oracle to collect Theseus' remains, bring them back to the city, and establish a suitable hero-cult for him. The problem with this had been that the Athenians had no idea where Theseus was buried, and the people of Scyros claimed not to know anything about the matter and refused them permission to undertake a search for the site. At the time in question, however, Cimon took a lot of care and the burial-place was eventually discovered. He put the bones on board his own personal trireme with a great deal of pomp and ceremony, and transported them back to Athens after an absence of almost 400 years. This was the main reason for his popularity in Athens.*

Another thing he is remembered for is the famous incident of his judging of the tragedies. It was the year when Sophocles, who was still a young man, put on his first play.* Since the audience was divided into quarrelsome factions supporting the various productions, the archon, Apsephion, did not cast lots to appoint the judges of the contest, but when Cimon and the other military commanders entered the theatre and made the traditional libations to the god, he stopped them from leaving and forced them to be sworn in and empanelled as judges, since there were ten of them, and one from each tribe. The eminence of the judges meant that the contest was conducted with even more determination to win than usual. When victory went to Sophocles, the story goes, Aeschylus was so hurt and offended that he stayed in Athens only a short while longer before angrily leaving for Sicily, where in fact he died: he is buried near Gela.

[9] Ion speaks of a time when he was still a young adult, newly arrived in Athens from Chios, and he was a fellow guest with Cimon at a dinner-party hosted by Laomedon. After the libations had been poured, Cimon was asked to sing, and did so quite pleasingly. His companions complimented him on having a greater range of abilities than Themistocles, who used to claim that he had never learnt how to sing or play the lyre, but knew instead how to increase a city's importance and wealth.* Later, during the drinking phase of the party, Cimon's accomplishments cropped up, as you might expect, in their conversation. Mention was made of the most important of these accomplishments, and then Cimon himself recounted a particular ruse which he regarded as the cleverest of his personal achievements. After Sestus and Byzantium, the allies had taken large numbers of Persian prisoners-of-war, and they asked Cimon to distribute the spoils. Cimon divided things into two categories, one consisting of the actual prisoners, the other of their jewellery and clothing. The allies protested that this was unfair, but Cimon told them to take whichever lot they wanted, and said that the Athenians would be happy with the one they left. Herophytus of Samos advised the allies to take the Persians' property rather than the Persians, and so they took the prisoners' effects

for themselves and left the prisoners for the Athenians. At the time
Cimon went on his way and everyone thought he had made a fool of
himself as a distributor of the spoils; after all, the allies carried off
golden anklets, necklaces, torques, robes and purple dye, while the
Athenians gained only the bodies of the prisoners, which had been
stripped of their effects and had never been trained for hard physical labour. Before long, however, the friends and relatives of the captives came down from Phrygia and Lydia and proceeded to ransom
every single one of them for large amounts of money. The upshot
was that this ransom money enabled Cimon to supply his fleet for
four months and still have a not inconsiderable amount left over for
the city.*

[10] Now that Cimon had plenty of money to finance his military
operations, he spent the money he was credited with having gained
in an honourable fashion from the enemy still more honourably on
the citizens of Athens. What he did was remove the fences surrounding
his properties, so that both visitors and his fellow citizens could help
themselves to his fruit if they felt like it, without worrying about any
repercussions, and also arrange for a meal to be provided every day
at his house—not a fancy meal, but enough to satisfy a lot of people
—to which anyone could come, if he was poor and if he wanted to,
and have a nourishing meal without any bother, so as to leave him
time to concentrate on his public duties. According to Aristotle, however, this daily meal was not designed for any and every Athenian
who wanted it, but only for people from the same deme as Cimon,
Laciadae.* Cimon also used to go around with a group of close friends,
all well-dressed young men, every single one of whom would swap
clothes with any elderly man Cimon met whose clothing was shabby.
This practice made a very good impression.

The same group also used to carry around huge quantities of cash,
and would go up to poor people of the better type in the city square
and quietly drop some coins into their hands. This is probably what
the comic poet Cratinus is alluding to in the following lines from his
Archilochuses:

> I too, Metrobius the scribe, used to pray the following prayer:
> To live out all the days of my life in the company of Cimon,
> That godlike man, a paragon of unselfishness,
> In every way the best and foremost of all the Greeks;
> I prayed that I might grow old and sleek sharing his table—
> But he has left and gone on before.

Also, Gorgias of Leontini says that Cimon became wealthy in order to put his wealth to use, and used it in order to earn respect; and again Critias, who was one of the Thirty, prays in one of his elegiac poems for

> The wealth of the Scopadae, the generosity of Cimon,
> And the victories of Arcesilas of Lacedaemon.*

It is true that Lichas the Spartiate, as we know, became well known throughout Greece for no other reason except that he used to feed the people who came to visit the Festival of Unarmed Dancing,* but Cimon's generosity surpassed even the unselfish kindness of Athenians of bygone days. The city has good reason to be proud of those Athenians of old, who not only gave the rest of Greece seed-corn,* but also showed men how to channel water from springs and how to light fires; but Cimon turned his home into a kind of town hall for public use,* and on his estates he made the first-fruits of his ripened crops and all the bounty of the seasons freely available for visitors to take and enjoy. In a sense, then, he made the legendary fellowship of the age of Cronus once more a feature of human life.* Those muckrakers who describe this as pandering to the rabble and as demagoguery are refuted by the man's general principles, which are those of a pro-Laconian aristocrat.* After all, it was Cimon who, with the help of Aristides, resisted Themistocles when he was increasing the power of the people beyond its proper limits, and who later fell out with Ephialtes when he was currying favour with the general populace by trying to dissolve the Council of the Areopagus;* and it was Cimon who, seeing that apart from Aristides and Ephialtes every politician in Athens was getting rich off profits meant for the public treasury, made sure that everything he did and said in the public domain was at his own expense and of the highest moral standards, and so kept himself free from the taint of bribery and corruption. In fact, there is a story that a Persian called Rhoesaces, who had defected from the king's cause, once came to Athens with a great deal of money, and was driven by the savagery of the informers to seek refuge at Cimon's house. He put two bowls by Cimon's door, filled respectively with silver and gold darics. The sight of the bowls made Cimon smile, and he asked the man whether he would prefer Cimon as a hired hand or as a friend. 'As a friend,' Rhoesaces replied. 'In that case,' said Cimon, 'go away, and take this money with you. Now that we are friends, I shall make use of it whenever I want to.'*

[11] The time came when although the allies were keeping up their tribute payments, they stopped providing the stipulated quotas of men and ships. They had had enough of military service and could see no reason for warfare, now that the Persians had left and were not causing them any trouble; they just wanted to work their land and get on with living quiet lives. So they stopped fitting out ships and sending troops.* Faced with this situation all the Athenian commanders except Cimon resorted to prosecution and punishment to force the allies do what they were supposed to do—which only served to make Athenian rule a painful and unpopular burden. During his period of command, however, Cimon pursued the opposite course. He never brought pressure to bear on any Greek state: if they refused to supply troops, he accepted money and unmanned ships from them instead. He let them give in to the lure of a life of ease and devote their time to their domestic business; he let them indulge in their folly and be men of peace—farmers and businessmen instead of soldiers. Where the Athenians were concerned, however, he used them in large numbers to man the fleet in shifts, and worked them hard out on military service. Consequently, before long he had used the money and wages provided by the allies to make the Athenians the masters of those who paid them. The point is that the Athenians were always at sea and constantly under arms; as a result of the allies' failure to undertake military service themselves, they were becoming seasoned and trained fighters. And so the allies acquired the habit of fearing and currying favour with the Athenians, and gradually became tribute-paying subjects instead of allies, and lost their freedom.

[12] As for the Great King himself, no one did more to humble him and curb his pride than Cimon. Even after his departure from Greece, Cimon did not let him be; hot on the Persians' heels, so to speak, before they could draw breath and make a stand he was sacking and destroying some places, and inducing others to defect and come over to the Greek side. In the end he completely cleared the coast of Asia from Ionia to Pamphylia of Persian military presence.*

When he learnt that the king's commanders were lying in wait near Pamphylia with a huge army and a sizeable fleet, he decided to try to make the whole sea west of the Chelidonian Islands too dangerous for Persian ships to enter at all. He put to sea from Cnidos and

Triopium with a fleet of 300 triremes. These had originally been state-of-the-art vessels constructed on Themistocles' orders for speed and manoeuvrability, but Cimon now widened them, and also provided each of them with a bridge connecting the decks, so that with a large complement of hoplites they would be more effective in any close combat with the enemy. He sailed against the city of Phaselis, whose inhabitants, despite being Greek, would not shelter his fleet and refused to secede from Persia, and set about ravaging its land and assaulting its walls. However, the Chians in his fleet, who had long-standing bonds of friendship with the Phaselites, tried to placate Cimon and were at the same time passing messages to the Phaselites by shooting arrows over the walls with small scrolls attached. In the end, they did succeed in making peace between the two sides, on condition that the people of Phaselis paid Cimon ten talents and provided a contingent to join his expedition against the Persians.

Ephorus says that the Persian fleet and land army had separate commanders—Tithraustes and Pherendates respectively—but according to Callisthenes it was Ariomandes the son of Gobryas who, as the commander-in-chief of the whole force, held the fleet at anchor off the mouth of the Eurymedon, but had no intention of engaging the Greeks, since he was waiting for eighty Phoenician ships which were on their way from Cyprus. Cimon wanted to join battle before these Phoenician ships arrived, so he put to sea, and was ready to force the issue if the enemy showed any reluctance to fight. At first, in an attempt to avoid being forced to join battle, the Persians ran for cover into the river, but the Athenians still bore down on them, so the Persians sailed out with their fleet of 600 or 350 ships (depending on whether you follow Phanodemus or Ephorus) to meet them. At sea, at any rate, the Persian performance did not measure up to their potential: they immediately turned around and made for dry land. The first to reach the shore abandoned their ships and fled for the protection of the land army which was drawn up near by, while the rest were overtaken by the Greeks and were destroyed along with their ships. This shows how many operational ships the Persians must have had in their fleet, because despite the fact that plenty will have escaped or been broken up, the Athenians still managed to capture 200 of them.

[13] The Persian land army moved down to the shore to meet the Greeks. Although Cimon was aware that to force a landing and lead his men against the Persians—to lead exhausted troops against a fresh

army which hugely outnumbered them—would be asking a great deal, nevertheless when he saw that his men were fired up by the strength and confidence that victory had given them, and were raring to get to grips with the enemy, he landed his hoplites, still hot from their struggle during the sea battle, and they charged into battle with a loud cry. The Persians stood their ground and offered spirited resistance, with the result that a fierce battle was joined, in which the casualties on the Athenian side included a number of brave men of great eminence and distinction. After a lengthy struggle the Athenians pushed the enemy back and the slaughter began, followed by the capture of both men and the Persian camp, which was well stocked with valuable property of all kinds.

So Cimon, like a superb athlete, carried off two prizes in a single day; and although with his land battle he had already overtaken the triumph of Salamis, and with his sea battle that of Plataea, he took part in yet another contest, on top of the victories he had already won. He learnt that the eighty Phoenician triremes which had missed the battle had put in at Hydrus, so he sailed there with all speed. The Phoenician commanders had as yet received no definite information about the main force, but were still filled with doubt and suspense— which only served to increase the shock of Cimon's attack, with the result that they lost all their ships and most of their men were killed as well.

These victories of Cimon's humbled the king's pride so much that he undertook, in the terms of the famous peace, always to keep at least a day's ride away from the Greek sea, and not to bring any long ship or bronze-rammed ship beyond the Cyanean Islands and the Chelidonian Islands. Callisthenes, however, denies that the Persian entered into an actual agreement to this effect, rather than just behaving this way in practice out of fear of another defeat like the last one; he adds that the king kept so far away from Greece that Pericles and Ephialtes were able to sail east of the Chelidonian Islands* with a fleet of fifty ships in Pericles' case, and of only thirty in Ephialtes' case, without encountering any naval opposition from the Persians.* However, among the decrees collected by Craterus there is a copy of a treaty in the right place, as if it had really happened. Moreover, they say that the Athenians built the Altar of Peace to celebrate this treaty, and heaped honours on Callias, who had been the Athenian representative.

The sale of the captured spoils from this campaign made the Athenian people so well off financially that they had enough money for, among other projects, building the south wall of the Acropolis. Again, although the Long Walls (the 'Legs', as they are known*) were not completed until later, yet when the original footings subsided into damp, marshy ground, it was Cimon, apparently, who was responsible for establishing them on a secure foundation, by financing out of his own pocket the dumping of a great deal of rubble and stones into the marshes until they became firm. He was also the first to embellish the city with the so-called cultivated and refined haunts, which would before long become so extremely popular. He planted plane trees in the city square, and transformed the Academy from a dry, unirrigated spot into a well-watered grove, which he equipped with obstacle-free racing-tracks and shady walks.

[14] Once some Persians were holding out in the Chersonese, and were appealing to the Thracians for help, without worrying about Cimon's presence, because of the tiny number of ships he had brought with him from Athens. However, he attacked them with four ships, captured their thirteen ships, and went on to expel the Persians, defeat the Thracians and annex the whole of the Chersonese for Athens. Later, when the people of Thasos had rebelled against Athens, he defeated them at sea, capturing thirty-three of their ships, and then blockaded the town into submission. He gained the goldmines on the mainland opposite the island for Athens, and he took control of the territory which had been under Thasian dominion.*

It was generally supposed that he could easily have gone on from there to invade Macedonia and take over a great deal of it, and when he refused to do so he was accused of taking bribes from King Alexander and was prosecuted on this charge by a coalition of his political enemies. In the course of the speech he made in his defence to the jurors, he pointed out that he was not, like some of his fellow citizens, the honorary representative of any rich city from Ionia or Thessaly, to be courted and plied with gifts; instead he represented the Lacedaemonians, whose simple and moderate lifestyle he admired and imitated, and while he held this lifestyle to be more precious than money, it made him proud to enrich the city with spoils taken from its enemies. When Stesimbrotus mentions this trial, he claims that Elpinice went to Pericles' house to plead for Cimon, since Pericles was the most determined of Cimon's prosecutors, and that Pericles smiled and said, 'You are an old woman, Elpinice—too old for a business like this.' Nevertheless, in the trial, Stesimbrotus goes on, Pericles turned out to be the most restrained of the prosecutors; in fact, he got up to speak only once, and seemed to be doing so merely for form's sake.*

[15] Anyway, Cimon was acquitted on this occasion, and for the rest of his political life, as long as he was personally present in Athens, he was able to control and check the general populace's assaults on the aristocratic party and attempts to divert all authority and power to itself. During his next naval expedition abroad, however, the common people lost all restraint: they overthrew the established political system and the traditional customs which had been observed until then. With Ephialtes at their head, they deprived the Council of the Areopagus of almost all its jurisdiction, put themselves in charge of the courts, and propelled the city into undiluted democracy. By then Pericles too had considerable influence as a populist.*

When Cimon returned, then, the abuses he found being heaped upon the honour of the council made him furious, and he tried to restore its juridical powers and to resuscitate the aristocratic government of Cleisthenes.* And so the populist leaders combined to denounce him, and tried to arouse the general populace against him by reviving the old slanders about his sister and accusing him of being pro-Laconian. This is the context of Eupolis' much-quoted lines about Cimon:

> He was all right—except for his boozing, his irresponsibility,
> And his occasional trips abroad to Lacedaemon,
> Leaving Elpinice alone in her bed at night.

However, if he was irresponsible and drunk when he captured all those cities and won so many victories, it obviously follows that no Greek before or after him could have surpassed his achievements if he had been sober and attentive!

[16] It is true that he was always pro-Laconian. (In fact he named one of his twin sons Lacedaemonius and the other Eleius. According to Stesimbrotus, their mother came from Cleitor,* and this is why Pericles was constantly casting aspersions on their mother's side of the family; according to Diodorus the geographer, however, these twins had the same mother as Cimon's third son, Thessalus—namely, Isodice, who was the daughter of Euryptolemus and granddaughter

of Megacles.*) And the Lacedaemonians for their part supported Cimon, since at the time in question they were at loggerheads with Themistocles and wanted to see this young man rise to a position of power and control in Athens. At first the Athenians were glad to see this, because the Spartiates' good will towards Cimon did them quite a bit of good as well, in the sense that although their power was just beginning to grow and they were busy developing their network of alliances, the Lacedaemonians tolerated the situation out of respect and affection for Cimon. In fact, Cimon was the Athenians' main negotiator when there was business to conduct with other Greeks, because of his ability to deal courteously with the allies and remain on good terms with the Lacedaemonians.

Later, when they were in a position of considerable power and they realized that Cimon was firmly attached to the Spartiates, they found his stance intolerable. He was constantly singing the praises of Lacedaemon to the Athenians, especially when he was trying to criticize them or stir them up. On these occasions, according to Stesimbrotus, he would habitually say: 'But the Lacedaemonians don't behave like that.' This used to generate resentment and even a degree of hostility from his fellow citizens.

The most cogent of the charges against him arose in the following circumstances. In the fourth year of the reign in Sparta of Archidamus the son of Zeuxidamus, a more severe earthquake than any previously recorded struck Lacedaemon. Gaping holes appeared in many places where the land had collapsed, the shocks broke off some of the peaks of Taygetus, and the city itself was completely destroyed, with only five houses left standing, and all the rest razed by the earthquake. It is said that shortly before the earthquake a hare appeared in the middle of the Colonnade, where youths and young men were exercising together; the young men ran out after the hare for fun, all oiled and naked as they were, and the gymnasium collapsed on top of the youths who had stayed behind, killing them all. To this day the place where they are buried is called the Earthquake Site.*

It did not take Archidamus long to appreciate that there was danger still to come as a result of the immediate disaster, and when he saw his subjects trying to rescue their most valuable possessions from their homes, he ordered the warning of an enemy attack to be sounded by trumpet, so that they would assemble under arms by his side in the shortest time possible. This was all that saved Sparta in her hour of crisis, because the helots swarmed in from all over the countryside with the intention of overwhelming any Spartiates who had survived. When they found the Spartiates armed and deployed for battle, however, they pulled back to their settlements and waged war openly with the Spartiates, and not only did they succeed in winning over quite large numbers of the perioeci, but at the same time the Messenians also came in on their side against the Spartiates.*

Under these circumstances the Lacedaemonians sent Periclidas to Athens to ask for help. This is the man Aristophanes mockingly portrays as sitting 'at our altars, pale-faced, red-clothed, begging for an army'.* Ephialtes objected to the request and protested against the idea of the Athenians aiding and restoring a city which was their rival, urging them to leave it levelled and let the pride of Sparta be trampled in the dust. Cimon, however, as Critias says, gave more importance to what was in the Lacedaemonians' interest than to increasing his native city's power and he persuaded the people of Athens to go out with a sizeable force of heavy infantry to help them. Ion preserves the actual expression Cimon used to particular effect to rouse the Athenians; he argued that they should 'not allow Greece to become lame, or Athens to lose its yoke-fellow'.

[17] While he was on his way back to Athens with the army, after having helped the Lacedaemonians, he was passing through Corinth, when Lachartus criticized him for bringing his army into Corinthian territory without asking their permission first; after all, he said, when people knock on a stranger's door, they do not enter until the owner has given them the go-ahead. 'But Lachartus,' Cimon said, 'you Corinthians didn't knock at the gates of Cleonae and Megara. You broke them down and forced your way in under arms, on the assumption that nothing stands in the way of the stronger party.' With this defiant reply to the Corinthian, he passed on his way through their land with his army.*

The Lacedaemonians appealed a second time to Athens, this time for help against the Messenian and helot stronghold in Ithome, but after their arrival they became nervous about the courage and brilliance the Athenians displayed and dismissed them on the grounds that they were fomenting revolution. The Athenians were the only ones of their allies that the Lacedaemonians treated this way, and when they got home they were furious.* They made no secret of the fact that they were taking their anger out on those with pro-Laconian sympathies, and they seized on a flimsy pretext to banish Cimon by ostracism for ten years, which was the prescribed length of time for ostracism.*

In the middle of Cimon's period of ostracism, when the Lacedaemonians pitched camp at Tanagra on their way back home after liberating Delphi from the Phocians, the Athenians came out to meet them in battle, and Cimon arrived with an armed retinue to join his tribe Oeneis, since he wanted to help his fellow citizens repel the Lacedaemonians. This news worried the Council of Five Hundred, and when his enemies loudly accused him of wanting to spread confusion in the ranks and pave the way for the Lacedaemonians to attack the city, the Council told the military commanders to refuse Cimon permission to fight. So he left, but not before he had asked Euthippus of Anaphlystus and all the rest of his comrades who were particularly suspected of being pro-Laconian to resist the enemy with all their might and so let their actions eliminate the suspicion from the minds of their fellow citizens. Euthippus and the others took Cimon's suit of armour and found a place for it in their ranks; in the battle they stayed close to one another and fell fighting bravely, all 100 of them, leaving the Athenians to miss them badly and to feel sorry for the unfair suspicions they had harboured against them.*

As a result of this, the Athenians soon shed their anger against Cimon as well, partly because, typically, they recalled all the good he had done them, and partly because events came to his assistance, in the sense that the Athenians had suffered a major defeat at Tanagra, and fully expected a Peloponnesian army to attack the following spring. So they recalled Cimon from his exile, and he returned in response to the decree which Pericles himself had proposed. And this just goes to show how in those days quarrels were conducted with civility, feelings were moderate, and people had no difficulty in restraining them if the public good was at stake; even ambition, which is the most dominant and powerful human emotion, used to be subordinate to national emergencies.

[18] As soon as he returned, Cimon reconciled the two cities with each other and brought the war to an end. And so there was peace, but Cimon realized that the Athenians were incapable of keeping still, and were eager for military expeditions, so as to be on the move and to expand their authority. However, he did not want them to annoy

any other Greek state, and he was worried that, if they sailed back and forth off the Aegean islands or the Peloponnese with a large fleet, they would bring down on the city the charge of fomenting civil unrest and would give the allies grounds for complaints. What he did, then, was outfit 300 triremes, with the intention of campaigning once more against Egypt and Cyprus. He had two objectives in mind: first, he wanted to give the Athenians practical experience of fighting the Persians, and, second, he wanted them to make an honest profit by bringing back to Greece the riches plundered from their natural enemies.*

Just at the time when the expedition was completely ready to leave, however, and the troops were on the point of boarding, Cimon had a dream in which an angry bitch was barking at him and, in a human voice mixed in with the barking, said to him: 'Go, for you will be doing both me and my pups a favour.' Now, this was a very difficult dream to interpret, but Astyphilus of Posidonia, a diviner who was a close friend of Cimon's, told him that the dream was foretelling his death. He analysed it as follows: when a dog barks at a person, that dog is an enemy, and the best favour one can do an enemy is to die; as for the mixed voice, this indicates, he said, that the enemy is Persian, because the Persian army consists of both Greek and non-Greek elements. Some time after this dream, Cimon was sacrificing to Dionysus, and when the diviner had cut open the victim, a swarm of ants gathered up the blood just as it was coagulating and carried it, little by little, over to Cimon. They proceeded to smear the blood on to his big toe, without Cimon noticing it for quite a while. Just as he did notice what was happening, the priest who had performed the sacrifice came up to him to show him that the liver lacked a head.*

It was out of the question for him to withdraw from the expedition, however, so he set sail and sent sixty of his ships to Egypt, while sailing with the rest to <. . .>,† where he won a sea battle against the Persian king's Phoenician and Cilician fleet, and then recovered the communities in the surrounding area and lay in wait, watching over things in Egypt. He had in mind nothing less than the complete destruction of the king's power, particularly because he had received information that Themistocles had risen in status and influence in Persia by promising the king that he would take command of the Persian army when the king launched his Greek offensive.* As the story goes, it was chiefly Themistocles' realization that he could never get the better of Cimon, who could do nothing wrong and was displaying outstanding qualities of leadership, that made him see the hopelessness of his prospects in Greece and led him to take his own life. Cimon, however, held his fleet off Cyprus and, because he was poised to initiate a major conflict, sent a delegation to the shrine of Ammon to put a secret question to the god.* No one knows what it was that this delegation went to ask, and the god did not reply to any question of theirs either. What happened was that as soon as they approached the shrine, the god told them to leave, on the grounds that Cimon was in fact already with him. On hearing this, the emissaries returned to the coast, and when they reached the Greek camp, which was then in Egypt, they discovered that Cimon was dead. And when they looked back to see how many days earlier the oracle had spoken to them, they realized that it was Cimon's death that had been alluded to, since he had already been with the gods.

[19] He was in the middle of besieging Citium when he died. Most sources say it was illness that carried him off, but some say it was a wound he had received while fighting the Persians. As he was dying he told his companions to conceal the fact of his death and sail back home straight away. And so they managed to get back home safely without either the enemy or the allies realizing what had happened, 'under Cimon's command,' as Phanodemus puts it, 'even though he had been dead for thirty days'.*

Cimon's death spelled the end of the days of glorious exploits by Greek commanders against the Persians. Afterwards, under the influence of demagogues and warmongers, the Greeks were turned against one another and, with no one to keep them apart, they clashed in a series of wars which gave Persia time to recover and which sapped Greece's strength to an incalculable degree. Many years were to pass before Agesilaus would campaign again in Asia. He briefly made war on the king's military governors in the coastal provinces, without achieving anything particularly outstanding or important, but then he was let down by a renewed outbreak of feuding and unrest in Greece.* So he withdrew, leaving the Persian tribute-collectors to roam among the communities of allies and friends, when in the time of Cimon's command not even a Persian horse was to be seen within 400 stades of the sea, and there was absolutely no chance of a messenger coming down to the coast.

That Cimon's remains were brought back to Attica is proved by the existence of the monuments which are still called the Cimoneia; however, the people of Citium also worship at 'Cimon's tomb', because, according to the orator Nausicrates, once during a time of famine and crop-failure the god told them not to overlook Cimon, but to revere and honour him as a superhuman being. So that is what the Greek leader was like.*

PERICLES

INTRODUCTION

Plato did not like Pericles. 'This is what I hear: Pericles made the Athenians idle, work-shy, garrulous, and mercenary, when he first introduced payments [for civic duties],' he has Socrates say in *Gorgias* (515e). Many shared Plato's opinion. The anti-democratic bias of most Greek and Roman writers tended to see Pericles as Plato did, a demagogue leading an unthinking populace by catering to its desires, and the view was shared by many in the eighteenth and nineteenth centuries. *Pericles* is Plutarch's answer to Plato: admittedly Pericles held power in a democracy, but he acted as an aristocrat, or better, a monarch, ruling the people firmly, through his own self-possession controlling the unruly emotions of the crowd.

Plutarch offers this tenth pair in his series of *Parallel Lives* as powerful portraits of two admirable statesmen, notable for their 'self-possession and integrity, and their ability to endure the foolishness of the populace and their colleagues' (*Per.* 2). An unusually explicit preface states the rationale behind these Lives. The mind has a capacity to be delighted and nourished by noble actions, and is moved to imitate them. While aesthetic beauty delights the viewer, it is only moral beauty as manifest in action that sets in motion 'an immediate urge to action'. This spirit of emulation is the goal of this pair of lives, in which the admirable political behaviour of Pericles and Fabius is presented to the reader.

Fabius, a distinguished member of the Roman senatorial oligarchy, in 217 BC was chosen dictator by the senate to stop Hannibal after the latter had won devastating victories over several Roman armies. By a controlled, restrained use of his army, he was able to blunt Hannibal's attack and give the Romans time to recover their strength and confidence. Pericles' greatest moment occurred when he preserved Athens from the invading Spartans by refusing to lead the Athenians out to defend their land (*Per.* 33). The two men, who most historians would say have nothing in common, are united in Plutarch's eyes by their self-possession, seen in their refusal to go along with the emotions of others, whether expressed by the Athenian populace, the Roman senate and people, or a colleague like Minucius, Fabius' second in command.

The structure of *Pericles* reinforces Plutarch's interpretation. In it he integrates chronological, topical, and rhetorical schemes. Viewed chronologically, there is a rough temporal sequence: Pericles' birth, his entry into public life, his rivalry with Cimon and with Thucydides son of Melesias, the crisis of 446, the Samian War, the Peloponnesian War, his dismissal and reinstatement, and his death. But many incidents are discussed out of sequence, especially his contacts with Anaxagoras, the building programme, and the campaigns treated in cc. 18–20, since there is also a topical ordering at work, presenting Pericles' family, formative influences, and character (3–6), his political style (7–8), his struggle with rivals (9–14), his qualities as a political and a military leader (15–17, 18–23), the great crises (24–35), and family life (36). Many other topics, such as Athens' glorious building programme (13) and Pericles' relationship with his mistress Aspasia (24), are subsumed under these.

The rhetorical challenge of demonstrating that the leader of the Athenian democracy in its heyday was in fact an admirably austere aristocrat led Plutarch to set out at the beginning of his Life the influence of Anaxagoras on Pericles' public behaviour, notion of the gods, and oratory (4–6, 8), and only afterwards (9) raise the problem of Pericles' success in manipulating the people to defeat and ostracize his overtly oligarchic rivals Cimon and Thucydides. In chapter 9, where Plutarch contrasts the view of Thucydides, that Pericles was in practice a monarch, with that of Plato, he sets the question for the reader: was Pericles a noble ruler or a base demagogue? The answer comes in the following chapters, but was already implicit in Plutarch's choice to set Pericles and Fabius side by side (2). In battling Cimon and Thucydides, Pericles' demagogic means of gaining power are justified by their own value (notably the success of the building programme) and by the way he exercised power once it was acquired. The middle sections (15–23) do not restrict themselves to one period, but give a survey of Pericles' qualities when in power: self-possessed, persuasive, and honest as a politician, visionary as a leader, cautious and successful as a general. The great moment of crisis, the outbreak of the war with Sparta and its allies, tests not only Pericles' resolution but the whole scheme of Plutarch's Life.

Plutarch hated civil war, and especially war among Greeks: yet Pericles bore the responsibility of urging war when it might have been avoided. In examining the possible reasons for this intransigence (30–2), Plutarch reports accusations of personal vendetta and Machiavellian expediency alongside Thucydides' argument that he was defending Athenian independence— and refuses to choose between them. Focusing rather on Pericles' conduct of the war itself, he celebrates his restraint of the Athenians' irrational desire to engage the enemy and his encouragement in their troubles (33–5), and ends with a recollection of his caution as a general (38) and a hymn to his self-possession, which made him, like Fabius, a sturdy bulwark that preserved the state (39).

At a time when emotions ran high in Greek cities, and in many cities of the empire, Plutarch's glorification of political leaders who restrained rather than inflamed their citizens spoke directly to the needs of the day. Pericles occurs frequently as an example in Plutarch's *Rules for Politicians*.

The message was appropriate at all levels, from the rivalries of local élites, to the struggles for the control of the empire. The example is no less necessary today. Yet Plutarch's Pericles, while self-possessed, is not a negative person: there is a breadth of vision shown in his encouragement of the Athenians in times of trouble, his ambitious plans for Athens (e.g. the Congress Decree, 17), and especially in his building programme, 'which all by itself demonstrates that Greece's much-vaunted ancient power and prosperity have not been misrepresented' (12), which contain 'an evergreen spirit and an unaging soul mingled together' (13).

Thucydides, our chief extant contemporary source for Pericles, provides the framework for cc. 22–35, but Plutarch supplements him with a wealth of contemporary and later material that makes this Life one of the most valuable to the historian. The memoirs of the poet Ion of Chios provide here, as in *Cimon*, valuable insights on the opinion of Pericles held among the upper class (5, 28) and Stesimbrotus' polemic preserves gossip on his sexual life and other matters (13, 36, 8, 26). Plutarch mines Aristophanes as well as the lost Athenian comic poets for jibes against Pericles (3, 4, 7, 8, 13, 16, 24, 26, 30, 33). He was familiar with the original plays and the commentaries to them that explained recondite allusions, and he would also have had access to reference works which collected allusions to famous figures. In addition he had access to texts of some of Pericles' decrees, perhaps in the collection made in the fourth century by Craterus. These decrees, moved by Pericles and approved by the Athenian Assembly, gave Plutarch direct access to Periclean policy, more authentic than the speeches incorporated in Thucydides' history (see 10, 17, 20, 25, 30 and 37; decrees by others are in 30 and 32). Of later authors Plutarch used Ephorus, Theopompus, Aristotle's *Constitution of the Samians*, Theophrastus, Duris of Samos, Plato, the Socratic writers Aeschines and Antisthenes (on Aspasia), and Heraclides of Pontus. To these he added his own observation, not only of the Acropolis buildings, but probably also of the bronze wolf at Delphi (21), the portrait statues of Pericles (3), and the shield of Athena Parthenos (31). He refers also to oral tradition 'in the philosophical schools' (35). The reference to 'the Megarians' who deny the murder of Anthemocritus (30) may be to his contemporaries, rather than to historians of Megara.

Since Thucydides offers us nothing on the personal life of Pericles and little on his career before 432 BC, the information collected by Plutarch on his political activity and the opposition that it generated is invaluable to our understanding of the fifth century. Without this Life, the expeditions to the Chersonese and Sinope would be forgotten, along with the Congress Decree and the decrees of Charinus, Glaucon, and Dracontides. We would not know that the Athenians elected Pericles general fifteen times consecutively, nor that in this period he was the object of constant attacks.

Plutarch sets Pericles in the risky world of partisan politics, and allows us to see a very human leader, a self-possessed orator of extraordinary power, who yet was called 'squill-head' and dismissed as a self-important boor, or vilified as a tyrant and lecher.

Commentaries to Pericles:

Podlecki, A., *Life of Pericles: A Companion to the Penguin Translation from The Rise and Fall of Athens* (Bristol: Bristol Classical Press, 1987).

Stadter, P. A., *A Commentary on Plutarch's Pericles* (Chapel Hill, University of North Carolina Press, 1989).

For a detailed narrative see:

Kagan, D., *The Outbreak of the Peloponnesian War* (Ithaca, NY: Cornell University Press, 1969).

—— *The Archidamian War* (Ithaca, NY: Cornell University Press, 1974).

For special topics:

Ameling, W., 'Plutarch, Perikles 12–14', *Historia*, 24 (1985), 47–63. Plutarch's presentation of the building programme.

Cawkwell, G. L., 'Thucydides' Judgement of Periclean Strategy', *Yale Classical Studies*, 24 (1975), 53–70.

Connor, W. R., *The New Politicians of Fifth-Century Athens* (Princeton: Princeton Univeristy Press, 1971). The shift in political behaviour in this period.

Dover, K. J., 'Anecdotes, Gossip and Scandal', in *The Greeks and Their Legacy* (Oxford: Blackwell, 1988), 45–52. On interpreting political scandal.

Henry, M. M., *Prisoner of History: Aspasia of Miletus and Her Biographical Tradition* (Oxford and New York: Oxford University Press, 1995).

Lewis, D. M., in *Cambridge Ancient History*, v, 2nd edn. (Cambridge: Cambridge University Press, 1992), 121–46, 370–401. Thoughtful, brief account of 450–429.

Pelling, C. B. R., 'Plutarch and Thucydides', in P. A. Stadter (ed.), *Plutarch and the Historical Tradition* (London: Routledge, 1992), 10–40. Examination of how Plutarch rewrites Thucydides.

Ste Croix, G. E. M. de, *The Origins of the Peloponnesian War* (London: Duckworth, 1972). Includes a thorough, though disputed, examination of the Megarian Decree.

Stadter, P. A., 'Plutarch's Comparison of Pericles and Fabius Maximus', *Greek, Roman and Byzantine Studies*, 16 (1975), 77–85.

—— 'The Rhetoric of Plutarch's *Pericles*', *Ancient Society*, 18 (1987), 251–269.

—— 'Pericles and the Intellectuals', *Illinois Classical Studies*, 16 (1991), 111–24. On Pericles' contact with the Sophists.

PERICLES

[1] Once, when Caesar* saw some wealthy visitors to Rome carrying young dogs and monkeys around on their laps and petting them, he apparently asked whether the women in their country did not produce children—a right royal rebuke of those who waste our innate capacity for love and affection on animals, when it is due to men. Now, since our minds have an innate capacity to enjoy learning and contemplation, does it not follow that it is reasonable to criticize people who waste this capacity on sights and sounds that do not deserve serious consideration, to the neglect of those that are fine and beneficial? For since the senses passively apprehend the impact of whatever comes their way, it is presumably inevitable that we will by these means see every phenomenon, whether or not there is any benefit to it; however, each of us has the capacity to *choose* to use his mind, to make a shift from time to time and to change direction with the greatest ease according to deliberate decision, and it therefore follows that we should go after what is best for us, so that we do not just see, but are also nourished by what we see. Just as colour is the proper object of the eye, and the brightness and charm of colour rekindles and feeds the sense of sight,* so we should steer our rational faculty towards the contemplation of things which it finds pleasing and which therefore encourage it to aspire to its proper good. These are to be found among deeds motivated by virtue, which imbue those who investigate them with a kind of admiration and a desire that stimulates one to emulation. After all, in other cases an urge to act does not immediately follow from admiration of an action; on the contrary, we often despise the workman while enjoying the work, as we like perfumes and dyes, but regard dyers and perfumers as mean and coarse.* That is why Antisthenes* spoke well when he said, on being told that Ismenias* was a good piper, 'But he's a bad man; otherwise he wouldn't be a good piper.' And again Philip* once asked his son, who was playing the lyre at a drinking-party with consummate and pleasing skill, 'Aren't you ashamed to be so good at the lyre?'—the point being that it is enough if a king finds the time to listen to people playing the lyre, and he does the Muses great honour simply by observing others competing in such pursuits.

[2] Working at mean tasks bears witness, in itself, to a person's indifference towards excellence: the labour he expends on things of no value demonstrates this. No promising youth is moved to want to be Phidias by the sight of the Zeus in Pisa, or to be Polyclitus by the sight of the Hera in Argos,* or to be Anacreon, Philemon, or Archilochus because he has enjoyed their poetry.* Enjoying a product and finding it pleasing do not necessarily mean that the person who made it deserves serious consideration. This is also why it does people no good to see the kinds of things which fail to promote emulative admiration or to cause a surge of energy which stimulates a desire and urge for assimilation. Actions arising out of virtue, however, immediately put one in a frame of mind such that one simultaneously admires the acts and desires to emulate the agents. We appreciate owning and enjoying the good things that come to us by chance, but we appreciate *doing* the good deeds which come to us from virtue; moreover, while we want to receive the former from others, we want others to receive the latter from us.* For anything noble actively attracts us to itself and instils in us an immediate urge to action; it does not build moral character in the spectator merely by means of a representation, but by giving him purpose through an account of the deed.*

And so I decided to carry on writing Lives and have composed this book, the tenth in the series, which includes the Lives of Pericles and of Fabius Maximus,* who fought so relentlessly against Hannibal. There are a number of similarities between the two men in respect of their virtues, but the most important traits they shared were self-possession and integrity, and their ability to endure the foolishness of the populace and their colleagues made them of particular value to their countries. The reader will be able to judge from the following account whether or not this assessment of mine hits the mark.

[3] Pericles belonged to the tribe Acamantis and deme Cholargus,* and came from the best family and stock on both his father's and his mother's side. Xanthippus, who defeated the Persian king's military commanders at the battle of Mycale, married Agariste, a descendant of Cleisthenes, who followed up his honourable expulsion of the Pisistratidae and dissolution of the tyranny by establishing a legal code and a political constitution that was admirably tempered to promote unanimity and ensure the preservation of the state.* In a recurrent dream Agariste imagined that she gave birth to a lion,* and then a few days later she gave birth to Pericles, who was a perfectly formed

Pericles also studied under Zeno of Elea, who was working as a natural scientist along the lines of Parmenides and had developed a particular refutational technique by means of which he could trap an opponent and use contradiction to reduce him to perplexity.* This is presumably also what Timon of Phleious is referring to in the following lines:

> O Zeno, you of the vast, inexhaustible power
> And the two-edged tongue, you who arrest everyone . . .

But the one whose association with Pericles lasted longest, who was particularly responsible for giving him authority and a sense of pride that was too solid for him to remain a mere demagogue, and who in general elevated and promoted his moral gravity, was Anaxagoras of Clazomenae—the Mind, as his contemporaries used to call him, perhaps because they were impressed with the great and exceptional intelligence he manifestly brought to bear on the study of natural science, or perhaps because he was the first to deny that either chance or necessity was the source of the orderly array of the universe, and instead established mind as something pure and unmixed which operates in the midst of all other things, which are mixed together, and separates out the homoeomerous substances.*

[5] Pericles was filled with unbounded admiration for this man and became saturated with so-called high-flown speculation about celestial phenomena. The first results of this were the dignified pride he apparently had, and a manner of speaking that was lofty and untainted by vulgar, unscrupulous trickery; then there were also things like the tranquillity of his features that never broke into laughter, his self-possessed gait, the way his clothing was arranged in such a way that it was never disturbed by any emotion while he was speaking, and his calm tone of voice, all of which made a remarkable impression on everyone. At any rate, on one occasion he had insults and abuse hurled at him by some crude and outrageous fellow in the city square, where he had pressing business to see to, and he endured it all day long and then went home in the evening, perfectly composed, with the man following him and calling him all kinds of names. By the time he got home it was dark, and just before going inside he told one of his slaves to take a torch and escort the man back to his house.

The poet Ion, however, says that Pericles had a presumptuous and rather arrogant way of dealing with other people, and that a great deal of disdain and contempt for others contaminated his haughtiness, while he commends Cimon for his tact, lack of formality, and elegance in social contexts. But let us ignore Ion, who always expected virtue, like a tragic production, to have a part for satyrs as well.* Faced with people disparaging Pericles' dignified manner as a manifestation of his thirst for popularity and his arrogance, Zeno urged them too to court popularity in some such way, on the grounds that even the pretence of noble traits subtly and imperceptibly results in a certain admiration of them and an adaptation to their ways.

[6] These were not the only advantages Pericles gained from his association with Anaxagoras. He is also held to have risen above superstition, which induces awe of heavenly phenomena in those who are ignorant of their causes. Such people are obsessed with things divine and are disturbed by their naivety in this domain—a naivety removed by natural science, which replaces timid and morbid superstition with the kind of secure piety that is supported by positive assumptions for the future.

There is a story that once the head of a single-horned ram was brought to Pericles from his country estate. When Lampon the diviner saw how the horn had grown firm and solid from the centre of the ram's forehead, he declared that although there were two dominant parties in the city, that of Thucydides and that of Pericles, power would devolve on to one person—the one on whose property the portent had occurred.* Anaxagoras, however, had the skull cut open and demonstrated that the brain had not filled the pan, but had slid from the cavity as a whole and gathered, pointed like an egg, in that part of the cavity where the root of the horn began. This immediately gained Anaxagoras the admiration of those who were present at the demonstration, but a short while later it was Lampon's turn, when Thucydides was overthrown and absolutely all the political affairs of the Athenian people passed into Pericles' hands.

In my opinion, it is perfectly possible that both the natural scientist and the diviner were right, in the sense that the one correctly interpreted the cause and the other the purpose. It was the job of the former to consider the circumstances under which the horn had arisen and how it had grown, and of the latter to declare the reason for the phenomenon and its significance. Those who claim that to disclose the cause is to dispose of the sign are failing to take into consideration that in doing away with the intrusion of the divine they are simultaneously doing away with artificial signs as well, such as the sounding of gongs, the light of beacons, and the shadows cast by the pointers of sundials; after all, in each of these cases it has taken some cause, some preparation, for them to function as signs. But this discussion probably belongs in another treatise.

[7] As a young man, Pericles was extremely wary of the Athenian people, because he was generally held to look like the tyrant Pisistratus, and old people used to remark how charming his voice was, and how fluent and rapid his speech was, and were amazed by the similarity. Since he was rich and from an illustrious family, and had very powerful friends, he was afraid of being ostracized and he steered clear of public life, while proving his excellence and courage on the battlefield. But with Aristides dead, Themistocles in exile, and Cimon often kept abroad by his campaigns,* Pericles enthusiastically espoused the popular cause and chose the side of the mass of poor people rather than that of the rich few, despite the fact that this ran contrary to his own nature, which was very far from being sympathetic to the common people. Nevertheless, motivated by the fear of being suspected of tyrannical ambitions, apparently, and by the realization that Cimon belonged to the aristocratic party and stood in exceptionally high favour with the upper classes, he won over the common people, as a way of safeguarding his position and of gaining power against Cimon. He also lost no time in adopting a changed way of life. The only street in the city where he could be seen walking was the one leading to the city square and the Council chamber; he stopped accepting invitations to dinner and gave up that kind of social intercourse and activity so completely that he never, throughout all the many years of his involvement in politics, went to have dinner at a friend's house.* The only exception was on the occasion of a wedding-feast given by his cousin Euryptolemus, when he attended until the libations had been poured and then immediately got up and left. The point is that conviviality tends to undermine authority and it is hard to maintain an appearance of gravity in the midst of familiar social intercourse; in the case of true virtue, however, it is the most obvious aspects that are the most admirable, and the daily life of good men is as remarkable to their companions as anything about them is to strangers.

Pericles also wanted to avoid the satiety that follows from continuous association, so he approached the Athenian people only at
intervals, as it were; he did not speak on every issue, nor did he constantly come forward to address the Assembly, but offered himself
—like the trireme *Salaminia*, as Critolaus puts it*—only in times of
crisis, while conducting the rest of his business through the agency
of friends and other speakers. One of these intermediaries is said to
have been Ephialtes,* who overthrew the power of the Council of the
Areopagus and, to use Plato's image, served the citizens of Athens
with plenty of undiluted freedom,* under the influence of which the
people behaved like an unruly horse, according to the comic poets,
and

> Stopped being prepared to obey orders,
> But nipped Euboea and mounted the islands.*†

[8] However, in tuning his manner of speaking to his way of life
and the extent of his pride, as if he were getting a musical instrument
ready for use, he often made use of Anaxagoras as an extra string and
tinged, so to speak, his rhetoric with natural science. For, as the divine
Plato says,* it was from natural science that 'he acquired this lofti-
ness of perspective and all-round effectiveness to add to his natural
ability', and once he had applied this as appropriate to the art of speaking, he became by far the best speaker in Athens. They say that this
is also why he received his famous epithet, although some think that
he was called 'Olympian' because of the buildings with which he
adorned the city, and others attribute the name to his political and
military power. In actual fact, it is not at all unlikely that the reputation was the combined result of a number of the man's qualities.
However, it is clear from the comedies produced by playwrights of
the time, who made him the target of a great many epithets, both
in fun and in earnest, that it was above all his manner of speaking
that gained him the nickname, since they describe him as 'thunder-
ing' and as 'emitting lightning' whenever he addressed the Athenian
people, and as 'carrying a terrible thunderbolt in his tongue'.* There
is also preserved a humorous *mot* of Thucydides the son of Melesias
about Pericles' skill at speaking. Thucydides' sympathies lay with the
upper classes, and he was Pericles' political rival for a very long time;
Archidamus, the king of the Lacedaemonians, asked him whether he
or Pericles was the better wrestler, and he replied, 'Suppose we're

wrestling and I throw him: he disputes the fall, wins the argument, and gets the spectators to change their minds!'

Nevertheless, Pericles himself† actually approached his speaking with caution; in fact, every time he walked up to the speaker's rostrum he used to offer up a prayer to the gods that not a single† word which was inappropriate to the matter at hand might accidentally spill out out of his mouth. Nothing of his remains in a written form except his decrees,* and only a very few sayings of his are preserved, as, for example, when he suggested the removal of Aegina as the eyesore of the Piraeus, or when he said he could see war bearing down on them from the Peloponnese. Again, when Sophocles, who was sharing with him the command of a naval expedition, praised a good-looking boy, he said, 'A military commander should keep his eyes clean, Sophocles, as well as his hands.' Stesimbrotus reports that in the course of his eulogy of those who had died in Samos, delivered at the speaker's rostrum, he described them as having become as immortal as the gods. 'For in fact,' he said, 'we cannot see the actual gods, but we deduce their immortality from the worship they receive and the benefits they confer.' But those who have died in defence of their country also have the same attributes, he said.

[9] Thucydides describes Pericles' government as quasi-aristocratic, when he says that it was 'nominally democracy, but actually rule by the leading man',* whereas many others say that at first he seduced the Athenian people with grants of land abroad, money for festivals, and financial handouts, that they were corrupted into bad habits by his policies at the time, and that they became extravagant and undisciplined instead of self-controlled and self-supporting.* We therefore need to refer to his actual deeds to consider the reasons for this change in him.

Originally, as I have already said, he had Cimon's reputation to contend with, so he curried popularity with the people. However, Cimon was better off financially, and made use of his money to win the favour of the poor: he used to lay on a meal every day for any Athenian citizen who wanted it and clothe elderly people, and he removed the fences around his properties so that people could pick the fruit if they liked.* Out-demagogued, then, by these manoeuvres of Cimon's he had recourse to the distribution of public funds, on the advice, according to Aristotle,* of Damonides from the deme Oa.† Before long he had bribed the general populace with money for festivals, fees for jury service, and other payments and grants, and then made use of the people against the Council of the Areopagus,* which he personally could not join because he had never been appointed by lot to the office of archon, thesmothete, king archon, or polemarch. These posts had been subject to appointment by lot since ancient times, and it was through them that those who passed the scrutiny were promoted to the Areopagus. That is why, once he had improved his position of strength with the people, he overthrew the Council of the Areopagus. The upshot was that through Ephialtes' agency it was deprived of almost all its jurisdiction, and Cimon was ostracized* for his pro-Laconian and anti-democratic tendencies, despite his unrivalled wealth and lineage, and despite all his glorious victories over the Persians and all the money and booty with which he had filled the city, as I have described in his Life. This goes to show the extent of Pericles' hold over the Athenian people.

[10] The legally stipulated period for banishment by ostracism was ten years, but before Cimon's time was up the Lacedaemonians invaded the district of Tanagra with a sizeable army and the Athenians immediately set out to meet them. Cimon therefore returned from exile and took up his position alongside other members of his tribe in one of the Athenian companies, with the intention of sharing his fellow citizen's danger and so letting his deeds acquit him of the charge of being pro-Laconian. A group of Pericles' friends, however, dismissed him on the grounds that he was an exile. This is generally taken to explain why Pericles fought with particular bravery in that battle; no one more conspicuously disregarded his personal safety than him. Apart from anyone else, every single one of Cimon's friends fell—and they were the ones whom Pericles had accused, along with Cimon, of being sympathetic to Sparta.* This defeat on the borders of Attica and the expectation that the campaigning season of the following year would bring a full-scale war combined to make the Athenians undergo a thorough change of heart, and they began to miss Cimon. When Pericles saw what was going on, he did not hesitate to gratify the desire of the common people: he personally drafted the decree and recalled the man. Once Cimon was back from exile,† he succeeded in making peace between the two cities, because the Lacedaemonians were as well disposed towards him as they were hostile towards Pericles and the other popular leaders.*

According to some sources, however, Pericles did not draft the decree recalling Cimon until the two of them had come to a secret agreement, using Elpinice, Cimon's sister, as an intermediary. The terms of the alleged agreement were that Cimon was to take a fleet of 200 ships abroad and was to have command of those on foreign service while attempting to annex the Persian king's territory, whereas Pericles was to have power in the city.* It is also generally held that Elpinice had helped Cimon by restraining Pericles on an earlier occasion too, when Cimon was on trial for his life. Pericles had been chosen by the people as one of the prosecutors,* and when Elpinice came and pleaded with him for Cimon he said with a smile, 'You're an old woman, Elpinice—too old for a business like this.'† Nevertheless, he got up to address the issue only once, to fulfil the formal requirements of his appointment, and by the end of the trial had caused fewer difficulties for Cimon than any of the other prosecutors.

How, then can we believe Idomeneus when he accuses Pericles of being so jealous and envious of the reputation of the popular leader Ephialtes that he assassinated him, although he was a friend and a colleague of the same political persuasion? No, he has raked up this charge from somewhere or other, as if he were gathering bile, and hurled it at Pericles. It may well be true that Pericles is not entirely without fault, but he had a noble pride and an ambitious mind, and these can harbour no such fierce and savage emotions. The fact is that the oligarchs were afraid of Ephialtes, who was inexorable in calling those who had wronged the Athenian people to account and in prosecuting them. So, as Aristotle records, his enemies plotted against him and got Aristodicus of Tanagra to kill him in secret.* As for Cimon, he died in Cyprus, where he was in command of an expedition.*

[11] The aristocratic party had been aware for some time that Pericles was the most prominent person in the city, but they still wanted there to be someone powerful† to resist him politically and to take the edge off his power, so that the government of Athens would not be a complete autocracy. They therefore put up Thucydides of the deme Alopece,* an equable man who was related by marriage to Cimon, to act as Pericles' political opponent. Thucydides was less of a soldier than Cimon, and less aloof as a politician; by staying in the city and getting to grips with Pericles at the speaker's rostrum, he soon brought the political system back to a position where the two parties

were evenly matched. What he did was stop the so-called good men and true of the upper classes being scattered here and there and mixed up among the general mass of people, with their gravity obscured by sheer numbers; instead he got them all to congregate in the same place, away from everyone else, and so enabled their collective power to become a serious force, and, as it were, a counterweight on the scale.*

There had been from the very beginning a kind of flaw, such as one might find in a piece of iron, festering below the surface and signalling the divergence between popular and aristocratic policies, and now the rivalry and competition between these two men sliced deeply into the city and separated out two distinct factions, called respectively 'the people' and 'the few'. At the time in question, then, Pericles made a particular point of letting the people have their head and began to design his policies with a view to their gratification; he was always thinking up something to put on in the city—a spectacle for general consumption, a public feast, a procession. He used a series of not entirely tasteless pleasures to keep control over the city,* and sent out sixty triremes a year on expeditions which lasted eight months and provided the large numbers of Athenian citizens who crewed the ships not only with wages, but also with practice and training at nautical skills. In addition he sent 1,000 settlers to the Chersonese, 500 to Naxos, 250 to Andros, 1,000 to Thrace to live alongside the Bisaltae, and others to Italy when Sybaris was being rebuilt as the colony they called Thurii. He did this to relieve the city of a crowd of unproductive and idle trouble-makers, to alleviate the poverty of the people, and to establish settlements near Athens' allies as a deterrent and defence against rebellion.*

[12] However, the provision of his which was the greatest source of pleasure and improvement for Athens, and the greatest source of astonishment for everyone else in the world, was that which all by itself confirms for Greece that her much-vaunted ancient power and prosperity have not been misrepresented—that is, the construction of the sacred buildings. Of all Pericles' policies, this was the one which his enemies particularly maligned and criticized time and again in the assemblies. 'The fame and reputation of the Athenian people are suffering,' they howled, 'because of the transference of the common Greek funds from Delos to our own keeping.* Moreover, Pericles has undermined the most plausible excuse we had to offer our critics, namely that the removal of the treasury from there had

been prompted by fear of the Persians, in the sense that we wanted to have it in a safe place where we could guard it. The Greeks regard it as outrageously arrogant treatment, as blatant tyranny, when they can see that we are using the funds they were forced to contribute for the military defence of Greece to gild and embellish our city, as if she were a vain woman adorning herself with costly marble, statues, and temples at 1,000 talents a time.'

In response Pericles used to tell the Athenian people that, since they were defending the allies and keeping the Persians at bay, they were not accountable to them for the money; the tribute the allies paid consisted only of money, not of horses, ships, or soldiers, and money, he claimed, belongs to its recipients, not its donors, as long as the recipients provide the services for which they are being paid. Moreover, he argued, once the city has been adequately supplied with military necessities, it needs to direct any surplus it has accumulated towards enterprises which when completed will bring eternal glory, and while in progress will provide immediate prosperity, in the sense that they will generate all kinds of work and a wide range of requirements, which by stimulating all the arts and crafts and getting every hand moving put almost the whole city in receipt of wages, so that the city is simultaneously being embellished and supported out of its own resources.

Campaigns abroad enabled those of the right age and degree of physical fitness to be well paid out of the common purse, but since Pericles did not like to see the crowd of disorganized artisans excluded from payment either, while wanting to avoid paying them for remaining unproductive and idle, he enthusiastically introduced before the Assembly impressive schemes for constructions, and plans for work that would employ a wide range of skills and take time to complete, so that those who stayed at home might have just as much of a reason to be paid out of public funds and to share in the general prosperity as those who were out at sea or on garrison duty or serving in the army. For since the materials involved were stone, bronze, ivory, gold, ebony, and cypress, and since the skilled workers needed to work with these materials and turn them into finished products were joiners, modellers, metal-workers, masons, gilders, ivory-softeners, painters, embroiderers, and embossers, and since there were also needed people to transport and deliver these materials—that is, merchants, sailors, and helmsmen for the sea, and for the land wagon-makers, keepers of pairs of oxen, muleteers, rope-makers, linen-weavers, leather-workers, road-makers, and quarrymen—and since each line of business deployed, as a commander does his army, a mass of unskilled and unspecialized hired labourers to act as the instrument and physical means of the service to be provided, then the requirements of these projects divided and distributed the surplus money to pretty well every age-group and type of person.

[13] For all the wonderful size, inimitable beauty and exceptional charm of the buildings that then began to arise, and for all the fine workmanship of the craftsmen, who were striving to surpass the limits of their craft, the most astonishing thing of all was the speed of progress. Whereas people imagined that each of them would take many successive generations, at least, to be completed, every one of them was finished within the prime of a single administration. There is a story that once when Agatharchus the painter was boasting about the speed and ease with which he created his figures, Zeuxis, who heard him, said, 'I take a long time over mine.'* And in fact it is true that dexterity and speed do not give a piece of art lasting weight and precision in conveying beauty, and that time invested in hard work during the production of a piece pays a dividend of strength manifest in its durability when completed. This is what makes Pericles' works even more impressive, because they have durability despite having been completed quickly. In terms of beauty each of them was a classic straight away at the time, but in terms of vigour each is a new and recent creation even today; and so a kind of freshness forms a constant bloom on them and keeps their appearance untouched by time, as if they contained an evergreen spirit and an unaging soul mingled together.

The general manager and supervisor of his works was Phidias, although important master builders and craftsmen were involved in them.* For instance, Callicrates and Ictinus were responsible for building the Parthenon, Coroebus made a start on the sanctuary of the mysteries at Eleusis (it was he who set the columns on the floor and connected them with architraves), and after his death Metagenes of the deme Xypete added the frieze and the upper level of columns, while Xenocles of the deme Cholargus capped the shrine with its lantern;* and it was Callicrates who won the contract for building the Long Wall, the construction of which Socrates says he personally heard Pericles proposing. Cratinus ridiculed the work on the Long Wall for its slow progress,* when he said:

> For a long time now it's been coming along fine
> In Pericles' speeches, but there's no change at all in fact.

The Odeum, with its banks of seats and numerous pillars inside, and its steep, sloping roof rising to a single peak, which is said to be a representation and a copy of the Persian king's tent, was another building constructed under the supervision of Pericles.* Hence Cratinus makes fun of him again in *The Thracian Women*, as follows:

> Here comes our squill-head Zeus,
> Wearing the Odeum on his head,
> Now that the ostracism is past.

Pericles was so ambitious for prestige that at the time of the building of the Odeum he passed a decree instituting a musical competition to be held as part of the Panathenaea* and arranged that he himself should be appointed to the Committee of Competition Supervisors, so that he could dictate how the competitors were to play the pipes or sing or play the lyre. The musical competitions were put on, both then and in later times, in the Odeum.

The Propylaea* on the Acropolis was completed within five years, with Mnesicles as the master builder. While it was being built something fantastic happened which showed that the goddess was not absent, but was co-operating in the work and helping to complete it: the most efficient and enthusiastic of the craftsmen slipped and fell from a great height, and was in such a bad way that the doctors gave up on him. Pericles was very depressed by the incident, but the goddess appeared to him in a dream and told him how to treat the man; by following her instructions, it did not take Pericles long, or cause him any difficulties, to cure the man. It was to commemorate this that he set up the bronze statue of Athena the Healer on the Acropolis near her altar; the altar, according to my sources, was there before.*

Phidias made the golden statue of the goddess, and his name can be found inscribed as its maker on the stele.* He was in charge of almost everything and, as I have already mentioned, was the general manager of all the craftsmen—a post he gained as a result of his friendship with Pericles. As well as making people jealous of Phidias, this proved to be another pretext for maligning Pericles, to the effect that Phidias arranged assignations at the building-sites† between Pericles and free-born women. The comic poets picked up the story and heaped a great deal of abuse on Pericles; they cast aspersions about him and the wife of Menippus, who was a friend of his and served as an officer in the army under him, and also about Pyrilampes and the birds he kept.* Since Pyrilampes was one of Pericles' friends, they accused him of offering his peacocks as bribes to the women with whom Pericles consorted. But why should it occasion surprise that people who make a living out of lechery periodically offer up slanderous abuse of their betters as a sacrifice to the malice of the common people, as if it were an evil deity, when even Stesimbrotus of Thasos went so far as to publish a shocking and disgusting suggestion about Pericles and his son's wife? It just goes to show how intractable the truth generally seems to be, and how difficult it is to hunt it down by research, when subsequent generations find the passage of time a hindrance to knowledge of the facts, and contemporary accounts of people's actions and lives twist and distort the truth out of either malicious hostility or crawling flattery.

[14] So the politicians who supported Thucydides were loudly denouncing Pericles for having squandered and wasted the tribute money. He therefore got up in the Assembly and asked the Athenian people whether they thought he had spent too much. When they said that he had spent far too much, he replied, 'In that case it should not be you who incur the cost, but me. I will have only my own name inscribed on the sacred buildings.' Perhaps they were impressed by his principled stand, or perhaps they did not want to let him have all the glory for the work, but at any rate their response to these words of his was to cry out that he was to draw money from the public funds and spend freely. Eventually, he took a chance and engaged Thucydides in a contest for ostracism—and succeeded not only in getting him banished, but also in overthrowing the opposing faction.*

[15] Now that there was an end to political feuding and the city had become absolutely seamless, so to speak, and unified, he brought into his domain Athens and all Athenian-related business; he took control of the revenues, military expeditions, the fleet, the islands, and the sea, and his considerable might and authority—defended as it was by subject races, friendships with kings, and alliances with dynasties—pervaded not only Greek lands, but also non-Greek territory. As a result he changed: he stopped being as subordinate to the people as he had been, or as ready to yield to and indulge the whims of the common people, which shift like the winds. In place of the florid and feeble mode of his previous relaxed and occasionally effeminate style

of popular leadership, he tuned his administration to aristocracy and kingship, and used it directly and unswervingly in the best interests of everyone. For the most part he led the people willingly, by persuading and instructing them, but sometimes, when they were especially recalcitrant, he reined them in and won them round, until they saw where their advantage lay and submitted to it; in other words he behaved exactly like a doctor who treats a complex and chronic illness by occasionally prescribing harmless pleasures, and at other times bitter but healing drugs. A wide variety of emotions had taken root, as was only to be expected in a rabble with such an enormous empire, and he alone had the ability to manage every single one of them in an appropriate fashion. His chief instruments were hope and fear: he used these as his rudders, so to speak, as he restrained the foolhardy elements among the people of Athens, and relieved and encouraged those who had lost heart. And so he demonstrated the truth of Plato's idea that rhetoric is a means of directing minds, and that the most important of its jobs is the scientific study of character and emotion, which are, so to speak, the pitches and strings of the mind, and require plucking and strumming in just the right way.* His success was based not merely on his ability as a speaker, but also, as Thucydides says, on the reputation his personal conduct had gained him: people trusted him, because he had proved himself to be totally incorruptible and beyond the reach of bribery.* And so he turned a great city into the greatest and richest city in the world, and acquired more power than a good many kings and tyrants, some of whom, in the case of their sons, actually bequeathed <more than they inherited, but>† he did not make his estate a single drachma richer than it had been when his father left it to him.*

[16] All the same, Thucydides has given a clear account of the extent of his power,* and the comic poets hint at it in their malicious fashion, when they describe his companions as 'new Pisistratidae'* and insist that he has to promise not to become a tyrant, on the grounds that there was a pre-eminence about him which was unsuited to and too oppressive for democracy. Teleclides says that the Athenians have passed into his hands

The revenue from cities, and the actual cities, to enslave or free as he chooses,
Their walls of stone, to build up or tear back down again,
Their treaties, forces, government, peace, wealth and prosperity.

And this was not the result of a temporary climax or the passing popularity of an administration that flourished for a brief season: Pericles' prominence lasted for forty years, among people like Ephialtes, Leocrates, Myronides, Cimon, Tolmides, and Thucydides.* After Thucydides' downfall and ostracism, he achieved through his annual appointment as one of the military commanders a supremacy and dominance that remained unbroken and uninterrupted for fifteen years.*

Throughout the period of his supremacy he kept himself invulnerable to bribery, although he was not averse to making money. In fact, because he was worried that the wealth that was legally his, by inheritance from his father, might disappear through neglect or cause him a lot of trouble and bother which he did not have the time for, he made what he considered to be the simplest and most precise arrangements for the management of his estates. He sold every single crop he produced in its entirety, and then bought from the market anything he needed to get on with living and making his way in the world. This made him unpopular with his sons when they came of age, and their wives found him a stingy provider; they complained about this daily and precisely budgeted expenditure, which meant that there was none of the kind of plenty normal in grand houses with enormous resources, and that all expenditure and income underwent a process of being counted and assessed. The person who maintained all this precise accounting for him was a house-slave called Euangelus, who was either outstandingly gifted or had been particularly well trained by Pericles in the sphere of estate management.

It may be that in this regard Pericles' behaviour clashed with the wise Anaxagoras,* who was so carried away by his high principles that he actually abandoned his estate and left the land uncultivated and fit only for sheep to graze, but it seems to me that the life of a philosopher, with his purely intellectual pursuits, is different from that of a politician. The noble use the one puts his mind to involves no tools and requires no external material, whereas the other applies his talents to human needs, and so for him wealth will sometimes prove to be not just a necessity, but something noble, as it was in Pericles' case, since he helped a great many poor people. And in fact there is a story that in his old age Anaxagoras lay all neglected and bundled up in his cloak, starving himself to death, while Pericles was busy. When news of what was going on reached Pericles, he ran in dismay straight to the man and pleaded with him in every way he could think of, since he was upset not for Anaxagoras' sake, but for his own, at the prospect of losing a political adviser of such calibre. So Anaxagoras unwrapped his head and told him, 'Pericles, even people who need a lamp pour oil in it.'

[17] When the Lacedaemonians started to show signs of irritation at Athens' increasing power, Pericles encouraged the Athenian people to entertain even more grandiose designs and to expect even greater things of themselves. He introduced a decree to the effect that all Greeks, wherever they lived in Europe or Asia, whether their settlement was large or small, should be invited to send representatives to a meeting to be held in Athens to discuss what to do about the Greek temples which had been burnt down by the Persians, and about the sacrificial rites they owed on behalf of Greece in fulfilment of pledges they had made to the gods during the fighting against Persia, and to try to decide how to make the sea safe for everyone to sail on in peace. For this purpose twenty men, picked from those who were over fifty years old, were dispatched; of these five took the invitation to the Ionian and Dorian Greeks in Asia, and to the inhabitants of the Aegean islands between Lesbos to the north and Rhodes to the south; five went to the Greek regions of the Hellespont and Thrace, as far as Byzantium; another five were sent to Boeotia, Phocis, and the Peloponnese, and then via the Locrians to the neighbouring mainland as far as Acarnania and Ambracia; and the remaining five made their way through Euboea to the Oetaeans, the Maliac Gulf, the Phthiotic Achaeans and Thessaly. Their mission was to convince people to come and play a part in the debates with a view to avoiding war and getting the Greeks to act in concert. It all came to nothing, however, and the gathering of the communities never took place, because the Lacedaemonians secretly opposed the plan—or so it is said—and the effort met with its first setback in the Peloponnese. Anyway, I have adduced this instance as evidence of Pericles' pride and lofty principles.*

[18] As a military commander, he was famous chiefly for his caution. He was never prepared to join battle when there was considerable uncertainty and risk, nor did he admire and model himself on those commanders who were acclaimed as great, but who enjoyed brilliant good fortune at the risk of their own lives. He was constantly telling his fellow citizens that if it were up to him they would remain

immortal for ever. Once, when he realized that Tolmides the son of Tolmaeus* was planning an invasion of Boeotia at quite the wrong time, on the strength of his earlier successes and the outstanding reputation his military exploits had won him, and had already convinced the best and most ambitious men of military age to serve as volunteers (and there were a thousand of them, let alone all the rest of the forces), he spoke in the Assembly in an attempt to restrain and dissuade him, and in the course of the speech came out with the memorable saying that if he would not take Pericles' advice, he could do no better than to wait for the wisest of all advisers, time. At the time this advice received only a moderate amount of attention, but a few days later, when news arrived of Tolmides' defeat in the battle of Coronea, and of the loss of a great many brave Athenians, including Tolmides himself, it brought him a great deal of fame and made people think well of him, as a man of intelligence and patriotism.*

[19] The most popular of his campaigns was the one on the Chersonese, since it turned out to be the salvation of the Greeks living there, in the first place because he brought 1,000 Athenian colonists and so revitalized the cities with a stock of good men, and in the second place because he barricaded the neck of the peninsula with fortifications and defences from sea to sea, which blocked off the raids of the Thracians who crowded about the Chersonese and put an end to the continual oppressive warfare with which the district was constantly burdened as a result of its proximity to non-Greek regions and because of the huge numbers of brigands who could be found both on and within its borders.*

However, what earned him admiration and fame abroad was his circumnavigation of the Peloponnese with a fleet of 100 ships which had put to sea at Pegae in Megarian territory.* He not only devastated a great deal of the coastal region, as Tolmides had done earlier, but also advanced quite a way inland with the hoplites from his fleet. His approach struck so much fear into the inhabitants that they took refuge inside their city walls, except in Nemea where the Sicyonians offered resistance and engaged him in battle—but he forced them into retreat and set up a trophy after the fight.* Then he recruited more troops from the Achaeans, who were friendly to him, put them on board his ships, and sailed with his fleet to the mainland on the opposite shore, where he overran Acarnania and pinned the inhabitants of Oeniadae inside the town. After laying waste and ravaging their land, he headed back home, having shown his enemies that he was a man to be feared, and his fellow citizens that he was a man of action—and yet could keep them safe, because the troops who took part in the expedition suffered no setbacks even as a result of chance.

[20] He once made a naval expedition into the Euxine Sea with a large and exceptionally well-equipped fleet,* where he saw to it that the Greek cities got what they wanted and treated them kindly, made the surrounding non-Greek tribes and their kings and chieftains aware of the extent of Athenian power, and proved their fearlessness and courage, in that they sailed wherever they wanted and made themselves masters of the whole sea, and left thirteen ships along with Lamachus and troops to help the people of Sinope against their tyrant Timesilaus. Once Timesilaus and his supporters had been overthrown, he got a decree passed to the effect that 600 Athenian volunteers would leave for Sinope and settle there alongside the Sinopians, taking over the houses and estates which had previously belonged to the tyrant and his men.

In general, however, he did not fall in with the impulses of his fellow citizens. Once, for instance, under the influence of their considerable military might and good fortune, they were spoiling to try once again to capture Egypt, and also to foment revolt in the coastal parts of the Persian empire, but he was not carried away by their enthusiasm.* Then again, quite a number of Athenians were already in the grip of that unfortunate and ill-fated lust for Sicily which was later fanned into a blaze by Alcibiades and his political colleagues;* there were even some for whom Tyrrhenia and Carthage were a dream —and a not unreasonable dream, given the extent of their existing dominion and the wave of success they were riding.

[21] But Pericles kept curbing this impetuosity and pruning their restlessness, and he tried to divert most of their resources to guarding and securing what they already had, since it was crucial, to his mind, to restrain the Lacedaemonians and since in general he tried to frustrate the Lacedaemonians, as he showed on a number of occasions, but above all by his actions in the Sacred War. The Lacedaemonians sent an army to Delphi and restored it from Phocian control to the Delphians, but no sooner had they left than Pericles sent an army there and reinstated the Phocians;* moreover, since the Lacedaemonians had inscribed their right of first consultation, which the Delphians had given them, on the forehead of the bronze wolf,

when he gained the same privilege for the Athenians he engraved it on the the same wolf,* on its right flank.

[22] The correctness of his policy of trying to keep Athenian resources confined within Greece was demonstrated by subsequent events. First the Euboeans revolted, and then, as soon as he had taken an army over to the island to meet the rebels, he received news that the Megarians had gone to war and that there was an army of Peloponnesians on the borders of Attica, under the leadership of Pleistonax the Spartan king.* So he withdrew his army from Euboea to deal with the war in Attica. He was not so rash as to respond to the challenge of such a large force of excellent hoplites and engage them in a hand-to-hand battle; instead once he noticed how young Pleistonax was, and how much he relied on one of his advisers, called Cleandridas (whom the ephors had sent along on this expedition, because of Pleistonax's youth, to act as his guardian and aide), he made a covert approach to Cleandridas. It did not take him long to corrupt him with bribes and prevail upon him to get the Peloponnesians to pull back from Attica. After the army had withdrawn and been disbanded, with all the various contingents returning to their home towns, the Lacedaemonians were so furious that they imposed a fine on the king—a fine which he could not pay in full, so that he left the country—and condemned Cleandridas to death, although he had already fled into exile. It was Cleandridas' son, Gylippus, who defeated the Athenians in Sicily.* Cleandridas' nature seems to have passed a fondness for money on to Gylippus as if it were an inherited disease, because he too was convicted of criminal behaviour and banished from Sparta in disgrace after succumbing to this weakness. But I have told this story in my *Life of Lysander*.*

[23] While defending his year of office as military commander, he recorded an expenditure of ten talents 'for necessities', and the people accepted this without taking it any further and without investigating what he was leaving unsaid.* Some writers, including the philosopher Theophrastus, have reported that every year ten talents found their way to Sparta from Pericles, and that he used this money to appease everyone in positions of authority and so to avert war; the object, they say, was not to buy peace, but time, in which he could make his preparations at his own pace and so wage war more efficiently.

He now wasted no time in turning his attention to the rebels. He took a fleet of fifty ships over to Euboea, with 5,000 heavy-armed men on board, and reduced the towns and cities on the island. He expelled from Chalcis the rich upper class known as the Horsebreeders, and, after evicting all the people of Hestiaea from their land, replaced them with Athenian colonists. He reserved this ruthless treatment for the Hestiaeans alone, because they had captured an Athenian ship and killed the crew.

[24] Later, during the thirty-year peace between the Athenians and Lacedaemonians, he got a decree passed to sanction his expedition to Samos,* on the pretext that although the islanders had been told to end their war with the Milesians, they had refused to do so. Since it is widely supposed that he undertook this action against the Samians to gratify Aspasia, this is an excellent occasion for considering the woman and trying to find out how she controlled the leading public figures of the day and got the philosophers to write about her in such glowing terms and at such length.* What powerful technique or abilities did she have? There is general agreement that she was a Milesian by birth and that her father was Axiochus. They also say that her campaigns against the most influential men of her day were a result of her admiration of an Ionian woman of ancient times called Thargelia, in the sense that Thargelia, who was a resourceful woman, as well as being beautiful and charming, cohabited with a great many Greek men and won all her partners over to the Persian cause, and so by means of these men, who were very powerful and important, she sowed the seeds of loyalty to the Persian cause in the Greek cities.

Now, some say that it was Aspasia's cleverness and political expertise that made Pericles think so highly of her; and in fact Socrates occasionally came to visit her with his disciples, and his closest friends brought their wives to her to listen to her speak, despite the fact that the business she ran was hardly decent or respectable, since she kept a house of young prostitutes.* Aeschines adds that Lysicles the sheep-dealer, a man of lowly and humble character, came to be the leader of Athens as a result of living with Aspasia after Pericles' death, and even though the beginning of Plato's *Menexenus* is not entirely serious, it still contains an element of historical fact when it states that it was Aspasia's rhetorical skill which was commonly supposed to be the reason why a number of Athenians spent time with her.*

Nevertheless, Pericles does seem to have been in love with Aspasia. His wife,* who was a relative of his, had previously been married to Hipponicus; her children were Callias 'the rich' by Hipponicus, and

Xanthippus and Paralus by Pericles. Later, since they were not finding living together agreeable, he gave her, with her consent, to someone else, while he himself took Aspasia, whom he loved very much.
In fact, it is said that every day, both as he left the house and as he
came back from the city square, he used to greet her with a kiss.

In the comedies she is called both the new Omphale and the new
Deianeira, and also Hera.* In the following lines Cratinus bluntly calls
her a concubine:

> And Buggery gave birth to that shameless concubine Aspasia,
> To be his Hera.

It also looks as though by her Pericles became the father of the
illegitimate son about whom, in Eupolis' play *The Demes*, he is made
to enquire:

> Is that bastard of mine alive?

To which Pyronides† replies:

> Yes, and would have been a man long ago,
> If he weren't shy about the stigma he inherited from the whore.

It is said that Aspasia became so famous and well known that even
Cyrus (the one who fought the Persian king for the sovereignty of
Persia*) changed the name of his favourite concubine from Milto to
Aspasia. Milto came originally from Phocaea, and her father was called
Hermotimus; after Cyrus' death in the battle, she was carried off to
the king, with whom she came to gain a great deal of influence. I
remembered this information about Milto while I was writing, and it
would have been unnatural, I would say, to reject it and ignore it.

[25] Pericles was accused of getting the decree passed authorizing
the war against Samos at Aspasia's request, to help the Milesians.
The Samians had the upper hand in the war between them and the
Milesians, which was being fought over Priene,* so when the Athenians ordered them to stop fighting and to submit the dispute to
arbitration in Athens, they refused. Pericles therefore took a fleet
to Samos, where he overthrew the oligarchic government, took fifty
of the leading men and the same number of boys hostages, and sent
them off to Lemnos. Now, it is said that each of the hostages offered
him a talent if he would spare him, and that those Samians who did
not want to see their city become a democracy offered him a great

deal of money as well. Moreover, Pissouthnes the Persian, who was sympathetic towards the Samian cause, sent him 10,000 gold staters, in an attempt to intercede for the city.* Nevertheless, Pericles refused to take any of this money; instead, he carried out his plans as regards the Samians, established a democratic system of government, and then sailed back to Athens. The Samians waited only for Pissouthnes to rescue the hostages for them, however, and then they revolted and generally prepared for war. So Pericles sailed out against them again —and they were no apathetic or cowering enemies, but had made up their minds to contest the mastery of the sea. A fierce sea battle took place near the island they call Tragiae,* in which Pericles won a brilliant victory, since his forty-four ships defeated a fleet of seventy, of which twenty were troop-carriers.

[26] Now that his victorious rout of the enemy fleet gave him control of the harbour, he began to besiege the Samians, who still somehow managed to summon up the courage to come out against him and fight in front of their city walls. When another, larger fleet arrived from Athens and the Samians were completely pinned inside, Pericles took sixty triremes and sailed into the outer sea. His objective, according to most writers, was to meet a Phoenician fleet which was coming to the help of the Samians and fight it out with them as far as possible from Samos, but Stesimbrotus proposes, implausibly, that the goal of the voyage was Cyprus.*

Anyway, whichever of these two was his reason, it looks as though he made a mistake, because once he had sailed away, Melissus the son of Ithagenes (a philosopher who at the time was the military commander of Samos) decided that the remaining ships were too few to be a threat and that the remaining commanders were too inexperienced, and he persuaded his fellow Samians to launch an attack on the Athenians. The Samians won the battle and, since they had taken a good many prisoners and destroyed large numbers of Athenian ships, they were able to make use of the sea to lay in essential military supplies that they had lacked before. Aristotle says that Pericles had also personally been defeated by Melissus in the earlier sea battle.*

The Samians used the Athenian prisoners to repay an insult: they tattooed owls on their foreheads in retaliation for the samaena the Athenians had tattooed on their prisoners. A samaena is a type of ship with a boar's-head prow; it is rather broad-beamed and paunch-like, so that it is good at crossing the open sea† at speed. Its name is derived from the fact that it first appeared in Samos, where the tyrant Polycrates had some built. Writers say that the following line of Aristophanes is an oblique reference to these tattoos:

The people of Samos have taken well to the imprint of letters.*

[27] Anyway, when Pericles heard that his forces had suffered a defeat he sailed to their assistance with all speed. He overcame Melissus' resistance, forced the enemy into retreat, and immediately set about walling them in, since he preferred to spend time and money conquering them and capturing the city rather than expose his fellow citizens to the risk of being wounded. After a while, however, it became difficult for him to restrain the Athenians, who were irritated by the delay and wanted to join battle, so he divided the whole army into eight sections and had them draw lots; whichever section picked the white bean he allowed to stand down and enjoy themselves, while the others continued with their effort. This is apparently why the expression 'white day' is used when people are enjoying a treat; the name is derived from the white bean.

Ephorus says that Pericles actually made use of siege engines, which were then impressive innovations, and that it was the engineer Artemon who supplied them. According to Ephorus, it was because Artemon had a bad leg and was carried around on a litter to see to those aspects of the construction which urgently required his attention that he was nicknamed 'the Conveyed'. However, Heraclides of Pontus disproves this suggestion by reference to Anacreon's poems where Artemon the Conveyed is mentioned many generations before these events of the Samian War. He describes Artemon as a man enfeebled by his luxurious lifestyle until he was so nervous about danger that he usually stayed in a sedentary position at home, with two slaves holding a bronze shield over his head to stop anything falling on him from above; if he was forced to go out anywhere, he says, he had himself carried around in a litter hanging close to the ground, which was the origin of his nickname, 'the Conveyed'.

[28] The Samians surrendered after eight months. Pericles demolished their defensive walls, impounded their fleet, and imposed a heavy fine on them; some of the fine they paid straight away, while the rest they undertook to pay at a stated time and gave hostages for in the meantime.* Duris of Samos exaggerates in tragic style when he accuses the Athenians and Pericles of behaving with considerable

savagery—a savagery which has gone unrecorded by Thucydides, Ephorus, and Aristotle. In fact, he seems to have gone so far as to lie when he says that Pericles actually had the Samian trierarchs and marines taken into the main square of Miletus and tied on to planks of wood, and that after they had been tortured there for ten days he gave orders that they were to be beaten to death by being clubbed on the head, and that their corpses were then to be cast out without any of the proper observances. But Duris tends to be incapable of keeping his account truthful even when no personal feeling is involved, and here he seems to have exaggerated his country's suffering to discredit the Athenians.*

On his return to Athens after the conquest of Samos, Pericles gave those who had died in the fighting a distinguished burial, and delivered the customary speech over their tombs.* The speech was widely admired, but as he was descending from the rostrum and accepting the greetings of all the other women, who were crowning him with garlands and chaplets as if he were a victorious athlete, Elpinice came up close to him and said, 'What a wonderful job you've done, Pericles! How well you deserve these garlands! After all, you have caused the deaths of large numbers of brave Athenians, and done so in a war fought not against the Phoenicians or the Persians, which was the kind of war my brother Cimon waged, but in subduing an allied city, a city of fellow Greeks.' Pericles, the story goes, quietly smiled at these words of Elpinice's and quoted Archilochus to her:

'An old woman like you should not anoint herself with perfume.'*

According to Ion, he was inordinately proud of his conquest of Samos, and used to boast that whereas Agamemnon had taken ten years to capture a foreign city, it had taken him nine months to defeat the most prominent and powerful people in Ionia.* In fact this evaluation of his achievement was not unjustified: the war really did hang in the balance and involve a high degree of risk. At any rate, Thucydides says that Samos came very close to depriving the Athenians of their control of the sea.*

[29] Some time later, when the Peloponnesian War was already beginning to heave and swell, Pericles persuaded the Athenian people to support the Corcyrans, who were under attack by the Corinthians, and so to bring over to their side an island furnished with a strong naval force, at a time when the Peloponnesians were all but at war

with them.* But when the people voted in favour of sending help, he sent Lacedaemonius the son of Cimon with only ten ships, as if he meant to humiliate him, because Cimon's house was on very good terms with the Lacedaemonians. So the reason he gave Lacedaemonius so few ships and sent him off against his will was to ensure that, if nothing important or outstanding was achieved under his leadership, he and his Laconian sympathies would be even more strongly denigrated. Besides, he generally tended to disparage Cimon's sons, arguing that even their names—Lacedaemonius, Thessalus, and Eleius—showed that they were not genuine Athenians, but aliens and foreigners;* moreover, it was commonly held that their mother was an Arcadian woman. In any case, Pericles was censured for these ten triremes; it was said that while providing those who needed it with little help he had furnished his critics with plenty of grounds for complaint. So he subsequently sent more ships to Corcyra, but they arrived too late for the battle.*

The Corinthians took offence at this Athenian expedition and denounced the Athenians in Lacedaemon, with the Megarians adding the charge that they were banned and excluded from all commerce with Athens and from every harbour which the Athenians controlled, and that this contravened their common rights and the pledges the Greeks had made to one another. Moreover, the Aeginetans considered that they were being wronged and harshly treated by the Athenians, and they used to complain in private to the Lacedaemonians, while lacking the courage to criticize the Athenians in public. Meanwhile the revolt and subsequent siege of Potidaea, a city that was subject to Athens despite being a Corinthian colony, hastened the advance of the war even more rapidly.*

Despite all this, delegations were constantly being sent to Athens and Archidamus, the Lacedaemonian king, was trying to resolve most of his allies' grievances and to calm them down. In these circumstances it seems unlikely that any of the other issues would have brought war down on the Athenians, if they had been persuaded to repeal the Megarian decree and settle their differences with them. So, because Pericles was the most ardent opponent of reconciliation, and urged the Athenian people not to relinquish their rivalry with Megara, he alone was responsible for the war.

[30] They say that once, when a delegation arrived in Athens from Lacedaemon to address these issues and Pericles had put forward as

an excuse a certain law forbidding the removal of the tablet on which the decree happened to have been written, a delegation member, a man called Polyalces, said, 'All right, then, don't remove the tablet—but turn it to face the wall. There's no law forbidding that.' Although this struck people as a clever suggestion, Pericles refused to give in at all.

It looks as though he had some kind of personal antipathy against the Megarians, but the charge he openly made against them in public was that they were appropriating the sacred meadow,* and he introduced a decree to the effect that a herald was to be sent on a mission to them and also to the Lacedaemonians, to denounce the Megarians. Now, this decree of Pericles' presented a reasonable and courteous claim to justice, but Anthemocritus, the herald who had been given this mission, was killed, and it was generally believed that the Megarians were responsible for his death.* After that, Charinus introduced another decree against them, that there should be a state of hostility towards Megara with no attempt at reconciliation by truce or heralds, that any Megarian who set foot on Attic soil was to be punished with death, that when the Athenian military commanders swore their traditional oath they were to add a pledge to invade Megarian territory twice a year, and that Anthemocritus should be buried next to the Thriasian Gate, which is now called the Double Gate.* The Megarians, however, deny that it was they who murdered Anthemocritus and try to lay responsibility for the decree at the door of Aspasia and Pericles. They refer to the following familiar and commonly cited lines from *The Acharnians*:

> Some young men, rather the worse for drink and party games,
> Went off to Megara and abducted a whore called Simaetha;
> Then the Megarians, fuming with hot air and garlic,
> Retaliated by abducting two of Aspasia's whores.*

[31] The original reasons for the decree are obscure, but everyone concurs in holding Pericles responsible for the fact that it was not repealed. The only variation is that some attribute his inflexibility to noble principles supported by reflection on the city's best interests, and say that he regarded the demand for the decree's cancellation as a test of the city's submissiveness and agreement to the demand as an admission of weakness, whereas others claim that his defiance of the Lacedaemonians stemmed from a kind of stubbornness and a combative concern to display Athens' strength.*

However, the worst of all the charges against him, and yet the one with the largest number of writers vouching for it, goes somewhat as follows.* Phidias the sculptor was, as I have said, commissioned to make the famous statue. As a friend of Pericles and someone with a great deal of influence over him, he acquired one group of enemies on his own account, simply because they were jealous of him; then there were others who used him to try to find out what kind of verdict the Athenian people would come to if they had to judge Pericles. This group persuaded Meno, one of Phidias' colleagues, to sit as a suppliant in the city square and request immunity from prosecution for informing and bringing a charge against Phidias. The Athenian people were receptive to his request and Phidias' trial took place before the Assembly. Theft was not proven, because right from the start Phidias had followed Pericles' advice and had made the gold as an extra layer fixed to the statue in such a way that it could all be taken off and weighed—which is exactly what Pericles insisted on Phidias' prosecutors doing on the occasion in question.* But the esteem in which his works of art were held brought an oppressive burden of envy down on Phidias, and people were particularly spiteful about the fact that in depicting the battle against the Amazons on the statue's shield he had engraved a figure somewhat resembling himself, as an old, bald-headed man holding a rock in the air with both hands, and had also included an excellent likeness of Pericles fighting an Amazon. The position of the hand, which is lifting a spear up in front of the figure's eyes,† has been skilfully designed as if it were meant to conceal the similarity, but it can still be glimpsed on either side of the spear. So Phidias was taken off to prison where he died of an illness, although according to some writers Pericles' enemies arranged for him to die of poisoning, in order to discredit Pericles.* In accordance with a proposal of Glaucon's, the Athenian people granted the informer, Meno, exemption from all obligations and made it one of the military commanders' jobs to ensure his safety.*

[32] At more or less the same time as this Aspasia was put on trial for impiety (Hermippus the comic poet was her prosecutor, and he also brought up the additional charge that she had arranged assignations in her house between Pericles and free-born women*), and Diopithes introduced a decree that anyone who did not pay due respect to supernatural phenomena or who offered to teach people about celestial phenomena should be impeached, which was supposed to cast

suspicion on Pericles by way of Anaxagoras.* The Athenian people
enthusiastically welcomed these slanders, and under these circumstances a decree proposed by Dracontides was passed, whereby
Pericles' financial accounts were to be deposited with the Executive
Committee, and the decision procedure for the case was to involve
the jurors picking up their voting pebbles from the altar on the
Acropolis.* However, Hagnon got this clause of the decree revoked,
and proposed instead that the case should be judged before 1,500 jurors,
whether one chose to describe it as a prosecution for theft and bribery,
or for malversation.

Pericles managed to secure Aspasia's acquittal as a result, according to Aeschines, of shedding copious tears for her during the trial
and of pleading with the jurors, and he was so worried about Anaxagoras that he sent him away from the city.† But in Phidias' case,
since he had clashed with the Athenian people, he fanned into flame
the imminent, smouldering war, hoping thereby to dissipate the charges
threatening him and to allay people's envy; for thanks to his gravity
and power it was to him alone that in times of crisis and danger the
city entrusted itself. So these are the reasons given to explain why he
did not allow the people to yield to the Lacedaemonians; the truth,
however, is uncertain.

[33] It occurred to the Lacedaemonians that if Pericles were
overthrown they would find the Athenians more compliant in all
respects, so they pushed the Athenians to rid themselves of the Cylonian
curse, liability to which had come down to Pericles from his mother's
side, as Thucydides tells us. However, the attempt backfired on its
initiators, because so far from falling under suspicion and being
discredited Pericles became even more trusted and respected by his
fellow citizens when they saw how bitterly their enemies hated and
feared him.* This is also the context in which to see Pericles' promise,
issued before Archidamus' invasion of Attica with the Peloponnesian army, that in the event of Archidamus devastating the whole
countryside but leaving his property alone, either because of the
guest-friendship between them or in order to give his enemies an
opportunity for slandering him, he would give both the land and
the buildings on his estates to the city.*

And so a huge army of Lacedaemonians and their allies, with King
Archidamus at their head, invaded Attica.* Laying waste to the land,
they advanced as far as Acharnae, where they established a camp, on

the assumption that the Athenians would not let them get away with it, but would be prompted by anger and pride to fight them. But the idea that they should join battle in defence of their city with 60,000 Peloponnesian and Boeotian hoplites (for that was the size of this first invading army) struck Pericles as outrageous. He proceeded to pacify those who were spoiling for a fight and were upset by what was happening, arguing that trees soon grow again even when they have been hacked and chopped, but that it is not easy to recover men once they have been killed. He refused to convene the Assembly,* since he was afraid of being forced to act against his better judgement; instead, as the helmsman of a ship caught in the open sea by a strong wind stows everything safely away and draws the sheets tight, and then relies on his skill rather than paying any attention to the tears and entreaties of the sea-sick and terrified passengers, so he battened down the city and thoroughly secured it with guards, and then relied on his own judgement, showing scant consideration for the outcries and complaints of the discontented. And yet he was under pressure from a great many quarters—from friends with their entreaties, from enemies with their threats and accusations—and the comic choruses were singing songs of mockery and humiliation, pouring scorn on his leadership for its cowardly surrender of the city's affairs to the enemy. Furthermore, Cleon was by now harassing him, and using the Athenians' anger at him as a stepping-stone towards popular leadership, as these anapaests composed by Hermippus show:*

> Why, king of the satyrs, why are you reluctant
> To take up a spear? No, all you give us
> Are brave words about the war,
> But you have the soul of Teles.
> Someone only has to sharpen a hand-held cleaver
> On a hard whetstone, and you gnash your teeth,
> Now that you've been bitten by the flashing fire of Cleon.

[34] Pericles, however, remained unmoved by any of this; he quietly submitted to the disrespect and hostility in a self-possessed manner. He sent a fleet of 100 ships to the Peloponnese, but did not accompany it himself; he remained at home administering the state, until the Peloponnesians left Attica. Then, in order to appease the common people, who were still† upset by the war, he won them over with distributions of money and introduced decrees authorizing

grants of land for settlers abroad: he evicted the entire population of Aegina, and held a lottery to decide which Athenians would receive grants of land on the island. The people could also find some consolation in their enemies' adversities; the expedition around the Peloponnese had devastated a great deal of land and razed a number of villages and small towns, and Pericles himself took a land force into Megarian territory and ravaged all of it.*

In other words, it was clear that although the Peloponnesians could inflict a great deal of damage on the Athenians by land, they would also suffer a great deal themselves from the sea; under these circumstances there can be no doubt that they would not have prolonged the war to the extent they did, but would soon have given up, as Pericles had foretold from the outset, if something supernatural had not intervened to thwart human calculations. As it was, the plague struck for the first time and ravaged the best of the Athenians' youth and resources. The people of Athens were afflicted by the plague not only physically, but also mentally; they became completely wild in their behaviour towards Pericles, and did their best to injure him, just as insane people try to hurt their doctor or their father. They behaved this way because they had been persuaded by his political enemies that the plague was caused by packing crowds of refugees from the countryside† into the city, where, at the height of summer, large numbers of people were being forced to stay all jumbled up together in huts and stifling tents, and to live an idle, indoor life instead of the healthy, outdoor life they were used to. The man responsible for all this, his enemies said, was Pericles: because of the war he had squeezed the rustic rabble inside the city walls and then made no use whatsoever of all these men, but left them, penned up like cattle, to infect one another with death, without providing them with any diversion or relief.*

[35] Since he wanted to make things better and at the same time to inflict some extra damage on the enemy, he fitted out 150 ships, put on board a sizeable and formidable force of infantry and cavalry, and made everything ready for an expedition which was to fill the Athenians with high hopes and their enemies with abject fear. But just when the ships were all manned and ready, and Pericles had even boarded his own trireme, an eclipse of the sun occurred, so that darkness replaced daylight. Everyone was terrified and took this to be a significant portent. Pericles saw that his helmsman was panic-stricken

and did not know what to do, so he held his cloak up until the man's eyes were covered and then asked him whether he thought what he was doing at all frightening or significant of anything frightening. 'No,' replied the man. 'Well,' said Pericles, 'what is the difference between the two cases? Only that in the case of the eclipse the darkness was caused by something larger than my cloak.' Anyway, that is the story one hears in the philosophical schools.*

So the expedition got under way, but it is generally held that Pericles failed to achieve anything to match the potential of the men and matériel at his disposal. Moreover, his siege of sacred Epidaurus, which served to arouse hopes of its capture, was foiled by the plague, which attacked and killed not only the Athenians, but also anyone who had any dealings at all with the army.* As a result of this failure the Athenians were exasperated with him, so he tried to console them and restore their morale. But he did not succeed in getting them to shed their anger or change their minds before they had taken their ballots in their hands to wield against him and made themselves his masters; they stripped him of his military command and imposed a fine on him, which different writers claim to have been between fifteen and fifty talents. The person recorded as prosecutor for the case was Cleon according to Idomeneus, Simmias according to Theophrastus, and Lacratides according to Heraclides of Pontus.*

[36] His public troubles were about to end, then, now that the common people had abandoned their fury, sting-like, as soon as they had struck at him. His domestic affairs were in a wretched state, however, since he had lost quite a few of his closest friends during the plague, and since his family had been troubled for some time by a feud. Xanthippus, the oldest of his legitimate sons, who was a spendthrift and had married a young, extravagant wife (the daughter of Tisander and granddaughter of Epilycus), resented his father's precision with money and the fact that he gave him a meagre allowance, a little at a time.* So he got in touch with one of his father's friends and borrowed money from him, pretending that the request actually came from Pericles. Later, when the friend asked for the repayment of the loan, Pericles not only refused, but also brought a suit against him as well. This made young Xanthippus cross, and he began to make rude remarks about his father. In the first place, he went around telling people, in a way designed to raise a laugh, what Pericles got up to at home and the conversations he used to have with the sophists.

For instance, when a competitor in the pentathlon accidentally hit Epitimius of Pharsalus with a javelin and killed him, Pericles spent a whole day discussing with Protagoras whether the javelin or the person who threw it or the organizers of the games should, speaking absolutely strictly, be held responsible for what had happened. Apart from this, there was also the slanderous story about his wife, which according to Stesimbrotus was spread around by Xanthippus himself.* Basically, the young man remained irreconcilably at odds with his father until his death—for Xanthippus died of the plague during the epidemic.

Pericles also lost his sister to the same disease, and the vast majority of his relatives and friends as well, including those who had been particularly helpful to him during his administration. However, he did not let these disasters make him give up or become a traitor to his lofty principles and noble detachment; in fact, no one saw him weeping, either when he was preparing any of his relatives for burial or at the tomb, at any rate until he also lost his remaining legitimate son, Paralus. Despite being crushed by this blow, he continued to try to hold true to his character and to maintain his detachment, but as he was laying a garland on the corpse he was overcome by emotion at the sight of his dead son, and he burst out into copious tears, although he had never done anything like that throughout the whole of his life.

[37] The city experimented with the other military commanders and politicians to see how well they conducted the war, but could find no one with enough countervailing weight or reliable gravity to take on such an important leadership. They began to miss him, and to invite him to take up a role as political or military leader. He was lying in a state of depression and grief at home, but was persuaded by Alcibiades and his other friends to return to public life. Once the people had apologized for their harsh treatment of him, and he had taken up the reins of government again and been appointed one of the military commanders, he asked for the law about illegitimate children to be repealed, despite the fact that he himself had been its original proposer. His reason for making this request was to stop his name and lineage from completely dying out for lack of an heir.

The circumstances of this law were as follows. Many years previously, when Pericles was at the height of his political power (and had, as I have said, legitimate children), he introduced a law that only people both of whose parents were Athenians should be Athenians themselves.* Now, when the 40,000 medimni of wheat presented by the king of Egypt to the people of Athens had to be divided up among the citizens, there was a rich crop of lawsuits under the terms of this law against illegitimate children who had until then been overlooked and ignored, and a large number of them also fell foul of informers. Just under 5,000 of them were convicted and sold into slavery,† while the number of those who passed the scrutiny, and so retained their citizenship and were judged to be genuine Athenians, was 14,040.*

Although it was a serious business that the law which had been enforced against so many people should now be repealed by the very person who had introduced it, the misfortune which was currently afflicting Pericles with regard to his household—and which looked like punishment for his famous disdain and haughtiness—moved the Athenians to pity. They thought that he had suffered just retribution and was asking a favour it was natural for a man to ask, so they let him enrol his illegitimate son among the members of his phratry,* and give him his own name. This was the man whom the Athenian people later put to death along with his fellow commanders after he had defeated the Peloponnesians in the sea battle of Arginusae.*

[38] It was at this time, apparently, that Pericles caught the plague. He did not suffer the usual acute or intense attack, but one which gradually wore out his body and undermined his proud spirit by means of a lingering and protracted illness that came and went.* At any rate, when in his *Ethics* Theophrastus raises the question whether people's characters are affected by their circumstances and whether physical illness can make them alter and degenerate from a virtuous state, he records that during his illness Pericles showed a visiting friend an amulet which had been hung around his neck by the womenfolk, as if to demonstrate what a terrible state he must be in to submit to this nonsense.

When he was close to death, the noblest Athenians and his surviving friends were sitting around his bed, and they fell to discussing the extent of his virtue and his abilities, which involved recounting his achievements and enumerating his trophies—he had set up nine trophies for Athens as a victorious military commander.* In carrying on this conversation with one another, they thought he had lost consciousness and could not understand them, but in fact he listened to everything, and then he spoke aloud and said that he was surprised at them. Why did they recall with admiration these things about him, when they were gifts of fortune available to everyone and had happened in the past to a great many military commanders? Why did they fail to mention the best and most important thing? 'And that', he said, 'is that no Athenian has put on mourning clothes because of me.'*

[39] He was remarkable, then, not only for his courtesy and self-possession, which he maintained throughout all the troubles and hostility that beset him, but also for his pride, in that he considered it a particularly noble aspect of his character that he had never used his enormous power to indulge either envy or passion, and had never treated any enemy as irreconcilable. And in my opinion there is one thing which makes that childish and pretentious nickname of his inoffensive and even appropriate: that the name 'Olympian' was applied to such a gracious character and to a man who during his lifetime exercised power in such a blameless and unblemished fashion. After all, we do hold that the gods have sovereignty and authority over things because they are so constituted as to be responsible for good and not for bad, contrary to the poets who confuse us with their stupid ideas and are convicted by their own fictions: in their attempt to imagine the most suitable surroundings for that which is blessed and immortal they call the putative abode of the gods a safe and stable seat, which experiences neither winds nor clouds, but is illuminated for ever and ever by a clear and gentle sky, shining with the clearest possible light,* and yet represent the gods themselves as riddled with confusion, malice, anger, and other emotions which are inappropriate even for men of intelligence. But this topic may well be thought to belong to another treatise.

Events soon gave the Athenians a clear sense of what they were missing in Pericles. Those who had resented his power while he was alive and felt that it had condemned them to obscurity tested out other politicians and popular leaders as soon as he was out of the way, and came to the conclusion that for all his aloofness there never had been a more moderate character, and that for all his self-possession there never had been anyone with a more impressive nature. So greatly was the state afflicted then with a rich crop and hoard of evil, which he had kept buried and whose dominance he had obstructed by keeping it weak and insignificant, that the offensive power he had wielded, which had previously been dubbed autocracy and tyranny, was seen to have been a source of safety and protection.

NICIAS

INTRODUCTION

How does one write about failure? What value can there be in a biography of a statesman whose career ends in a crushing defeat? And how can a writer retell effectively a story already told brilliantly, incomparably, by a classic historian six centuries before? The Life of Nicias, the Athenian general who was pushed into leading the great Athenian expedition against Syracuse and saw it end in total disaster, presented these challenges: the result is an unusual and valuable Life, original and more negative than we have seen so far.

Nicias and its pair *Crassus* unfold parallel trajectories: wealth, success, disaster. The Roman Crassus was extraordinarily wealthy, an ambitious politician, and twice consul. A close associate and rival of Pompey and Caesar, with whom he formed a political alliance, the so-called first triumvirate, in 60 BC, he attempted to emulate the military success of these men. In 54 BC he led an expedition against the Parthians beyond Rome's eastern frontier. In the following year his troops were hemmed in near Carrhae and routed; soon after he was killed and his head sent to the Parthian king. Nicias' exploitation of the Athenian silver mines brought him great wealth, and he had a series of military successes before he was chosen, against his will, one of the commanders of the Sicilian Expedition. The pair of Lives, then, is a study in how previous successes do not guarantee future victories.

However, the Lives focus not on fortune but on character: despite the similarities in their life pattern, Plutarch sees the two men as very different. Crassus was greedy, a powerful orator, irreligious, ambitious, reckless—in every way asserting his presence and his desire for power and recognition. Nicias was just the opposite: generous, a poor orator, extremely attentive to the gods, respectful and yielding to others, cautious.

The overriding characteristic which Plutarch recognizes in Nicias is timidity: a timidity towards the Athenians, towards the gods, towards his good luck. The theme emerges in the early chapters. Although one of 'the three best citizens of Athens' and an opponent of the demagogue Cleon, he was 'naturally faint-hearted and unconfident': on campaign he was fearful but lucky; when at home 'his jitteriness and susceptibilty to confusion' pleased the people, because he seemed afraid of them (2). His generosity in public display was motivated by his superstitious attitude towards all things divine (4). In his narrative, Plutarch constantly reinforces this aspect of Nicias' character with his own commentary and the materials he uses to supplement Thucydides. Thus he includes the Delian religious mission and the mockery of the comic poets (3–4) and reinforces our understanding of Nicias' fears by listing what other Athenian leaders had suffered at the hands of the populace: fines, exile, even being driven to suicide (6). He denounces Nicias' culpable resignation of his position as commander (8) and his 'excessive caution and hesitation' once he had been made a leader of the Sicilian expedition (14). Although Nicias was generous with his money and often showed courage and resourcefulness (3, 16–18), Plutarch continues to highlight his timidity, which culminates in his overreaction to the eclipse and his acceptance of a full month's delay before the army moved (23). In the *Comparison* with Crassus, Plutarch again crticizes the folly of yielding command to Cleon (*Comp.* 3), and even makes his surrender to Gylippus an act of cowardice, although Thucydides (7. 85) had made it an effort to prevent the slaughter of his men. Thucydides had portrayed Nicias as a far-sighted but uncertain leader, able to see the dangers of the expedition, but unable to persuade the Athenians, or once on the expedition, to overcome difficulties he had foreseen. In the end, he was 'of the Greeks in my day least deserving of the fate he came to, because of his complete exercise of what is considered excellence' (7. 86. 5). Plutarch, intent also on the contrast with the rash, assertive Crassus, pushes the matter much farther: Nicias is an example of the man who wants to play a public role, but will not assert himself against those who oppose him. His superstition is just one aspect of his general diffidence, which destroyed the man himself and the army he was leading.

Thucydides, a contemporary of the events, devoted two books to the expedition (6–7), surpassing, as Plutarch states, 'even his own high standards of effectiveness, vividness, and variety' (*Nic.* 1). Not only was Thucydides an outstanding historian, in Plutarch's day he was a model of Attic style, taught in every school, and his vocabulary and vividness were imitated in exercises and speeches. Plutarch explains in his first chapter that he chooses a role different from the historian Timaeus: he will not try to improve upon Thucydides—a course which led Timaeus to make himself ridiculous—but will present briefly the essentials of the story, because they reveal Nicias' character. In fact, most of the Life is based upon Thucydides' narrative. Unlike other Lives, Plutarch had no information on the family and early training of Nicias, and there are rather few anecdotes. The greater part of the Life (cc. 12–30) is devoted to the Sicilian expedition,[1] and the account sticks close to that of Thucydides. Earlier passages, especially the stories of Cleon at Sphacteria and of Alcibiades tricking the Spartan ambassadors (7–8, 10), also derive from him. To allow easy comparison of the two narratives, I have regularly indicated in the notes the parallel passages in the historian.

---

[1] In the same way, the Parthian campaign occupies a large part of *Crassus* (16–33).

A number of other sources are cited in the Life. The most important is Philistus, a Syracusan historian who was about 15 years old when the Athenians attacked his city. Plutarch refers to him in the first chapter, and cites him at 19 and 28, in both cases seeming to prefer Philistus and Thucydides against Timaeus, a third-century historian of Sicily. These two Sicilian authors must furnish many of the stories and incidents with which Plutarch supplements Thucydides.

At the end of his preface Plutarch notes three other sources: 'facts which may have been mentioned here and there by other writers or which can be found recorded on ancient votive offerings or in decrees, but which are unnoticed by most people.' Here he calls attention to the variety of historical materials which he uses in this Life. Note especially his full account of the mission to the sanctuary of Apollo on Delos (3), perhaps derived from the inscribed stone set up by Nicias, and the quotations from comedy in cc. 4, 8, and 11. Pasiphon, author of Socratic dialogues, is an extremely obscure writer, cited because he speaks of Nicias (4). The stories of Euripides' popularity in Sicily (29) come from the literary tradition, and are similar to those in Satyrus' *Life of Euripides*. Plutarch may have seen personally some of the objects he mentions, such as the small statue of Athena on the Acropolis (the Palladium), the choregic tripods of Nicias, the fallen colossal statue of Apollo erected by the Naxians (3), and the Herm of Andocides (13). From others he learned of the 'shield of Nicias' on display in Syracuse (28). Plutarch, a priest at Delphi himself, and author of treatises on oracles, superstition, and other religious concerns, offers special information on divination: the role of Nicias' adviser Hiero (4), the omens before the expedition (13), Nicias' diviner Stilbides (23), and the standard interpretation of eclipses (23), as well as a discussion of the state of knowledge regarding eclipses in Nicias' day (23). This last notice is important, because it makes clear that Nicias did not have the kind of philosophical training that gave Pericles his self-possession and freedom from superstition (*Per.* 4–9, 35). Although a Greek, Nicias did not possess a Greek philosophical education.[2]

The historical value of *Nicias* depends in large part on its extensive use of Thucydides, a contemporary and extremely perceptive observer of people and political power. The material Plutarch adds provides an invaluable supplement. Chapter 3, for instance is excellent evidence both of Athenian religious practice and its political importance. He often avoids alluding to Thucydides' insights at important moments, preferring to introduce the same points on other occasions, and encourage us to see them in a fresh

---

[2] Nor, apparently, did Crassus: his training was in rhetoric, which he saw only as necessary for dealing with his fellow citizens. Later in life he kept near him the Academic philosopher Alexander, but treated him badly (*Crass.* 6).

light. In this Life, his presentation of Nicias' character requires that his relations with the Athenian people be simplified. Most of the account of his fears appears in the early chapters. Unlike Thucydides, he sees Nicias' choice of campaigns as motivated by fear (6) and by changing Thucydides' indirect citation of the people's challenge to Cleon to a direct quote, he makes it indicate more directly that Nicias is following their lead (7). Thucydides suggests that Nicias misreads his enemies or the people; Plutarch focuses on his weakness toward them. With this groundwork, the account of the Sicilian expedition turns more towards Nicias' vacillation and the fear induced by the eclipse, and makes less than Thucydides did of Nicias' continuing fear of the Athenians' wrath. The parallel episodes in *Alcibiades* take on greater complexity, because Alcibiades' relation with the populace is more complex. Although worried by Alcibiades' erratic behaviour, they are also charmed by it. They are pleased rather by Nicias' timidity towards them (2), and their reaction is either praise or censure. Politicians who live by opinion polls are not foreign to our own time: they rarely emerge as great leaders.

Plutarch, although he uses Thucydides as his fundamental source and expects his audience to be familiar with his account, presents a view of Nicias quite different from the earlier historian: this is indeed a good and sober man caught up in an expedition of which he foresaw the dangers, but also a man who, by his constant fear of what the gods or the Athenians might do to him, was hampered from either gaining victory or saving his army from disaster.

Green, P., *Armada from Athens* (Garden City, NY: Doubleday, 1970). An account of the Sicilian Expedition.

Kagan, D., *The Peace of Nicias and the Sicilian Expedition* (Ithaca, NY: Cornell University Press, 1981). A detailed historical narrative.

Nikolaidis, A. G., 'Is Plutarch Fair to Nicias?', *Illinois Classical Studies*, 13 (1988), 319–33.

O'Brien, D., 'Derived Light and Eclipses in the Fifth Century', *Journal of Hellenic Studies*, 88 (1968), 114–27. Fifth-century knowledge of eclipses.

Pearson, L., *The Greek Historians of the West: Timaeus and his Predecessors* (Atlanta: Scholars Press, 1987). Treats Philistus and Timaeus.

Pelling, C. B. R., 'Plutarch and Thucydides', in P. A. Stadter (ed.), *Plutarch and the Historical Tradition* (London: Routledge 1992), 10–40.

Powell, C. A., 'Religion and the Sicilian Expedition', *Historia*, 28 (1979), 15–31.

Titchener, F., 'Why did Plutarch write about Nicias?', *Ancient History Bulletin*, 5 (1991), 153–8.

Westlake, H. D., *Individuals in Thucydides* (Cambridge: Cambridge University Press, 1968). Chapters on Nicias and Alcibiades.

NICIAS

[1] Since I find much to recommend a comparison between Nicias and Crassus, and between the Sicilian and Parthian expeditions, I should immediately tender on my behalf an earnest entreaty to the readers of this treatise, to allay any suspicions they might have that my attitude towards the inimitable narrative published by Thucydides, whose account of the Sicilian expedition surpassed even his own high standards of effectiveness, vividness, and variety, is the same as that of Timaeus, who hoped not only to write with more skill than Thucydides, but also to show how utterly ordinary and amateurish Philistus' account was.* As a result, he forces his history along through the middle of conflicts, sea battles, and speeches, which had been successfully dealt with by these writers, and thereby shows himself to be not even, in Pindar's words, 'a foot-soldier marching beside a Lydian chariot', but altogether one who came late to intellectual pursuits and was still a callow novice—in other words, he revealed himself to be, in the words of Diphilus, 'a coarse man, stuffed with Sicilian lard'. Moreover, he constantly descends to the level of Xenarchus,* as, for instance, when he says that in his opinion it did not augur well for the Athenians that, of their military commanders, it was the one whose name is cognate with victory who initially refused to take command of the expedition, and when he says that the mutilation of the herms was the gods' way of warning the Athenians that their worst military setbacks would be due to Hermocrates the son of Hermon; or again, when he says that it was perfectly reasonable for Heracles to aid the Syracusans, because it was Core who handed Cerberus over to him, and be angry with the Athenians, because they were trying to protect the Segestans, whose ancestors had been Trojans, whose city he had sacked because of the wrong done him by Laomedon.*

Presumably it was the same diligence that led Timaeus to come up with the idea of writing as he did, and also led him to correct Philistus' language and find fault with Plato and Aristotle. In my view, however, jealous rivalry with other authors over diction is petty pedantry—not to say downright stupidity if the rival is a work of inimitable quality. At any rate, while I could not simply omit the events described by Thucydides and Philistus, especially since they determine my subject's personality and disposition, which were revealed† by the number and enormity of the disasters that befell him, I have touched briefly on the essentials—enough to avoid gaining a reputation for carelessness and indolence—while trying to collect the facts which may have been mentioned here and there by other writers or which can be found recorded on ancient votive offerings or in decrees, but which are unnoticed by most people.* My purpose, however, was not to gather meaningless historical data, but to record data which promote the understanding of character and personality.

[2] So the first thing I may allow myself to say about Nicias has already been said by Aristotle: that the three best citizens of Athens, men who demonstrated the goodwill and affection of a father towards the general populace, were Nicias the son of Niceratus, Thucydides the son of Melesias, and Theramenes the son of Hagnon.* This assessment applies less to Theramenes, however, than to the other two; since he was a native of Ceos rather than Athens he has been criticized for inferior lineage, and his fickleness, in constantly vacillating from one political party to the other, earned him the nickname of 'Buskin'.* Of the other two, Thucydides was the elder, and as the champion of the upper classes often opposed the popularist policies of Pericles; Nicias, who was younger, had acquired a certain standing even during Pericles' lifetime, in so far as he had been elected military commander along with Pericles and had often held office on his own as well, but no sooner had Pericles died than he was elevated to the leadership, particularly by the wealthy notables of Athenian society, who made him their antidote against Cleon's crass effrontery, but that is not to say that he was not popular enough with the people for them to further his ambitions too.* For although Cleon had gained a great deal of power 'by pampering the people and giving them plenty of paid work', they could see through his attempts to flatter them and discern his self-seeking ambition, arrogance and effrontery, and they tended to back Nicias. His lofty manner was blended with a certain caution, rather than being harsh or overbearing, so that it was actually his apparent fear of the people that made him a popular leader! Despite being naturally faint-hearted and unconfident, in warfare he had hidden his timidity under a cloak of good fortune (for he was uniformly successful as a military commander), and in politics his jitteriness and susceptibility to confusion when faced with informers* were generally held to be democratic features, and increased† his power

quite a bit, since they earned him the goodwill of the Athenian people, who fear those who find them beneath contempt† and promote those who fear them. After all, the greatest compliment that can be paid the people by their superiors is not to be despised by them.

[3] Pericles used true virtue and his powers as a speaker to govern the city, and could deal with the rabble without resorting to affectation or specious rhetoric;* Nicias, however, was deficient in these respects, but was enormously wealthy, so he used his wealth to win the leadership of the people. Since he lacked the confidence to match Cleon's tactics of using unscrupulous and flattering trickery to handle the Athenian people, he tried to win them over by laying on extravaganzas such as dramatic and athletic competitions, which he made more stylish, and on which he spent more money, than any of his predecessors and contemporaries. Moreover, of his dedicatory offerings, there were still standing in my day not only the Palladium on the Acropolis, which has lost its gilding, but also, in the precinct of the temple of Dionysus, the shrine which lay under the tripods he had won as an impresario.* For whenever he was an impresario, which was often, he never suffered defeat, but always won. There is a story that during one of his dramatic productions a house-slave of his—a very tall and exceptionally good-looking young man, not yet old enough to grow a beard—came forward to make a speech, dressed up in the costume of Dionysus; the Athenians greeted the delightful spectacle with prolonged applause, and afterwards Nicias stood up and said that it was wrong, in his opinion, for a person who had been consecrated to a god to be a slave, and he gave the young man his freedom.

The extravaganzas he arranged on Delos have also gone down in history as magnificent affairs, appropriate to the god. The choruses which the various communities used to send to sing in honour of the god had tended to arrive at the island haphazardly, and a crowd of people would meet the ships as soon as they docked and get them to perform in a completely disorganized fashion, hurriedly and chaotically, while they were in the middle of disembarking, putting on their garlands and changing their clothes. However, when Nicias was in charge of the mission, he landed on Rheneia with the chorus, the sacrificial victims and all the rest of their equipment, and then during the night he bridged the strait between Rheneia and Delos (which is not wide*) with a pontoon bridge he had brought, which had been made to measure in Athens and gorgeously decorated with gilded and dyed materials, and with garlands and tapestries. At daybreak the next day he led the procession in honour of the god and the lavishly arrayed chorus, singing its songs, across the bridge and on to Delos. After the sacrificial rites, the competition and the banquets were over, he set up the famous bronze palm-tree as an offering to the god, and bought for 10,000 drachmas an estate which he consecrated to the god; the income from this estate the people of Delos were to spend on a sacrificial banquet at which they would pray to the gods for countless blessings for Nicias. He actually inscribed these instructions on a block of stone, which he left on Delos to act as the guardian, so to speak, of his endowment. The famous palm-tree, however, was broken by the winds; it fell on to the huge statue erected by the people of Naxos and knocked it over.

[4] Vulgar ostentation, with a view to enhancing his reputation and satisfying his ambition, obviously played an important part in all this, but to judge by the rest of the man's personality and character this way of bidding for popular favour and the leadership of the people was a symptom of religious sensibility. He was one of those people who are powerfully impressed by supernatural events, and, as Thucydides says, he was 'addicted to divination'.* In one of his dialogues Pasiphon says that he used to sacrifice to the gods every day, and that he kept a diviner in his household, ostensibly so that he could enquire whenever he liked about public matters, but in fact the majority of his questions were about his own private affairs, and especially about his silver mines. He owned a number of mines in the district of Laurium, which were extremely profitable, but quite dangerous to work; he maintained a sizeable workforce of slaves there, and had most of his capital in silver coin.* He was therefore surrounded by quite large numbers of people, who kept asking him for handouts. They received them too, because he used to give money to people who could do him harm just as much as he did to people who deserved his benevolence, with the upshot that, to generalize, bad men made money from his timidity and good men from his generosity.

The comic poets are another source of evidence for all this. Teleclides composed the following lines about one of the informers:

> So Charicles gave him a mina to stop him telling
> How it was no womb but a wallet that gave him birth—
> Him, his mother's first-born. And Nicias the son of Niceratus
> Gave him four minas. Now, although I know perfectly well
> Why he gave him the four minas, I'm not going to say,
> Because he's a friend of mine—but he strikes me as a sensible man.

And the subject of Eupolis' comedy *Maricas* ushers on to the stage an inoffensive pauper and says:

A. So how long is it since you met Nicias?
B. Never, till I saw him just now, standing in the city square.
A. Ha! The man admits he's seen Nicias.
  But why would he have seen him, if not to betray him?
C. Did you hear that, comrades?
  Nicias has been caught in the act.
B. What are you up to? You're crazy.
  Why would you make trouble for such a good man?

And Aristophanes has Cleon come up with the following threat:

I'll shout down the speakers and upset Nicias.*

Phrynichus also alludes to his timidity and nervousness in these lines:

I'm perfectly well aware that he was a brave Athenian;
He wouldn't have gone around all diffident, as Nicias does.

[5] He was so worried about informers that he would never take his meals with any of his fellow citizens or get involved in discussions or pass the time of day with them. In fact, he did not really have time for this kind of activity: when he was in office he used to stay in the commanders' rooms until after dark, and he was always the first to arrive and the last to leave the Council. And if he had no public business to conduct, he made himself inaccessible and reclusive by staying at home with his doors closed, while his friends used to go up to the people who had come to his door and apologize on his behalf, saying that even then he was busy with some urgent state matters.*

The person who particularly helped him act out this dramatic role, clothe himself in authority, and gain prestige was Hiero, a man who had been raised in Nicias' household and had received from Nicias a thorough grounding in literacy and music. Hiero used to make out that he was the son of Dionysius 'the Bronze', as he was known, whose poems are extant; later, as the leader of the colonizing expedition to Italy, he founded Thurii.* Anyway, it was this Hiero who acted as Nicias' agent in his secret dealings with diviners, and who also used to spread among the Athenian people stories of what an overworked and wretched life the state affairs of Athens caused Nicias to live. 'Even when he's taking a bath,' he would say, 'or eating a meal, some political matter always crops up. He's so busy taking care of public business that he neglects his own private concerns, and he rarely gets to bed before the dead of the night. That's why he's so run down physically, and is so grumpy and antisocial with his friends. In fact, during his time in politics he has lost his friends as well as his money, whereas other politicians use their public careers to win friends and make themselves rich, so that they can have a good time and treat politics as a trivial pastime.'

Nicias' life really was like that, and as a result he could honestly apply to himself Agamemnon's words:

> My life may be ruled
> By authority, but I am in fact a slave to the rabble.*

[6] He noticed that while the Athenian people would occasionally make use of the expertise of powerful speakers or exceptional thinkers, their permanent attitude towards cleverness was one of suspicion and wariness, and they tried to keep such people in their place, without letting them get too proud or earn too great a reputation. This manifested in the fining of Pericles, the ostracism of Damon, the general distrust of Antiphon of the deme Rhamnus, and above all in what happened to Paches the conqueror of Lesbos: he was in the middle of giving an account of his term as military commander when he drew his sword, right there in the courtroom, and killed himself.* Nicias therefore tried to evade problematic or lengthy commands, and whenever he went out on an expedition himself, he made safety his primary concern; consequently he was, of course, usually successful. However, he did not attribute his successes in the slightest to his own skill or abilities or courage, but gave the credit to fortune and so, to avoid envy, gave up some of the glory by taking refuge in the realm of the divine.

The wisdom of his approach was confirmed by events, because although the city suffered many major defeats in those days, he was involved in absolutely none of them. Calliades and Xenophon were the military commanders for the Athenian defeat by the people of Chalcidice in Thrace, the Aetolian disaster happened during Demosthenes' term of office, Hippocrates was in command when the Athenians lost 1,000 of their troops at Delium, and Pericles received most of the blame for the plague, on the grounds that he had confined the rabble from the countryside within the city because of the war, and that the plague was the result of their relocation and their unfamiliar way of life.* Nicias, however, remained free of blame for any of these events; moreover, as a military commander, he captured Cythera, an island in a good position off the coast of Laconia which had been settled by Lacedaemonians; he captured and annexed a number of towns in Thrace which had rebelled against Athens; he pinned the Megarians inside their city and went straight on to gain control of the island of Minoa, which he then used a little later as a base from which to take Nisaea; and, having landed an army in Corinthian territory, he defeated the Corinthians in battle and inflicted heavy losses on them, including their commander, Lycophron.*

It so happened that at the end of this battle the bodies of two of his men were overlooked during the collection of the dead and left behind. As soon as this came to his attention, he stopped his fleet from setting sail and sent a herald to the enemy to ask whether they could be collected. Now, according to tradition and established practice, the side which was granted the right to collect the bodies of its dead under a truce was considered to forfeit any claim to victory, and if they obtained this right they were not allowed to set up a trophy. The thinking behind this custom was that it is those who are in possession of the field who are the victors, and that those who ask for a favour are not in possession of the field because they are not in a position just to take what they want. Nevertheless, Nicias would rather have submitted to giving up the glory of the victory than have left two of his fellow citizens unburied.* He also devastated the coastline of Laconia, routed any Lacedaemonians who resisted him, captured Thyrea, which had been held by the Aeginetans, and brought his prisoners back alive to Athens.*

[7] Demosthenes' fortification of Pylos led to a concerted Peloponnesian attack on the place by both land and sea, but the battle left about 400 Spartiate troops trapped on the island of Sphacteria.* The Athenians did not underestimate the importance of capturing these men, but a number of factors made blockading the island difficult and problematic. In the first place, there was little fresh water in the region, and secondly the shipping of supplies around the Peloponnese was long and costly in summer, and likely to be risky if not completely impossible in winter. So the Athenians were discontented and were regretting having dismissed a Lacedaemonian delegation which had come to them to discuss a truce and terms for peace. They had rejected the offer as a result of Cleon's opposition, and Cleon had opposed

it mainly because of Nicias. He was Nicias' political enemy and when he saw how enthusiastic Nicias was in his dealings with the Lacedaemonians, he persuaded the Athenian people to vote against the truce. So when the blockade was starting to drag on, and they heard about the terrible difficulties under which their troops were operating, they were angry with Cleon.*

Cleon tried to divert the blame on to Nicias. He accused him of being so timid and irresolute that he was letting the Spartiates slip out of his grasp and claimed that, if *he* had been in command, they would not have held out for such a long time. At this point it occurred to the Athenians to say, 'It's not too late. Why don't you take a fleet and get the men yourself?' Nicias stood up and resigned his command of the expedition to Pylos in Cleon's favour; he went on to suggest that Cleon take as large a force as he wanted and, rather than boasting in mere words which involved no risk, actually come up with some significant achievement for Athens. Now, Cleon had not expected anything like this, and at first, in his confusion, he tried to draw back. But provoked by the Athenians' insistence and Nicias' taunts, he became fired with ambition: he accepted the command and also declared that within twenty days of setting sail he would either kill the Spartiates there or bring them back alive to Athens. The Athenians were more inclined to laugh long and loud at this than believe him, because they had learnt from other occasions to treat his capricious impetuosity as a rather good joke.* For instance, there is a story that once, when the Assembly was in session, he kept the people waiting in their seats up on the hill for a long time, and when at last he did arrive late in the day, wearing his garlands for dinner, he asked them to adjourn the Assembly until the next day. 'I'm busy today,' he explained. 'I'm having some guests round for dinner, and I've already sacrificed to the gods.' The Athenians, it is said, burst out laughing, and then got up and dissolved the Assembly.

[8] This time, however, Cleon was lucky. He did an excellent job as commander of the operation, along with Demosthenes, and within the specified time he brought back as prisoners of war all the Spartiates who had surrendered and so survived the battle.* Nicias' reputation suffered dreadfully as a result of Cleon's success. For a soldier to abandon his shield is bad enough, but it seemed somehow worse, more disgraceful, for Nicias to have voluntarily resigned his command out of timidity, and to have handed over to his political

enemy the opportunity to achieve such an important success by voting himself out of office. Aristophanes—to quote him again—mocks
Nicias for this in *Birds*, in lines which go somewhat as follows:

> Right, yes, it's certainly time for us to stop
> Drowsing and procrastiniciating!*

And in the *Farmers* he says:

A. I want to get back to my farm.
B. Who's stopping you?
A. All of you. But I'll give you 1,000 drachmas
   If you let me resign my office.
B. It's a deal. That'll be 2,000 with what we got from Nicias.

And the fact is that Nicias did do the city, as well as himself, quite
a bit of harm, in making it possible for Cleon to increase his reputation and power so much that he entered upon a phase of insolent pride
and ungovernable boldness, during which he inflicted upon the city
various disasters (one of the primary victims of which was Nicias
himself), not the least of which was that he stripped the rostrum of
its decorum, since he was the first to raise his voice to raucous levels
during his public speeches, pull his cloak open, slap his thigh, and
pace around while speaking.* In other words, he conditioned Athens'
politicians to regard proper behaviour with indifference and disdain—
and it was this that before long threw all the city's affairs into chaos.

[9] This was also more or less the time when Alcibiades too was
beginning to graft himself on to the Athenians. He was not as complete a demagogue as Cleon, but, as the soil of Egypt is said to be
fertile enough to bear at one and the same time 'many healing herbs,
and many harmful, all together',* so Alcibiades' nature contained currents that flowed strongly and flamboyantly in both directions and
therefore initiated major innovations for both good and bad. Even after
he was free of Cleon, therefore, Nicias did not have the opportunity
to relieve and alleviate the city from all its troubles. He managed to
set matters on the road to safety, but was then forcibly driven off course
and back to war by the overwhelming torrent of Alcibiades' ambition.*

Here is what happened. The chief opponents of peace for Greece
were Cleon and Brasidas; after all, the war disguised the iniquity of
one of them, to whom it provided opportunities for serious crimes,
and emphasized the excellence of the other, to whom it provided

opportunities for major successes. As soon as these two men had both fallen at Amphipolis in a single battle,* Nicias ascertained that the Spartiates had desired peace for a long time, and that the Athenians were no longer so confident about their prospects in the war—that both sides were relaxed, so to speak, with their hands deliberately hanging loose by their sides—and he set in motion actions designed to bring the two cities together in friendship, to free and relieve the rest of Greece from its troubles, and so to secure for the future his reputation for success. He found the rich, the elderly, and the majority of those who worked the land inclined from the start towards peace, and once he had held private meetings with many of the rest, at which he educated them and blunted their desire for war, then he gave the Spartiates grounds for hope, and encouraged and urged them to keep to the ways of peace. They already knew him as a decent man, especially because he had shown concern for the welfare of the men who had been captured at Pylos and imprisoned in Athens, and had lightened their misfortune by treating them humanely, so they trusted him. The two sides had previously arranged a kind of armistice for a year, during which they had held meetings and once again tasted the pleasures of security, leisure, and the company of guest-friends and relatives, and so had come to miss a life without the stain of war and were happy to hear choruses singing lines such as 'May my spear be laid aside for spiders to weave their webs around',* and to remember the saying that in times of peace men are woken by cocks, not trumpets. So they denounced and censured those who said that the war was fated to last thrice nine years, and in this frame of mind they met for thorough discussions and concluded a peace treaty.* Most people took this to mean that their troubles were definitely over, and Nicias was a frequent topic of conversation. They described him as a favourite of the gods, and said that the gods had rewarded his piety by attaching his name to an unparalleled and exceptional blessing. They really did regard the peace as the work of Nicias, just as they considered the war the work of Pericles. The one was held to have involved the Greeks in calamitous disasters, for no very good reason, while the other managed to persuade them to forget all their terrible injuries and become friends. And that is why even today this peace is called 'the Peace of Nicias'.

[10] Under the terms of the treaty, each side was to restore the land and communities they held which belonged to the other side, and also

return their prisoners of war, with the side which was to effect this restoration first being chosen by lot; but Theophrastus records that Nicias used bribery covertly to arrange that the lot would fall on the Lacedaemonians first. And when it looked as though the Corinthians and Boeotians, who were not happy with the proceedings, would revive the war with their accusations and criticisms, Nicias persuaded the Athenians and Lacedaemonians to supplement the peace treaty with their famous alliance, which would act as an authoritative bond between the two states, and so increase their ability to deter would-be rebels and their confidence in each other.*

Faced with these proceedings, Alcibiades, who was naturally inclined to find inactivity irksome, and was also irritated by the Lacedaemonians' high-handed disregard of himself in favour of Nicias, to whom they were loyally attached, registered his immediate opposition to the peace. At first his objections got him nowhere, but before long he noticed that the Athenians were starting to feel less kindly towards the Lacedaemonians; they thought that they were contravening the terms of the treaty by having entered into an alliance with the Boeotians, by having failed to restore Panactum to them with its fortifications intact, and by having failed to return Amphipolis at all.* So Alcibiades latched on to these grievances one by one and set about stirring up the anger of the Athenian people about them. In the end he arranged for an official delegation to be sent from Argos, and he tried to broker an alliance between Argos and Athens, but a plenipotentiary delegation arrived from Lacedaemon, and at its preliminary meeting with the Council impressed the members with the apparent justice of all the proposals it had come to present. Alcibiades became worried that the Lacedaemonian envoys would win round the Assembly too with the same proposals, so he double-crossed them.* He promised to give them his complete co-operation, provided that they denied, even when questioned, that they had come with full powers of negotiation; that, he said, was the way for them to achieve their goals. They were convinced, and they shifted their allegiance from Nicias to him.

After he had introduced them to the Assembly, the first question he asked them was whether they had come with full powers to negotiate on any issue that might arise. They said that they had not, and then, contrary to their expectations, he changed tack: he proceeded to call on the members of the Council to testify to what the delegates had told them earlier, and then he went on to tell the assembled Athenians not to pay any attention to people who were so obviously liars, let alone trust them, when they contradicted themselves from one moment to the next. The Lacedaemonians were of course shocked by the turn of events, and Nicias was too upset and astonished to have anything to say. The Athenian people immediately set about summoning the Argive delegation and were poised to conclude an alliance with them, but a slight earthquake came to Nicias' rescue by interrupting the proceedings and ending that session of the Assembly. On the next day the Assembly convened again, and after a great deal of effort and argument Nicias finally succeeded in persuading them to put off their business with the Argives and send him on a mission to the Lacedaemonians, which he promised would work out for the best.

However, although he was basically treated with respect in Sparta, as a man of integrity and as someone who had done a lot for them, he achieved none of his aims, but was defeated by the pro-Boeotian party there. When he returned to Athens, on top of the disparagement and defamation he had to endure, he was actually afraid of what the Athenians might do to him. They were distressed and irritated by the fact that they had let him persuade them to return so many important men; for the prisoners they had taken at Pylos belonged to the leading families of Sparta, and counted the most influential members of Lacedaemonian society among their friends and relatives.* But the Athenians did not deal very harshly with him in their anger; instead, they elected Alcibiades to the post of military commander, entered into an alliance not just with the Argives, but also with the Mantineans and Eleans, who had seceded from the Lacedaemonians, and sent raiders into Pylos to plunder Laconia. And the upshot of all this was that they re-established a state of war.*

[11] The feud between Alcibiades and Nicias flourished and the process of ostracism was set in motion.* This was a measure the Athenian people used to take from time to time, to send into exile for a period of ten years, by voting with a sherd, a single individual who had either generally acquired such a reputation that he was an object of suspicion, or who was so rich that he was an object of envy. It was a time of considerable turmoil and danger for both parties, since one or the other of them was bound to endure exile as a result of the ostracism. In Alcibiades' case, people were disgusted by his life and feared his boldness, as I have explained in more detail in his Life; in

Nicias' case, his wealth inspired envy, but the main problem lay with his way of life, which was not open or democratic, but antisocial and oligarchic, and struck people as weird; moreover, they found him an irritant, since he had often in the past opposed their wishes and forced them to follow the course of expediency rather than predilection. Basically, the contest was between the younger generation, who wanted war, and the older generation, who wanted peace, with one side wielding the sherd against Nicias and the other against Alcibiades.

'But in times of civil strife even criminals become respectable.'* And so on that occasion the division of the Athenians into two factions made room for the worst kind of unscrupulous crook, one of whom was Hyperbolus of the deme Perithoedae. He was a man with bravado which had no basis in power, but who came to power on the basis of his bravado, and who brought the city into disrespect because of the respect he received in the city. At that time Hyperbolus considered himself to be beyond the reach of ostracism (in so far as he was more likely to be a candidate for the pillory) and he assumed that, once one of Nicias and Alcibiades had gone into exile, he would become the political rival of the survivor. He made no secret of the fact that their feud delighted him and that he was stirring the Athenian people up against both of them. Once Nicias and Alcibiades became aware of Hyperbolus' iniquity, they held secret talks, as a result of which they combined their two parties into a single faction, and successfully saw to it that Hyperbolus rather than either of them was the one who was sent into exile by the ostracism!

In the short term, the Athenian people enjoyed this and thought it a good joke, but subsequently they came to regret the fact that, as they saw it, the institution had been demeaned by being applied to a person who did not deserve it. They thought that even punishment has a certain dignity, or rather that exile by ostracism was a punishment for Thucydides, Aristides, and people of their calibre, but in Hyperbolus' case was an honour and an occasion for boasting, since as a result of his iniquity he had shared an experience with men of the highest virtue. Hence Plato the comic poet makes the following comment about him in one of his plays:

> And yet he suffered no less than his conduct deserved,
> But more than he and his tattoos deserved,*
> For ostracism was not invented for the likes of him.

The upshot was that no one at all was ever ostracized after Hyperbolus: he was the last, while Hipparchus of the deme Cholargus, a relative of the tyrant, was the first.*

Fortune is an inscrutable matter, incapable of comprehension by the rational mind. If Nicias had taken Alcibiades on and run the risk of ostracism, he would either have won and lived safely in Athens with Alcibiades in exile, or he would have lost and gone into exile himself before the disasters which finally overwhelmed him, with his reputation as a brilliant military commander intact. I am perfectly well aware of Theophrastus' claim that Hyperbolus was ostracized when Phaeax, not Nicias, was Alcibiades' rival, but I have followed the version given by the majority of my sources.*

[12] In any case, it was Nicias who objected to the idea of sending an army to Sicily, which was what a delegation sent to Athens from Segesta and Leontini was trying to persuade the Athenians to do, but he was defeated by Alcibiades' ambitious designs.* Even before the Assembly had met at all, Alcibiades had corrupted the majority of the people with his assurances and his arguments, and won them over to his cause so thoroughly that as the young men sat in the wrestling-schools, and the old men in their workshops and alcoves, they used to sketch maps of Sicily, including the properties of the sea off the island, and mark the harbours and natural features on the stretch of its coastline which faces Libya. For they did not regard Sicily as an ultimate prize of the war so much as a base of operations, from where, they imagined, they could set out to take on the Carthaginians and gain control of Libya and the whole of the sea east of the Pillars of Heracles. Given that this was what the majority had in mind, Nicias found few people to support his resistance to the plan, and those he found were not men of influence. The men of substance were frightened of appearing to be trying to avoid their financial obligations and their duty to equip triremes, so they kept quiet against their better judgement.

Nicias persevered, however, and refused to give up. Even after the Athenians had voted in favour of war and had elected him the commander-in-chief, with Alcibiades and Lamachus as his colleagues,* he stood up when the Assembly reconvened, tried to get them to change their minds, and protested the decision; in the end he accused Alcibiades of trying to satisfy his own personal greed and ambition by forcing the city to undertake a difficult, dangerous war overseas.

But he got nowhere. In fact, he succeeded only in increasing people's estimation of his value to the project because of his experience; they thought the risks would be considerably diminished once his caution was blended with Alcibiades' daring and Lamachus' recklessness, and so he made them feel all the more confident in their decision. For Demostratus, the demagogue who was doing the most to arouse the Athenians' enthusiasm for the war, stood up and said that he would stop Nicias making any more excuses.* He proposed a decree to the effect that the military commanders should have unconditional powers to decide, not just on the field of battle but there in Athens too, about the planning and conduct of the campaign, and persuaded the people to vote the decree into law.

[13] There is said, however, to have been considerable opposition to the campaign from the priests too; but Alcibiades found other diviners and published the claim, derived from some supposedly ancient oracles, that the Athenians would win great fame in Sicily. He was also helped when some envoys returned from the shrine of Ammon* with an oracle to the effect that every single Syracusan would fall into Athenian hands; but the envoys suppressed oracles with the opposite import because they did not want to jinx the expedition. For even obvious and unambiguous portents could do nothing to deter the Athenians. There was the mutilation of the herms, for instance, when in the course of a single night every herm had its extremities broken off; the only herm to escape damage was the one known as the Herm of Andocides, which was dedicated by the Aegeid tribe, and stood in front of what was then Andocides' house.* Then there was what happened at the Altar of the Twelve Gods: a man suddenly leapt up to the altar, stood astride it, and castrated himself with a stone.

In Delphi there was a dedicatory offering set up by Athens from the prizes for valour won by Athenians in the Persian Wars—a golden Palladium mounted on a bronze palm-tree. For a number of days crows perched on the statue and mutilated it, and also pecked the golden fruit off the palm-tree and dropped it on to the ground. The Athenians claimed that this was a story made up by the people of Delphi and that they had been put up to it by the Syracusans, but when an oracle commanded them to fetch the priestess of Athena from Clazomenae, they sent for the woman—and her name was Peace! This was apparently the gods' way of advising the city to keep the peace for the time being.

Perhaps he was alarmed by these omens, or perhaps it was just his human intelligence that led him to dread the expedition, but anyway Meton the astronomer,* who had been appointed an officer in the army, pretended to be mad and burnt his house down. Another version of the story makes no mention of any pretence of insanity, but claims that he burnt down his house one night and then presented himself in the city square in his wretched state and asked his fellow citizens, in view of this calamity, to release his son from active service, who was about to sail to Sicily in command of a trireme. And the philosopher Socrates' divine sign revealed to him, in its usual symbolic fashion, among other things that the expedition would bring about the destruction of Athens. He told his friends and acquaintances, and the story became widely known.*

Quite a few people were also disturbed by the timing of the dispatch of the fleet. The women were celebrating the festival of Adonis at the time, and all over the city they were preparing statuettes of the god for burial, giving them funerals and mourning over them.* Consequently, anyone who was inclined to find this kind of thing significant felt some misgivings, and became afraid that this famous armed force, for all its brilliance and vitality, might soon wither away.

[14] That Nicias should have opposed the decision about the expedition and not changed his mind under the influence of either optimism or amazement at the size of his command shows that he was a man of integrity who knew his own mind. However, once he had got nowhere either in his attempts to convince the Athenians to abandon the war or in his requests to be relieved of the command— once the Athenian people had, so to speak, picked him up, taken him and deposited him at the head of the expeditionary force—then his excessive caution and hesitation were out of place. It was no longer appropriate for him to look back to shore from his ship, like a child, or to repeat and dwell so often on his failure to have won the people over by the force of his arguments that he actually took the edge off his colleagues' enthusiasm and sapped their energy for action. He should have grappled and closed with the enemy without delay, and learnt what fortune had in store for him in actual conflict. Instead, with Lamachus recommending that they sail straight for Syracuse and engage the enemy as close as possible to his city, and with Alcibiades suggesting that they first get the Syracusans' allies to secede and then proceed against the Syracusans themselves, he argued against them

and in favour of quietly sailing along the Sicilian coastline and cir-
cumnavigating the island to show the islanders how well armed they
were and the size of their fleet, and then sailing back to Athens, after
leaving a portion of their force for the Segestans. All this weakened
his men's resolution and lowered their morale.*

A short while later, the Athenians recalled Alcibiades to stand trial,
leaving Nicias nominally the joint commander with Lamachus, but
in fact in sole command.* From then on he did nothing but stay
in one place, or cruise around aimlessly, or make plans, until his
men's optimistic energy went into decline, and the dismay and fear
which the sight of his forces had originally inspired in the enemy
trickled away.

Before Alcibiades' departure, a fleet of sixty ships did sail for
Syracuse. While the bulk of the fleet remained in formation out at
sea off the harbour, a squadron of ten ships rowed in to reconnoitre
and had a crier call out to the people of Leontini with instructions to
return home.* This squadron captured an enemy vessel with a cargo
of tablets on which the Syracusans had inscribed a list of their citizen body, broken down into tribes. These tablets had stood some
way from the city, in the precinct of the temple of Olympian Zeus,
but they had been required at that time to help determine and draw
up a list of those who were of military age. After their capture by the
Athenians, they were taken to the staff officers, and when it became
obvious how many names there were on them the diviners became
worried in case these tablets might turn out to constitute the necessity predicted by the oracle that every single Syracusan would fall into
Athenian hands. Others, however, maintain that this prophecy was
in fact fulfilled for the Athenians later, when Callippus of Athens killed
Dion and gained control of Syracuse.*

[15] Not long after this Alcibiades left Sicily, and then Nicias
had absolute power. Although Lamachus was a man of courage and
integrity, and gave unsparingly of himself in battle, he was so poor
and pinched that every time he went out on campaign he charged the
Athenians a small amount of money for his clothing and footwear.
Nicias, however, owed his importance and authority above all to his
wealth and prestige. There is a story that once he and his fellow commanders were in a meeting in the commanders' office, and he invited
Sophocles the poet to give his opinion first on the matter they were
discussing, on the grounds that he was the oldest of the commanders;

'I may be the oldest,' Sophocles is supposed to have replied, 'but you are the most senior.'

And so on the occasion in question too he made himself Lamachus' master, even though he was less skilled in military matters. He persisted in using his forces cautiously and hesitantly; not only did his practice of keeping a good distance from them on his cruises around Sicily raise the enemy's morale, but also his attack on the tiny community of Hybla, which was broken off before he had captured the place, made him completely contemptible in their eyes. Eventually he returned to Catana without having achieved anything apart from overrunning the non-Greek territory of Hyccara, which is said to have been the place where Laïs the courtesan, who was still a young girl at the time, was bought as one of a group of prisoners of war, and from where she came to the Peloponnese.*

[16] At the end of summer, he learnt that the Syracusans were feeling so confident that they were going to take the initiative and make an attack on his forces; moreover, by this time the Syracusan cavalry was in the habit of riding up to the Athenian camp and insolently asking whether they had come to settle with the people of Catana or to resettle the people of Leontini. So Nicias finally launched an attack by sea on Syracuse. He wanted his men to establish a position there in complete safety, without being harassed by the enemy, so he surreptitiously sent an agent from Catana to tell the Syracusans that if they wanted to find the Athenian camp deserted and to capture the Athenians' weapons, they should come to Catana in full strength on a certain specified day, because with the Athenians spending most of their time away from the camp in the town, the pro-Syracusan Catanaeans had decided to take the approach of the Syracusan army as a signal to seize the camp gates and set fire to the beached Athenian fleet; there were plenty of people involved in the conspiracy, the message concluded, and they were only waiting for the Syracusan army to come.

This was Nicias' best tactical manoeuvre in Sicily. He drew off the whole enemy army and ensured that the city was more or less undefended, while he put to sea from Catana, took over the enemy's harbours, and secured for his camp a piece of land which would in his opinion enable him to minimize the damage he would sustain from those elements of the enemy's forces where he fell short, while offering an unimpeded field of action for the forces he could rely on.* As soon as the Syracusans returned from Catana and drew up their army in front of the city, Nicias led the Athenians out against them and defeated them. Syracusan losses were not extensive, however, because as they fell back their cavalry stopped Nicias' men pursuing them, and all Nicias could manage was to destroy and break up the bridges over the river. This made it possible for Hermocrates* to console his Syracusan troops by saying that the lengths Nicias went to as a commander to avoid battle made him ridiculous; it was as if he had sailed all that way for some other purpose, not fighting. All the same, Nicias did succeed in frightening and alarming the Syracusans enough for them to replace the fifteen commanders they had at the time with three others, to whom the Syracusan people gave solemn assurances that they would let them have full power, free from interference.

The temple of Olympian Zeus was near by, and the Athenians intended to take it over, because it contained a large number of golden and silver dedicatory offerings. However, Nicias deliberately waited until it was too late, and let the Syracusans send troops in to defend it, because he could see no advantage to his men stealing the temple's treasures: it would not do the state any good, and he himself would be blamed for the sacrilege.

He completely failed to profit from his famous victory, of which so much was being made. After an interval of a few days, he withdrew once again to Naxos* and saw the winter out there, spending a great deal of money on his vast army, but achieving little in his negotiations with the few Sicels who had abandoned the Syracusans and come over to his side. Consequently, Syracusan morale was restored, and they marched out to Catana, where they laid waste to the land and burnt the Athenian camp to the ground.* Everyone blamed Nicias for all this, and accused him of having spent so much time thinking and hesitating and being careful that he wasted every opportunity he had to actually get something done. After all, no one could have found fault with him when he acted: once he had decided to do something, he was energetic and effective. It was just that he was usually too hesitant and timid to make the final decision to do anything.

[17] However, when he mobilized his troops once more against Syracuse, his tactics were so successful, and he moved with such speed (while also not endangering his men), that before anyone was aware of his presence he had put in at Thapsus with his fleet, landed his men, launched a surprise attack on Epipolae, and occupied it. Then

he proceeded to defeat the élite troops who were sent to relieve Epipolae, killing 300 of them, and he even succeeded in routing the Syracusan cavalry, which was supposed to be invincible.* But there was one thing above all which terrified the Sicilians and astonished the Greeks, and that was the rapidity with which he constructed a wall enclosing Syracuse, a city which is at least as big as Athens, and is surrounded by terrain which is less amenable to the task of building a surrounding wall of that size, because of its unevenness, its juxtaposition to the sea, and its proximity to marshland. But he only just failed to complete the task, and this was a man who did not enjoy the kind of good health needed for concerns of that scale, but who suffered from a kidney ailment, which may fairly be said to be responsible for the small part of the work that was left undone.* What they did succeed in doing is remarkable testimony to the dedication of the commander and the fortitude of his men. After their defeat and annihilation, Euripides composed an epitaph for them, in which he wrote as follows:

> Eight times those who lie here defeated the Syracusans,
> Man to man, when neither side was favoured by the gods.

In actual fact, it is arguable that the Syracusans were defeated by them more than eight times, until, as Euripides rightly says, thanks to the gods or to fortune the tide turned against the Athenians, just when their power had peaked.

[18] Despite his poor state of health, Nicias took part in most of his army's activities. On one occasion, however, when he was in a particularly bad way, he was laid up in bed in the fort, attended by a few slaves, while Lamachus and the army were fighting the Syracusans, who were trying to run a wall out from the city towards the one the Athenians were building, to intersect with it and prevent its completion. The Athenians defeated the Syracusans, but in so doing got involved in a somewhat disorderly pursuit, in the course of which Lamachus became cut off from the rest of the Athenian army and bore the brunt of a charge from the Syracusan cavalry. The leader of the Syracusan cavalry, an excellent and courageous fighter called Callicrates, challenged Lamachus to single combat. The challenge was accepted, and Lamachus stepped forward to face him. He was the first to be wounded, but then he wounded Callicrates back, and the two men fell and died together. The Syracusans took possession

of Lamachus' body and armour and bore them off the field, but then charged towards the Athenian fortifications, where Nicias was. Although there was no one there to assist him, the emergency impelled Nicias out of bed. Once he had taken stock of the danger, he told his attendants to fetch all the pieces of wood which happened to be piled in front of the fortifications ready for the siege-engines, and the siege-engines themselves, and set fire to them. This thwarted the Syracusans, and saved not only Nicias, but the Athenian fortifications and all their equipment, because at the sight of the huge wall of flame that flared up in their path, the Syracusans pulled back.*

So Nicias was the only one of the original commanders left, but he was extremely optimistic. Towns and cities were beginning to rebel against the Syracusans, and ships laden with grain came to his camp from all over the place, since there was a general move to join his side now that things were going well for him; some Syracusans had even approached him several times already about the possibility of a deal, since they had given up hope for their city. Moreover, when Gylippus, who was on his way from Lacedaemon to help the Syracusans, heard about how the Athenians were walling the city in and causing the Syracusans all kinds of difficulties, he assumed that Sicily was lost, and although he carried on with his journey, he did so with the intention of protecting the communities of Italy—if he could, since the Athenians were rapidly gaining a firm reputation for carrying all before them and for having a commander who was too lucky and intelligent to be defeated in battle.*

The immediate effect of all this on Nicias himself was an uncharacteristic degree of confidence in view of the apparently unstoppable surge of good fortune he was enjoying at the time.* In particular, he was encouraged by the secret talks he was having with the Syracusans who had approached him to regard the city as more or less negotiated into his hands. Consequently he paid no attention to the approach of Gylippus' fleet, and failed even to post guards at the appropriate time.† Finding himself completely disregarded and disdained, then, Gylippus sailed through the straits without Nicias knowing anything about it, landed at the opposite end of the island from Syracuse, and gathered together a sizeable army.* Even the Syracusans were unaware of his presence; they were not expecting him, and so they had even convened a general assembly to discuss coming to terms with Nicias. In fact, some people were already making their way there, thinking that they should reach a settlement before the city was completely walled in. For there really was not much work left to be done, and all the material needed for the building of the wall was piled up in place.

[19] At this critical juncture, with danger looming, Gongylus, who had come from Corinth, reached Syracuse with a single trireme. Everyone flocked to meet him, of course, and he told them of Gylippus' imminent arrival and of the fleet that was on its way to help them. At first they were not entirely sure whether or not to believe him, but then a messenger came from Gylippus, suggesting that they join up with him. With their morale high, they put on their armour and took up their weapons. No sooner had Gylippus marched up than he deployed his men in battle formation and advanced against the Athenians, but when Nicias had his men too form up opposite them, Gylippus got his troops to lay down their arms and he sent a herald to offer the Athenians safe passage if they would leave Sicily. Nicias did not even deign to reply, but some of his soldiers asked the herald scornfully whether the arrival of just one Laconian cloak and staff had suddenly bolstered the Syracusans' affairs to such an extent that they held the Athenians in contempt, when the Athenians had kept 300 men, each of whom was far stronger and longer-haired than Gylippus, tied up in prison before returning them to the Lacedaemonians.*

Now, Timaeus claims that the Sicilians did not think at all highly of Gylippus either, not just subsequently, when they realized how avaricious and mean he was, but even at first sight, since they found his cloak and long hair ridiculous. However, he himself goes on to say that as soon as Gylippus appeared men flew in his direction in large numbers, like birds to an owl,* and volunteered their support in his campaign. This is the more accurate of his two statements, because in fact people saw his staff and his cloak as symbols of the dignity of Sparta and rallied around them. Moreover, it is not just Thucydides who attributes the final victory to him alone, but also Philistus, who was a Syracusan and witnessed these events at first hand.*

Although the Athenians won the first battle and killed a few Syracusans, as well as Gongylus of Corinth, on the following day Gylippus showed the value of experience. He had the same weaponry, horses, and terrain at his disposal, but he employed them differently, and he defeated the Athenians by varying his tactics. Once the

Athenians had retreated into their camp, he halted the Syracusans and, with the same stones and timber the Athenians had brought up for their own use, he built a Syracusan wall where there was a gap and cut off the Athenians' wall, which meant that it would do the Athenians no good to win a battle.* By now the Syracusans were in a more positive frame of mind, and they began to make their ships ready for battle, while their own and their auxiliaries' cavalry patrolled the countryside taking large numbers of prisoners. Meanwhile Gylippus made personal visits to the island's towns and cities to rouse them to action, and he managed to unite them all in an alliance based on solid loyalty to him and support for his cause. The upshot of all this was that Nicias reverted to his original thoughts about the situation; his awareness of the change in the state of affairs depressed him, and he wrote to the Athenians recommending that they either send another army or recall this one from Sicily, and requesting that in any case he should be relieved of his command on the grounds of ill health.*

[20] The Athenians had been planning to send further forces to Sicily even before Nicias' request arrived, but the most prominent politicians of the city, who were disconcerted by his success, had kept delaying the project out of envy; but this time, at any rate, there was no reluctance to send reinforcements. Demosthenes was to set sail with a large fleet once winter was over, while Eurymedon sailed on ahead of him while it was still winter, taking money and the news that among his officers there Euthydemus and Menander had been chosen to share the command with him.*

Meanwhile, however, Nicias was suddenly attacked by land and sea. The sea battle went badly for him at first, but he still repulsed the enemy fleet and sank many of their ships. However, he did not manage to get help to his land army on time, and Plemmyrium fell to Gylippus' surprise attack. Plemmyrium had been used to store equipment for the fleet and a great deal of money; all of this fell into Gylippus' hands, and he also killed or captured quite a large number of men. But the most serious thing was that he deprived Nicias of an easy route for his supplies. While the Athenians had held Plemmyrium, their supplies had been safely and quickly transported past the promontory, but now that they had lost it, the transportation of supplies became difficult, and involved fighting off the enemy, who kept a squadron of ships at anchor there.*

Moreover, the Syracusans felt that their defeat at sea had not been due to the Athenians' superior strength, but to the fact that they had allowed their ships to lose formation when they were pursuing the Athenian fleet. So they were all for giving it another go, with more conspicuous success this time, and were making their preparations accordingly. Nicias, however, was reluctant to meet the enemy at sea; he said it would be sheer stupidity to fight with forces that were out-numbered and poorly supplied when Demosthenes was speeding their way with a huge fleet and fresh troops. However, Menander and Euthy-demus, recently promoted and ambitious, wanted to outshine the other two commanders: they wanted to accomplish something glorious before Demosthenes had a chance to, and to do better than Nicias. But they cloaked their ambition under talk of the city's reputation, which, they argued, would be completely ruined and lost if they let a Syracusan attack by sea unnerve them. So they forced through a decision to meet the enemy at sea, but when it came to it they were outwitted by the Corinthian captain Ariston, as Thucydides has recorded, in the business with the midday meal, and then defeated by superior numbers, with heavy losses. Furthermore, Nicias became extremely depressed by the fact that he had not only done badly when he was in sole command, but was now also having to suffer the consequences of his colleagues' mistakes.*

[21] Just then Demosthenes appeared off the harbours in a magnificent show of strength which dismayed the enemy. He had brought seventy-three ships, with 5,000 hoplites on board, and at least 3,000 others armed with javelins, bows, and slings. With his array of weaponry, with the figureheads on his ships, and the number of men employed in calling the time for the rowers and playing the pipes, he presented a fine display, designed to strike fear into the enemy.* As was to be expected, the Syracusans were once again plunged into a state of abject terror, since they could see no release or reprieve from their troubles, but only useless toil and and pointless self-destruction. However, the presence of these reinforcements did not cheer Nicias up for long: at their first meeting, Demosthenes argued for engaging the enemy immediately—for them to risk all in battle as soon as possible, and either take Syracuse or sail back home to Athens.* His impulsive daring frightened and perturbed Nicias, who pleaded for a course of action that was neither desperate nor foolish, arguing that delay worked against the enemy, because they were now short of money

and their allies would not remain loyal for long, but would turn to him again to discuss terms, as they had done before, if they were in dire straits.

The point is that there were a fair number of people in Syracuse who were in secret communication with Nicias and were urging him to wait, on the grounds that the Syracusans were already so exhausted by the war and fed up with Gylippus that it would take only a slight increase in their exigencies for them to give up completely. In his talks with his colleagues Nicias hinted at some of this, but did not feel he could talk about it openly, and the upshot was that he gave them an impression of timidity. They argued that this was simply a re-emergence of his familiar old habits of hesitating, delaying, and quibbling over details, and claimed that in relying on these traits he had already drained the energy out of the expedition by refusing to engage the enemy as soon as he had arrived, and by letting himself instead grow stale and earn the enemy's contempt. So they sided with Demosthenes, and Nicias was reluctantly forced to go along with their plans.

Demosthenes took the land army and launched a night attack on Epipolae.* He took the enemy by surprise, killed some of them before they were aware of his presence, and then drove back others who had begun to defend themselves. On he went without waiting, spurred on by his victory, until he came up against the Boeotians, who were the first enemy contingent to have grouped together. Yelling out loud, they charged the Athenians with spears levelled and inflicted heavy losses on them. In no time at all panic and confusion spread throughout the whole Athenian army. The part that was still winning soon collided with the part that was trying to retreat, while those who were advancing and bearing forward from the rear were beaten back by their terrified comrades, until the whole army became tangled up with itself and fugitives were mistaken for pursuers, friends for enemies. The Athenians found themselves in an appalling and catastrophic mess as a result of the chaos of men milling around all together in fear and uncertainty, combined with the impossibility of trusting their sight on a night which was neither wholly dark nor light, but which, as was only to be expected, given that the moon was now low in the sky and was partially obscured by the mass of weaponry and by figures moving across its face, failed to make shapes clear and so to terrified minds made what was familiar an object of suspicion. It also so happened that they had the moon behind them, which meant that they cast their shadows forward on to their own men, and so obscured the number and brightness of their weapons, whereas the reflection of their opponents' shields in the moonlight made them appear more numerous than they were, and increased the dazzle of their armour. In the end, the Athenians gave way and then the enemy attacked them from all sides; as they fled they were killed either by the enemy or by their own side, while others fell to their deaths off the cliffs. When day dawned, the cavalry caught and killed the scattered and straying fugitives. Two thousand men lost their lives, and hardly any of the survivors saved their weapons along with their lives.

[22] Although it did not entirely surprise him, Nicias was disheartened by this disaster, which he blamed on Demosthenes' rashness. Demosthenes claimed that this had nothing to do with it and suggested that they leave the island as soon as possible, arguing that no more reinforcements would come, and that they could not defeat the enemy with their current resources, especially since, even if they did have the upper hand, they would have to move camp off the island, away from their present site, which had never been a hospitable and healthy place for an army to encamp; they had been told as much before, and now they could see that at this time of year it was deadly. It was the beginning of autumn, a lot of their men were already ill, and morale was low throughout the camp.

Nicias was unhappy with talk of retreating and leaving the island, not because he was blasé about the Syracusans, but because he was more afraid of the Athenians with their lawsuits and informers. He used to say that he expected nothing terrible to happen to him there, but that if it did, he preferred death at the hands of his enemies to death at the hands of his fellow citizens—quite the opposite sentiment from that expressed at a later date by Leon of Byzantium, who was to tell his fellow citizens, 'I would rather be killed by you than alongside you.' However, he said that they would discuss the site and location of a new camp when they had the time.

In response, Demosthenes stopped trying to force the issue, since his previous plan had been a failure too. This made others think it was because Nicias had high hopes of his friends inside the city that he so strongly resisted the idea of retreat, and so they all went along with his recommendation.* But later, after another army had come to reinforce the Syracusans, and when the Athenians were worse affected by disease, even Nicias agreed to a change of location, and he ordered his troops to get ready to leave the island.

[23] However, just when everything was ready for carrying out this plan, and the enemy were completely off their guard, since they were not expecting anything like this, there was a lunar eclipse one night.* Nicias and those of his men who were ignorant or superstitious enough to be impressed by such things were terrified. The overshadowing of the sun towards the end of the month was by this time understood even by the common people to be some kind of effect of the moon, but it was hard for them to grasp what body the moon itself could encounter and how, especially when it was full, it could suddenly lose its light and vary its colouring so much. This struck them as a weird phenomenon, and as a divinely sent portent of some major disaster or other.*

The first person to have committed to writing a particularly clear and supremely bold account of the illumination and overshadowing of the moon was Anaxagoras,* but he was not an ancient authority, and his work had not become well known; it was still too dangerous to talk about it openly, and it circulated among only a few people, who regarded it with caution rather than confidence. For there was widespread intolerance of natural scientists—'airheads', as they were called at the time—on the grounds that they reduced the divine to unthinking causes, blind forces, and necessary effects. Protagoras was banished from Athens, Pericles only just managed to rescue Anaxagoras from prison, and even though Socrates had nothing to do with this kind of speculation he was killed for his devotion to learning. It was only later, thanks to Plato, whose way of life earned him an untarnished reputation and who made natural forces subject to divine principles, that this kind of teaching lost its bad reputation and became available to everyone. At any rate, Plato's friend Dion was not disturbed by a lunar eclipse that occurred just as he was about to set sail from Zacynthos on his campaign against Dionysius: he put to sea, landed at Syracuse, and drove out the tyrant.*

At the time in question, however, Nicias did not even have the advantage of a professional diviner, because his close friend Stilbides, who had usually quelled his superstition, had died a short time before. After all, as Philochorus says, the sign was not adverse for people who were retreating, but was very auspicious, since concealment is just what risky undertakings need, whereas light is inimical to them. Besides, as Autocleides emphasized in his *Commentaries*, it was normal to watch out for solar and lunar phenomena for only three days, whereas Nicias persuaded the Athenians to wait for a whole lunar cycle. It was as if he did not see that the moon's pristine brilliance was restored as soon as it passed beyond the region of the sky where the earth acted as a barrier and cast a shadow.*

[24] He ignored almost everything else and spent his time on sacrifices and divination, without moving, until in a combined assault the enemy invested the Athenian fortifications and camp by land, while surrounding and blockading the harbour with their fleet.* As if they did not have enough troubles with the enemy troops in their triremes, teenagers would embark on their fishing-boats or row up in their skiffs and taunt and insult the Athenians. One day, one of these lads, a boy called Heraclides, whose parents were eminent Syracusans, found himself with his boat out ahead of the others, and with an Attic ship in hot pursuit and on the point of catching him. The boy's uncle, a man called Pollichus, was so afraid for his nephew that he rowed out to intercept the Attic ship with the ten triremes under his command, and then his fellow commanders, who were concerned in their turn for Pollichus' safety, launched their ships too. A fierce sea battle took place, which the Syracusans won, inflicting heavy losses on the Athenians. Among the dead was Eurymedon.*

Remaining where they were was no longer acceptable to the Athenians. They loudly implored their commanders to retreat by land—which was the only option left to them, since straight after their victory in the sea battle the Syracusans had built a boom across the channel out of the harbour and closed it off.* However, Nicias refused to take this course of action, on the grounds that the idea of abandoning all their transport ships and nearly 200 triremes was unthinkable. Instead he manned 110 of the triremes—the others had no oars—with the pick of his foot-soldiers and his best javelin-throwers, and stationed the rest of the army along the shore. This involved abandoning the large camp and the fortifications which had connected it with the temple of Heracles,* and this meant that although the Syracusans had not been performing their usual sacrifices to Heracles, their priests and commanders now went up to the temple and carried out the sacrificial rites then, while their triremes were being fitted out and manned.

[25] When the diviners told the Syracusans that the entrails fore-told a glorious victory, provided that they did not initiate the fighting, but remained on the defensive—after all, they said, Heracles won all his battles by defending himself against opponents who attacked him first—they launched their fleet.* The ensuing sea battle was by far the most important and fierce of the whole campaign, and one in which the spectators suffered as much emotional turmoil as those who were taking part in it, since they could survey the whole action and see how rapidly and unexpectedly things chopped and changed. It was difficult to tell which did the Athenians more harm, their own or the enemy's equipment. Their ships were heavy and all crowded together, and they were attacked from all sides by light vessels; they had stones fired at them, which do an equal amount of damage at whatever angle they strike, whereas they were replying with javelins and arrows, whose flight was disturbed by the motion of the waves, so that they did not always land point first. The tactics used by the Syracusans were taught them by the Corinthian captain Ariston, who fought with determination throughout the battle, only to be killed just as the Syracusans began to gain the upper hand.*

The Athenian fleet was so thoroughly routed and destroyed that there was no longer any question of them fleeing the island by sea. When they saw that it was also going to be no easy matter for them to win through to safety by land, they did nothing to stop the enemy dragging away any ships that remained near by, and they did not ask for a truce to collect their dead either, because they were more upset about the prospect of abandoning their sick and wounded, who were right before their eyes, than about leaving their dead unburied. In fact, they felt themselves to be worse off than their dead, because they still had to face more hardship before inevitably meeting the same fate.

[26] The Athenians decided to leave that night. Now, the Syra-cusan people were busy with sacrificial rites and drinking, in celebra-tion not only of the victory but also of the festival of Heracles, so Gylippus despaired of either persuading them or bullying them to get to their feet just then and attack the departing enemy. However, without consulting anyone else, Hermocrates came up with a plan to trick Nicias. He dispatched some of his companions to Nicias, who, pretending that they had been sent by the same group who had in the past frequently been in secret communication with Nicias, advised him not to set out during the night because the Syracusans

had occupied his escape routes in anticipation of the Athenian retreat and were lying in wait for him. Outwitted by Hermocrates, Nicias waited—and so guaranteed that the enemy would really inflict on him the fate he had been tricked into fearing. For the Syracusans set out early the next day, occupied the awkward points of the road, barricaded the fords, demolished the bridges, and posted their cavalry where the ground was smooth and level, so that wherever the Athenians found themselves, they could not move without a battle.*

The Athenians waited the whole of that day and the following night, and then set out with so much weeping and wailing at their lack of supplies and the fact that they were abandoning companions and friends that one might have thought they were leaving their homeland, not a hostile country. For all their misery, however, they were inclined to regard their present troubles as easier to bear than what they foresaw in the future. The camp was filled with terrible scenes, but no sight was more pitiful than Nicias himself, wasted by his illness, and reduced to an inadequate diet of essentials only and to the bare minimum required to maintain his body, when because of his illness he actually needed a lot. Despite his weakness, however, he continued not only to act, but to work at a pace which many of the fit men in the camp could scarcely endure, and it was obvious to everyone that he was not persisting in his tasks for his own sake, or even just because he was clinging to life, but that he was refusing to give up hope, and was doing so for their sakes. While everyone else fell to weeping and complaining out of fear and distress, it was clear that on the occasions when he too had no choice but to succumb to grief, he was driven to it by awareness of the gap between the shame and disgrace to which his expedition had now come and the size and glory of the achievements he had originally hoped for. It was not only the sight of him that moved men to pity; they were even more inclined to regard his lot as ill deserved when they remembered how in his speeches he had warned them not to undertake the expedition. And the realization that someone who stood as high in the gods' favour as Nicias did, and who had performed so many remarkable services for the gods, was faring no better than the worst and most insignificant soldier in the army made them despair of seeing divine intervention on their behalf.*

[27] Nicias, however, tried to show by his tone of voice, his expression, and the way he greeted others, that he was not being got down by the grim situation, and throughout the eight days of the

march, with enemy missiles raining down on them and taking their
toll, he kept the forces who were under his command undefeated, until
Demosthenes and his division of the army were captured, after they
had fallen behind during the fighting and been surrounded on the
country estate belonging to Polyzelus. Demosthenes himself drew
his sword and tried to commit suicide, but the wound was not fatal,
and the enemy soon closed in on him and took him prisoner.* The
Syracusans then rode up to Nicias and told him the news. He sent
horsemen to check and, once he was sure that Demosthenes' half
of the army had indeed been captured, he decided to try to negotiate a truce with Gylippus, whereby the Syracusans would let the
Athenians leave Sicily in exchange for hostages to assure the future
payment of the Syracusans' wartime expenses. The Syracusans, however, not only spurned his offer, but angrily and arrogantly threatened
and insulted the Athenians, and, despite the fact that the Athenians
had by now completely run out of all military necessities, continued
to pelt them with missiles. Nevertheless, Nicias held out through
that night and the following day, by the end of which they had
advanced under the hail of missiles to the Asinarus river. There the
enemy made a concerted attack which drove some of the Athenians
into the waters of the river, while others, without waiting to be forced
in, hurled themselves into the water to quench their thirst; and then
the slaughter† became particularly terrible and savage, with men being
cut down in the river even as they were trying to take a drink.*

Eventually, Nicias hurled himself at Gylippus' feet and said,
'Gylippus, have mercy in your hour of victory! I do not seek pity
for myself, since I have in the past enjoyed fame and prestige for my
glorious achievements, but for my fellow Athenians. Remember that
the fortunes of war are shared by both sides, and that while good fortune was theirs the Athenians did not make it an opportunity to deal
harshly and cruelly with you.' So Nicias spoke, and Gylippus was moved
a little, by his appearance as much as his words. He knew that the
Lacedaemonians had been treated well by him when the terms of the
peace had been arranged, and he thought it would add considerably
to his prestige for him to bring back home alive the commanders who
had opposed him. So he raised Nicias up from the ground, told him
not to worry, and gave orders that the others were to be taken alive.
However, the orders passed slowly through the ranks, and in the end
the slaughtered vastly outnumbered the survivors, even taking into

account the numbers of prisoners who were secretly kept alive by Syracusan soldiers.*

Once the Syracusans had herded together all the prisoners they were prepared to disclose, they festooned the tallest and finest trees on the river bank with the arms and armour they had captured, and then rode into the city, with garlands on their heads and their own horses magnificently adorned, while they had cropped the manes and tails of those they had taken from the enemy.* Thanks to their unparalleled tenacity, and by drawing on the deepest reserves of commitment and courage, they had successfully won the most complete victory in the most remarkable conflict ever fought by Greeks against Greeks.*

[28] A general assembly of the entire Syracusan population and of their allies was convened, at which the popular leader Eurycles proposed, first, that the anniversary of Nicias' capture (that is, the 26th of the month they call Carneius, which the Athenians call Metageitnion*) should be kept as a holiday, on which they should perform sacrifices and have a rest from work, and that the festival should be called the Asinaria, after the river; and, second, that while they should sell the Athenians' slaves and the bulk of their allies, they should confine in the quarries their allies from Sicily and all the actual Athenians except the commanders, who should be put to death.

The Syracusans endorsed Eurycles' proposal. Hermocrates' argument that proper use of victory improved even on victory was noisily shouted down, and when Gylippus asked them to spare the Athenian commanders, so that he could take them alive to Sparta, the Syracusans, grown arrogant in their success, heaped abuse on him. What exacerbated their attitude towards Gylippus was that throughout the war they had found his harshness and the Laconian nature of his leadership hard to bear, and, according to Timaeus, that they had become aware of a certain meanness and rapacity in him—an inherited defect which not only led to his father Cleandridas being banished for accepting bribes, but Gylippus himself was banished in the deepest disgrace for removing thirty of the 1,000 talents which Lysander had sent to Sparta and hiding them in the roof of his house, as an informer revealed. But I have given more details of this affair in my *Life of Lysander*.*

Timaeus claims that Demosthenes and Nicias were not put to death on the orders of the Syracusans, which is what Philistus and Thucydides say,* but that Hermocrates got word to them while the assembly was still in session and that they committed suicide with the connivance of one of their guards. Their bodies, however, he adds, were thrown out by the prison gates and lay there in full view for anyone to see who wanted to. I am told that even now there is in Syracuse a shield on display in a temple, which is said to be the shield of Nicias; it consists of a skilful blend of gold and purple, hammered into an interlocking design.

[29] Most of the Athenians died in the quarries of disease and inadequate food, their daily ration being two cotylae of barley and one of water.* Quite a few of them, however, were sold after having been secretly kept alive, or managed to pass themselves off as slaves, in which case they were sold as slaves after being tattooed with a horse on their foreheads, since there were those who were prepared to endure even this in addition to being sold into slavery.* In due course their tact and modest demeanour stood them in good stead, because they were either given their freedom before long, or they remained with their owners as respected members of the household.

Some of the Athenians were also saved thanks to Euripides. Apparently the Greeks in Sicily were keener on his poetry than any other non-mainland Greeks, and longed to hear it. They would learn by heart the occasional small specimens and samples that reached the island through visitors and one of their great pleasures was to share them with one another. Anyway, the story goes that at the time in question many of the survivors who made it back home greeted Euripides warmly when they met him, and told him either that they had been released from slavery for having taught their owners all they could remember of his verses, or, in some cases, that when they were wandering about after the battle they were given food and water for singing some of his songs.* If this is true, there is no need to doubt another story. Some Caunians were once trying to bring their ship into the harbour to escape some pirate vessels. At first the Syracusans refused to let them in, and actually prevented them from entering. Later, however, they asked whether the Caunians knew any of Euripides' songs. The Caunians said they did, and *then* the Syracusans let them in and helped them beach their ship.*

[30] It is said that the Athenians were inclined to disbelieve the news of the disaster, and particularly because of the way it arrived. Apparently a stranger landed in Piraeus, sat down in a barber's shop, and proceeded to talk about what had happened as if the Athenians

already knew about it. The barber listened to what the stranger had to say, and then, before he could tell anyone else, ran at top speed to the city, rushed up to the archons, and immediately made the news public knowledge. It was, of course, greeted with amazement and consternation. The archons convened an assembly and brought the man in. When he was asked who he had heard the news from, his reply was ambiguous, and people decided that he had made the story up to cause a commotion in the city. He was strapped on to the wheel and tortured for a long time, until messengers arrived with accurate information about the whole catastrophe. That is how difficult it was for them to believe that Nicias had suffered the fate which he had often warned them about.

ALCIBIADES

INTRODUCTION

Few heroes capture the imagination as Alcibiades does: brilliant, handsome, wealthy, he is also mercurial, outrageous, infuriating. He is a prominent figure in Thucydides' history, Aristophanes' comedies, Plato's dialogues, and the speeches of the orators. Loved and hated, admired and feared, his life challenged all of Plutarch's art, and evoked an extraordinary response. For while a figure of history, Alcibiades also represented to Plutarch, as he had for Plato, the outstanding pupil, whose gifts, if properly channelled by philosophy, would produce something close to the philosopher king.

Alcibiades is one of only three Greek Lives which come second in their pair. The Roman parallel, *Coriolanus*, is set in the first half of the fifth century BC, when Rome was still fighting its immediate neighbours in Italy, and divided by continual quarrels between the people and the patricians. Coriolanus is presented as a noble and brave man, but lacking in the kind of Hellenic education which would have smoothed his rough edges and taught him to deal with others. He angrily opposes the populace, is exiled, and returns at the head of an enemy army to besiege his city. His is a simple, powerful character, full of raw emotion: Shakespeare created from the Life his tragedy of the same name.

This Roman Life prepares for the more complex portrait of Alcibiades, Coriolanus' opposite in many ways. Not only was Alcibiades born into the most cultivated city in Greece, and the object of impassioned attention by Socrates, he had the gift of persuasion and charm which made the people love him and laugh at his irregularities—such as bringing a quail into the assembly (10). Where Coriolanus scorned the populace, Alcibiades adapted himself to it, and manipulated it as a flatterer. For Plutarch considers flattery Alcibiades' complete adaptability to those he is with (23 and note), and explicitly states that Alcibiades and Tissaphernes are two flatterers trying to win over each other (24). Aristotle had set the virtue of friendliness as the mean between surliness and flattery (*Nichomachean Ethics* 2. 6): the two men in this pair of lives are examples of the extremes. While both men have great ambition, Coriolanus is a model of harsh rigidity, Alcibiades of variability and change (2). The *Comparison* which follows the two Lives notes Alcibiades' brilliance, flexibility, and affability, but concludes that Coriolanus 'for his temperance and superiority to money should be paralleled to the best and most honest of the Greeks, not certainly to Alcibiades, who was outrageous in this respect and totally contemptuous of what is good' (*Comp.* 5).

The accounts of Alcibiades in Plato's dialogues and the writings of other students of Socrates, and the numerous anecdotes told of him in other writers, allowed Plutarch to divide the Life into two parts. The first (1–16) presents a free-flowing series of achronological anecdotes, loosely set in Alcibiades' younger years, but organized more by topics than time. In order they present his ambition (2), his love affairs and the attempt of Socrates to win him over from self-serving admirers (3–6), his bravery and outrageousness (7–8), and his early involvement in politics (10–15). The final chapter of this section (16) sets the problem for the reader: 'But along with [Alcibiades'] statesmanship, eloquence, pride, and ingenuity went, by contrast, a luxurious lifestyle, over-indulgence in drink and sex, effeminacy of dress . . . and incredible extravagance.' The city loves him and hates him. The misanthrope Timon embraces him, because he will ruin Athens. Then as now, 'people could not make up their minds what to think about Alcibiades'.

The second and longer part follows Alcibiades' political career from the Sicilian Expedition in 415 to his death in Persian territory c.404. He convinces the Athenians, over the objections of Nicias, to attempt the conquest of Sicily (17–18), but then is charged in a double outrage, the mutilation of the herms and the parody of the Mysteries, and is recalled, flees into exile, and is condemned to death (19–22). This success and reversal sets a pattern in Plutarch's narrative which will be regularly repeated. In the following chapters, we see success at Sparta, then rejection and flight (23–4); success with Tissaphernes, later followed by his arrest (24, 27), success with the Athenians on Samos and recall to Athens, and then rejection and exile once more (26–34, 35–7). Plutarch picks up and develops more explicitly the dynamic identified by Thucydides in Alcibiades' relationship with Athens: 'Most people became frightened at a quality in him which was beyond the normal and showed itself both in the lawlessness of his private life and habits and in the spirit in which he acted on all occasions. They thought that he was aiming at becoming a dictator, and so they turned against him' (6. 15. 4, cf. cc. 6 and 16). The instability in Alcibiades' character both echoes and evokes an instability in those who deal with him. In politics as in his earlier love affairs, people wish to enjoy what he can offer them, and thus will put up for a time with his impudence, but they also distrust him and are ready to turn against him. They support his self-aggrandizement only as long as they see it as helping their own. When they suspect it does not, he is brutally rejected. Nevertheless, he can rise to be a great leader, as he does with the fleet on Samos, when for a time he abandons flattery (26). It is finally Critias, the aristocrat who had proposed his recall in 411, supported by the Spartans whom he had helped against Athens, who insists with Lysander in 404 that he must be killed (33, 38). The accounts of his death show again the two sides of his character (39). In the first,

Alcibiades fights bravely against the murderers that his political enemies have sent, and is buried with loving care; in the second he is killed by the angry relatives of a noble woman whom he has seduced.

Both Thucydides and Plato saw Alcibiades as someone who was unable to realize his tremendous potential. Plutarch supplements the historical account of the one and the Socratic and philosophical focus of the other from numerous other sources, some significant, some minor. In Thucydides, Alcibiades first appears at 5. 43. 2 (420 BC) and continues prominent until the work breaks off in 411. Plato treats him especially in *Symposium* 217b–221b, where Alcibiades gives an account of his relation with Socrates, and in *Alcibiades I*, in which Socrates and Alcibiades discuss his ambition and his educational needs. Also important are the speech of the orator Andocides *On the Mysteries*, where he explains his own role in the events of 415, and a speech *Against Alcibiades* falsely attributed to Andocides. Isocrates' speech *On the Team* defending Alcibiades' son is also used. Plutarch's reference to Duris, Theopompus, Ephorus, and Xenophon (32) indicates that he consulted these four fourth-century historians for at least the part of the life not treated by Thucydides, but since they were standard historians, he probably used them for earlier events as well. A four-page passage in the late writer Athenaeus on the luxurious life of Alcibiades, containing several of the anecdotes reported by Plutarch, reminds us that ancient readers often were fascinated by the details of his life (as with others of the rich and powerful) without asking that they be integrated into his political and military career.[1]

Plutarch combines the austere analysis of Thucydides with some of the titillating detail of contemporary invectives, fleshing out a portrait of a complex man interacting on several levels with a complex society. He is at his best in changing the emphasis of an account to shed new light on his subject, as is seen most clearly in the first part of the Life, where he lays the groundwork for his portrait. The presentation of historical events is also subtly adjusted. Thus his version of the ostracism of Hyperbolus (13) differs from that in *Nic*. 11, focusing attention on Alcibiades. This and the tricking of the Spartan ambassadors which follows (14) are given in reverse order, as part of the timeless sequence establishing Alcibiades' character. The first episode defines him by contrasting him with other leaders, the conservative Nicias and the demagogues Phaeax and Hyperbolus, whom he manipulates to protect himself. The second shows him again manipulating Spartans and Nicias, confusing them with half-truths and a

---

[1] Although he cites the Roman author Nepos in some Roman Lives, Plutarch does not cite his *Life of Alcibiades* (nor those of Themistocles and Cimon), no doubt because he considered Greek sources more informed and reliable. Nor does he cite Satyrus, who wrote about Alcibiades, perhaps in his lost *Lives*.

willingness to act contrary to custom and to his own stated purpose. Plutarch employs similar procedures throughout the second half of the Life, as a careful comparison with Thucydides, for example, reveals.

Alcibiades provides many anecdotes and names not in Thucydides. More important, it forces us to think more directly on the role of an individual's choices of goals and lifestyle in judging his political career. It is significant that Socrates plays an important part in the early chapters of the Life, then disappears. Socrates, finding Alcibiades 'in a state of complete promiscuity and presumptuousness', attempted to 'teach him humility and restraint' (6). It became all too apparent that he didn't succeed, and Alcibiades and Athens suffered the consequences.

General:

Hatzfeld, J., *Alcibiade, étude sur l'histoire d'Athènes à la fin du Ve siècle* (Paris: Presses Universitaires de France, 1940). The standard biography.

Kagan D., *The Peace of Nicias and the Sicilian Expedition* (Ithaca, NY: Cornell University Press, 1981). A detailed historical narrative to 413.

—— *The Fall of the Athenian Empire* (Ithaca, NY: Cornell University Press, 1987). A detailed historical narrative, 413–404.

Alcibiades in Thucydides:

Bloedow, E. F., *Alcibiades Reexamined* (*Hermes* Einzelschrift 21, Wiesbaden: Steiner, 1973).

Brunt, P. A., 'Thucydides and Alcibiades', *Revue des études grecques*, 65 (1952), 59–96.

Forde, S., *The Ambition to Rule: Alcibiades and the Politics of Imperialism in Thucydides* (Ithaca, NY, and London: Cornell University Press, 1989).

Special Studies:

Dover, K. J., excursus on the Herms affair, in A. W. Gomme, A. Andrewes, K. J. Dover, *Historical Commentary to Thucydides* (Oxford: Clarendon Press, 1970), iv. 264–88.

Gray, V. J., 'The Value of Diodorus Siculus for the Years 411–386 BC', *Hermes*, 115 (1987), 72–89.

Osborne, R., 'The Erection and Mutilation of the Hermai', *Proceedings of the Cambridge Philological Society*, 31 (1985), 47–73.

Pelling, C. B. R., 'Plutarch and Thucydides', in P. A. Stadter (ed.), *Plutarch and the Historical Tradition* (London: Routledge, 1992), 10–40.

Russell, D. A., *Plutarch* (London: Duckworth, 1972), c. 7, 'Alcibiades, or the Flatterer: an Analysis', 117–29.

—— 'Plutarch, *Alcibiades* 1–16', in B. Scardigli (ed.), *Essays on Plutarch's Lives* (Oxford: Clarendon Press, 1995), 191–207 (repr. of *Proceedings of the Cambridge Philological Society*, 12 (1966), 37–47).

ALCIBIADES

[1] Alcibiades' family-line is supposed to have been founded by Eurysaces the son of Ajax, and on his mother's side he was an Alcmaeonid, since his mother was Deinomache the daughter of Megacles. His father, Cleinias, was famous for the part he played in the sea battle at Artemisium in a trireme he had equipped at his own expense, and died later at Coronea in a battle against the Boeotians. Pericles and Ariphron, the sons of Xanthippus, who were closely related to Alcibiades, then became his guardians.*

It is said that his fame is due in no small part to the fact that Socrates befriended him and was kindly disposed towards him, and this does seem to be true. After all, Nicias, Demosthenes, Lamachus, Phormio, Thrasybulus, and Theramenes were Alcibiades' contemporaries and were famous at the time, but there is no trace even of the names of any of their mothers. Where Alcibiades is concerned, however, we know the names not only of his mother, but also of his wet-nurse (a Laconian woman called Amycla) and his tutor (Zopyrus). Antisthenes has recorded the first name, Plato the second.*

As for Alcibiades' good looks, perhaps all that needs to be said is that they bloomed in his childhood, in his youth, and when he was grown up too; however old he was and whatever phase of physical growth he was at, the attractiveness and charm afforded him by his good looks never left him. Euripides' notion that anyone beautiful remains beautiful in their autumn is not universally true, but Alcibiades is one of the few people to whom it does apply, because of his natural beauty and physical perfection. Even his lisp suited his voice, it is said, and made his conversation charmingly persuasive. Aristophanes also mentions this lisp of his, in the passage where he makes fun of Theorus by saying:

A. Then Alcibiades said to me in his lisping voice:
   'Look at Theolus in a laven's head! What a thing to blandish!'
B. Yes, Theorus certainly blandishes! Alcibiades and his lisp have got that right!*

And when Archippus is making fun of Alcibiades' son he says, 'He wants people to think he's exactly like his father, so he minces along with his cloak trailing behind him, tilts his head to one side and speaks with a pronounced lisp.'

[2] In later life his character became noticeably very inconsistent and changeable, which is perhaps not surprising given the importance of the enterprises he was engaged on and the ups and downs of his fortunes. He had a highly passionate nature, and his most powerful motivation was the desire to compete, and to come first. Some of his childhood sayings make this clear. Once, for instance, he was hard pressed at wrestling and was in danger of being thrown. In order to prevent this happening, he shifted the grip of the boy who was giving him a hard time to within reach of his mouth and was on the point of biting right through his arms. The other boy let go of him and said, 'You bite like a woman, Alcibiades.' 'No, I don't,' Alcibiades replied. 'I bite like a lion.'

While he was still a small boy, he was playing dice in an alley and, just as it was his turn to throw, a cart laden with goods approached. The first thing he tried was to tell the driver of the pair of oxen to wait, because his throw was about to land in the path of the cart. The rude driver did not listen, however, but continued driving the cart along. All the other boys got out of the way, but Alcibiades threw himself face down in front of the oxen, stretched himself out on the ground, and told the driver to carry on if he wanted to. Faced with this situation, the man was frightened and reined in his oxen, while the shocked spectators called out and ran in a group towards Alcibiades.

During his school days, he was generally quite good at obeying his teachers, but he refused to learn the pipes on the grounds that it was not appropriate for a person of noble and free birth.* He argued that there was no disfigurement and distortion of the appearance proper to a free man in wielding a plectrum and playing the lyre, but that when a person set pipes to his mouth and started to blow even his close friends would find it pretty difficult to recognize his features. Besides, he said, the lyre can accompany the voice and singing of its player, whereas the pipes muzzle and obstruct a person and rob him of his ability to express himself in words. 'So let's leave the pipes to the children of Thebans,' he said, 'because they don't know how to make conversation. As for us Athenians, however, our fathers tell us that Athena is the founder of our city and Apollo is our patron— and she discarded the pipes, while he flayed the piper!'* With this combination of light-hearted tone and serious intent Alcibiades got not only himself off learning the pipes, but his fellow pupils too, because they soon heard that Alcibiades detested pipe-playing and ridiculed anyone who was learning to play them, and had good reasons for doing so. The upshot was that pipe-playing was dropped from the list of subjects studied by free men and was held in complete contempt.

[3] In an invective, Antiphon has recorded a number of uncomplimentary stories about Alcibiades,* one of which is that, during his teens, he ran away from home to one of his lovers, a man called Democrates. Ariphron wanted to have him publicly pronounced a missing person, but Pericles stopped him by saying, 'If he's dead, the public announcement will bring his discovery forward only one day; but if he's safe and sound, it will damage him for the rest of his life.' Another story Antiphon tells is that once, in Sibyrtius' wrestling-ground, Alcibiades hit one of his servants with a piece of wood and killed him. But we should probably discount these stories, since the person telling them admits that it is his enmity towards Alcibiades which prompts him to retail uncomplimentary facts about him.

[4] Soon a large number of high-born men began to gather around him and follow him around. Most of them made no secret of the fact that they were cultivating him because they had been overwhelmed by his dazzling youthful charms. However, the fact that Socrates was in love with him strongly suggests that the boy was endowed with a natural aptitude for virtue.* Socrates saw Alcibiades' physical good looks as the brilliant external manifestation of this excellence, and he worried about the boy's wealth and social standing, and about the fact that masses of people from Athens and from both allied and other cities abroad were employing flattery and favouritism to pre-empt his affections. So Socrates set out to protect him against these influences; he could not just stand by and watch a blossoming tree wastefully destroy its own fruit. For fortune has surrounded and enclosed no one so thoroughly with the so-called good things of life that he cannot be pierced by the shafts of philosophy and reached by the stinging candour of reasoned argument.* And Alcibiades was no exception. Although he had been spoiled all his life, and although those whose only reason for being in his company was to indulge him tried to stop him listening to anyone who might correct him and discipline him, nevertheless his innate excellence led him to recognize Socrates, and

he shunned his rich and eminent lovers in favour of associating with Socrates. He soon became close to Socrates and heard arguments from a lover who was not hunting after unmanly pleasure and was not begging him for kisses and caresses, but was trying to expose the unsoundness of his mind and was harrying his vain and foolish pride. And then 'he crouched down in fear, like a defeated cock, with wing aslant',* and he believed that Socrates' mission really was a way of carrying out the gods' wishes by looking after young men and keeping them free from corruption.* He began to despise himself and admire Socrates; he began to value Socrates' kindness and feel humble because of his goodness. And so, without realizing it, he gained (to borrow Plato's phrase) 'a counter-love which is a reflection of love given', and then everyone was astonished to see that, while he ate and exercised with Socrates, and shared his tent on campaigns, he was cruel and intractable to the rest of his lovers.* In fact, he occasionally behaved downright imperiously with them, as he did with Anytus the son of Anthemion.*

Anytus was a lover of Alcibiades. He was having some guest-friends round for dinner and he invited Alcibiades too, but he refused the invitation. Instead, he got drunk at home with some friends and then they all went in a drunken crowd to Anytus' house. Alcibiades stood in the doorway of the dining-room, and when he noticed that the tables were laden with silver and gold cups, he ordered his servants to take half of them and carry them back to his house. Then he went away, without even bothering to come into the room. Anytus' guests angrily accused Alcibiades of treating him in a disrespectful and high-handed manner, but Anytus replied, 'No, he behaved with moderation and kindness. He could have taken all the cups, but he's left us half of them.'*

[5] He treated all his other lovers the same way as well, with the single exception of a resident alien.* The story goes that this man, who was not well off, sold everything he owned, brought Alcibiades the sum he realized, which was 100 staters, and begged him to accept it. Alcibiades laughed with delight at what the man had done and invited him to dinner. After giving him an excellent meal and treating him with kindness, he returned his money and ordered him to take part the next day in the auction for the right to collect the public taxes, and to outbid everyone else.* The man protested that this would cost a great many talents, but Alcibiades, who in fact held a

private grudge against the tax-farmers, threatened to thrash him if he refused to do it. So the next day the resident alien went to the city square and bid an extra talent. When the tax-farmers gathered angrily around him and told him to name his guarantor, expecting him not to have one, the man began to back down in consternation—until Alcibiades, who was standing some way off, said to the archons, 'Put my name down. He's a friend of mine. I'll be his guarantor.' This utterly confounded all the tax-farmers, who generally used the income from the second set of taxes to pay off the debt owed for the first, and therefore seemed to be completely stuck. So they offered the man money and begged him to withdraw his bid, but Alcibiades got him to hold out for a talent, and it was only when they offered him a talent that he told him to take the money and withdraw. So much for the story of how he helped *this* man, at any rate.*

[6] However, against all the odds and despite the number and importance of his rivals, Socrates with his love did tend to subdue Alcibiades, who had sufficient innate excellence for Socrates' arguments to get through to him, wrench his heart, and start the tears flowing. But he also sometimes surrendered to his flatterers and all the delights they held out, and then he would give Socrates the slip and be hunted down, for all the world like a runaway slave, because Socrates was the only one of his lovers he respected and feared, while he had nothing but contempt for the rest. Cleanthes used to say that although he used to take his beloved by the ears and subdue him, the boy's body offered his rivals a great many grips which he refused to touch, meaning his stomach, genitals, and throat.* And Alcibiades was certainly liable to give in to the temptations of pleasure, as is also suggested by the 'lawlessness in respect of his bodily regimen' which Thucydides attributes to him.* Nevertheless, it was actually by pandering to his ambitious longing for recognition that his corrupters set him prematurely on the road of high endeavour; they convinced him that as soon as he took up politics, he would not merely eclipse all the other military commanders and popular leaders, but would gain more power and prestige among the Greeks than even Pericles enjoyed. Just as iron, then, is softened in the fire, but is hardened again by cold and reconstitutes its own compact nature, so time and again Socrates took him back in a state of complete promiscuity and presumptuousness, and by force of argument would pull him together and teach him humility and restraint, by showing him how great his flaws were and how far he was from virtue.*

[7] Once, when he was scarcely more than a boy, he went up to a teacher and asked for a book of Homer. When the man said that he had nothing by Homer, Alcibiades punched him and walked on by. Another teacher said that he had a Homer corrected by himself. 'What!' exclaimed Alcibiades. 'You're teaching reading and writing, when you're capable of correcting Homer? Why aren't you teaching young men?'* He once went to Pericles' house, because he wanted a meeting with him, but was told that he was busy trying to work out how to give the Athenian people an account of his term of office. 'What!' he exclaimed. 'Wouldn't it be better for him to try to work out how *not* to give such an account?'*

During the campaign against Potidaea, when he was still a young adult, he was assigned Socrates as his tent-mate and companion on the battlefield. A fierce engagement took place in which both men displayed great bravery, and when Alcibiades fell wounded, Socrates stood over him, kept the enemy at bay, and manifestly, in plain view of everyone, saved him along with his arms and armour. By all rights, then, the prize for valour should have gone to Socrates, but because of his high rank in society the commanders were obviously very eager for Alcibiades to have the glory. Wanting to increase Alcibiades' ambitious determination to succeed, at least where noble pursuits were concerned, Socrates took the lead in testifying to the lad's bravery and in insisting that they award him the garland and the suit of armour.* Again, during the Athenian retreat at the battle of Delium, Alcibiades spotted Socrates pulling back with a few comrades, and despite the fact that he was on horseback while Socrates was on foot, he refused to ride on by, but escorted him and defended him on all sides, although the enemy were harassing the Athenians and killing a lot of them. But this happened when he was older.*

[8] Hipponicus, the father of Callias, was, thanks to his wealth and lineage, a well-known and influential man, but Alcibiades once punched him without having any real reason such as anger or a quarrel to do so, but just for fun, because he had made a bet with his friends that he would. This preposterous action became the talk of the town, and everyone of course shared the common feeling of outrage, but early the next day Alcibiades went to Hipponicus' house and knocked on the door. Once he had gained admission to his presence, he took off his cloak, exposing his body, and told Hipponicus to thrash him in punishment. But Hipponicus calmed down and forgave him, and later let him marry his daughter Hipparete.*

However, some authors say that, rather than Hipponicus, it was
his son Callias who gave Hipparete to Alcibiades, with a dowry of ten
talents, and that Alcibiades subsequently extracted a further ten talents from Callias after Hipparete had given birth to a child, claiming
that this was what they had agreed, if children were born. Callias was
so afraid of Alcibiades' intriguing that he stood up before the people of
Athens and offered to bequeath his money and property to them in
the event of his dying without offspring.* Hipparete was a well-behaved
and affectionate wife, but the marriage became unbearable to her
because of Alcibiades' liaisons with both foreign and native Athenian
courtesans, and she moved out of the house and went to live with her
brother. This did not worry Alcibiades, who just continued to treat
her with disrespect. Hipparete had to lodge the petition for divorce
with the archon in her own person, rather than through proxies.
But when she arrived to see to this business as the law required,
Alcibiades came up, grabbed hold of her, and took her back home with
him—and although he passed right through the city square, no one
dared to oppose him or take her away from him.* She stayed with
him, however, until her death, which happened a short while later,
while Alcibiades was on a voyage to Ephesus. This violent behaviour
of his did not really strike people as showing scant regard for the laws
or as being harsh, because in all probability the law has the wife who
wants a divorce put in a public appearance in person precisely to give
the husband a chance of meeting her and restraining her.*

[9] He had a remarkably large and attractive dog, which had cost
him seventy minas;* its tail was particularly fine, but he cut it off.
When his close friends told him off for this and warned him that everyone was laying into him and saying bad things about him because of
the dog, he laughed and said, 'That's exactly what I wanted to happen. I'm perfectly happy for the Athenians to be chattering about this:
it will stop them saying anything worse about me.'

[10] His first entry into public life was apparently connected with
a donation he made to the state, rather than being part of a deliberate plan. He happened to be passing when a loud noise came from
the Athenian people in the Assembly, and he asked what the reason
for it was; on being told that someone had donated some money, he
went forward and donated some himself. The Athenians were so
pleased that they applauded and shouted out loud—but Alcibiades
had forgotten about a quail he was carrying in his cloak. The bird

took fright and escaped, which made the Athenians shout even louder. Lots of people stood up and joined in trying to catch the bird, but it was Antiochus the helmsman who caught it and gave it back, which endeared him to Alcibiades a great deal.*

Although great doors to political life were opened to him by his birth, wealth, and courage in battle, and although he had an extensive network of friends and family, more than anything else he expected the support of the common people to be won by his pleasing rhetorical style. That he was a capable orator is vouched for not only by the comic poets, but by the most capable orator of all, who remarks, in his speech *Against Midias*, on various of Alcibiades' features, including his great skill at speaking.* However, if Theophrastus is to be trusted (and he is the most learned and studious of the philosophers), Alcibiades was particularly good at grasping and understanding the essential points of an issue, but then tried to find not only the perfect argument, but also the perfect words and phrases with which to express himself, and since a large vocabulary was not one of his gifts, he often used to hesitate, fall silent in the middle of a speech, and interrupt the flow, while searching for an elusive expression, before picking up the threads again and proceeding with caution.

[11] Everyone heard about his horse farms; they were famous not just in themselves, but also for the number of chariots they supported. For no one else—no king, let alone any other private citizen—had ever entered seven chariots in the Olympic Games. He was the only one to have done so, and the fact that he came first, second, and fourth (or third, according to Euripides—it is Thucydides who says fourth) means that he gained more, in terms of distinction and renown, than anyone can ever have hoped to have achieved in these games.* Euripides' ode goes as follows:

> I am full of admiration for you, Cleinias' son.
> Victory is fair, but the fairest victory of all,
> And never before won by any Greek,
> Is to take the first three places in the chariot-race,
> And to step down unwearied, crowned with the olive
> Of Zeus, to become a subject for the town-crier.*†

[12] Moreover, the splendour of the occasion was highlighted further by the competitiveness of various communities. The Ephesians erected a magnificently decorated tent for him, the town of Chios

provided fodder for his horses and sacrificial animals galore, the Lesbians gave him wine and everything else he would need for the lavish entertainment of large numbers of guests.* However, his notorious determination to succeed did lead to a malicious rumour, or possibly a vindictive act on his part, which was talked about even more than his successes. The story goes that there was in Athens a man called Diomedes,* a man of some distinction and a friend of Alcibiades, who wanted to win a victory at Olympia; he heard that the Argives had a publicly owned chariot and, knowing that Alcibiades had a lot of influence and friends in Argos, he persuaded him to buy it. Having bought it, however, Alcibiades had it registered for the games in his own name, and simply ignored Diomedes, who furiously called on gods and men to witness how he was being treated. It looks as though the business led to a lawsuit: Isocrates has written a speech *On the Team of Horses* in defence of Alcibiades' son, in which the plaintiff is Tisias, not Diomedes.

[13] No sooner had he embarked on a political career than he hum- iliated all the other popular leaders and found himself in competition with Phaeax the son of Erasistratus and Nicias the son of Niceratus —and this while he was still a young adult.* Nicias was already quite elderly and had the reputation of being an extremely fine military com- mander, but Phaeax was, like himself, just beginning to win support at the time, and though he came from a distinguished family, he was basically Alcibiades' inferior, especially when it came to delivering speeches. He had the reputation of being an affable and persuasive person in private conversation, but incapable of winning contests in public. He had, in Eupolis' words, 'an unrivalled gift of the gab, but not of speaking'. There is actually extant a speech of Phaeax *Against Alcibiades* which contains, among other things, the assertion that Alcibiades used all the many gold and silver ceremonial utensils owned by the city in his daily life as if they were his own.*

There was a man called Hyperbolus of the deme Perithoedae, also mentioned by Thucydides as a man of little worth,* whom all the comic poets without exception constantly ridiculed and made fun of in their productions. However, he had such contempt for the views of others that his bad reputation left him unmoved and unconcerned—an atti- tude that some call courageous adventurousness, though it is actually empty-headed effrontery. No one liked him, but the common people often made use of him when they wanted to defame and harass those with high social status. Anyway, at the time in question, at Hyperbolus' instigation, the Athenians were about to wield their vote in an ostracism; this was a measure, designed to placate their envy rather than any possible fear, they periodically employed to curb the most outstandingly popular and powerful man in the city and send him into exile. Once it became clear that there were three possible candidates, one of whom would suffer the effects of the ostracism vote, Alcibiades combined the disparate factions and, after holding talks with Nicias, arranged things so that the ostracism backfired on to Hyperbolus. Some say, however, that it was Phaeax, not Nicias, with whom Alcibiades held talks, and that it was after gaining the support of Phaeax's party that he got Hyperbolus banished. Hyperbolus could hardly have anticipated being banished, because this form of punishment had never before fallen on anyone unimportant and obscure, as Plato the comic poet also implies when he says, after mentioning Hyperbolus:

> And yet he suffered no less than his conduct deserved,
> But more than he and his tattoos deserved,
> For ostracism was not invented for the likes of him.

However, I have written down at greater length elsewhere the results of my research into this business.*

[14] The admiration Nicias won from Athens' enemies irritated Alcibiades just as much as the respect paid him by his fellow citizens. For although Alcibiades was the Lacedaemonian representative in Athens and had looked after the interests of the men captured at Pylos, Nicias was chiefly responsible for the Lacedaemonians obtaining peace and recovering the prisoners, and so the Lacedaemonians felt a great deal of affection for him.* Moreover, the Greeks used to say that it was Pericles who had brought them into conflict and Nicias who had put an end to the war; in fact the most common name for the peace was 'the Peace of Nicias'. All this made Alcibiades exceedingly irritated and he spitefully began to try to find ways to undermine the peace treaty.

First, because he was aware that the Argives loathed and feared the Spartiates and were looking for an escape-route, he secretly led them to hope for an alliance with Athens, and the messages he sent and talks he held with the leading democrats of the city motivated them to put an end to their attitude of fear and submission to the

Lacedaemonians, and instead to look expectantly to the Athenians, who were close to changing their minds and abandoning the peace.

Second, when the Athenians were angry at the Lacedaemonians for entering into an alliance with the Boeotians and for returning Panactum to Athens with its fortifications demolished rather than intact, Alcibiades proceeded to exacerbate things even more. He was constantly jeering at Nicias and accusing him, with considerable plausibility, of having been reluctant to capture the enemy troops trapped on Sphacteria himself during his period of military command, and then, once others had done so, of having set them free and returned them as a favour to the Spartans; as if that were not enough, he said, Nicias, out of loyalty to the Lacedaemonians, did nothing to dissuade them from forming a coalition with the Boeotians or even the Corinthians, and yet whenever anyone in Greece wanted to get on good terms with the Athenians and enter into an alliance with them, he made it hard for them to do so, unless the Lacedaemonians approved.*

These attacks did Nicias considerable harm, but just then the tide of fortune seemed to turn in his favour and a delegation arrived from Lacedaemon with a set of reasonable proposals from the government there and with, as they claimed, full powers to negotiate any solution which was fair and which would help to bring the two sides together. The Council gave them a favourable hearing, and the next day the people were due to convene in Assembly, but Alcibiades, who was afraid of what might happen there, arranged a meeting between himself and the Lacedaemonian delegates. At this meeting he said, 'What's up with you Spartiates? How can you be so blind? You must appreciate that while it is the Council's way to be lenient and kind whenever a delegation appears before it, the Athenian people have such high pretensions and ambitions that if you tell them you have come here as a plenipotentiary delegation, they'll coldly tell you what they want to happen, and pressure you until things go their way. You really shouldn't be so naive. If you want to make the Athenians easy to deal with, and if you'd rather not be forced to adopt unwelcome terms, you must pretend that you don't have full powers of negotiation, and discuss the rights and wrongs of the situation with them. And I'll co-operate with you, as a favour to the Lacedaemonians.' And so, once he had given them pledges in earnest of the truth of his words, he won them away from Nicias; they trusted him completely and were deeply impressed with his ingenuity and resourcefulness, which they judged to be quite extraordinary.

The next day the people convened and the delegates were introduced. Alcibiades asked them, with perfect politeness, what their status was as a delegation, and they replied that they were not plenipotentiary. Alcibiades immediately proceeded to lay into them in a loud and angry tone of voice, as if he were the victim, not the perpetrator of sharp practice. He called them untrustworthy liars and described their mission and their words as spurious. The members of the Council were indignant, the assembled people were furious, and Nicias was astounded and embarrassed at the delegates' change of tack, since he had no idea of the fraudulent deception that had taken place.*

[15] Now that the Lacedaemonian initiative had been repulsed in this way, and once he had been appointed to the post of military commander, Alcibiades lost no time in concluding an alliance between Athens and Argos, Mantinea, and Elis.* Although no one approved of the means he used to accomplish this, it was a significant achievement, since he created divisions and turmoil throughout almost all the Peloponnese, made it possible for vast numbers of men to muster and all face the Lacedaemonians at Mantinea on a single day, and ensured that the battle, along with its threat to Athens, took place as far away from Athens as it could, in a place where victory brought the Lacedaemonians no significant additional advantage, and where, had they been defeated, the position of Lacedaemon would have been precarious.*

Straight after the battle, the thousand-strong oligarchy at Argos set about overthrowing the democracy there and making the city subject to the Lacedaemonians, and the dissolution of the democracy was completed with the arrival of Lacedaemonian troops. But the common people armed themselves and gained the upper hand again. Alcibiades went to them, and once he had helped make sure that their victory was secure, he persuaded them to run their long walls down to the sea and so to make their city wholly dependent on Athenian power by having it joined to the sea. He even brought builders and masons from Athens, and he displayed such wholehearted commitment to their cause that he won as much gratitude and power for himself as he did for his state.*

The same thing happened at Patrae: he also persuaded the people there to join their town to the sea with long walls. When someone warned them that the Athenians would swallow them up, Alcibiades replied, 'That may be so, but they'll do so little by little, starting with the feet, whereas the Lacedaemonians will gulp you down head first and all at once!'*

However, he also advised the Athenians to appreciate the importance of the land—that is, to confirm by their actual practice the pledge regularly undertaken by Athenian young men on the threshold of adulthood in the sanctuary of Agraulus, who swear to regard wheat, barley, the vine, the fig-tree, and the olive as the boundaries of Attica, and so are trained to treat all arable, fertile land as their own.*

[16] But along with his statesmanship, eloquence, pride, and ingenuity went, by contrast, a luxurious lifestyle, over-indulgence in drink and sex, effeminacy of dress—he would trail his purple-dyed clothing through the city square—and incredible extravagance. For instance, he had the decks of his triremes altered so that he could lay his bedclothes on cords rather than on bare boards and so have a softer bed to sleep on, and he had a shield made, with golden tracery, which bore, instead of an ancestral device, an image of Eros holding a thunderbolt. Faced with all these aspects of his behaviour, the notable men of Athens combined feelings of abhorrence and disgust with fear of his haughty and lawless attitude, which struck them as tyrannical in its excessiveness.* As for the common people, their feelings towards him have been well summed up by Aristophanes in the following line:

They miss him, hate him, want him to be with them.

And again, but this time more forcefully because of the metaphor:

It's best not to keep a lion in the city,
But if you do, pander to his moods.*

And in fact the donations he made, the choruses he financed, the superlative extravaganzas he put on for the city,* the fame of his ancestors, his eloquence, his physical good looks and fitness, and his experience and prowess in war made the people of Athens tolerate and make allowances for everything else about him. They were constantly finding blatant euphemisms for his faults and attributing them to youthful high spirits and his determination to succeed. For instance, there was the time when he kept the artist Agatharchus locked up until

he had decorated his house with paintings, when he gave him a present and let him go; and once he took a stick to a rival impresario
called Taureas because he was so determined to win the competition;
or again, he picked a woman from among the Melian prisoners of
war, installed her in his house, and brought up a child she bore him.
They described this as an act of kindness, but the problem was that
he was more responsible than anyone for the slaughter of all the adult
male inhabitants of Melos, since he had spoken out in support of the
decree.*

When Aristophon depicted a personified Nemea, seated and holding Alcibiades in her arms, people were delighted and flocked to see
the painting, but the older members of society found this abhorrent
too, on the grounds that it was the kind of thing a tyrant might do
and showed scant regard for custom and the laws. The general feeling also was that Archestratus had hit the mark when he said that
Greece could not have endured two Alcibiadeses.*

Once Timon the misanthrope met Alcibiades returning flushed with
success from the Assembly, with a crowd of people around him.
Unusually, he did not pass him by or get out of the way, as he did
with other people, but walked right up to him, greeted him, and said,
'Keep up the good work, young man! The more power you get, the
more harm you'll do this lot.'* The basic reaction to this was either
laughter or abuse, but Timon's words did make others really stop and
think. This shows how, due to his innate inconsistency, people could
not make up their minds what to think about Alcibiades.

[17] Even during Pericles' lifetime, the Athenians had coveted Sicily,
and after his death they tried to gain control of it. From time to time
they sent what they described as 'missions to relieve and reinforce
the victims of Syracusan aggression', which actually constituted a process of laying stepping-stones for the larger expedition.* But the person who fanned this smouldering desire of theirs into full flame and
convinced them not to set about the task gradually or by halves, but
to send out a large fleet and overrun the island, was Alcibiades. But
however high he raised the common people's hopes, he himself was
aiming even higher: he regarded Sicily as the initial objective in a campaign which would fulfil his aspirations, not, as everyone else did, as
an end in itself. So while Nicias was trying to persuade the Athenian
people not to go, on the grounds that the capture of Syracuse would
prove too much for them, Alcibiades was dreaming of Carthage and

Libya, and then, after the annexation of these places, of taking over
Italy and the Peloponnese. He tended to think of Sicily as little more
than an entry-point into the war. The young men of the city were
immediately carried away by these hopes of his, while their elders filled
their ears with plenty of wonderful tales about the expedition; the
upshot was that in the wrestling-schools and alcoves people could commonly be seen sitting and mapping out the shape of Sicily and the
position of Libya and Carthage.*

However, Socrates the philosopher and Meton the astronomer are
said to have been pessimistic about the outcome of this expedition
for Athens. Socrates was probably forewarned by his usual divine sign,
and Meton—whose apprehension about the future was prompted either
by his calculations or by the results of divination of some kind—
pretended to have gone mad, grabbed a blazing torch, and came close
to setting fire to his own house. Some say that Meton's insanity was
not faked, and that he did burn down his house one night, and then
came before the people the next day and pleaded with them, in view
of the great calamity that had befallen him, to release his son from
serving on the expedition. At any rate, he did succeed in duping his
fellow citizens and getting his way.*

[18] Nicias was reluctantly elected military commander; what put
him off the position above all was the colleague he was faced with.
For the Athenians imagined that the war would go better for them
if they sent Alcibiades on his way diluted, and blended his rashness
with Nicias' caution. The third commander was Lamachus, a man
who despite his advanced years had the reputation of being just as
fiery and fond of taking military risks as Alcibiades. Nicias seized
the opportunity presented by the debate about the size and details
of the equipment to try once again to raise objections and stop the
war, but Alcibiades' responses carried the day, and an orator called
Demostratus argued for a decree he proposed, to the effect that the
military commanders should have unconditional powers to decide about
the equipment and about the whole war.*

After the people had voted this decree into existence, and just when
the fleet was poised and ready to set sail, a number of unfortunate
things happened, including the festival of Adonis, which fell at that
time. All over the city the women were preparing statuettes of the
god for burial in a way which closely resembled the treatment of human
corpses, and were beating their breasts, just as they would at a funeral,

and chanting dirges. Then there was the mutilation of the herms, when in the course of a single night every herm had its facial extremities broken off; this disturbed a great many people, even if they were normally inclined to be indifferent to such things.* There was a suggestion that the Corinthians had done it—Syracuse being a Corinthian colony—in the hope that the portent might get the Athenians to delay or even abandon all thoughts of the war, but the common people were unaffected either by this argument or by another which said that there was nothing ominous about the affair at all, but that it was just the kind of thing that tends to happen under the influence of undiluted wine, when undisciplined young men get carried away beyond fun and into violence. Instead, they reacted with anger and fear to what had happened, and imagined that it was a daring move on the part of a band of conspirators with far-reaching objectives, and they conducted a relentless investigation into every possibility, with both the Council and the Assembly meeting repeatedly within the space of a few days to discuss the matter.

[19] Meanwhile, the popular leader Androcles produced some slaves and resident aliens who accused Alcibiades and a group of his friends of mutilating other statues, and of parodying the Mysteries when drunk. They said that the Herald was played by someone called Theodorus, the Torch-bearer by Poulytion, the High Priest by Alcibiades, and that other friends of his who were there had acted as Watchers and been nominated as Initiates.* These were the charges contained in the impeachment brought by Thessalus the son of Cimon, which accused Alcibiades of impiety towards the two goddesses.* The people of Athens were bitterly angry with Alcibiades, and Androcles, who was one of Alcibiades' main enemies, fanned the flames of their anger. At first Alcibiades was concerned, but then he realized that he had the loyalty of all the soldiers and sailors on the ships destined for Sicily, and when he heard the 1,000-strong contingent of Argive and Mantinean hoplites openly declaring that if it were not for Alcibiades they would not be undertaking this long overseas expedition, and that if anyone were to treat him unfairly they would not hesitate to leave, he felt more positive about the future and he seized the opportunity to defend himself.* As a result, it was the turn of his enemies to be discouraged; they were afraid that the Athenians would let the fact that they needed Alcibiades take the edge off their anger when it came to judging him.

They therefore devised a plan whereby certain speakers who were not known to be hostile to Alcibiades, but who hated him just as much as those who openly professed their enmity, would stand up in the Assembly and argue that it was absurd for someone who had been put in absolute command of such an enormous force, and whose army and allies were all assembled, to let the critical moment pass by while they were casting lots for places on the jury and filling the water-clocks.* 'No,' they said, 'let him sail now, and we wish him all the best. But when the war has been brought to a successful conclusion, let him return and defend himself. The laws won't change between then and now.'

Alcibiades was well aware of the malice behind this proposed delay, so he came forward and argued that it would be terrible for him to be sent off at the head of such an enormous force, leaving unresolved accusations and slanders behind him; he said that if he could not secure an acquittal he ought to be put to death, but that if he did, if he proved his innocence, he ought to be able to proceed against the enemy without any fear that back home information was being laid against him.*

[20] The Athenians were not convinced by these arguments, however, and ordered him to set sail. So he and his fellow commanders put to sea with a remarkable armada, including just short of 140 triremes, 5,100 heavy-armed troops, and about 1,300 archers, slingers, and light-armed troops.* After they had landed in Italy and captured Rhegium, Alcibiades put forward a strategic plan for the conduct of the campaign, which was opposed by Nicias, but endorsed by Lamachus, and so they sailed to Sicily. In Sicily Alcibiades won Catana over to their side, but achieved nothing else, because he was immediately summoned home by the Athenians to stand trial.*

As I have already said, at first it was just a case of certain vague suspicions and slanders against Alcibiades being aired by slaves and resident aliens, but later, while he was away, his enemies put more effort into their attacks; they linked the violence done to the herms and the business with the Mysteries, and made out that they had both been done by a single group of conspirators whose aim was to overthrow the government. Consequently, anyone who was accused of anything at all connected to these two cases was cast into prison without a trial, and the Athenians became irritated with themselves for failing to pass judgement and come to a verdict about Alcibiades at the time, considering how important the charges were. Meanwhile,

any of Alcibiades' relatives, friends or intimates who fell foul of the
Athenians while they were angry with Alcibiades found them harsher
than usual. Thucydides failed to name the people who denounced
Alcibiades, but according to others they were Diocleides and Teucer.*
One of these sources is the comic poet Phrynichus, who has this to
say in one of his plays:

> A. Precious Hermes, please take care not to fall and hurt yourself,
>   Or you'll give another Diocleides, with mischief on his mind,
>   The chance to spread malicious rumours.
> B. All right, I'll be careful. I've no desire
>   To reward Teucer, that bloodthirsty foreigner!

The information they lodged was, however, totally unreliable and
unsound. When one of the informants was asked how he had recognized the faces of the mutilators of the herms, he replied that he saw
them by the light of the moon—which made his whole story uncon-
vincing, because the crime was committed on the last day of the
month.* Even this, however, although it disturbed anyone with any
intelligence, failed to make the common people feel more lenient when
considering the charges. They simply carried on as they had started,
gaily casting anyone who was denounced into prison.

[21] One of the people who was imprisoned and held in custody to await trial was Andocides the orator, who was a descendant
of Odysseus, according to the historian Hellanicus. Andocides was
generally held to be anti-democratic and in favour of oligarchy, but
the main thing that made him a suspect in the mutilation of the herms
was that the tall herm near his house, which had been erected and
dedicated by the Aegeid tribe, was almost the only one of the few really
conspicuous statues to remain unharmed. That is why to this day it
is known as the Herm of Andocides, which is the name everyone gives
it, despite the contradictory evidence of the inscription it bears.*

It so happened that Andocides became particularly close friends
with one of the people who was in prison with him on the same charge
—a man called Timaeus, who did not have the same social standing
as Andocides, but was exceptionally intelligent and daring. Timaeus
convinced Andocides to turn state's evidence against himself and
a few others. He pointed out that if Andocides confessed he would,
according to the terms of the people's decree, be immune from punishment, whereas no one could ever tell what the verdict was going

to be in a trial, and influential people like him had more to fear than anyone else. Given that the same charge was involved, it was better to tell a lie and save one's life, he argued, than to suffer the ignominy of death; besides, taking the common good into consideration, it was all right to sacrifice a few dubious characters and save a large number of good men from the effects of the people's anger. Andocides was won over by Timaeus' arguments and recommendations; he informed against himself and some others, and while the decree gave him immunity from punishment, all those he named lost their lives, unless they fled into exile. In order to make his story more plausible, Andocides also included among the people he named some of his own slaves.*

The Athenian people were not completely mollified by this, however. On the contrary, now that they had resolved the issue of the mutilators of the herms, they hurled themselves with even more vehemence against Alcibiades; it was as if their anger now had the freedom to express itself more fully. In the end they sent the *Salaminia* to fetch him home, with instructions—sensible instructions, in this case—not to use physical violence or lay hands on him, but just to ask him, as reasonably as they could, to come with them to stand trial and to try to convince the Athenian people of his innocence. The last thing they wanted was for the army to get edgy or even mutinous in enemy territory, which Alcibiades could easily have engineered had he chosen to, because the men's morale dropped with his departure.* They anticipated a long, drawn-out, sluggish war under Nicias' leadership, now that the person who stirred things up had been removed. For Lamachus may have been belligerent and brave, but his poverty meant that he lacked standing and authority.*

[22] No sooner had Alcibiades sailed away than he snatched Messana from the Athenians' grasp. There were people there who were on the point of surrendering the city to the Athenians, but Alcibiades knew who they were; he gave unambiguous information about them to the pro-Syracusans in the town, and so made sure that the matter came to nothing. When he reached Thurii, he went ashore and hid himself to escape his pursuers.* Someone recognized him and said, 'Alcibiades, don't you trust your fatherland?' 'Basically, yes,' he replied. 'But where my life is concerned I wouldn't trust even my mother not to mistake a black pebble for a white one when she comes to cast her vote.' And later, when he heard that Athens had condemned him to death, he said, 'I'll show them that I'm alive.'

Here is the text of the impeachment the Athenians brought against him:

Thessalus the son of Cimon, of the deme Laciadae, charges Alcibiades the son of Cleinias, of the deme Scambonidae, of crimes against the two goddesses, in that he did parody the Mysteries and make them the subject of a show put on for friends of his in his house, while dressed in garments resembling those the High Priest wears when he shows the sacred objects, and calling himself the High Priest, Poulytion the Torch-bearer, Theodorus of the deme Phegaea the Herald, and the rest of his friends who were there Initiates and Watchers, contrary to the laws and institutions of the Eumolpidae, the Heralds, and the priests of Eleusis.*

They found him guilty *in absentia*, confiscated his property, and also decreed that he should be publicly cursed by all the priests and priestesses in the city. It is said that Theano, the daughter of Meno, of the deme Agryle, was the only one to object to this decree; she declared that she was a priestess for prayers, not for curses.*

[23] After escaping from Thurii, Alcibiades immediately made his way to the Peloponnese, and spent some time in Argos, with these decrees and verdicts hanging heavily over him. Since he was afraid of his enemies and had completely given up on his native country, he sent a message to Sparta, asking for asylum and promising to render them the kind of service and assistance that would outweigh the harm he had done them before when they were on opposite sides. The Spartiates enthusiastically granted this request and welcomed him in Sparta. The first thing he did, as soon as he arrived, was arouse the Lacedaemonians to action over Syracuse: they had been hesitating, and had put off sending help to the Syracusans, but he got them interested in sending an expeditionary force under Gylippus to crush the Athenian army there. Secondly, he got them to start up the war against the Athenians in Greece. Thirdly, and most importantly, he persuaded them to fortify Decelea, which played a more crucial part than anything else in bringing about the destruction and downfall of Athens.*

At Sparta, in public as well as in private, he became a well-known and much-admired figure. During this period he gained influence over the common people there, and held them spellbound by adopting a Laconian style of life. When they saw him with his hair in need of a close cut, bathing in cold water, accustomed to coarse bread, and supping broth, they seriously doubted whether this was a man who had ever had a cook in his house, or set eyes on a perfumer, or could endure the touch of Milesian wool. The point is that, of the many skills Alcibiades possessed, we hear in particular of one which was a useful tool for captivating men, and that was that he could assimilate and adapt himself to their habits and lifestyles. He could change more abruptly than a chameleon. The only difference between him and a chameleon was that whereas a chameleon apparently finds it totally impossible to assimilate itself to the colour white, whether Alcibiades found himself in the company of good men or bad, there was nothing he could not imitate and no habit he could not acquire. In Sparta he took exercise, lived frugally, and wore a frown on his face; in Ionia he was fastidious, companionable, and easy-living; in Thrace he went in for hard drinking and hard riding; when he was with the satrap Tissaphernes he outdid the Persians, for all their magnificence, with his pomp and extravagance.* It was not that he actually changed personality so readily, or that his character was infinitely mutable, but that when his real self was going to upset the people he was with, he assumed and took refuge in whatever appearance and image was appropriate for them. At any rate, as far as externals were concerned, in Lacedaemon one would have said, ' "You are no son of Achilles, but the man himself," ' a true product of Lycurgan training; but as far as his real feelings and behaviour were concerned, one would have cried, ' "She is the same woman she always was!" '*

For while King Agis was out of the country on campaign, Alcibiades seduced his wife Timaea so thoroughly that not only did she get pregnant with his child, but she did not even deny it. The boy that she gave birth to was called Leotychidas in public, but in private the child's name, as whispered by the mother to her friends and serving-women, was Alcibiades. That is how infatuated the woman was.* As for Alcibiades, he used to say, in his wilful fashion, that it was not defiance or lust that had led him to do it, but rather because he wanted to have his descendants rule over the Lacedaemonians. Plenty of people told Agis what was going on, and as time went by he came to believe them, because there had been an earthquake and he had run in terror out of his wife's bedroom and away from her, and then had not slept with her again for ten months. Since Leotychidas was born at the end of this period, Agis declared that he was no son of his—and that is why Leotychidas was later refused the kingship.*

[24] After the Athenian catastrophe in Sicily the Chians, Lesbians, and Cyzicans all sent delegations at the same time to Sparta with

a view to rebelling against Athens. Although the Boeotians were co-operating with the Lesbians, and Pharnabazus was supporting the Cyzicans, at Alcibiades' instigation the Lacedaemonians chose to help the Chians first.* He even went over there in person. He succeeded in fomenting rebellion throughout almost the whole of Ionia and, through constantly working in conjunction with the Lacedaemonian military commanders, did a great deal of harm to Athenian interests. However, he had an enemy in Agis, whose hostility was due not just to his troubles with his wife, but also to his resentment of the reputation Alcibiades was acquiring for being responsible for almost everything that happened, and certainly for nearly all the successes; and, prompted by their envy, the most influential and ambitious of the other Spartiates had also had enough of Alcibiades. So they prevailed on the authorities in Sparta to send a message to their commanders in Ionia, ordering Alcibiades' death.*

By surreptitious means, Alcibiades received advance warning of what was going on.* Fearing for his life, he continued to co-operate with the Lacedaemonians in all their enterprises, but he made absolutely sure that he kept out of their hands, and for safety's sake he entrusted himself to Tissaphernes, the satrap of the Persian king. Before long there was no one Tissaphernes admired or valued more. The Persian was a devious and malicious man, who felt no qualms about doing wrong, and he was impressed by Alcibiades' versatility and extraordinary ingenuity. No one, whatever his character or temperament, could fail to be touched and captivated by Alcibiades' charisma, if he spent time and lived with him on a daily basis; even those who feared and envied him found themselves enjoying his company and warming to him once they were with him and could actually see him. At any rate, although Tissaphernes felt as savage a hatred of Greeks as any Persian, he was so won over by Alcibiades' blandishments that he outdid him in flattering him back. He declared that the most beautiful walled garden he had, which was graced with lawns and refreshing pools, and dotted with exceptional haunts and places of resort prepared in a manner fit for a king, should be named 'Alcibiades'— and that is the name by which everyone continued to refer to it for a long time.

[25] So Alcibiades abandoned the Spartan cause because they had turned against him and because of the threat posed by Agis, and set about maligning and defaming them to Tissaphernes. He did not want

him to be too ready to help them, and thereby destroy the Athenians, but preferred him to let them have a miserly amount of support, so that they would gradually get into difficulties and be worn down; in this way, he argued, both sides would exhaust each other and fall into the Persian king's hands.* Tissaphernes was easily convinced by this, and made no secret of his admiration and approval of Alcibiades. This had the consequence that Greeks on both sides looked up to him, and, now that they were suffering at his hands, the Athenians also began to regret the decisions they had made in his case. Moreover, Alcibiades too had reasons to be worried and apprehensive: the destruction of Athens might mean that he would fall into the clutches of the Lacedaemonians, who hated him.

Now, at the time in question almost all the Athenian forces were stationed on Samos. They were using the island as a naval base from which to regain rebel states and protect others, and they somehow still contrived to be a match for their enemies at sea. However, they were worried about Tissaphernes and his 150 Phoenician triremes, which were said to be due any day, and whose arrival would spell doom for the city. Alcibiades was aware of these fears, and he sent a secret message to the Athenian leaders on Samos, in which he held out the prospect of gaining Tissaphernes' support for their side. This had nothing to do, he said, with trying to curry favour with the common people, whom he did not trust anyway; he was doing it for the aristocrats, to see if they had what it took to prove their courage, stop the common people lording it over them, take matters into their own hands, and save Athens.

Everyone was very interested in what Alcibiades was saying, except for one of the military commanders, Phrynichus of the deme Deirades, who suspected, quite rightly, that Alcibiades had just as much or little use for an oligarchic government as he did for a democratic one— that he was only looking for some way to return to Athens, and was using complaints against the people as a means of flattering and ingratiating himself with the aristocrats. He therefore spoke out against Alcibiades, but he lost the argument.* Now that his enmity towards Alcibiades was out in the open, he sent a secret message to Astyochus, the commander of the enemy fleet, warning him about Alcibiades and suggesting that he arrest him as a renegade. What he did not know, however, was that this was in fact a case of one traitor talking to another. Astyochus was in awe of Tissaphernes and, seeing that Alcibiades was high in his favour, he informed them both of Phrynichus' message.

Alcibiades lost no time in sending men to Samos to denounce Phrynichus, who, finding all his colleagues united in their fury against him, could see no escape from his predicament and tried to alleviate the problems created by one misdeed by committing another, worse one. He sent another message to Astyochus, in which he told him off for revealing the contents of his first message, and promised to put the Athenian fleet and camp in his hands. But the Athenians came to no harm from Phrynichus' treachery, because Astyochus betrayed him yet again: he told Alcibiades what Phrynichus was up to this time as well.

Phrynichus, however, had expected this and, anticipating a second denunciation from Alcibiades, pre-empted him by telling the Athenians that the enemy were about to send a fleet to attack the island, and advising them to man their ships and fortify their camp. The Athenians were in the middle of doing this when a second letter came from Alcibiades, telling them to keep an eye on Phrynichus, as he was planning to betray their naval base to the enemy. They did not trust this information, and assumed that Alcibiades, with his inside knowledge of the enemy's armament and intentions, was using the letter to discredit Phrynichus by telling lies about him.* Later, however, when one of the border guards called Hermon stabbed Phrynichus to death in the city square with a dagger, in the ensuing trial the Athenians found Phrynichus, although he was dead, guilty of treason, and rewarded Hermon and his accomplices with garlands.*

[26] At the time in question, however, Alcibiades' supporters gained the upper hand on Samos and sent Pisander to Athens to try to bring about a coup; he was to encourage the men of power to overthrow the democracy and form a government, with the argument that only then would Alcibiades bring Tissaphernes over to their side and get him to enter into an alliance with them.* This was how the instigators justified and excused their establishment of the oligarchy, but when they grew strong enough to take control of affairs, the Five Thousand (as they were called, although they were actually Four Hundred) completely ignored Alcibiades. Their war effort was also rather half-hearted, partly because they were not yet sure of their fellow citizens, who had not made up their minds about the change of government, and partly because they thought the Lacedaemonians

would be more lenient towards them, since they always looked favourably upon oligarchies.* The common people in Athens were cowed into a reluctant state of inactivity by the frequency with which those who openly opposed the Four Hundred were put to death, but when the rank and file in Samos heard what was going on in Athens, they were furious and wanted nothing more than to sail for Piraeus without delay. They sent for Alcibiades, put him in supreme command, and urged him to lead them on an expedition to overthrow the tyrants.*

If anyone else had suddenly been raised to power by popular favour, what would he have experienced? What would he have tended to do? He would immediately have thought it his job to do everything he could to please, and nothing to oppose, the people who had just saved him from the life of a wandering fugitive and appointed him to lead and command a mighty fleet and army, with powerful resources. But not Alcibiades. Instead, as befitted a great leader, he resisted their angry impulses and stopped them making a grave mistake. On this occasion, at least, it is undeniable that he proved to be the saviour of the city. For if they had just put to sea and sailed back home, not only would they have enabled their enemies to gain the whole of Ionia, the Hellespont and the Aegean islands without meeting any resistance, but they would also have pitched Athenians against Athenians, and made the city itself a theatre of war. It was thanks to Alcibiades, more than anyone else, that this did not happen. He not only gave convincing reasons for not setting sail in his speeches to the assembled troops, but he also approached people individually, and either pleaded with them or curbed their enthusiasm. He was assisted in this task by Thrasybulus of Steiris, who used to go around with him and bellow out his instructions; apparently, no Athenian had a louder voice.*

Another important thing Alcibiades did, in addition to this, was that he undertook either to bring the Phoenician ships, which the Persian king had dispatched and the Lacedaemonians were expecting, over to the Athenian side, or at least to make sure that they did not join the Lacedaemonians, and promptly set sail from Samos to see to this. The Phoenician ships were sighted off Aspendus, but although it was Tissaphernes who let the Lacedaemonians down by not taking them any further, Alcibiades was credited by both sides with having got them to turn back. The Lacedaemonians were particularly vehement in their accusations, claiming that Alcibiades had told Tissaphernes to stand back and let the Greeks destroy one another. At any rate, it was clear that whichever side was joined by such a large force would completely ruin the other side's chances of gaining control of the sea.*

[27] Later, with Alcibiades' friends wholeheartedly co-operating with the democrats, the Four Hundred were overthrown. The Athenians now wanted Alcibiades to return from exile, and urged him to do so, but he had no desire to come back empty-handed, without having achieved anything, and with his restoration accomplished thanks merely to pity and popularity; he wanted to come back in a blaze of glory. So the first thing he did was set sail with a few ships from Samos and patrol the sea off Cnidos and Cos.* While he was there he heard that the entire Lacedaemonian fleet, under Mindarus the Spartiate, had pulled back into the Hellespont with the Athenians in pursuit, so he quickly set out to help his fellow commanders. As luck would have it, he managed to arrive with his eighteen triremes at the precise moment when both sides had committed their entire naval resources to a battle off Abydos, and had been engaged in a fierce struggle all day, with one side winning here, the other side there. The sight of his ships gave both sides the wrong idea, in the sense that it raised the morale of the Lacedaemonians and disheartened the Athenians, but he lost no time in hoisting the Athenian standard on his flagship and heading straight for those Peloponnesians who had gained the upper hand and were forcing their opponents into retreat. He scattered them and drove them ashore, but continued after them until he rammed and disabled their ships. The crews swam to land, where Pharnabazus with his infantry came to their help and protected the ships stranded along the coast. But in the end the Athenians captured thirty enemy ships, recovered their own, and erected a victory trophy.*

Now, Alcibiades felt a strong competitive urge to take advantage of the outstanding success he had won to show off to Tissaphernes. He supplied himself with tokens of guest-friendship and with gifts, and made his way there at the head of a princely retinue. Things did not turn out as he expected, however. The Lacedaemonians had for a long time been criticizing Tissaphernes, and he had become afraid that the Persian king would find fault with him. Alcibiades' arrival therefore struck him as very opportune: he arrested him and imprisoned him in Sardis, hoping that this offence would serve to dispel the criticisms.*

[28] Thirty days later, however, Alcibiades somehow managed to get hold of a horse and break away from his guards. He escaped to Clazomenae, made things worse for Tissaphernes by spreading the rumour that he had been released by him, and then took a boat to rejoin the Athenian forces. Once he was there, he found out that Mindarus had combined with Pharnabazus, and that they were in Cyzicus. He delivered a stirring speech to the Athenians, telling them that they would now not only have to fight on sea and on land, but even besiege the enemy in his fortresses, because there was no money to pay them unless they won every battle they undertook, whatever kind of warfare it involved. Then he got them to board their ships and brought the fleet in at Proconnesus,* where he gave orders that all fishing-boats were to be kept within their perimeter and closely watched, to stop the enemy having any way of getting advance notice of his approach.

It so happened, also, that there was a sudden heavy rainstorm, and the thunder and darkness helped his plans to go undetected. In fact, he not only took the enemy by surprise, but even the Athenians had become resigned to the prospect of not fighting when he ordered them to board their ships, and they put to sea. After a short while, the darkness cleared, and the Peloponnesian ships could be seen hovering in front of the harbour of Cyzicus. Alcibiades was worried that if they caught sight of the size of his force too early they might have time to take refuge ashore, so he ordered his fellow commanders to sail on at a gentle pace, so that they fell behind, while he took forty ships, let himself be seen, and challenged the enemy to battle. The Peloponnesians were completely taken in by the trick. They sailed out to attack what they took to be a pitifully small number of ships, and before long the two sides were locked in battle. In the middle of the fight the remainder of the Athenian ships bore down on them, and the Peloponnesians fled in terror. Alcibiades broke through their lines with twenty of his fastest ships, put in to land, and ordered his men to disembark. They attacked the Peloponnesians as they tried to escape ashore from their boats, and inflicted heavy losses on them. Mindarus and Pharnabazus came up to help the Peloponnesian crews, but Alcibiades defeated them too. Mindarus died fighting bravely, but Pharnabazus managed to escape. The Athenians gained possession of the bodies of large numbers of the enemy, along with their arms and armour, and captured their entire fleet.* Pharnabazus abandoned Cyzicus to its fate, and the city fell to the Athenians as well, with the loss of the Peloponnesian troops stationed there. And so the Athenians had not only secured the Hellespont, but had, by main force, driven the Lacedaemonians entirely off the seas. They also intercepted a typic- ally Laconic dispatch to the ephors informing them of the disaster: 'Ships lost. Mindarus dead. Men starving. No idea what to do.'*

[29] Alcibiades' troops were now so brimming with confidence and self-importance that they refused to fraternize with the rest of the army, which had often been defeated, while they remained undefeated. For it was not long since Thrasyllus had taken a beating at Ephesus and, much to the Athenians' shame, the Ephesians had erected a bronze trophy. So the men who had been serving with Alcibiades taunted Thrasyllus' men with this, while boasting of their own prowess and that of their commander, and refused either to exercise along with them or to share the same patch of ground in the encamp- ment. However, when a sizeable body of cavalry and infantry under Pharnabazus attacked Thrasyllus' men, who had been carrying out a raid into the territory of Abydos, Alcibiades came out to reinforce them, and together they forced the enemy back and hunted them down until darkness fell. And so the two forces worked together, and returned to camp on good terms with each other and in high spirits. On the next day, Alcibiades set up a trophy and plundered Pharnabazus' territory without anyone daring to put up any resistance. But he released some captive priests and priestesses without ransom.*

While he was on his way to fight the people of Chalcedon, who had revolted from Athens and accepted a Lacedaemonian garrison and harmost, he heard that they had collected all their flocks and herds from the countryside and taken them for safe keeping to the Bithynians, with whom they had friendly relations, so he led his army to the borders of Bithynia instead, and sent a herald on ahead to lay charges against the Bithynians. They were so frightened that they gave him the flocks and herds and entered into a pact of friend- ship with him.*

[30] When he was in the middle of building a siege wall all the way around Chalcedon from sea to sea, Pharnabazus arrived with the inten- tion of raising the siege, and at the same time the Lacedaemonian harmost, Hippocrates, sallied forth from the city at the head of the

troops he had there with him to engage the Athenians. But Alcibiades drew his men up in a formation which enabled them to face both armies at once, forced Pharnabazus to take to his heels in an ignominious fashion, and overcame Hippocrates, killing him and a great many of his men in the process.*

Next, he sailed in person to the Hellespont to raise money. While he was there, he captured Selymbria, with extraordinary lack of concern for his own safety. The signal agreed on between himself and the Selymbrians who were betraying the city to him was that they would show a torch in the middle of the night, but they were forced to do so early, because they were concerned about one of their accomplices, who had suddenly changed his mind. So the torch was raised before the Athenian army was ready. Alcibiades collected about thirty men and sprinted for the walls, ordering the rest to follow as soon as they could. The gate was opened for him and he dashed inside, at the head of his thirty men, who had now been reinforced by twenty light-armed foot-soldiers. Just inside the gate, however, he found himself faced by the people of Selymbria, armed and advancing towards him. He was obviously doomed if he put up a fight, and yet his desire to win made the idea of running away intolerable, since in all his campaigns down to that day he had never known defeat, so he had the trumpet call for silence, and then had one of his company issue a formal statement to the effect that the Selymbrians were not to bear arms against Athenians. This proclamation took the edge off some of the Selymbrians' appetite for battle, because they supposed that the whole Athenian army had entered the city, while others began to find the prospect of a peaceful settlement more attractive. The two sides got together and negotiated with each other, and while they were doing so the main bulk of Alcibiades' army arrived. He judged, quite rightly, that the Selymbrians were inclining towards peace, but he was afraid that his Thracian troops might sack the city—there were a lot of them, and their admiration and loyalty towards Alcibiades made them fanatical soldiers—so he sent all of them out of the city, and then, at the Selymbrians' request, left the city completely unharmed. All he did, before leaving, was extract some money from them and install a garrison in the city.*

[31] Meanwhile, the commanders who were besieging Chalcedon had concluded a treaty with Pharnabazus, the terms of which were that on receipt of some money, and on the condition that the people

of Chalcedon resumed their status as subjects of Athens, Pharnabazus' territory was to be left alone; Pharnabazus was also to provide an escort and safe passage for an Athenian delegation to the Persian king. So when Alcibiades returned, Pharnabazus demanded that he too give his solemn word to honour the agreement, but Alcibiades refused to do so until Pharnabazus had done so first.*

Once pledges had been given and received, Alcibiades' next target was Byzantium, which had seceded from Athens. He built a siege wall around the city, but then Anaxilaus, Lycurgus, and a few others undertook to hand the city over to him, provided that he left it unharmed afterwards. So he spread a rumour that developments in Ionia called him away and sailed off with his whole fleet in broad daylight—only to return at night. He himself went ashore with his hoplites, approached the city walls, and waited quietly, while his fleet launched an assault on the harbour and forced their way in, with the crews shouting for all they were worth and making a great deal of noise and commotion. The unexpectedness of the attack terrified the Byzantines, and at the same time gave the pro-Athenians in the city the chance to let Alcibiades safely in, because everyone had gone to the harbour to resist the Athenian fleet. However, Byzantium was not surrendered without a fight. There were Peloponnesian, Boeotian, and Megarian troops stationed in the city, who managed to repel the troops from the Athenian fleet and force them back on board their ships, and who then realized that there were Athenians inside the city, took up battle stations and advanced to attack them. A fierce fight followed, but Alcibiades won—he commanded the right wing, with Theramenes on the left—and took about 300 of the surviving enemy troops prisoner.

After the battle no one from Byzantium was killed or sent into exile, since those were the terms of the agreement on the basis of which the men had betrayed the city to Alcibiades: they were not concerned to reserve any special treatment for themselves. And that is why, during his defence in Lacedaemon on the charge of treason, Anaxilaus could demonstrate in his speech that he had not acted at all dishonourably. He pointed out that he was a Byzantine, not a Lacedaemonian, and that it was Byzantium, not Sparta, whose perilous state had confronted him. There was a siege wall built around the city, no one could get through, and the Peloponnesians and Boeotians were consuming all the food there was in the city, while the people of

Byzantium—men, women, and children—were going hungry. He argued that he had therefore not betrayed his city to the enemy, but rescued it from the horrors of war, and that in doing so he had followed the example of the best Lacedaemonians of the past, for whom the good of their country was the only unequivocal criterion of what was noble and moral. This argument won the admiration of the Lacedaemonians, and they acquitted the defendants.*

[32] By now, however, Alcibiades had a strong desire to see his homeland, and an even stronger desire to be seen by his fellow citizens, since he had won so many victories over their enemies, and so he put to sea. His own Attic triremes were decked from stem to stern with shields and other spoils of war, and had plenty of captured triremes in tow, as well as a cargo of an even larger number of figureheads from ships he had defeated and destroyed. The number of enemy triremes in both categories amounted to at least 200.*

Duris of Samos, who claims to be a descendant of Alcibiades, goes into more detail. He says that Chrysogonus, the victor at the Pythian Games, played the pipes for the rowers, and that the tragic actor Callippides called the time, both wearing their full competition costume—straight-cut tunics, elegant robes and all—and that the flagship entered the harbour under a purple sail. He makes it sound as though Alcibiades were gadding about after a drinking-party. But these details are not recorded by Theopompus, Ephorus, or Xenophon, nor is it likely that he would have behaved in such a wilful manner when he was returning from exile and after having been in so much trouble.* In fact, he was very nervous as he came in to land, and after the ship had been beached he did not disembark until from where he stood on the deck he could see that his cousin Euryptolemus was there, along with a great many other friends and relatives, welcoming him back home and inviting him ashore.*

Once he was ashore, however, people hardly even noticed any of the other military commanders they met, but ran and crowded round him, calling out to him, greeting him, accompanying him on his way, and crowning him with garlands if they could get close to him, while those who could not watched him from a distance, and the older men pointed him out to the younger ones.* But the city also found the occasion a bitter-sweet mixture of tears and smiles, as people remembered and compared their present good fortune with their former misfortunes, and reflected that they would not have failed in Sicily, nor would any of their other hopes have been dashed, if only they had left Alcibiades in charge of their affairs at the time, and in command of that expeditionary force. After all, they thought, a short while ago Athens had just about been driven from the seas, on land it was barely in control of its own outskirts, and it was torn by internal schisms, and yet now Alcibiades had taken these wretched, dejected remnants and resurrected the city to such an extent that not only had he restored its mastery of the seas, but on land he had also enabled it to conquer its enemies all over the world.*

[33] The decree for his recall had been ratified some time earlier. The motion was proposed by Critias the son of Callaeschrus;* we have his own words to verify this, when in one of his elegiac poems he reminds Alcibiades of the favour as follows:

> As for the decision to bring you home, it was I who spoke out
> Before all the people and, having proposed it, brought it to pass.
> Upon these words the seal of my tongue is set.

At the time of his return, then, the people convened in the Assembly and Alcibiades stepped up to address them. He spoke with sorrow and anguish of his sufferings, but he hardly blamed the Athenian people for them at all, and then only moderately; instead, he attributed the whole business to his own bad luck and to a spiteful deity. He spent most of the time talking about his fellow citizens' hopes for the future and boosting their morale. After his speech, he was crowned with garlands of gold, and was elected to the post of military commander with full powers on land and sea.* They also voted to restore his property to him, and decreed that the Eumolpidae and the Heralds were to revoke the curses they had spoken against him in accordance with the people's instructions. All the other priests revoked their curses, except for Theodorus, the High Priest, who said, 'No, I never prayed that he would suffer harm—provided he does no wrong to the city.'

[34] So Alcibiades was doing spectacularly well. However, the timing of his return disturbed some people. The landing of his ship coincided with the day when Athena's Plynteria were being performed; this is the ceremony carried out in secret by the Praxiergidae on the twenty-fifth of Thargelion, which involves taking off the goddess's robes and covering her image. Consequently, the Athenians regard this day as one of most unlucky in the calendar and refuse to carry

out business of any kind on it. So the goddess was taken to be hiding herself from Alcibiades and rejecting him, rather than receiving him back in a kindly or welcoming fashion.*

Nevertheless, everything was going Alcibiades' way, and a fleet of 100 triremes was being fitted out for another expedition he planned to make. But then he was seized by a noble ambition which kept him in Athens until the time of the Mysteries. Ever since Decelea had been fortified and by their presence there the enemy had controlled the approaches to Eleusis, the rites had been conducted in a chaotic fashion: the procession went by sea, and sacrifices, dances, and a number of the rites which are performed en route to Eleusis, when they parade out of the city with Iacchus, had to be omitted.* It therefore struck Alcibiades as a good idea, bearing in mind how it would enhance not only his piety in the eyes of the gods, but also his reputation among men, to restore the traditional form to the rites, by having his infantry escort and guard the ceremony past the enemy. This, he thought, would either thoroughly embarrass and humiliate Agis, if the king chose to do nothing, or would enable him to fight a sacred battle, with the approval of the gods, in a supremely holy and crucial cause, and to do so within sight of his native city, with all his fellow citizens there to witness his courage.

Once he had decided to go ahead, he told the Eumolpidae and the Heralds of his plans. At dawn on the day of the procession, he posted lookouts in the hills and sent out an advance guard. Then he mustered the priests, the initiates, and their sponsors, provided them with a protective screen of armed men, and led them out in a calm, silent procession. On this occasion he made the post of military commander which he held such an awesome and majestic spectacle that he was described, by those who did not begrudge him his success, as a high priest and a sponsor of initiates, as much as a military commander.* No enemy troops dared to attack the procession, and he led it safely back again to Athens. He felt elated and proud, and the whole affair also raised the morale of the army, which felt that under his command they were invincible and irresistible. He became so popular with the lower, poorer classes that they conceived a passionate longing for him to rule over them as tyrant; some people even brought the issue up in their speeches and approached him to suggest it as a way of reaching a place where the envy of others could have no affect on him, where he could do away with decrees and laws and the idle chatterers who were ruining the city, and so act and administer the city's affairs without fear of the informers.*†

[35] We do not know what Alcibiades himself thought about tyranny, but the most powerful Athenians were concerned enough to hurry him off on his expedition as quickly as possible. They got everything he wanted ratified by decree, including the colleagues of his choice, and so he sailed away. At Andros, however, although his attack on the island was successful in that he defeated the inhabitants and the Lacedaemonian contingent there, he did not take the town, and this became the first of the fresh charges levelled against him by his enemies.*

Alcibiades seems to be a clear case of someone destroyed by his own reputation. His successes had made his daring and resourcefulness so well known that any failure prompted people to wonder whether he had really tried. They never doubted his ability; if he really tried, they thought, nothing would be impossible for him. So they expected to hear that Chios had fallen too, and the whole of the rest of Ionia, and were therefore irritated when they heard that he had not managed to accomplish everything as quickly or instantaneously as they wanted. They did not stop to consider that he was short of money, and that therefore, as he was fighting people who had a powerful financial backer in the Persian king, he often had to make trips away from the scene of the action, leaving the army to its own devices, to raise money for wages and provisions. In fact, this was the context within which the final charge against him arose. Here is what happened.

Lysander, who had been sent out by the Lacedaemonians to take command of their fleet, was giving his men four obols a day, instead of the standard three, out of money he had been given by Cyrus, whereas Alcibiades was pinched to pay even the daily allowance of three obols, so he sailed away on a fund-raising mission to Caria. The person he left in charge of the fleet was Antiochus, a man of undistinguished birth who was a skilful helmsman, but basically not a very intelligent man. Although Alcibiades had left him with instructions not to engage the enemy even if they sailed out against him, he became so arrogant and disdainful that he manned two triremes (his own and one other), went over to Ephesus, and sailed past the prows of the enemy ships, making coarse gestures and calling out rude comments to them. At first Lysander launched just a few ships to chase him away, but when the Athenians came to Antiochus' assistance, he launched his whole fleet and inflicted a defeat on them. Antiochus himself was among the casualties, a great many Athenian ships and men were captured, and Lysander erected a trophy. As soon as Alcibiades heard what had happened, he returned to Samos, put to sea with his entire fleet and tried to provoke Lysander to fight; but Lysander was perfectly content with his victory and refused to come out against him.*

[36] One of the people serving with the Athenian army on Samos who disliked Alcibiades was Thrasybulus the son of Thraso.* He felt particularly bitter, and he set sail for Athens to denounce him. He aroused people's feelings there and made a speech in the Assembly in which he claimed that it was Alcibiades who had spoiled their chances and caused the loss of the ships by his wilful attitude towards his position and by leaving in command men who had wormed their way into his confidence by carousing and gossiping with him; he had abandoned his command, Thrasybulus said, so that he could cruise around collecting money without a care in the world, and indulge in drinking sessions and liaisons with courtesans in Abydos and Ionia, while the enemy fleet lay at anchor near by. His enemies also found grounds for complaint in the stronghold he had built in Thrace, near Bisanthe, which they claimed was a bolt-hole in case he was either unwilling or unable to live in his native country.*

The Athenians found these accusations convincing and elected other military commanders as a way of showing the anger and rancour they felt towards him. When Alcibiades heard about this, he became afraid, and he left the camp on Samos once and for all. He put together a force of mercenaries and made war on his own account against those Thracian tribes which remained outside the Persian king's dominion. He collected a great deal of money by ransoming prisoners, and also made things safe for the neighbouring Greek settlements, so that they did not have to worry about being raided by the barbarian tribesmen.*

The Athenian commanders—Tydeus, Menander, and Adeimantus —who were stationed at Aegospotami with all the ships the Athenians had at the time gathered there, invariably sailed at daybreak to Lampsacus, where Lysander had berthed his fleet, and tried to provoke him to come out and fight them. Then they would turn around and go back again, and spend the rest of the day in careless disarray, since they did not think much of their enemy. Alcibiades was based near them, and he could not just ignore this behaviour and not do something about it. He rode over on his horse and tried to explain things to the Athenian commanders. He pointed out that their anchorage was no good, since there was no proper harbour there, and no settlements either, so that they had to go all the way to Sestus to get supplies, and suggested that they not let their crews disperse and roam around wherever they wanted when they were on land, while there was a sizeable enemy fleet anchored near by, which was trained to move silently into action without needing orders from more than one man.

[37] The Athenian commanders ignored this advice of Alcibiades', and also his suggestion that they move their anchorage to Sestus; in fact, Tydeus even rudely told him to leave. 'Others are in command now,' he said, 'not you.'* Alcibiades left with the distinct impression that there was treachery afoot, and he told acquaintances from the Athenian encampment, who went with him some of the way, that if the commanders had not been so rude to him, he would within a few days have forced the Lacedaemonians either to have taken on the Athenian fleet despite their reluctance to do so, or to have abandoned their ships. Some people thought that this was just vain boasting, but others thought it quite possible, if he had struck at the Lacedaemonians by land with a large force of Thracian javelineers and horsemen, and thrown their camp into confusion.

Events soon proved that his assessment of the Athenians' mistakes was perfectly correct. When Lysander suddenly launched an unexpected attack, only eight Athenian triremes escaped with Conon, while the rest, which numbered not far short of 200, were captured and towed away. Three thousand men from the ships were taken alive by Lysander and then massacred—and before long he took Athens as well, put the Athenian fleet to the torch, and demolished the Long Walls.*

After this, Alcibiades was so afraid of the Lacedaemonians, who were by now the masters of land and sea, that he moved to Bithynia, taking a great deal of valuable property with him, and sending a great deal more on ahead by ship, but leaving even more behind in the stronghold where he had been living. In Bithynia he again lost quite a bit of his property, and his land was raided by the local Thracians, so he decided to go up to the court of Artaxerxes. He thought he would prove himself to be just as useful to the king as Themistocles had been, if the king was prepared to put him to the test, while having a better excuse for being there. For he was not going to offer his services to the king and ask him for resources so that he could attack his fellow citizens, as Themistocles had, but so that he could defend his country against its enemies. It seemed to him that Pharnabazus was the best person to guarantee him safe passage and facilitate his journey up to Artaxerxes, so he went to Pharnabazus in Phrygia and spent some time with him as an honoured member of his court.*

[38] The Athenians found it hard enough to bear the loss of their supremacy, but when Lysander also deprived them of their freedom by putting the city in the hands of the Thirty,* they came to understand things and, now that they had lost, to entertain ideas they had ignored when they were capable of saving themselves. They looked back with remorse over all their mistakes and misjudgements, and now considered that the most stupid thing they had done was get angry with Alcibiades the second time. He had been cast aside through no fault of his own; they had got angry because a junior officer had lost a few ships in a shameful fashion, and, to their more lasting shame, had deprived the city of its best and most skilful military commander. Yet even in these circumstances some faint hope was reviving that all was not quite lost for the city as long as Alcibiades remained alive. 'Last time,' they thought, 'he couldn't stand spending his exile in passive inactivity, and this time too, if he still has the means, he won't let the Lacedaemonians get away with their arrogant brutality or the Thirty with their abuse of power.' Nor was it irrational for the common people to have these dreams, when even the Thirty found themselves concerned, and were prompted to make enquiries about him, and to take the greatest interest in his actions and intentions.

In the end, Critias tried to explain to Lysander that, if Athens were a democracy, the Lacedaemonians' dominion over Greece would not be secure, and that although the Athenians were not allowing the oligarchy to disturb their self-possession and self-satisfaction† in the slightest, yet as long as Alcibiades was alive he would not let them do nothing about the present situation. However, Lysander was not convinced by these arguments until a *skytalē** arrived from the Lacedaemonian authorities ordering him to get rid of Alcibiades, perhaps because they too were worried about his initiative and endeavour, or perhaps because they wanted to gratify Agis.

[39] So Lysander sent a message to Pharnabazus ordering him to do the deed, and Pharnabazus gave the job to his brother Bagaeus and his uncle Susamithras. Now, at the time Alcibiades was living in a

village in Phrygia, and he had Timandra the courtesan with him. One night he had a dream in which he was dressed in Timandra's clothes, and she was cradling his head in her arms while she made up his face like a woman's with eye-liner and white lead.* Others say that in his dream he saw Bagaeus cutting off his head and his body burning, but they agree that the dream happened not long before his death.

The men sent to kill him did not dare to enter the house, but surrounded it and set it on fire. When Alcibiades noticed the fire, he picked up nearly all his clothes and bedding, threw them on to the flames, and then, wrapping his cloak around his left arm and holding his drawn dagger in his right hand, he dashed out of the house before the clothing caught fire. He was unharmed by the fire, and when the foreign assassins saw him they scattered. Not one of them stood his ground against him or came up to fight him hand to hand; they kept their distance and hurled javelins and fired arrows at him instead. So this is how he met his death. After the assassins had left, Timandra collected his body for burial. She wrapped her own clothes around the body to cover it, and gave him the most splendid and ambitious funeral she could under the circumstances.* This is the woman who is said to have been the mother of Laïs—Laïs of Corinth, as she was called, although she actually came from Hyccara, a town in Sicily, where she became a prisoner of war.*

Some writers basically agree with this account of Alcibiades' death, but say that responsibility for it lies not with Pharnabazus or Lysander or the Lacedaemonians, but with Alcibiades himself. They say that he had seduced a woman from a notable family and had her living with him; it was her brothers, on this account, who were driven by their fury at his high-handed behaviour to come one night and set fire to the house where he was staying, and who shot him down, as I have described, when he sprinted through the flames.

AGESILAUS

INTRODUCTION

Agesilaus became Eurypontid king of Sparta in 400, at the age of 44. Sparta seemed at the height of its power: for a century the leader of the Peloponnesian League, it had just defeated Athens in the 27-year Peloponnesian War and now controlled the islands and Greek cities of the Aegean. In the forty years of his reign, all this was to change. Despite his generally successful expedition against Persia, major allies united to oppose Sparta in the Corinthian War, which broke out in 395. The war eventually was ended by the Peace of Antalcidas, imposed by the Persians, with the agreement of Sparta, in 386. Continuing tensions finally resulted in a Spartan attempt to put Thebes in its place by force. The Spartan army was disastrously defeated at the battle of Leuctra in 371. In the years which followed, Sparta saw its homeland ravaged, and Messenia, one half of its territory and a major source of its wealth, split off and made independent. Sparta suffered another major loss at the battle of Mantinea in 362, and Agesilaus in his eighties was forced to take service leading a mercenary army in Egypt to win money to defend his city. He died in 360 on his way home, a king who despite— or because of—his forceful personality, political influence, and military genius had presided over the complete collapse of Sparta as a major Greek power.

As Plutarch unfolds the course of the king's life, he asks the reader to consider the qualities Agesilaus displays while interacting with the political, social, and economic realities of his time. Following his normal practice, he attempts to understand the complex character of the individual by his actions, and to reveal the basis of both his weaknesses and his strengths. This Life, however, is unusually ambivalent about its subject. Plutarch can write, in the words of Theopompus, that there was 'no one alive to compare with him in power and fame' (10), yet also note the resentment of the Spartan allies and of the Spartans themselves against his policies (e.g. 26, 30). A regular alternation of praise and blame forces readers to engage actively in moral judgement, looking for some clear standard of value. While he offers no introduction to the *Agesilaus–Pompey* pair, the first paragraphs on Agesilaus (1–4) introduce in a simple form the themes which will be developed in the two lives. The Spartan training which, unlike most kings, Agesilaus underwent, taught him to obey and made him more congenial to the other Spartiates. His ambition was thrown into relief by his lameness, which might have given him an excuse for holding back. The powerful assistance of his older lover Lysander allowed him to claim the throne after his brother's death, despite the son's traditional right to succeed. He became king, despite the warning of an oracle, which tied 'lame kingship' to 'long and unexpected disasters'. Ambition, subservience, charm, friendship used for political power: although this Life has no section on youth and education—Agesilaus is a mature man when he appears —the foundation has been laid for a portrait. At the same time, the oracle indicates that the king's fate is also Sparta's: the city's greatness hangs in the balance.

The same mixture of qualities is found in *Pompey*.[1] The external parallels are obvious: both were famous commanders, were much admired by their contemporaries, fought in Asia Minor, and died in Egypt. Both were helped to power by controversial, unscrupulous leaders, Lysander and Sulla (whom Plutarch joined in another pair of Lives); both were defeated by better men, Epaminondas and Caesar. Their personalities are united by qualities of simplicity, loyalty to higher authority (the Spartan Council of Elders and the ephors; the Roman senate) and to their friends. The ambition of both drove them to wage civil war rather than fight against external enemies: Plutarch clearly parallels Agesilaus' constant wars against other Greeks, especially Thebes, with Pompey's fight with Caesar for preeminence. In reading *Agesilaus*, then, it is necessary always to have *Pompey* in mind.[2] In each Life, the hero also in a way represents the regime of which he is leader. *Pompey* is the major Life, almost twice as long, and ties the end of the Roman Republic to the strengths and failings of one man. *Agesilaus*, through the life of its protagonist, looks at the collapse of the Spartan state ideally imagined by Lycurgus.

In books eight and nine of his *Republic*, a passage well known to Plutarch, Plato gives a justly famous account of the different stages of constitutional decay from his ideal state, and the characteristic personal types to which they correspond. The first stage is the timarchic constitution (547b-551a), which, Plato says, 'corresponds to the Spartan system' (545a). Although only a slight falling from the ideal in comparison with the other types, there are serious problems, represented by making the spirited element superior to the intellectual. The product is a society where ambition is dominant and victory is all, where there is a secret desire for money, and where intellectual training is subordinate to physical exercise and military pursuits. In particular, Plato writes, the timarchic man will 'be excessively submissive to authority, and ambitiously eager for authority himself' (549a). All this reflects not only important traits of Sparta in Plato's day

---

[1] Cf. H. Heftner, *Plutarch und der Aufstieg des Pompeius* (Frankfurt-on-Main: Peter Lang, 1995), 19–22.

[2] See the translation of this Life in the selection of Roman Lives in the Oxford World's Classics.

(cf. Cartledge, *Agesilaos*, 402), but in particular the portrait which Plutarch creates of Agesilaus, who is 'passionately competitive' not only among the youth (2) but throughout his life,[3] but also subservient to the ephors and elders, especially in his return to Greece in 394. Plato's timarchic society is the first stage in the breakdown of the unity of the ideal state. Plutarch's statement that some philosophers—not Plato—considered strife essential is meant to recognize the role of competition in the Lycurgan system. Nevertheless, he warns the reader: 'excessive rivalry is not just bad, but extremely risky for states' (5). This rivalry in fact was to bring disaster to both Sparta and Rome. *Agesilaus* thus is a thought-provoking examination not just of a man, but of a state. It is not Agesilaus' leg alone which is lame, but his character, and his society.

The structure of the Life follows the sequence of historical events, but focuses on Agesilaus' attitudes more than on military conflicts.

1. Introduction (1–5). As already stated, this presents Agesilaus' character and accession, and ends with a note on competition.

2. The expedition to Asia, 396–94 (6–14). Agesilaus' sacrifice at Aulis indicates his desire to emulate Agamemnon, but also is the beginning of his hostility to the Thebans (6). His conflict with Lysander reveals his determination to pursue his own glory, even at the expense of his patron and former lover. The destructive potential of this conflict should not be underrated: if Lysander had lived, Plutarch says, he would have caused a major upheaval at Sparta (8). In fact, in pairing Lysander with Sulla in his *Parallel Lives*, Plutarch suggests that the conflict at Sparta might have been similar to that of Marius and Sulla at Rome. The rest of this section strikes a positive note: the victory at Sardis over Tissaphernes reveals Agesilaus' tactical skill, whereas the novelistic scenes set in Phrygia bring out his personal charm, his simplicity, and his strong erotic feelings, which he nevertheless keeps under control. He is a good friend and a dangerous enemy.

3. The Corinthian War, 394–391 (15–21). Agesilaus obediently returns to aid Sparta in its war against its former allies. Plutarch's feelings are ambivalent: it was noble to return home, but fighting among Greeks is really civil war (15). That is, a decision virtuous in the abstract can be mistaken in a given context. Agesilaus would have done better to imitate Cimon, and fight the Persians rather than fellow Greeks.[4] Although his victory at Coronea is determined more by 'the heat of his passion and desire for victory' (18)

---

[3] For his ambition (*philotimia*), cf. the particular statements at *Ages.* 2, 3, 5, 7, 8, 18, 20, 21, 23, 29, 32, 33, and 36; for his competitiveness (*philonikia*), at 2, 4, 5, 7, 11, 18, 23, 26, 33, 34.

[4] Later, of course, Alexander pursues the route of barbarian conquest to its furthest limit.

than by reason, his simplicity and forebearance win him favour at home, and his power is at its height (21). This point is parallel to Pompey's acme in 61 (*Pomp.* 45).

4. The conflict with Thebes, 390–362 (22–35), including the end of the Corinthian War (22–3). This major section can be divided into three segments.

(*a*) 390–377 (22–7) Confident in his success, Agesilaus ignores the Theban envoys, and immediately is brought up short by the Spartan defeat at Lechaeum (22). The defeat is a presage of future events. The victories of Conon and Pharnabazus force Sparta to negotiate with Persia for the Peace of Antalcidas (23). In the Peace, the Spartans renounce all that Agesilaus had gained in Asia Minor, handing the Greek cities of Asia over to Persia, and make Persia the arbiter of Greek affairs. Agesilaus is moved to accept the peace by his desire to weaken Thebes, as is shown by his support for the impious and treacherous seizure of the citadel of Thebes in 382. His attachment to his son and his son's lover leads him to protect Sphodrias, setting the Athenians to war against Sparta. Exasperated with Cleombrotus' caution, in 377 he invades Boeotia and is defeated; on his return he suffers an attack of phlebitis which keeps him from taking an active part in politics for several years.

(*b*) 371 (27–30) Jumping ahead to 371, Plutarch shows Agesilaus reacting angrily to Epaminondas' reasonable arguments on peace terms. Agesilaus removes Thebes from the peace agreement and immediately has Cleombrotus attack Thebes. Thebes wins decisively at Leuctra. The discipline of the Spartans when they hear the news is impressive, but does not conceal the disaster. Agesilaus' policy of competitiveness and anger —in Platonic thinking, features of a passionate man, acting without the control of reason (cf. *Rep.* 548c, 549b)—leads to the Theban victory, and the Spartans regret their decision to choose a lame king. Perhaps the oracle was true. Nevertheless Agesilaus' qualities and reputation are such that they choose him to deal with the constitutional crisis created by the fact that a substantial percentage of the citizen body had not obeyed the Spartan code at Leuctra.

(*c*) 370–362 (31–5) Agesilaus' resourceful defence of Sparta from Theban attack cannot hide the fact that this is the first time that an invader had been seen in the country in 600 years. The wailing of the women and attempts at rebellion testify to the collapse of Lycurgan ideal: 'all it took was one error for the scales to tilt and bring the state's prosperity crashing down' (33). The loss of Messenia and the defeat at Mantinea (34–5) confirm the end of Spartan dominance, although Agesilaus refuses to accept it.

5. Coda: Mercenary service in Egypt and death, 360 (36–40). Agesilaus in his eighties is a shadow of his former self. His wretched simplicity when

he meets the king's officers is pitiable when compared with the nobility of his earlier encounter with Pharnabazus. The Egyptians are wrong to laugh, for he is a great man, as his tactical skill in rescuing Nectanebis will prove, yet his situation reflects also the situation of Sparta. Agesilaus' code of always putting Sparta first—and his irrational anger at his treatment—now permits him to justify the betrayal of Tachos, whom he had come to serve, for the greater promises of Nectanebis. In his last lines Plutarch points ahead to Agis IV, the most noble and energetic of Agesilaus' descendants, who would attempt to revive at Sparta the ancient Lycurgan ways a century and a quarter later.

Agesilaus' actions, because of his central role in Greek affairs, had been recorded by a number of historians, most notably Xenophon. This Athenian, after he and the 10,000 Greek mercenaries had fought their way through Persian territory back to the Aegean coast, joined the Spartan forces in Asia Minor and later, when Agesilaus received the command of the army there, the two became friends. Xenophon's *History of Greece*, covering the period 411–362, is sympathetic to Sparta and to Agesilaus, although the overall theme is the inability of any city, whether Athens, Sparta, or Thebes, to rule an empire justly and wisely. Sparta's capture of the citadel of Thebes in particular is seen as a horrible offence against morality, which brought its own punishment (*Hell.* 5. 4. 1). Xenophon omits a great deal, and employs well-developed scenes and dialogues rather than historical analysis to make his points, but his closeness to events and to Agesilaus make him a valuable source for us. Xenophon also composed a short encomium of the king, *Agesilaus*, after his death, and a pamphlet, *Constitution of the Lacedaemonians*, which describes the Lycurgan constitution and laments its fall into disuse. Plutarch used at first hand and extensively the *History of Greece*, and to a lesser extent the other works.[5] He also cites other standard or lesser known fourth-century historians: Theopompus, Callisthenes, Duris, Hieronymus, Dicaearchus, Dioscurides.[6] He undoubtedly used the historian Ephorus, whom he frequently cites in other works, though he does not name him in this Life. It is probable that he also knew the anonymous history, preserved only on papyrus, which we call *Hellenica Oxyrhynchia*. Aristotle's *Constitution of the Lacedaemonians* had been a major source for *Lycurgus*; there is no doubt that it was used here as well. The result is that Plutarch frequently is able to supplement or correct the account we read in Xenophon.[7] He will regularly revise Xenophon's information and

[5] Xenophon's *Symposium* is cited at 29.

[6] Xenophon is cited in 18, 19 (bis), 29 and 34; Theopompus at 10, 31, 32, and 33; Callisthenes at 34; Duris at 3; Hieronymus at 13; Dicaearchus at 19; and Dioscurides at 35.

[7] Cf. e.g. 16–17 (Agesilaus' march from the Hellespont), 24 (details of Sphodrias' march), 27 (Epaminondas' speech), 28 (Agesilaus' anger).

present it in his own terms, as for example the arrival of the news of Leuctra at Sparta (29). Since Xenophon's *History of Greece* stops at the battle of Mantinea, Plutarch also provides the fullest account of the Egyptian campaign of Agesilaus. Plutarch had a thorough familiarity with this period, dating back to his first years at school, which was reinforced by the work he did for other related Lives: *Lysander, Pelopidas, Epaminondas*, and *Artaxerxes*.[8]

The biographer also drew on his own experience and autopsy. He was thoroughly familiar with the Boeotian landscape around his own home of Chaeronea, and knew the battlefield of Leuctra and the sanctuary of Athena near Coronea (19). His own sense of Boeotian solidarity and enormous admiration for Epaminondas colour his account, most obviously when Epaminondas confronts Agesilaus in c. 27. He visited Sparta, where he had friends such as Callicrates, who could tell him of the tradition concerning his ancestor Anticrates, the Spartan who killed Epaminondas (35), and where he conducted his own researches in the records of Sparta to find the names of the wife and daughters of the king (19).

Poetic quotations heighten the rhetoric of key moments, most notably at c. 15, where he makes his own the impassioned cry of Andromache from the *Trojan Women*: 'What clever Greeks, to have devised atrocities worthy of barbarians!'[9]

Plutarch's sources were the best available. His distinguishing characteristic here as elsewhere is that he passes over military or diplomatic history (most battles are treated in a sentence or two) to focus on small signs of character: Agesilaus' difficulty with the kiss of Megabates, or his straddling a hobby horse when playing with his son. Yet the narrative is historically as well as psychologically important. Using the insight into the sociology of the Spartan state in the fourth century offered by Plato and developed by his own keen observation of people, Plutarch presents a sensitive and sympathetic picture of the virtues and the failings of the Spartan system, combined in the great and flawed man who presided over its collapse.

Buckler, J., *The Theban Hegemony 371–362 BC* (Cambridge, Mass., and London: Harvard University Press, 1980). A detailed history.

Cartledge, P., *Agesilaos and the Crisis of Sparta* (London: Duckworth, 1987). A full presentation of the collapse of Sparta during Agesilaus' reign, with a special emphasis on Spartan society.

Cawkwell, G., 'Agesilaus and Sparta', *Classical Quarterly*, 26 (1976), 62–84. Review of Agesilaus' reign, looking for the reasons for the decline of Sparta.

---

[8] Although he cites the Roman Cornelius Nepos in other lives, Nepos' *Agesilaus* is a negligible work and there would have been no reason for Plutarch to use it.

[9] Cf. also 1 (Simonides), 5 and 9 (Homer), 14 (Timotheus).

Hamilton, C. D., *Agesilaus and the Failure of Spartan Hegemony* (Ithaca, NY, and London: Cornell University Press, 1991). A study of the role of Agesilaus in the failure of Spartan hegemony.

—— 'Plutarch's "Life of Agesilaus"', *ANRW* II.33.6 (1992), 4201–21.

Hillman, T. P., 'Authorial Statements, Narrative, and Character in Plutarch's Agesilaus–Pompey', *Greek Roman and Byzantine Studies*, 35 (1994), 255–80. Plutarch's statements in the two Lives on their use of friends.

Michell, H., *Sparta* (Cambridge: Cambridge University Press, 1952). A general history.

Shipley, D. R., *Plutarch's Life of Agesilaus. Response to Sources in the Presentation of Character. Greek Text, Commentary, and Bibliography* (Oxford: Clarendon Press, 1997). A full commentary.

AGESILAUS

[1] After an illustrious reign over the Lacedaemonians Archidamus the son of Zeuxidamus left on his death two sons—Agis,* whose mother was an eminent woman called Lampido, and Agesilaus, who was much younger, and whose mother was Eupolia the daughter of Melesippidas. The kingship belonged by law to Agis, so the expectation was that Agesilaus would spend his life without any rank, and he was therefore put through what is known in Lacedaemon as the 'training'—a programme which forces one to live a tough and demanding life, but which educates young men in obedience.* So the reason, we hear, why Simonides described Sparta as 'the tamer of men' was because more than any other state its customs were designed to instil obedience in its citizens and make them subject to its laws, as if they were horses to be tamed from a very early age. Anyway, heirs to the throne are not required to undergo this training, but one of Agesilaus' many distinctions was that he had acquired a thorough grounding in obedience before he came to rule. This explains why he was far more congenial to his subjects than any other king: on top of his innate qualities as a king and a leader he gained from the training the common touch of ordinary human kindness.

[2] While he was a member of one of the so-called 'herds' of boys who were being brought up together, his lover was Lysander, who was deeply impressed with the boy's natural self-composure.* Although Agesilaus was highly and passionately competitive when he was in the company of young men, with a desire to be first in everything, and although he had an assertiveness and intensity which no one could resist or overpower, he was at the same time so obedient and even-tempered that he did everything he was told to do, motivated not by fear of punishment but by a sense of honour. By the same token he was more distressed by criticism than he was oppressed by hardship.

As for the deformity in his leg, the charms of his youthful physique disguised it, and the fact that he put up with it lightly and cheerfully —he was the first to tease and make fun of himself—went a long way towards offsetting the misfortune. In fact, the deformity threw his ambition into relief, since he refused to let his lameness act as an excuse for giving up, however exhausting the activity he was faced with. We have no likenesses of him, since he himself vetoed them: in fact, even as he lay dying he gave orders that no statue or painting was to be made of him.* He is said to have been a small man, rather unprepossessing in appearance. However, his high spirits and his cheerful good humour in every eventuality, which was never accompanied by an offensive or hurtful tone of voice or look, made him more lovable, even in his old age, than attractive young men in the bloom of youth. But, as Theophrastus records, the ephors fined Archidamus for having married a small woman, saying, 'She will bear us kinglets rather than kings.'

[3] Be that as it may, it was during the reign of Agis that Alcibiades arrived in Lacedaemon from Sicily as an exile, and before he had spent much time in the city he was accused of having an affair with the king's wife, Timaea.* When she gave birth to a child, Agis refused to acknowledge it and claimed that Alcibiades was the father. According to Duris, Timaea was not particularly upset at this; in fact, when she was at home, in an undertone in front of her helot slaves she actually used to call the child Alcibiades, rather than Leotychidas. Moreover, Duris goes on, Alcibiades claimed that his affair with Timaea was not motivated by defiance, but because he wanted the Spartiates to be ruled by his descendants. Anyway, this led to Alcibiades' surreptitious departure from Lacedaemon, because he was afraid of Agis. The boy remained suspect in Agis' eyes for a long time, and never received the recognition due to a legitimate son of a king, until when Agis was ill Leotychidas prostrated himself weeping before him and persuaded him to declare in front of a number of witnesses that he was his son.

Nevertheless, after Agis' death Lysander, who by this time had defeated the Athenians at sea* and was the most powerful person in Sparta, began to press Agesilaus' claim to the throne, using Leotychidas' illegitimacy to argue that the throne should not be his. This aim of his met widespread and wholehearted support in Sparta from people who were impressed by Agesilaus' qualities and liked the fact that he had been brought up with them and had shared in their training programme. However, there was an oracle-monger in Sparta called Diopithes, who had an excellent collection of ancient oracles and was generally held to be outstandingly knowledgeable about divine matters, and he said that it was wrong for a lame man to become king of Lacedaemon and during the trial cited the following oracle:*

Beware, Sparta, for all your proud boasts, lest at the height
Of your sound-footed progress your offshoot is lame kingship.
For then you will be gripped by long and unexpected disasters
And the man-destroying, overwhelming billows of war.

Lysander's response to this was to argue that if the Spartiates were
really worried about the oracle they should beware of Leotychidas.
The god, he claimed, was not concerned about the possibility of someone with a bad foot becoming king; what mattered to him was the
possibility of someone who was illegitimate and not a descendant of
Heracles coming to the throne: this is what he meant by a 'lame kingship'. And Agesilaus said that Poseidon had given damning evidence
of Leotychidas' illegitimacy when an earthquake of his drove Agis from
his bedroom, and then more than ten months had passed before
Leotychidas was born.*

[4] So this is how Agesilaus came to be king. He immediately gained
Agis' property as well, since Leotychidas had been banished because
of his illegitimacy. But seeing that his relatives on his mother's side
were terribly poor, despite their respectability, he divided half of the
property among them, thereby ensuring that his inheritance secured
him loyalty and a good reputation instead of envy and hostility.*

Xenophon says that his constant readiness to carry out his country's orders brought him a great deal of power, until he could do what
he wanted.* To be specific, this was the situation. At that time supreme
political power was in the hands of the ephors and the elders. The
ephors held office for only one year, while the elders kept their position for life; these bodies were formed, as I have explained in my *Life
of Lycurgus*, to stop the kings having absolute power.* Hence, from
the time of their institution onwards, the kings were always at odds
with them, and each king inherited this ancient, traditional feud.
Agesilaus, however, took the opposite course: instead of battling and
clashing with them, he set out to win their favour. He never did anything on his own initiative without asking their permission; if he was
summoned to a meeting with them he hurried there on the double;
if he happened to be sitting on the royal throne doing business when
the ephors came in, he used to stand up to greet them; and whenever a new elder was appointed Agesilaus acknowledged his merits
by sending him a cloak and an ox. All this made it look as though he
was respecting and even enhancing the dignity of the positions held
by the ephors and elders, but in fact he was subtly increasing his

own power and gaining for the kingship extra authority which was conceded to him out of goodwill.

[5] In his dealings with the rest of his fellow citizens it would be harder to fault his behaviour as an enemy than it would his behaviour as a friend. He never harmed his enemies unfairly, but he did have a tendency to help his friends when they were doing wrong; and although he would have felt ashamed if he failed to acknowledge his enemies when they were in the right, he not only found it impossible to criticize his friends when they were in the wrong, but even took pride in helping them and sharing in their offences. He could not see how there could be anything wrong in friends helping one another out. Then again, when his opponents had bad luck, he was the first to offer his condolences and he had no hesitation in lending them his support if they wanted it. As a result he won universal popularity and allegiance. This drew the attention of the ephors, who became worried about how powerful he was and fined him on the grounds that he was making the citizens his own, when they should belong to the state.*

The natural scientists believe that if discord and strife were to disappear from the universe, the heavenly bodies would come to a standstill and the concord of everything with everything else would mean the end of creation and change.* Similarly, it seems that the Laconian lawgiver injected an element of conflict and rivalry into his constitution* as a stimulus towards virtue, since he wanted good men to find some point of difference always arising between them, so that they were constantly competing among themselves. For in his opinion it was wrong to describe as 'agreement' the kind of compliance which simply gives way to an untested point of view, without making any effort or putting up a fight. Some people are of the opinion that Homer certainly grasped this point as well, since he would not have portrayed Agamemnon as pleased when Odysseus and Achilles fell to abusing each other 'with violent words',* if he did not think that it was substantially in the common interest for the best men to compete and quarrel with one another. However, the idea needs some qualification before one can accept it, because excessive rivalry is not just bad, but extremely risky for states.

[6] Not long after Agesilaus had succeeded to the throne, reports arrived from Asia that the Persian king was preparing a massive fleet to drive the Lacedaemonians from the sea.* Lysander wanted to be

sent to Asia again so that he could help his friends there, because as a result of their mismanagement and brutality they were being thrown out and killed by the inhabitants of the cities where he had left them as rulers and governors. So he persuaded Agesilaus to undertake the expedition on behalf of Greece and suggested that he fight as far away as possible from the mainland, by crossing over to Asia and anticipating the Persians' plans. At the same time he sent messages to his friends in Asia asking them to get word to Lacedaemon that they wanted Agesilaus as their commander. So Agesilaus presented himself before the assembly and agreed to take charge of the war, provided that they would assign him thirty Spartiates as his officers and advisers, an élite unit of 2,000 ex-helots,* and a contingent of 6,000 allied troops. Thanks to Lysander's support, his requests were speedily approved by the Lacedaemonians, and they lost no time in sending Agesilaus on his way, with Lysander chief among the thirty Spartiates he took with him. Lysander owed his position not just to his personal fame and influence, but also to the friendship of Agesilaus, who felt more indebted to him for his help in gaining him this command than he did for his help in gaining him the kingdom.

While the troops were assembling at Geraestus, Agesilaus went down to the coast at Aulis along with his friends and took quarters there for the night.* During the night he had a dream in which he heard someone saying: 'Lacedaemonian king, you are surely aware that no one has ever been given the command of all Greece at once except in earlier times Agamemnon and now you. The troops under your command are identical to his, you are fighting the same enemy, and you are setting out to war from the same place; it is therefore only right that you should make the same sacrifice to the goddess as he did here before setting sail.'* These words immediately reminded Agesilaus how at the instigation of the diviners Agamemnon had sacrificed his daughter. But Agesilaus was not worried. He got out of bed, told his friends about the dream, and explained that he would honour the goddess with a sacrifice which it would not be inappropriate for her, as a goddess, to find pleasing, but that he would not imitate the heartlessness of his predecessor. So he took a hind and decked it with garlands. Now, he gave orders that the sacrifice was to be carried out by his own diviner, but this contravened the usual practice, which was for the appointed Boeotian official to do the job, and when the Boeotarchs* heard what was going on they were livid.

They sent some of their assistants to tell Agesilaus not to perform an illegal sacrifice in contravention of Boeotian tradition, and these men not only delivered their message, but also tossed the thighs of the victim off the altar.* Agesilaus sailed away in an unsettled state of mind, then, because he was furious with the Thebans and was also filled with gloom at the omen, which he took to mean that his mission would not be completed and that his expedition would fail to achieve its proper objectives.

[7] No sooner had he reached Ephesus than the high regard in which Lysander was held and his influence began to prove a source of irritation and annoyance to Agesilaus. There were always people flocking to Lysander's door, and everyone followed him around and sought his favour, as if the command of the expedition belonged to Agesilaus in name and appearance alone, because that was what the law required, whereas in reality all responsibility, power, and effectiveness lay with Lysander.* No commander on service in Asia ever won as much glory or inspired as much fear as Lysander, and no man ever proved a greater benefactor to his friends or a greater bane to his enemies. All this was still fresh in people's minds, and moreover Agesilaus' plain, simple, and unpretentious way of dealing with people did not compare well in their eyes with the intensity, brusqueness, and curtness which Lysander retained from before, and so they fawned totally on Lysander and ignored everyone else. In the first place, this led to discontent on the part of the rest of the Spartiates, who found themselves being treated as Lysander's subordinates rather than as the king's advisers. In the second place, even though Agesilaus was not the kind to resent or grudge someone else's high standing, he was highly ambitious and competitive, and so he began to be afraid that any brilliant successes he might achieve would be attributed to Lysander because of his reputation.

What he did, then, was this. First, he resisted Lysander's suggestions, put all the projects he was most enthusiastic about on hold, and did nothing about them, while pursuing alternative courses of action instead. Second, if it came to his attention that any of those who came to him with requests had been listening to Lysander's advice, he sent them away empty-handed, and by the same token, when it came to adjudicating cases, any people Lysander disparaged were sure to come off best, while on the other hand it was a struggle for those whom he was obviously committed to helping to avoid being fined. None of this happened at random intervals, but so uniformly that it was obviously a deliberate policy, and when Lysander realized what was behind it he made no attempt to hide the truth from his friends. He told them that they were being slighted because of him, and advised them to go and try to ingratiate themselves with the king and those who had more influence with the king than he did.

[8] But even these actions and words of Lysander's seemed to Agesilaus designed to make people resentful of him, so because he wanted to deliver a more severe reprimand, he gave Lysander the job of carving the meat at public feasts,* and on one occasion, the story goes, remarked in front of a large number of people, 'Dismiss these petitioners now. Let them go and try to get around my meat-carver.' Lysander was saddened by all this and said to him, 'You certainly know how to humble your friends, Agesilaus.' 'Absolutely,' Agesilaus replied. 'At any rate, when they want to be more powerful than me.' So Lysander said, 'Your words may well be better than my actions. But give me a job and a posting where I can be useful to you without bothering you.'*

So he was sent to the Hellespont, where from the territory governed by Pharnabazus he managed to bring over to Agesilaus' side a Persian called Spithridates, along with a great deal of money and 200 horsemen.* But he never forgave Agesilaus: he remained angry with him for the rest of his life, and tried to think up schemes whereby he could deprive the two royal houses of the kingship and restore entitlement to the throne to all Spartiates equally. And he might well have succeeded in causing a major upheaval, all because of his quarrel with Agesilaus, if his plans had not been cut short by his death while campaigning in Boeotia.* This is an example of how ambitious people can do more harm than good in a state, if they fail to restrain themselves. For even though Lysander was undoubtedly a nuisance, and went too far in gratifying his ambition, Agesilaus must surely have been aware of an alternative, less objectionable way of correcting the faults of such an eminent and ambitious man. In fact, it rather looks as though both of them suffered from the same emotional flaw, which would not let one of them acknowledge the authority of his commander or the other endure the neglect of his close friend.

[9] At first Tissaphernes* was afraid of Agesilaus and entered into a treaty with him whereby he was to detach the Greek cities from the Persian king's empire and hand them over to Agesilaus. Later,

however, once he was convinced that he had sufficient military resources, he declared war, and Agesilaus gladly took up the challenge, because he had high hopes of his expedition. Given that Xenophon and the Ten Thousand had fought their way through to the sea, defeating the king whenever they wanted,* Agesilaus could not bear the thought of failing to give the Greeks a victory to remember him by, when he was in command of the Lacedaemonians, who were supreme on land and sea. So he immediately offset Tissaphernes' treachery with a legitimate trick of his own, and made it seem as though he was planning to march to Caria.* However, once Tissaphernes had assembled his troops there, he set out and invaded Phrygia,* where he captured a great many towns and cities, and took possession of vast sums of money. In this way he showed his friends the difference between violating a treaty and outwitting one's enemy: the former shows contempt for the gods, while the latter, as well as being legitimate, entails considerable glory and results in profit and all its consequent pleasures.

Since he was outnumbered by the enemy's cavalry, and since the livers of his sacrificial victims were without lobes,* he withdrew back to Ephesus and set about forming a cavalry contingent. What he did was tell the wealthy men in his army that they had a choice between serving in the cavalry themselves, or, if they did not want to do that, providing a horse and a substitute rider. A lot of them took this alternative option, and Agesilaus soon had a sizeable force of militarily effective cavalrymen rather than cowardly hoplites. He thought Agamemnon had been right to release a cowardly rich man from active service and accept a good mare instead.*

Once, when at his orders the quartermasters responsible for selling the booty stripped some prisoners of their clothes before offering them for sale, there were plenty of people interested in buying the clothing, but the naked bodies of the Persians, who were all pale and soft because of their indoor lifestyle, they found ridiculous, and could see no use or value in them. So Agesilaus came up and said, 'Here you see the men you're fighting, and here you see the objects you're fighting for.'*

[10] After the winter, when an invasion of enemy territory was feasible once more, Agesilaus announced that he was going to march up into Lydia, and although this time he was not trying to mislead Tissaphernes, the Persian completely fooled himself: the earlier trick had made him suspicious of Agesilaus, and he thought that *this* time

Agesilaus really was going to attack Caria, because the terrain there was not suitable for cavalry and Agesilaus was far weaker than him in that department. But when Agesilaus kept his word and arrived on the plain of Sardis, Tissaphernes had to retrace his route from Caria to reinforce his troops there. On his way through the plain he came across Greeks plundering the region in disarray and killed large numbers of them with his cavalry. Agesilaus realized that whereas he was at full strength, the enemy infantry had not yet arrived, so he felt that now was the time to join battle. He combined his peltasts with his cavalry and ordered them to advance with all speed and engage the enemy, while he was right behind them, bringing up the hoplites. The Persians were put to flight and the Greeks followed them, captured their camp, and inflicted heavy losses on them.*

The consequences of this battle for the Greeks were, first, that they could raid the king's territory with impunity, and, second, that they got to see Tissaphernes—a loathsome man, deeply hated by the Greeks—receive his just deserts, since immediately after the battle the Persian king sent Tithraustes to arrest him. After beheading Tissaphernes, Tithraustes demanded that Agesilaus enter into a peace treaty with him and return home, and sent messengers to him with an offer of money. Agesilaus replied that only his city had the authority to make peace, and that rather than making himself rich he preferred to enrich his troops; besides, he added, the Greeks think that the proper thing to take from an enemy is booty, not gifts. However, he did want to show some appreciation of the fact that Tithraustes had punished Tissaphernes, the common enemy of the Greeks, so he had his army decamp to Phrygia, taking from Tithraustes thirty talents to cover his expenses en route.

A *skytalē** reached him in mid-journey from the government at home, telling him to assume command of the fleet as well—a unique honour in the history of Sparta. There was, by common consent, no one alive to compare with him in power and fame, as even Theopompus says somewhere, though he prided himself more on his moral qualities than his command. However, it is generally agreed that he made a mistake in appointing Pisander to take charge of the fleet at that time, because there were older and more experienced men at hand, and he was not thinking of the best interests of his country when he gave Pisander the command of the fleet, but was respecting family ties and gratifying his wife, who was Pisander's sister.

[11] Meanwhile, he stationed his troops in the province governed by Pharnabazus, where supplies were readily available for his army and he also collected a great deal of money. While he was there he advanced as far as Paphlagonia and entered into an alliance with Cotys, the king of the Paphlagonians, who wanted to be on good terms with such an outstanding and reliable man.* Now, ever since Spithridates had seceded from Pharnabazus and come over to Agesilaus, he used to accompany him on all his journeys and expeditions—along with his exceptionally good-looking young son, Megabates, with whom Agesilaus was passionately in love, and also a beautiful daughter of marriageable age. At Agesilaus' instigation, Cotys took Spithridates' daughter to be his wife, and in return gave Agesilaus 1,000 horsemen and 2,000 peltasts.*

Agesilaus then pulled back to Phrygia, Pharnabazus' domain, and devastated the countryside. Pharnabazus refused to face him in battle and had no confidence in his strongholds either; he kept the bulk of his most valuable and precious things with him and spent the whole time retreating and slipping away out of Agesilaus' reach, constantly changing his base from one part of the country to another, until Spithridates, who had been tracking his movements, got Herippidas the Spartiate to join him in an attack on his camp. The camp fell and Spithridates took possession of all Pharnabazus' valuables, but this proved only to be an occasion for Herippidas to keep a strict eye on the spoils, and he forced Spithridates' men to give back everything they had taken. His constant inspections and investigations made Spithridates so angry that he took the Paphlagonians back to Sardis with him. This incident is said to have made Agesilaus absolutely livid. He was furious at the loss of Spithridates, who was a good man, and the quite sizeable force he had taken with him, and he was ashamed that people would accuse him of being petty and mean, a charge he was always anxious to prove that he and his country did not deserve.*

Apart from these public reasons, he was also terribly tormented by his love for the boy, which had gradually worked its way deep inside him. When the boy was there with him, however, he tried valiantly to control his desires, and once even turned aside when Megabates came up to him as if to embrace and kiss him.* Megabates was so embarrassed that he never tried again and from then on always kept his distance when addressing Agesilaus, but this upset Agesilaus too, and he regretted having spurned his kiss. He pretended to be surprised and wondered aloud why Megabates did not show his affection for him with a kiss. 'It's your fault,' his close friends said. 'You were the coward who was too frightened to stand your ground when the attractive young man offered you a kiss. But even now he might be persuaded to come within kissing range. Just make sure you don't lose your nerve again.' Agesilaus thought about it for a while in silence and then said, 'No, I don't want you to convince him to kiss me.† I think I'd prefer to fight the battle of the kiss all over again than possess all the gold I've ever seen.'* That was how he behaved when Megabates was there with him, but after he had gone the fire of his passion was so strong that it is hard to say whether he would have been able to resist a kiss had Megabates suddenly reappeared.

[12] After this, Pharnabazus wanted to have a conference with Agesilaus. The meeting was arranged by Apollophanes of Cyzicus, who was a guest-friend of both men. Agesilaus and his entourage arrived at the designated place first, and he sat down in some shade where the grass was growing thickly and waited there for Pharnabazus. When Pharnabazus arrived, soft cushions and embroidered rugs were spread on the ground for him, but with Agesilaus lying there like that he felt embarrassed, so he reclined on the grassy ground too, just as he was, even though the clothes he was wearing were incredibly delicate and finely dyed. Once they had greeted each other, Pharnabazus started on a long list of grievances which were perfectly fair, seeing that he had often been of enormous help to the Lacedaemonians during their war against the Athenians,* and now here they were destroying his land. Agesilaus noticed that the Spartiates he had brought with him kept their eyes fixed on the ground in shame and confusion, since they were aware of the justice of Pharnabazus' complaints, so he said, 'Previously, Pharnabazus, we were on good terms with the king, so we treated him as a friend, but now that we're enemies, we treat him as an enemy. Since you obviously want to be one of the king's chattels, then of course we hurt him through you. But from the moment you decide to become a friend and ally of the Greeks rather than preferring the name of slave to the king, you will see this army, these weapons and ships, and all of us protect your property—and your freedom, in the absence of which no human possession is fine or desirable.'

At this, Pharnabazus spoke plainly to Agesilaus. 'Personally,' he said, 'if the king were to send someone out to replace me as his commander,

I'd come over to your side; but if he entrusts the command to me, then I'll act in his best interests and do all I can to resist you and hurt you.' This response delighted Agesilaus and as the two men got to their feet, he took Pharnabazus' hand in his and said, 'We need men like you as our friends rather than our enemies, Pharnabazus. I hope it happens one day.'*

[13] As Pharnabazus and his entourage were leaving, his son let the others get ahead and then ran up to Agesilaus with a smile. 'I'd like you to be my guest-friend, Agesilaus,' he said, and gave him the spear he was carrying. Agesilaus accepted the gift, and was delighted with the boy's friendly bearing. He cast his eyes over his companions to see if anyone had anything which would make a gift suitable for a fine-looking and generous boy, so that he could give him something in return, and as soon as he noticed that the horse belonging to his scribe, Idaeus, was fitted out with ornamental cheek-pieces, he stripped them off the horse and gave them to the boy. Subsequently, he never forgot this incident. Later, in fact, when this son of Pharnabazus was uprooted from his home by his brothers and arrived in the Peloponnese as an exile, he took very good care of him. He even helped him to a certain extent in his love life. The Persian was in love with a young athlete from Athens, who was in danger of being ruled out of the Olympic Games because of his height and ruggedness, so he turned to Agesilaus and asked him to help the boy. Agesilaus was happy to do even this favour for him, and although it was far from easy he did eventually bring the matter to a successful conclusion.*

Although on the whole Agesilaus was correct and conventional, he thought that inflexible probity in matters involving friends was merely an excuse for not helping out. For instance, in a letter to Hidrieus of Caria* he is supposed to have written: 'If Nicias is innocent, acquit him; if guilty, acquit him for my sake. Acquit him, anyway.' This is typical of Agesilaus' behaviour in most cases where his friends were concerned, but sometimes he took advantage of a situation to further his own aims. He proved this when once he was having to move quarters in somewhat of a hurry, and he left his sick boyfriend behind. The boy pleaded with him and called out to him as he was leaving, but Agesilaus turned around and said that it was hard to combine compassion and prudence. We have this story on the authority of the philosopher Hieronymus.

[14] By the end of the second year of his command,* Agesilaus was beginning to be talked about even in inland Asia, and had become a larger-than-life figure, widely known for the disciplined, simple, and modest way he lived. For instance, when he was travelling, he used to pitch his tent at night away from everyone else within the compounds of the most holy sanctuaries, so that he would have the gods to watch over and witness those aspects of life which few of our fellow human beings see us doing. And in an army of so many thousands, one would have been hard put to find a poorer straw mattress than Agesilaus'.* When he was faced with heat and cold, it was as if he were unique in his natural ability to take advantage of the weather however it was constituted by the god on any particular occasion. It gave the Greeks living in Asia particular pleasure to see how the Persian satraps and military governors, who had for so long been intolerably overbearing, and had been made dissolute by wealth and luxury, trembled and grovelled before a man who went around in a simple cloak, and how it took just one brief, Laconic sentence from him for them to change their ways in conformity with his wishes. Many men, in fact, were moved to quote the line of Timotheus: 'Ares is lord: Greece has no fear of gold.'

[15] Asia was now in turmoil, with many places drifting towards revolution, but Agesilaus brought concord to the cities there and restored a proper state of order to their governments without having to assassinate or banish anyone. Then he resolved to advance further inland than he had before—to move the theatre of war away from the Greek coast and make the Persian king's own person and his prosperity in Ecbatana and Susa the focus of the fighting. Above all, he intended to strip the king of his leisure and make it impossible for him to sit in comfort on his throne, arbitrating between warring Greek states and corrupting their popular leaders.* But just then the Spartiate Epicydidas came to him with news that Sparta had become embroiled in a serious war in Greece, and that the ephors were ordering him to return and help his countrymen at home.

'What clever Greeks, to have devised atrocities worthy of barbarians!'* How else could one describe the terrible envy which then made Greeks organize themselves into hostile cliques and forces? They arrested Fortune on her upward flight, and diverted back on to themselves weaponry and war which had only recently been uprooted from

Greece and turned to face foreign lands. I for one cannot agree with
Demaratus of Corinth's assertion that the Greeks who had not seen
Alexander sitting on Darius' throne had missed a rare treat;* in fact,
I think that in all likelihood they might have wept at the realization
that Alexander and his Macedonians were simply the heirs of the
Greeks of the time who squandered the lives of their commanders on
the battlefields of Leuctra, Coronea, Corinth, and Arcadia.*

Agesilaus, however, never did anything nobler or greater than returning home then; it was a perfect example of obedience and morality.
Hannibal was already in trouble and on the point of being driven
out of Italy, yet he found it extremely difficult to obey the summons
to return to attend to the war at home;* Alexander even resorted to
mockery when he heard about the battle between Antipater and Agis,
and said, 'Apparently, gentlemen, while we've been defeating Darius
here a battle of mice has taken place back home in Arcadia.'* Consider,
then, how fortunate Sparta was in Agesilaus' respect for his country
and scrupulous observance of the laws. As soon as the *skytalē* arrived,
he gave up and set aside the supreme position of ascendancy and
power he had already gained, and all the high hopes leading him on
to further greatness, and sailed back home straight away 'with his task
unfulfilled'.* His departure left his allies to appreciate how much they
needed him, and showed how completely wrong Erasistratus the son
of Phaeax was to say that of the Lacedaemonians and the Athenians,
the former were the better men in the public sphere and the latter in
the private sphere.* For while Agesilaus proved himself to be without equal as a king and a military commander, the companions and
friends who knew him in his private capacity found him even more
impressive and appealing. Persian coins were stamped with the figure
of an archer, and Agesilaus said as he was breaking camp that the king
had used 30,000 archers to drive him out of Asia, since this was how
much money had been send to Athens and Thebes and distributed
to the popular leaders there. And so the people of Athens and
Thebes were at war with the Spartiates.*

[16] As he was making his way through Thrace, after crossing the
Hellespont, he made no demands on any of the native peoples, but
sent messengers to each of them, to ask whether he should expect a
friendly or hostile reception as he passed through their land. All the
native tribes gave him a friendly reception and escorted him on his
way, except the Trochalians, as they are called. This was a tribe to

which even Xerxes had given gifts, we hear, and now they demanded 100 talents of silver and the same number of women as a fee for Agesilaus' passage through their territory. Agesilaus responded with scorn, challenging them just to come and take what they wanted, and continued onward. The Trochalians drew themselves up in battle formation and came out against him, but Agesilaus routed them and inflicted heavy losses on them.*

He sent the same question to the Macedonian king, who replied that he would think about it. 'Fine,' Agesilaus said. 'He can think about it while we continue on our way.' This bold move so astonished and worried the king that he told Agesilaus he could expect to be treated as a friend on his march through Macedonia. The Thessalians had entered into a treaty of alliance with his enemies, so he devastated their territory, but he sent Xenocles and Scythes to Larissa to try to win the friendship of the people there—who promptly arrested and imprisoned these representatives of his. Everyone around Agesilaus was furious and thought he should establish his army near the city and lay siege to it, but he said that he would rather have either of these men safe than gain the whole of Thessaly, so he recovered them under a truce.*

This behaviour of Agesilaus' will probably seem less surprising in view of the fact that when he heard that a major battle had taken place at Corinth,* with a disproportionately large number of losses on the enemy side compared with the extremely few Spartiates who had been killed, it was plain to see that the news did not make him happy or proud. Instead he heaved a great sigh and said, 'Alas, poor Greece! By her own hands she has destroyed enough men to have defeated in battle, were they alive, a combined force of all the easterners at once.'* However, when a Pharsalian force of 500 horsemen was harassing and injuring his army, he ordered his men into the attack, routed the Pharsalians, and set up a trophy at the foot of Mount Narthacium. He was particularly pleased with this victory because with nothing but a cavalry force of his own making he had defeated the people whose chief source of pride was their horsemanship.*

[17] While he was in this region an ephor called Diphridas arrived from Sparta, with orders that he was immediately to invade Boeotia. Now, Agesilaus had been planning to do this anyway, but only when he had a larger army at his disposal. There was no question of his disobeying the magistrates, however. He therefore told his men that

the day for which they had come from Asia was at hand, and he also sent for two divisions of troops who were stationed at Corinth. As a mark of honour, the Spartans back home in the city issued a proclamation asking for volunteers from among the young men to enlist and help the king. They all signed up without any hesitation, and the magistrates selected the fifty fittest and strongest and sent them to join Agesilaus.

Agesilaus passed through the Gates* and made his way through Phocis, which was friendly territory. Shortly after he had entered Boeotia and encamped near Chaeronea, there was a partial eclipse of the sun, which coincided with news reaching him of Pisander's death during the defeat of his fleet off Cnidos by Pharnabazus and Conon.* He was of course deeply upset by the news, not only because he had lost a good man, but also because of the danger Sparta now faced; nevertheless, he did not want his men to march into battle with morale and confidence at a low ebb, so he told the messengers who had come from the coast to lie and say that they had won the sea battle. Then he appeared in public wearing a garland, and after performing the sacrifices appropriate to receiving good news, he sent portions of the victims to his friends.*

[18] So Agesilaus continued on his way. When he came within sight of the enemy, which was at Coronea, he drew his men up in battle formation, giving the left wing to the Orchomenians, while he himself took charge of the right. On the opposite side the Thebans held the right wing themselves, with the Argives on the left. Xenophon says that this was the most remarkable battle of his day, and he was there in person, fighting on Agesilaus' side, since he had crossed over with him from Asia.* The first clash did not involve much in the way of resistance and fighting: the Thebans soon routed the Orchomenians, while Agesilaus did the same to the Argives. However, both sides turned back on hearing that their respective left wings had been forced into retreat. At this point an easy victory was within Agesilaus' grasp, if he had been prepared to resist meeting the Thebans head on and had attacked them in the rear as they came past him. But in the heat of his passion and desire for victory he went straight for them, with the intention of pushing them back by main force. The Thebans resisted just as vigorously as he attacked, and the fighting was fierce all the way along the line, although it was fiercest at the point where Agesilaus himself was stationed, surrounded by his fifty

volunteers, whose determination seems to have been just what was needed to save the king's life. They fought with fanatical energy and disregard for their own safety. It was impossible for them to keep him unhurt; he was wounded many times by spears and swords which penetrated his armour and reached his body. But they just managed to snatch him away alive by forming a barrier in front of him, where they killed and died in large numbers. Since it proved too hard to force the Thebans back directly, they had no choice but to do what they had been reluctant to do in the first place. That is, they separated into two parts, opening up a gap through the middle of their ranks, and then, when the Thebans had broken through the gap and were proceeding in some disarray, they ran up behind them and attacked them from both sides. They failed to rout the Thebans, however, who withdrew to Mount Helicon, proud of the fact that their unit, at least, had remained undefeated in the fighting.

[19] Although Agesilaus was in considerable pain from all his wounds, he refused to retire to his tent until he had been taken on a stretcher to the battle-lines and had seen the bodies of the dead brought within the defensive perimeter. He also gave orders that none of the enemy troops who had taken refuge in the sanctuary were to be harmed. The battle had taken place close to the temple of Athena Itonia, in front of which is a trophy which the Boeotians had set up long before, when a Boeotian army under Sparto had defeated the Athenians and killed Tolmides.*

At dawn the next day Agesilaus wanted to find out whether the Thebans would offer battle. With his men wearing garlands and the pipers playing their pipes, he got his troops to set up and decorate a trophy as if victory had been theirs. The Thebans sent heralds to ask permission to collect their dead, and he agreed to a truce. Reassured, then, that he had indeed won,* he travelled to Delphi, where the Pythian Games were being held. While he was there, he took part in the procession in honour of the god, and dedicated 100 talents of spoils—a tenth of what he had brought from Asia.*

On his return home, he immediately won the affection and admiration of his fellow citizens for his conduct and his lifestyle, because unlike most commanders he did not come back from abroad a changed man, entranced by foreign customs, dissatisfied with things at home, and chafing under the domestic yoke. Instead, he felt as much respect and regard for the situation there as those of his fellows who had never crossed the Eurotas. He did not alter his eating or bathing habits; he treated his wife the same way; he did not change the style of his arms and armour or the furniture in his house; in fact, he even left the doors to his house as they were, despite the fact that they were so ancient that they looked as if they were the very ones which Aristodamus had hung.* And Xenophon tells us that his daughter's *kannathron* was no more magnificent than anyone else's—a *kannathron* being a wooden float carved in the shape of a griffin or a goat-stag on which young girls ride in processions there.* Xenophon did not write down the name of Agesilaus' daughter, and Dicaearchus expresses his annoyance that the names of neither Agesilaus' daughter nor Epaminondas' mother are known. However, I found in the Laconian archives that Agesilaus' wife was called Cleora, and his daughters Eupolia and Hippolyta. And one can still see his spear in Lacedaemon, which is no different from anyone else's.*

[20] However, because he noticed that some of his fellow citizens were giving themselves airs and were puffed up with pride because they bred horses, he persuaded his sister Cynisca to enter a chariot in the Olympic Games.* The point was to show the Greeks that victory in the Games was not a sign of manly virtue, but merely the result of having money to spend.

One of the favoured members of his circle at this time was the philosopher Xenophon, and Agesilaus told him to get his sons to come to Lacedaemon and bring them up there, so that they would learn the most important lesson of all, namely how to obey and how to command.*

After Lysander's death, Agesilaus discovered that there was a sizeable party in existence whose purpose was to oppose him, and that Lysander had formed it immediately after returning from Asia. He therefore set out to uncover what Lysander had been like, as a citizen of Sparta, during his lifetime, and he found a speech which Lysander had left behind on a papyrus roll. The speech, which had been composed by Cleon of Halicarnassus, was all about revolution and political change, and Lysander had been planning to take it and deliver it before the people of Sparta. Agesilaus wanted to make the speech public knowledge, but one of the elders read it and found its ingenuity alarming, so he advised Agesilaus not to dig Lysander up again, but to bury the speech along with him. Agesilaus agreed that this was a good idea, and kept quiet.*

He did nothing to harm his opponents openly, but as the occasion arose he arranged for them to be sent away from the city to take up a command or govern a district, to expose their worthlessness and greed in positions of power. Then, however, when they were on trial, he would come to their aid and support their defence, and so make them his friends instead of enemies, and win them over to his side, until he had no opponents left.

As for the other king, Agesipolis, not only was he the son of an exile, but he was still far from full adulthood; moreover, he was inherently even-tempered and unassuming, so he played little part in public life.* Nevertheless, Agesilaus set about establishing his influence over him too. Whenever the Spartan kings are resident in the country, they go and eat together in the same *phidition*. Now, Agesilaus was aware that Agesipolis, like himself, had strong homoerotic instincts, so he always used to introduce into their conversations the topic of alluring boys, encourage the young man to share his own passions and fall in love with the same boys, and help him in his affairs. There is nothing disgraceful about homoerotic affairs in Lacedaemon; in fact, as I have explained in my *Life of Lycurgus*, they are highly moral, and are used to arouse noble ambitions and motivate the quest for virtue.*

[21] So Agesilaus gained enormous power in Sparta. He then arranged for Teleutias, his half-brother on his mother's side, to take command of the fleet, and mounted a campaign against Corinth, in which he took the city's long walls by land while Teleutias at sea <captured the enemy fleet and dockyards>.*† Now, the Argives were in control of Corinth at the time. It was the time of the Isthmian Festival, and the Argives had just finished performing the sacrifices to the god when the arrival of the Lacedaemonians caused them to abandon all their paraphernalia and flee. Although Agesilaus refused to take charge of the games, which is what the Corinthian exiles in his entourage asked him to do, he stayed and provided security for them while they held the games and celebrated the festival. Later, however, after Agesilaus had left, the Isthmian Games were held again by the Argives, and some contestants won all over again, while others went down in the records as having won the first time but not the second.* Agesilaus declared that this showed the Argives to be self-convicted cowards, because despite the fact that they obviously considered the right to manage the games a matter of considerable importance and seriousness, they lacked the courage to fight for it.

For himself, he thought it best to act with some restraint in all these matters. He used to respect the choral and athletic competitions in Lacedaemon, and would always attend them with a great deal of enthusiasm and interest, and without failing to put in an appearance at any contest involving boys or girls;* but he hardly seemed to know even the first thing about matters which he saw impressing everyone else. Once, in fact, the tragic actor Callippides, who was very famous and well known throughout Greece and was universally admired, first came up to and addressed Agesilaus, and then presumptuously pushed his way into the crowd of people who were walking around with Agesilaus at the time and began to draw attention to himself, expecting Agesilaus to make friendly overtures towards him. Eventually he said, 'Don't you recognize me, my lord?' Agesilaus looked hard at him and said, 'Yes, aren't you Callippides the showman?'—which is how the Lacedaemonians refer to actors in plays.* On another occasion, when he was invited to hear a man imitating a nightingale, he said, 'I've heard the real thing.'* The doctor Menecrates was so successful in a number of cases which had been pronounced hopeless that he was given the nickname 'Zeus'—a name which he had the bad taste to use. Once, in fact, he went so far as to begin a letter to Agesilaus as follows: 'Menecrates Zeus sends his greetings to Agesilaus.' So Agesilaus wrote back: 'Agesilaus sends his wishes for a speedy recovery to Menecrates.'*

[22] Another thing he did during his time in and around Corinth was capture the Heraeum. As he was watching his soldiers plundering the temple of its spoils, a delegation arrived from Thebes to sue for peace. But he had always hated Thebes, and this just gave him a good opportunity, as far as he was concerned, to show his utter contempt for the place, so when the delegates presented themselves before him he pretended that he could not see them or hear them. But he soon got his come-uppance, because the Theban delegation had not yet left when news arrived of the annihilation of the Lacedaemonian division by Iphicrates. This was the worst disaster the Lacedaemonians had suffered for a long time: not only did they lose a lot of good men, but they were hoplites and Lacedaemonians, while they were defeated by peltasts and mercenaries.*

Agesilaus immediately leapt into action and wanted to go to their assistance, but when he learnt that they had already been wiped out, he returned to the Heraeum. This time he granted the Boeotians an audience and was ready to negotiate with them, but they repaid him for his insulting behaviour by making no further mention of peace, and demanding safe passage to Corinth instead. Agesilaus lost his temper and said, 'If you want to see your friends elated at their success, you'll be able to do so in safety tomorrow.' And the next day he took them with him when he went out to devastate the countryside around Corinth and advanced right up to the city itself. Now that he had demonstrated that the Corinthians did not have the courage to offer him any resistance, he dismissed the Theban delegation. He personally picked up the survivors from the decimated division and took them back to Lacedaemon. During this journey he tended to break camp before daybreak and pitch camp after dark, so that any Arcadians who hated them and wished them harm should not be able to gloat over them.*

Next, as a favour to the Achaeans, he crossed over to Acarnania on a joint expedition with them. He carried off a lot of booty there, and defeated the Acarnanians in battle. When the Achaeans asked him to spend the winter there in order to rob the enemy of the chance to sow their fields, he replied that he would do the opposite of what they were suggesting, because the enemy would be more likely to want to avoid war the next summer if their fields were all sown. And events proved him right: when the Acarnanians were warned that another expedition was being mounted against them, they came to terms with the Achaeans.*

[23] Conon and Pharnabazus, with the Persian fleet, had made themselves masters of the sea* and were raiding the coastal districts of Laconia; moreover, the Athenian walls had been rebuilt with money donated by Pharnabazus.* Under these circumstances, the Lacedaemonians decided that it would be a good idea to make peace with the Persian king.* They sent Antalcidas to Tiribazus and, in a criminal act of horrendous proportions, handed the Asian Greeks over to the Persian king. Now, it was precisely these Greeks on whose behalf Agesilaus had gone to war, so he could have no part in this infamous act. Antalcidas was a political opponent of his, and set about securing the peace treaty on any terms because he was convinced that the war increased Agesilaus' power and enhanced his reputation and importance. Nevertheless, when someone suggested that the Lacedaemonians were siding with the Persians, Agesilaus replied that it was more a case of the Persians siding with the Lacedaemonians. Moreover, by

threatening to declare war on any Greeks who refused to accept the peace, he forced them all to abide by whatever terms the Persian king decided to impose. This was aimed primarily at the Thebans, the idea being to weaken them by giving the rest of Boeotia self-determination.

Later events made it clear that this was his policy. For instance, when Phoebidas committed the outrage of seizing the Cadmeia while there was a peace treaty in force,* there was public outcry through-out Greece and the Spartiates were furious. In an attempt to cast suspicion on Agesilaus, his enemies angrily asked Phoebidas who had put him up to the deed, but Agesilaus had no hesitation in taking Phoebidas' part and stated, for all to hear, that the only consideration was whether there was any practical benefit to be gained from the actual deed, since it is was perfectly acceptable for someone to act independently, without carrying out anyone's orders, if it was to the advantage of Lacedaemon.* In theory, however, his constant refrain was that justice was the chief virtue, on the grounds that without justice there was nothing to be gained from courage, for instance, and that, if everyone were just, courage would be obsolete. When he heard people say, 'It is the Great King's pleasure that such-and-such hap-pens,' his response was, 'Is he any greater a man than me? Only if he is more just.'* In other words, he thought—quite rightly and correctly—that justice was the royal measure, so to speak, by which one should assess how much greater one ruler is than another. After the peace treaty had been concluded, the Persian king sent him a letter proposing that the two of them become guest-friends on a personal basis, but Agesilaus rejected the suggestion: the public friendship would do, he said, and as long as it remained in force they would have no need of a personal relationship.*

However, he did not always keep to these principles in practice; he was often carried away by his ambition and competitiveness, particularly when it came to dealing with the Thebans. And so he not only protected Phoebidas, but even persuaded the city to take responsibility for his crime and to occupy the Cadmeia on its own authority. He also got them to make Archias and Leontiadas, the people who had let Phoebidas into the city so that he could seize the acropolis, the political and administrative leaders of Thebes.*

[24] All this gave rise to the suspicion that Phoebidas had merely been an agent of Agesilaus, who had planned the whole business, and few people would have disputed the allegation after his subsequent

actions. For when the Thebans drove the garrison out and liberated their city, Agesilaus charged them with the murder of Archias and Leontiadas—men who had used their position as polemarchs to rule as tyrants—and declared war on them.* Cleombrotus, who had come to the throne after Agesipolis' death,* was sent to Boeotia with an army. Agesilaus turned down this command on the grounds that he was forty years past the age at which military service begins, and was therefore legally exempt from active service.* But in fact what inhibited him was the prospect of being seen making war on the Thebans on account of their tyrants, when he had just finished fighting the Phleiasians on behalf of their exiles.*

There was a Spartan called Sphodrias, a political opponent of Agesilaus, who had been appointed to the position of harmost at Thespiae. He was a man of no little courage and determination, but was always brimming with hope rather than good sense, and wanted to make a big name for himself. He thought about what a famous celebrity Phoebidas had become as a result of his bold strike in Thebes, and became convinced that he would achieve something even more admirable and glorious if he took it upon himself to launch a surprise attack on the Piraeus from the landward side, seize it, and so deprive the Athenians of their access to the sea. Pelopidas and Melon, the Boeotarchs,* are said to have been the originators of the plan, and to have made the first approach to Sphodrias. The men they secretly sent to him pretended to be Spartan sympathizers, and kept on singing Sphodrias' praises and making much of him, saying that he was the only one who could pull off such an important coup, until they induced and incited him to undertake something that was just as much an act of criminal aggression as what Phoebidas had done, but which was carried out with less daring and attended by less luck. First, daybreak found him still on the Thriasian Plain, when he had hoped to attack the Piraeus during the night; then, apparently, his men were appalled and terrified by the sight of light pouring from some of the sanctuaries at Eleusis; and finally Sphodrias himself lost his nerve and began to doubt his ability to capture the Piraeus. So he let his men raid the countryside a little and then withdrew ignominiously and ingloriously back to Thespiae.*

As a result of all this, a delegation was dispatched to Sparta from Athens to denounce Sphodrias, but they found that the magistrates there had no need of anyone to lodge a complaint against him, because they had already indicted him on a capital charge. Sphodrias, how-ever, was determined not to stand trial, because he was afraid of what his fellow citizens might do in their anger. They had lost the moral high ground to the Athenians, and they wanted to give the Athenians the impression that they too were Sphodrias' victims rather than his colleagues.

[25] Now, Sphodrias had a son called Cleonymus, a good-looking boy still, whose lover was Archidamus, the son of King Agesilaus.* At the time in question, although Archidamus naturally shared the boy's anxieties about the danger he was in because of his father, he could not be seen doing anything to help him, since Sphodrias was one of Agesilaus' political opponents. Cleonymus came to him in tears and begged him to mollify Agesilaus, because there was no one he and his father had more cause to fear. For three or four days Archidamus hung around Agesilaus, but was too embarrassed and frightened to say anything. Eventually, however, with the trial loom-ing, he summoned up the courage to tell him that Cleonymus had asked him to do something to help his father. Even though Agesilaus had known that Archidamus was Cleonymus' lover, he had let the affair continue, because from a very early age Cleonymus had shown particular promise of turning out well. However, at the time he gave his son no reason to expect that his appeal would produce any favourable result or incline him towards leniency; all he said, before leaving, was that he would think about what it was right and proper for him to do. Feeling that he had let Cleonymus down, Archida-mus stopped going to see him, although he had previously been in the habit of doing so many times a day. This in turn meant that Cleony-mus and Sphodrias became even more depressed about Sphodrias' prospects, until in conversation with them one of Agesilaus' friends, Etymocles, revealed the way Agesilaus' mind was working, which was that while he utterly condemned what Sphodrias had done, he con-sidered him to be basically a man of calibre and believed that the city needed men like him in the army. This was what Agesilaus used to say about the trial whenever the matter came up, because he wanted his son to be happy. The upshot was that Cleonymus immediately appreciated Archidamus' efforts, and Sphodrias' friends gained enough confidence to come to his support.*

Agesilaus was in fact extraordinarily fond of children. There is a famous story about how when his children were young he joined in

their games and used to ride about on a stick at home, pretending
that it was a horse. When he was seen by one of his friends he asked
him to say nothing, until he had children of his own.*

[26] After Sphodrias' acquittal, with the Athenians getting ready
to go to war, Agesilaus was very severely criticized for having apparently obstructed the course of justice at the trial, and implicated the
city in crimes of such enormity against fellow Greeks, all in order to
gratify the ridiculous desires of a child. Moreover, when it came to
his attention that Cleombrotus was not prosecuting the war against
Thebes with any great enthusiasm, he ignored the law he had previously relied on where the expedition was concerned, and invaded
Boeotia himself.* He inflicted some damage on the Thebans, but
also suffered some setbacks in return, so much so that when he was
wounded during this campaign Antalcidas said to him, 'What an
excellent way the Thebans have found to pay you for the lessons you
gave them when they had neither the inclination nor the expertise
to fight!' For our sources do claim that in actual fact the Thebans'
military expertise improved at that time beyond all recognition, as a
result of all the exercise, so to speak, they gained during the many
campaigns the Lacedaemonians fought against them. This was why
in one of his three rhetras, as they are known, Lycurgus in ancient
times had forbidden repeated campaigns against the same enemy, to
stop them acquiring military expertise.*

The allies of the Lacedaemonians also resented Agesilaus' intention to destroy the Thebans when there was no public wrong to be
redressed and he was merely indulging his own anger and competitiveness. They said that under these circumstances they were not prepared to die for the Lacedaemonians year after year, following them
around here and there, especially since there were so many of them
and so few Lacedaemonians. This, we hear, was when Agesilaus came
up with the following trick to try to disprove their numerical superiority. He got all the allies to sit down together whatever their place
of origin, while he got the Lacedaemonians to sit down by themselves
away from all the others. Then he called out, first for all potters to
stand up, then the metal-workers once the potters were standing,
followed by the wood-workers, the builders, and so on for each
category of job. By the end, almost every single one of the allies was
on his feet, but none of the Lacedaemonians was, because they are
not allowed to learn and work at any manual trade.* At this point

Agesilaus laughed and said, 'Gentlemen, do you see how many more soldiers we send out into the field than you?'

[27] Once when he was in Megara, on his way back from campaigning in Thebes, he was walking up towards the civic offices on the acropolis when he suddenly got a severe and painful cramp in his good leg. Later, the leg swelled up and seemed to become congested with blood and extremely inflamed. A Syracusan doctor opened the vein below the ankle, which relieved the pain, but blood poured out at such a rate that the flow could not be stopped. Agesilaus lost consciousness and came critically close to losing his life, but this stopped the flow of blood. He was taken back to Lacedaemon, where for a long time he was very weak and in no condition to undertake military expeditions.*

This coincided with a period when the Spartiates met with many setbacks on land and sea. The worst was the battle of Tegyra, where for the first time they were defeated in a pitched battle by the Thebans.* There was a general move towards establishing a universal peace, and a conference was held in Lacedaemon, attended by delegates from all over Greece, to sort out the terms. One of the delegates was Epaminondas, a man who was highly respected for his culture and his learning, but whose abilities as a military commander remained untested at the time.* He noticed that all the other delegates were inclined to let Agesilaus have his way, but he was the only one with the self-confidence to speak his mind. He delivered a speech containing proposals designed to benefit Greece as a whole, rather than Thebes alone, in which he proved that the war made Sparta more powerful at the expense of everyone else's misery, and called on the Greeks to procure peace for themselves on terms of equality and justice. For a lasting peace would be secured, he said, only if everyone was equal.*

[28] It was clear to Agesilaus that the delegates were incredibly impressed with what Epaminondas was saying and were listening closely to him, so he asked him if he considered that self-determination for Boeotia was covered by the terms 'equality and justice'. Epaminondas promptly and defiantly shot a question back at Agesilaus, and asked him whether in his opinion self-determination for Laconia was just. At this, Agesilaus angrily leapt to his feet and told him to tell them unequivocally whether he would grant Boeotia self-determination, but Epaminondas just repeated his first question again, and asked him whether he would grant Laconia self-determination. Agesilaus was now

in such a rage that, relishing the excuse, he immediately erased the name of the Thebans from the peace accord and declared war on them. He told all the rest of the delegates to leave, now that they and the Lacedaemonians were on good terms, and to let peace take care of their reconcilable problems and war their irreconcilable ones, since it had not been possible to clear up and put an end to all their disputes.*

Now, it so happened that Cleombrotus was in Phocis with an army at the time, so the ephors immediately sent a dispatch ordering him to lead his men in an attack on Thebes, and also sent messages around their various allies, rallying them for the war.* The allies were far from enthusiastic, and resented the war, but they did not yet have the confidence to oppose or disobey the Spartans. There were several bad omens, as described in my *Life of Epaminondas*,* and Prothoüs of Laconia argued against the advisability of the campaign, but Agesilaus refused to give way and made sure that the war went ahead. He assumed that, with the whole of Greece united on the Lacedaemonian side and the Thebans excluded from the treaty, it was a good opportunity to teach them a lesson. However, the timing of the campaign shows that it was prompted by anger rather than sober calculation, because the treaty was made in Lacedaemon on the fourteenth of Scirophorion and they were defeated at Leuctra on the fifth of Hecatombaeon, only twenty-one days later. A thousand Lacedaemonians died in the battle, including King Cleombrotus and the pick of the Spartiates by his side. Among them, we hear, was Cleonymus, the handsome son of Sphodrias, who was struck down three times while defending the king, but got back up on his feet each time until he was finally killed fighting the Thebans.*

[29] The Lacedaemonians had met with an unexpected defeat and the Thebans with a victory they could not have anticipated—a victory the like of which had never been seen in any battle of Greeks against Greeks—yet the courage of the losers was just as admirable and impressive as that of the winners. Xenophon is right to say that there is always something worth recording in even the casual remarks and comments good men pass for fun at a party;* but there is something even more worth noting and observing in good men, and that is what they say and do to preserve their dignity in the face of misfortune. Sparta was in the middle of a festival—the Festival of Unarmed Dancing*—and so was filled with visitors from abroad, with the choral competition

being held in the theatre, when messengers arrived from Leuctra with news of the disaster. Although it was immediately obvious that their cause was ruined and that they had lost their position of supremacy, the ephors refused to allow the city to interrupt the dances or alter the festival programme; they notified the families of the dead by sending messengers to their homes, while they themselves remained to direct the spectacle and the choral competition. By the next day the names of the living and the dead were common knowledge. The fathers, relatives, and friends of the dead went down into the city square and greeted one another with cheerful faces, full of pride and joy,† while the families of the survivors stayed at home with their womenfolk as though they were in mourning, and if one of them had to appear in public, his demeanour, voice and looks all gave an impression of dejection and despondency. What one could see or hear about the women was even more striking: those who were expecting their sons back alive from the battle were depressed and taciturn, while those with sons on the casualty list made their way straight to the sanctuaries, and visited one another's homes in cheerful high spirits.*

[30] However, when their allies began to desert them and Epaminondas, flushed from recent victories, was expected to invade the Peloponnese, then most Lacedaemonians looked at Agesilaus' lameness and remembered the oracles. Their morale plummeted and they were terrified by the thought that the gods were behind the city's troubles because they had banished the sound-footed king in favour of a lame cripple, which was exactly what the god had been telling them to beware of and be on their guard against.* But apart from this, his power, excellent qualities, and reputation were so great that they not only continued to treat him as their king, and rely on him for military leadership in times of war, but even regarded him as the healer and mediator of internal political problems. For instance, the time came when they were reluctant to apply the penalties prescribed by law to those who had shown cowardice in battle (for whom the Lacedaemonian name is *tresantes*), because there were so many of them, and they were men of such power and influence, that they were afraid of them engineering a political coup. Not only are *tresantes* forbidden to hold any political office, but intermarriage with one of their families is also considered a disgrace, and anyone who wants to can strike any of them he meets. They have to put up with going around in an unkempt and shabby state, wearing cloaks patched with variously

coloured bits of material, with half of their moustaches shaved and half left to grow.*

Anyway, they did not like the idea of leaving large numbers of *tresantes* in the city at a time when the city was desperately short of fighting men, so they gave Agesilaus legislative powers. He managed to avoid adding or subtracting or altering a word of the laws. When he came before the Lacedaemonian people, he simply stated that the laws had to be allowed to sleep for that one day, but that from the next day onwards they were to be authoritative. This enabled him to preserve the city's laws and at the same time to avoid disenfranchizing the *tresantes*.

As a way of doing something about the low morale and despondency prevalent among the young men of Lacedaemon, he invaded Arcadia. He was very careful not to meet the enemy in open battle, but he overran Mantinean territory and captured a small town there, which made his fellow citizens feel more optimistic and cheerful, and they began to think that their situation was not completely desperate.*

[31] After this, Epaminondas arrived in Laconia at the head of a force of Boeotians and their allies consisting of at least 40,000 hoplites. Counting also the large numbers of light-armed troops and unarmed marauders who accompanied them, the total number of men in the invading army which came down into Laconia was 70,000.* It was at least 600 years since the Dorians had settled in Lacedaemon, and this was the first foreign army, in all that time, to be seen in their country, because until then no one had dared to invade. But now they invaded a land which had never before been ravaged or despoiled, burning and plundering their way up to the banks of the Eurotas and the city, and no one came out against them, because Agesilaus would not let the Lacedaemonians fight against what Theopompus describes as 'a rushing torrent of war'. He concentrated his hoplites around the central and most important parts of the city, and put up with the threats and taunts of the Thebans, who called on him by name and challenged him to fight for his country, since it was he who had kindled the flames of war and so was responsible for its troubles. No less distressing for Agesilaus was the situation inside the city, which was filled with noise and shouting and aimless running to and fro: the older men were infuriated at what was happening, and the women, who found it impossible to stay calm, were driven frantic by the cries emanating from the enemy camp and the sight of the watchfires there.* He was also

tormented by the prospect for his reputation, given that he had taken over the city when it was at the height of its powers and influence, and had presided over the collapse of its reputation and the suppression of its proud boast—one which he himself had often made—that the womenfolk of Laconia had never seen the smoke of an enemy's fire. There is a story that during an argument with Antalcidas* about courage an Athenian said, 'But we've often chased you away from the Cephisus,' and Antalcidas replied, 'Yes, but we've never chased you away from the Eurotas.' A similar reply was given by a less famous Spartiate to an Argive: when the Argive said, 'Plenty of your men lie buried in the Argolid,' the Spartiate replied, 'Yes, but none of your men lie buried in Laconia.'

[32] At the time we are talking about, however, Antalcidas, who was an ephor, is said to have been so terrified that he secretly sent his sons away to Cythera. When the enemy tried to cross the river and force their way into the city, Agesilaus abandoned the rest of it and deployed his troops in defence of the high ground in the centre. The Eurotas was as deep and as strong at the time as it ever is, since there had been a snowfall, and the Thebans found it particularly troublesome and awkward, not so much because of the swiftness of its current as because of the coldness of the water. As Epaminondas was advancing on the city at the head of his phalanx, he was pointed out to Agesilaus who apparently watched him for a long time, keeping his eyes fixed on him wherever he went, and then said merely, 'There goes a man who wants to achieve great things.' Epaminondas was determined to join battle inside the city and to set up a trophy there, but he did not have the strength to dislodge Agesilaus and could not lure him out either, so he withdrew and proceeded to lay waste the countryside.*

Meanwhile, in Lacedaemon about 200 treacherous and worthless men banded together and seized the Issorium, a well-protected and easily defended spot where the sanctuary of Artemis is. The Lacedaemonians wanted to rush them straight away, but Agesilaus was worried about the possibility of a mutiny among the troops and told them to do nothing, while he went up to the Issorium in person, without any armour and with only a single slave in attendance. As he approached he called out that they must have misheard his orders, since they were not supposed to assemble on the Issorium, or to stay together: some were to go over there (he pointed to another spot), while others went elsewhere in the city. The insurgents were delighted to hear this because it made them think that Agesilaus did not know what was going on, and they split up and went off to the various places he had ordered them. Agesilaus immediately called up other troops and occupied the Issorium; then he had about fifteen of the group arrested and put to death during the night. An informer told him about another conspiracy, a larger one, involving a group of Spartiate men who met in secret in a house to plot revolution. There was no way he could bring them to trial at a time of such confusion, but at the same time he could not afford simply to ignore their scheming. So after consulting the ephors, Agesilaus had these men too put to death without letting the case come to court, despite the fact that previously no Spartiate had ever been executed without a trial.* Moreover, large numbers of the perioeci and helots who had been conscripted into the army were escaping from the city and going over to the enemy, and this was causing Lacedaemonian morale to sink to new depths. So Agesilaus told his slaves to go every morning to the barracks, collect the arms and armour left behind by the deserters, and hide them, to disguise the number of men who were leaving.*

Various reasons have been given to explain the Theban withdrawal from Laconia. Most writers attribute it to the fact that they had already been there for three months and had ravaged most of the countryside, and then there was a period of atrocious weather and the Arcadians began to leave in disorderly dribs and drabs. Theopompus, however, adds that after the Boeotarchs had decided to leave a Spartiate called Phrixus came to them from Agesilaus with ten talents to cover the costs of their retreat, so that they ended up carrying out a plan they had long been committed to, with their expenses met by the enemy as well.

[33] I cannot imagine how this story escaped the notice of every single writer except Theopompus. But they all agree that the safety of Sparta at this time was due to the fact that Agesilaus laid aside his inherent competitive determination to succeed and desire for victory, and managed matters cautiously. But he could not enable Sparta to recover the power and position it had lost after its defeat. The city was like a person who may be healthy, but who has followed too strict and rigid a regimen throughout his life: all it took was one error for the scales to tilt and bring the state's prosperity crashing down. There is nothing surprising about this. The Spartan constitution was

perfectly designed for promoting moral excellence, peace, and unanimity, but they made it support an empire and a position of supremacy won by force, which, in Lycurgus' opinion, made no contribution at all to the prosperity of a state, and so they fell.*

Agesilaus now renounced military service because of his age, but his son Archidamus, with help which had come from the tyrant in Sicily, defeated the Arcadians in the 'tearless battle', so called because no one on his side was killed, while there were a great many losses on the enemy side.* This victory gave convincing proof of the weakness of the city. Previously they had regarded defeating their enemies as so ordinary and natural an event for them that there had been no public victory-offering sacrificed to the gods except a cock, participation in the battle had not been an excuse for boasting, and hearing about the victory had not been the occasion for any particular rejoicing. In fact, even after the battle of Mantinea, which Thucydides has described,* the magistrates sent the person who first told them of the victory nothing more than a piece of meat from his *phidition* as the reward due a bearer of good news.* But now, when news of the battle reached the city, and as Archidamus himself drew near, no one could restrain himself. His father was the first to greet him, with tears of joy on his face, and he was followed by the chief magistrates, while most of the older men and the women went down to the river, raising their hands to heaven and giving thanks to the gods, as if Sparta had thrown off its degrading reproach and could once more see the bright light of day. For it is said that before this the men had felt so ashamed of the defeats they had suffered that they had not even been able to look their wives in the face.

[34] However, when Messene was rebuilt by Epaminondas and its former citizens flocked there from all directions, the Lacedaemonians could not find the courage to resist what was happening or the resources to prevent it.* They took out their anger and resentment on Agesilaus, because for so long they had reaped the benefit of controlling a country which was as big as Laconia and as fertile as anywhere in Greece, and now, during his reign, they had lost it. This explains why Agesilaus rejected the Theban peace offer. He was not prepared formally to cede the territory to those who held it in actuality, but he continued to pit himself against the Thebans, and the upshot was that he not only failed to recover Messenia, but came close to losing Sparta as well, thanks to Epaminondas' superior military strategy. Here is what happened.

When the Mantineans rebelled against the Thebans, Agesilaus responded to their request for help by leading an expeditionary force out of Lacedaemon with a view to attacking the Thebans.* As soon as Epaminondas found out that Agesilaus was on his way, he broke camp in the middle of the night, without the Mantineans noticing anything, and led his army away from Tegea in an attack on Lacedaemon itself. He slipped past Agesilaus and came very close to suddenly seizing the undefended city. But Euthynus of Thespiae, according to Callisthenes (or a Cretan, according to Xenophon), told Agesilaus, who quickly sent a horseman on ahead to warn those who were in the city, and then arrived back in Sparta himself not long afterwards. A short while later the Thebans crossed the Eurotas and began to attack the city, but Agesilaus put up an unusually spirited defence for someone of his age. Unlike the last time, he did not see the situation as calling for caution and defensive measures, but rather for recklessness and daring. Although he had never trusted in or relied on such tactics before, on this occasion they were all he used to repel the danger. He snatched the city out of Epaminondas' grasp and set up a victory trophy, thereby showing the children and the womenfolk of the city that the Lacedaemonians were repaying their country in the noblest possible fashion for the upbringing it had given them. This applied especially to Archidamus, who was conspicuous in the fighting for his courage and agility, as he ran swiftly through the streets to the trouble spots, and wherever he went he and his few companions stood firm against the enemy.

Isadas the son of Phoebidas* put on a magnificent display of bravery, in my opinion, and one which impressed his enemies as much as his fellow citizens. He was extremely handsome and tall, and was at that age, just between childhood and adulthood, when a person's physical charms are at their most alluring. He had just finished anointing his body with oil, so not only was he not wearing protective armour, but he did not even have any clothes on. He dashed out of his house with a spear in one hand and a sword in the other and pushed his way through the thick of the fighting to where he would find plenty of opponents, every single one of whom he struck down and killed. Not one of them managed to wound him, so perhaps his courage earned him the protection of some god, or perhaps his enemies took him to be too tall and brilliant to be a mere human being. It is said that the ephors first crowned him with a garland in recognition of his exploits, and then imposed a fine of 1,000 drachmas on him, for being foolhardy enough to risk his life without the protection of armour.

[35] A few days later the two sides met in battle near Mantinea.* Epaminondas had already overwhelmed the front ranks of the Lacedae-monians, but he was still pressing hard on their heels, when a Laconian called Anticrates stood his ground against him and struck him down, with a spear according to Dioscorides, but the Lacedaemonians even now call Anticrates' descendants 'the Swordsmen', which implies that he struck him with a sword. They had been so afraid of Epaminondas while he was alive that, as a way of expressing the extent of their admira-tion and appreciation, they conferred on Anticrates certain prerogat-ives and rewards, including exemption from taxes in perpetuity, a right which Callicrates, one of Anticrates' descendants, still holds today.*

After the battle and the death of Epaminondas, the Greeks set about making peace among themselves, but Agesilaus tried to exclude the Messenians from the oath, on the grounds that they were stateless. All the rest of the Greeks accepted the Messenians, however, and saw no problem with them giving their oath, so the Lacedaemonians uni-laterally withdrew from the proceedings and remained in a state of war, since they hoped to recover Messenia.* Agesilaus therefore gained a reputation for being impetuous and unyielding, and for having an insatiable appetite for war, since he was doing all he could to under-mine and hinder the general peace. Moreover, lack of funds forced him to lay the financial burden on his friends in Sparta, by borrowing and soliciting contributions from them. At a time when he should have been seizing the opportunity he had been presented with to put an end to Sparta's troubles, and when he had thrown away their great empire in its entirety, with its cities and mastery of land and sea, he was getting all worked up about the goods and revenues of Messene.

[36] His reputation suffered even further when he offered himself as a military commander to Tachos of Egypt.* People did not think it right that a man who had once been judged to be without a rival, and who had been known throughout the world, should lend his body and hire out his name and reputation to work, in effect, as a paid cap-tain of mercenaries for a foreigner who had risen up in revolt against his king. Agesilaus was now past eighty years of age, and his body was covered in scars from old wounds. Even if he had again accepted the noble and admirable position of commander-in-chief fighting to free the Greeks from tyranny, it would still have been possible to find

fault with his drive and determination in some respects. For what is good has its own proper time and season; in fact, to generalize, it is observance of due measure that constitutes the difference between the good and the bad. As far as Agesilaus was concerned, however, this was not a consideration, and he did not regard any form of public service as beneath his dignity. On the contrary, he thought it would be inappropriate for him to live in the city without doing anything, but just sitting and waiting for death. So he recruited mercenaries with the money Tachos sent him, manned ships, and put to sea, taking thirty Spartiate advisers with him as before.*

As soon as he landed in Egypt the king's chief officers and governors came up to the ship to show their respect for him. His arrival had also generated a great deal of interest and been keenly anticipated all over Egypt, because the name of Agesilaus was so well known, and a huge crowd of people gathered to come and see him. Instead of a splendid display with all sorts of paraphernalia, they found an old, slightly built, unremarkable man lying on some grass on the seashore, wearing a coarse, cheap cloak, and at the sight they began to laugh scornfully and make jokes. They said that this was a perfect example of the saying about the mountain being in labour and then producing a mouse. They found his behaviour even more eccentric and odd. When gifts of welcome were fetched and carried over to him, he accepted the flour, calves, and geese, but made as if to reject the dried fruits, pastries, and perfumes. They insisted, and begged him to accept them, so he told them to take them and give them to his helots.* However, according to Theophrastus, he liked the papyrus they used for weaving garlands, because it made such neat and simple garlands, and when he was leaving Egypt he asked the king to give him some.

[37] Now, however, when he met up with Tachos, who was getting ready for his campaign, he was not given charge of the whole army, as he had expected, but only of the mercenaries, while Chabrias of Athens* was put in command of the fleet and Tachos himself was commander-in-chief. Agesilaus was annoyed about this, and there were further irritations in store for him, because he had to endure the Egyptian's lies and vanity, which was hard for him. He did in fact sail with him on an expedition against the Phoenicians, during which he deferred to him and put up with him, although it went against both his dignity and his nature to do so; but when the opportunity for a change presented itself, he took it.

Tachos' cousin Nectanebis, who was in command of part of the army, rose up in rebellion, and when the Egyptians proclaimed him king, he sent messengers to Agesilaus, asking for his support. He also approached Chabrias with the same request, and promised to reward both of them if they joined him. When Tachos found out what was going on and begged the two Greeks to stay with him, Chabrias tried to get Agesilaus to remain on good terms with Tachos. He argued with him and tried to calm his anger, but Agesilaus said, 'Chabrias, you came here of your own free choice, so you can do whatever you personally think best, but I was seconded to the Egyptians as a military commander by my country, and it would be wrong for me to fight against the very people I was sent to help, unless my country changes its instructions to me.' As well as saying this, however, he sent men to Sparta to denounce Tachos and endorse Nectanebis. The two Egyptians also sent agents to Sparta to appeal for help, with Tachos reminding the Lacedaemonians how long he had been their ally and friend, and Nectanebis promising to outdo Tachos in his loyalty and commitment to Sparta's cause.

The Lacedaemonians listened to both sides of the argument and then made a public response to the Egyptians in which they said that it would be Agesilaus' responsibility to decide what to do about these matters. Meanwhile, in a letter to him they told him to make sure that Sparta's interests were served by whatever he did. Under these circumstances, Agesilaus took his mercenaries and changed sides from Tachos to Nectanebis, using Sparta's interests as a pretext for this inexplicable and appalling act. After all, stripped of this excuse, his action can only be described as treachery. But it is typically Lacedaemonian to think of goodness primarily in terms of their country's interests; they have no conception or understanding of justice except as what they think will enhance Sparta.*

[38] Tachos, deserted by his mercenaries, fled into exile.* But Nectanebis' claim to the throne was challenged by a rival from Mendes,* who rose up in revolt against him and was proclaimed king. The new king gathered together an army of 100,000 men and advanced towards Nectanebis' position. Nectanebis tried to convince Agesilaus that there was nothing to worry about, arguing that for all their numbers the enemy troops were no more than a mixed rabble of artisans, so inexperienced in war that they could safely be treated with disdain. But Agesilaus said, 'It is precisely their inexperience and

ignorance that worry me, not their numbers. It may prove difficult to trick them. The point of tricks is that they bring the unexpected to bear on people who are geared up to defend themselves against what they anticipate and expect. But it's impossible to trick someone who is not expecting or anticipating anything from you at all, just as in a wrestling match it's impossible to throw someone off balance unless he's in motion.'

Later, the Mendesian also approached Agesilaus and tried to win him over. Nectanebis was alarmed at this, and when Agesilaus told him he should join battle as soon as possible, and not wage a war of attrition against men who might have no experience of conflict, but who had the numerical superiority to encircle him, contain him within a trench, and then have the edge on him and seize the initiative in many respects, this increased Nectanebis' suspicions and fears about him so much that he retreated back to a city with strong defences and a high surrounding wall. Agesilaus found Nectanebis' lack of confidence in him galling and irritating, but since he could not bear the thought of changing allegiance again and joining the other side, or of going home without having achieved anything at all, he accompanied Nectanebis into his stronghold.

[39] When the enemy came up to the city, however, and began to dig a trench around it, the Egyptian changed his mind and, rather than facing the awful prospect of a siege, he now wanted to engage the enemy in battle—a plan with which the Greeks were all in favour, since there was no food in the place. But Agesilaus argued against the idea and stopped Nectanebis carrying it out, which made the Egyptians even more critical of him than they had been before. They called him a traitor to the king's cause, but he calmly endured their calumny and watched out for the right time to put into effect the following scheme. The enemy were running a deep trench around the outside of the city wall, with the intention of completely enclosing them inside it. When the two ends of the trench were quite close to meeting, so that the city would be completely surrounded, Agesilaus waited until the evening and then told the Greeks to arm themselves. He went to the Egyptian and said, 'Now is the time, young man, for us to win our safety. I kept silent until the actual moment was at hand, in case something happened to ruin our chances. We have the enemy themselves, and all the hard work they have undertaken, to thank for our safety. They have got so far with digging their trench that the

completed part will impede them, because of their large numbers, while the gap between the two ends of the trench is just the right size to make it possible for us to fight them on fair and equal terms. If you really want to prove your courage, join us as we race into the attack, and you will save yourself and your men. We will rout those of the enemy troops who meet us head on, and the trench will stop the rest doing us any harm.'

Nectanebis was most impressed with Agesilaus' cleverness. He surrounded himself with Greek weaponry, charged into the attack, and overwhelmed any of the enemy who stood in his way. As soon as Agesilaus found that Nectanebis trusted him, he used on the enemy the same tactics once more, like a feint in wrestling. By sometimes retreating a little way and giving ground to the enemy, and sometimes wheeling round to face them, he bottled the whole mass of them up in a place which had deep irrigation channels flowing by on both sides. Then he filled the entire space between these channels with the head of his phalanx, and so ensured that his men faced an equal number of the enemy, who could not employ any outflanking or encircling manoeuvres. After resisting for a short while the enemy were routed with huge losses; any survivors who escaped scattered and melted away.

[40] After this the Egyptian had nothing to worry about and his affairs prospered. He had become very fond of Agesilaus and, for friendship's sake, asked him to stay and see the winter out there with him. But Agesilaus was anxious to set out for the war back home, since he knew that Sparta was short of money and was trying to maintain a mercenary force. Nectanebis therefore gave him a magnificent send-off as a mark of respect and gave him, apart from various privileges and personal gifts, 230 talents of silver for the war. Since it was now winter, Agesilaus kept his ships close to the coastline. In the course of his journey past Libya, he reached an uninhabited place called Menelaus' Haven,* where he died. He was 83 years old, and had been a king of Sparta for forty-one years. For more than thirty years of his reign, there was no one to compare with him for power and influence: he had been regarded as the leader and king of almost all Greece, up until the battle of Leuctra.

The Laconian way of dealing with the bodies of those who died abroad was simply to bury them and leave them where they were, except in the case of kings, whose bodies were brought home. So the Spartiates who were with him coated his body with wax, since there was no honey available,* and took him back to Lacedaemon. The throne passed to his son, Archidamus, and remained in his family down to the time of Agis, who was killed by Leonidas while trying to restore the ancient constitution. Agis was the fifth in descent from Agesilaus.*

ALEXANDER

INTRODUCTION

Less than 33 years old when he died, Alexander in the space of thirteen years had led his Macedonian army on a mission of conquest which brought under his power peoples from the Danube to the Nile and the Indus. The strategic, tactical, and logistic skill of the king and his comrades, the sheer force of will, marked the history of the Mediterranean and south-west Asia permanently. Between the crossing of the Hellespont in 334 BC and the return from the Punjab in 326 he fought three major set battles against the Persians and one with an Indian king, took innumerable cities, sometimes after immensely difficult sieges, battled mountain tribes, and overcame obstacles of every sort. Plutarch, however, directs his attention not to these military achievements, but to the man behind them. What qualities did Alexander show in the few years of his life, and how can we evaluate his character and his actions?

Julius Caesar is the parallel figure: this juxtaposition indicates that Plutarch is interested not only in the figure of the conqueror, but in that of the ruler, one who brings the world, or most of it, under his control. Caesar not only conquered, but won supreme power at Rome, defeating even Pompey, the other great Roman commander who might have been compared with the Macedonian. Alexander and Caesar shared a driving ambition, military genius, betrayal by their friends, and untimely death. Both were accused of demanding too many honours, but both seemed so extraordinary as to be above the human plane. Both men, in their different ways, serve as models and warnings for the Roman emperors of Plutarch's day. In particular, Plutarch may have thought of Trajan, who admired Alexander, led victorious armies, and added the provinces of Dacia, Arabia, Armenia, Mesopotamia, and Assyria to the empire. In these Lives, Plutarch does not question conquest in itself—in fact, he recognizes its heroic aspect—but he stresses that the real worth of an individual is measured by other criteria.

Despite his disclaimer that he will not write history, this Life is one of the longest which we have. The canvas is vast and there were many stories of Alexander. We may divide the life into sections:

1. (1–10, 356–336): his birth, natural qualities, education, and adolescence, until the death of his father, Philip II. The stories connected with his birth establish a heroic tone, and later chapters indicate the inborn 'spiritedness' which is at the basis of his character and report early signs of his genius.

2. (11–23, 336–333): his accession, repression of the tribes south of the Danube and of Greece, and first victories against the Persians at the Granicus and Issus. The section confirms his military genius, while treating personal themes such as his sorrow for the destruction of Thebes (13), his admiration for philosophy (14), and his notion of kingship (21–3).

3. (24–8, 333–331): Alexander's conquest of Egypt and visit to the oracle of Ammon at Siwah. Plutarch explores the question of Alexander's relation to godhead.

4. (29–42, 331–330): the battle of Gaugamela, the conquest of Babylonia and Persis, and the death of Darius. Alexander is at his peak, conqueror of the Persian empire, 'king of Asia'.

5. (43–56, 330–327): after the death of Darius, Alexander adopts Persian attire, and his relations with the Macedonians deteriorate, as seen in the execution of Philotas, the killing of Clitus, the debate on prostration, and the Pages' Conspiracy.

6. (57–66, 327–25): the invasion of India, the battle with Porus, and the mutiny at the Hyphasis River (modern Beas). Alexander finds a limit in the weariness of his men. His journey down the Indus to the Indian ocean.

7. (66–77, 325–323): Alexander returns to Susa and Babylon, is troubled by omens of his death, and dies. The immediate aftermath of his death.

Plutarch's normal pattern is to recount briefly a few events, then to expand on their import with anecdotes touching upon aspects of Alexander's character suggested by the events. Thus, the victory at Issus, his first defeat of Darius, is treated in one sentence, but the battle is surrounded by anecdotes illustrating Alexander's character, in particular his attitude towards kingship and the need for self-restraint (18–23). The procedure is far from simple, since often Plutarch slides smoothly between event and anecdote, and the anecdotes frequently stand in place of the event. To illustrate: the march from Gaza to Siwah in the Egyptian desert is never narrated, but the reader, by a series of anecdotes relating to Homer and the foundation of Alexandria, is brought from Gaza to Alexandria and to Siwah (25–6).

Plutarch seems to abandon chronological sequence for the fifth section of the Life, between the death of Darius in 330 and the invasion of India in 327. Alexander's adoption of Persian garb falls in the narrative soon after Darius' death. The initiative provoked a strong reaction in the army and Plutarch uses it as a springboard for an anecdote sequence on the tensions between the king and his Macedonian followers. One after another the reader encounters the trial and death of Philotas, the murder of Clitus, the rebukes of Callisthenes, the argument over prostration, and the Pages' Conspiracy. These are all historical events, yet they are told without indications of chronology and with an emphasis on Alexander's character, exploring whether power has destroyed his self-control and his warm relations with his companions. When the narrative resumes, Alexander is ready to invade India, and it is spring 327. Even then, Plutarch inserts further incidents arranged without regard to chronology on the topic of Alexander's exertions on the road to glory (57–58).

In reading the many anecdotes in this Life, it is necesary to be alert to the underlying implications of the stories. Before Alexander tames Bucephalas (6), he rebukes the horse's trainers for not knowing how to deal with a noble but fiery animal. Alexander himself had a fiery temperament, full of heat and enthusiasm, but could not be controlled by his tutors (4–5). After seeing Alexander tame Bucephalas, his father Philip immediately hired Aristotle to be his tutor, employing a great philosopher to educate his child. The fiery nature of both Bucephalas and Alexander had to learn to submit to reason, as in the myth of Plato's *Phaedrus* the spirited horse of the soul had to be directed by reason and not be allowed thoughtlessly to follow the passions of its yokemate. For Plutarch, in this as in his other Lives, an education in philosophy and self-restraint is what allows a human to develop his nature in the best way.

Alexander's nature was to pursue glory enthusiastically. By tracking Alexander's behaviour through the Life, Plutarch permits the reader to evaluate how he has responded to the challenges his nature faced in a historical context. Plutarch's portrait is basically positive, and he sees many fine moments and traits in Alexander's life, but there are numerous darker incidents, which impress on us the difficulty of combining power and virtue, and the danger of extraordinary ambition. Something of this idea is suggested immediately after the battle of Gaugamela, when Alexander is proclaimed king of Asia. Plutarch inserts here the report of the discovery near Babylon of naphtha (35), which the Macedonians found both wonderful and destructive: Plutarch speculates that it might have been the substance used by Medea to burn king Creon and his daughter with unquenchable flames. Beneath the speculation lies an intimation that Alexander's fiery nature can be both admirable and destructive.

Central to this Life as to *Caesar* is the hero's relation to his comrades. Caesar died assassinated by his fellow senators; Alexander suspected conspiracies from Philotas and the Pages, and in a drunken brawl killed Clitus, a man who had saved his life. Plutarch sets these events in a larger context, of Macedonian drinking (and Philip trying to kill his son, 9), of Alexander's trust in his doctor (19)[1] and generosity toward his friends (39–42), and of the hostility between Hephaestion and Craterus (47).

---

[1] Echoed, interestingly enough, in an anecdote of Trajan's trust in an adviser told by Dio Cassius, 68. 15. 3²–16.1ª.

Important too was the effect of Anaxarchus and other flatterers at court, who encouraged Alexander that he could do no wrong (23, 52). The implication is that one's very friends and supporters can lead a well-minded person astray. In Platonic terms, their passions are like the passionate horse of the *Phaedrus* myth, which by their unruliness can cause the spirited horse to ignore reason's rein.

In addition, the heavy cloud of omens which darken more and more the final quarter of the Life remind Alexander and the reader of that most certain barrier to all man's plans, death. Alexander can conquer all obstacles, but one never yields, and waits for him: Bucephelas dies, and the Brahman Calanus, and his dear friend Hephaestion. Omens foreshadow the end in diverse ways. Alexander's only hope is that through his labours and conquests he may win a kind of immortality as Heracles and Achilles did, whether by being honoured as a god, or through lasting fame.[2]

The historians of Alexander were without number, but all of those contemporary or close to him have been lost (on these, see Pearson, *Lost Histories*). Our narrative sources are all from the imperial period: besides Plutarch, they are Diodorus Siculus book 17, Quintus Curtius, Arrian's *Anabasis* and *Indica*, and Justin's epitome of Pompeius Trogus. This is not the place to go into the controversies over the relative value of these accounts. Plutarch was undoubtedly familiar with sources contemporary to Alexander, and cites twenty-four writers by name. However, citations usually serve to highlight an isolated fact, not to define the source of a narrative, and other historians that are not named probably were used as well. Three authors stand out for being cited six times: Aristobulus, who accompanied the expedition, although he probably wrote many years later; Chares, the court chamberlain who wrote anecdotal memoirs; and Onesicritus, who had been a pupil of the Cynic Diogenes of Sinope and served as head steersman of Alexander's fleet, and did not hesitate to retell the charming if false story of the visit of the Amazon queen to Alexander. Callisthenes, who also figures as an actor in the narrative (52–5), accompanied the expedition until his death and wrote a heroicizing account of Alexander. He is cited four times. Cleitarchus, the author of a rather romanticizing and sensational account which strongly influenced Diodorus and Curtius, is cited only once by Plutarch, in a list of citations concerning the visit of the Amazon queen (46), but his stories occur several times in the narrative. Plutarch's most distinctive source was a collection of Alexander's letters which he quotes some thirty times, and clearly believed to be authentic. Most modern historians have been sceptical, considering many if not all forgeries. However, as with the laws and poems of Solon and the decrees of Pericles,

---

[2] In the corresponding Life, Caesar's death also is foreshadowed by omens, and after his death he is declared a god by the Roman senate (*Caes.* 67).

Plutarch felt that he had contemporary documents of extraordinary value in establishing the character of his protagonist. He regularly uses these letters to correct the accounts of other historians, and quotes one at length on the battle with Porus (60). A second documentary source, an official diary, is cited for Alexander's last days (76, cf. 22) This is also cited by Arrian, but again the authenticity of the document is uncertain.

The historical value of the Life is not in the account of military events, which were not of central interest to Plutarch, but in the number and variety of stories which bring to life the world of Alexander, from the initial uneasy relation with his father to the protocol surrounding the king's last days. Contemporary writers reported many of these items, large and small, and Plutarch preserves them for us. Our other sources take more interest in battle tactics, though none give substantial attention to administrative, logistic, or strategic plans which were central to Alexander's achievement. Nor do any consider the conquest from the point of view of the conquered. I have not usually indicated parallel ancient accounts or disagreements in the notes: these are fully presented in Hamilton's commentary and Brunt and Bosworth's works on Arrian, as are the units and formations employed in the battles.

Plutarch's most significant contribution is his own effort at drawing a sensitive, persuasive portrait of a man who has always seemed larger than life. His exploration of the facets of his character as they took shape under the pressure of political and military power, false and true friends, and Alexander's own spirited nature fascinates the reader. When *Alexander* is combined with *Caesar* (translated in the companion volume to this), the pair provide a thoughtful narrative investigation of the pitfalls of supreme power, and the qualities which might help one to resist them. Plutarch in the course of a long life had seen how a series of Roman emperors had wielded power, and in his *Lives of the Caesars* had narrated their faults, and perhaps their virtues. In *Alexander–Caesar* he pairs two lives of special interest to Trajan, offering the help of philosophy on that most intractable problem, the governance of states. We do not know whether Trajan ever saw Plutarch's book, but its value remains for all who read it.

On Alexander the Great:

Bosworth, A. B., *Conquest and Empire: The Reign of Alexander the Great* (Cambridge: Cambridge University Press, 1988). A detailed narrative.

Brunt, P. A., *Arrian: History of Alexander and Indica*, i–ii (Cambridge, Mass.: Harvard University Press (Loeb Classical Library), 1976–83). The least sensational of the extant Alexander historians, with notes and lengthy appendices on historical topics.

Bieber, M., *Alexander the Great in Greek and Roman Art* (Chicago: University of Chicago Press, 1964). A guide to the portraiture of Alexander.

Engels, D. W., *Alexander the Great and the Logistics of the Macedonian Army* (Berkeley and Los Angeles: University of California Press, 1978). An investigation of the logistical aspect of the campaign.

Fuller, J. F. C., *The Generalship of Alexander the Great* (New Brunswick: Rutgers University Press, 1960). A review of the major battles and sieges from a military standpoint.

Hammond, N. G. L., *Alexander the Great: King, Commander and Statesman* (Park Ridge, NJ: Noges Press, 1980). A life of Alexander.

Lane Fox, R., *Alexander the Great* (London: Futura Publications, 1973). A life of Alexander.

Wilcken, U., *Alexander the Great*, with preface, notes and bibliography by E. N. Borza (New York: Norton, 1967). A life of Alexander.

On Plutarch's Alexander:

Hamilton, J. R., *Plutarch: Alexander. A Commentary* (Oxford: Clarendon Press, 1969).

Hammond, N. G. L., *Sources for Alexander the Great: An Analysis of Plutarch's Life of Alexander and of Arrian's Anabasis* (Cambridge: Cambridge University Press, 1993).

Mossman, J., 'Tragedy and Epic in Plutarch's Alexander', *Journal of Hellenic Studies*, 108 (1988), 83–93.

Pearson, L., *The Lost Histories of Alexander the Great* (American Philological Association, Philological Monographs, 1960).

Sansone, D., 'Plutarch, Alexander, and the Discovery of Naphtha', *Greek, Roman and Byzantine Studies*, 21 (1980), 63–74. On *Alexander* 35.

Stadter, P. A., 'Anecdotes and the Thematic Structure of Plutarchean Biography', in J. A. Fernández Delgado and F. Pordomingo Pardo (eds.), *Estudios sobre Plutarco, IV. Aspectos formales* (Madrid: Ediciones Clásicas, 1996), 1–13.

ALEXANDER

[1] In this book I will write the biographies of King Alexander and of Caesar—the Caesar who overthrew Pompey.* Now, given the number of their exploits available to me, the only preamble I shall make is to beg the reader not to complain if I fail to relate all of them or to deal exhaustively with a particular famous one, but keep my account brief. I am not writing history but biography, and the most outstanding exploits do not always have the property of revealing the goodness or badness of the agent; often, in fact, a casual action, the odd phrase, or a jest reveals character better than battles involving the loss of thousands upon thousands of lives, huge troop movements, and whole cities besieged. And so, just as a painter reproduces his subject's likeness by concentrating on the face and the expression of the eyes, by means of which character is revealed, and pays hardly any attention to the rest of the body, I must be allowed to devote more time to those aspects which indicate a person's mind and to use these to portray the life of each of my subjects, while leaving their major exploits and battles to others.*

[2] As regards Alexander's lineage, it has been reliably established that on his father's side he was descended from Heracles via Caranus and on his mother's side from Aeacus via Neoptolemus.* We also hear that after Philip had been initiated on Samothrace along with Olympias, he fell passionately in love with her, and although he was only a young adult and she was an orphan, he went right ahead and betrothed himself to her, once he had gained the consent of her brother Arybbas.* On the night before they were to be locked into the bridal chamber together,* the bride had a dream in which, following a clap of thunder, her womb was struck by a thunderbolt; this started a vigorous fire which then burst into flames and spread all over the place before dying down. And later, after they were married, Philip dreamt that he was pressing a seal on his wife's womb, and that the emblem on the seal was the figure of a lion. Although all his other diviners viewed the dream with suspicion and interpreted it as meaning that Philip needed to protect his marriage more securely, Aristander of Telmessus* said that the woman was pregnant, since no one puts a seal on anything empty, and that the child she was

carrying was impatient and lion-like. Moreover, a snake was once seen stretched out alongside Olympias' body while she was asleep, and they say that it was this incident more than anything that cooled Philip's passion and affection until he even stopped coming to her bed very often, perhaps because he was afraid that she would cast spells over him and drug him, or perhaps he refused to have sex with her on religious grounds, because she was the partner of a higher being.* However, there is another version of this story, as follows. It is a long-standing tradition in this part of the world for all the women to be involved in the Orphic and Dionysian rites. The female practition-ers are called Clodones and Mimallones, and there is a great deal of similarity between what they do and the practices of the Edonian and Thracian women on Mount Haemus (from whom, apparently, the word *thrēskeuein* came to be applied to extravagant and over-elaborate ceremonies*). Olympias, it is said, outdid the other women in her efforts to achieve possession by the god and used to exhibit her inspira-tion in a wilder fashion: she would introduce great tame snakes into the meetings, which used to terrify the men by crawling out of the ivy and the ritual baskets and coiling themselves around the women's wands and garlands.*

[3] Be that as it may, the story goes that after the portent Philip sent Chaeron of Megalopolis to Delphi and he returned with an oracle from the god, instructing Philip to offer more sacrifices and honour to Ammon than to any other god, and adding that he was to lose whichever of his eyes he had applied to the chink in the door to glimpse the god in the guise of a snake sleeping with his wife.* Also, according to Eratosthenes, when Alexander was setting out on his eastern campaign, Olympias accompanied him during the pro-cession, told him in private the secret of his birth, and urged him to entertain ambitions worthy of his parentage. Others, however, main-tain that she repudiated the idea on religious grounds and said, 'I wish Alexander would stop getting me into trouble with Hera.'*

Anyway, Alexander was born during the first quarter of the month Hecatombaeon (or Loüs, to give it its Macedonian name), on the sixth, which was the day when the temple of Artemis at Ephesus was destroyed by fire.* It was in reference to this that Hegesias of Magnesia made a statement of sufficient frigidity to have extinguished that great conflagration: it is not surprising, he said, that the temple was burnt down, since Artemis was busy delivering Alexander.

However, there happened to be a number of Magi resident in Ephesus at the time, and they all interpreted what had happened to the temple as an omen of further disaster; they ran to and fro, pummelling their faces and crying that Asia's ruin and perdition had been born that day.*

Philip had just succeeded in capturing Potidaea and three messages reached him more or less simultaneously. The first reported the defeat of the Illyrians by Parmenio in a great battle, the second brought news of his victory at the Olympic Games in the horse race, and the third told him of Alexander's birth. He was already delighted with all this, of course, but his diviners raised his spirits even higher by declaring that since the boy's birth coincided with three victories he would be invincible.

[4] His physical features can be seen particularly clearly in the statues of Lysippus, who was, in fact, the only sculptor Alexander regarded as good enough to portray him. Lysippus has perfectly captured what many of Alexander's successors and friends tried to imitate, the way he held his neck cocked with a slight inclination to the left, and his melting gaze.* Apelles' famous picture, 'The Wielder of the Thunderbolt',† has not accurately reproduced his complexion, but makes him too dark and swarthy. He had a pale complexion, they say, and his skin used to take on a ruddy tinge especially around the chest and face. Moreover, his skin used to emit a delightful odour and, as I have read in Aristoxenus' *Memoirs*, his mouth and whole body used to be bathed in a fragrance which filled his clothes. This was perhaps due to the unusually hot and fiery blend of the humours in his body; at any rate, according to Theophrastus, fragrance is a result of the coction of liquids by heat.* That is why most spices, and certainly those with the nicest scents, grow in the dry and fiery places of the world: the sun draws off the moisture, which lies like a source of corruption on the surface of the bodies of the plants. It was the heat of Alexander's body, presumably, which gave him his fondness for drink, and also made him impatient.

Even as a child, however, his self-restraint was apparent in his stubborn disregard for physical pleasures and the composure with which he approached them, which contrasted with his intensity and impetuosity in other respects; moroever, his ambitious desire for recognition gave his mind a certain dignity and detachment beyond his years. For he did not feel attracted towards recognition *tout court*, whatever its source, as Philip did, with his tendency to preen himself on his rhetorical skill like a sophist and to engrave his successes at Olympia in the chariot-race on his coins.* On the contrary, when people in Alexander's retinue asked him whether he might like to compete in the foot-race at the Olympic Games, since he was a fast runner, he said, 'Yes, if I could have kings to compete against.' By and large, he seems to have been against athletes; at any rate, although he instituted a great many tragic and musical competitions (for both the pipes and the lyre), and also rhapsodic contests, games involving all kinds of hunting, and quarterstaff matches, he showed no interest in offering prizes for boxing or pancration.*

[5] Once, when Philip was out of the country, Alexander received the members of a delegation from the Persian king and came to be on very good terms with them. He won them over with his friendliness, and because rather than asking any childish or trivial questions he tried to find out how long the roads were in Persia and the nature of the route into the interior, whether or not the king was inclined to go to war, and what martial ability and military resources the Persians had. They were so impressed that they regarded Philip's well-known ingenuity as nothing compared to his son's eagerness for high endeavour.

Anyway, Alexander never used to greet the news that Philip had captured an important city or won a famous victory with particular delight; instead he used to say to his friends, 'Lads, my father's going to pre-empt me in everything. By the time he's finished, there'll be nothing important left for me to present to the world, no splendid victories to be won with your help.' Since he had set his sights on excellence and fame, rather than pleasure and wealth, he thought that the more he received from his father, the less he would accomplish by himself. And so, since the strengthening of Macedonia's position meant, to his mind, that more and more achievements were being squandered on his father, he did not want him to bequeath an empire which would afford him wealth, luxury, and enjoyment, but one which would provide him with conflicts, wars, and opportunities for distinction.

We hear, of course, of a great many people who were concerned with his welfare, as instructors, tutors, and teachers, but chief among them was Leonidas, a man of stern temperament and a relative of Olympias.* Although he himself did not mind the title of tutor, since he thought that the job involved noble and admirable work, other people called him Alexander's instructor and mentor because of his moral gravity and his kinship to the boy. However, the person who assumed both the mannerisms and the title of tutor was Lysimachus, an Acarnanian by birth, who was basically a man of no culture, but won favour by his habit of referring to himself as Phoenix, Alexander as Achilles, and Philip as Peleus,* and became second in importance to Leonidas.

[6] When Philonicus of Thessaly brought Bucephalas to Philip with an asking price of thirteen talents, they went down to the plain to assess the horse and found him to be, apparently, intractable and quite unmanageable. He refused to accept anybody on his back or to submit to the commands of any of Philip's companions, but just kept resisting them all. Philip was starting to get annoyed and to tell Philonicus to take the horse away, on the grounds that he was wild and uncontrollable, but Alexander, who was there, said, 'What a horse they are losing! And all because they are too inexperienced and feeble to manage him!'

At first Philip made no reply, but then, when Alexander kept on interrupting him and showing how deeply upset he was, he said, 'Who are you to criticize your elders? Do you think you know more than them or can manage horses better?'

'Yes,' Alexander replied, 'I do think I could manage *this* horse better than others have done.'

'If you don't succeed in doing so, what penalty are you prepared to pay for your cheek?'

'I guarantee to pay the price of the horse,' he said.

There was laughter at this, but as soon as the two of them had settled the terms of the wager Alexander ran over to the horse, took hold of the reins, and turned him to face the sun—apparently because he had noticed that the horse was made jittery by the sight of his shadow stretching out and jerking about in front of him. He ran alongside the horse for a short while, caressing him, until he saw that he was bursting with energy and that his spirit was up, at which point he unhurriedly shrugged off his cloak, jumped up, and sat safely astride him. Then he pulled a little on the bit with the reins and kept him in check without hitting him or tearing his mouth. When he saw that the horse was no longer a threat and was eager for a gallop, he gave him his head, urging him on more stridently now, and kicking with his heels. At first Philip and his companions were in an agony of silent suspense, but when Alexander made a perfect turn and started back jubilant and triumphant, everyone else cried out loud, but his father—so we are told—actually shed tears of joy, and when Alexander had dismounted he kissed him on the head and said, 'Son, you had better try to find a kingdom you fit: Macedonia is too small for you.'

[7] Now, Philip could see that although Alexander was stubborn when it came to resisting compulsion, he was easily led by reasoned argument to the proper course of action, so he not only tried for his own part to use persuasion rather than order him about, but also, because he did not entirely trust the teachers of cultural studies and the usual curriculum to take care of him and educate† him well (since education was, in his opinion, a matter of considerable importance and, as Sophocles puts it, 'a job for bridles a-plenty and rudders too'*), he sent for the most famous and learned of the philosophers, Aristotle. The fee he paid him was noble and appropriate: Aristotle's home town, Stagira, had been depopulated by Philip, and its inhabitants had scattered far and wide or been sold into slavery, but he now brought them back and resettled the town again.*

Philip gave Aristotle and Alexander, as a place of resort where they could go and study, the sanctuary of the Nymphs at Mieza, where even now people point out the stone seats and shady walks Aristotle used to frequent.* It looks as though Alexander not only received from Aristotle his ethical and political doctrines, but also took in his more profound, secret teachings, which Aristotle's successors used to call the 'oral' and 'esoteric' teachings and did not offer to the public. For later, during his campaign over in Asia, he heard that some aspects of this secret teaching had been published by Aristotle in books, and he wrote him a candid letter in defence of philosophy, the text of which is as follows: 'Greetings from Alexander to Aristotle. It is wrong of you to have published your oral doctrines. How am I to stand out from everyone else if the ideas which constituted my education become common property? I would rather be distinguished by my knowledge of these excellent teachings than by my power. Farewell.' In his response, Aristotle encouraged this ambition of Alexander's and tried to justify what he had done with these teachings by saying that they both were and were not public knowledge. And it is in fact true that his treatise on metaphysics† is useless for either teaching or learning, but was originally written as an *aide-mémoire* for those already trained in the subject.*

[8] I imagine that Aristotle was chiefly responsible for giving Alexander his interest in medicine as well, which extended beyond mere fascination with the theory, because he helped his friends when they were ill: as we can tell from his letters, he prescribed certain treatments and regimens for them. He was also interested in literature, studious, and fond of reading. He regarded and referred to the *Iliad* as a handbook on warfare, and carried about with him Aristotle's recension of the text, which he called 'the *Iliad* of the casket' and always kept under his pillow along with his dagger, according to Onesicritus. When he was deep in Asia and had no access to any other books, he told Harpalus* to send him some, and Harpalus sent him Philistus' works,* a lot of tragedies by Euripides, Sophocles, and Aeschylus, and the dithyrambic poetry of Telestes and Philoxenus.

Although at first he admired Aristotle and felt just as much affection for him as for his father, as he himself used to say, on the grounds that while his father gave him life, Aristotle gave him the gift of putting that life to good use, he later came to view him with some suspicion. It never reached the point where he actually did him harm, but the fact that his acts of kindness towards Aristotle failed to exhibit their original intensity and warmth is sufficient proof of his estrangement from him. But the passionate attraction towards philosophy which he had had all his life, both as an innate gift and as a product of his education, never left him, as we can tell from his respect for Anaxarchus, the fifty talents he sent Xenocrates, and his great interest in Dandamis and Calanus.*

[9] While Philip was away on a campaign against Byzantium, Alexander was appointed regent of Macedonia in his absence, despite being only sixteen years old, and given responsibility for the royal seal. During his period of office, some of the Maedians rose up in rebellion against Macedonia; Alexander defeated them, captured their main settlement, expelled all the natives from it, brought in a mixed population of soldiers and civilians, and renamed the place Alexandropolis. He also went and took part in the battle of Chaeronea against the Greeks, and is said to have led the charge against the Theban Sacred Band. Even today one is shown an ancient oak growing next to the Cephisus which is called 'Alexander's Oak' because he pitched his tent against it; it is quite close to the communal grave of the Macedonian dead.*

These exploits of his made Philip extremely proud of his son, of course; in fact, he did not even mind the Macedonians describing Alexander as their king and Philip as their commander. But troubles at home, when as a result of Philip's marriages and love-affairs a kind of infection spread from the women's quarters to the whole kingdom, caused a great many recriminations and fierce quarrels between father and son, which Olympias, who was a jealous and vituperative woman, spitefully exacerbated by egging Alexander on. The most open quarrel was provoked by Attalus on the occasion of Philip's wedding to Cleopatra, a young woman whom Philip had married after falling in love with her when she was still a girl despite being past the age for such things.* Attalus was Cleopatra's uncle, and he drunkenly called on the Macedonians to pray to the gods for a legitimate heir to the throne to be born to Philip and Cleopatra. This irritated Alexander, who said, 'So, scum, you consider me a bastard, do you?', and threw a cup at him. Philip got up to attack Alexander and drew his sword, but luckily for both of them his anger and the wine he had drunk made him stumble and fall. Alexander taunted him and said, 'Gentlemen, there lies the man who was getting ready to cross over from Europe to Asia, but who trips up on his way over to one couch from another!' After this drunken brawl Alexander took Olympias and set her up in Epirus, while he stayed among the Illyrians.*

While he was there, Demaratus of Corinth,* who was a guest-friend of the household and a man who was used to speaking his mind, came to visit Philip. Once the preliminary greetings and expressions of affection were over, Philip asked about the state of inter-Greek *entente cordiale*. 'It is really very good of you, Philip,' said Demaratus, 'to express concern for Greece when your own household is overrun, thanks to you, with so much conflict and trouble.' This brought Philip to his senses; he sent messengers to Alexander and with Demaratus' help persuaded him to return home.

[10] As an incentive for Philip to enter into an alliance with him, Pixodarus, the satrap of Caria, wanted to marry his eldest daughter to Philip's son Arrhidaeus, and he sent Aristocritus to Macedonia to see to the matter. Once again stories and lies began to reach Alexander's ears from his friends and his mother, to the effect that Philip was planning to use an illustrious marriage and important state affairs to promote Arrhidaeus and settle the kingdom on him. Alexander found the stories disturbing, so he sent the tragic actor,

Thessalus, to Caria,* to talk to Pixodarus and convince him that
he ought to ignore the illegitimate son, who was also weak in the
head, and think instead about contracting a marriage alliance with
Alexander. This idea was far more attractive to Pixodarus than his
earlier scheme, but when Philip realized <what was going on, he
entered>† Alexander's room (taking with him one of Alexander's close
friends, Philotas the son of Parmenio), berated his son with harsh
words, and accused him of betraying his high birth and his felicitous
position by finding attractive the prospect of becoming the son-in-
law of someone who was not only a mere Carian, but was a slave to
a foreign king. Philip dealt with Thessalus by writing to the Corinthians and demanding that they return him to Macedonia in chains,
and he banished several of Alexander's Companions from Macedonia
—Harpalus and Nearchus, and also Erigyius and Ptolemy—though
they were later recalled by Alexander and held in the highest honour
by him.*

    When Pausanias, who had been assaulted at the instigation of Attalus
and Cleopatra, murdered Philip for failing to recompense him, most
of the blame attached itself to Olympias, on the grounds that she had
encouraged the young man in his anger and incited him to do the deed,
but Alexander did not come out of the affair spotless either.* It is said
that once, after the assault, Pausanias happened to meet Alexander;
when he started complaining, Alexander quoted the line from the
Medea, 'The giver of the bride, the groom and the bride too'.*
However, he did in fact hunt down Pausanias' accomplices and
punish them, and he was furious with Olympias for the brutal way
she dealt with Cleopatra when he was once out of the country.*

    [11] The kingdom that Alexander inherited at the age of twenty
was surrounded on all sides by bitter resentment, deep hatred, and
danger. Not only were the native tribes on his borders chafing at their
lack of freedom and missing their traditional monarchies, but also,
although Philip had gained control of Greece by force of arms, he
had not had the time to tame the people and accustom them, so to
speak, to the Macedonian yoke; all he had done was make things different and unsettled, and then leave them, due to his inexperience,
in a state of considerable commotion and instability. The Macedonians were concerned about the critical situation and thought that
Alexander should ignore Greece altogether, without using any extra
force there, while attempting to win back the revolting native tribes

by conciliatory moves and to appease their rebellious feelings before they really got started. Alexander, however, adopted the opposite approach and resolved to win safety and security for Macedonia by bold and confident gestures, in the belief that if he were seen to relax his proud stance at all, he would be set upon by all his enemies.*

So he took an army and swiftly overran the country up to the Danube, which put an end to any rebellious stirrings among the native tribes and brought the wars there to an end, and he defeated King Syrmus of the Triballians in a major engagement.* Then, as soon as he heard that the Thebans had risen up against him and that the Athenians had joined them, he led his army through the pass of Thermopylae, asserting that he wanted Demosthenes, who had dismissively called him a child when he was in Illyrian and Triballian territory, and a youth when he had reached Thessaly, to see before the walls of Athens that he was a man. He drew close to Thebes, but wanted to give them a chance even then to repent of what they had done, so he demanded the surrender of Phoenix and Prothytes, and proclaimed a pardon for anyone who came over to his side. But the Thebans responded by demanding, in their turn, that Alexander should surrender Philotas and Antipater, and they proclaimed that anyone who wanted to help them liberate Greece should join their ranks; and so Alexander committed his troops to war.

The Thebans fought with courage and determination, and excelled themselves against an enemy who vastly outnumbered them, but when the Macedonian garrison also came down from the Cadmeia and attacked them in the rear, they were surrounded. Most of the Theban soldiers fell in the actual battle, and the city was captured, plundered, and razed to the ground, mainly because Alexander expected the Greeks to be terrified at the enormity of the disaster and to cower in fear, but also as a specious way of gratifying his allies' grievances, since the Phocians and Plataeans had complained to him about the Thebans. He separated out priests, all those who were guest-friends of Macedonians, Pindar's descendants, and everyone who had voted against insurrection, and sold the rest into slavery. About 30,000 were sold into slavery, while over 6,000 had died in the battle.*

[12] Here is one out of many examples of the kind of savagery that afflicted the city at this time. Some Thracians broke into a house belonging to Timocleia, a well-respected and virtuous woman, and while his men were looting the building, the leader raped her and

defiled her, and then demanded to know if she had gold or silver hidden anywhere. She said that she had, took him out alone into the garden and pointed to the well, where, she said, she had thrown her most valuable possessions when the city's fall was imminent. As the Thracian leant over and peered down the well, she came up behind him and pushed him in, and then hurled a great many stones down on top of him until he was dead. When she was brought before Alexander in chains by the Thracians, he could tell straight away from her demeanour and the way she walked that she was a woman of dignity and self-assurance, because she showed no fear or concern as her captors led her in. When Alexander asked her who she was, she replied that she was the sister of Theagenes, the Theban commander who had deployed his men against Philip in defence of the liberty of Greece and had fallen at Chaeronea. Alexander was impressed with the way she replied, as well as with what she had done, and told her that both she and her children could have their freedom and leave.*

[13] He also came to terms with the Athenians, despite the fact that they were deeply troubled by the catastrophe that had befallen Thebes. In fact, although the celebration of the Mysteries was under way, they were so upset that they abandoned it;* they also showed nothing but kindness to any Theban refugees who sought safety in Athens. Nevertheless, perhaps because, like a lion, his anger was sated, or perhaps because he wanted to offset an act of terrible and grim ferocity with one of clemency, he not only dropped all the charges against them, but even told the Athenians to take good care of themselves, because if anything should happen to him, they would be the rulers of Greece. However, on more than one occasion later the Theban disaster is said to have caused him remorse and to have made him treat quite a few people with greater leniency. At any rate, he used to say that both the business with Clitus, which happened when he was drunk, and the cowardice of the Macedonians when they were up against the Indians, which robbed his expedition and his glory of their crowning achievement, were due to the vengeful anger of Dionysus;* and later, whenever any of the Theban survivors came to him with a petition, he granted it. Anyway, that is what happened to Thebes.

[14] Following a conference held by the Greeks at the Isthmus, at which they decided to join Alexander's expedition against Persia, he was formally put in charge.* A great many people—not only

politicians, but philosophers too—gained audiences with him to tender their congratulations, and he hoped that Diogenes of Sinope, who was living in Corinth at the time, would follow their example. Diogenes, however, continued to live an untroubled life in Craneium, without paying the slightest attention to Alexander, so Alexander paid him a visit and found him relaxing in the sun. Diogenes raised himself up a bit when the huge crowd of people appeared and looked at Alexander, who greeted him and asked him if there was anything he wanted. 'Yes,' replied Diogenes, 'move aside a little, out of my sunlight.' The story goes that Alexander was so struck at being held in such contempt, and so impressed with the man's haughty detachment, that while the members of his retinue were ridiculing and mocking Diogenes as they left, he said, 'But as for me, if I were not Alexander, I would be Diogenes.'*

He went to Delphi, because he wanted to hear what the god had to say about his proposed expedition to the East, but his visit happened to coincide with a run of inauspicious days, when the delivery of oracles is traditionally forbidden. At first he merely sent for the prophetess, but when she refused to officiate and cited tradition by way of explanation, he went up to her residence himself and started to drag her against her will towards the temple, whereupon, apparently overcome by his forcefulness, she said, 'You are invincible, my son.' On hearing this, Alexander declared that this was the only prophecy he needed—that she had given him the response he wanted.

A number of supernatural portents marked the start of his eastern expedition. For instance, at about that time, the wooden statue of Orpheus at Leibethra (it was made out of cypress wood, in fact) sweated profusely. Everyone was frightened at this omen, but Aristander told Alexander not to worry, because his achievements would form the theme of songs and tales, and would cost poets and musicians a great deal of sweat and toil to celebrate in verse.

[15] The most conservative estimates of the size of his army make it consist of 30,000 foot-soldiers and 4,000 mounted troops; the most generous make it 43,000 foot-soldiers and 5,000 cavalrymen. To provide this army with supplies he had, according to Aristobulus, no more than seventy talents; Duris claims that he had enough food for only thirty days, and Onesicritus adds that he was 200 talents in debt as well.* But although he set out with such meagre and restricted resources, he did not board his ship until he had discovered how things

stood with his Companions, and had given one of them a farm, another a village, and another the income from some hamlet or harbour. After he had used up and distributed almost all the royal properties, Perdiccas asked, 'But what are you leaving for yourself, my lord?' 'My hopes,' he replied. 'All right,' said Perdiccas, 'then that's what *we*'ll have too; after all, we're joining you on this expedition.' Then he refused to accept the property that had been assigned him, and some other friends of Alexander's followed his example. But Alexander was happy to gratify anyone who accepted his offer and who wanted what he was giving, and in this way he distributed and gave away most of his Macedonian properties. This goes to show how determined he was, and how he prepared himself mentally for his expedition.*

And so he crossed the Hellespont.* At Troy, he offered up a sacrifice to Athena and poured libations to the heroes. At Achilles' tombstone,† he anointed himself with plenty of oil, ran a foot-race, naked as custom demands, with his friends, and crowned the tombstone with a garland, pronouncing Achilles fortunate for the true friend he found during his lifetime and the great herald he found after his death.* While he was walking about and seeing the sights of the city, someone asked him if he would like to see Alexander's lyre; he replied that he had not the slightest interest in that lyre, but was looking for the one Achilles had used to sing of the glorious achievements of brave men.*

[16] Meanwhile, since Darius' commanders had gathered together a considerable army and deployed it at the crossing of the river Granicus,* it was presumably going to be necessary to fight at the gateway to Asia, so to speak, for the right to enter the Persian empire.† However, most of the Macedonians were concerned about the depth of the river and the unevenness and ruggedness of the further bank which they would have to make their way up in the thick of battle, and some were also of the opinion that they should not break with the tradition that in the month of Daesius Macedonian kings generally do not go out to war. However, he sorted out the latter objection by telling them to treat the month as a second Artemision,* and when Parmenio tried to stop him fighting a decisive battle, on the grounds that it was too late in the day, he said that the Hellespont would be embarrassed to see him afraid of the Granicus after having succeeded in crossing it, and he plunged into the river with thirteen cavalry squadrons.

Since he was riding towards an enemy armed with missiles and making for precipitous terrain which was defended by both armed men and cavalry, and since the current was strong enough to sweep men away and overwhelm them, this seemed to be an insane tactic, reckless and ill-advised. Nevertheless, he persevered with the crossing and, albeit with a great deal of difficulty, gained the opposite bank, which was wet and treacherously muddy—whereupon he was immediately forced to fight in disarray and to take on wave after wave of assailants, before he could get the men who were crossing the river into some kind of order. The enemy yelled as they charged into the attack, matching horse against horse, wielding their spears and then their swords when their spears were broken. Alexander himself was a particular target, for he was easily recognizable by his shield and by the amazingly tall white plumes which flanked the crest of his helmet. At one point he was hit by a javelin, which pierced the joint of his breastplate, but he came to no harm. Then Rhoesaces and Spithridates, two high-ranking officers, bore down on him simultaneously. He evaded Spithridates and got in the first blow against Rhoesaces, but his spear snapped on his breastplate, so without further ado he turned to his sword. While he was engaged with Rhoesaces, Spithridates rode up on his blind side, reared up straight away on his horse, and brought a Persian sword down on his head. He sheared off the crest and one of the plumes, and the helmet only just managed to withstand the blow—in fact, the flat of the sword touched the ends of the hairs on Alexander's head. Spithridates was raising himself up again for another blow,† but before he could strike Clitus the Black ran him through with his spear. At the same moment Rhoesaces fell too, cut down by Alexander's sword.*

While the cavalry engagement was hanging precariously in the balance like this, the Macedonian heavy-armed troops were crossing the river, and the foot-soldiers from both sides joined battle. The Persians, however, did not put up a very spirited resistance and before long all of them had turned and fled, with the exception of the Greek mercenaries, who grouped together at a certain hill and begged Alexander for mercy. In response, guided by anger rather than reason, he led a charge against them. Alexander lost his horse to the thrust of a sword through the ribs (but he was on a different horse, not Bucephalas), and it was in this fight that the Macedonians ran the greatest risk and sustained their heaviest losses in terms of numbers of men killed or wounded, because they were up against desperate men who were skilled fighters.

It is said that 20,000 foot-soldiers and 2,500 horsemen died on the Persian side, while, according to Aristobulus, losses among Alexander's men amounted to thirty-four dead, of whom nine were foot-soldiers. Alexander commissioned bronze statues of the dead, which Lysippus sculpted.* He wanted the Greeks to feel involved in the victory, so, apart from sending the Athenians in particular 300 of the shields he had captured, he also had the rest of the spoils inscribed for general appreciation with a highly ambitious legend: 'Alexander the son of Philip and all the Greeks except the Lacedaemonians dedicate this booty won from the natives of Asia.'* But he sent almost all the items such as cups and purple-dyed garments that he took from the Persians to his mother.

[17] This battle immediately brought about substantial changes in Alexander's affairs: even Sardis, the bulwark of Persian mastery of the sea, surrendered to him, and he annexed various other places as well. The only cities that offered any resistance were Halicarnassus and Miletus, but he captured them by force of arms and subdued all the territory around them. But then he was undecided about what to do next. He was often attracted to the idea of meeting Darius and gambling everything on the outcome of the encounter, but he also often thought he should undergo a training programme first, so to speak, and build up his strength on the affairs and resources of the coast, before heading inland to face Darius.*

Near the city of Xanthus in Lycia there is a spring which is said to have overflowed its banks and changed course at this time, apparently without anything causing it do so, and in the process to have brought up from its depths a bronze tablet with ancient writing on it, which made it clear that the Persian empire would be overthrown and brought to an end by Greeks. This gave Alexander fresh heart, and he hurriedly set about clearing up the coastal region as far as Phoenicia and Cilicia. His rapid progress through Pamphylia has turned out to provide a number of historians with material for vivid and high-flown language; they claim that the sea providentially made way for Alexander, although it generally surged in from the open sea and hardly ever revealed the faint and exposed paths that run under the cliffs and gullies of the mountainside.† In fact, Menander makes a joke about this miracle in one of his comedies:

> What an Alexandrine situation this is! Anyone I look for
> Will appear as if by magic, and of course if I have to cross
> Some place through the sea, it'll open up for me.*

However, in his letters Alexander himself makes no mention of anything supernatural like this, but just says that he set out from Phaselis and made his way through the country along the Ladder, as the road is called. This also explains why he spent several days in Phaselis. During his stay there he noticed that a statue of Theodectes, who was a citizen of Phaselis, had been set up in the main square after his death, and one day, drunk after his evening meal, he led a band of revellers there and tossed quite a few of their garlands on to the statue's head—a nice, if flippant, way of thanking the man for the time they had spent together after he had been introduced to him by Aristotle and philosophy.*

[18] Next he put down a rebellion among the Pisidians and conquered Phrygia.* When the city of Gordium capitulated to him (this is the city which is said to have been the capital of Midas' kingdom in the olden days), he saw the famous cart with its lashing made out of the bark of a cornel tree, and heard the story which the natives there believe, that whoever undid the knot was destined to become the ruler of the whole world. Most writers say that since the ends of the knot were hidden, and since the strands were twisted and turned over and under one another time and time again, Alexander could not find a way to undo it, and so he cut through the knot with his sword until a number of ends were exposed. However, Aristobulus says that he undid it very easily, by removing from the pole the dowel, as it is called, which joined the lashing to the cart, and then pulling the yoke away from under the cart.

He went on to annex Paphlagonia and Cappadocia.* When he heard of the death of Memnon, who of all Darius' commanders on the coast was the one who had been likely to make a great deal of trouble for him and cause him countless setbacks and delays, he felt even more positive about his prospects for marching towards the interior.* In any case, Darius was already on his way down from Susa, with his confidence boosted not just by the size of his army (he had 600,000 men under him*), but also by a dream which the Magi had interpreted in a manner designed to please him rather than to accord with probability. In the dream he saw the Macedonian infantry consumed by a raging fire and himself being waited on by Alexander, who was dressed in the clothing he, Darius, had been accustomed to wear in days gone by, when he was the king's courier; then Alexander seemed to pass into the precinct of Bel and disappear. All this was apparently the god's way of suggesting that Macedonian affairs were destined to become brilliant and glorious, and that Alexander would gain control of Asia (just as Darius had when he stopped being the royal courier and became king), but before long would die at the height of his fame.

[19] Darius was even more encouraged by the length of Alexander's stay in Cilicia, which he took to be a sign of cowardice. In fact, however, it was the result of an illness, which some writers attribute to exhaustion, others to his having bathed in the river Cydnus and caught a chill. Most of his doctors lacked the confidence to treat him; they thought that the risks of the treatment outweighed any help it could provide, and they were afraid of the criticism failure would earn them from the Macedonians. However, Philip of Acarnania saw that Alexander was in a bad way and trusted in his friendship; he could not bear the idea of not making absolutely every effort to help him, even if the cost were to prove to be his life, and did not see why he should stay out of danger when Alexander was in danger, so he prepared a medicine and persuaded him to drink it, however unpleasant he might find it, since he was so eager to regain his strength for the war.*

Meanwhile Parmenio sent Alexander a letter from the camp in which he advised him to be on his guard against Philip, on the grounds that he had been suborned by an offer from Darius of vast sums of money, and even marriage to his daughter, to murder Alexander. Alexander read the letter and then put it under his pillow, without having shown it to any of his friends. When the time for Philip's appointment with Alexander arrived, and he came in with his associates, carrying the medicine in a cup, Alexander handed the letter over to him while happily accepting the potion without the slightest hesitation. The ensuing scene was wonderful and worthy of the stage: one of them was reading the letter and the other drinking the potion, and then they both looked at each other, but not with the same significance, since Alexander was displaying his goodwill and trust in Philip with his cheerful and open countenance, while Philip was distraught at the accusation, and alternated between calling on the gods with his hands raised to heaven and throwing himself down by Alexander's couch with words of encouragement and the advice to listen to his instructions. For at first the drug proved too powerful for Alexander's body and, so to speak, expelled and submerged his energy, with the result that he lost the power of speech and grew very faint, with a near total loss of use of his senses. Philip soon brought him back round, however, and once he had recovered he showed himself to the Macedonians, who could not regain their morale until they had actually seen Alexander.

[20] In Darius' army there was a Macedonian exile called Amyntas who knew Alexander quite well. When he saw that Darius was intending to march to meet Alexander within the confines of the mountains, he begged him to stay where he was and fight on the broad, open plains, since his army vastly outnumbered Alexander's. When Darius replied that he was worried about the enemy running away before he had made contact with them, and that he did not want Alexander to escape, Amyntas said, 'Well, you can put your mind at rest on this score, at any rate, my lord. He will come against you; in fact, he's probably on his way already.'*

However, Darius was not convinced that Amyntas was right, so he mobilized his troops and made his way into Cilicia. Meanwhile, Alexander was marching into Syria to meet him. But they missed each other in the night, so they turned their armies around again—a piece of good fortune that delighted Alexander, and he hurried on to meet Darius in the mountains, while Darius was just as eager to extract his forces from the mountain passes and get back to the place he had used earlier for an encampment.* For by now he realized that he had done himself a disservice by advancing into country which was unsuitable for cavalry manoeuvres because of the sea and the mountains, which had a river—the Pinarus—running through the middle of it, and which was so frequently broken up that it favoured the small numbers of the enemy force.

So fortune provided Alexander with the battle site, but his tactics made a more important contribution towards victory than the provisions of fortune. Given the fact that he was so greatly outnumbered by the foreigners, he did not give them a chance to surround his army, but he outflanked their left wing with his right wing, which was under his personal command, got on their flank, and routed the Persians ranged against him. He was so prominent in the fighting that he was wounded in the thigh by a sword. Chares says that it was Darius who wounded him—that the two of them met in hand-to-hand combat—but in his letter to Antipater about the battle Alexander does not say who wounded him, only that he had been wounded in the thigh by a dagger, and that no serious harm came to him as a result of the wound.*

Although he won an outstanding victory and killed over 110,000 enemy troops, he failed to capture Darius, who fled with a head start of four or five stades, but he did capture his chariot and his bow before turning back from the pursuit. He found his Macedonian troops plundering the Persian camp of its riches, which were extraordinarily plentiful, despite the fact that the enemy had come to the battle lightly equipped and had left most of their baggage in Damascus. They had kept Darius' tent for him, which was filled with magnificent slaves and furniture, and a great deal of money. He lost no time in stripping off his armour and heading for the bath, saying, 'Let's go and wash the sweat of battle off in Darius' bath.' But one of his Companions said, 'No, in *Alexander's* bath. The losers' possessions must pass to the victor, and that should be acknowledged in the way we speak.' When Alexander saw the bowls, pitchers, wash-basins, and perfume-jars, all of gold and elaborately wrought, when he smelt how marvellously the forechamber was scented with aromatic herbs and spices, and when he passed from there into a tent which was quite remarkable for its height and size, and for its gorgeous couch and tables, not to mention the actual food served up on them, he looked at his Companions and said, 'This, I suppose, is what it was to be a king.'

[21] As he was settling down to eat his evening meal, someone told him that among the prisoners were Darius' mother, his wife, and two of his unmarried daughters, and that at the sight of Darius' chariot and bow and arrows they had struck their breasts and burst out into tears of grief, because they assumed that Darius had been killed. After a long pause, feeling more strongly about their misfortune than he did about his own good fortune, Alexander sent Leonnatus with instructions to tell them not only that Darius was still alive, but that there was no reason for them to be frightened of him; it was true, he said, that he was fighting Darius for supremacy over Asia, but they would have everything that they had come to expect during Darius' rule. The women appreciated how merciful and compassionate these words were, but his actions proved even more kind. He gave them permission to bury any Persians they wanted, and to use clothing and

jewellery from the spoils for this purpose; he let them keep all the
attendants and tokens of prestige they had formerly possessed, and
they even enjoyed a larger allowance than they had previously been
given. But the noblest and most kingly favour these high-born and
virtuous women received from him while they were his prisoners was
that he protected them from hearing even the slightest hint or implication of anything that would cause them shame; they lived such a
secluded and isolated life that it was as though they were being looked
after in the hallowed young women's quarters of some temple rather
than in an enemy camp. And yet it is said that there was no queen
on earth who could approach Darius' wife in beauty—that she was
a match, then, for Darius himself, who was more handsome and tall
than any other man alive—and that the daughters took after their
parents. Alexander, however, considered the ability to conquer his
enemies less important for a king than the ability to control himself,
so he did not lay a finger on them. In fact, before his marriage the
only woman he was intimate with was Barsine, who was the widow
of Memnon and was captured at Damascus. Since Barsine had been
brought up in the Greek fashion, was a good woman—and was, besides,
the granddaughter, via her father Artabazus, of a king's daughter—
Alexander decided (at Parmenio's instigation, according to Aristobulus) to take her as his mistress, seeing that she was beautiful and
had nobility to match her beauty.*† But faced with the exceptional
beauty and stature of these other captive women, Alexander merely
used to remark, as a joke, that Persian women are a torment to the
eyes.* But he used to match their physical beauty with a beautiful
demonstration of self-control and restraint, and pass them by as though
they were no more than lifeless statues.

[22] Also, when Philoxenus, the military governor on the coast, wrote
to ask whether he wanted to buy two extraordinarily good-looking
boys who were being offered for sale by a man called Theodorus of
Tarentum, who was staying with him, Alexander was furious. In a
raised voice he asked his friends over and over again what baseness
Philoxenus could possibly have observed in him that he should spend
his time procuring such shameful creatures for him, and he wrote a
long, rude letter back to Philoxenus in which he told him to send
Theodorus and his wares to perdition. He also once rebuked Hagnon
in no uncertain terms for having written offering to buy and bring
him Crobylus, a young man who was highly thought of in Corinth.

When he heard that two Macedonians called Damon and Timo-theus, who were serving under Parmenio, had seduced the wives of some mercenaries, he wrote to Parmenio with orders that, if they were found guilty, their punishment should be death, on the grounds that they were no better than wild beasts whose sole purpose in life is the ruination of human beings. In this letter he also wrote about himself, and I quote: 'In my own case, no one could accuse me of even listen-ing to talk of the beauty of Darius' wife, let alone seeing her or want-ing to see her.' And he used to say that there was nothing better than sleep and sex for reminding him that he was not a god, presumably on the assumption that both tiredness and pleasure arise from the same flaw in our nature.*

He was also very self-controlled about food. One out of many ex-amples of this is his remark to Ada, whom he referred to as 'mother' and made queen of Caria.* She used to express her fondness for him by sending him lots of savouries and pastries every day, and even-tually sent him the best chefs and pastry-cooks she knew. But he told her he had no need of any of them, because he already had better cooks, given him by his tutor Leonidas—a night's marching to get him ready for the morning meal, and short rations to prepare him for the evening meal. 'And Leonidas also used to come and open the chests where I kept my bedding and clothing,' he said, 'to make sure my mother hadn't put some delicacy or extravagance in there.'*

[23] He also had less of a penchant for wine than was generally thought. He gained this reputation because he dragged out the time he took over each cup, but it was time spent talking rather than drink-ing, since he was constantly presiding over some lengthy conversa-tion or other, at any rate when he had plenty of time. When action was called for, unlike other commanders he was not detained by wine, sleep, some trivial pursuit or other, marriage, or a show—as is proved by his life, which for all its brevity he packed with exploit after major exploit. When he had time on his hands, however, he would get up and sacrifice to the gods, and then immediately sit down to eat his morning meal. Then he would go on to spend the day hunting or arranging his affairs or teaching some aspect of warfare or reading. If he was on a leisurely journey he would try to improve his archery during it, or practise mounting and dismounting from a moving chariot; as we can learn from the Royal Diary, he also often used to hunt foxes and birds for fun.* Once he had found quarters for the

night, he would ask his bakers and cooks, while he was busy with bathing or washing, whether they had everything they needed for his evening meal. He used to take to his couch and eat his evening meal late, after dark, and take an astonishing amount of care and consideration at the table to make sure that everyone got equal—and equally generous—portions. As I have already said, he would prolong the after-dinner drinking with conversation. Although he was basically better company than any other monarch, and had all the social graces, during these conversations he tended to flaunt his achievements in a disagreeable manner and become too boastful. And not only did he indulge in self-glorification, but he also allowed himself to be ridden by flatterers, who made things difficult for any particularly refined people present, because they had no desire to try to beat the flatterers at their own game and yet did not want to lag behind in praising Alexander; they found the first option degrading, but the second was risky. After he had finished drinking, he would wash, and then go to sleep, often until midday, but occasionally for the whole of the next day.

He was also self-controlled where savouries were concerned. In fact, when especially rare fruits and fish were brought to him from the coast he used to have them sent to each of his Companions, often until he was the only one left with nothing. But his evening meals were magnificent affairs, and the cost of them increased along with his successes, until in the end it reached 10,000 drachmas. It stopped there, however, and this was the stipulated amount which those who entertained Alexander were to spend.*

[24] After the battle of Issus he sent a contingent to Damascus and seized the Persians' money, baggage, children, and wives.* The Thessalian cavalry did particularly well from the booty: they had fought exceptionally well in the battle and Alexander sent them on this mission on purpose, because he wanted them to do well out of the booty. But there was more than enough to go round everyone else in the army as well, and after this first taste of gold and silver and women and an eastern way of life, the Macedonians raced like hounds which have found the scent to pursue and track down Persian wealth.

However, Alexander decided that he should first gain control of the coast. As soon as he arrived there, the various kings of Cyprus came and surrendered to him, and all of Phoenicia did the same, except Tyre. During the seven-month siege of Tyre,* in which he used earthworks and siege-engines by land and a fleet of 200 triremes on the seaward side, he had a dream in which Heracles, standing on the city wall, reached out his right hand to him in greeting and spoke his name.* Meanwhile a number of Tyrians dreamt that Apollo told them that he was leaving them and going to join Alexander, since he did not like what was happening in the city. The people of Tyre treated the god as if he were a common mortal caught in the act of deserting to the enemy: they tied ropes around his cult statue and nailed it down to its base, calling him a collaborator with Alexander. Alexander had another dream in which a satyr seemed to tease him from a distance and then eluded him when he tried to catch him, but eventually surrendered after Alexander had run around after him, pleading with him over and over again to give up. His diviners split the word up and told him, plausibly, '*Tyre* will be *yours*.'* One is shown a spring there and told that it is near where Alexander had his dream of the satyr.

While the siege was in progress, Alexander led a campaign against the Arabians who live around the Anti-Lebanon range. During this campaign he exposed himself to considerable danger, thanks to his tutor Lysimachus, who insisted on accompanying him, saying that he was no less brave or any older than Phoenix.* When the expeditionary force got near the mountains they abandoned their horses and continued on foot, and while the others went on a good way ahead, Alexander refused to leave Lysimachus, who was too tired to keep up. Even though night was drawing in and the enemy were close by, he stayed behind to encourage and support him. Before he knew it, he had become separated from the main body of the army and was left with only a few men. It was dark and bitterly cold, and the terrain where they bivouaced was harsh. Then he saw, not far away, a number of enemy campfires dotted about. Since he had no doubts about his fitness, and was used to constantly encouraging the Macedonians when they got into difficulties by exerting himself, he ran over to the nearest fire, stabbed two of the Arabians who were grouped around it with his dagger, stole a brand, and brought it back to his men. They lit a good-sized fire, scared some of the enemy into immediate flight, and later routed others who attacked them. After that they spent the rest of the night in their camp without further danger. The source for these events is Chares.

[25] Here is how the siege came to an end. There came a period when the bulk of the army was resting, on Alexander's orders, after

all the fighting they had been doing, and he used to lead just a few
men in attacks on the city walls to keep the pressure on the enemy.
Then Aristander the diviner made a sacrifice and when he saw the
omens he declared with some confidence to those who were present that the city would certainly fall that month. This provoked
sceptical laughter, since it was already the last day of the month, but
Alexander did not like to see Aristander in a predicament, and always
supported his commitment to his predictions. He therefore gave instructions that the day was no longer to be counted as the thirtieth of the
month, but the twenty-eighth instead,* and then he got the trumpeters
to sound the attack and made an assault on the walls in greater strength
than he had originally intended. A spectacular fight developed, and
not even the troops who had remained behind in the camp could resist
joining in, but ran over to help their comrades. At that point the Tyrians
gave up, and so Alexander did take the city on that day.

Later, while he was laying siege to Gaza, the largest city in Syria,*
a lump of earth, which had been dropped from a bird flying in the
sky, fell on to his shoulder. The bird then landed on one of the siege-
engines and accidentally got caught in the network of sinews they were
using to tighten and twist the ropes. This omen too turned out just
as Aristander predicted: Alexander was wounded in the shoulder,
but took the city. He sent a great deal of the booty to Olympias,
Cleopatra, and his friends, but he also had 500 talents of frankincense
and 100 of myrrh transported back for his tutor, Leonidas, in memory
of an incident from his childhood which had sown the seeds of aspira-
tion. Apparently, during a sacrificial ritual, Alexander had scooped up
incense with both hands and burnt it as an offering on the fire, and
Leonidas had said to him, 'Alexander, when you've conquered the
land which produces incense, you'll be able to burn it this extravagantly, but for the time being go easy with what you've got.' So now
Alexander wrote to Leonidas: 'I have sent you frankincense and myrrh
in abundance, so that you don't have to stint the gods any more.'*

[26] When he was brought a casket which was, in the estimation
of those who had appropriated Darius' property and baggage, the
most valuable item there, he asked his friends what they thought was
important enough to be kept in it. Various suggestions were made,
but he himself said that he would put the *Iliad* there for safe keeping.*
This story is vouched for by quite a few reliable sources. And if there
is truth in what the people of Alexandria say, on the authority of

Heraclides, Homer was no sleeping partner on his campaign, but made a positive contribution. For they say that after he had conquered Egypt, he wanted to found, as a memorial, a major, populous Greek city, named after himself, and on the advice of his chief engineers he already had a site more or less measured out and enclosed, but then one night while asleep he had an amazing dream in which a grey-haired, distinguished-looking man came up to him and quoted the following lines:

> Now, there is a certain island in the restless, churning sea
> Lying before Egypt: Pharos is the name men give it.*

So he got up straight away and went to Pharos, which in those days was still an island a little north of the Canobic mouth of the Nile, although now it has been connected to the mainland by a causeway.† When he saw the place—a spit of land like a moderately wide isthmus between a large lake and the sea, which ends in a large natural harbour—he appreciated its exceptionally favourable situation and declared that Homer had turned out to be as clever an engineer as he was remarkable in other fields, and he commanded his designers to draw up the plans for the city, making it conform to the topography of the place. There was no chalk to hand, so they took some barley and on a level patch of dark soil they marked out a rounded hollow whose inner arc was extended by straight lines, which uniformly contracted the size of the area from its fringe upwards, so to speak, until the whole thing was the shape of a military cloak. Their royal master was delighted with the design, but suddenly a vast number of birds from the river and the lake, of all kinds and sizes—so many that it was as if a cloud passed across the sky—swooped down on to the place and devoured every last grain of barley. Even Alexander found this omen disturbing, but the diviners told him that there was no cause for alarm, because the city founded here by him would be self-sufficient to a very high degree and would supply the needs of all kinds of men, so he told his overseers to get on with the work.

Meanwhile, he himself set out on the long, tough, and arduous journey to the shrine of Ammon.* There are two reasons why the journey is dangerous: the first is the unavailability of water, which means that the route actually passes through desert for quite a few days, and the second is the possibility of a fierce south wind descending on travellers as they are passing over an immense area of deep sand—as in the famous story of how long ago, in the case of Cambyses' army, this wind whipped up a huge heap of sand until the plain was a surging sea, buried 50,000 men, and killed them.* Almost without exception, Alexander's advisers took all this into consideration, but it was never easy to get Alexander to change his mind once he had decided on a course of action. By yielding to his assaults, fortune had strengthened his determination, and his passionate nature boosted his ambition until he became invincible against things,† and not only his enemies, but even places and opportunities succumbed to his will.

[27] At any rate, the help he luckily received from the god during this journey when the going was difficult has met with more credence than the oracles the god subsequently delivered—or rather, in a sense the oracles have gained credibility because of these lucky events. In the first place, heavy rain and persistent showers from Zeus not only relieved them of the fear of thirst, but also smothered the dryness of the sand until it became moist and compact, and so purified the air and made it easy to breathe. Again, when the markers which the guides were following were obliterated, and the travellers were wandering aimlessly around and getting separated from one another in their ignorance of which way to go, some crows appeared and took on the role of expedition leaders: they would fly swiftly on ahead as long as the party stayed with them, and would wait for them if the others fell behind and slowed down. But the most astonishing thing, as reported by Callisthenes, is that the birds used their cries to recall any members of the party who went astray during the night and cawed until they had got them back on to the tracks left by the rest of the party in its journey.*

Once he had passed through the desert and reached his destination, the prophet of Ammon gave him the god's greetings in terms implying that the god was his father. When Alexander asked whether any of his father's assassins had escaped him, the spokesman told him not to speak such sacrilegious words, because he had no mortal father, so Alexander changed the question and asked whether he had punished all of *Philip's* assassins. Then he turned to his empire and asked whether it was the god's will that he should rule over the whole world. The god replied that such was his will, and that Philip had been paid the full quota of justice, and Alexander presented the god with magnificent offerings and the men with money.

This is the account most writers give of the god's prophecies, but Alexander himself in a letter to his mother says that he received some secret oracles which he would tell her and her alone when he returned. Some writers say that the prophet wanted, out of politeness, to address Alexander in Greek with the words '*O paidion*', 'My son', but, not being a Greek-speaker, made a mistake with a sigma at the ending and said '*O paidios*' instead, susbtituting a sigma for the nu. Alexander, they say, was delighted with this slip in pronunciation, and word got out that the god had addressed him as the son of Zeus, *pai Dios*.*

It is also said that while he was in Egypt he attended a lecture by the philosopher Psammon and was particularly ready to accept his argument that since the ruling and dominant part of anyone is divine, it follows that all men are ruled by the god. However, the story goes on, he himself had an even better and more philosophical idea on this matter, when he said that while the god is the common father of all men, he regards men of exceptional virtue as peculiarly his own.

[28] He generally behaved haughtily towards non-Greeks and made it seem as though he was fully convinced of his divine birth and parentage, but kept his assumption of divinity within reasonable bounds and did not overdo it when he was dealing with Greeks. All the same, in a letter to the Athenians about Samos he said, 'I cannot have given you that free and illustrious city; you received it from the person who was then your master and who was called my father'—that is, Philip. But on a later occasion, when he had been wounded by an arrow and was in great pain, he said, 'What you see flowing here, my friends, is blood and not "ichor, which flows in the veins of the blessed gods".'*

Once there was a huge clap of thunder which terrified everyone. Anaxarchus the sophist* was there and he asked Alexander, 'Could you, as the son of Zeus, do that?' Alexander laughed and said, 'No, I don't want to frighten my friends, which is what you would have me do, when you cast aspersions on my banquets because you see the table laden with fish rather than satraps' heads.' For we hear that once, when Alexander sent some little fish to Hephaestion, Anaxarchus really did say that, as if he were disparaging and mocking those who wear themselves out and risk their lives in the pursuit of fame and fortune when they have little or no advantage over others in terms of pleasure or satisfaction.* Anyway, it is clear from what I have said that Alexander had not actually become affected or puffed up, but used belief in his divinity to dominate others.

[29] After returning to Phoenicia from Egypt,* he discharged his duties to the gods with sacrificial rituals, processions, and competitions for both dithyrambic and tragic choruses which were spectacular not only for their trappings, but also for the degree of rivalry between the competing companies. For the impresarios were the kings of Cyprus, performing exactly the same function as is performed at Athens by those who are chosen by lot from the tribes, and they proved remarkably competitive and eager to outdo one another. The contest between Nicocreon of Salamis and Pasicrates of Soli was especially fierce. Both of them were assigned for their productions the most famous actors—Athenodorus for Pasicrates, and for Nicocreon Thessalus, one of whose greatest fans was Alexander himself. However, Alexander did not reveal his interest in Thessalus until the votes had been counted and Athenodorus had been declared the winner. But then, apparently, as he was on his way out of the theatre, he remarked that although he approved of the judges' decision, he would happily have given up a part of his kingdom in order not to have seen Thessalus beaten. Nevertheless, when Athenodorus, who had been sentenced by the Athenians to pay a fine for failing to appear at the Dionysia, asked Alexander to write a letter to them about his case, although he refused to do so, he did send them the fine at his own expense. Also, when Lycon of Scarphe was having a good day at the theatre and inserted into the comedy in which he was acting a line containing a request for ten talents, Alexander laughed and gave him the money.

Darius wrote Alexander a letter, and sent a delegation of his friends as well, to ask him to accept 10,000 talents as a ransom for the prisoners, to keep all the land west of the Euphrates, to marry one of his daughters, and to enter into a treaty of friendship and alliance with him.* Alexander told his Companions about the offer, and Parmenio said, 'If I were Alexander, I'd accept it.' 'So would I, for sure,' replied Alexander, 'if I were Parmenio.'* And in his letter back to Darius he said that if Darius came to him, he would be treated with every courtesy, but that otherwise he, Alexander, would presently be marching against him.

[30] Before long, however, he had cause for regret, when Darius' wife died in childbirth.* It was easy to see that he was upset at having lost such an excellent opportunity to display his kindness, and he spared no expense in her funeral rites. Now, one of the eunuchs of her bed-chamber (for they had been taken prisoner along with the

women) escaped from the encampment and made his way on horse-back to Darius. When the eunuch, whose name was Tireos, told Darius the news about his wife's death, Darius struck his head in grief and cried out, 'Alas for the guardian spirit of the Persian people, if it is fated that the king's sister-wife should be taken prisoner, and as if that were not enough that she should also have died without gaining a royal funeral!'

But the eunuch replied, 'My lord, as far as her funeral is concerned, and the question whether she received all the honour that was her due, you have no cause to find fault with the wretched spirit of the Persian people. My mistress Stateira, while she was alive, and your mother and children, did not lack any of the blessings and advantages they had enjoyed before, except the opportunity to see the light of your countenance, whose splendour I pray the Lord Oromazes may cause to shine once more. Moreover, in death, she not only received the full array of funeral ornaments, but was even honoured with the tears of your enemies. For Alexander is as kind in victory as he is terrible in battle.'

In his grief and distress, these words filled Darius with absurdly misguided suspicions. He drew the eunuch deeper into the tent and said, 'If you have not joined the fortune of the Persians in siding with the Macedonians—if I, Darius, am still your master—tell me, as you revere the great light of Mithras and the right hand of your king, was the evil that befell Stateira for which I am now shedding tears not the least of it? Did I suffer more pitiful wrongs while she was still alive? Would my misfortune not have been more compatible with my honour if I had met with a savage, grim enemy? For what proper relation-ship between a young man and the wife of his enemy could lead him to pay her so much honour?'

Even while he was still speaking, Tireos had thrown himself down at his feet and begged him not to say such terrible things, things which wronged Alexander, demeaned his dead sister-wife, and robbed him-self of the greatest consolation for his misfortunes—the idea that he was being beaten by a man who could rise above human nature; he said that Darius should even admire Alexander for a display of restraint in dealing with the Persians' womenfolk that surpassed the courage he had displayed in dealing with the Persians themselves. Leaving the eunuch still swearing awesome oaths to guarantee the truth of what he had been saying, and giving further examples of Alexander's restraint and noble principles, Darius went out to his companions and, with his hands raised to heaven, spoke the following prayer: 'Gods of my race and my kingdom, I pray above all that, by your leave, I may recover the Persian empire and see it once more established in as good and sound a state as when I received it, so that, once I have defeated Alexander, I may repay him for the favours he has done me, in the hour of my misfortune, concerning those whom I hold dearest. But if in fact the moment of destiny has come—the moment owed to the equilibration and mutability of things—and it is time for Persian dominance to cease, I pray that no man may sit on the throne of Cyrus unless it be Alexander.' The majority of my sources record these events and speeches as I have written them down.

[31] Alexander gained control over all the territory west of the Euphrates and then marched to meet Darius, who was coming down against him with an army of a million men.* During this march one of Alexander's Companions, thinking it a laughing matter, told him that for fun the camp-followers had divided themselves into two groups, and appointed a person to command and lead each of the groups, one of whom they called Alexander, the other Darius. They had started by throwing lumps of soil at one another, then moved on to using their fists, and by the time the fight had been broken up, which had not been easy since there were a lot of people involved, in the heat of their desire for victory they had gone as far as wielding sticks and stones. When Alexander heard this he ordered the leaders themselves to fight each other in single combat. He himself gave arms and armour to the one called 'Alexander', while Philotas did the same for 'Darius'. The army watched the duel, and everyone regarded the result as an omen for the future. The two fought fiercely, but 'Alexander' won, and received as a reward twelve villages and the right to wear Persian clothing. This story has been recorded for us by Eratosthenes.

The great battle against Darius did not in fact take place at Arbela, as most writers say, but at Gaugamela.* The word apparently means 'home of the camel',* and gained its name when an ancient king escaped from his enemies on the back of a dromedary, and then settled the animal there, gave the job of looking after it to some villages, and set aside some of his revenues for its upkeep. Be that as it may, there was an eclipse of the moon of the month Boedromion round about the time of the beginning of the celebration of the Mysteries at Athens,*

and on the eleventh night after the eclipse, with the two armies
visible to each other, whereas Darius kept his army at battle stations
and held a review of his troops by torchlight, Alexander let his
Macedonians rest, while he himself was busy performing certain secret
rituals and sacrificing to the god Fear in front of his tent, along with
his diviner, Aristander. When the older men among his Companions,
particularly Parmenio, saw the whole plain between the Niphates range
and the Gordyaean mountains lit up by the Persians' fires, and heard
the confused hubbub of voices and the noises echoing from the enemy
camp as if from some vast sea, they were astounded at the huge
numbers facing them and, after talking things over among themselves,
came to the conclusion that it would be extremely difficult for them
to engage and repel an enemy force of this size in broad daylight. So
they approached the king, once he had finished with his sacrifices, and
tried to persuade him to attack the enemy during the night and so to
conceal the most fearful aspect of the coming battle under a blanket
of darkness. Alexander gave a celebrated reply to this advice—'I am
not a thief, to steal my victory,' he said—but it struck some people
as a childish and foolish response, and they thought he was being
flippant in the face of terrible danger. His reply seemed to others, however, to indicate that he was not dismayed by the situation and had
correctly judged the future, in the sense that he would not give Darius
a pretext for summoning up the courage for another attempt if he lost
this time, by blaming his defeat on the night and the darkness, as he
had blamed Alexander's previous victory over him on the mountains,
the narrowness of the passes, and the sea. After all, they reasoned,
as long as Darius could draw on the enormous resources of the vast
territory at his disposal, he would never stop fighting because he had
run out of weapons or men; no, he would do so only when he had
lost his pride and confidence, and this would happen only when the
point had been brought forcibly home to him by a crushing defeat
in broad daylight.

[32] Alexander lay down in his tent, once the men had left, and is
said to have spent the rest of the night so much more soundly asleep
than usual that in the morning, when his officers came to his tent,†
they were surprised to find him still asleep, and they issued orders
on their own initiative that the men were to take their morning meal
before doing anything else. Then, given the urgency of the occasion,
Parmenio entered the tent, stood by Alexander's couch, and spoke

his name two or three times. When he had woken him up like this, he asked him how he could possibly sleep as if he had already won, instead of being on the point of fighting the most important battle of his life. Alexander smiled and said, 'What do you mean? Don't you think victory is already ours, now that we no longer have to wander around in a huge, desolate land in pursuit of Darius, while he refuses to take us on?'

Nor was it only before the battle that he demonstrated his calibre and showed how serenely confident he was in his assessment of the situation: he did the same during the actual fighting too. On the left wing, where Parmenio was in command, the battle turned and heaved against them when the Bactrian cavalry burst violently into the Macedonian ranks with a terrific roar and Mazaeus sent horsemen around the outside of the Macedonian infantry to attack the men posted to defend the baggage. These two manoeuvres panicked Parmenio into sending messengers to Alexander to tell him that camp and baggage were lost unless he moved a strong body of men immediately from the front to help those in the rear. Now, this happened to be exactly the moment when Alexander was signalling the men around him to attack. After listening to the message delivered by Parmenio's men, he described Parmenio's behaviour as overhasty and irrational, and said that his discomposure had made him forget that in any battle the winners are going to gain their enemies' possessions as well, while the losers had to forget about their valuables and their slaves, and make sure only that they died fighting with honour and glory.

After sending this message back to Parmenio, he proceeded to put his helmet on, but he had been wearing the rest of his armour ever since leaving his tent. He wore a belted Sicilian undergarment and on top of this a breastplate consisting of two layers of linen, which he had found among the booty captured at the battle of Issus. His helmet, the work of Theophilus, was made out of iron, but it gleamed as though it were pure silver; attached to it there was a neckpiece, also of iron, and set with precious stones. He had a marvellously well-tempered sword, of incredible lightness, which was a gift from the king of Citium, and he was such a highly trained swordsman that a sword was invariably the weapon he chose to use during battles. He was wearing a cloak which did not quite go with the rest of his gear, since it was of a more elaborate design. It was the work of Helicon, a weaver from former times, and had been presented to Alexander by the city

of Rhodes as a mark of respect. It was another item he always used
to wear into battle.* As long as he was merely riding past his men,
and perhaps slightly rearranging the infantry lines, or offering some
encouragement or advice, or conducting a review, he would use a different horse, and spare Bucephalas, who was now past his prime; but
whenever he was going into action Bucephalas would be brought
up, and as soon as Alexander had swapped horses he would begin
the attack.

[33] On this occasion he addressed the Thessalians and other Greeks
at length, until they reassured him by shouting for him to lead them
against the Persians. Then he shifted his spear into his left hand, leaving his right hand free to invoke the gods. According to Callisthenes,
he called on the gods to defend and support his Greek troops, seeing that he really was the son of Zeus. Meanwhile, Aristander the
diviner, wearing a white robe and crowned with a golden garland,
rode in front of the lines, pointing out to them an eagle which hovered
high in the sky over Alexander's head and directed its flight straight
at the enemy. This sight boosted the troops' morale a great deal, and
then, after speaking words of encouragement and assurance to one
another, the infantry phalanx rolled on like a flood after the cavalry,
which was charging at full speed against the enemy. The Persians gave
way before the front lines had clashed, and a fierce pursuit began, with
Alexander herding the defeated enemy into the centre where Darius
was.* For he had caught sight of Darius in the distance—just a glimpse
deep into the centre of the ranks of the Royal Cavalry deployed to
protect him—a tall, fine figure of a man, standing on a high chariot,
and protected by many magnificent horsemen who were drawn up in
a very tight defensive formation around his chariot. But the awful sight
of Alexander near at hand, driving the retreating troops into the ranks
of those who had maintained their positions, terrified most of the royal
guards, and they scattered. The bravest of them, however, the crack
troops, were cut down in front of the king and fell on top of one another
until they formed a barrier against the Macedonians' charge, entwin-
ing themselves in their death throes about the men and horses.

With all these horrors before his eyes, and with the troops deployed
to protect him being pushed back against him, Darius tried to turn
his chariot around and drive away. This was not easy, however, since
the wheels locked as they became entangled with the massed corpses,
and the horses, terrified† at the number of the dead, refused to go

on, and began to rear and plunge so much that the charioteer was beginning to lose control. So Darius abandoned his chariot and his armour, and fled, apparently, on the back of a horse which had recently given birth. But it is generally held that he would not have escaped if further horsemen had not come from Parmenio and called Alexander away, on the grounds that a considerable body of enemy troops still held together there and were continuing to resist.

Parmenio is commonly criticized as having been sluggish and ineffective in this battle, perhaps because he was by then too old and tired for acts of daring, or perhaps, as Callisthenes says, because he resented and found oppressive the unbridled arrogance of Alexander's power. At any rate, at the time in question Alexander was so irritated by his summons that he did not tell his men the truth. Instead he made out that he was glutted with the slaughter and, using the bad light as an excuse as well, had the trumpeters sound the recall. And as he was riding up to the danger area, he was informed that the enemy had been utterly defeated and put to flight.

[34] Given its outcome, this battle was generally believed to mark the complete overthrow of the Persian empire, and Alexander was proclaimed king of Asia. He made magnificent sacrifices to the gods and rewarded his friends with fortunes, estates, and military commands. Because he was anxious to win the favour of the Greeks, he wrote an open letter pointing out that all tyrants had been deposed and that they now enjoyed political freedom. He also wrote to the Plataeans in particular, promising to rebuild their city because their forefathers had allowed the Greeks to locate their fight for freedom on Plataean territory. And he sent a portion of the spoils to the people of Croton in Italy, as a mark of respect for the determination and bravery of the athlete Phayllus. For during the Persian Wars, when everyone else in Italy rejected the Greeks' requests for help, he fitted out a ship at his own expense and sailed to Salamis to play his part in the battle.*† These acts of Alexander's show how he favoured all forms of bravery, and how he felt protective and supportive of noble deeds.

[35] Next he attacked Babylonia, and soon subdued the whole country. What he found most astonishing there was the chasm of fire in Adiabene,*† where flames constantly shoot up into the air like a fiery fountain, and the stream of naphtha which is so extensive that it forms a lake quite close to the chasm. Naphtha is basically similar to asphalt, except that it is so sensitive to fire that it is ignited, even

before a flame has touched it, just by the radiance around the flame, and often sets fire to the intervening air as well. In order to demonstrate its qualities and power, the Babylonians lightly sprinkled the street leading up to Alexander's quarters with the substance, and then stood at one end of the street and applied their torches—for night was drawing in—to the moistened spots. The first spots caught fire straight away, and the fire spread too quickly for the eye to follow; as quick as thought, it shot down to the other end until there was an unbroken wall of fire all the way down the street.

There was a man called Athenophanes, who came from Athens, and was one of those whose job it was to tend to the king's body while he was being oiled and bathed, and to divert his mind with suitable relaxing pleasantries. At the time in question a young boy called Stephanus, who was particularly, even ridiculously, ugly, but had a beautiful singing voice, was also in attendance on Alexander in the bathroom, and Athenophanes said, 'Shall we take some of that substance, my lord, and conduct an experiment with it on Stephanus? If it sets fire to him without being extinguished, I would have to say that there is nothing that can withstand it and that its power is truly formidable.' For some reason the boy also enthusiastically offered himself for the experiment, and as soon as he had smeared the substance on himself and handled it, flames burst out all over his body, and he was so completely covered with fire that Alexander became completely panic-stricken with fear. Luckily there were lots of people there with bowls of water in their hands for his bath, otherwise the boy would have been beyond help and the flames would have spread. Even as things were his body was so completely on fire that they only just managed to extinguish the flames, and afterwards he was in a terrible state.

It is quite plausible, then, for some people, in trying to salvage the veracity of the myth, to say that this is the substance Medea smeared on the crown and the cloak, as portrayed in the tragedy.* They argue that it was not the crown and the cloak that started the fire, and that it did not start spontaneously either, but that a flame was brought near them and then a rapid attraction and connection, imperceptible to the senses, took place. The rays and emanations which proceed from a flame that is some distance away usually do no more than impart light and heat to things, but in the case of objects which have an airy dryness or a sufficiently oily moisture they gather, combust, and rapidly transform the material. There has been considerable discussion about the origin of <naphtha . . .>,† or whether, on the contrary, the liquid which acts as a fuel for the flame flows out of the ground, which has an oily and combustible nature. For Babylonia is so very fiery that grains of barley often jump out of the ground and are hurled up into the air, as if the places where this happens throbbed with inflammation; and during the hot season the people there sleep on skins filled with water. When Harpalus was left in charge of the country, he was keen to embellish the palace gardens and walks with Greek plants, and whereas he managed to get other plants to take, ivy was the only one the soil always rejected and killed: ivy thrives in cool soil, and therefore could not survive in soil with a fiery composition. But perhaps impatient readers will complain less at digressions like this if they do not go on for too long.*

[36] When Alexander took control of Susa,* he found 40,000 talents of coined money in the palace, as well as countless furnishings and valuables, including, according to my sources, 5,000 talents of purple cloth from Hermione, which still had a fresh, bright colour, despite having been lying in storage for 190 years.* The reason for this, they say, is that honey was used when dyeing the purple-dyed cloths, and white olive-oil on the white cloths, since honey and white olive-oil also retain their brilliance and gleaming appearance after that many years. Moreover, according to Dinon, the Persian kings used to have water fetched from the Nile and the Danube and stored up along with everything else in their treasury, or *gaza*, as a way of confirming the extent of their empire and their mastery over the whole world.

[37] Persia is a difficult country to get into, owing to the ruggedness of the country, and it was guarded by crack Persian troops, since Darius had taken refuge there.* So Alexander found a guide who showed him a roundabout way in which involved only a slight detour. The guide was bilingual, since his father was Lycian and his mother Persian, and it was this, they say, that the Pythia had predicted in a prophecy she gave when Alexander was still a child, to the effect that a Lycian would be Alexander's guide on his march against the Persians.*

A terrible massacre of prisoners took place there.† Alexander himself writes in a letter that, since he thought it would be to his advantage, he gave the command for the people to be slaughtered.* He found as much coined money there as at Susa, and they say that it took 10,000 pairs of mules and 5,000 camels to transport all the rest of the furnishings and valuables out of the city. When Alexander saw a colossal statue of Xerxes, which had been rudely knocked over by the press of the huge numbers of people forcing their way into the palace, he stood by it and said, as if he were talking to a living person, 'Shall I leave you lying there, to pay for your expedition against Greece, or shall I wake you up because of your noble self-assurance and excellence in other respects?' Eventually, after pondering the matter in silence for quite a while, he left the statue lying there and walked on. He wanted to give his troops a break—and it was wintertime, anyway —so he spent four months in Persepolis.* It is said that the first time he sat on the royal throne under the golden canopy, Demaratus of Corinth, a loyal old family friend of his, burst into tears, as old men will, and declared that the Greeks who had died before they could see Alexander seated on Darius' throne had missed a rare treat.

[38] Later, just when he was about to set out against Darius, he happened to get involved in a heavy drinking party with his Companions, at which even women were present, having been invited to meet their lovers. The most famous of these women was Thaïs, a courtesan who originally came from Attica, and was there with Ptolemy, who later became king.* As the drinking went on, partly as a graceful way of complimenting Alexander and partly to amuse him, she was induced to deliver a speech which was in keeping with the customs of her native country, but was too high-flown for her. She said that although the high life they were enjoying that day in the extraordinary palace of the Persian kings made her exhausting travels through Asia seem worthwhile, she would still prefer for them to celebrate by burning down Xerxes' residence, since he had destroyed Athens by fire;* and she said that she wanted to start the fire herself, with Alexander merely looking on, so that word might get around that the women in Alexander's entourage had avenged Greece more thoroughly than all his fine commanders with their battles on sea and land.

Her words were greeted with tumultuous applause, and Alexander, won over by the enthusiastic prompting of his Companions, leapt to his feet and led the way, with a garland on his head and a torch in his hand. The others followed him with cries of drunken merriment and surrounded the palace, and they were joined by some other Macedonians who had heard what was going on and ran up with torches. Their mood was good, because they hoped that burning the palace to the ground was the act of someone who was thinking of home and was not intending to live in foreign lands. But although some accounts claim that this is how it happened, others say it was a premeditated act. In any case, everyone agrees that Alexander soon changed his mind and ordered the fire extinguished.

[39] Alexander was born very generous, and became even more so as his affairs prospered.* He was also blessed with kindness, without which no gift is really welcome. I will mention a few instances. Once when Ariston, the commander of the Paeonians, had killed one of the enemy, he brought the man's head to Alexander to show it off to him, and he said, 'It is a Paeonian custom, my lord, for this gift to be rewarded with a golden cup.' Alexander laughed and said, 'Yes, an empty cup, but I'll give you one full of wine.'*

On another occasion one of the Macedonian rank and file was driving a mule which was carrying some of the king's gold, and when the beast became too tired to continue, the man hoisted the load on to his shoulders and proceeded to carry it himself. Alexander happened to see the man struggling along and had the situation explained to him, and so, when the man was about to put the load down, he said, 'Don't give up. Just keep on going to your tent, and take the gold there for yourself.'

He was usually more annoyed by people refusing gifts than by people asking him for something. In a letter to Phocion he said that in the future he would not treat him as a friend if he rejected his gifts.* Serapion, one of the young lads Alexander used to play ball with, never got any presents because he never asked him for any, and he in his turn, when he joined in their games, never threw the ball to Alexander. Eventually Alexander said, 'Why don't you give me the ball?' 'Because you don't ask for it,' Serapion replied. Alexander laughed at this and gave him a lot of presents.

There was a fairly cultured crowd of people with whom Alexander used to drink and tell jokes, and one of them, Proteas, once seemed to have incurred his anger. Proteas' friends apologized for him, and Proteas himself pleaded with him with tears in his eyes, until Alexander said he forgave him—at which point Proteas said, 'In that case, my lord, first give me something to prove it.' And Alexander arranged for him to be given five talents.

That his friends and bodyguards used to give themselves considerable airs over the valuable presents he gave them is proved by a letter from Olympias to Alexander in which she says, 'You should find some other way to do your friends good and show them how highly you think of them,† because at the moment you're making them all your kingly equals, and while you're guaranteeing them plenty of friends, you're leaving yourself none.' Olympias often wrote to him like this, and he used to keep her letters secret, except that once, when Hephaestion also read, as he usually did, a letter that had been left open, Alexander did not stop him, but slipped off his ring and applied the seal to his lips. And he once offered one of the sons of Mazaeus (who had been the most influential person in Darius' court) an additional, larger province to govern, even though he already had one; Mazaeus' son refused, however, and said, 'My lord, previously there used to be only one Darius, but now you have made many Alexanders.'

It is said that he gave Parmenio Bagoas' residence, in which people say there were found 1,000 talents' worth of clothing,* and he wrote to Antipater warning him of plots against his life, and recommending that he keep bodyguards by him. He sent his mother a great many presents, but he refused to let her meddle in his affairs or interfere with his strategies; when she scolded him for this, he remained unruffled by her anger. Once, however, when Antipater wrote him a long letter complaining about her, he remarked, after reading it, that Antipater was unaware that a single tear shed by a mother erases 10,000 letters.

[40] When Alexander noticed that his courtiers had become spoiled by luxurious living and were vulgarly flaunting the extravagance of their lifestyles—for instance, Hagnon of Teos used to wear silver nails in his boots, Leonnatus had the dust he used for his exercising transported by camel train from Egypt, Philotas owned hunting-nets 100 stades long, they infinitely preferred myrrh to oil as an unguent before going to be scraped clean, and they surrounded themselves with masseurs and chamberlains—he criticized them gently and reasonably.* He found it astonishing, he said, that people who had fought so many major battles could forget that working for others makes for a better night's rest than being worked for by others, and could fail to appreciate, from a comparison between their own lives and those of the Persians, that, on a scale from slavery to kingship, wallowing in luxury was way down at the bottom and hard work was way up at the top. 'And yet,' he went on, 'how can anyone look after a horse on his own, or work on a spear or a helmet, if he has grown unaccustomed

to using his hands on his very own body? Don't you realize', he added, 'that there's no point in our winning unless we avoid imitating the losers?'

And so he pushed himself to work even harder. He exposed himself to hardship and danger at war and out hunting—so much so that a Laconian ambassador who had watched him kill a huge lion said, 'Well fought, Alexander! You gambled with the lion for your kingdom!' This is the hunt depicted by the group of statues dedicated by Craterus at Delphi; he commissioned Lysippus and Leochares between them to make bronze figures of the lion and the hounds, of the king taking on the lion, and of himself coming to help.*

[41] Although Alexander continued to risk his life in the pursuit of excellence for himself and in trying to motivate the rest of his men to seek it too, their wealth and their pretensions had by now made his friends want only a life of luxurious ease, and they resented Alexander's campaigns and expeditions so much that it gradually got to the point where they would curse him and malign him.* At first he remained perfectly calm about this, saying that a king was bound to have people wish him harm when he was trying to do them good, and even the slightest favours he did his close friends showed how much he continued to like and value them. Here are a few examples, to prove the point.

In a letter to Peucestas he told him off for having written to tell everyone else apart from him that he had been bitten by a bear, and said, 'But write to me now, and tell me how you are and whether any of the people you'd gone hunting with left you in the lurch—in which case I'll punish them.' Once when Hephaestion was away on some business Alexander wrote and told him how Craterus had been accidentally wounded in the thigh by Perdiccas' spear when they were hunting mongooses for fun. After Peucestas recovered from an illness, Alexander wrote to Alexippus the doctor to thank him. When Craterus was ill, Alexander not only personally performed certain sacrifices for him, as a result of a dream he had, but told him to follow his example as well; he also wrote to the doctor, Pausanias, who wanted to use hellebore on Craterus, partly to express his anxiety and partly to advise him how to use the drug. He imprisoned the first people to bring him news of Harpalus' flight and desertion, who were called Ephialtes and Cissus, because he assumed that they were lying to get Harpalus into trouble.

Once, when Alexander was having the invalids and veterans sent back home, Eurylochus of Aegae got himself included on the sick-list even though he had nothing wrong with him, and when he was caught he confessed that he was in love with Telesippa and was try-ing to follow her to the coast, since she was leaving. Alexander asked about her family, and when he heard that she was a free-born cour-tesan, he said, 'Well, Eurylochus, I'll help you pursue Telesippa, but we must be sure to win her round by arguments or presents since she is from a free-born family.'

[42] For his friends he also wrote the kind of letter one can scarcely believe he would have had time for. When a slave belonging to Seleucus* ran away to Cilicia, for instance, he wrote giving orders for him to be hunted down; in another letter he praised Peucestas for apprehending Nicon, a slave belonging to Craterus, and in another to Megabyzus he talked about how to deal with a house-slave of his who had taken refuge in the sanctuary, telling him to entice the slave outside the sanctuary, if possible, and then apprehend him, but not to touch him inside the sanctuary.

It is said that when he first began judging capital cases he used to listen to the prosecutor's speech with a hand placed over one of his ears, so that it might be kept unsullied and unbiased for the defendant. Later, however, all the accusations he had heard began to make him less tolerant, since there were enough true ones to have paved the way for the false ones and given them credibility. Above all, abuse would drive him mad and make him harsh and implacable, because he loved his reputation more than his life and his kingdom.

At the time in question, then, he marched out against Darius, with the intention of engaging him in yet another battle, but when he heard that he had been arrested by Bessus,* he dismissed his Thessalian troops and sent them home, after distributing among them a bonus of 2,000 talents on top of their pay. His pursuit of Darius proved so long and arduous—they rode 3,300 stades in eleven days—that most of his men fell by the wayside, thanks particularly to the short-age of water.*† This was the point at which he came across some Macedonians carrying skins of water from the river on their mules; it was midday, and as soon as they noticed that he was desperately thirsty, they filled a helmet with water and brought it to him. He asked them who the water they were carrying was for. 'For our sons,' they said. 'But as long as you are alive we can always have other sons, even if we lose the ones we've got at the moment.' This made him accept the helmet, but then he looked around and saw that all the horsemen in the vicinity were craning their necks and staring at him expectantly, so he gave the helmet back without drinking from it. He thanked the men for their kindness, and said, 'If I'm the only one to get a drink, it will have a bad effect on the morale of my men.' At this display of his self-control and noble principles, the horsemen shouted out for him to lead the way, and whipped their horses into action. As long as they had such a king, they said, he could trust them not to feel tired or thirsty or even to consider themselves mortal at all.

[43] The same commitment to the task infused the whole army, but it is said that Alexander was accompanied by only sixty men when he burst into the enemy camp. They rode over piles of discarded silver and gold, past carts laden with women and children which had been abandoned by their drivers and left to wander aimlessly, and concentrated on chasing the men who had got away first, because they supposed that Darius would be among them. Eventually he was found lying in a wagon, his body riddled with javelin wounds, close to death. Nevertheless, he asked for something to drink and took a drink of cold water. Then he said to Polystratus, the person who had given him the water, 'My misfortunes can get no worse than this, that I cannot return this favour you have done me. But Alexander will repay you for your good turn, and the gods will repay Alexander for his kindness towards my mother, wife, and children. Here, take my hand: I offer it to him through you.' With these words he grasped Polystratus' hand and died.

When Alexander arrived and saw what had happened, he took off his own cloak and used it to cover and wrap the body, without attempting to disguise his grief. And later, once he had tracked Bessus down, he scattered his body, like slingshot, in various directions. Two upright trees were bent down until they met, and a part of Bessus' body was tied on to each of the trees, which were then released, so that as each tree sprang back up it took with it the part of Bessus' body that was attached to it. At the time in question, however, he sent Darius' mother her son's corpse, adorned with a king's regalia, and let his brother Exathres join the ranks of his Companions.*

[44] Meanwhile he took the pick of his fighting force and went down into Hyrcania, where he saw a gulf of the open sea which looked as though it was at least as big as the Euxine Sea, but was less salty than

the other sea. His enquiries brought him no clear information about it, and his best guess was that it was an overflow from Lake Maeotis. Long before Alexander's expedition, however, natural scientists were aware of the truth and as a result of their researches reported that this is the most northerly of the four gulfs which run in from the outer sea, and is known as both the Hyrcanian Sea and the Caspian Sea.*

While he was in this part of the world some native tribesmen ambushed the attendants of Alexander's horse Bucephalas and captured it. Alexander's fury knew no bounds, and he sent a messenger threatening to kill them all, including their children and womenfolk, unless they sent the horse back to him. But when they did come, and not only brought the horse with them, but surrendered their towns to him as well, he treated all of them with kindness and gave those who had captured Bucephalas ransom-money.*

[45] Next he marched into Parthian territory,* and it was here, during a lull in the fighting, that he first wore non-Greek clothing, perhaps because he wanted to associate himself with local customs, on the grounds that the sight of what is familiar and congenial goes a long way towards winning people over, or perhaps this was a sly attempt to get the Macedonians to adopt the practice of prostration, by gradually getting them used to putting up with changes in his way of life. However, he did not approve of the famous Median style of clothing, which is so thoroughly alien to Greek tastes, and he did not take to trousers or *kandys* or *tiara*, but adopted a kind of balanced blend of Persian and Median clothing, which was more simple than the latter and more stately than the former.* At first he used to wear these clothes only when meeting non-Greeks and when he was with his Companions at home, but then he began to be seen by ordinary people in these clothes when out riding and when holding audiences. His fellow Macedonians did not like to see him dressed like this, but they were so impressed with his outstanding qualities in other respects that they thought they should let him get away with some things which pleased him or increased his prestige. For despite the fact that, in addition to all the other wounds he had received, he had recently been hit in the shin by an arrow which splintered and dislocated the shin-bone, and on another occasion had been hit on the neck by a stone, which had caused his sight to become clouded and to remain so for quite a long time, he did not stop taking serious risks with his life, and in fact he crossed the river Orexartes (mistaking it

for the Tanaïs), routed an army of Scythians, and chased them for
100 stades—all while suffering from dysentery.*

[46] It was after he had crossed the Orexartes that the queen of the
Amazons paid him a visit—a visit that is recorded in most writers,
such as Cleitarchus, Polyclitus, Onesicritus, Antigenes, and Ister. But
Aristobulus and Chares the Chamberlain are joined by Hecataeus of
Eretria, Ptolemy, Anticlides, Philon of Thebes, Philip of Theangela,
Philip of Chalcis, and Duris of Samos in claiming that this visit is
a fiction. And it looks as though Alexander supports them, because
he wrote a very precise and detailed letter to Antipater in which he
says that the Scythian king offered him his daughter in marriage, but
he does not mention any Amazon. And there is a story that many
years later Onesicritus was reading the fourth book of his history of
Lysimachus, who had become king by then, and when he came to
the bit about the Amazon, which is contained in this book, Lysimachus
smiled gently and said, 'And where was I at the time?' Anyway, our
admiration for Alexander will not be decreased if we disbelieve the
story of the Amazon or increased if we believe it.*

[47] Alexander was worried about his troops refusing to continue
with the campaign, so leaving the main body where it was, and taking
only the best of them—20,000 foot-soldiers and 3,000 cavalrymen
—with him into Hyrcania,* he won them over† by telling them that
at the moment the easterners could see them face to face,† but that
if all they did was cause havoc in Asia and then leave, the enemy would
regard them as no better than women and not hesitate to attack them.
Nevertheless, he left it up to them to leave if they wanted to, and asked
that if they did so they should testify that in his attempt to make the
whole world subject to the Macedonians, he had been left behind with
his friends and those who were prepared to continue with the campaign.† This is almost a verbatim quote from a letter of his to Antipater,
and he goes on to say that after he had finished speaking they all
shouted out loud, calling on him to take them wherever he wanted
in the world. Once these élite troops had met this test of their loyalty, it proved easy to win over the main body of the army, which
readily followed his lead.

After this, then, he began to assimilate his way of life even more
closely with that of the locals, and also tried to get them to adopt
Macedonian customs. He was of the opinion that while he was away
on a lengthy expedition political stability would follow from fusion

and co-operation, achieved through goodwill, rather than from the use of force. This is also why he issued instructions that 30,000 selected children were to learn Greek and to be trained in the use of Macedonian weaponry, and appointed a large number of people to oversee this project.* Moreover, although what happened with Rhoxane occurred because he fell in love with her beauty and grace when he saw her dancing at a banquet, the marriage was also held to fit in quite well with the policy he was pursuing.* For the easterners were reassured by the bond the marriage formed, and they particularly appreciated the self-restraint he demonstrated in refusing to lay a finger even on the only woman he ever fell for until it had been sanctioned by law.

Moreover, when he saw that among his closest friends Hephaestion approved of what he was doing and joined him in modifying his habits, whereas Craterus stuck to the traditional ways, he used Hephaestion for conducting business with foreigners, and Craterus for Greeks and Macedonians.* And, to put it succinctly, he loved Hephaestion best, but respected Craterus most; he was constantly saying that in his opinion while Hephaestion was loyal to Alexander, Craterus was loyal to the king. This helps to explain why there was bad feeling festering between the two of them, so that they often clashed. Once, in fact, while they were in India, they even got into a fight, with drawn swords, and their friends were taking sides and coming up to help, when Alexander rode up and told Hephaestion off in front of everyone, calling him a reckless, crazy fool for failing to understand that Hephaestion without Alexander was nothing. After also giving Craterus a severe dressing-down in private, he brought the two of them together and had them make friends again, and he called on Ammon and all the other gods to witness that although these were the two men he loved most in the world, if he found them quarrelling again he would kill them both, or at least the one who started the quarrel. After this, we are told, neither of them said or did anything to offend the other, even as a joke.

[48] Philotas the son of Parmenio was one of the most highly respected Macedonians, with a reputation for bravery and endurance, and for being second only to Alexander himself in his generosity and loyalty towards his companions.* At any rate, there is a story that on being asked for some money by one of his close friends, he ordered it to be given to him, but the steward told him that he had none to give. 'What?' said Philotas. 'Not even a cup or a cloak?' However, his

haughty pride, opulence, concern for bodily comfort, and lifestyle were offensive in a private citizen, and also his affectation of lofty aloofness was awkward in its clumsy vulgarity and speciousness. All this only made him an object of suspicion and envy; and even Parmenio felt compelled to say to him once, 'Please don't make so much of yourself, my son.'

Now, Alexander had in fact been hearing bad things about Philotas for very many years. For after Darius' defeat in Cilicia and the seizure of the property in Damascus,* there was found among the prisoners of war, who were brought into the Macedonian camp, an attractive woman called Antigone, who came originally from Pydna. She became the property of Philotas. Now, he used to speak freely to her, as young men will to a lover when they are under the influence of wine, in a self-important and boastful fashion, and in telling her the great importance of his own and his father's achievements, he used to say that it was thanks to them that Alexander, whom he described as a callow youth, was enjoying the title of ruler. Antigone told this to one of her close friends, and he of course told somebody else, until eventually the tale reached Craterus, who got the woman and secretly took her to see Alexander. When he heard what she had to say, he told her to carry on meeting Philotas and to come and tell him everything she found out from him.

[49] Philotas had no idea that this trap was being set for him, and during his times together with Antigone he would often, in his anger and pride, criticize the king and express disapproval of him. In spite of the incontestable evidence that had come his way against Philotas, Alexander restrained himself and put up with it without saying or doing anything, perhaps because he felt he could confidently rely on Parmenio's loyalty, or perhaps because he was afraid of Philotas' and Parmenio's reputation and power.

Now, at this point in time, a Macedonian from Chalaestra called Dimnus† was plotting against Alexander's life, and he invited a young man called Nicomachus, with whom he was in love, to join the conspiracy. Nicomachus refused, and told his brother Cebalinus about the enterprise, whereupon Cebalinus went to Philotas and asked him to get them a audience with Alexander, because they had urgent and important news to communicate to him. Philotas, however, for reasons that are obscure, did not take them to see Alexander, on the grounds that the king was busy with other, more important matters.

In fact, he turned them down twice. They now became suspicious of Philotas and turned to someone else instead, who got them in to see Alexander. They started by denouncing Dimnus, and then they gradually revealed that Philotas had twice done nothing about it when they were trying to obtain an audience with him. This made Alexander furious, and when Dimnus resisted arrest and was killed by the man Alexander had sent to take him into custody, the thought that proof of the intrigue had been lost worried him even more. In his bitter rage against Philotas he attracted to himself those who had hated Philotas for a long time, who now spoke their minds and said that the king was not making much of an effort if he imagined that Dimnus, a man from Chalaestra, would undertake such a bold enterprise all by himself; they said that he was no more than a hired hand, or rather a tool set to work by a greater agency, and that the the source of the plot should be sought among those who had the most to gain from its concealment.

Once the king had opened his ears to this kind of argument and insinuation, Philotas' enemies began to denounce him in countless ways, and the outcome was that he was arrested and questioned, with the Companions standing by during the torture, while Alexander listened from behind a curtain which had been stretched across as a divider. And they say that when Philotas pitifully and miserably begged Hephaestion for mercy, Alexander said, 'How could anyone as feeble and cowardly as you, Philotas, have taken on such a formidable task?' No sooner was Philotas dead than Alexander sent men to Media and had Parmenio killed too—Parmenio, who had been Philip's colleague in many great victories, who had been almost the only one of Alexander's older friends to have encouraged him to invade Asia, who had given the lives of two of the three sons of his who were on active service, and who was now murdered along with the third of these sons.* These measures of Alexander's made a number of his friends afraid of him, especially Antipater, who entered into secret negotiations with the Aetolians and exchanged pledges with them. Aetolian fear of Alexander stemmed from the time they had razed Oeniadae and he had said, on hearing about it, that the Aetolians would not be punished by the sons of Oeniadae, but by him.*

[50] Soon after this there occurred the business with Clitus too,* and although at first sight it might seem more savage than what happened to Philotas, if we consider both the cause and the circumstances

we find that the act was not premeditated, but was a kind of unfortunate accident for Alexander that took place when his drunken anger furnished Clitus' spirit* with an excuse. Here is what happened. Some fruit from Greece was brought up from the coast to Alexander, and he was most impressed with how fresh and attractive it was, so he called Clitus because he wanted to show him the fruit and give him some. Clitus happened to be in the middle of performing a sacrifice at the time, but he left it and came over—with three of the consecrated sheep following him. When Alexander heard about this, he consulted his diviners, Aristander and Cleomenes of Laconia, who said that it was a bad omen, and so he ordered sacrifices to be carried out without delay to avert any danger from Clitus. For in fact, two nights earlier, he had had a strange dream, in which Clitus and Parmenio's sons were seated together all dressed in black, and all dead. However, the sacrifices for Clitus had not yet been performed when he hurried to come and have dinner with Alexander, who had sacrificed to the Dioscuri.*

A vigorous drinking-session was initiated, and songs by a certain Pranichus (or Pierion, on some accounts) were sung, which had been composed to embarrass and mock the Macedonian commanders who had recently been defeated by an eastern army. The older men protested and rebuked both the poet and the singer, but Alexander and his friends were enjoying the song and told the man to continue. Clitus, who was drunk by then and was in any case bad-tempered and insubordinate, was particularly angry. He said that abusing Macedonians in front of non-Greeks and enemies* was wrong, even if they had met with a piece of bad luck, and that they were much braver than the ones who were doing the laughing. Alexander retorted that for Clitus to make cowardice out to be a piece of bad luck was no more than special pleading. Clitus stood up and said, 'Well, this "cowardice" kept you safe once, for all your divine parentage, when you left your back exposed to Spithridates' sword, and it was Macedonian blood and these wounds of mine that made you grand enough to disown Philip and call yourself a son of Ammon!'

[51] Alexander was furious. 'Damn you!' he hissed. 'Do you think you're going to get away with it every time you talk like that about me and set the Macedonians at one another's throats?'

'I'm not getting away with it even now, Alexander,' Clitus replied. 'Look at how I'm rewarded for all my troubles. The lucky ones are

those who have already died, to my mind, because they didn't live to
see us Macedonians flogged with Median rods and having to beg
Persians for an audience with our king.'

At these candid words of Clitus', Alexander's friends got to their
feet too and hurled abuse at him, while the older men present tried
to calm things down. But Alexander turned to Xenodochus of Cardia
and Artemius of Colophon and said, 'Don't you get the impression
that the Greeks strut around among the Macedonians like demi-gods
among animals?'

Clitus refused to back down, and he told Alexander to say what he
wanted to say for all to hear,† or alternatively not to invite to dinner
men who were free and spoke their mind, but to surround himself
with foreigners and slaves, who would prostrate themselves before his
Persian belt and pure white tunic. At this Alexander could no longer
contain his anger. He picked up one of the apples that was lying on
the table, threw it at Clitus, and hit him with it. Then he began to
cast about for his sword, but one of his bodyguards, a man called
Aristophanes, quickly removed it before he could lay his hands on
it. Everyone else stood around him and begged him to calm down,
but he leapt to his feet and called out in Macedonian for the Shield-
bearers, which was a prearranged signal indicating serious trouble;
then he ordered the trumpeter to sound the alarm and punched him
when he hesitated and refused to do so. Afterwards, then, this trumpeter was congratulated for the crucial part he played in preventing
the camp being thrown into confusion.

Clitus was still seething, but his friends just managed to push
him out of the dining-room. He started to come in by another door,
insolently and brashly quoting the following lines from Euripides'
Andromache: 'Alas! What evil customs rule in Greece . . .'*† This was
when Alexander grabbed a spear from one of the guards, and as Clitus
stepped towards him while drawing aside the curtain which covered
the door he ran him through. As soon as Clitus fell to the ground
with a gasp and a bellow of pain, Alexander's anger vanished. When
he came to himself and saw his friends standing speechless, he pulled
the spear from Clitus' body before anyone could stop him and made
as if to stab himself in the throat—but was stopped by his bodyguards,
who pinioned his hands and carried him struggling into his bedroom.

[52] A night of bitter tears followed, and the next day, worn out
by his cries of grief, he lay without saying a thing, sighing deeply.

His friends were worried by his silence and insisted on coming in to see him. He ignored what they all said, but when Aristander the diviner reminded him of the dream he had had about Clitus and of the portent, as if to suggest that it had all been fated for a long time, he seemed to relax, so they brought in the philosopher Callisthenes, a relative of Aristotle's, and Anaxarchus of Abdera.* While Callisthenes tried to deal with his suffering by tactful and gentle means, using euphemisms and circumlocutions to avoid giving pain, Anaxarchus, who had always had an idiosyncratic way of going about philosophy, and had acquired a reputation for despising and belittling convention, shouted out, as soon as he was in the room: 'Look at Alexander, the idol of all the world! Here he lies prostrate with grief, as afraid of people's rules and criticism as a slave, when people should really regard him as their rule and standard of right and wrong, since by his victories he has gained the right of rulership and authority, and need never be enslaved and cowed by superficial opinion. Don't you realize', he concluded, 'why Zeus has Justice and Right seated beside him? It is to ensure that every action performed by anyone in a position of authority is right and just.'

Anaxarchus may have alleviated the king's pain with this kind of argument, but he also considerably increased his conceit and his inclination to disregard rules. Moreover, he succeeded in making himself incredibly popular, while putting Alexander off Callisthenes, whose company was in any case too exacting to be pleasant. There is a story that once at dinner there was a discussion about the climate and the weather, and when Anaxarchus started to raise objections and argue against Callisthenes, who was siding with the view that it was more cold and stormy there than in Greece, Callisthenes said, 'But you have to admit that it's colder here than there. After all, you used to go through winter there wearing only a thin cloak, but here you lie down for your meals with three blankets on top of you.'* This, of course, only added to Anaxarchus' irritation with Callisthenes.

[53] Callisthenes used to annoy all the other sophists and flatterers as well, who did not like to see that the young men found his discourses interesting, and that the older men found the way he lived just as attractive. In fact, his life was so orderly, dignified, and self-sufficient that it tended to confirm the reason given for his trip abroad—that he had made his way inland to Alexander because he wanted to bring his fellow citizens back home and repopulate the country of his birth.*

Not only did the way others admired him make him an object of resentment, but he himself also sometimes supplied his detractors with ammunition to use against him, in that he would usually refuse invitations to dinner, and when he was in company his serious and silent manner made it seem as though he disapproved and disliked what was going on. Once, in fact, Alexander said about him, ' "I can't stand a clever man who doesn't apply his intelligence to himself." '*

We are told that once at one of Alexander's dinners, to which he had invited a great many guests, Callisthenes was ordered, during the drinking session, to give a speech eulogizing the Macedonians, and he spoke so eloquently on the topic that everyone gave him a standing ovation and threw their garlands at him. So Alexander quoted Euripides, 'Speaking well is no great problem, given good material for one's speech,'* and went on to say: 'Why don't you prove your eloquence by giving a speech criticizing the Macedonians, to teach them their faults so that they can improve?' And so the man set about his palinode and turned to outspoken and detailed criticism of the Macedonians. After showing that Greek feuding was the cause of Philip's rise to power, he said: ' "But in times of civil strife even criminals become respectable." '* This made the Macedonians hate him, with a deep and bitter hatred, and Alexander said that Callisthenes had not proved his ingenuity so much as his ill will towards the Macedonians.

[54] We have this story on the authority of Hermippus, who says that Stroebus, the slave who read aloud to Callisthenes, told it to Aristotle. And, Hermippus adds, when Callisthenes realized that the king was angry with him, as he was leaving he muttered two or three times under his breath the line 'Patroclus too is dead, who was a far braver man than you.'* So Aristotle seems to have hit the mark in saying that Callisthenes was a capable and powerful speaker, but lacked common sense.

Nevertheless, by his vehement objection on philosophical grounds to the act of prostration*—he was the only one openly to discuss the issues which were secretly alarming all the best and oldest Macedonians—he averted the practice and so saved the Greeks from serious humiliation, and Alexander from even worse dishonour. This cost him his life, however, since he was generally thought to have used force rather than persuasion on the king. Chares of Mitylene says that once during a symposium, after drinking from a bowl, Alexander handed it to one of his friends, who stood up to face the hearth, drank from the bowl, prostrated himself before Alexander, and then kissed him, before resuming his place on his couch. Everyone else did the same one after another, and then the bowl reached Callisthenes. Alexander was not watching what he was doing, but was talking to Hephaestion. After drinking, Callisthenes went over to kiss him—but Demetrius, whose surname was Phidon, said, 'My lord, don't kiss him: he's the only one who hasn't prostrated himself before you.' When Alexander refused to kiss him, Callisthenes said in a loud voice: 'All right, then, I'll go away, a kiss worse off than before.'

[55] The first consequence of the tension developing between Alexander and Callisthenes was that Hephaestion was believed when he said that Callisthenes had promised him he would prostrate himself before Alexander, and had then gone back on his word. Secondly, people like Lysimachus and Hagnon stuck close to Alexander and claimed that the haughty way the sophist went around smacked of the intention to overthrow the monarchy, and that young men flocked to him and followed him around as if he were the only free man to be found among all those countless thousands of people. In this context, when the conspiracy of Hermolaus and his associates came to light,* the accusations Callisthenes' enemies made against him seemed plausible. They said that when Hermolaus had asked him how he could become the most famous person in the world, Callisthenes had replied, 'By killing the most famous person in the world.' They also said that he had encouraged Hermolaus in his attempt by telling him not to be put off by the golden couch, but to remember that he was approaching a man, who was capable of falling ill and being wounded. And yet even when pressed to the limit not one of Hermolaus' accomplices denounced Callisthenes. In fact, in the letters he wrote immediately after the event to Craterus, Attalus, and Alcetas, Alexander himself says that under torture the youths confessed that they had made this attempt by themselves and that no one else had been in on the plot. In a later letter to Antipater, however, he accuses Callisthenes of complicity and says, 'The youths were stoned to death by the Macedonians, but I shall punish the sophist myself, along with those who sent him and those who harbour in their cities men who intrigue against me.' These words are an unequivocal expression of his feelings about Aristotle, since Callisthenes, as a relative (his mother Hera was Aristotle's cousin), had been brought up in Aristotle's home.

As for Callisthenes' death, some say that he was hanged by Alexander, and others that he was imprisoned and died of disease, but Chares says that after his arrest he was kept in prison for seven months so that he could be tried before the congress with Aristotle present, but that round about the time when Alexander was wounded in India, Callisthenes died a vastly overweight, louse-ridden man.*

[56] But this happened later. Meanwhile, Demaratus of Corinth, who was by now getting on in age, conceived the ambition to make the journey up into Asia to see Alexander, and having done so declared that the Greeks who had died before they could see Alexander seated on Darius' throne had missed a rare treat.* However, he did not get to enjoy the king's goodwill towards him for long, because he died after a debilitating illness. He received a magnificent funeral, and the army raised as a memorial of his death a mound eighty cubits high and with an enormous base. His remains were taken down to the coast on a spectacularly decorated four-horse chariot.

[57] Alexander was poised to set out across the mountains into India, but he could see that his army was by now bogged down by the weight of all the booty they had taken. At dawn one day, therefore, after the baggage had been packed on to the carts, he began by burning the booty belonging to him and to the Companions, and then gave orders to set fire to his men's takings.* In the end, the deed proved to be considerably less imposing and formidable in the execution than it was in the planning. For only a few men found it unwelcome, while the majority set to with a will. Shouting and cheering, they shared essentials with those who needed them, and burnt and destroyed with their own hands anything that was superfluous. Their enthusiasm filled Alexander with energy and resolution, and in any case by this stage of his career his men had come to fear him, as an implacable punisher of wrongdoing. There was, for instance, the occasion when one of his Companions, a man called Menander to whom Alexander had given command of a military outpost, refused to stay where he had been posted, and Alexander killed him; then there was Orsodates, a Persian who rose up in revolt against him, whom Alexander personally shot with his bow.

When a sheep gave birth to a lamb with a mark on its head which in both shape and colouring was like a *tiara* with testicles on either side of it, Alexander found the portent disgusting and had himself purified by the Babylonians whom he invariably kept around for this kind of purpose. He told his friends that he was not worried for his own sake, but for theirs, in case after his death the gods might confer power on an ignoble and impotent man. However, a more promising portent occurred, and Alexander's spirits lifted. Proxenus, the Macedonian whose job it was to supervise those who took care of the king's furnishings, was excavating a site for Alexander's tent beside the river Oxus when he uncovered a spring of oily and fatty liquid. When they skimmed the surface off, it immediately bubbled up pure and translucent, apparently identical to olive-oil in smell and taste, and completely indistinguishable as far as its brightness and oily texture were concerned. And yet this was a country where there were no olive-trees growing. The water of the Oxus itself is also said to be very soft, and consequently to make one's skin sleek if one bathes in it. In any case, a letter of Alexander's to Antipater shows how incredibly pleased he was at the portent: he counted it one of the most important omens the god had ever given him. His diviners, however, interpreted the portent as signifying a campaign in which glory would be won by a great deal of effort and hard work, since oil is a gift from the god to men for the relief of their weariness.*

[58] And so Alexander was often in dangerous situations during battles, and sustained serious wounds, but it was the shortage of essential supplies and the severity of the weather that took the greatest toll of the army. But Alexander was determined that fortune would fall to daring, strength to courage: he was convinced that there was no position so impregnable that it could keep brave men out, and none so secure that it could keep cowards safe. It is said that during the siege of Sisimithres' stronghold,* which was built on a such a sheer and inaccessible rock that his men despaired of taking it, Alexander asked Oxyartes what kind of man Sisimithres was. When Oxyartes replied that he was a terrible coward, Alexander said, 'So you for one are saying that we can take this rock, since it is insecure at the top.' And in fact he did succeed in taking the rock by scaring Sisimithres. During his assault on another rock,* just as precipitous, with a detachment of younger Macedonians, he said to one of them, whose name was Alexander, 'Well, we expect to see *you* fight bravely because of your name.' And when the young man died fighting brilliantly, Alexander's grief knew no bounds.

When the Macedonians were reluctant to advance on the city of Nysa,* because there was a deep river by it, Alexander stood on the

river-bank and said, 'What an utter fool I am! Why did I never learn
to swim?' And he was ready to try to cross even though he was carrying his shield.† After he had called a halt to the fighting, a delegation came from the besieged stronghold to ask for terms; first of
all, they were astonished to find him unkempt and still wearing his
armour, and then, when a pillow was brought for him, he told the
oldest member of the delegation, a man called Acouphis, to take it
for his seat. Acouphis, impressed by his self-possession and kindness,
asked him what it would take for them to be on good terms with him.
'I'd like to see them make you their ruler,' Alexander replied, 'and
send me their 100 best men.' Acouphis laughed and said, 'But I'll be
doing a better job as ruler, my lord, if I send you my worst men, not
my best.'

[59] Taxiles' kingdom in India is said to have been as large as
Egypt and to have contained excellent land, both for livestock and
arable farming.* He is also supposed to have been a man of considerable intelligence. When he met Alexander, after they had exchanged
greetings he said, 'Why do we have to fight and make war on each
other, Alexander? It's not as if you have come to steal our water or
essential foods, which are the only things men with any sense should
feel compelled to fight for. As for other forms of wealth and what
men call possessions, if I'm better off than you in these things, I'll
happily do you a good turn, and if I'm worse off, I have no objection
to being in a position to thank you for any good turn you do me.'

Alexander liked the man a great deal. He took him by the hand
and said, 'Do you really think these welcoming words of yours can
avert a battle arising from our meeting? No, I won't let you prevail.
I shall fight to the bitter end, pitching my generosity against yours, to
make sure that you don't get the better of me in kindness.' Eventually,
after he had received a great many gifts and had given even more,
Alexander presented Taxiles with 1,000 talents of coined money—
which really upset his friends, but went a long way towards disarm-
ing the hostility of many of the natives.

The best fighters among the Indians were mercenaries whose strenu-
ous defence of various cities which called them in did Alexander a
great deal of harm. Once, after he had entered into a truce with them
at one of these cities, he ambushed them on the road as they were
leaving and annihilated them all. This act of his is like a stain on his
military achievements, since he generally fought in accordance with

the rules of war and behaved as a king should.* The philosophers also made his life just as difficult as these mercenaries, by vilifying any kings who joined him and inciting the populations of autonomous cities to rebel against him. So he hanged a great many of them too.*

[60] He himself has described the course of his battle against Porus in his letters.* He says that the Hydaspes flowed between the two armies and that Porus kept his elephants permanently stationed on the opposite bank† to guard the crossing. Under these circumstances, then, he had his men make a great deal of random noise every day as they went about their business in the camp, so that the enemy would get used to it and not view it as a reason for alarm. Then on a stormy, moonless night he took an infantry detachment and the pick of his cavalry quite a way from the enemy, and crossed over to a small island in the river. While he was there the rain started pelting down, and his troops were struck by frequent thunderbolts and buffeted by high winds. Although he could see that some of his men were being burnt to death by the thunderbolts, he set out from the island and began to make his way over to the opposite bank. But the Hydaspes had been whipped up and swollen by the storm and, as it rushed down, it gouged a deep channel and quite a bit of its water began to flow down this new channel. His men could find no sure footing on the ground between the two currents since it was slippery and broken up. It was at this point, we hear, that he said, 'Men of Athens, you'll probably find incredible the terrible dangers I face in order to win your good opinion.'*

But that is from Onesicritus. Alexander himself says that they abandoned their rafts and crossed the channel in their armour, wading through chest-high water. After they had crossed he had the cavalry ride twenty stades ahead of the infantry, his idea being that if the enemy attacked with their cavalry he would easily overcome them, and if they mobilized their infantry his own infantry would arrive before theirs did. And in fact one of these two possibilities did happen: he was attacked by a force consisting of 1,000 horsemen and sixty chariots, and he routed them, capturing all the chariots and killing 400 of the horsemen. Porus now realized that Alexander himself had crossed the river, and he advanced towards him with his whole army, except for a small force he left behind to stop any Macedonians who tried to use the crossing. Alexander's chief worries were the elephants and the sheer size of the enemy army, so while he charged one of the wings, he ordered Coenus to lead the Macedonian right wing into the attack. The enemy was routed, and on both sides the troops who were pushed back retreated towards the elephants and became crowded together at the centre. From then on, for seven hours or more until the enemy finally gave up, the battle was fought at close quarters.

This is the account of the battle given by its prime mover in his letters. Most writers agree that Porus was four and a half cubits tall, and that because of his height and massive body he fitted his elephant just as well as a horseman does his horse—and this despite the fact that his was the largest elephant in the army. This elephant also showed astonishing intelligence and concern for its royal master: while he was still safe and sound, the creature bravely warded off and beat back attackers, but once it sensed that he was failing because of the number of times he had been struck by missiles and wounded, it became afraid that he might slip off. It calmly lowered itself down on to its knees, and then gently took hold of each of the spears with its trunk and pulled them out of his body.

Porus was taken prisoner, and when Alexander asked him how he should treat him, he replied, 'As a king should.' Alexander went on to ask him if he had anything else to add, but he said, ' "As a king should" covers everything.' So Alexander not only let him rule over his former kingdom with the title of satrap, but also gave him extra territory, once he had subdued its autonomous inhabitants,† which is said to have included fifteen tribes, 5,000 notable towns, and countless villages. He also made one of his Companions, Philip, the satrap of another piece of land three times the size of this satrapy of Porus'.

[61] Another thing that happened after the battle against Porus was that Bucephalas died—not immediately afterwards, but some time later. He died, according to most writers, from wounds for which he was undergoing treatment, but Onesicritus says that he died of old age, a broken down old horse, aged thirty at the time of his death. Alexander took his death very hard, since he felt exactly as though he had lost a close and loyal friend, and he founded in his memory a city on the banks of the Hydaspes, which he called Bucephalia. There is also a story that when Alexander lost a dog he loved called Peritas, which he personally had brought up, he founded a city named after it. Sotion says he heard this from Potamon of Lesbos.*

[62] Now, the battle against Porus took the edge off the Macedonians' appetite for war and checked their advance further into

India. It had not been easy for them to repel Porus, who had taken to the field with 20,000 foot-soldiers and 2,000 cavalrymen, and so they strongly resisted the pressure coming from Alexander to cross the Ganges as well—a river, they discovered, which was thirty-two stades wide and 100 fathoms deep, and whose further shores were covered with huge numbers of armed men, horses, and elephants. For they were hearing reports that the kings of the Gandaritae and the Praesians were waiting for them with 80,000 horsemen, 200,000 foot-soldiers, 8,000 chariots, and 6,000 war elephants. Nor do these reports seem to have been exaggerated, because Sandrocottus,† who reigned there not long after this, gave Seleucus 500 elephants, and overran and conquered the whole of India with an army of 600,000 men.*

At first, then, Alexander shut himself up in his tent and lay there in sullen anger, refusing to feel any gratitude for what he had already achieved unless he could cross the Ganges as well; in fact, to his way of thinking, pulling back from there was the same as admitting defeat. But his friends gave him plausible reasons for not feeling so bad, men from his army stood by the entrance to his tent with tears and pro-testations, and between them they implored him to change his mind. Eventually he relented and began to break camp, and while doing so came up with a number of tricks and subterfuges designed to influence the Indians' impressions of him. For instance, he had an unusually large suit of armour made, and oversized horses' mangers and par-ticularly heavy bits, all of which he left behind, scattered here and there as if casually cast aside. He also set up altars to the gods, which are still used for sacred purposes by the kings of the Praesians when they cross the river: they perform sacrifices in the Greek manner at them. Sandrocottus, who was then just a young man, actually saw Alexander, and he often used to say in later years that Alexander very nearly had the country handed over to him, since the king at the time was hated and despised for his iniquity and low birth.

[63] Next Alexander had large numbers of rafts and oared ferry-boats built and began to make his way at a leisurely pace down the rivers, because he wanted to see the outer sea.* Not that the voyage was entirely idle or unwarlike, however: he used to land and attack the settlements he came across. All of them, without exception, fell to him, but when he took on the people known as the Mallians, who have the reputation of being the best fighters in India, he came very close to being cut down. After sweeping the defenders off the walls

with a hail of missiles, a ladder was placed against the wall and he was the first up it, but then the ladder was broken and he found himself exposed to the missiles of the Indians who lined the bottom of the wall below him. Despite being almost alone he crouched down and leapt into the middle of the enemy, and luckily landed on his feet. As he brandished his weapons, the Indians saw it as a flash of flame and an apparition moving in front of his body, and so at first they fled and scattered. But when they saw that he was supported by only two Shield-bearers, they rushed up, and while he defended himself against those who fought him at close range, trying to pierce his armour and wound him with their swords and spears, one of them stood back a little and fired an arrow from his bow with such energy and force that it penetrated his breastplate and lodged in his ribcage. The force of the blow pushed Alexander back and he sank to his knees, while his assailant charged up with his Indian dagger drawn, and Peucestas and Limnaeus defended their king. Both of them sustained wounds, which proved fatal for Limnaeus, but Peucestas held out, and Alexander killed the Indian. However, he had received a number of wounds, and finally a blow on the neck from a club forced him to rest his back against the wall, with his eyes still fixed on his enemies. Meanwhile his Macedonian troops had formed a solid mass around him and, now unconscious of his surroundings, he was snatched away and taken to his tent. In no time at all a rumour had arisen in the camp that Alexander had been killed, but, although it was a difficult and time-consuming task, they sawed off the wooden shaft of the arrow, so that they could then ease off the breastplate and get down to cutting out the head of the arrow, which was embedded in one of his ribs, and is said to have been three fingers wide and four long. During its removal, therefore, Alexander passed out and came very close to death, but he pulled through. Even after he was out of danger, he remained weak for a long time and had to keep to a regimen and a course of treatment, but outside his tent he could hear his men clamouring in their desire to catch sight of him, so he got a cloak and went out to them. Then, after sacrificing to the gods, he boarded his ship again and continued on his way down river, conquering plenty of territory and major cities on his way.

[64] He captured the ten Gymnosophists who had been the ring-leaders behind Sabbas' rebellion and had therefore done the Macedonians a very great deal of harm.* They were reputed to have the ability

to answer questions cleverly and pithily, so Alexander put difficult questions to them, with the warning that he would first kill the first one to give a wrong answer, and then the rest, one after another, on the same principle. He started with the oldest one, and asked him whether, in his opinion, the living or the dead were more numerous: 'The living,' he said, 'because the dead no longer exist.' The second was asked whether the earth or the sea produced larger creatures: 'The earth,' he said, 'since the sea is part of the earth.' The third was asked which animal was the greatest nuisance: 'An animal as yet undiscovered by man,' he replied. The fourth was asked why he had persuaded Sabbas to revolt, and he replied: 'Because I wanted him either to live an honourable life or to die an honourable death.' The fifth was asked which came first, in his opinion, day or night: 'Day,' he said, 'by a day.' And when the king looked puzzled, he added that hard questions are bound to have hard answers. So Alexander moved on to the sixth Gymnosophist and asked him how a man could best win popularity: 'By being extremely powerful,' he said, 'without being an object of fear.'

That left three Gymnosophists. One was asked how a man might become a god: 'By doing something', he answered, 'that a man cannot do.' The next one was asked which was stronger, life or death: 'Life,' he said, 'because it carries so much suffering.' And the last one was asked how long a man should live: 'Until he has stopped considering death preferable to life,' he replied. So then Alexander turned to the judge and told him to deliver his verdict. He said that they had each given a worse answer than the one before. 'In that case,' Alexander said, 'you will be the first to die for giving this verdict.' But he said, 'No, my lord, unless you were lying when you said that the first to die would be the one who gave the worst answer.'

[65] He gave these Gymnosophists gifts and let them go, but there were others who were particularly highly regarded and lived in peace and isolation. He sent Onesicritus, a philosopher who was a follower of Diogenes the Cynic, to ask them to pay him a visit. Onesicritus tells us that Calanus dealt with him brusquely and rudely, ordering him to strip naked before listening to what he had to say, and telling him that otherwise he would not talk to him even if he had been sent from Zeus. Dandamis, however, was more even-tempered: he listened while Onesicritus spoke about Socrates, Pythagoras, and Diogenes, and then remarked that for all their obvious natural talents, they had

lived in too much awe of convention. Other writers claim, however, that Dandamis said absolutely nothing except: 'Why did Alexander bother to come all the way here?'

However, Taxiles did manage to persuade Calanus to pay Alexander a visit. Calanus' real name was Sphines, but since he greeted people he met in the Indian language and said '*Kale*' instead of 'Hello', he came to be called Calanus by the Greeks. This is the man who is also said to have given Alexander a famous illustration of government. He threw a dry and shrivelled hide on to the ground and stepped on the edge of it, which pressed it down there, but made it rise up everywhere else; then he went all the way around the edge, flattening each bit in turn and showing what happened. Finally, he stood in the middle of the hide, and that checked it and kept the whole hide still. This was meant to be a vivid demonstration of how important it was for Alexander to put pressure on the middle of his empire and not travel far away from it.

[66] His voyage down the rivers to the sea took seven months. After emerging into the Ocean with his fleet, he sailed back to an island which he called Scilloustis (although others knew it as Psiltoucis), where he landed and made a sacrifice to the gods. He carried out a survey of the open sea and of as much of the shoreline as was accessible, and then, after praying that no one might ever beat his record and go further than he had gone in this expedition, he turned back.* He ordered the fleet to sail along the coast, keeping India on their right, and he put Nearchus in overall command, with Onesicritus as chief helmsman.* Meanwhile, he himself made his way by land through the territory of the Oreitae, where things could not have gone worse for him. He lost so many men that by the time he left India his fighting force had been reduced by more than three-quarters—and this was an army which had once consisted of 120,000 foot-soldiers and about 15,000 cavalrymen. But serious illnesses, inadequate food, scorching heat, and above all starvation carried them off, since they were crossing an uncultivated land, inhabited by people who eked out a miserable existence with the few wretched sheep they owned —sheep they usually fed on seafish, and which therefore had offensive, foul-smelling flesh. At last, after sixty days, they made their way across this region and reached Gedrosia, where they immediately had more than enough of everything, supplied by the nearest satraps and kings.*

[67] After recruiting fresh troops from Gedrosia, then, he set out on a riotous seven-day journey through Carmania. He himself was pulled along at an easy pace by eight horses, on a dais fixed on a tall, conspicuous, oblong scaffold, feasting continuously with his Companions, day and night. He was followed by an enormous train of wagons, each with some means of protecting its passengers from the sun—either purple-dyed or embroidered canopies, or boughs which were kept constantly green and fresh. These carts carried the rest of his friends and the officers of his army, all of whom wore garlands and were drinking. There was not a shield or helmet or pike to be seen, but all the way along the road there were soldiers ladling wine out of huge jars and vats with bowls, cups, and beakers, and drinking to one another's health, some doing so even while they marched along, others lying by the side of the road. The whole place resounded with the frequent strains of wind-pipes and reed-pipes, of song and lyre, and with the shrieks of Bacchic women. They accompanied their disorderly and meandering progress with games of Bacchic licence, as if the god himself were present and were leading the drunken procession.

And when Alexander reached the palace of Gedrosia,* he again gave his army a break while he celebrated a festival with a public procession. There is a story that he was watching a choral competition, rather the worse for drink, and his beloved, Bagoas, after winning the dancing contest, made his way through the audience, still in his costume, and sat down beside him. At this sight the Macedonians applauded and called out for Alexander to kiss him, until he put his arms around him and gave him a loving kiss.

[68] While he was here Nearchus came up to see him.* Alexander listened with delight to his account of his voyage, and became enthusiastic about the prospect of himself taking a large fleet and sailing down the Euphrates, around the coasts of Arabia and Libya, and through the Pillars of Heracles into the inner sea. He got to the stage of having all kinds of ships under construction at Thapsacus, with sailors and helmsmen pouring in from all over the place, but the difficulty of his return journey so far, the wound he had received in Mallia, and rumours of the heavy losses his army had sustained, raised doubts about whether he would survive the planned expedition. These doubts encouraged rebellion among the subject peoples, and caused his military governors and satraps to act with gross injustice, greed,

and brutality, until the whole of the empire was riddled with turmoil and instability.* Olympias and Cleopatra had even fallen out with Antipater and divided his principality between them, with Olympias taking Epirus and Cleopatra Macedonia. When Alexander heard about this he remarked that Olympias had made the wiser choice, because the Macedonians would not put up with being ruled by a woman.*

So Alexander ordered Nearchus to put to sea again, since he had made up his mind to fill the whole coastline with settlements,† while he himself went down and punished those of his military governors who had abused their powers. He personally killed Oxyartes, one of the sons of Aboulites, by running him through with a pike, and when Aboulites failed to furnish him with provisions, but brought him 3,000 talents of coined money instead, he gave orders that the money was to be offered to the horses. When they refused to touch it, he said, 'What use are these provisions of yours to us?', and threw Aboulites into prison.

[69] The first thing he did in Persia was pay the womenfolk their money, in accordance with the custom by which whenever Persian kings arrive in the country they give some gold to every woman there. This explains why some of them apparently did not go there very often, and Ochus not even once: he was so mean that he preferred voluntary self-exile from the country of his birth.

Secondly, when he discovered that the tomb of Cyrus had been broken into, he had the person who had committed the crime put to death, even though the culprit was an eminent Macedonian from Pella called Poulomachus. After reading the inscription on the tomb, he had a Greek version transcribed underneath the original. This is how the Greek version reads: 'Sir, whoever you may be and wherever you may be from, know that I am Cyrus, who gained the Persians their empire. Therefore do not begrudge me this earth which covers my body: it is not so very much.' This reminder of the uncertainty and instability of things profoundly moved Alexander.*

It was here that Calanus, who had been suffering for a short while from an intestinal disorder, asked for his funeral pyre to be built. After riding to the pyre on horseback, he offered up a prayer, purified himself with a sprinkling of water, and consecrated some of his hair, before climbing up on to the pyre. He greeted the Macedonians who were present, urged them to have a good day, suggested that they join the king for some drinks—and told them that he would soon be seeing the king in Babylon. Then he lay down and covered his head. The approach of the flames did not make him move; he stayed exactly as he was when he lay down, and made an acceptable sacrifice of himself in accordance with the traditional practice of the sophists of his country. Many years later in Athens another Indian, when meeting with Caesar, did the same as Calanus, and even today people point out his tomb, which is called 'The Tomb of the Indian'.*

[70] After leaving the funeral pyre, Alexander called a lot of his friends and officers from the army together for a banquet, and proposed that they should hold a contest in drinking undiluted wine, with a garland for the winner. Promachus managed to down four choes, which was the largest quantity, so he received the prize of a garland, which was a talent in weight, but he lasted only another three days before dying. In fact, according to Chares, forty-one of the others died from the after-effects of the drink as well, when severe cold followed upon their drinking.*

At Susa he arranged a mass marriage of his Companions. He himself took Stateira, Darius' daughter, for his wife, and in assigning his men their brides he tried to match excellence with excellence. Then he held a wedding-feast not only for them, but also for any Macedonians who had got married earlier. According to my sources, there were 9,000 guests at the feast, and not only was every single one given a gold drinking-bowl for the libations, but everything else was on just as spectacular and astonishing a scale. And Alexander paid the creditors off for any of them who were in debt, which cost him in all 9,870 talents. When Antigenes the one-eyed got himself falsely listed as a debtor and produced someone who claimed that he had lent him money against his bank, Alexander paid the man back the money, but then, when the deception was found out, he was so angry that he banished Antigenes from his court and stripped him of his command. However, Antigenes was a brilliant soldier, and while still a young man, during Philip's siege of Perinthus, despite having been wounded in the eye by a bolt from a catapult, he refused to let the bolt be removed or to rest until he had pushed the enemy back and pinned them inside the walls. On the occasion in question, then, his shame at being disgraced knew no bounds, and it was clear that his grief and depression were going to make him do away with himself. Alexander did not want to see that happen, however, so he forgave him and told him to keep the money.

[71] The 30,000 boys he had left to be trained and educated* had developed manly physiques and handsome features, and also displayed remarkable skill and agility in their exercises. Alexander himself was delighted with their progress, but his men were worried and depressed, because they thought the king would pay them less attention. So when he sent the sick and disabled back down to the coast, they called it a foul insult for him first to make the fullest possible use of people, and then to discard them in disgrace and toss them back to their home-lands and parents, just because they were no longer the men he had recruited. They asked him why he did not send them all away and regard all Macedonians as useless now that he had these young blades to help him sweep across the world and bring it all under his control.

This made Alexander furious. In his rage he cursed them thor-oughly, dismissed his guards, and brought in Persians to do the job instead, using them to make up his units of bodyguards and atten-dants. When the Macedonians saw him being escorted by Persians, while they were excluded and reviled, they were humbled, and after talking the matter over came to the conclusion that they had been driven almost out of their minds by jealous anger. In the end they came to their senses and, without carrying arms or wearing armour over their tunics, went to Alexander's tent. With cries and tears of grief, they put themselves in his hands and asked him to deal with them as their iniquity and ingratitude deserved, but he refused to accept their petition, although in fact his attitude had already begun to soften. They would not go away, however: they stayed just as they were by his tent for two days and nights, without lessening their lamentations or their appeals to their lord and master. On the third day he emerged from his tent and when he saw their pitiful and wretched state he wept for a long time before gently telling them off and speaking kindly to them. Then he dismissed those who were *hors de combat*, after giving them magnificent gifts, and told Antipater in a letter that they should have the right to wear garlands and have the front seats whenever any public games were being held or there was a production at a theatre. He also made the sons of those who had died stipendiary orphans.*

[72] At Ecbatana in Media,* as soon as he had dealt with matters that needed his urgent attention he became involved once again with theatrical productions and public festivals, since 3,000 performers had arrived from Greece. Sometime around then Hephaestion contracted

a fever, but with a young man's impatience he refused to submit to a strict regime. As soon as the doctor, Glaucus, had left, he went to the theatre and ate a morning meal of boiled chicken, accompanied by a large cooler of wine, whereupon he was taken ill, and died a short while later.

Alexander went out of his mind with grief at his death. He immediately gave orders that all horses and mules were to be shorn as a sign of mourning, and that the fortifications of the cities thereabouts were to be dismantled; he had the wretched doctor impaled on a stake, and banned playing the pipes and all music in the camp for a considerable period of time, until he received an oracle from Ammon, telling him to worship Hephaestion as a hero and to institute sacrificial rituals in his honour. He used warfare as a means of consolation, and went out after men as if he were going out hunting. So he not only conquered the Cossaeans, but slaughtered all the adult male inhabitants, and described this massacre as an offering to Hephaestion. He planned to spend thousands upon thousands of talents on his tomb and on an elaborate funeral, and since he wanted to get more than his money's worth in terms of craftsmanship and originality of design, he was desperate to get as the architect Stasicrates, who was breaking new ground with structures displaying splendour, boldness, and ostentation. For instance, at a previous meeting between the two men Stasicrates had said that there was no mountain better suited than Athos in Thrace for being given the form and shape of a man, and so, if Alexander gave him the go-ahead, he would turn Athos into an effigy of him that would surpass all others in terms of endurance and prominence, holding in its left hand a city of 10,000 inhabitants, and dispensing with its right hand a mighty river whose waters would flow into the sea. Alexander had turned down this offer, but now he was busy working with his architects to develop and devise far more extraordinary and expensive projects.

[73] Alexander next set out for Babylon.* *En route* there he was rejoined by Nearchus, who had completed his voyage into the Euphrates from the great sea, and Nearchus told him of the advice some Chaldeans he had met had given him, to the effect that Alexander should keep away from Babylon. Alexander ignored this advice, however, and continued on his way—and then, just as he reached the city walls, he saw a large number of crows wheeling about in the air and striking at one another, and some of the crows fell dead at his

feet. Next, on receiving a report that Apollodorus, the military governor of Babylon, had commissioned a sacrifice to try to see what the future held for Alexander, he summoned the diviner, Pythagoras, who made no attempt to deny that he had performed the rite. When Alexander asked him what the entrails had been like and received the reply that the liver had had no lobe, he exclaimed, 'Ah! What a powerful omen!' He did not punish Pythagoras, however, and he regretted having ignored Nearchus' advice. In fact, he spent most of the time camped outside Babylon or cruising up and down the Euphrates.

There were also a number of other omens that worried him. For instance, the largest and most handsome lion in his menagerie was set upon and kicked to death by a tame donkey. And once he had stripped to oil himself for a ball-game, and when the time came for him to get his clothes again, the young men he had been playing with saw a man sitting in silence on Alexander's throne, wearing the royal diadem and robes. When he was asked who he was, there was a long pause before he pulled himself together at last and said that his name was Dionysius and that he came from Messene. He went on to tell them that he had been brought there from the coast, because he had been accused of some crime or other, and had been in prison for a long time; then a short while ago, he said, Sarapis had come and released him from his chains and brought him there, with instructions to take the robes and the diadem and sit down without saying a word.

[74] After hearing the man's story, Alexander did away with him, as the diviners recommended, but he remained depressed—no longer confident of the favour of the gods and suspicious of his friends. He was especially afraid of Antipater and his sons.* One of these sons, Iolas, was his chief cup-bearer, but the other, Cassander, had only recently joined him, and when he saw some easterners prostrating themselves before Alexander, he could not stop himself laughing, because he had been brought up in the Greek manner and had never seen anything like that before. Alexander lost his temper, grabbed hold of Cassander's hair violently with both hands, and pounded his head against the wall. On another occasion, when Cassander wanted to respond to some men who were lodging complaints against Antipater, Alexander interrupted him and said, 'What do you mean? Do you think people would make such a long journey if they had no genuine

grievances and just wanted to lie?' Cassander said that the very fact
that they had travelled so far from the evidence proved that they were
lying, but Alexander laughed at him and said, 'This is just another
one of those sophisms you followers of Aristotle have devised for
arguing either side of a case, but you'll suffer for it if I find that
you've done these men the slightest wrong.'

In short, it is said that fear of Alexander took hold of Cassander's
mind with such terrible force and became so deeply embedded there
that many years later, when he was king of Macedonia and master of
Greece, he was walking around Delphi looking at the statues, when
he suddenly glimpsed a statue of Alexander and became so terrified
that his body shuddered and trembled, he nearly fainted at the sight,
and it took a long time for him to recover.*

[75] Anyway, now that Alexander had abandoned himself to superstition, there was no unusual or odd event, however insignificant, that
did not appear to his troubled and terrified mind to be an ominous
portent. All over the palace people could be found performing sacrifices,
ritual purifications, and divinations—and filling Alexander with inane
fear. This shows that while contemptuous doubt of the supernatural
is an awful thing, superstition is terrible as well: like water, it always
finds it way down to the lowest level and <. . .>†*

Nevertheless, when he received the oracles from the god about
Hephaestion, he set aside his grief and turned once more to sacrificial
feasts and drinking. Once he gave a spectacular banquet in honour
of Nearchus, and then, although he had taken his customary bath
before going to bed, when Medius asked him to a drunken party, he
accepted the invitation. After spending the whole night and the next
day there drinking, he began to feel feverish. The fever was not brought
on by his having drained Heracles' goblet nor did it follow a sudden
pain in the back as if he had been stabbed by a spear, even though
both these stories can be found in authors who felt obliged to write
as if they were creating the tragic and emotive finale of a great drama.
And Aristobulus says that he had a severe fever, and that as a result
of his raging thirst he drank some wine, after which delirium set in,
and he died on the thirtieth of Daesius.*

[76] Here, however, is the account of his illness recorded in the
Royal Diary.* On the eighteenth of Daesius he slept in the bathroom
because of his fever. The next day, after bathing, he went back to his
bedroom and spent the day playing dice with Medius. In the evening

he took his bath, performed the sacrificial rites to the gods, ate a light meal, and had a fever throughout the night. On the twentieth, he had another bath, made a sacrifice as usual to the gods, and passed the time on a couch in the bathroom, listening to Nearchus' tales of his voyage and the great sea. On the twenty-first he did the same again, but was running a worse fever; he passed an uncomfortable night and was extremely feverish the next day. He had his bed moved to beside the large swimming-pool, where he lay and had a discussion with his commanders about the lack of officers in some regiments, and how they should go about assessing men to fill the vacancies. On the twenty-fourth he was extremely feverish and had to be carried outside to perform his sacrifices, and he told his staff officers to wait in the palace courtyard, while the regimental commanders and the commanders of the units of 500 were to spend the night outside the palace. On the twenty-fifth he was carried to the palace on the other side of the river, where he got a little sleep, but the fever did not abate. When his officers came in to see him, they found him incapable of talking, and the same thing happened again on the twenty-sixth. Under these circumstances the Macedonians believed that he had died, and they came crying and shouting to his door; they threatened the Companions until they had no choice but to open the doors for them, and then one by one, dressed only in their tunics, they all filed passed his couch. It was also on this day that Python and Seleucus were sent to the sanctuary of Sarapis to ask if they should bring Alexander there, but the god told them to leave him where he was. And then he died late in the afternoon of the twenty-eighth.

[77] This is an almost verbatim transcript of the account in the Royal Diary. No one had any suspicion at the time that Alexander had been poisoned, but five years later, apparently, on the strength of information she had been given, Olympias had a large number of men put to death, and scattered the remains of Iolas' body, on the grounds that it was he who had administered the poison.*

There are some writers who claim that Aristotle put Antipater up to the deed, and that the collection of the poison was entirely Aristotle's doing. They say that they have this on the authority of a certain Hagnothemis, who in his turn heard it from King Antigonus. The alleged poison was freezing-cold water from a certain cliff in Nonacris which† people gather in the same way one collects delicate dew, and store in a donkey's hoof, which is the only container that can keep it in, since it is so cold and acidic that it eats its way through everything else.* However, most writers take the story about the poisoning to be nothing but a fabrication, and it is strong support for their case that throughout the period when Alexander's officers were quarrelling among themselves,* which lasted quite a few days, his body lay untended in various warm, unventilated spots, but stayed fresh and unblemished, without showing any signs of decay.

Now, Rhoxane happened to be pregnant, which made the Macedonians especially proud of her, but she was jealous of Stateira. She used a forged letter to trick her into coming, and once she had got her there she killed her and her sister, threw the bodies into a well, and filled it in. Perdiccas was in on the plot and helped her carry it out, because immediately following Alexander's death he was the one who gained the most power, by attracting the support of Arrhidaeus, who was, so to speak, a cipher of kingship, since his mother was an undistinguished commoner called Philinna, and an illness had made him weak in the head. This was neither an accident nor congenital: as a boy, they say, his cleverness and natural gifts were plain to see, but then his mind became ruined when he was poisoned by Olympias.*

APPENDIX

Measures of Money, Weight, Capacity, Length

(All figures are approximate)

Money and Weight (Greek coinage was in general worth its weight)
1 talent = 60 minas = 6,000 drachmas = 36,000 obols
These weighed, according to the common Attic–Euboic standard:
1 obol = 0.7 g.
1 drachma = 4.3 g.
1 mina = 433 g. (15 oz.)
1 talent = 26 kg. (57 lb.)
There was also in circulation a stater (or 'standard', sometimes called a daric after Darius I).

Capacity, liquid
1 amphora ('jar') = 12 choes ('pitchers') = 144 cotylae ('cups') = 864 cyathi ('spoons')
1 cyathus = 45 ml.
1 cotyle = 270 ml. (0.5 pt.)
1 chous = 3.25 l. (5.7 pt.)
1 amphora = 39 l. (68.6 pt., 8.6 gal.)

Capacity, dry
1 medimnus = 48 choenices = 192 cotylae
1 cotyle = 270 ml. (0.5 pt.)
1 choenix = 1.1 l. (1.9 pt.)
1 medimnus = 51.8 l. (91.2 pt., 11.4 gal., 1.5 bushels)

Length/Distance (Attic scale)
1 foot = 29.6 cm. (11.65 in.)
1 cubit = 1.5 Greek feet or 44.4 cm. (17.5 in.)
1 fathom = 6 Greek feet or 1.8 m. (5 ft. 10 in.)
1 stade = 600 Greek feet or 177.6 m. (582.7 ft.)

EXPLANATORY NOTES

THE PARALLEL LIVES

Given in the order of the tripartite edition, with abbreviations.

Theseus–Romulus	Thes.–Rom.
Solon–Publicola	Sol.–Pub.
Themistocles–Camillus	Them.–Cam.
Aristides–Cato the Elder	Arist.–CMaj.
Cimon–Lucullus	Cim.–Luc.
Pericles–Fabius Maximus	Per.–Fab.
Nicias–Crassus	Nic.–Cras.
Coriolanus–Alcibiades	Cor.–Alc.
Demosthenes–Cicero	Dem.–Cic.
Phocion–Cato the Younger	Phoc.–CMin.
Dion–Brutus	Dion–Brut.
Aemilius Paullus–Timoleon	Aem.–Tim.
Sertorius–Eumenes	Sert.–Eum.
Philopoemen–Flamininus	Phil.–Flam.
Pelopidas–Marcellus	Pel.–Marc.
Alexander–Caesar	Alex.–Caes.
Demetrius–Antony	Demtr.–Ant.
Pyrrhus–Marius	Pyr.–Mar.
Agis and Cleomenes–Tiberius and Gaius Gracchus	Ag.Cl.–Grac.
Lycurgus–Numa	Lyc.–Num.
Lysander–Sulla	Lys.–Sull.
Agesilaus–Pompey	Ages.–Pomp.

Imperial Lives

Galba, Otho	Galb., Oth.

Independent Lives

Aratus, Artaxerxes	Arat., Artax.

PLUTARCH'S SOURCES

Plutarch's sources for these lives are the major historians of the period, Herodotus (*Solon, Themistocles*), Thucydides (*Themistocles, Pericles, Nicias, Alcibiades*), Xenophon (*Alcibiades, Agesilaus*), Ephorus (*Pericles, Agesilaus*), the historians of Alexander the Great, various lost historians, and Aristotle's *Constitutions of Sparta* and *Athens* (*Lycurgus, Solon*). Contemporary sources include the *rhetrae* ascribed to Lycurgus, Solon's law code and poems, the decrees of Pericles, and citations from the comic poets.

Most of the writers that Plutarch cites are no longer extant. The Index of Literary and Historical Sources Cited provides a complete list of the authors cited in these lives, with a brief identifying note. Further information can usually be found in *Oxford Classical Dictionary*, third edition, 1996. In the notes I have also cited Diodorus Siculus, a first-century AD historian (available in English in the Loeb Library, Cambridge, Mass., and London: Harvard University Press and Heinemann) and Greek inscriptions from C. W. Fornara (ed.), *Archaic Times to the End of the Peloponnesian War*, second edition (*Translated Documents of Greece and Rome*, i; Baltimore and London: Johns Hopkins University Press, 1988).

LYCURGUS

9 *the Olympic truce*: Iphitus of Elis was said to be the founder of the Olympic Games in historical times. The traditional date was 776 BC. A time of truce throughout the Greek world was established for the games, so that contestants and spectators could participate safely. For Lycurgus' role, see c. 23.

name inscribed on it: a reference to Aristotle's lost *Constitution of the Lacedaemonians*, cited frequently in this Life.

time of the Heraclidae: Xenophon, *Constitution of the Lacedaemonians* 10.

witnesses on their side: this whole paragraph is a warning to the reader of the unreliability of the tradition on Lycurgus. Plutarch does not conceive him as a historical figure in the same way as he does Themistocles or Pericles.

descendant of Heracles: the twin lines of Spartan kings, the Agiads and the Eurypontids, were traced back to Heracles, whose immediate descendants, the Heraclidae, were thought to have conquered the Peloponnesus. Our earliest list of the kings is in Herodotus, 7. 204 (Agiad line) and 8. 131 (Eurypontid line), which differs considerably from Plutarch's account. As Plutarch shows, the early parts of these king lists were quite unstable. Herodotus 1. 65 makes Lycurgus an Agiad and regent for his nephew Leobotas, though Plutarch makes him a Eurypontid and regent for Charilaus.

10 *Spartiates*: the full citizens of Sparta, a very limited group. The following story of Soüs is a pre-Lycurgan example of Spartan self-control and endurance.

enslaved the helots: the helots were the conquered people of Messenia and Laconia, held on the land as state serfs and assigned to the members of the Spartiate class. For their treatment cf. cc. 24 and 28. They revolted in the 460s (cf. *Cim.* 16–17); the Thebans freed those in Messenia in 369 (*Ages.* 34). Plutarch here puts this conquest well before Lycurgus.

11 *were delighted*: Charilaus means 'delight of the people'.

men of the island: the constitutions of the Cretan cities were admired by philosophers, and were thought to have much in common with the Spartan constitution, especially in the use of common messes.

Thales: a Cretan poet, also called Thaletas, not to be confused with the pre-Socratic philosopher from Miletus. Plato had argued in the *Republic* for the importance of musical education, and Plutarch notes that the musical theorist Damon was an adviser to Pericles (*Per.* 4). Cf. Campbell, *Greek Lyric* II (Cambridge, Mass., and London: Harvard University Press 1988), 320–9 (this reference is no. 6).

12 *Creophylus*: a shadowy figure, reported as being follower, friend, or son-in-law of Homer. Modern scholars now place Homer *c*.725–700, much later than the dates Plutarch gives for Lycurgus.

from all the others: cf. Hdt. 2. 164–8.

craftsmen no part in it: on the exclusion of Spartiates from the crafts, see c. 24.

son of Hipparchus: the Gymnosophists, or naked wise men, were Brahmans encountered by Alexander many centuries later: cf. *Alex.* 64–5.

13 *rather than a man*: a similar oracle is recorded by Herodotus 1. 65.

the Bronze House: the shrine of Athena, located on the acropolis of Sparta. In the fifth century, the regent Pausanias fled there when he was about to be arrested (cf. Thuc. 1. 134).

affairs of the moment: Plato, *Laws* 691e. The medical notion of the feverish body politic which is cured by the wise legislator is repeated in *Numa* 8, referring to Plato, *Republic* 372e. The kings and twenty-eight elders (*gerontes*) comprised the council, or *gerousia*. It was seen as parallel to the Roman senate, a body of older men who would advise the kings and limit the action of the citizen assembly. For its powers, see c. 6; for the electoral process, c. 26.

14 *Sphaerus*: a Stoic philosopher, who influenced the Spartan king Cleomenes III (cf. Plut. *Cleom.* 3; note Cleomenes' use of the history of Lycurgus' takeover to justify his own action, *Cleom.* 10). He wrote works on the Spartan constitution and on Lycurgus and Socrates.

twenty-eight elders: twenty-eight equals the sum of its factors (1 + 2 + 4 + 7 + 14). The number thirty is specified also in the Great Rhetra which follows.

rest with the people: this text, often called the Great Rhetra, is in the Doric dialect and, although corrupt (especially in the last sentence, which some reconstruct 'the people has the power to respond and decide') and of disputed meaning, is generally accepted as a pre-classical Spartan document. Plutarch probably found it in Aristotle's lost *Constitution*, which may also have given the explanations which follow.

14 *council-hall*: in early times, an open-air meeting would be usual, but later in most Greek cities special council chambers were built, and theatres were often used for assemblies.

15 *Polydorus and Theopompus*: c.760–700 BC.

straight rhetras: Tyrtaeus, a seventh-century elegiac poet, celebrated the Spartan system. This passage is extracted from his poem 'Good government' (*Eunomia*), F4 West.

mixed constitution: that is, one combining monarchy (the kingship), oligarchy (the elders), and democracy (the assembly).

office of the ephorate: Plato, *Laws* 692a. The ephors were a board of five men elected annually by the Spartiates, and came to have significant power. Plutarch here follows the earlier chronology, which places Lycurgus c.880, and the beginning of the ephorate c.750. Xenophon attributed the ephorate to Lycurgus, *Lac. Const.* 8; Plutarch seems to follow Aristotle (cf. *Politics* 1313ª26).

allocation of land: that is, in the legendary division among the Heraclidae, Argos and Messenia received richer land.

16 *perioeci*: communities of free non-Spartiates living in Laconia and Messenia.

9,000 plots: these totals double those made in the redistribution proposed by King Agis IV (cf. Plut. *Agis* 8), and are suspicious precisely for that reason (Messenia, half of Sparta's land, had been lost in 362).

amount of fruit: a medimnus equals about 52 litres, or about 1½ bushels. Presumably the man's greater amount is to support other dependants as well as himself: he is expected to supply only 12 medimni a year to the common mess (12).

17 *cattle to transport it*: Plutarch is anachronistic here, since there was no coinage in early Greece. However, long after other states began to issue coinage, Sparta continued using iron spits, down to the third century BC. Remains of such spits have been found in Laconian sanctuaries, although we cannot be certain they were used for money rather than other purposes. 1 mina may be taken as equal to 600 obols, the coin equivalent of spits: 10 minas, the equivalent of a few gold coins, would be 6,000 spits.

superfluous professions: contrast Numa's and Solon's encouragement of trade (*Numa* 17, and *Comp. Lyc.–Num.* 2; *Solon* 22).

18 *truly blind*: Wealth, personified as a god, was often called blind because he favoured the wrong people.

19 *'eating' (edōdē)*: the origin and form of the word were much debated in antiquity, and our manuscripts often have *philitia* for *phiditia*. Modern scholars are uncertain: the connection with *pheido* is possible. Plutarch, however, encourages the reader to think of a connection with friendship.

savouries: that is, roughly 52 litres or 1½ bushels of grain, 26 litres of wine, 2.2 kilos of cheese, and 1.1 kilo of figs. (A chous was about 3.25 litres, a mina about 433 grams, close to a pound.) 'Savouries' would be anything else to give flavour to this.

19 *polemarchs fined him*: this was probably Agis II, who defeated the Athenians at Mantinea in 418. The polemarchs were six senior officers immediately subordinate to the king. They ate with the king while on campaign.

20 *a holed ballot*: normal Athenian voting procedure in the courts used a solid ballot for acquittal, a pierced one for condemnation.

famous black broth: the black broth was an acquired taste. Alcibiades showed his adaptability by eating it with relish when in Sparta, cf. *Alc.* 23.

drink this broth: this story is told of Dionysius of Syracuse at *Spartan Sayings* 236f.

21 *Epaminondas*: the Theban general, much admired by Plutarch, who defeated the Spartans at Leuctra (371) and Mantinea (362). Cf. *Ages.* 27–35.

Leotychidas: Eurypontid king in the late seventh century. The anecdote is told of Agesilaus in Asia at *Spartan Sayings* 210d–e.

expertise to fight: this was Agesilaus' invasion of 378. Cf. *Ages.* 26. Antalcidas was a prominent Spartan of the period.

22 *from the god*: the word 'rhetra' itself simply means 'something said', and generally applies to a compact or agreement: Plutarch suggests that it implied a divine ordinance.

the title of Mistress: a similar thought is found in Aristotle, *Politics* 1269^{b}32–1270^{a}8, although Plutarch must refer to the lost *Constitution of the Lacedaemonians*. In the *Politics*, Aristotle speaks especially of the situation in his own day.

naked: note that the word *gumnos*, while it usually means 'naked, without clothes' (the normal way in which men exercised, for example), can also mean 'without one's usual clothes or equipment', and thus still with some covering. For example, when vase painters depicted the popular scene of Peleus wrestling with Atalanta, they regularly showed her with a pair of tight pants, and occasionally with a halter. On the other hand, male and female acrobats are regularly shown naked. On Spartan female nudity, cf. P. Cartledge, 'Spartan Wives: Liberation or License?', *Classical Quarterly*, 31 (1981), 91–2. Plutarch explains one type of nakedness, the high slit gown, revealing the thigh, at *Comp. Lyc.–Num.* 3, quoting also poets who commented on this, and suggests that Lycurgus' practices may have made the women too masculine.

Gorgo the wife of Leonidas did: the famous daughter of King Cleomenes and wife of King Leonidas, who fell with the 300 Spartans at Thermopylae. She is mentioned by Herodotus (5. 48, 51; 7. 239), and is the subject of several anecdotes, including this one, in *Spartan Sayings* 240d–e.

23 *Plato*: Plato, *Republic* 5. 458d. The whole passage discusses the training of women alongside men, a Spartan practice of which Plato approved, at least in theory.

Festival of Unarmed Dancing: the Gymnopaideia, a major festival, involving a choral singing competition of youths, mature men, and older men (cf. 21, and *Ages.* 29). In the mid-second century AD it was a major tourist attraction: cf. Pausanias 3.11.9, P. Cartledge and A. Spawforth *Hellenistic and Roman Sparta: A Tale of Two Cities* (London and New York: Routledge, 1989), 193–4.

23 *Dercyllidas*: a Spartan commander active from 411 to 389 against Athens and Persia.

24 *others just as fine*: Herodotus tells a rather less edifying story of how the sixth-century king Ariston wanted to have children by the wife of a friend (6. 61–2).

25 *adulterer in Sparta*: this Geradas (called Geradatas at *Spartan Sayings* 228b–c) is not otherwise known. In *Comp. Lyc.–Num.* 3 Plutarch sets the Lycurgan and Roman systems of raising women and of marriage side by side.

was convened: the *leskhē* was a meeting place for the men: cf. 25.

Laconian woman: cf. *Alc.* 1.

Plato records: Plato, *Alcibiades* 1. 122b, cf. Plut. *Alc.* 1. Pericles was the guardian of Alcibiades.

26 *herds*: the use of this word, *agelē*, for groups of boys at Sparta is distinctively Plutarchan. It does not reflect the normal usage of his own times (see N. M. Kennell, *The Gymnasium of Virtue: Education and Culture in Ancient Sparta* (Chapel Hill: University of North Carolina Press, 1995) 38 and 107–8).

warming properties: the plant was a kind of thistle.

'boy-herder': the Spartan name, *paidonomos*, for the official responsible for training of the youth. According to Xenophon, *Lac. Const.* 2, they had authority to punish the boys severely, having a staff of young men with whips for the purpose. In Plutarch's day a new term, *patronomos*, was in use.

27 *'near eirens'*: this passage has caused some difficulty to interpreters, but it seems likely that the boys' period, at least in Plutarch's day, ran to age 19, and the next year the youths received the title *eiren*. See Kennell, *Gymnasium of Virtue*, 36.

bravery and cunning: Aristotle, on the other hand, rather sharply comments that Lycurgus' training made the boys like animals (*Politics* 1338^{b}9–16).

shaping agent: for the ancient Greeks, and especially for Aristotle, the male supplied the shaping force, the female the raw material, of the embryo. Ancient doctors tried to avoid excessive weight gain in pregnancy as much as modern, but for different reasons.

claws and teeth: this vivid story seems to reflect an exemplary tale told to Spartan boys. Cf. Kennell, *Gymnasium of Virtue*, 122.

Artemis Orthia: this important Spartan sanctuary, on the west bank of the Eurotas river, was excavated by British archaeologists early in the twentieth century (cf. P. Cartledge, *Sparta and Lakonia, A Regional History, 1300–362 BC* (London: Routledge and Kegan Paul, 1979), 357–61). The whipping ritual has aroused much discussion. Xenophon, *Lac. Const.* 2, describes a ritual where boys snatch as many cheeses as they can from this altar while others are whipping them (perhaps alluded to also by Plato, *Laws* 633b–c, 'certain grabbings in the midst of blows'). The ritual described by Plutarch (which he does not ascribe to Lycurgus) seems to be an archaicizing reconstruction, demonstrating that ancient Spartan toughness continued. It was much commented on in Roman times. Boys were flogged in a contest of endurance, and victors set up honorary inscriptions for themselves, some of which are still preserved. Some have interpreted 'dying' as merely 'passing out'. This may be modern squeamishness, but it seems unlikely that Plutarch would have approved of the children of his Spartan friends dying in this way. Plutarch writes 'we have seen', which may imply not just himself, but also his friends at Sparta over a number of years. Cf. also Plut. *Arist.* 17, a reference to a different whipping ritual, perhaps that described by Xenophon. For a discussion, see Kennell, *Gymnasium of Virtue*, 70–4, 149–61.

28 *improve their beloved*: Plutarch presents a highly idealized 'Platonic' view of Spartan pederasty, as he does also in *Agesilaus*. The reality, in this as in other aspects of Plutarch's account, would have been less philosophic. For a view of the political and social background of the practice, see P. Cartledge, 'The Politics of Spartan Pederasty', *Proceedings of the Cambridge Philological Society*, 207, NS 27 (1981), 17–36. For Plutarch's attitude, see P. Stadter, ' "Subject to the Erotic": Male Sexual Behaviour in Plutarch', in Doreen Innes, Harry Hines, and Christopher Pelling (eds.), *Ethics and Rhetoric: Classical Essays for Donald Russell on his Seventy-fifth Birthday* (Oxford, 1995), 221–36. For Athens, cf. *Alc.* 4–5 and 4 note. Cf. also *Cim.* 1.

enemies with them: according to *Spartan Sayings* 216c and *Sayings of Kings and Commanders* 191e, this Athenian was the orator Demades, and this Agis would be Agis III, who reigned in the 330s BC.

29 *raising a hand*: raising the hand was a sign of surrender or defeat. Cf. *Spartan Sayings* 228d.

others like them: the letters were surely spurious, as Plutarch no doubt knew. Many collections of fictional letters of famous personages circulated in antiquity, a number of which survive. Plutarch uses them (and the sayings, also apocryphal) here because they fit his idea of the man.

Leonidas: the Agiad king killed at Thermopylae in 480.

when to speak: the story perhaps refers to Hecataeus of Abdera (or Teos), a student of the sceptic Pyrrho, and Archidamus IV, king *c.*305–275.

Demaratus: Eurypontid king, who was dethroned, went into exile, and accompanied the army of Xerxes in 480 BC.

Agis: probably Agis II, Eurypontid king *c.*427–400.

Theopompus: Eurypontid king *c.*700.

Pleistonax: Agiad king 459–409 (in exile, 446–427).

30 *Ares*: the god of war.

devotion to exercise: an extraordinary example of the lengths to which Plutarch goes to portray the Spartans as 'philosophical': the word here for 'devotion to the intellect' is in fact the verb *philosophein*, literally, 'to philosophize'. However, he follows in the steps of Plato, who has Socrates make a similar comment (*Protagoras* 342e).

cowards: a technical term at Sparta, the *tresantes*, or 'those who have run away'. They are chastised in a poem of Tyrtaeus to which Plutarch probably refers (F 11 West: 'all courage of men who are *tresantes* is lost: no one could succeed in saying each bad thing which comes to a man, if he should learn shameful behaviour'), and as a class they were deprived of citizen rights (cf. *Ages.* 30, and Xen. *Lac. Const.* 9).

31 *advanced on the enemy*: the Spartans had special songs in anapaestic rhythm, called *embatēria*, for this purpose.

most cultured: literally, 'the most devoted to the Muses', that is to all aspects of *mousikē*: song, dance, music, etc. This whole passage attempts to counterbalance the common view of Sparta as a purely militaristic culture.

the Laconian poet: Alcman, of the late seventh century.

sleek and well combed: the practice made famous when they were observed combing their hair before the battle at Thermopylae against the Persians (Hdt. 7. 208).

32 *phalanx*: the heavy-armed infantry formation of close-ordered soldiers several ranks deep.

Ode to Castor: Castor and Pollux, the twin sons of Zeus, were patrons of the Spartan army.

the prize was a garland: this was a limited circle of the most prestigious games: in classical times, the Olympian, Pythian, Nemean, and Isthmian games. Games in which monetary prizes were awarded were considered of less standing.

standing their ground: this Spartan practice was already noted by Thucydides, 5. 73.

33 *mentioned earlier*: see c. 8.

for not working: Dracon was said to have established the death penalty for idleness. Solon repealed this, but had the Areopagus establish penalties for not working: see *Solon* 17 and 22.

out on campaign: note that in this list Plutarch deliberately downplays military training, which he encompasses under 'exercises'.

34 *as they called them*: cf. c. 16.

castigation and reproof: the social pressure of this 'light-hearted' criticism could be intense: men committed suicide rather than endure it.

Three Hundred: an élite group, called *Hippeis* or Horsemen, cf. *Spartan Sayings* 231b and Xen. *Lac. Const.* 4. Pedaritus was a governor (harmost) on Chios, and fell in action there in 411: see Thuc. 8. 28 ff.

34 *Polystratidas*: otherwise unknown; at *Spartan Sayings* 231f he is called Polycratidas.

   better than him in Sparta: Brasidas was a leading Spartan general in the first phase of the Peloponnesian War, responsible for winning Amphipolis from the Athenians. He was killed in battle in 422, and honoured at Amphipolis with a tomb within the city. See Thuc. 4. 78–5. 11.

   as already mentioned: c. 5.

35 *shouting the winner*: Thucydides (1. 87) describes a similar method of making a decision at Sparta. Aristotle called this system 'childish' (*Politics* 2, 1271ª10).

36 *died in childbirth*: all these regulations contrast with the normal practices for Greek burial. 'Died in childbirth' is an emendation suggested by some inscriptions: the manuscripts are unclear, but seem to refer to a priestess.

   valuable moral lessons: Thuc. 2. 39, from Pericles' funeral oration: an early allusion to this practice of expelling strangers (*xenēlasia*).

   Aristotle: here and below Plutarch probably refers to the *Constitution of the Lacedaemonians*: there is not a similar reference in the *Politics*. Plutarch's account of the *krypteia* here is the fullest extant. The practice is extraordinary, but the use of terror to control a subject population is often attractive. We do not know the scale or frequency of this practice. At *Cleomenes* 28 Plutarch mentions a magistrate in charge of the *krypteia*. It is treated as an initiation ritual for young men by P. Vidal-Naquet, *The Black Hunter* (Baltimore: Johns Hopkins University Press, 1986), 106–28, esp. 112–14. For a brief account, see H. Michell, *Sparta* (Cambridge: Cambridge University Press, 1952), 162–4; P. Cartledge, *Agesilaos and the Crisis of Sparta* (London: Duckworth, 1987), 30–2.

   Plato: *Laws* 633b.

37 *met their deaths*: Thuc. 4. 80. The connection with the *krypteia* is Plutarch's deduction.

   would not approve: the Thebans invaded Laconia several times in the years between the battles of Leuctra and Mantinea, 371–362 BC, as described in *Agesilaus*.

   brink of destruction: in the mid-460s: see Thuc. 1. 101–2.

38 *supported as well*: cf. the Delphic pronouncement reported in c. 5. The word he uses to describe the *krypteia*, *miaros*, means not only morally 'disgusting' but 'ritually polluted', something of which a god would not approve.

   Plato: *Timaeus* 37c.

39 *Agis the son of Archidamus*: the Eurypontid king, 427–400 BC. In this case, Plutarch thinks of the earlier chronology, placing Lycurgus *c*.900. On the relation between training of the young and stability, see also *Comp. Lyc.–Numa* 4.

   and with luxury: Lysander, the Spartan naval commander who forced Athens to surrender in 404 BC, also opened the wealth of the Athenian empire in

the Aegean to the Spartans. On his career, see Plutarch's *Lysander* and
cf. *Ages.* 2–8 and 20; for its effect on Sparta, cf. *Lys.* 16–17.

39 *skytalē*: a staff of office: cf. note to *Alc.* 38.

orderly array: Plutarch, like Aristotle (*Hist. Anim.* 553ª25, 629ª3), speaks
of the leader of the bees as being male, not female.

40 *living in Asia*: Gylippus aided the Syracusans against the Athenians in
414–413 BC (Thuc. 7). Brasidas helped the Thracians throw off the
Athenians (cf. note to c. 25). Lysander (see above), Callicratidas (cf. Xen.
Hellenica 1. 6), and King Agesilaus (see Plutarch's *Life*) were commanders
in Asia Minor and along the Aegean coast between 408 and 395. Plutarch
suppresses here the fact that Gylippus ran into trouble in Syracuse for
penny-pinching, and later was expelled from Sparta for taking public money
(cf. *Nic.* 28 and *Lys.* 16).

Stratonicus' joke: a fourth-century cithara-player, famous for his witticisms.

beaten up their tutor: the Thebans invaded the Peloponnese and defeated
the Spartans at the battle of Leuctra in 371.

virtue and internal unanimity: cf. Plato, *Republic* 4.

words and ideas: all three wrote *Republics* (Greek *politeiai*) imagining ideal
regimes. Diogenes of Sinope was the fourth-century founder of the Cynic
school, who went looking for an honest man with a lantern; Zeno founded
Stoicism in the late fourth century.

41 *ended his days in Crete*: the circumstances of Lycurgus' death are as unreliable as all else about him. Cirrha is a port on the Corinthian Gulf near
Delphi.

Antiorus: according to Pausanias (3. 16. 6), the son's name was Eucosmus
(i.e. well-ordered).

say about Lycurgus: Plutarch ends by recalling the long duration of
Lycurgus' reforms, which set him apart from Numa, whose *Life* follows
immediately.

SOLON

46 *Didymus the grammarian*: Plutarch often begins a Life with a citation: here
he indicates his familiarity with the learned discussions of Solon's laws.

Euphorion: this would have been a very obscure reference to any of
Plutarch's readers. He uses it as a springboard to talk of Solon's family
and relation to the future tyrant Pisistratus.

Codrus: a legendary king of Athens.

Zeus' fire: Euripides, *Bacchae* 8. For such homosexual relations between
an older man and a youth, see *Alc.* 4 note.

fist-fight: Sophocles, *Women of Trachis* 441.

torches: the Academy was a grove used for exercising, and later the home
of Plato's school, so the statue would have been well known. Pausanias

(1. 30. 1) saw it; Athenaeus (13. 609d) quotes the inscription and says it was set up by Charmus, who was the lover of Hippias, Pisistratus' son.

47 *knowledge*: Herodotus 1. 29 says he travelled for 'seeing' as well as to avoid changing his laws.

disgrace: Hesiod, *Works and Days* 311.

Massalia: Protis was a merchant of Phocea credited with founding Massalia, modern Marseilles.

trip there: Thales was said to have made a killing in the olive trade (Aristotle, *Pol.* 1. 1259ᵃ6); Plutarch is our only source for the others.

48 *sages*: the so-called Seven Sages, which included not only philosophic wise men like Solon, Thales of Miletus, and Bias of Priene, but tyrants and rulers of cities, such as Periander of Corinth, named in the next chapter, and Pittacus of Lesbos. Thales was the most famous for scientific philosophy, including prediction of a solar eclipse. Plutarch wrote a fictional dialogue about one of their gatherings, hosted by Periander, *The Banquet of the Seven Sages*, in which he included Anacharsis the Scythian (cf. c. 5), a brother of the Scythian king and famous for his travels (cf. Herodotus 4. 76–7).

49 *Bathycles*: the story was a popular one which survives in several variants, and Plutarch apparently knew even more. Some used legendary motifs (Helen's tripod), others more historical (Herodotus mentioned Croesus' dedications at Delphi; Bathycles was a famous sculptor). As with Delphi's response to Socrates' friend Chaerephon (Plato, *Apology* 21a), it forced one to consider who was wisest: the sages recognized that it is not any one of them, but the god.

51 *illness and medicines*: cf. Pericles' weakness when dying, *Per.* 38.

dog or a horse: on such substitution of affection, cf. *Per.* 1.

rest of their lives: cf. Plutarch's own *Consolation to My Wife* on the death of their daughter, following upon the death of two of their four sons, and his admiration for Pericles' self-control, *Per.* 36.

lay claim to Salamis: the rich island of Salamis lay off the coast of Attica and of Megara, the city just west of Athens. From the time of Solon, Salamis was under Athens' control. The date of the Megarian War (*Sol.* 8–10) is uncertain: Plutarch places it before Solon's archonship, but Herodotus connects it with Pisistratus, not Solon (1. 59), a date which Aristotle, *Constitution of the Athenians* (hereafter cited by its common abbreviation, *Athpol.*) 17. 2 says is chronologically impossible. Modern scholars are divided. The law referred to here is mentioned by Demosthenes, *On the False Embassy* 252, who praises Solon's bravery in defying it.

52 *felt cap on his head*: the reason for this felt cap is disputed: it may have been usually worn at night, or when sick, and thus an indication of Solon's madness. The word is an emendation: the manuscripts have 'small square' i.e. a brick or a bandage, which is not impossible.

Cape Colias: south-east of Piraeus and Phalerum, the modern Hagios Kosmas, and site of ancient sanctuaries of Aphrodite and Demeter.

53 *Periphemus and Cychreus*: in Greece, 'heroes' were men (some legendary, some historical) who were given special honours as great men who even when dead had power to help those who honoured them. Victories are often associated with such special attention. Cimon brought the bones of Theseus to Athens for heroic honours (*Cim.* 8), and an oracle advised Alexander to honour his friend Hephaestion as a hero (*Alex.* 72).

stationed: *Iliad* 2. 557–8.

54 *four corpses*: our archaeological evidence does not support either contention: every burial ground seems to have its own orientation, and the Athenians regularly used family tombs.

Cleomenes: this list of names is not preserved elsewhere. Some scholars think that this Cleomenes is the Spartan king who ruled at the end of the sixth century, long after Solon, others put the arbitration in Solon's day.

defend the god: a reference to the so-called first Sacred War, fought against the port city of Cirrha, on the Corinthian Gulf, by the members of the Amphictyonic League, states of central Greece which administered the sanctuary at Delphi, at some date before Solon's archonship *c.*594 BC.

Athenian commander: we have no information on the records at Delphi cited by Plutarch, a priest at Delphi for years.

55 *wives*: this unsuccessful conspiracy, led by Cylon, perhaps occurred in 632 or 624 BC. The conspirators were trapped on the Acropolis by the Athenians, led by Megacles, who was one of the nine archons or chief magistrates, perhaps the one simply called archon, who gave his name to the year. Cf. also Hdt. 5. 71, Thuc. 1. 126. Megacles was a member of the Alcmaeonid family, and an ancestor of Pericles, whom the Spartans accused of being accursed (*Per.* 33, Thuc. 1. 127).

found guilty: the prosecutor Myron is named also at Aristotle, *Athpol.* 1.

off Salamis: Nisaea was a port town in Megarian territory.

'New Coures': we know very little of Epimenides, except that the stories, like this one, connect him with religious wisdom. The Couretes were legendary Cretans responsible for the care of Zeus when he was a baby. Both the nymph mother and the connection with the Couretes emphasize his close contact with the gods.

for his legislation: cf. the similar role of Thales of Crete with Lycurgus, *Lyc.* 4.

56 *very own teeth*: this prophecy about Munychia was perhaps ascribed to Epimenides after the Macedonian Antipater fortified it with a permanent garrison in 322 BC.

olive tree: the olive was a gift of Athena to Athens, and the original tree, considered especially sacred, was preserved on the Acropolis, cf. Hdt. 8. 55.

gain power: Herodotus (1. 59) and Aristotle (*Athpol.* 13. 4) connect this geographical division of factions with the times of Pisistratus, not Solon: cf. c. 29 and note.

56 *tyranny*: in sixth-century Greece, political tensions often resulted in the establishment of a single ruler, or strong man, called a *tyrannos*. Plutarch highlights Solon's refusal to become tyrant, and his inability to stop Pisistratus from becoming one.

hired hands: Plutarch explains the terms *hektēmoroi* (cf. Aristotle *Athpol.* 2) and *thētes*. The exact status of the *hektēmoroi* and their role in the economy is much debated. They would perhaps have owned land, but had an obligation to the local lord. The thetes supported themselves as day labourers.

57 *make laws*: Solon's archonship is usually dated to 594/3 BC, but the reform powers Plutarch mentions (in agreement with Aristotle, *Athpol.* 5. 2) may have been separate or additional to the archonship. Plutarch treats first the 'alleviation' and the political problems it caused (14–16), then his other reforms (17–24), but need not imply a long period of time between the stages. In *Athpol.* 5–10, the reforms are all seen as part of his role as 'archon and arbitrator'.

58 *tyrant over them*: Pittacus, one of the seven sages, was vilified as tyrant of Mytilene by the poet Alcaeus, although his office according to Aristotle (*Politics* 3, 1285ᵃ29) was elective. Tynnondas is otherwise unknown, unless he is the same as a certain Tynnes of Chalcis.

59 *person as collateral*: the reform is often called by its Greek name, *seisach-theia*, literally, 'shaking off of burdens'. It seems to have had two facets: the 'freeing of the land' from obligations (*hektēmoroi* are not mentioned after Solon) and the ban on enslaving a citizen for debt, including restoring to Attica those who had been enslaved and sold abroad. But the precise nature of the reform is debated, as it was in ancient times. Cf. *Athpol.* 6.

Androtion: Androtion attempted to describe Solon's changes as being relatively slight, but his explanation in terms of money values is certainly wrong, since coinage did not come to Athens before 560. Solon may have reformed weights and measures, but there is little scholarly agreement on this.

in the slightest: on this re-evaluation, see Aristotle, *Athpol.* 10. 1–2, who however says the rate had been 70, not 73 drachmas to the mina.

now is free: Aristotle, *Athpol.* quotes 27 lines of this poem.

60 *debt-cheats*: the story of Solon's friends is also in Aristotle, *Athpol.* 6. 2, though without their names and the expression 'debt-cheats', *chreokopidai*. There are problems with the whole story: such borrowing and purchase of land at short notice would be difficult before coinage; and descendants (Conon, Alcibiades, and Callias) of the three men named were all prominent towards the end of the fifth century: the story may have been invented to discredit them.

as Lycurgus had done: cf. Plutarch's *Lycurgus*. The following paragraph is a significant analysis by Plutarch of the differences between the political situations of the two lawgivers. The problem of situation is addressed further in the parallel Life, *Publicola*: see Solon: Introduction.

60 *their foe*: this and the following are from poems more fully quoted in Aristotle, *Athpol.* 12.

61 *temple-robbery and homicide*: Draco was a real lawgiver, if very shadowy both to the Athenians and to us, whose laws were famous for their severity. Cf. Aristotle, *Athpol.* 4 (apparently a later addition to the work), which dates his law-code to the archonship of Aristaechmus, *c.*621/20 BC.

62 *act as jurors*: the classes were respectively the *Pentekosiomedimnoi*, the *Hippada teleountes* or simply *Hippeis*, the *Zeugitai*, and the *Thētes*, cf. Aristotle, *Athpol.* 7. 3–4. *Zeugitai*, literally 'Yokemen', alternatively might mean hoplites (armoured infantry), referring to their standing close together in battle. A medimnus at Athens measured about 52 litres, or 1.5 bushels. 'Wet or dry' would commonly refer to wine, olive oil, or grain. Cf. the references to Spartan income at *Lyc.* 8 and 12. The citizen jurors sat as courts (there was no judge to rule on law) in numbers from 200 to as many as 6,000. Solon redistributed the offices by property rather than birth, and gave some political role to every citizen.

masters of the laws: as both Plutarch and Aristotle note, the citizen's right to serve on the courts was to prove extremely important. Cf. Aristotle, *Athpol.* 9. 2.

prosecute him: Athenian law for most cases did not have a public prosecutor; instead the individual citizens had to initiate prosecution, a procedure which proved to be one of the major features of the developed democracy. In Solon's day its use was probably still quite limited in practice, but it did mean that enforcement of Solon's code was in the hands of the citizens.

63 *general population*: the two councils, the Areopagus Council, formed of ex-magistrates serving for life, and the Council of 400 elected annually (changed by Cleisthenes at the end of the century to 500), often called by its Greek name, *boulē*, are the two bodies which restricted to some degree the action of the Assembly of male citizens. In 462, the Areopagus was weakened by Pericles and Ephialtes (cf. *Per.* 9). As Plutarch goes on to say, the Areopagus pre-existed Solon. Cf. Aristotle, *Athpol.* 8. 4.

ephetae: another group of magistrates involved in homicide cases. In Aristotle's day they worked with the king archon (cf. Aristotle, *Athpol.* 57. 4).

disenfranchised: cf. Aristotle, *Athpol.* 8. 5.

64 *relatives of his*: in Athenian law, an heiress (*epiklēros*) was an unmarried woman who had inherited the property of her family, and it was considered necessary for her to marry with and have an heir by her closest relative, to conserve the property in the family. This law of Solon dealt with the particular problem of an impotent husband (who Plutarch apparently assumes is a relative of the heiress, so that her new partner will also be a member of her family). The verb used by Solon, 'have sex with' (*opuesthai*), does not specify whether this is to be a legitimate second marriage or a special exception.

64 *eating a quince*: the quince was associated with marriage, perhaps because its many seeds suggested fertility. In his *Advice on Marriage* 138d Plutarch also speaks of the sweetness it leaves in the mouth.

estrangement: Solon's law would have been directed towards assuring an heir, but Plutarch emphasizes his own interest in a harmonious marriage, in which he thought affectionate sexual relations had an important part (cf. his *Advice on Marriage* and *Eroticus*, trans. D. Russell, in *Plutarch, Selected Essays and Dialogues* (Oxford: Oxford University Press, 1993)).

out of the question: this would be Dionysius the Elder, tyrant of Syracuse in the early fourth century.

for marriage: from a lost play, not Sophocles' *Philoctetes*.

65 *powers of a woman*: this provision was the cause of some trouble, since it opened the way to challenges in court. It was often cited by the orators, and was repealed by the Thirty in 404/403: cf. Aristotle, *Athpol.* 35. 2.

66 *Superintendents of Women*: similar offices regulating female behaviour existed in many cities: Aristotle said they were normal in oligarchic regimes (*Politics* 4, 1300ᵃ4–6). It is not clear whether by 'our laws' Plutarch means those of Chaeronea, or contemporary Athens (of which Plutarch was also a citizen).

twice the number: from a lost tragedy.

area of expertise: another comparison between Lycurgus and Solon as lawgivers. The Spartans had subjugated those they had conquered to be a kind of serfs called helots, who farmed the land and acted as servants. Only the Spartans themselves were considered citizens. Cf. *Lyc.* 2 note.

67 *ox and a sheep*: Plutarch's comment on the change of monetary value leads him into a note on Solonian monetary equivalences and on farming in Attica.

Aegicorians: these are the names of the four pre-Cleisthenic tribes, which Plutarch interprets etymologically (incorrectly, according to modern scholars).

68 *four stades*: 4 stades = *c*.700m. (*c*.2,400 ft.).

twice a day: a total of *c*.40 litres. Cf. *Lyc.* 12 note.

fig-informer: in Greek, a *sykophantēs* (cf. English 'sycophant') or malicious prosecutor.

could rely on: grants of citizenship in Greece were rare, so that this represented an unusual initiative to encourage artisans. Resident aliens or metics came to play an important role in the Athenian economy.

69 *table-sharing*: the members of the Council on service at any given time were provided a meal in their quarters, to which state guests were also invited. Others were also honoured with an invitation: victorious generals, Olympic victors, and civic benefactors.

for 100 years: so also Aristotle, *Athpol.* 7. 2. Herodotus 1. 29 says for ten years.

69 *rest were called 'tables'*: the Greek terms are *axones* and *kyrbeis*: cf. Aristotle, *Athpol.* 7. 1. There has been much speculation on their shape and mode of display: for one recent interpretation that the *axones* and *kyrbeis* were two publications of the laws, one by Solon in the Prytany quarters (the *axones*, on horizontal rotating axes) and the other by Pisistratus in the agora (the *kyrbeis*, triangular bronze pillars), see N. Robertson, *Historia*, 35 (1986), 147–76. This argument would mean that Plutarch is in error here. See also the fragments of an inscription from Sicily on lead, apparently meant to be revolved horizontally, as we imagine the *axones*: G. Nenci, 'La κύρβις Selinuntina', *Annali della Scuola Normale di Pisa*, 3rd ser. 24 (1994), 459–66.

golden statue: the oath of all nine archons (cf. Aristotle, *Athpol.* 7. 1, 55. 1), including the six *thesmothētai* was taken on a special stone, which has now been found in the Athenian agora, in front of the Stoa of the Basileus (King). The oath to dedicate a life-size statue at Delphi is also found in Plato, *Phaedrus* 235d.

behaviour of the moon: the Attic lunar calendar counted the day of the new moon, as Plutarch describes, as 'old and new', and the last ten days as 'tenth of the declining moon', 'ninth . . .', etc. The Homeric verse is found at *Od.* 14. 162, 19. 307.

70 *travels*: Herodotus 1. 29 gives the excuse as observation, Aristotle, *Athpol.* 11. 1 both business and observation.

form of a poem: cf. Plato, *Timaeus* 21c–23d, *Critias* 108d, who refers to Saïs but does not give the names of the priests, which are found only here and must be from another source. In the *Timaeus* and *Critias* Plato unfolds the story of Atlantis told by the Egyptian priests to Solon: 9,000 years before, the island in the Ocean had had a marvellous but warlike civilization, which attacked the Athens of that time, and was defeated. Afterwards Atlantis sank into the sea. On Solon and Atlantis, see c. 31.

called Aepeia: this story of the renaming probably gives a false etymology: Assyrian documents of the seventh century already call the town Sillu.

71 *fiction*: chronology indeed seems to make it impossible: Solon was archon in 594/3, and Croesus was king of Lydia *c.*560–546. Attempts to move the two dates closer have not been successful. Solon does not mention Croesus in his poems. If he visited Lydia, it would have been at the court of an earlier king; but Herodotus may have invented the entire story of their meeting (1. 29–34) to create a paradigmatic encounter of Athenian sage and oriental prince. Ancient chronographers were not reliable, however, and Plutarch is not completely unreasonable in disregarding them to create a scene central to the whole Life: cf. Introduction.

72 *painless death*: the stories of Tellus and of Cleobis and Biton are in Herodotus.

utmost honesty: Aesop is a shadowy figure, said to have lived in Solon's day (in the *Dinner of the Seven Sages* 150a, Plutarch introduces him as a speaker, recently sent by Croesus to Delphi). The fables ascribed to him are all late, but may reflect early stories. This anecdote is not reported elsewhere.

73 *educated another*: the two preceding paragraphs paraphrase Hdt. 1. 86–88. 1.

Pisistratus: cf. 13. 2, Hdt. 1. 59, and Aristotle, *Athpol.* 13. 4. Plutarch repeats the account of factional division placed by Herodotus and Aristotle before Pisistratus' attempt at power.

74 *Thespis*: the traditional inventor of tragedy, whose first competition is placed *c*.534. The scene with Solon is probably invented.

on a cart: cf. Hdt. 1. 59.

fellow citizens: the reference is to Odysseus' disguise as a beggar when he was planning how to deal with the suitors of his wife.

75 *thinking is vain*: Solon's opposition is found also in Aristotle, *Athpol.* 14. 2, with the following quote on being either wiser and better, and the armour at the door, though the proposer is named Aristion.

76 *peacefulness of the city*: cf. c. 22. Herodotus 2. 177 says that Solon took the idea from Amasis of Egypt.

legend of Atlantis: in Plato's dialogues *Timaeus* and *Critias*, the story of Atlantis is ascribed to Solon. His lack of leisure is mentioned at *Timaeus* 21c.

right of kinship: Plato, according to Diogenes Laertius 3. 1, was descended from Solon's brother.

77 *fine products*: the reference is to Plato's *Critias*, which begins the story of Atlantis but soon breaks off.

that of Comias: respectively, the years 561/60 and 560/59.

Aristotle the philosopher: the notice was in a work now lost.

THEMISTOCLES

82 *future distinction*: the beginning is abrupt, and some have suggested that an introductory paragraph such as those found in the first Life of many other pairs has been lost. But not all pairs have formal introductions, as the *Solon* shows.

tribe Leontis: after the constitutional reforms of Cleisthenes at the end of the sixth century, the citizen body of Athens was divided into ten units called tribes, and some 139 local districts called demes. These were the basis of many aspects of political life. In naming an Athenian, writers often include the deme, as in c. 2, Mnesiphilus of Phrearrhii.

Halicarnassus: since women were seldom mentioned in Athens, and then most often to denigrate a politician, we cannot sort out the truth about Themistocles' mother, nor what the allegation of 'illegitimacy' might mean. It would not have been unusual for an Athenian of good family to have married a foreign woman at this time, though a law of 451 made the children of such unions illegitimate.

84 *public arena too*: for such homosexual relations (and rivalries) between an older man and a youth, see *Alc.* 4 note. Ariston also was from Ceos, and perhaps had special information—or bias.

against the Persians: the Athenians, led by Miltiades, defeated the Persians at Marathon in 490 BC.

85 *sea against Xerxes*: the Laurium silver mines near Cape Sunium were some of the richest in the Greek world, and had a notable effect on the Athenian economy. The war with the island of Aegina, an important naval power at this time, had been simmering for some time, but broke out in the years between 490 and the invasion of Xerxes in 480.

quote Plato: Plato, *Laws* 706c.

subduing them: Plutarch refers to Xerxes' return to Persia after his defeat at Salamis in 480; Mardonius was left to fight and lose at Plataea in 479.

86 *donated food*: Plutarch may be thinking of the custom that, for a party among friends, all the friends might contribute food. Thus selling some would seem extraordinarily cheap.

path to his door: Epicles is otherwise unknown.

pretentiousness: this competition with Cimon would be later, after Themistocles' success at Salamis, so the pretentiousness would consist in trying to rival Cimon's inherited status with the new riches gained from the spoils.

Adeimantus: the name of the archon Adeimantus permits us to date this play by Phrynichus to 477/6. By this time Themistocles was famous, and the production of a play a standard duty of a wealthy citizen.

people favours: the poet Simonides was notoriously stingy. Although Plutarch does not, his source most probably punned on the two meanings of *nomos*, melody and law.

by ostracism: ostracism was the practice of reducing political conflict by banishing from the state for ten years, without loss of property, a politician selected by a special vote. Each year the Assembly decided whether to vote to ostracize someone. Originally used against friends of the expelled tyrants, it fell upon a number of prominent politicians, including besides Aristides Themistocles (22), Cimon (*Cim.* 16, *Per.* 9), Thucydides the son of Melesias (*Per.* 14), and Pericles' friend Damon (*Per.* 4). Voting was done by scratching the name of the person to be ostracized on a sherd of a broken pot (ostracon: Greek, *ostrakon*): thousands of these have been discovered at Athens, with all the names above, as well as other names both famous and obscure. See M. Lang, *The Athenian Agora XXV: Ostraka* (Princeton, 1990). The practice ended with the ostracism of Hyperbolus in 417 (*Nic.* 11, *Alc.* 13).

87 *ambition out of him*: only Plutarch tells this story of Epicydes.

earth and water: before invading Greece, both Darius in 491 and Xerxes in 481 sent ambassadors demanding the surrender of earth and water as symbols of submission.

87 *give to the Greeks*: the incident of Arthmius of Zelea was referred to often by later orators. The details are unclear, but scholars think that it belongs after the Persian Wars. The mover of the decree may have been Cimon, not Themistocles.

in this regard: according to Herodotus 9. 9, the advice of Cheileos of Tegea in Arcadia for the Spartans to support the Athenians was given, not in 480, but in 479, before the battle of Plataea.

with the enemy: the Greek army was at Tempe *c.* April–May 480. Cf. Hdt. 7. 173.

guard the strait: Cape Artemisium is the northernmost tip of the island of Euboea (cf. c. 8). For the campaign at sea of summer 480, cf. Hdt. 7. 175–7, 183, 188–95; 8. 1–23. The naval battle at Artemisium paralleled the more famous land battle at Thermopylae, and according to Herodotus was fought on the same day. Eurybiades was the Spartan commander at Artemisium and Salamis, and overall commander of the Greek fleet.

88 *Sciathos*: Sciathos is an island north-east of Cape Artemisium, and Aphetae was opposite it on the mainland, near Cape Sepias.

Eurybiades: Hdt. 8. 4–5. In *Herodotus' Malice* 867bc, Plutarch criticizes Herodotus for reporting this story; here Plutarch adds a detail, the name of the Euboean envoy, Pelagon.

Themistocles' plans: Architeles' identity, and that of the sacred ship, are uncertain. He perhaps was a Corinthian, not an Athenian.

89 *land routes*: the Spartan king Leonidas and his 300 warriors defending the pass at Thermopylae were defeated by the Persians.

90 *suspicion of the Ionians*: cf. Hdt. 8. 22. The Ionians considered themselves colonists and descendants of the Athenians.

ancestral tombs: the evacuation of Attica had long been considered, and represented an extraordinary initiative. An inscription, the 'Themistocles Decree', discovered in Troezen in 1959 is probably a third-century copy with revisions of the actual decree moved by Themistocles, perhaps in the spring of 480. The text (Fornara, no. 55) and its historical implications have been much discussed since. Plutarch refers to the decree in c. 10.

portents and oracles: here Plutarch refers to the famous crane, or *machina*, used to hoist over the stage the god who would resolve the plot. The snake story is in Hdt. 8. 41; the oracle of the wooden wall in 7. 140–3.

91 *that he could*: the 'Themistocles Decree': see c. 9 note.

by Nicagoras: the decree of Nicagoras of Troezen is mentioned by the orator Hyperides, 3. 32–3. Troezen is in the Peloponnese, across the Saronic Gulf from Athens, and south-east from Epidaurus.

Aristotle says: Aristotle, *Athpol.* 23. 1.

92 *banished by ostracism*: cf. c. 5.

bon mots by Themistocles: cf. Hdt. 8. 59, 61.

Phaleric Gulf: just off Phalerum, on the west coast of Attica.

402   *Explanatory Notes*

93 *business with Sicinnus*: cf. Hdt. 8. 75. For the following battle of Salamis, see Hdt. 8. 83–95.

mentioned earlier: cc. 5 and 11.

94 *writings as well*: Phanias' story of human sacrifice, like others of his, appears pure fiction, although Plutarch repeats the story in *Aristides* 9. 1–2. Dionysus did have the cult-name Eater of Raw Flesh in some places; and Euripides' *Bacchae* shows the maenads tearing to pieces first animals, then the king of Thebes himself.

stands the count: Aeschylus, *Persians* 336–8.

95 *Piraeus*: Socles' deme is uncertain, since Piraeus is an emendation. Other editors suggest Pallene, or leave the text undeciphered.

for Xerxes: the story is not found in Herodotus, though he says Ameinias was recognized for his courage (8. 93).

on the triremes: the story is found in Hdt. 8. 65.

96 *Apollo at Phlya*: according to Hdt. 8. 11 and 84, Lycomedes took the first ship at Artemisium, whereas Ameinias rammed the first ship at Salamis. Plutarch may have erred in putting Lycomedes at Salamis, unless he got this information from Simonides' poem on the battle (see below). He has already mentioned Simonides and the Lycomidae shrine at Phyla in c. 1. He may have seen the dedication.

quote Simonides: Simonides wrote long poems on the battles of Artemisium, Salamis, and Plataea. Recently discovered fragments of the Plataea poem show that they could be both detailed and heroicizing.

97 *losing everything*: in Hdt. 8. 108–10, the debate on destroying the bridge is set on Andros. After Eurybiades opposes the plan, Themistocles shifts tactics with the Athenians, and sends Sicinnus, not Arnaces, to Xerxes.

as far as the border: Hdt. 8. 93 (Aegina), 123–4 (Themistocles). Plutarch improves Herodotus' story by making not the majority, but every general give Themistocles second place.

Olympic Games: probably the Olympic Games of 476 are meant, since those of 480 preceded the battle.

98 *you were from Athens*: Seriphos is a tiny Aegean island, famous for its insignificance.

merely tricked them: for the majority story, see Thuc. 1. 90–2, who however does not mention Polyarchus. For the Spartan ephors, see *Lyc.* 7 and note.

99 *Aristophanes puts it*: Aristophanes, *Knights* 815.

worked the land: the Pnyx was the hill where the Athenian Assembly met. There is archaeological evidence that the orientation of the meeting-place was changed in the late fifth century, the time when the Thirty Tyrants ruled Athens after its defeat by Sparta.

100 *powerful states*: the Amphictyonic League was a group of Greek states responsible for protecting Apollo's shrine at Delphi. This story is not otherwise known.

100 *him any money*: Hdt. 8. 111, but Plutarch changes the names of the gods, without changing the meaning of the names. Herodotus places the story immediately after the battle of Salamis, when Andros would have still been under Persian control; Plutarch uses it as a story to illustrate the resentment created by his treatment of the islanders after they had joined the Athenian alliance.

101 *Themistocles' death*: Pausanias is the Spartan commander and victor at Plataea; Leotychidas and Xanthippus the Spartan and Athenian victors at the battle of Mycale. Leto is the goddess mother of Apollo and Artemis.

   heroic temperament: blocks from this shrine of Artemis were found in Athens in 1958. A portrait bust of Roman date, labelled 'Themistocles', has been found, and may be a copy of a fifth-century original (on this and other portraits, see F. J. Frost, *Plutarch's Themistocles: A Historical Commentary* (Princeton: Princeton University Press, 1980), 184–5).

102 *loss of status*: on ostracism, cf. note to c. 5. The date of the ostracism is uncertain: perhaps 472 or 471 BC. Almost 2,300 ostraca bearing Themistocles' name have been found.

   a handle against him: the stories of the downfalls of Pausanias and Themistocles are given by Thucydides, 1. 128–38, but Plutarch adds Pausanias' communications with Themistocles, Themistocles' letter to Athens, the version of Stesimbrotus, and other material.

103 *giving Themistocles up*: formal supplication was a recognized procedure which created certain obligations for the person supplicated. The Molossian procedure already seemed archaic when Thucydides described it, 1. 136.

   competition: Hiero at the time was tyrant of Syracuse in Sicily.

104 *Asian coastline*: Pydna is in Macedonia. The Athenians were besieging the island of Naxos about 468 BC. One Plutarch manuscript reads Thasos, besieged about 465, but this is contrary to our text of Thucydides 1. 137.

   on his head: 200 talents was an extraordinary sum, more than the fortune of the wealthiest Greek.

   several days hiding: in Diodorus 11. 56. 4, this man is given the name Lysitheides. The 'men from up country' would have been Persian nobles.

105 *had his audience*: a famous chronological crux, still fought over, though most scholars now accept Thucydides' statement (1. 137). Xerxes died in 465.

106 *their best men*: Ahriman was the evil principle of Zoroastrianism, Ormuzd the good, as Plutarch knew: cf. his *Isis and Osiris* 369d–370b.

107 *between the two men*: Demaratus, the deposed Spartan king, is famous as the counsellor of Xerxes in Herodotus, 7. 101–4, 209, 234–7, 8. 65. This story was told by the third-century historian Phylarchus, where Plutarch may have found it: cf. c. 32.

108 *bedding and clothing*: Thuc. 1. 138 lists the first three cities. 'Savouries' are any condiment or meat you eat with bread.

   Mother of the Gods: the Anatolian goddess also known as Cybele, Dindymene, or the Great Mother, often associated with one or more lions.

108 *Sardis*: the capital of Lydia.

109 *control of the sea*: Egypt revolted from Persia *c*.460; Cimon controlled the sea for Athens before he was ostracized *c*.461, and from his recall (perhaps soon after the battle of Tanagra, 457) to his death off Cyprus *c*.450: cf. *Cimon* 18. Themistocles would have died about 460.

110 *some writers say*: bull's blood is in fact not poisonous, and Thucydides (1. 138) seems right in saying he died of illness rather than poison.

Themistocles' children: for a chart of Themistocles' family, see Frost, *Commentary*, 231. Plato names Cleophantus at *Meno* 93d.

made the story up: the monument in Magnesia is mentioned by Thucydides, 1. 138, and appears on a second-century AD Roman coin. Andocides' oration does not survive. Phylarchus was often criticized for overdramatizing his history.

111 *Ammonius the philosopher*: a Platonist, the teacher of Plutarch, mentioned by him in many works.

CIMON

118 *non-Greek inhabitants*: Opheltas was the son of Penelaus, a leader of the Boeotian contingent at Troy (cf. Pausanias 9. 5. 8), and perhaps Plutarch considered him an ancestor of his family (cf. his *On the Delay of Divine Punishment*, 558a). Chaeronea, Plutarch's home town, was on the route from Thessaly into Boeotia. Peripoltas is otherwise unknown.

Persian invasions and wars against the Galatians: i.e. 480–479 BC and 279 BC.

insignificance and poverty: this Roman billeting was in the winter of 88–87 BC, during the war against Mithridates, when L. Licinius Lucullus was proquaestor of Cornelius Sulla, who was besieging Athens. In the following year Chaeronea was the site of a major battle. While it was sometimes acceptable for a teenage youth of good family to allow himself to be the favourite of an older man, such behaviour would be considered shameful in a mature young man. Damon was past the normal age for such relations. Cf. *Alc*. 4 note.

119 *made him gymnasiarch*: this office, literally in charge of athletic training, was regularly a post of distinction held by a member of the local élite, who was responsible for the good order of the city. Damon merited it by his birth, but not by his behaviour.

120 *foreigners*: Plutarch says *barbarous*, emphasizing that both leaders fought wars outside their own civilization, Greek or Graeco-Roman.

to Cimon himself: Plutarch's citation of these two poets in this chapter, like his reference to Stesimbrotus, shows his interest in using contemporary sources.

Cimoneia: the name given to the funeral monuments of the family. Cf. c. 19.

121 *Stesimbrotus has written*: the tragedy of Euripides is not known.

122 *worthy of Marathon*: his father Miltiades had been the victorious general at the battle of Marathon, 490 BC.

123 *ingenuity and adventurousness*: the rivalry of Themistocles and Aristides is treated more fully in Plutarch's *Themistocles* (in this volume) and *Aristides*.

Pausanias and the Lacedaemonians: the Persians retreated in 479 BC, after the battle of Plataea. Pausanias was deposed as commander of the Greek fleet in the Aegean and leader of the alliance against Persia in 478. This permitted the Athenians to establish an alliance of cities around the Aegean, which developed into an empire. Cf. Thuc. 1. 94–7, 128–34.

doom for men: Pausanias was in Byzantium in 478, and returned to control it for an uncertain period, perhaps a number of years.

124 *stone herms*: the herms were pillar-statues erected to Hermes: this was a monumental series, with inscriptions. For private herms, cf. *Nic*. 13 with note and *Alc*. 18.

disciplined prowess: the reference is to Athens' contingent in the Trojan War, led by Menestheus.

125 *give it back*: for the Amphictyonic League, see *Them*. 20 note.

126 *popularity in Athens*: Theseus, the legendary king of Athens, was revered as the founder of the democracy and the one who made Athens strong. On the enduring power of such heroes, see *Solon* 9 note.

first play: at the Festival of Dionysus of 468 BC.

importance and wealth: cf. *Them*. 2.

127 *for the city*: the occasion described here probably occurred after the capture of Byzantium in 478.

Laciadae: Aristotle, *Athpol*. 27. 3. Plutarch also uses the lost historian Theopompus for this anecdote, which is repeated in *Per*. 9.

128 *Arcesilas of Lacedaemon*: the Scopadae were a powerful Thessalian clan of the sixth century; Arcesilas of Sparta won two Olympic victories with his horses in the mid-fifth century, as well as numerous lesser ones.

Festival of Unarmed Dancing: the generosity of Lichas, son of the Arcesilas mentioned by Critias in the preceding quote, had been mentioned by Xenophon, *Mem*. 1. 2. 61. On the festival, see *Lyc*. 15 and note.

seed-corn: the mythical mission of the Athenian Triptolemus to teach the sowing of grain to other Greek cities was a traditional source of pride to Athenians.

for public use: the Athenians regularly entertained state guests and specially honoured citizens, such as Olympic victors, in the town hall. See *Sol*. 24 note.

of human life: the golden age, when Cronus was chief god before he was deposed by Zeus: cf. Hesiod, *Works and Days* 109–20.

pro-Lacedaemonian aristocrat: contrast *Per*. 9, where Cimon's generosity is seen more as a political move to win the people's favour.

128 *the Areopagus*: on Ephialtes and the Areopagus, see below, c. 15, and *Per.* 9.

129 *I want to*: Rhoesaces is otherwise unknown. Apparently he was a target of lawsuits by those who hoped to gain politically or materially from them. Darics were coins issued by Persia; they got their name from King Darius, whose face appeared on them.

sending troops: this significant step is briefly mentioned by Thucydides, 1. 99.

Persian military presence: i.e. all the western and southern coast of Asia Minor. The account which follows is our fullest of the Eurymedon campaign and battle (*c.*468 BC). The Eurymedon river, now Köprüçayi or Pazarçavi, flows into the Gulf of Antalya.

131 *Chelidonian Islands*: the very existence of this so-called Peace of Callias was (as Plutarch notes) and is disputed; its date is variously placed in the 460s, soon after Eurymedon, or *c.*449, after Cimon's victory near Cyprus (see c. 18). See Introduction, p. 113. The area covered by the Peace ran from the Bosporus in the north to Phaselis on the southern coast of Asia Minor.

from the Persians: Ephialtes was the democratic leader, an associate of Pericles in reforming the Areopagus Council (see c. 15). This notice indicates that he was a general in command of a fleet.

132 *as they are known*: the Long Walls ran from Athens to the harbour town of Piraeus, rendering Athens safe from a land invasion.

Thasian dominion: the Chersonese or Gallipoli peninsula had before the Persian Wars been under the control of Cimon's father Miltiades. Thasos' rebellion took two years to put down, *c.*465–463, cf. Thuc. 1. 100–1. Only Plutarch mentions Cimon's role.

133 *for form's sake*: Stesimbrotus suggests that Elpinice was hoping to charm or seduce Pericles; there is a pun in the Greek for 'like this', which may mean 'important as this is' or 'proper to younger people as this is'.

as a populist: this reform of the Areopagus Council engineered by Ephialtes and Pericles is considered a major step in the establishment of unrestricted democracy at Athens. Cf. *Per.* 9. Cimon's 'naval expedition' is puzzling and may be an error: other sources suggest that he had gone to the aid of the Spartans at Ithome (cf. cc. 16–17), which would most naturally have been by land.

government of Cleisthenes: Cleisthenes had introduced a less radical democracy at Athens in 508, after the expulsion of the tyrants.

Cleitor: a small town in Arcadia, in the Peloponnese. One name may be not Eleius (i.e. of Elis) but Oulius, and therefore would have Athenian and Ionian connections.

134 *of Megacles*: the names of her father and grandfather reveal that Isodice was a member of the Alcmaeonid family and thus related to Pericles: cf. *Per.* 3.

Earthquake Site: the date of the earthquake and the consequent revolt of the helots (cf. *Lyc.* 2 note) is disputed, but lies probably in the period 465–462. The revolt lasted ten years (Thuc. 1. 103. 1).

135 *against the Spartiates*: the perioeci, or 'neighbours', were free Laconians without Spartiate citizen rights. Thucydides (1. 101. 2) names two communities which joined the revolt. The Messenians were the helots of Messene, which was freed from Spartiate control in the fourth century (cf. *Ages.* 34).

begging for an army: Aristophanes, *Lysistrata* 1137–44.

with his army: apparently Corinth had recently attacked these two cities whose territory bordered hers, Megara on the east, towards Athens, and Cleonae on the south-west, towards Argos.

they were furious: for Sparta's rejection of the Athenians' aid, see Thuc. 1. 102. Plutarch may be making two expeditions out of one, as our other sources know only one.

136 *time for ostracism*: in 461. For ostracism, see note to *Them.* 5. The exact period of Cimon's ostracism, especially whether he returned before the end of the ten years, as stated by Plutarch, is much disputed.

harboured against them: the battle of Tanagra was fought in Boeotia in 458 or 457 BC. The Athenians lost. Cf. Thuc. 1. 107–8. In *Per.* 10, the friends of Pericles are responsible for not allowing Cimon to fight. Plutarch does not mention the major Athenian victory at Oenophyta two months later.

137 *their natural enemies*: there had been a major expedition to help an Egyptian revolt against Persia in 458–453 (Thuc. 1. 104, 109–10). The present expedition probably dates to 451 and 450. Persia at this time controlled the Mediterranean coast from Lebanon south, as well as Egypt and Cyprus.

lacked a head: damage to the liver of a sacrificial animal was a sign of grave danger: cf. *Ages.* 9 and *Alex.* 73. This sequence of progressively more serious and clear portents is found in several Lives, especially before death. See F. Brenk, *In Mist Apparelled: Religious Themes in Plutarch's Moralia and Lives* (Leiden, 1977), 184–213.

his Greek offensive: cf. *Them.* 31.

138 *question to the god*: this shrine was at the oasis of Siwah, in the Libyan desert, consulted also by Alexander, *Alex.* 26–7.

for thirty days: Citium is on Cyprus.

unrest in Greece: cf. *Ages.* 6–15.

139 *So that is what the Greek leader was like*: these words provide a link to the Life of Lucullus, the Roman paired with Cimon.

PERICLES

144 *Caesar*: probably Augustus Caesar, who was given to such comments (cf. Suetonius, *Aug.* 34, 42).

sense of sight: the theory of sight implied, found in Plato, *Timaeus* 45b–e and elsewhere, imagines that the fire in the eye emits a stream, which is strengthened when it is reinforced by the light outside, so as to form a perception of the object. This analogy between sight and intellect is Platonic: cf. especially *Republic* 507b–508d, 509a–511e.

144 *mean and coarse*: Plutarch shared the traditional aristocratic bias against manual labour, particularly those which, as here, dirtied the worker.

Antisthenes: the follower of Socrates and author of Socratic dialogues.

Ismenias: a Theban aristocrat, famous for his skill on the *aulos*, a reed instrument related to the oboe (though often translated 'flute').

Philip: Philip II, king of Macedon and father of Alexander the Great. The lyre was used to accompany oneself singing, as a guitar today.

145 *Pisa . . . Argos*: famous examples of artistic excellence: the colossal gold and ivory statues of Zeus in the temple at Olympia (near Pisa in the Peloponnese), created by Phidias, the sculptor of the Parthenon (see below, c. 13), and of Hera in her temple at Argos, by Polyclitus, Phidias' contemporary and famous also for his Spearbearer (Doryphorus) and Filletbinder (Diadoumenos).

poetry: three poets best known for their lascivious and satiric content. Anacreon (sixth century) wrote erotic lyric, Philemon (third/second century) comedy, and Archilochus (seventh century) elegiac and iambic poetry, among which his biting invective was notorious.

from us: the contrast is between what philosophers, Plutarch among them, considered goods dependent on events outside our control (health, family, wealth, etc.), and those produced by virtuous action (acts showing justice, self-control, bravery, etc.).

the deed: this expresses in compressed form Plutarch's idea behind the *Parallel Lives*: to inspire his readers through these works to make a conscious choice to practise virtue in their own lives.

Fabius Maximus: on Fabius, see Pericles: Introduction.

Cholargus: on the use of tribe and deme to identify an Athenian under the democracy, cf. *Them.* 1 note.

state: Xanthippus was commander of the Athenians at the battle of Mycale (479 BC). His wife Agariste was actually not a descendant but a niece of Cleisthenes. This Cleisthenes came from the distinguished family of the Alcmaeonids, who were largely responsible for expelling the sons of the tyrant Pisistratus, Hippias and his brother Hipparchus, from Athens in 510. He later introduced a series of reforms which laid the basis for the fifth-century democracy.

lion: cf. Hdt. 6. 131.

146 *deformity*: various busts copied from a bronze statue of Pericles by Cresilas have been preserved, including one in the British Museum. The head wears a helmet, which from its angle might be thought to conceal an oddly shaped head. See G. Richter, *The Portraits of the Greeks* (London, 1965), i. 102–4 and plates 429–47. From the evidence of the recently discovered bronze Riace statues, elongation of the head was a standard feature of helmeted statues, probably to help the helmets stay on better.

146 *Pythoclides*: Damon was a musical theorist and adviser to Pericles. The Aristotle passage (F 364) is not preserved, but Plato the philosopher mentions Pythoclides (*Protagoras* 316e).

pro-tyrannical schemer: on ostracism, see *Them.* 5 note. The date is unknown.

Plato: the comic poet, not the philosopher.

147 *to perplexity*: Zeno of Elea in Italy, was a pre-Socratic philosopher, student of Parmenides, and famous for his paradoxes.

homoeomerous substances: Anaxagoras, we think, envisioned Mind as the chief agent of order in the universe and the 'homoeomerous substances' as the tiny elements, indistinguishable to the eye, which, when sorted out, become different types of matter. See W. K. C. Guthrie, *History of Greek Philosophy* (Cambridge: Cambridge University Press, 1965–81), ii. 325–6. The periods of his stays in Athens are uncertain. Cf. also cc. 16, 32.

148 *satyrs as well*: at Athens, a tragic poet would present at one time a set of four plays: three tragedies followed by a satyr play, that is, a much lighter play in which the wine-loving and boisterous satyrs, followers of Dionysus, made up the chorus.

had occurred: Lampon was a diviner or seer, involved in the foundation of the city of Thurii and other political matters. This Thucydides is not the historian but Thucydides son of Melesias, a political rival of Pericles, who succeeded Cimon in upholding traditional aristocratic privilege. After he was ostracized about 443 BC, Pericles apparently had no organized opposition. Cf. cc. 8, 11, 14.

149 *by his campaigns*: all three Athenian statesmen are subjects of Plutarchan Lives, two, Themistocles and Cimon, in this volume.

friend's house: Pericles' avoidance of typical aristocratic gatherings, previously the source of political influence, began a new kind of politics at Athens, based both on rhetoric and greater attention to financial administration: see W. R. Connor, *The New Politicians of Fifth-Century Athens* (Princeton: Princeton University Press, 1971).

150 *Critolaus puts it*: the *Salaminia* was an official ship, used for special state business.

Ephialtes: cf c. 9.

undiluted freedom: cf. Plato, *Republic* 562c, 'In its thirst for freedom, a democratically governed community might get leaders who aren't any good at serving wine. It gets drunk on excessive quantities of undiluted freedom . . .' (trans. Waterfield, Oxford World's Classics, 303).

islands: Euboea, long subject to Athens, had attempted to revolt in 446 (see c. 22) and been put down; the islands are the subject states of the Delian League, founded in 478 after the Persian Wars and made into an Athenian empire in subsequent years.

Plato says: a free quotation of Plato, *Phaedrus* 270a, already echoed in c. 5.

since they describe . . . tongue: the first two quotations are from Aristophanes, *Acharnians* 531; the third from an unknown comic poet. All compare

Pericles with Zeus, the wielder of the thunderbolt, who is often called 'Olympian'.

151 *decrees*: Plutarch refers to a number of these decrees in the course of the Life: see Pericles: Introduction.

leading man: Thuc. 2. 65.

self-supporting: this view was represented by Plato, as well as many later authors: cf. *Gorgias* 515e, Pericles, when he first introduced payments for civic duties, made the Athenians 'idle, work-shy, garrulous, and mercenary'.

if they liked: Cimon not only came from a wealthy family, but had won enormous booty by his victories over the Persians: see *Cim.* 10. Plutarch's account derives from Aristotle, *Athpol.* 27. 3–4 and Theopompus.

Aristotle: *Athpol.* 27. 4. Damonides was the father of Damon (cf. c. 4), and also an adviser to Pericles, though some emend the text to make Damon the adviser here.

152 *Areopagus*: the oldest council of Athens (cf. *Sol.* 19), at this time composed of those who had been archons, that is, held one of the magistracies named by Plutarch: archon, king archon, polemarch, or one of the six members of the judicial committee (*thesmothētai*). The extent and nature of these reforms is controversial, but the council's prerogatives were undoubtedly lessened. It was felt as a major anti-aristocratic and pro-democratic reform, since power was transferred from an élite body to citizen courts.

ostracized: probably early in 461. See *Cim.* 15.

Sparta: the battle of Tanagra in Boeotia came about, probably in 458, when the Athenians opposed a Spartan army which had assisted the town of Doris, and now was returning through Boeotia. Both sides suffered heavy casualties: see Thuc. 1. 107 and *Cim.* 17. Thucydides states that some anti-democratic conspirators at Athens hoped to use the Spartans to end the democracy. Only Plutarch (here and *Cim.* 17) says that Cimon was on the battlefield.

leaders: whether Cimon was in fact recalled early from ostracism and what the date would be are in dispute: Theopompus said he was recalled before five years were up. Thuc. 1. 112 speaks of a five-year treaty, which is often dated to 451. Plutarch may be telescoping events. Cf. also *Cim.* 17.

153 *city*: the story, not in *Cimon*, gives an example of Pericles' gift of compromise. Thuc. 1. 112 also mentions the 200 ships; *Cim.* 18, 300.

prosecutors: in *Cim.* 14, Stesimbrotus is given as the source for the story, which is there dated after the siege of Thasos, *c*.463/2.

secret: Aristotle, *Athpol.* 25. 4. Aristodicus is otherwise unknown.

expedition: cf. Thuc. 1. 112.

of the deme Alopece: i.e. Thucydides son of Melesias: cf. c. 6 note.

154 *counterweight on the scale*: Thucydides probably got his supporters to sit together in one place in the assembly, so that they could voice their support as a block when issues were being debated or voted on.

154 *control over the city*: Plutarch apparently is referring to the theatre productions of the Dionysiac festivals, as well as to other festivals, which we
know were expanded at this period.

rebellion: the naval figures are hard to reconcile with our other evidence,
but may nevertheless give an indication of the normal activity of the Athenian
navy. This is the fullest list of Athenian colonies that we have, though it omits
others mentioned below, such as those to Hestiaea, to Sinope and Amisus,
to Aegina, and to Astacus (cc. 23, 20, 33). The colony among the Bisaltae
is probably Amphipolis (cf. Thuc. 4. 102), not Brea as often suggested.

to our own keeping: the treasury for the Delian League, containing money
collected from the subject states, was transferred in 454 BC from Delos to
Athens.

156 *I take a long time over mine*: Agatharchus and Zeuxis were both famous
painters; Agatharchus was said to have been held prisoner by Alcibiades
(*Alc.* 16).

were involved in them: Phidias gained his reputation as an outstanding
sculptor for his two colossal gold and ivory statues, one of Athena in
the Parthenon (see below) and the other of Zeus at Olympia. Only in this
chapter is he given any larger role in the Periclean building programme
than that of sculptor of the Parthenos statue. We do not know Plutarch's
source or its reliability, but it is surely wrong to take Plutarch's words at
face value and treat Phidias as chief architect and master of public works
for the whole project. In what follows, Plutarch gives valuable information on the various architects of the building programme.

lantern: the hall of the mysteries at Eleusis (*telestērion*) was remarkable in
size, *c*.51 metres square, designed for large crowds of initiates. Plutarch's
statement on the different stages of the building and their architects is the
most explicit we possess, but does not mention Ictinus, who is named by
Vitruvius (7 pref. 16) and Strabo (9. 1. 2).

slow progress: the Long Walls connected Athens to the harbour town
of Piraeus, which meant that in the event of a siege, Athens could be
supplied by sea. The part of the project mentioned here may belong to
c.445–443. For Socrates' statement, cf. Plato, *Gorgias* 455e.

157 *supervision of Pericles*: the Odeum was an enormous music hall, some
62.4 × 68.6 m., on the slopes of the Acropolis next to the theatre of
Dionysus, with ten rows of nine columns each. It was used both for
musical contests and law courts.

Panathenaea: a major festival in honour of Athena, held every year, and
with special pomp every fourth year. Besides the music contests, there were
processions, athletic competitions, and horse races.

Propylaea: the monumental gateway to the Acropolis, and the most famous
Periclean building after the Parthenon.

was there before: The inscribed base of this statue has been found beside
the south-east wall of the Propylaea. (See the photo in J. Travlos, *Pictorial
Dictionary of Ancient Athens*. (New York: Praeger, 1971).)

157 *stele*: perhaps the inscribed slab marking the dedication of the statue.

158 *birds he kept*: Pyrilampes on his return from an embassy to Persia brought
back peacocks which became famous in the city. Since an ordinary cock
was a regular love-gift, a peacock would have been quite impressive.

faction: Thucydides' ostracism is calculated to have been in 443, allowing
fifteen years for Pericles' unrivalled ascendancy before his death in 429/8
(cf. *Per.* 16). Some sixty-four ostracon sherds bearing Thucydides' name
have been found.

159 *right way*: Plato, *Phaedrus* 271c, 270c–d.

bribery: Thuc. 2. 65. 8.

left it to him: the Greek text here is corrupt, though the general meaning
is clear enough: Pericles did not increase his patrimony when he could have
done so easily.

power: Plutarch refers especially to Thucydides' evaluation of Pericles at
2. 65. 8–10.

new Pisistratidae: referring to the sixth-century Athenian tyrant Pisistratus
and his sons Hippias and Hipparchus: cf. *Per.* 3 and note, *Solon* 29–31.

160 *Ephialtes . . . Thucydides*: all were famous generals and statesmen: Ephialtes,
above cc. 7, 9, and *Cim.* 13; Leocrates a general at Plataea (479) and later
at Aegina (early 450s); Myronides a general at Plataea and victor over
the Boeotians at Oenophyta (*c.*458). For Cimon, see his Life and above
cc. 9–10.

fifteen years: here Plutarch marks Pericles' period as leader without rival
in Athens. The position he held, military commander (*stratēgos*, often translated general), was as one of a body of ten equals, elected annually. Thus
he had to be reconfirmed as one of the commanders each year, but he was
able to use the position to maintain his sway over the city. Only Plutarch
speaks of fifteen consecutive years, and we do not know where he got the
figure. The reference to forty years in the preceding sentence would take
Pericles' prominence as statesman back to *c.*468, much earlier than many
modern historians would accept.

wise Anaxagoras: for Anaxagoras, cf. cc. 4–5.

161 *lofty principles*: this chapter of Plutarch is our only source for this important document, the so-called 'Congress Decree', whose authenticity, date,
and nature are subjects of continuing controversy. Those who accept the
decree as authentic usually place it in the early 440s, just before the Periclean
building programme gets under way. Whereas Thucydides reported
Pericles' speeches, especially the funeral oration (2. 35–46) to reveal his
vision for Athens, Plutarch chooses this decree, of whose panhellenic vision
he would have approved.

162 *Tolmides the son of Tolmaeus*: Tolmides was a general, famous for his expedition around the Peloponnese in 456/5 (Thuc. 1. 108). The root of
his and his father's name, *tolm-*, means 'daring', which perhaps reinforces
Plutarch's point.

162 *patriotism*: the Athenians after preliminary successes were defeated by the Boeotians at Coronea in 447 or 446, and thus lost control of Boeotia (Thuc. 1. 113).

borders: both the campaign and the settlement in the Hellespontine Chersonese (the Gallipoli peninsula) probably belong to 447 BC.

Megarian territory: this campaign in the Corinthian Gulf (not actually a circumnavigation of the Peloponnese) took place in 455 or 454: cf. Thuc. 1. 111.

after the fight: Greek armies regularly erected a trophy, or pile of captured armour, at the site of a victory, where the enemy had turned to flight.

163 *well-equipped fleet*: this expedition to the Black Sea, otherwise unrecorded, probably belongs to the 430s BC. It indicates an initiative in the area of which Thucydides and other writers are silent, although we know of extensive Athenian trade there.

enthusiasm: the first naval expedition to Egypt, in the 450s, ended in disaster (cf. Thuc. 1. 104, 109–10). Plutarch here may refer to Cimon's dispatch of ships to Egypt just before his death (*Cim*. 18, Thuc. 1. 112), or to another undocumented occasion.

colleagues: for the Athenian expedition against Sicily, which ended in disaster in 413, see *Nic*. 12–28, *Alc*. 17–19.

Phocians: Delphi was in the territory of Phocis, but received special treatment. This was probably in 448 BC. Cf. Thuc. 1. 112.

164 *same wolf*: Pausanias (10. 14. 7) says he saw this wolf near the great altar at Delphi. Plutarch, a priest at Delphi for many years, would have been familiar with it.

the Spartan king: for the revolts of Euboea and Megara, and the Spartan threat to Attica, all in 446 BC, Plutarch closely follows Thuc. 1. 114, supplemented with Ephorus' account of the bribe to Cleandridas. The loss of Euboea and the invasion made the moment extremely dangerous for Athens.

Sicily: for Gylippus in Sicily, see *Nic*. 19, 21, 26–8, and Thuc. 7.

Lysander: *Lys*. 16.

unsaid: Plutarch here thinks of the accounting given by each magistrate at Athens at the end of his term. The expression 'for necessities' was still remembered by Athenians years later: Aristophanes builds a joke on it in *Clouds* 858–9.

165 *Samos*: Samos, one of the strongest cities of the Delian League, revolted against Athens' domination in 440, and was put down in a hard-fought war which revealed Athens' strength and her willingness to use it: cf. below cc. 25–8 and Thuc. 1. 115–17.

at such length: Plutarch's chapter on Aspasia, though frustratingly patchy, is our fullest account of this fascinating woman. Her intelligence and relation to Pericles are central to works of several of the Socratic philosophers: Plato's *Menexenus*, in which Socrates purports to have learned from Aspasia a funeral speech she had written for Pericles, and two lost works, both entitled *Aspasia*, by Aeschines of Sphettus and by Antisthenes, contemporaries of Plato. As Plutarch shows, she was also mentioned in comedy. On Aspasia and her legend, see M. M. Henry, *Prisoner of History: Aspasia of Miletus and her Biographical Tradition* (Oxford and New York: Oxford University Press, 1995).

165 *prostitutes*: although many modern scholars disagree, Plutarch clearly did not consider Aspasia's activities respectable. He nevertheless tries to present her influence on Pericles under the two headings of political expertise and love. The nature of Pericles' legal relationship with Aspasia is uncertain. After the passage of his citizenship law (see c. 37), he could not have contracted a regular marriage with her, since she was not an Athenian citizen. Her role as an intelligent woman associated with an extremely powerful politician, in a society which did not encourage women to participate in public life, means that statements about her are very difficult to interpret.

time with her: Plato, *Menex*. 235e.

His wife: this woman remains anonymous, though some have suggested that she is Deinomache, mother of Alcibiades. The order of her marriages is difficult to fit with the estimated ages of her children, but Plutarch may be correct in saying that she married Hipponicus first.

166 *Hera*: Omphale was a legendary queen of Lydia, to whom Heracles was made subject as punishment: she made him work wool; Hera was the consort of Zeus. Pericles is alluded to in the figures of Heracles and Zeus.

sovereignty of Persia: Cyrus the younger, whose expedition against his brother King Artaxerxes is described by Xenophon in the first book of his *Anabasis*. Cf. *Alc*. 35, *Artax*. 2–8.

fought over Priene: Plutarch's account of the war is founded on Thuc. 1. 115–17, but with many additions. Miletus and Priene were on the mainland opposite Samos. Thucydides well brings out the gradual escalation as Athens reacts with more and more force to Samos' continuing opposition. An inscription (Fornara no. 113) preserves summaries of the Athenian expenses for the war.

167 *intercede for the city*: the Persian satrap at Sardis, whose territory was adjacent to Samos. A stater was a Persian coin: see Appendix.

Tragiae: modern Agathonisi, some 12 miles south of Samos.

Cyprus: the Phoenician fleet was the navy of the Persian empire, and might have been sent at the request of Pissouthnes; Thucydides notes that the Samians had also sent for them (1. 116). Stesimbrotus may have thought that Pericles would wait for the Phoenicians at Cyprus.

Aristotle . . . sea-battle: probably from Aristotle's lost *Constitution of the Samians*.

168 *letters*: tattooing (not branding, as frequently translated) was also employed by the Persians to mark rebels (Hdt. 7. 233), by the Syracusans on their

Athenian prisoners (*Nic.* 29), and by private masters for runaway slaves. Plutarch however seems to have reversed the fact: the Athenians would have tattooed the Samians with an owl, symbol of Athens, and the Samians would have retaliated with the samaena. Aristophanes' *Babylonians*, from which this line comes, is not preserved.

168 *in the meantime*: Samos surrendered in early 439, unusually quickly for such a strong city. Sources place the reparations as high as 1,200 talents.

169 *discredit the Athenians*: Plutarch may be right about Duris' prejudice against the Athenians, but the punishment described, exposure on a plank, was usual for traitors and a wide class of criminals. Cf. Hdt. 9. 120, and the fates of Prometheus in the *Prometheus Bound* and of Euripides' relative in Aristophanes' *Thesmophoriazusae*.

speech over their tombs: this speech was famous, Stesimbrotus (cf. c. 8) and Aristotle (*Rhetoric* 1. 7, 1365ª31–3) recall phrases.

perfume: Archilochus of Paros wrote strongly personal and frequently abusive iambic and elegiac poetry. Pericles suggests that Elpinice does not understand her position, and can no longer rely on her beauty to get her way.

Ionia: the comparison of a contemporary war with the Trojan War seems pretentious, but was a commonplace of poetry and history: cf. Hdt. 1. 4, Thuc. 1. 9–11, Xen. *Hell.* 3. 4. 3–4, and the newly discovered fragment of Simonides' elegy on the battle of Plataea. Cf. also *Ages.* 6, Agesilaus' sacrifice at Aulis.

control of the sea: Thuc. 8. 76.

170 *at war with them*: in 433 BC. Cf. Thuc. 1. 31–55; for Lacedaemonius, cf. Thuc. 1. 45, naming also the other two commanders sent with him, and the inscription giving the expenses of the squadron, Fornara no. 126.

aliens and foreigners: the names allude to respectively the states of Lacedaemon (Sparta), Thessaly, and Elis (but cf. *Cim.* 16 note).

too late for the battle: but in time to save the day for the Corcyraeans: cf. Thuc. 1. 50–1.

rapidly: for these complaints to the Spartans in 432, see Thuc. 1. 67.

171 *the sacred meadow*: a piece of land on the border of Megara and Athens, sacred to the goddesses Demeter and Persephone honoured at Eleusis.

responsible for his death: Plutarch's account of the circumstances of the decrees relating to Megara is unique, and depends on his use of a collection of decrees not otherwise cited. It is difficult to reconcile with the much less detailed account of Thucydides, for whom the so-called 'Megarian Decree', that is, the one blocking access to the harbours and agora of Athens, was just a pretext for the Spartans to open hostilities. Plutarch instead speaks of several decrees, of which this 'reasonable and courteous decree' is the first in time, presented in a flashback exploring the reasons for Pericles' intransigence. It is then followed, after Anthemocritus' death, by the Charinus Decree, which seems identical to Thucydides' Megarian Decree and to the one which the Megarians protested in Sparta (c. 29), though many scholars argue that the Charinus Decree is separate from and followed the 'Megarian Decree'.

171 *gate, which is now called the Double Gate*: this decree, declaring a state of hostility with Megara and forbidding Megarians to set foot on Attic soil, seems to be a fuller summary of Thucydides' Megarian Decree, enacted shortly before the meeting in Sparta in 432. The Spartans, however, did not decide at once to treat this as a rupture of the treaty and a cause of war between the Athenians and the Peloponnesian League. That at some point the Athenians began to invade Megara twice a year is clear from Thucydides 4. 66. Anthemocritus is not mentioned by Thucydides, but his tomb just outside the walls was a landmark: cf. the quote from the fourth century orator Isaeus in Harpocration s.v. Anthemocritus, and Pausanias 1. 36. 3.

Aspasia's whores: the Megarians (either Megarian historians, or contemporary Megarians) argue that the reason for the 'Megarian Decree' was not Anthemocritus' death, but Apsasia's whores, citing Aristophanes, *Acharnians* 524–7, part of the explanation that Dicaeopolis gives for the cause of the war.

strength: the first reason gives a paraphrase of what Thucydides ascribes to Pericles' first speech, 1. 140; the second is not found in any extant writer, although something similar is found in Plutarch, *Herodotus' Malice* 856a, 'wishing to reduce the sense of superiority of the Peloponnesians and yield in no way to the Spartans'.

172 *as follows*: this 'worst charge' combines the account of Ephorus (cf. Diodorus 12. 38–40) on the attacks against Phidias with other new material (the decree of immunity for Phidias' accuser and the indictments of c. 32). Phidias' trial presumably took place not long after the completion of the Parthenos statue in 438/7.

occasion in question: the gold and ivory plates of this kind of statue were attached to a wooden core, and so could be removed. It is doubtful that Pericles had thought it would be necessary to do so. The moulds for similar plates used on the statue of Zeus at Olympia have been found in Phidias' workshop there.

to discredit Pericles: in fact, Phidias seems to have gone to Olympia to work on the statue there, as traces in his workshop reveal and the Athenian historian Philochorus reports. Phidias apparently was condemned in spite of Pericles' defence, and had to flee from Athens.

to ensure his safety: apparently Plutarch had seen the decree moved by Glaucon granting Meno his privileges.

free-born women: some scholars doubt this prosecution, thinking instead Hermippus brought up the question in one of his plays, and later historians treated the matter as a fact. The charge of impiety may be based on Aspasia's purported profession of prostitute or procurer, since such persons were excluded from religious sanctuaries and rites.

173 *Anaxagoras*: again, Plutarch seems to have access to Diopithes' decree. This is important evidence for the religious climate at Athens, but hard to interpret. There were a number of stories in circulation about the trial of Anaxagoras in antiquity. The date is also in dispute, but it seems best to place it, as Plutarch does, in proximity to Phidias' trial. The wording of Diopithes' law is similar to the indictment of Socrates, although this may be because Plutarch is influenced by Plato's *Apology*.

Acropolis: the special procedure is meant to impress upon the jurors the sacred importance of their vote when there were strong reasons for not voting justly (cf. *Them.* 17).

feared him: this notice is a paraphrase of Thuc. 1. 127. 1. Now that Plutarch has finished treating the reasons for Pericles' intransigence over the Megarian Decree, he returns to Thucydides' narrative, picking up with the embassies before the war. On the curse on the Alcmaeonids, going back to Cylon's attempt to seize the tyranny in the seventh century, see *Sol.* 12.

estates to the city: cf. Thuc. 2. 13. In the parallel Life of Fabius Maximus, Hannibal causes trouble for Fabius by sparing his land while he ravaged the rest, *Fab.* 7.

Attica: in May 431 BC, cf. Thuc. 2. 19. The number of men that Plutarch gives, 60,000, is impossibly large.

174 *Assembly*: the generals had the authority to convene the Assembly for a crisis, but Pericles chose not to use it.

Hermippus show: Cleon became prominent after Pericles' death, urging on the war against the Peloponnesians until his death at Amphipolis in 422. Thucydides despised him as a demagogue; Aristophanes mocks his ranting, greed, and lack of scruples, especially in his *Knights*. Cf. *Nicias* 7 and 9. The comic poet Hermippus has the chorus address Pericles.

175 *all of it*: these actions are all in summer 431. Cf. Thuc. 2. 23, 25, 27, 30, 31.

relief: the plague hit Athens in spring 430. Cf. Thuc. 2. 47–54.

176 *philosophical schools*: according to Thucydides (2. 28) this eclipse actually occurred in Aug. 431, but Plutarch associates it with Pericles' command of 430, presumably because this combination fits better the story of the cloak. Plutarch knew that Anaxagoras had explained eclipses as shadows: cf. *Nic.* 23. It reinforces Plutarch's notion of Pericles as a rational leader.

the army: Plutarch conflates the campaign against Epidaurus led by Pericles with the subsequent reinforcement of the troops at the siege of Potidaea, which resulted in the spread of the plague to those forces: cf. Thuc. 2. 56, 58.

Heraclides of Pontus: Pericles was probably dismissed from office in late summer 430. Plutarch here supplements Thuc. 2. 65 from other writers.

a little at a time: on Pericles' stringent domestic regime, cf. c. 16.

177 *Xanthippus himself*: the story is mentioned already at the end of c. 13. Plutarch refuses to say more, leaving the details of Stesimbrotus' slander in silence.

178 *Athenians themselves*: this citizenship law was carried in 451/50, cf. Aristotle, *Athpol.* 26. 4. It established a standard qualification for citizenship, but also restricted the citizen body and separated it more sharply from foreigners, including the large number of resident aliens (metics) at Athens. Effectively, it meant that marriages with non-Athenians were no longer recognized as a means of begetting citizen children or continuing one's family. The motivation for the law is controversial: Aristotle speaks of the size of the citizen body; moderns of discouraging aristocratic alliances with families of other states, a desire for racial purity, or unwillingness to share the privileges and monetary rewards of empire—such as the grain distribution mentioned below.

the number . . . was 14,040: the grain distribution probably was in 445/4, as explained in ancient notes to Aristophanes, *Wasps* 718, which refers to a prosecution for being a non-citizen and falsely getting grain. The Egyptian king probably was hoping for Athenian help against the Persians. The number of people denied citizenship seems very large, but we have little to go on: this may have been an extremely emotional issue. Slavery was the normal penalty for pretending to be a citizen. A medimnus was about 52 litres; this would have been over 2,000 cubic metres or 60,000 bushels.

his phratry: the phratry was an association at Athens, intermediate between deme and tribe, united by real or fictitious kinship, religious ties, and civil duties. Membership in a phratry was considered evidence of citizenship.

Arginusae: in 406 BC: cf. Xen. *Hell.* 1. 6. 28–7. 35.

came and went: Plutarch's description suggests that it was not the plague at all, but another illness.

commander: on trophies, cf. c. 19 note.

179 *mourning clothes because of me*: Plutarch thus emphasizes Pericles' unwillingness to encourage factional fighting among the citizens. Many died in the wars he supported.

clearest possible light: a paraphrase of Homer's description of Olympus, *Od.* 6. 42–5.

NICIAS

184 *Philistus' account was*: on these three writers, see Nicias: Introduction.

Xenarchus: a Sicilian writer of farcical comedies.

Laomedon: Plutarch finds Timaeus' rhetorical attempt to give serious meaning to play on words and to myth disastrous stylistically. Nicias is derived from *nikē*, victory; the herms were pillars dedicated to Hermes, whose name is the base of Hermocrates and Hermon. Hermocrates was a Sicilian leader:

see cc. 16, 26, 28. Heracles went down to the underworld, of which Persephone (here called Core) was queen, to capture the dog Cerberus, and Persephone was a patron goddess of Sicily. Heracles was said to have sacked Troy, before the Trojan war (cf. Homer, *Il.* 5. 639–43), when King Laomedon refused to pay him for ridding his land of a monster. For Segesta's request for aid, see c. 12. Note that Plutarch presumes that his readers are familiar with the story of the Sicilian expedition.

185 *unnoticed by most people*: cf. Nicias: Introduction.

Theramenes the son of Hagnon: this judgement is found in Aristotle, *Athpol.* 28. 5, who restricts it to 'those after the older ones', that is after Cimon. The three were leaders who appealed to the élite more than the populace. Note that Plutarch gives no account of Nicias' life prior to entering politics, presumably because he had no information. On Thucydides son of Melesias (not the historian), see *Per.* 8, 11, 14.

Buskin: a large boot, worn by tragic actors, which could be worn on either foot, and thus a fitting nickname for a fence-straddler. Theramenes was a major figure in the oligarchic revolution of 411 and in the reign of the Thirty in 404/3; he was executed by the Thirty in 403.

ambitions too: Pericles died in 429 BC. Cleon rapidly emerged as a powerful popular leader, despised by the Athenian élite, mocked viciously by Aristophanes in his *Knights*, and made a villain by Thucydides. For his opposition to Nicias, see cc. 7–8.

informers: men who took advantage of the law permitting any individual to prosecute wrongdoing (cf. *Sol.* c. 18) to harass prominent figures, for financial or political gain.

186 *specious rhetoric*: cf. *Per.* 8, 15, Thuc. 2. 65.

impresario: the Palladium was a small statue of Athena; the shrine apparently served as a base for the tripods, which Nicias had won as a producer of choral or dramatic contests. However, an inscription tells us that the shrine under the tripods was built in 320/19 by another Nicias. The duty of paying the expenses of a dramatic or musical production was one of the most significant expenses of a wealthy citizen. The following passage gives an idea of the expenses which might be incurred in another kind of civic service, support for a chorus sent to Delos, an island in the Aegean sacred to Apollo.

not wide: about 700 m.

187 *addicted to divination*: Thuc. 7. 50. 4.

in silver coin: the silver mines at Laurium were an important source of wealth for Athens: Themistocles had used the money from one strike to build up the Athenian navy (*Them.* 4). They were let out to be worked to private entrepreneurs like Nicias: Xenophon, *Ways and Means* 4. 14 says that he had 1,000 slaves that he rented for work in the mines, rendering 10 talents per year. Plutarch probably is mistaken in saying that Nicias actually owned mines.

188 *upset Nicias*: *Knights* 358.

state matters: cf. also Pericles' dedication to state business over personal, *Per.* 7.

founded Thurii: little else is known of this Hiero. His father Dionysius was a politician and elegiac poet, and helped found Thurii *c*.443 BC.

189 *slave to the rabble*: Euripides, *Iphigeneia in Aulis* 449–50. The quotation encapsulates an important aspect of Plutarch's interpretation of Nicias.

killed himself: Pericles was fined and deposed from office in 430 (*Per.* 35, Thuc. 2. 65); Damon was ostracized as a friend of Pericles (*Per.* 4). Antiphon was condemned to death after the revolution of 411 (Thuc. 8. 68. 2); Paches, who retook Mytilene in 427 after its revolt, committed suicide in court (cf. *Aristid.* 26). This is one of several lists of outstanding leaders who fell foul of the democracy. Plutarch does not mention the three generals who arranged a treaty in Sicily in 424: on their return two were exiled, and the third fined (Thuc. 4. 65).

190 *unfamiliar way of life*: Callias and Xenophon were defeated in 430 BC (Thuc. 2. 79); Hippocrates in 424 (Thuc. 4. 100–1; Plato says Socrates and Alcibiades were present at Delium, *Symp.* 220d–221a). For Pericles and the plague, cf. *Per.* 34–5, Thuc. 2. 65.

commander, Lycophron: Nicias captured Cythera in 424 (cf. Thuc. 4. 53–4); the Thracian towns in 423 (cf. Thuc. 4. 129–31); Minoa in 427 (cf. Thuc. 3. 51). Plutarch misunderstands Thucydides and thinks that Nisaea was taken at the same time: in fact it fell in 424 to Hippocrates and Demosthenes: cf. Thuc. 4. 66. Nicias defeated the Corinthians in 425: cf. Thuc. 4. 42–4. Plutarch orders the victories by importance, not chronology, and omits the less significant campaign of Nicias against Melos, Locris, and Tanagra in 426 (Thuc. 3. 91).

citizens unburied: Thucydides mentions sending for the two bodies, but not the implications of the request. Plutarch saves the item which reveals character for last.

back alive to Athens: the Aeginetans who had been expelled by the Athenians from Aegina in 431 (cf. *Per.* 34) were settled at Thyrea, on the border between Laconia and Argos. Nicias took it in 424: Thuc. 4. 56–7.

island of Sphacteria: in 425 some Spartans were trapped on the island of Sphacteria, which closes the bay of Pylos or Navarino on the west coast of the Peloponnese: cf. Thuc. 4. 3–23, 26–7.

191 *angry with Cleon*: the negotiations with Sparta are described in Thuc. 4. 17–23; the Athenian discontent in Thuc. 4. 27.

good joke: cf. Thuc. 4. 28.

survived the battle: 292 hoplites were captured, including about 120 Spartiates. Cf. Thuc. 4. 29–41.

192 *procrastiniciating*: Aristophanes, *Birds* 639–40, where the word *mellonikian* plays on Nicias' name. The *Farmers* no longer survives.

192 *while speaking*: cf. Aristotle, *Athpol*. 28. 3: 'Cleon . . . seems especially to have corrupted the populace with his energy, and was the first to shout on the rostrum and abuse his opponents and speak with his cloak wrapped around his waist.' Plutarch remarks on the similar behaviour of Gaius Gracchus, *Gracch*. 2.

all together: Homer, *Od*. 4. 230.

Alcibiades' ambition: Alcibiades was a dynamic young politician: see his Life in this volume. For what follows, cf. *Alc*. 14 ff.

193 *in a single battle*: in October 422, cf. Thuc. 5. 10. Brasidas was a Spartan general.

webs around: from Euripides' lost *Erechtheus*.

peace treaty: in April 421. Cf. Thuc. 5. 17–19, where the text of the treaty is given. Nicias is one of those swearing the oath for Athens. The reference to 'thrice nine years' recalls Thuc. 5. 26. 4. The peace in fact broke down in 414, and the war went on to 404, twenty-seven years after it began in 431.

194 *each other*: the Corinthians and Boeotians refused to sign the treaty. The alliance between Athens and Sparta was concluded soon after the peace: cf. Thuc. 5. 22–4.

Amphipolis at all: cf. Thuc. 5. 35, 39. Panactum and Amphipolis had been captured from Athens by the Peloponnesians.

double-crossed them: the story also in *Alc*. 14 and Thuc. 5. 43–6. The Council (cf. *Sol*. 19 note) heard ambassadors before presenting them to the Assembly.

195 *friends and relatives*: cf. Thuc. 5. 15.

state of war: Plutarch strongly compresses Thucydides' narrative. Thucydides reports the treaty with Argos, Mantinea, and Elis (also partially preserved on stone) at 5. 47, Alcibiades' election as general for 419/18 at 5. 52, and the attacks on Laconia from Pylos (in 416) at 5. 115; but the Spartans openly resumed the war only in 414 (6. 105). Mantinea and Elis had been members of Sparta's Peloponnesian League.

set in motion: this vote for ostracism probably took place in 417. The story is also told in *Alc*. 13. On ostracism, see also *Them*. 5 note. Plutarch here emphasizes the social rather than the political aspect of the process.

196 *become respectable*: a favourite proverb of Plutarch's, quoted also at *Alex*. 53, *Sulla* 39, and *On Brotherly Love* 479a.

tattoos deserved: runaway slaves were sometimes marked with tattoos: cf. *Per*. 26.

197 *the first*: Hipparchus was a relative of the tyrant Hippias, perhaps his grandson. Cf. Aristotle, *Athpol*. 22. 4, who correctly gives Hipparchus' deme as Collytus, not Cholargus.

majority of my sources: cf. on Phaeax, a minor politician, also *Alc*. 13. We have ostraca with Phaeax's name, so he may have also been a 'candidate' at the ostracism.

197 *ambitious designs*: for Athenian interest in Sicily and the debate in spring 415 leading to the decision to send an expedition, see Thuc. 6. 1–26 and *Alc.* 17–18. Two Sicilian cities, Segesta and Leontini (allies of Athens), asked that Athens intervene in the island: Athens accepted, with the ambition of conquering the whole island, including its chief city Syracuse. The exact dates of the departure of the expedition are disputed: it may have set sail in early June, and arrived in Sicily in late July of 415.

as his colleagues: Lamachus was an experienced, much older commander. Commander-in-chief is not correct: the commanders were equal colleagues.

198 *any more excuses*: Demostratus is not mentioned in Thuc. 6. 26, but his role in the debate is mentioned by Aristophanes, *Lysistrata* 391–6. Plutarch may have seen the text of the decree moved by him, in the collection of Craterus or another source.

shrine of Ammon: at the oasis of Siwah, in Egypt: cf. *Alex.* 26–7.

Andocides' house: the shock to the city caused by the mutilation of the herms (stone pillars fitted with an erect phallus and sacred to Hermes), which stood at street corners and the entrances to houses, is described by Thucydides, 6. 27–9, 60–2 cf. *Alc.* 18. Alcibiades was thought by many to be one of those responsible: cf. *Alc.* 18–20. The orator Andocides was involved in the affair: cf. *Alc.* 21 and his speech *On the Mysteries*. Both Thuc. 6. 27 and *Alc.* 18 speak of violence to the *prosopa*, faces, but a joke in Aristophanes, *Lysistrata* 1094, indicates that many phalluses were broken off.

199 *Meton the astronomer*: Meton was known for calculating a nineteen-year cycle which could regularize the relation between the solar year and the lunar months.

became widely known: Socrates' sign, which warned him not to do things, is described in Plato's *Apology*. The stories of Socrates and Meton are also found at *Alc.* 17, but are not otherwise known.

mourning over them: at this festival the women mourned for Adonis (the young man beloved by Aphrodite who was struck down in his youth), so that the resolution to send the army was punctuated by the women's cries and laments from the rooftops: cf. Aristophanes, *Lysistrata* 387–98.

200 *lowered their morale*: Plutarch summarizes the generals' discussion once they arrived at Rhegium in Italy (Reggio Calabria), cf. Thuc. 6. 47–9, but adds his own harsh judgement of Nicias' behaviour.

in sole command: Alcibiades was recalled to stand trial for his alleged participation in the mutilation of the herms, perhaps in early August 415: cf. *Alc.* 20, Thuc. 6. 53. Thucydides does not mention Lamachus again until his death in the next year, 6. 101.

return home: cf. Thuc. 6. 50. 4. The following episode of the citizen tablets is found only in Plutarch, and is presumably from Philistus.

control of Syracuse: in 354 BC: cf. Plut. *Dion* 54–7.

201 *to the Peloponnese*: for the Sicilian towns of Hybla and Hyccara: cf. Thuc. 6. 62. Catana (modern Catania) served as a base for the attack on Syracuse. Laïs became a famous courtesan at Corinth: cf. *Alc.* 39.

he could rely on: cf. Thuc. 6. 64–6.

202 *Hermocrates*: the leader of the Syracusan forces.

to Naxos: another city on the east coast of Sicily.

to the ground: cf. Thuc. 6. 75. 2. The Sicels were the indigenous people of Sicily, most of whom lived inland.

203 *invincible*: cf. Thuc. 6. 97. The Epipolae is a plateau overlooking the old city of Syracuse on the north-west; it was captured in summer 414.

that was left undone: cf. Thuc. 6. 98. Thucydides refers to Nicias' kidney ailment at 7. 15. 1.

204 *Syracusans pulled back*: cf. Thuc. 6. 101–2. Thucydides mentions Lamachus' death, but not the fight with Callicrates, which might come from Philistus.

defeated in battle: Gylippus had been sent by the Spartans on the advice of Alcibiades: cf. *Alc.* 23 and Thuc. 6. 93.

enjoying at the time: Plutarch says that Crassus showed an equally uncharacteristic boastful self-assurance after receiving the province of Syria, from which he expected to launch his Parthian campaign (*Cras.* 16).

a sizeable army: Gylippus landed first at Himera, on the north coast of Sicily, and after collecting an army, arrived in Syracuse in late summer 414 (Thuc. 7. 1–3).

205 *to the Lacedaemonians*: the Athenians refer to the prisoners from Pylos, c. 8. The plain cloak (*tribōn*) was the usual Spartan dress (cf. *Lyc.* 30); the staff a symbol of office. Spartan men, unlike the other Greeks, wore their hair long (cf. *Lyc.* 22).

like birds to an owl: a proverb: smaller birds will attack an owl when it is seen in daylight.

at first hand: on the three historians, see Nicias: Introduction.

206 *no good to win a battle*: Gylippus' wall cut across the Athenian one, so that the Athenians could no longer surround the city with their wall: cf. Thuc. 7. 5–6, 11.

grounds of ill health: cf. the letter of Nicias to the Athenians in Thuc. 7. 11–15, written in the winter of 414–413.

command with him: Demosthenes was a highly successful commander, active also at Pylos (cf. c. 7), the others were experienced leaders. Cf. Thuc. 7. 16.

at anchor there: cf. Thuc. 7. 4. 4: 'Plemmyrium is the promontory opposite the city, which by sticking out makes the mouth of the large harbour narrow, and if it should be fortified, Nicias thought the transport of supplies would be easier.' It was captured by the Athenians after the arrival of Gylippus, and lost in the first half of summer 413.

207 *colleagues' mistakes*: in this famous episode, Thuc. 7. 39–40, the Syracusans tricked the Athenian sailors into beaching their ships and dispersing for their meal, then attacked them unawares.

strike fear into the enemy: Demosthenes arrived in July 413.

sail back home to Athens: for Demosthenes' reasoning, cf. Thuc. 7. 42. 1–5.

208 *night attack on Epipolae*: the attack is described in a memorable and moving passage by Thucydides, 7. 42. 6–45.

209 *recommendation*: cf. the conference of generals in Thuc. 7. 47–9.

210 *lunar eclipse one night*: cf. Thuc. 7. 50. 4. The eclipse took place 27 August 413.

some major disaster or other: a solar eclipse must occur at the new moon, that is at the end of the lunar month; a lunar eclipse always occurs at the full moon, in the middle of the month. At *Per.* 35, Pericles explains a solar eclipse to astonished sailors.

Anaxagoras: the philosopher and adviser to Pericles: cf. *Per.* 4.

drove out the tyrant: Dion expelled the tyrant Dionysius in 357. Cf. *Dion* 24.

211 *cast a shadow*: both Philochorus and Autocleides were experts on religious matters. According to Thuc. 7. 50. 4, the seers with the expedition had recommended waiting for twenty-seven days.

with their fleet: cf. Thuc. 7. 51–4. The fortifications were those on the Epipolae.

Eurymedon: Eurymedon died in the second battle in the harbour: cf. Thuc. 7. 52. 2. The story of Heraclides and Pollichus is found only in Plutarch. The source is presumably Sicilian, either Philistus or Timaeus. The reference to Heracles here and below (the temple of Heracles) favour Timaeus (cf. c. 1).

closed it off: cf. Thuc. 7. 59. 3.

temple of Heracles: this temple, and the walls which connected it to the Athenian camp, are not mentioned by Thucydides. The 110 triremes and the abandonment of the upper fortification is found in Thuc. 7. 60. 3–4; the troops stationed along the shore at 7. 69. 3. All this is preparation for the third or great battle in the harbour.

212 *launched their fleet*: again, as with the night battle on Epipolae, Plutarch is acutely aware that in describing the great battle in the harbour he is paraphrasing one of the most dramatic passages in Thucydides (7. 69–71).

gain the upper hand: Ariston of Corinth (cf. c. 20) is not mentioned by Thucydides in connection with this battle.

213 *without a battle*: cf. Thuc. 7. 73–4.

on their behalf: cf. Thuc. 7. 75.

214 *took him prisoner*: cf. Thuc. 7. 81–2. Thucydides does not mention either the estate of Polyzelus or Demosthenes' attempt at suicide.

trying to take a drink: cf. Thuc. 7. 83–4. The Asinarus river is the modern Assinaro or Fiumara di Noto, approximately 28 km. (17 miles) south of Syracuse.

215 *Syracusan soldiers*: cf. Thuc. 7. 85. It is noteworthy that Plutarch puts in Nicias' mouth his appeal to Gylippus, but not the speeches given him by Thucydides at 7. 77, nor indeed does he quote directly any of the other of Nicias' speeches in Thucydides. The words emphasize Nicias' abject surrender, which is criticized in *Comparison* 5. Here, however, Nicias' words also recall his own past glory, the Athenians' (and his) generous treatment of the Spartans, and the mutability of fortune.

taken from the enemy: this full description is not found in Thuc. 7. 86.

Greeks against Greeks: cf. Thuc. 7. 87. 5: 'This action was the greatest of this war, and in my opinion the greatest of which we hear in Greek history: to the conquerors the most remarkable, and to those destroyed the most unfortunate, for they were defeated utterly and completely, their sufferings were enormous and their loss total; soldiers, navy, everything were destroyed, and from many, only a few returned.'

Metageitnion: we do not know the precise count of days from the eclipse (cf. c. 23), which would have occurred in the middle of the lunar month. This date would be either about eleven days later, or 41 days later, so that the date in current reckoning would be 7 September or 7 October, 413. But lunar months were subject to modification, so the date remains uncertain. This information and most of the rest of the chapter is not in Thucydides.

Life of Lysander: cf. *Lys.* 16; *Per.* 22.

Philistus and Thucydides say: Thuc. 7. 86. Suicide would have been a more acceptable death. At his death, Thucydides writes: 'He was the least worthy of the Greeks of my time to come to such ill fortune, since his whole way of life was directed toward what is considered excellence.' Given the facts of Nicias' life, the meaning of this phrase has been much disputed. It is best however, not to take it as irony, but as a regret for the unseemly death of an admirable man.

216 *one of water*: i.e. about a ½ litre of barley, and a ¼ litre of water.

sold into slavery: for such tattooing, cf. also *Per.* 26. The horse was an emblem of Syracuse.

some of his songs: this story of the popularity of Euripides' songs makes a strange parallel with the ending of the *Crassus* (33), in which Crassus' severed head is used to represent the head of the dead Pentheus in a performance of Euripides' *Bacchae*.

beach their ship: Caunus is a city on the south-west corner of Asia Minor, and was tributary to Athens in the fifth century.

ALCIBIADES

222 *became his guardians*: Ajax was the Trojan war hero, from Salamis, from whom the Eupatrids, Alcibiades' father's family, traced descent (cf. Plato, *Alc. 1.* 121a–b, Deinomache is named at 105d, 123c). The Cleinias who fought at Artemisium (cf. Hdt. 8. 17) was probably not Alcibiades' father but his great uncle, since the two battles were thirty-three years apart. His father Cleinias died at Coronea in 447 or 446 (cf. *Per.* 18). For the Alcmaeonid family, to which Pericles also belonged through his mother Agariste, see notes to *Per.* 3 and 33. The exact relation of Deinomache to Agariste, and thus of Pericles to Alcibiades, is uncertain: Agariste may have been Deinomache's aunt, and Pericles her first cousin.

Plato the second: Alcibiades figured in several Platonic dialogues as well as those by other Socratics, such as Xenophon and Antisthenes. Zopyrus, the slave companion who took him to school, is mentioned by Plato in *Alc. 1.* 122b; the work of Antisthenes is not preserved. His wife's name was Hipparete: cf. c. 8. The men named are all distinguished generals: Nicias, Lamachus, and Demosthenes fought in Sicily, and Thrasybulus and Theramenes in the Aegean. Phormio belongs to an earlier period: he was a general at Potidaea and in the Gulf of Corinth, and probably died *c*.428.

got that right: Aristophanes, *Wasps* 44–6. Alcibiades said *kolax* for *korax*, i.e. flatterer for raven. The following quote is from the fifth-century comic writer Archippus, whose plays are now lost.

223 *noble and free birth*: this refusal is mentioned by Plato, *Alc. 1.* 106e.

flayed the piper: well-born Thebans played the pipes: cf. Ismenias of Thebes (*Per.* 1). Athena, according to the story, rejected the pipes because they made her cheeks puff out and look ugly; Marsyas the satyr, a piper, challenged Apollo to a contest: when he lost, Apollo flayed him.

224 *stories about Alcibiades*: this work is not extant, and it is unclear whether it belongs to Antiphon of Rhamnous, the orator and politician admired by Thucydides (cf. Thuc. 8. 68), or the sophist of the same name, if they are indeed different people.

aptitude for virtue: in upper-class Athenian society, it was the custom for an older man to court a handsome youth, until the boy grew up, cf. *Sol.* 1, *Them.* 3. For Sparta, cf. *Lyc.* 18, and *Agesilaus*; for later times, *Cim.* 1. The relation was unequal, the man being the lover, the youth the beloved, and was expected to include a physical relationship. Alcibiades' beauty made him particularly desirable, but Plutarch, like Plato, presumes that Socrates is interested only in his soul, unlike his other lovers.

reasoned argument: this is a neat expression of one aspect of the programme of Plutarch's *Lives*: to penetrate the barriers of luxury, distraction, and ambition which keep his readers from applying philosophy to their lives.

225 *with wing aslant*: the image is drawn from cockfighting; the line is quoted from one of two poets named Phrynichus, either the tragedian or the comic poet. The comic poet is cited at c. 20.

225 *free from corruption*: Plutarch alludes to the indictment against Socrates, that he did not honour the gods of the city, introduced new gods, and corrupted the youth. In c. 6, Plutarch will note that it is really his flatterers who corrupt Alcibiades, not Socrates.

rest of his lovers: Plato, *Phaedrus* 255d. He is said to have shared Socrates' tent at Potidaea: cf. c. 7.

Anytus the son of Anthemion: Anytus was a politician active in the restoration of the democracy in 403, and one of the prosecutors of Socrates in 399.

half of them: Athenaeus 534e ascribes the same anecdote to the third-century biographer Satyrus, who adds that Alcibiades then gave the silver to a friend in need, Thrasyllus.

resident alien: Athens welcomed foreign merchants and artisans as a means of strengthening the economy (cf. *Sol.* 24). However, in the fifth century they were not allowed to become Athenian citizens, but remained resident aliens (or metics), under the patronage of an Athenian. Here Alcibiades seems to take on the role of patron for this alien.

outbid everyone else: there is a version of this story also in Proclus, *On Plato's Alc.* 1. 110. The rights to collect certain taxes, including the tax on metics, were farmed out by a board of magistrates, the *polētai*: cf. *Athpol.* 47. On the battle for bids, cf. Andocides, *On the Mysteries* 133–4, where Andocides takes credit for bidding 36 against the tax farmers' 30 talents.

226 *helped this man, at any rate*: the man offered Alcibiades 100 staters or 200 drachmas; he came away with a talent, that is 6,000 drachmas. Proclus says the profit was 10 talents on 100 drachmas.

stomach, genitals, and throat: Cleanthes, a leading third-century Stoic philosopher, refers to the same problem in teaching young men that Socrates had: the counter-influence of food, sex, and wine.

attributes to him: Thuc. 6. 15, the famous passage where Thucydides analyses the effect of Alcibiades' lifestyle on his political role: see Alcibiades: Introduction and c. 16.

far ... from virtue: the whole chapter is very much influenced in language and thought by the speech of Alcibiades about his love for Socrates in Plato, *Symposium*, esp. 215e–216b, as well as by Plato's *Alc.* 1. Cf. D. A. Russell, 'Plutarch, *Alcibiades* 1–16', in B. Scardigli (ed.), *Essays on Plutarch's Lives* (Oxford: Clarendon Press, 1995), 196–7.

227 *teaching young men*: Homer was considered the basis of Greek education, and to contain all the values important to live a noble life.

give such an account: this story is regularly connected with the account of why Pericles started the Peloponnesian War: cf. Diodorus 12. 38. Alcibiades would have been quite young, about 13 or 14: but the anecdote is surely apocryphal.

suit of armour: the campaign against Potidaea was at the beginning of the Peloponnesian War, 432–430, cf. Thuc. 1. 56–66, 2. 58, 70; this battle was apparently that described in Thuc. 1. 62–3. The story is given by Plato at *Symposium* 220de, part of Alcibiades' speech in praise of Socrates. However, the description of the award (the garland and suit of armour) appears only in an oration of Isocrates (16. 29). Socrates' presence at the battle is also mentioned in Plato, *Charmides* 153a–c. Alcibiades would have been 20 or a bit more.

227 *when he was older*: the Athenians were defeated by the Boeotians at Delium on the Boeotian frontier in 424 (Thuc. 4. 96–7). The story is told by Alcibiades at Plato, *Symposium* 221a, and was referred to by Antisthenes, and Socrates' brave presence was recalled also by Plato at *Laches* 181b. However, the historicity of these exploits of Socrates with Alcibiades reported in philosophic dialogue was questioned even in antiquity (Athenaeus 5. 215c–216c).

his daughter Hipparete: Hipponicus and his son Callias were among the richest men in Athens; Hipponicus had died sometime before 421, perhaps at Delium in 424, as stated in pseudo-Andocides, 4 (*Against Alcibiades*) 13.

228 *dying without offspring*: cf. pseudo-Andocides 4. 13–14.

away from him: cf. pseudo-Andocides 4. 15.

restraining her: for some of Plutarch's ideas on Athens' marriage laws, cf. *Sol.* 20. In his *Advice on Marriage* he urged harmonious and caring relations between husband and wife, and he disapproved of divorce and second marriages (ibid. 144a).

seventy minas: i.e. 7,000 drachmas or over a talent: a very large sum. The source of the anecdote is unknown.

229 *a great deal*: citizens were occasionally asked to make voluntary donations to the polis. Proclus in his commentary on Plato's *Alc.* 1. 110 says the sum contributed was ten talents, 'when he was still a child'. Quails were used as love-gifts and as fighting animals; Plutarch recalls the story also at *Rules for Politicians* 799d. Antiochus later misused Alcibiades' trust at the battle of Notium (c. 35). The source of this anecdote also is unknown.

skill at speaking: Demosthenes 21. 145.

achieved in these games: Thuc. 6. 16. 2, cf. Isocrates 16. 34. Horse-raising was quite expensive, and chariot racing a royal sport; famous competitors were the Sicilian tyrants Hiero and Gelon, for example. Earlier, Cimon the son of Stesagoras had won fame for owning an extraordinary team which won three Olympic victories in three consecutive games. Alcibiades pursued this sport, like everything else, in the grand style. For a contrasting view of the importance of such victories, see *Ages.* 20.

town-crier: Plutarch again cites this victory song at *Dem.* 1, where he questions whether it is actually by Euripides.

230 *numbers of guests*: these arrangements, reported also in pseudo-Andocides 4. 30 and Athenaeus 12. 534d, were for the Olympic Games.

230 *Diomedes*: on the Diomedes incident, cf. pseudo-Andocides 4. 26, Diodorus
13. 74 (neither of which mention Argos). The team which Alcibiades bought
from Argos was described in Isocrates' speech *On the Team* (no. 16), where
Tisias is the plaintiff and sues Alcibiades' son, arguing that Alcibiades robbed
him of the team: it is possible that Tisias is Diomedes' son or had some
other relation to the quarrel. It seems unlikely that Plutarch has confounded
two separate cases.

a young adult: the account of the ostracism which follows is usually dated
to 417, so Alcibiades would have been roughly 33. Nicias was about
60. The story of Hyperbolus' ostracism is told with slightly more detail
in *Nic.* 11; cf. the text and notes there.

as if they were his own: the speech is evidently pseudo-Andocides 4: this
item is found at 4. 29.

of little worth: cf. Thuc. 8. 73.

231 *I have written . . . into this business*: i.e. in *Nic.* 11.

affection for him: the desire to recover the Spartan citizens who had been
captured at Pylos in 424 (cf. *Nicias* 8) was a major impetus to Sparta to
negotiate a peace. On Alcibiades' efforts, cf. Thuc. 5. 43. 2; on Nicias being
largely responsible for the peace cf. Thuc. 5. 43. 2 and 46. 4, and *Nic.* 9–10.

232 *unless the Lacedaemonians approved*: these attacks on Nicias are not docu-
mented in Thucydides or elsewhere, and probably represent Plutarch's
amplification based on what he thought Alcibiades would have said.

233 *had taken place*: on these negotiations of 420, cf. Thuc. 5. 42–5, *Nic.* 10.
Plutarch transfers Alcibiades' words to the Spartans from indirect to direct
speech. Here Plutarch omits the earthquake which delayed the decision
for a day, which was reported in *Nic.* 10 and Thuc. 5. 45: the focus is on
Alcibiades' success, not Nicias' efforts. In *Nic.* 10, the incident was placed
before Hyperbolus' ostracism.

Argos, Mantinea, and Elis: cf. Thuc. 5. 46–7. The alliance was made in
420; we possess a fragment of an inscribed text of the decree. Thucydides
first mentions Alcibiades as general at 5. 52, 419 BC.

would have been precarious: the Spartans won the battle of Mantinea in 418:
cf. Thuc. 5. 66–74.

did for his state: for the change of government in Argos and their treaty
with Sparta in winter 418–417, cf. Thuc. 76–81. For the re-establishment
of the democracy in the following summer, though with no mention of
Alcibiades, cf. Thuc. 5. 81–2. Alcibiades is mentioned as helping Argos
in summer 416 (Thuc. 5. 84).

234 *all at once*: cf. Thuc. 5. 52, for 419, though without the anecdote.

as their own: a fourth-century inscription containing a version of this
'Oath of the ephebes' has been discovered: M. N. Tod, *Greek Historical
Inscriptions*, ii (1948), 204. At the end is a list of gods they were to
swear by, followed by 'boundaries of the fatherland, wheat, barley, vines,

olive-trees, fig-trees'. Plutarch (like Cicero, *De republica* 3. 15) interprets the plants as in apposition with 'boundaries', defining them. This understanding is not accepted by modern scholars, but apparently was common in antiquity. These young men, called *ephēboi*, were between 18 and 20, just come of age, and training to be soldiers.

234 *tyrannical in its excessiveness*: cf. Thuc. 6. 15. 4: 'For most people became frightened at a quality in him which was beyond the normal and showed itself both in the lawlessness of his private life and habits and in the spirit in which he acted on all occasions. They thought that he was aiming at becoming a dictator, and so they turned against him' (trans. Warner). Plutarch changes Thucydides' 'most people' to 'the notable men', whom he opposes to the 'common people' who follow.

his moods: from Aristophanes' *Frogs*, produced in 405 when Alcibiades was in exile for the second time. First Euripides, in the underworld, explains how Athens feels about Alcibiades (1425), then Aeschylus answers the question, what Athens should do with him (1432–3).

extravaganzas he put on for the city: wealthy Athenians were regularly required to put on dramatic and choral productions and other public celebrations, called liturgies: the more generous and ambitious would spend freely on these to win favour. Cf. Nicias' religious embassy to Delos, *Nic.* 3.

235 *support of the decree*: the island of Melos had been besieged and destroyed in 416 for refusing to join the Athenian empire. The adult males were killed and the women and children sold into slavery (Thuc. 5. 116). Thucydides' depiction of the debate between Melians and Athenians before the siege is a powerful study of imperialism and foolhardiness, Thuc. 5. 85–114. The three anecdotes of Agatharchus, Taureas, and the Melian woman are told in the same order by pseudo-Andocides, *Against Alcibiades* 17, 20, 22.

two Alcibiadeses: at *Lysander* 19, Plutarch says that this comment is reported by Theophrastus. This Archestratus is probably the commander at Potidaea in 431, cf. Thuc. 1. 57. 6.

the more harm you'll do this lot: Timon was a famous misanthrope, mentioned by Aristophanes (*Birds* 1509, *Lysistrata* 809–15), and briefly sketched by Plutarch in *Antony* 70.

larger expedition: cf. *Per.* 20 and the expedition of 427–424 described in Thuc. 3 and 4.

236 *Libya and Carthage*: Plutarch artfully summarizes in a few sentences Thucydides' account of Athenian interest in Sicily, the debate between Nicias and Alcibiades, and Athenian eagerness to sail (cf. Thuc. 6. 6–24), treated in more detail in *Nic.* 12.

getting his way: on Socrates and Meton, cf. *Nic.* 13. Socrates' refusal to participate in the expedition suggests his own rejection of Alcibiades' aims.

about the whole war: cf. Thuc. 6. 25–6, *Nic.* 12.

237 *indifferent to such things*: on this mass mutilation, which greatly disturbed the Athenians, see *Nic.* 13, Thuc. 6. 27.

nominated as Initiates: Thuc. 8. 65. 2 names Androcles as one of the prime instigators of Alcibiades' banishment. The mystery cult of Demeter and Persephone at Eleusis was a major feature of Athenian religious life, and consisted of sacred rites, open to initiates, which promised happiness after death. They were not to be revealed to others.

the two goddesses: Thessalus is the son of the general Cimon, subject of the Life in this volume. His indictment, which was brought only after Alcibiades sailed for Sicily, is quoted in c. 22. The two goddesses are Demeter and Persephone.

defend himself: on these hoplites, cf. Thuc. 6. 29. 3 and 61. 5.

238 *water-clocks*: speeches before a court were limited in duration, and timed by water-clocks. Cf. the photos of a pot used as such a clock, found in the Athenian agora, in M. Lang, *The Athenian Citizen* (Princeton: American School of Classical Studies, Agora Picture Book no. 4, 1960), and J. Camps, *The Athenian Agora Guide*, 4th edn. (1990), 244–5. This clock ran for about six minutes.

laid against him: cf. Thuc. 6. 29. Plutarch has dramatized the scene, putting the words of Alcibiades' opponents in direct speech.

light-armed troops: Plutarch gives the round figures not for when they sailed (Thuc. 6. 31), but when all the forces united at Corcyra (6. 43). For the course of the expedition before Alcibiades was recalled, see also *Nic.* 14.

to stand trial: cf. Thuc. 6. 47–52.

239 *Diocleides and Teucer*: our source for these two, besides Plutarch, is the speech of Andocides, *On the Mysteries*, esp. 35, 37–9.

last day of the month: since the Attic calendar followed the moon, the last day of the month was always the new moon, and therefore dark. Andocides *Myst.* 38 gives this man as Diocleides. The contradiction noted by Plutarch is also reported by Diodorus, 13. 2. 3–4. Some scholars (e.g. K. J. Dover, *Historical Commentary to Thucydides* (Oxford: Clarendon Press, 1970), iv. 275) reject this as applying to the parody of the mysteries, not the mutilation of the herms, and think that the night was a full moon.

inscription it bears: cf. Andocides, *Myst.* 62. Plutarch may well have seen this herm.

240 *some of his own slaves*: cf. Thuc. 6. 60 and Andocides, *Myst.* 48 ff., where, however, the man urging this action to Andocides is his nephew Charmides, not this Timaeus, who is otherwise unknown. Andocides' conduct invites comparison with that of Alcibiades.

dropped with his departure: the *Salaminia* was one of two special ships used on state business: cf. also *Per.* 7. For the request to return and worries about morale, cf. Thuc. 6. 53, 61. 4–5.

240 *standing and authority*: the course of the Sicilian war after Alcibiades' departure is treated in *Nic.* 15–27.

escape his pursuers: Messana: Thuc. 6. 74. 1; Thurii: Thuc. 6. 61–7. The following anecdote is found only in Plutarch.

241 *priests of Eleusis*: cf. c. 19. This indictment is solely for the parody of the Mysteries. It probably is authentic, perhaps from the collection of documents made by Craterus in the fourth century. Note however that here the parody was said to have been performed in Alcibiades' house, whereas elsewhere it was in the house of Poulytion (cf. Isocrates, *On the Team*, 6). There is no distinction of religious and secular jurisdiction.

not for curses: inscriptions have been discovered belonging to a large monument recording the sale of the property confiscated from the mockers of the mysteries and set up near the Eleusinium in the Athenian market: see Fornara, no. 147. Alcibiades is among those listed.

downfall of Athens: cf. Thuc. 6. 88. 9–93. The visit to Argos is in Isocrates, *On the Team* 9, but not in Thucydides. Decelea was a village in north-east Attica, close to the Boeotian border, and was occupied by the Spartans from 413 to the end of the war. Gylippus was successful in defeating Nicias in Sicily: see *Nicias*.

242 *pomp and extravagance*: cf. the biographer Satyrus quoted at Athenaeus 12. 534b: 'In Ionia he appeared more luxurious than the Ionians, in Thebes with his body-building and exercising more Boeotian than the Thebans, in Thessaly with his horse-raising and charioteering more horsy than the Aleuadae, in Sparta he beat the Laconians in practicising temperance and frugality, and he surpassed the Thracians in hard drinking.' Plutarch characterizes this adaptability as a trait of the great flatterers and demagogues, and especially of Alcibiades: cf. *How to Tell a Flatterer from a Friend* 52b–e, 'A horned owl, apparently, is caught as it tries to copy a human being and move and dance along with him; a flatterer, on the other hand, is the one who inveigles others and leads them into the trap, by playing a variety of parts: he dances and sings with one person, but wrestles and rolls in the dust with another . . . The point is further illustrated by the actions of the greatest flatterers and demagogues, of whom the most outstanding was Alcibiades: in Athens, he had fun, bred horses and lived a witty and elegant life; in Sparta, he had a crew cut, wore a thin cloak, and washed in cold water; in Thrace, he drank and was aggressive; and when he arrived at Tissaphernes' court, he adopted the soft life of luxurious indulgence and pretension. By this process of assimilation and adaptation, he kept on ingratiating himself with everyone and currying their favour.' (Translation by R. Waterfield, who emends the manuscripts' 'ape' to 'horned owl' to fit other passages.) The tradition of considering demagogues as flatterers goes back at least to Plato's *Gorgias* (463b ff.).

she always was: the first quote, from a lost tragedy and referring to Neoptolemus, the son of Achilles, recalls the ideal of heroic virtue (cf. also *How to Tell a Flatterer* 51c); the second, from Euripides' *Orestes* 129, is the warning of Electra that Helen has not changed her character. Lycurgus was credited with designing the Spartan way of life: cf. Plutarch's Life in this collection.

242 *how infatuated the woman was*: in *Ages*. 3, Plutarch ascribes this story to the fourth-century historian Duris of Samos.

later refused the kingship: cf. Xen. *Hellenica* 3. 3. 2 and Plut. *Ages*. 3, *Lys*, 22; ironically alluded to by Plato, *Alcibiades* 1. 121b–c. Xenophon has Agesilaus tell Leotychidas that the earthquake drove out Leotychidas' father, but leaves ambiguous whether he is speaking of the true father (Alcibiades) or the supposed father (Agis): Plutarch opts for the latter here and in *Agesilaus*.

243 *help the Chians first*: in winter 413/12, after the Athenian expedition was destroyed at Syracuse (cf. *Nic*. 23–30), the islands of Chios and Lesbos, as well as Euboea, and the city of Cyzicus on the Propontis (Sea of Marmora) were treating with Sparta. Thucydides says that Chios was favoured because Alcibiades had a formal tie of friendship with Endius, one of the ephors (Thuc. 8. 5–6). Pharnabazus and Tissaphernes were competing Persian satraps on the coast of Asia Minor, the first to the north, based in Dascyleum on the Propontis, and the second further south, at Sardis in Lydia. It was Persian policy to take advantage of the war to regain the Greek cities of Ionia (along the Aegean coast) which had been in its possession before the Persian Wars, but for most of the century had been under Athenian control.

Alcibiades' death: cf. Thuc. 8. 11–14, 17, 26, 45. Plutarch condenses drastically.

what was going on: one story had it that Timaea, the wife of Agis, warned him: Justin 5. 2. But Endius or other Spartan friends might have passed the word.

244 *Persian king's hands*: cf. Thuc. 8. 46. 1.

lost the argument: cf. Thuc. 8. 48. 2–3.

245 *telling lies about him*: cf. Thuc. 8. 50–1. This is winter 412/11; Plutarch follows Thucydides closely.

accomplices with garlands: in autumn 411: cf. Thuc. 8. 92, who says only that the assassin was one of the border guards, though he names Hermon as a commander of the guards. Two non-Athenians, Thrasybulus and Apollodorus, were identified by the orator Lysias (13. 71). An inscription records the honours given by the Athenians in spring 409 to Thrasybulus, along with others, and orders an inquiry into the voting for the honours paid Apollodorus (Fornara no. 155).

alliance with them: cf. Thuc. 8. 49.

246 *oligarchies*: this oligarchic coup of 411 at Athens is described by various sources, of which Thuc. 8. 63–98 and Aristotle, *Athpol*. 29–33 are the most important. Apparently the Four Hundred were a tight group which at first governed on its own, while winning support with talk of a larger body of

5,000; the Four Hundred were driven from power later in 411, and the Five Thousand (defined as all who could provide themselves with heavy armour) governed for a time until the full democracy was re-established (cf. Thuc. 8. 89–97). The conflict of the sources, especially on the relative role of the two groups, has made a precise account impossible to establish.

246 *overthrow the tyrants*: the fleet at Samos refused to accept the oligarchy, and continued as a kind of democratic government in exile until the oligarchy at Athens collapsed. They recalled Alcibiades to Samos, elected him a general, and made him their leader (cf. Thuc. 8. 81–2. 1).

louder voice: cf. Thuc. 8. 86, including the words: 'This was when Alcibiades first seems to have helped the city more than anyone else . . . Only he was able to restrain the crowd.' On Thrasybulus' activity, cf. Thuc. 8. 81. 1.

247 *control of the sea*: cf. Thuc. 8. 87. Aspendus is on the southern coast of Asia Minor.

off Cnidos and Cos: i.e. in the strait at the south-west corner of Asia Minor, to meet any Persian ships which might try to move into the Aegean.

victory trophy: the battle of Abydos (on the Hellespont), winter 411/10. Cf. Xen. *Hell.* 1. 1. 4–8, Diodorus 13. 45–6. (Thucydides' narrative breaks off at this point.) In cc. 27–8, after the period off Cnidos, the theatre of action is the Hellespont, the time autumn 411 and spring 410.

248 *dispel the criticisms*: cf. Xen. *Hell.* 1. 1. 9–10.

Proconnesus: an island in the Propontis, near Cyzicus.

249 *captured their entire fleet*: the battle of Cyzicus, 410, a great victory for Athens: cf. Xen. *Hell.* 1. 1. 14–18, Diod. 13. 40. Events between the battle of Cyzicus and the battle of Arginusae in 406 are not securely dated to year, therefore in the notes that follow two possible figures will be given. Scholars have argued for particular dating schemes. See A. Andrewes in *Cambridge Ancient History*, 2nd edn., v. 503–5; P. Krentz, *Xenophon Hellenika I–II*. 3. 10, 11–14.

No idea what to do: The identical Laconian dialect text is in Xen. *Hell.* 1. 1.23.

without ransom: cf. Xen. *Hell.* 1. 2. 7–10, 15–17. It is winter 410/9 or 409/8.
pact of friendship with him: cf. Xen. *Hell.* 1. 3. 2–4.

250 *in the process*: cf. *Xen. Hell.* 1. 3. 5–7. The Spartans had established Spartan governors (harmosts) in the cities which came under their control.

garrison in the city: Xen. *Hell.* 1. 3. 10 and Diod. 13. 66. 4 mention the fall of Selymbria, a city on the north shore of the Propontis (409 or 408), but do not tell this story of how it fell. It may have been in Diodorus' usual source, Ephorus. A decree ratifying the treaty with Selymbria in 407 is preserved on stone, including a resolution of Alcibiades: Fornara no. 162.

251 *had done so first*: cf. Xen. *Hell.* 1. 3. 8–13.

252 *acquitted the defendants*: Byzantium fell in 409 or 408 BC. Cf. Xen. *Hell.* 1. 3. 14–22. The account of Anaxilaus' behaviour creates an implicit comparison with that of Alcibiades.

at least 200: Alcibiades returned in 408 or 407. Cf. Diod. 13. 68. 3. Xen. *Hell.* 1. 4. 8–19 describes Alcibiades' return home. Plutarch uses Xenophon selectively, omitting e.g. the gathering of booty and careful island-hopping by which Alcibiades approached Athens, and rearranging the placement of detail, most notably moving mention of the Plynteria festival from Alcibiades' entrance into the harbour to the overview in c. 34. He also adds items from other sources, including no doubt Theopompus and Ephorus, mentioned below.

in so much trouble: Duris tended to embellish his history dramatically (cf. *Per.* 28), whereas Xen. *Hell.* 1. 4. 12 mentions none of this. Cf. the same description in Athenaeus 12. 535. As at *Per.* 28, Plutarch tests the historian's account against his own idea of what the man would do.

inviting him ashore: cf. Xen. *Hell.* 1. 4. 18–19.

the younger ones: cf. Diod. 13. 69.

253 *all over the world*: a good example of authorial comment put in the minds of participants. Xenophon does something similar at *Hell.* 1. 4. 13–17.

son of Callaeschrus: Critias, a leading member of the oligarchic faction, relative of Plato, and author of tragedies and elegies, in 404 became the chief of the Thirty, who ruled Athens for Sparta. His decree had been moved in 411, under the rule of the Four Hundred.

on land and sea: cf. Xen. *Hell.* 1. 4. 20.

254 *or welcoming fashion*: cf. Xen. *Hell.* 1. 2. 12. At the Plynteria, the old wooden statue of Athena was ceremonially washed by the priestly family of the Praxiergidae. The date would be sometime in May 408 or 407.

had to be omitted: the Spartans had held Decelea since 413, when Alcibiades had recommended it (cf. c. 23). The procession of the initiates from Athens to Eleusis in September was a major religious occasion. The god Dionysus was invoked under the special title Iacchus. Xen. *Hell.* 1. 4. 20 briefly mentions this initiative of Alcibiades.

a military commander: thus Alcibiades was given the titles of two officers in the Eleusinian Mysteries, one of which, the high priest, he was accused of having parodied in 415 (cf. c. 22).

255 *fear of the informers*: critics of the democracy regularly attacked its profusion of laws, irresponsible demagogues, and vexatious informers: they had been attacked also in the oligarchic revolution of 411. The rule of a strong man or tyrant was one way to control these faults.

by his enemies: cf. Xen. *Hell.* 1. 4. 21–2, with precise information on the force sent against Andros.

256 *come out against him*: the battle of Notium (near Ephesus), 407 or 406. Cf. Xen. *Hell.* 1. 5. 11–15, Diod. 13. 71–2, *Hellenica Oxyrhynchia* 8. 1–4

(ed. and trans. by P. R. McKechnie and S. J. Kern (Warminister: Aris and Phillips, 1988)), and Plut. *Lys.* 5. 1–4. Our accounts vary considerably: Plutarch is close to Xenophon. Cyrus was the Persian king's younger son, sent in 408 or 407 as satrap in Lydia and general commander of the Persian forces in western Asia Minor, at the same time Lysander took over as Spartan naval commander.

256 *son of Thraso*: to be distinguished from the more famous Thrasybulus son of Lycus, mentioned in c. 26, who helped re-establish the democracy in 403.

his native country: on Alcibiades' numerous liaisons, cf. Athenaeus 12. 534e–535c and 13. 574d–e: Plutarch is more restrained. Bisanthe was on the north shore of the Propontis. Nepos, *Alc.* 7. 4 names this and other forts belonging to Alcibiades.

barbarian tribesmen: cf. Xen. *Hell.* 1. 5. 16–17, and the different account of Diod. 13. 73–4. The generals are those of the Attic year 406/5. This change may be the result of the regular annual election, although Plut. *Lys.* 5 and Nepos, *Alc.* 7 seem to state that Alcibiades and the other generals were replaced before their term was out.

257 *not you*: cf. Xen. *Hell.* 2. 1. 25–6, Plut. *Lys.* 10.

demolished the Long Walls: Lysander's crushing victory in the battle of Aegospotami (on the north shore of the Hellespont) in summer 405 led immediately to the siege of Athens and its capitulation in 404. This was the end of the Peloponnesian War, begun in 431. Plutarch skips events not related to Alcibiades, including the Athenian victory at Arginusae in 406. The generals at Aegospotami are not those who replaced Alcibiades in 406. Aegospotami: Xen. *Hell.* 2. 1. 16–30; Plut. *Lys.* 9–11. Surrender of Athens: Xen. *Hell.* 2. 2. 19–32; Plut. *Lys.* 14; Diod. 14. 3. 2; cf. Andocides, *On the Peace* 11–12.

258 *of his court*: cf. Diod. 14. 11, Nepos, *Alc.* 9. On Themistocles' success in Persia, see Plut. *Them.* 27–31.

hands of the Thirty: the Thirty, or Thirty Tyrants, was a junta set up by Lysander to rule Athens in 404; it was led by Critias. Their lawless violence led to their overthrow in 403. Cf. Xen. *Hell.* 2. 3–4, Aristotle, *Athpol.* 34–7.

skytalē: at *Lys.* 19 Plutarch explains the word *skytalē* as a Spartan coded message, written on a strip wrapped around a staff, which could only be read by the holder of an identical staff. Although this is the standard explanation in Plutarch's day (cf. also Aulus Gellius 17. 9) and later, down to modern times, there are strong doubts whether in the classical period such a method was ever used: cf. Thomas Kelly, 'The Spartan Skytale', in J. W. Eadie and J. Ober (eds.), *The Craft of the Ancient Historian: Essays in Honour of Chester G. Starr* (Lanham, Md.: University Press of America, 1985), 141–69. Presumably a Spartan officer simply carried a staff of office which confirmed his message.

259 *and white lead*: women used white lead on the face as make-up. Cf. e.g. Aristophanes, *Women in the Assembly* 878, 929, and the discussion in Xenophon, *Household Management* 10.

under the circumstances: cf. Diod. 14. 11 and Nepos, *Alc.* 10. 2–6 (another reason for Alcibiades' removal: he had information of Cyrus' plan to dethrone his elder brother, which Diodorus ascribes to Ephorus), Athenaeus 13. 574e–f.

prisoner-of-war: cf. *Nic.* 15.

AGESILAUS

267 *Agis*: Agis II, Eurypontid king 427–400, son of Archidamus II, king 469–427.

men in obedience: the Spartan training system, or *agōgē*, is described in some detail in *Lyc.* 14–23.

natural self-composure: on these 'herds', or *agelai*, see *Lyc.* 16. For mature lovers of young men at Sparta, see *Lyc.* 18 and note. Agesilaus' erotic interests run through the Life: cf. 11, 20, 25.

268 *made of him*: Plutarch regularly describes the physical appearance of his subject, and refers to portraits when available (e.g. *Per.* 3, *Alex.* 4).

king's wife, Timaea: cf. *Alc.* 23. The child was named Leotychidas.

the Athenians at sea: Lysander's victory at Aegospotami in 405 allowed him to besiege Athens with his fleet; it surrendered in 404. Agis died in 400.

following oracle: Plutarch cites this in *Why are Delphic Oracles No Longer Given in Verse?* 399b as an example of a quite specific and truthful oracle. Xen. *Hell.* 3. 3. 2 mentions Diopithes and the oracle, but does not quote it. The effect at this point in the biography is to raise a question about the kingship of Agesilaus (which interpretation is correct?) and the danger for Sparta if the wrong choice is made.

269 *Leotychidas was born*: Poseidon was god of earthquakes as well as of the sea. Xenophon develops the confrontation in a dialogue, *Hell.* 3. 3. 2.

envy and hostility: cf. Xen. *Ages.* 4. 5.

do what he wanted: Xen. *Ages.* 6. 4.

absolute power: cf. *Lyc.* 5–7.

270 *belong to the state*: this is considered false by P. Cartledge, *Agesilaos and the Crisis of Sparta* (London: Duckworth, 1987), 144 (according to Xen. *Ages.* 6. 8, he was 'never fined by the citizens').

creation and change: Plutarch is thinking of the early philosophers Heraclitus, who wrote (*Fragmente der Vorsokratiker*[6], F 53) 'War is the father of all, and the king of all', and Empedocles, who saw strife and love as the two fundamental principles of the world. The philosophical position reflects the tension within the personalities of Agesilaus and Pompey between friendliness and competition, which will shape both their careers.

270 *rivalry into his constitution*: here Plutarch's words 'conflict and rivalry' (*philonikon kai philotimon*) are the same as those which Plato's Socrates uses to categorize the first stage in the decline of the ideal constitution: 'the competitive and ambitious person who corresponds to the Spartan system' (*Republic* 545a, cf. 548c). Plato goes on to describe the weaknesses of this stage in 547b–551a.

violent words: Homer, *Od.* 8. 77. It had been predicted that if the two quarrelled, the Greek army at Troy would win. Plutarch here chooses not to mention the other, destructive, quarrel, between Odysseus and Ajax, which resulted in the suicide of Ajax (cf. *Od.* 11. 543–64 and Sophocles' *Ajax*).

from the sea: Agesilaus became king in 400; he sailed to Asia in 396 BC.

271 *2,000 ex-helots*: i.e. *neodamodeis*, helots manumitted expressly to serve as soldiers, and not incorporated into full citizenship. Cf. Cartledge, *Agesilaos*, 39–40. This policy, which began in the 420s, reflected a decline in the Spartiate population and a need for more military manpower. On the helots, see *Lyc.* 2 note.

there for the night: Geraestus is the promontory and port on the south tip of the island of Euboea; Aulis is on the mainland in Boeotia, at the narrowest point of the strait between Euboea and the mainland, and is the city from which the Greek fleet under Agamemnon was said to have sailed against Troy. Agamemnon had sacrificed his daughter Iphigeneia to Artemis to receive a favourable wind.

before setting sail: this dream is not in Xenophon, but fits a type common in ancient authors. Cf. especially the dream of Pelopidas before Leuctra (*Pel.* 21), which also asked for a human sacrifice, and the review of other such requests, including the dream of Agesilaus, with the suggestion that his expedition failed because he refused the sacrifice. Others, however, rejected that interpretation. The view that the gods wish such sacrifices is rejected in *Oracles in Decline* 417c. Here we do not know whether it in fact happened, or was invented by a later writer (perhaps as a narrative device in explaining his decision to sacrifice), or by Agesilaus himself to enhance his mission.

Boeotarchs: the Boeotarchs were part of the federal government of Boeotia, an elected commission of commanders from the cities of Boeotia; Thebes had two commanders, as well as an additional two from its dependencies. Cf. the account given (for the year 395) in *Hellenica Oxyrhynchia* 16 (McKechnie and Kern, 83).

272 *tossed the thighs of the victim off the altar*: cf. Xen. *Hell.* 3. 4. 3–4, some of whose words Plutarch repeats. However, Xenophon does not give the justification that Plutarch does, that this sacrifice contravened Boeotian tradition. This act seems to be the beginning of Agesilaus' implacable hostility towards the Thebans.

lay with Lysander: for these events see also Xen. *Hell.* 3. 4. 7–10, Plut. *Lys.* 23. Lysander had been extremely popular with the Greeks of Asia Minor on his earlier command. On Agesilaus' treatment of Lysander, and the dependence of regal power on personal influence, cf. Cartledge, *Agesilaos*, 152–3. Plutarch's treatment in *Lysander* differs from that in *Agesilaus*: there it is envy, and not ambition, which motivates the king.

273 *the meat at public feasts*: the post would normally be considered an honour, but the honour was far less than that to which Lysander was accustomed.

without bothering you: Plutarch here and in *Lys.* 23 refines a dialogue already present in Xen. *Hell.* 3. 4. 9.

200 horsemen: Pharnabazus was the Persian satrap (governor) of the territory in the north-west corner of Asia Minor, along the Hellespont. He appears also in *Alcibiades*. For the story of Spithridates, cf. Xen. *Hell.* 3. 4. 10.

campaigning in Boeotia: on Lysander's plans for drastic reform of the Spartan state, which might have made him sole king, see *Lys.* 24–6, Cartledge, *Agesilaos*, 94–7. They are briefly mentioned below at 23. Lysander died in a rash attack on Haliartus in Boeotia in 395 (cf. *Lys.* 28).

Tissaphernes: the Persian satrap at Sardis in Lydia, who had earlier helped first the Athenians (influenced by Alcibiades), then the Spartans, in the Peloponnesian War: cf. *Alc.* 23–8.

274 *whenever they wanted*: this is the famous expedition, from 401 to 399, described by Xenophon in his *Anabasis*.

Caria: in the south-western corner of Asia Minor.

Phrygia: Hellespontine Phrygia, the territory of Pharnabazus.

without lobes: the cavalry defeat is described by Xenophon at *Hell.* 3. 4. 13–14; the faulty sacrifices (the missing lobe was considered ominous) at *Hell.* 3. 4. 15.

a good mare instead: cf. Homer, *Il.* 23. 295–9: Agamemnon allowed Anchisiades to remain at home, accepting a mare in recompense. Xenophon praises this initiative of Agesilaus' at *Ages.* 1. 23–4.

you 're fighting for: cf. Xen. *Hell.* 3. 4. 19. Plutarch tells a similar story about Cimon, though it has a different point, that the captive men can bring valuable ransom, though they look worthless (*Cim.* 9).

275 *heavy losses on them*: the battle of Sardis, 395 BC. Cf. Xen. *Hell.* 2. 4. 20–4, *Ages*, 1. 28–32, Diod. 14. 80. 1–8.

skytalē: cf. note to Alc. 38.

276 *reliable man*: roughly, Paphlagonia was the land between the Sangarius and the Halys rivers. The king's name is variously reported in our manuscripts: Cotys in Plutarch, but Otys in Xen. *Hell.* 4. 1.3, Gyes in *Hell. Oxy.* 17, Thys in Theopompus, and Thuys in Nepos, *Datames* 2. 2.

2,000 peltasts: cf. Xen. *Hell.* 4. 1. 4–15 gives a vivid account with dialogue of these negotiations.

did not deserve: Plutarch summarizes Xen. *Hell.* 4. 1. 1–28. According to Xenophon (4. 1. 28), 'For Agesilaus, no event of the campaign was more grievous than the departure of Spithridates, Mitridates, and the Paphlagonians.'

276 *and kiss him*: according to Xen. *Ages*. 5. 4, this was a sign of respect used in Persia. Agesilaus found it sexually enticing and threatening to his self-control.

277 *all the gold I've ever seen*: Xenophon's version of the story, not found in *Hell.* but in *Ages*. 5. 4–5, is told in a rather different manner from Plutarch, who shows the other Spartans mocking the king for un-Spartan cowardice. Cf. also the different version in *Spartan Sayings* 209de. The following sentence is Plutarch's own interpretation.

against the Athenians: during the last phase of the Peloponnesian War, after 413, when Persia decided to help the Spartans.

278 *happens one day*: the scene of this chapter derives from the fine account in Xen., *Hell.* 4. 1. 29–38.

successful conclusion: cf. Xen. *Hell.* 4. 1. 39–40.

Hidrieus of Caria: Hidrieus or Idrieus, one of the Hecatomonid dynasty of Caria and brother of Mausolus, was satrap of Caria 351–344 BC. This message, if authentic, would have been sent him during his brother's reign.

279 *of his command*: Spring 394.

than Agesilaus': cf. Xen. *Ages*. 5. 2.

their popular leaders: Plutarch presents Agesilaus (following Xen. *Ages*. 1. 36) as aiming at destroying Persian rule as Alexander later did. Ecbatana and Susa were two capitals of the Persian empire, which had interfered so strongly in the Peloponnesian War, and would continue to dictate terms to Greece in the following decades. Plutarch shows Agesilaus' awareness of the destructiveness of Persian influence in the anecdote at the end of this chapter.

worthy of barbarians: a line from Euripides' *Trojan Women* (764), spoken by Andromache.

280 *a rare treat*: cf. *Alex*. 37. 7 and 56. 1.

Leuctra, Coronea, Corinth and Arcadia: battles of Greeks against Greeks fought respectively in 371 (see c. 28), 394 (18), 394 (16), and 362 (35).

the war at home: Hannibal in 203 was in South Italy when Scipio's invasion of Africa forced the Carthaginians to summon him home.

home in Arcadia: the battle between Agis III of Sparta and Antipater, Alexander's regent in Macedonia, in 331 at Megalopolis. The witticism of Alexander is not reported elsewhere.

task unfulfilled: a quote from Homer, *Il.* 4. 175, setting Agesilaus in a heroic context by recalling the expedition against Troy.

private sphere: Erasistratus was son of the Athenian demagogue Phaeax, and lived in the fourth century.

280 *war with the Spartiates*: this is the so-called Corinthian War, which had begun in 395, and had already occasioned the death of Lysander at the battle of Haliartus in Boeotia.

281 *heavy losses on them*: this encounter is not recorded elsewhere. The name in our manuscript, Trochalians, is unknown, and perhaps should be emended to Trallians, who were a Thracian people.

under a truce: Xenocles and Scythes had been counsellors to Agesilaus in 396 (*Hell*. 3. 4. 20), but this incident is otherwise unknown.

at Corinth: the battle of Nemea, 394: see Xen. *Hell*. 4. 2. 14–23.

all the easterners at once: Xen. *Hell*. 4. 3. 1–2 presents a quite different dialogue with Dercyllidas, who brought him the news. This account comes from Xen. *Ages*. 7. 5. Eight Spartiates had died, but almost 10,000 men from other cities.

their horsemanship: cf. Xen. *Hell*. 4. 3. 9. Agesilaus had formed the cavalry squadron in Ephesus: cf. c. 9.

282 *the Gates*: i.e. the pass of Thermopylae (the Hot Gates, named after the hot springs there).

Pharnabazus and Conon: the eclipse (cf. Xen. *Hell*. 4. 3. 10) took place on 14 August 394. The battle of Cnidos, in which Pharnabazus, helped by the Athenian commander Conon, defeated the Spartan fleet under Agesilaus' brother-in-law Pisander (cf. 10), marked the end of Spartan naval power.

to his friends: cf. Xen. *Hell*. 4. 3. 10–14.

with him from Asia: cf. Xen. *Hell*. 4. 3. 16 and *Ages*. 2. 9. The battle, with Agesilaus' unusual decision to confront the fleeing Thebans head on, is described by Xenophon, *Hell*. 4. 3. 15–20, *Ages*. 2. 9–14. Plutarch's account is more emotionally charged. Plutarch himself, one must remember, was a Boeotian, and proud of the Thebans' courage. Xenophon does not mention the fifty men sent from Sparta (cf. 17), who save Agesilaus in the battle.

283 *killed Tolmides*: the battle of Coronea of 447: cf. *Per*. 18.

had indeed won: according to Greek custom, the victor in a set battle was the side which controlled the battlefield and set up a trophy: asking for permission to bury one's dead was an admission of defeat, therefore.

brought from Asia: the quadrennial Pythian games at Delphi were usually held in September. The size of the tithe reminds the reader of Agesilaus' successes in Asia, and intimates the tremendously disruptive effect his return with this loot will have in Sparta. We are also to think of Pompey's return in triumph from the Mithridatic Wars (*Pomp*. 45).

284 *which Aristodamus had hung*: cf. Xen. *Ages*. 8. 7. Aristodamus was a legendary figure, placed a few generations after Heracles. Cf. *Lyc*. 1.

processions there: cf. Xen. *Ages*. 8. 7. Plutarch adds the description of the *kannathron*, which is not in Xenophon.

284 *anyone else's*: an extremely important testimonial to Plutarch's historical curiosity. Plutarch refers to archives (*anagraphai*). A Spartan inscription, of Trajanic date, contemporary with Plutarch, refers to an archive building (*grammatophulakeion*, *IG* 5. 1. 20a, 3–4), in which records of victors were kept, and there was an office of archive-keeper. Plutarch had friends among the Spartan élite, and probably visited there on more than one occasion (cf. e.g. 35, and *Lyc.* 18). The spear could have been preserved as a dedication in a temple, although it seems unlikely. Dicaearchus is the fourth-century Peripatetic philosopher who wrote *On the Laws at Sparta* and a kind of Greek history, *Life of Greece*.

in the Olympic Games: cf. Xen. *Ages.* 9. 6, making the same point. She clearly was an extraordinary woman. This victory is mentioned as a first for women both in entering and in winning in the chariot race by Pausanias, 3. 8. 1; cf. 3. 15. 1 (a hero-shrine of Cynisca), 5. 12. 5 and 6. 1. 6–7 (a bronze statue group of Cynisca and her chariot, team, and driver). Cf. also the inscribed epigram in honour of Cynisca at Olympia, *IG* 5, 1564, *Anth. Pal.* 13. 16. See the general comments on her chariot-racing activity and Agesilaus' position in Cartledge, *Agesilaos*, 149–50.

how to command: cf. also Diogenes Laertius, *Lives of the Philosophers*, who ascribes this notice to a certain Diocles. Xenophon does not mention this, nor the fact that his son Gryllus died fighting in the Athenian cavalry troop which had come to help the Spartans in the battle of Mantinea, 362.

kept quiet: for Lysander's revolutionary agenda, see *Lys.* 24–6.

285 *played little part in public life*: Agesipolis I, the son of Pausanias, who though king had gone into exile at Tegea after Lysander's defeat at Haliartus in 395, reigned from 395 to 380.

quest for virtue: cf. *Lyc.* 17 and 18.

dockyards: in 391 BC. Cf. Xen. *Hell.* 4. 4. 19; *Ages.* 2. 17. For the events of 391–390 in Corinth, as far as they can be understood from Xenophon's somewhat unclear narrative, see Cartledge, *Agesilaos*, 222–4.

not the second: cf. Xen. *Hell.* 4. 5. 1–2. These are the games of 390, and should immediately precede the events of c. 22.

286 *boys or girls*: on these contests, cf. *Lyc.* 14.

actors in plays: in Greek, *deikeliktas*, a Spartan word for stage performers. Tragic actors had reached exceptional prominence in this period: cf. the competitions staged for Alexander the Great, *Alex.* 29.

the real thing: the saying is also ascribed to Lycurgus, *Lyc.* 12.

recovery to Menecrates: Agesilaus makes a witty play on the modes of salutation used for a letter. Menecrates uses the standard, 'be of good cheer' (*chairein*); the king replies with the less common, but here quite apposite, 'be of good health' (*hygiainein*). Athenaeus reports a variety of anecdotes about Menecrates, including a similar exchange of letters, which he credits to Philip of Macedon (7. 289a–290b).

286 *peltasts and mercenaries*: in 390 BC. The whole scene at the Heraeum is presented quite dramatically by Xen. *Hell.* 4. 5. 5–10; the disaster which befell the Spartan *mora* equally vividly at 4. 5. 11–17. The sanctuary was that of Hera Akraia on a promontory north of Corinth, not far from Peraeum; the defeat took place at Lechaeum, the port of Corinth. The shift from the arrogance of military power to humbling defeat in Xenophon's narrative clearly impressed Plutarch; he saw a similar moment in *Pompey* 38, when Pompey's overconfidence in distributing booty is punished by *nemesis*. The defeat at Lechaeum was extraordinary: a battalion of about 600 Spartan hoplites was ambushed by a combined force of hoplites and light-armed peltasts commanded by the Athenian Iphicrates. The peltasts were able to wound the Spartans with their javelins, but then scamper away as the heavily armed Spartans tried to chase them. As this happened time and again, the Spartans were beaten down, and eventually lost 250 of the 600 men. The battle showed the effectiveness of light-armed troops against the traditional hoplite when properly used, and also meant a significant loss of Spartan manpower. Plutarch presumes his reader is familiar with the story.

287 *gloat over them*: cf. Xen. *Hell.* 4. 5. 9–10 and 18.

with the Achaeans: on this campaign of 389, cf. Xen. *Hell.* 4. 6. 1–7. 1, *Ages.* 2. 20. The greatest threat to a city was to ravage its crop of grain before it could be harvested.

masters of the sea: a reference to the consequences of their victory over the Spartans at Cnidos in 394: cf. 17.

donated by Pharnabazus: cf. Xen. *Hell.* 4. 8. 9–10.

Persian king: the so-called Peace of Antalcidas, of 386. The negotiations are described by Xen. *Hell.* 4. 8. 12–16, 5. 1. 6, 5. 1. 25–32; a short statement of the king's terms appears at 5. 1. 33. All the cities of the Asian mainland were to be subject to Persia, and all Greek cities were to be independent (a clause aimed at ending Thebes' domination of the cities of Boeotia).

288 *treaty in force*: in 382 Phoebidas, who was leading an army through Boeotia to support Spartan operations in Thrace, was offered the chance of seizing the Cadmeia, the citadel of Thebes, by Leontiadas, a Theban sympathetic to Sparta. He immediately occupied the citadel, stationed a garrison there, and established Leontiadas and his friends in power. Cf. Xen. *Hell.* 5. 2. 25–31, Diod. 15. 20. 2, and Plut. *Pel.* 5.

advantage of Lacedaemon: for the discussion at Sparta, cf. Xen. *Hell.* 5. 2. 32–6. Plutarch, *Pel.* 6, reports that Phoebidas was fined 100,000 drachmas or 16⅔ talents, a sizeable sum.

Only if he is more just: quoted by Plutarch also in *Progress in Virtue* 78d and *Self-Praise without Offence* 545a.

personal relationship: cf. Xen. *Ages.* 8. 4.

288 *leaders of Thebes*: although Xenophon does not mention him at this point, Plutarch associates Archias with Leontiadas, so that he is not just a later member of the junta: cf. *Pel.* 5.

289 *declared war on them*: the liberation of Thebes in 379 was a glorious moment in Boeotian history, and celebrated by Plutarch in *Pel.* 7–14 and in an unusual philosophical/historical dialogue, *Socrates' Sign* (575a–598f). Xenophon's account is *Hell.* 5. 4. 1–12.

Agesipolis' death: Agesipolis died in 380: Xen. *Hell.* 5. 3. 18–19.

active service: cf. Xen. *Hell.* 5. 4. 13. Agesilaus would have been about 66.

on behalf of their exiles: for Agesilaus' support of the exiles' return to Phleious, a small city south-west of Corinth, cf. Xen. *Hell.* 5. 2. 8–10, 5. 3. 10–17, 21–5.

the Boeotarchs: Pelopidas was the great Theban general and friend of Epaminondas, celebrated in a Life by Plutarch. At *Pel.* 14. 2 Plutarch says that another Boeotarch, Gorgidas, rather than Menon, aided Pelopidas in the scheme. For the Boeotarchs, cf. c. 6 note.

back to Thespiae: Sphodrias' abortive raid began from Thespiae, a town of Boeotia north of Plataea, went over the mountains into Attica and arrived as far as the Thriasian Plain between Eleusis and Athens before retreating. Cf. Xen. *Hell.* 5. 4. 20–5 (suggesting that some Thebans had bribed Sphodrias to get the Athenians on their side) and Plut. *Pel.* 14.

290 *son of King Agesilaus*: Archidamus III, who succeeded Agesilaus as king, 360–338, plays a prominent part also in cc. 33–4.

come to his support: this paragraph simplifies the rather sentimental dialogue version in Xen. *Hell.* 5. 4. 24–34, focusing on Archidamus' relation to his father.

291 *children of his own*: this kind of scene is rarely found in Greek literature. Valerius Maximus 8. 8 ext. 1 describes a similar scene of Socrates playing horse. The anecdote may derive from a work on seriousness and play by the Stoic Athenodorus of Tarsus: it belongs to that sort of philosophical tradition.

invaded Boeotia himself: for the law, cf. 24. The invasion was in 378: cf. Xen. *Hell.* 5. 4. 35–41. He led a second invasion in 377, *Hell.* 5. 4. 47–56. Plutarch prefers to consider the effect of the Spartan wars in improving Thebes' military skills. Cf. the similar passage in *Pel.* 15.

military expertise: cf. *Lyc.* 13. There is also a parallel to Pompey's help to Caesar, which Caesar used against him (*Pomp.* 46).

manual trade: for this ban on crafts among the Spartiates, cf. *Lyc.* 24.

292 *military expeditions*: cf. Xen. *Hell.* 5. 4. 58. Recall that Agesilaus was lame in one leg from birth. On this occasion in 377 BC he may have suffered thrombophlebitis (inflammation resulting from a blood clot in a vein).

defeated . . . by the Thebans: in 375 Pelopidas destroyed two Spartan battalions (*moras*): cf. *Pel.* 16–17.

292 *untested at the time*: Plutarch's *Life of Epaminondas*, now lost, was the first of the series of *Parallel Lives*. He speaks of him at length in *Pelopidas* and in *Socrates' Sign*. For Plutarch he is the exemplary figure of a military leader steeped in philosophy. He and Pelopidas were the chief engineers of Thebes' rise to power, especially in the victories over Sparta at Leuctra (371) and Mantinea (362), mentioned in the following chapters. The congress at Sparta took place in 371: Plutarch's narrative has moved rapidly over the intervening years.

everyone was equal: Xen. *Hell.* 6. 3 reports the speeches of the Athenians in favour of peace, but does not mention Epaminondas. Cf. however, Nepos, *Epaminondas* 6. 4.

293 *all their disputes*: Xenophon mentions only the Theban refusal to sign unless for the Boeotians as a whole, *Hell.* 6. 3. 19–20. Thebes' policy in this period was that it had a right to act as leader of the Boeotian confederacy; Spartan policy denied this and insisted that all cities should be independent. Plutarch's account gives Agesilaus' anger as the main cause of the disagreement and the disastrous battle which followed.

rallying them for the war: cf. Xen. *Hell.* 6. 4. 1–3. According to *Pel.* 20, Cleombrotus had 10,000 hoplites and 1,000 cavalrymen.

Life of Epaminondas: the Life is lost, but for some omens, cf. *Pel.* 20 and Xen. *Hell.* 6. 4. 7.

fighting the Thebans: for the battle of Leuctra (18 Aug. 371), which established the Thebans as the most powerful army in Greece, see *Pel.* 20–3, Xen. *Hell.* 6. 4. 3–15, Diod. 15. 51–6. The Theban tactics of combining cavalry with a massively deep hoplite formation destroyed Cleombrotus' more traditional formation. Cf. J. Buckler, *The Theban Hegemony 371–362 BC* (Cambridge, Mass., and London: Harvard University Press, 1980), 54–66; Cartledge, *Agesilaos*, 236–41.

fun at a party: Xen. *Symposium* 1. 1.

Festival of Unarmed Dancing: the Gymnopaideia, one of the major Spartan festivals: cf. *Lyc.* 15.

294 *cheerful high spirits*: cf. Xen. *Hell.* 6. 4. 16. The paradoxical notion is that the relatives of the dead rejoice that they have died for their country, the others are ashamed that their relatives have escaped and returned safely.

be on their guard against: the oracle is quoted in c. 3. The thought is further developed in *Comp. Ages.–Pomp.* 1 and 2, where Plutarch speaks as if the gods had clearly warned the Spartans not to choose Agesilaus king.

295 *half left to grow*: on the *tresantes*, cf. also *Lyc.* 21, Xen. *Constitution of the Lacedaemonians* 9. 4–6, and Cartledge, *Agesilaos*, 179 and 214. Presumably anyone who left his position would be so defined, so that all the returning soldiers would be in this position. Unlike the Three Hundred with Leonidas at Thermopylae, they had chosen to survive. The dishonour suffered by Aristodemus, the one man who by chance survived Thermopylae, but was called a *tresas*, is recalled by Herodotus, 7. 231 and 9. 71. Cf. also

the treatment of the Spartans captured at Sphacteria in 425 when they returned, Thuc. 5. 34. 2.

295 *completely desperate*: late autumn and winter 370. Cf. the full account of Xen. *Hell.* 6. 5. 10–21.

Laconia was 70,000: in winter 370/69: cf. *Pel.* 24, Xen. *Hell.* 6. 5. 25–32, 50, *Ages.* 2. 24.

watchfires there: cf. Xen. *Hell.* 6. 5. 28.

296 *Antalcidas*: cf. cc. 23 and 26.

lay waste the countryside: on Agesilaus' defence of the unwalled city, cf. Cartledge, *Agesilaos*, 232–5.

297 *executed without a trial*: these revolutionary movements among the Spartans themselves are not narrated by Xenophon, but are mentioned in Nepos, *Ages.* 6. 2–3. Cf. also Cartledge, *Agesilaos*, 164 and E. David, 'Revolutionary Agitation in Sparta after Leuctra', *Athenaeum*, NS 58 (1980), 299–308.

who were leaving: cf. Xen. *Hell.* 6. 5. 28–9, 32. Perioeci (neighbours) were a class of freemen of Laconia and Messenia, who had none of the political rights of the Spartiates.

298 *and so they fell*: cf. the encomium of Lycurgus' constitutional regime at *Lyc.* 30–1, where the particular cause of decline is made Lysander's introduction of large sums of money at the end of the Peloponnesian War (cf. *Lys.* 2, 16, 17, 30).

on the enemy side: Agesilaus was 75 in 369. The tyrant Dionysius I of Syracuse sent ships and other aid to the Spartans to use against Thebes in 369 and 368 (Xen. *Hell.* 7. 1. 20, 28). For the campaign and victory at Eutresia in 368, see Xen. *Hell.* 7. 1. 28–32. The battle was the first significant land victory in over twenty years, but was unable to block the creation of the new Arcadian city of Megalopolis.

Thucydides has described: the battle was in 418: see Thuc. 5. 64–74.

bearer of good news: on the *phidition*, see *Lyc.* 12.

resources to prevent it: as a result of the campaign of 369, Epaminondas was able to liberate Messenia from Spartan domination (thus depriving the Spartan state of half its land mass) and establish its major city, Messene. This action was the worst to befall Sparta, and it never recovered.

299 *attacking the Thebans*: the Thebans marched against Mantinea in 362: cf. Xen. *Hell.* 7. 5. 1–9. For Epaminondas' attack on Sparta, cf. *Hell.* 7. 5. 10–13.

Phoebidas: for Phoebidas, cf. c. 23.

300 *battle near Mantinea*: this major battle took place in 362 just after Epaminondas' attack on Sparta. Xenophon concludes his history with it: *Hell.* 7. 5. 18–27. Thebes won, but the death of Epaminondas meant the end of Theban military dominance: as Xenophon writes (7. 5. 27), 'There

was even more confusion and disturbance than there had been previously.' According to Plutarch, *The Glory of Athens* 350a, it was fought on 12 Skirophorion, that is in June or July 362. Cf. Buckler, *Theban Hegemony*, 213–19.

300 *still holds today*: Plutarch uses his own acquaintance with Callicrates at Sparta to argue a historical point against Dioscorides and to establish the honours given to Anticrates and his descendants. Dioscorides, cited also in *Lyc.* 11, wrote a *Constitution of Sparta*.

recover Messenia: Sparta never was able to achieve this goal.

Tachos of Egypt: the Pharaoh Tachos took the throne in 361, and joined with other satraps in a revolt against the Persian king Artaxerxes (Diod. 15. 90–3). Agesilaus sailed in spring 360. In addition to Plutarch and Diodorus, cf. also Xen. *Ages.* 2. 28–31 and Nepos, *Ages.* 8.

301 *with him as before*: Agesilaus also had taken 30 advisers to Asia in 396 (c. 6).

give them to his helots: as in c. 12, there is a strong contrast between oriental luxury and Spartan simplicity, but then Agesilaus was in the prime of his youth and success, now he is aged and weak.

Chabrias of Athens: a successful Athenian and mercenary commander on land and sea for many years; he died in battle in his sixties in 357/6.

302 *enhance Sparta*: Agesilaus' decision is defended in Xenophon's encomium, *Ages.* 2. 30–1. Plutarch reaffirms his position in *Comp. Ages.–Pomp.* 5: Agesilaus went to Egypt 'neither honourably nor of necessity, but for money to use to fight Greeks, earned by commanding for barbarians . . . he was trusted, but he abandoned [Tachos] and crossed over to the enemies of those whom he had sailed to aid'.

fled into exile: according to Diodorus, Tachos was pardoned by the Persian king Artaxerxes and sent back to Egypt to deal with the rebels.

Mendes: a city in the Nile delta.

304 *Menelaus' Haven*: the story was that Menelaus of Sparta, on returning from the Trojan War, had stopped in Egypt. So Agesilaus dies in a place with a Spartan connection, and one which recalls his initial desire to emulate Agamemnon as he sailed to Asia (6).

305 *no honey available*: Diodorus 15. 93. 6, on the other hand, says they used honey, the usual method of embalming. Plutarch chooses not to mention the special honours connected with a king's burial at Sparta (mentioned passingly at Xen. *Ages.* 11. 16, but cf. Hdt. 6. 58, Cartledge, *Agesilaos*, 331–43).

in descent from Agesilaus: Agis IV reigned 244–241. Plutarch devoted an unusual set of four Lives to Agis IV and Cleomenes III of Sparta paired with Tiberius and Gaius Gracchus. Agis IV would attempt a revolution to restore in some measure the Lycurgan constitution.

ALEXANDER

312 *Pompey*: Julius Caesar. See Alexander: Introduction and Plutarch's *Caesar* in our companion Roman volume.

others: a famous statement of Plutarch's purpose in the *Lives*, which must be read in the context of the military fame of the two men and the unusual length of this pair of lives. Observation of behaviour and words permits moral evaluation, quite apart from the historical significance of what is studied. Implicit in Plutarch's choice of subjects, however, is that the moral behaviour of major historical actors has greater significance to the reader than that of lesser persons. The comparison of the biographer to the painter is common in Plutarch: cf. *Cim.* 2.

Neoptolemus: Caranus first appears as an ancestor in the historian Theopompus in the fourth century BC. Neoptolemus, son of Achilles (who was grandson of Aeacus), was said to have settled in Molossia (modern north-west Greece) on returning from Troy and founded the dynasty of kings there. This genealogy establishes Alexander's connection with major Greek heroes.

Arybbas: the mystery cult on Samothrace (in the north Aegean) was famous. The exact date of the meeting is debated: Philip was born in 382, Olympias in 375, and Alexander in 356. Arybbas was actually Olympias' uncle: the error may be Plutarch's, or our manuscripts'.

together: on the wedding night the bride was led into the bedroom, and the bridegroom locked the door.

Telmessus: a diviner, who later accompanied Alexander in Asia.

313 *higher being*: all these omens point to divine parentage for Alexander, a topic which resurfaces often in the Life: cf. esp. 27–8.

ceremonies: the word *thrēskeuin*, to revel wildly, was derived, probably falsely, from the region of Thrace.

garlands: Plutarch suggests that the snake-in-the-bed story might have arisen from Olympias' snake-handling. Stories of Dionysiac frenzy among women were often repeated (most famously in Euripides' *Bacchae*, written in Macedonia); Macedonian and Thracian women were thought to be particularly given to this behaviour.

with his wife: Philip was struck in the eye by an arrow at Methone in 354 BC.

with Hera: i.e. by accusing her of adultery with Zeus, Hera's husband.

fire: about 20 July 356. There were several successive temples of Artemis at Ephesus.

314 *that day*: Artemis was goddess of childbirth: Plutarch finds Hegesias' expression 'frigid', i.e. affected and inappropriate.

melting gaze: see the works by Richter and Schwarzenberg in the bibliography.

314 *liquids by heat*: a fragrant odour characterized the gods and heroes. Here Plutarch uses physical theory to explain both Alexander's body temperature and his personality. The theme of Alexander's fieriness continues throughout the Life. See Alexander: Introduction and the article by Sansone listed there.

315 *on his coins*: for these coins, see C. H. V. Sutherland, *Art in Coinage* (London, 1955), 72–3, *Sylloge Nummorum Graecorum*, v, *Ashmolean Museum, Oxford*, pt. III: *Macedonia* (London, 1976), plates 46–65; and M. J. Price, *The Coinage in the Name of Alexander the Great and Philip Arrhidaeus: A British Museum Catalogue* (2 vols., Zurich and London, 1991).

boxing or pancration: the pancration was an athletic competition combining wrestling, boxing, and kick-fighting.

Olympias: for Leonidas' severity see cc. 22 and 25.

316 *Philip as Peleus*: Phoenix and Peleus were respectively the older mentor and father of Achilles. On Phoenix, cf. Homer, *Il.* 9. 432–96.

317 *rudders too*: from a lost play.

resettled the town again: Stagira was destroyed in 350; it is not known when it was restored. Plutarch admires Aristotle for working not for money but for the good of his fellow citizens. He joined the court in 342.

used to frequent: Mieza was about 40 km. from the capital, Pella, near modern Naoussa. Plutarch may have visited the site.

318 *subject*: our texts of Aristotle are all based on lecture notes not published by Aristotle; his published works have been lost, except for the *Constitution of the Athenians* (*Athpol.*), found on a papyrus first published in 1891.

Harpalus: a boyhood friend, later put in charge of finances. He lived in great luxury, but in 324 fled from Babylon to Athens, to escape Alexander's return from the East.

Philistus' works: Plutarch used Philistus, the historian of Sicily, for *Nicias* (cf. *Nic.* 1).

Dandamis and Calanus: cf. *Alex.* 28, 65, 69. Xenocrates, the second head of the Academy, is not mentioned again in the Life, but often elsewhere: cf. Plutarch's *Fortune and Virtue in Alexander the Great* 331e, 333b.

Macedonian dead: in the battle of Chaeronea, 338 BC, Philip decisively defeated the Greek cities, and soon after established himself as 'leader' of Greece. Plutarch knew the historical sites around his native town very well. The communal grave has been discovered and excavated: see W. K. Pritchett, *American Journal of Archaeology*, 62 (1958), 307–11. The Sacred Band was an élite force of 300 Thebans noted for its bravery. He also described accurately the second battle of Chaeronea in 86 BC: see his *Sulla* 19.

319 *past the age for such things*: Philip married Cleopatra in 337. Plutarch strongly disapproved of older men taking young wives, but Philip was polygamous, taking at least seven wives, for diplomatic as well as personal reasons. Three

were called queens: Olympias, Phila, and Cleopatra. Cleopatra belonged to the Macedonian nobility and so represented a challenge to Olympias and Alexander. Satyrus treated the marriage in his life of Philip, and may be the source of Plutarch: cf. Athenaeus 13. 557b–e.

319 *stayed among the Illyrians*: this must have been a major family fight. Olympias returned to her native country, and Alexander, the crown prince, went into exile.

Demaratus of Corinth: Demaratus was one of the leaders of the Macedonian party in Corinth, fought at the Granicus as a Companion of Alexander, and was later at Susa.

320 *Thessalus, to Caria*: actors were not uncommonly used in diplomatic negotiations in this period.

honour by him: the Pixodarus affair, which probably preceded Philip's marriage with Cleopatra, also reveals serious dissension in the royal household: Philip did not take being crossed lightly. All four friends became very prominent later, Harpalus as finance minister, Nearchus as satrap and commander of Alexander's Indus fleet; Erigyius as cavalry commander, and Ptolemy as a Companion and special forces commander and later king of Egypt. Thessalus, however, was not sent to Macedonia by the Corinthians.

spotless either: it is typical of Plutarch's style to put the assassination of Philip (October, or perhaps June, 336) into a subordinate clause. The reasons for the murder, and the various people at court who might have been involved, have been endlessly debated. Alexander was accused of having a role, but this seems unlikely. In any case, Alexander immediately had a number of prominent figures and potential rivals executed.

the bride too: Euripides, *Medea* 288: Medea lists who must die: Creon, her husband Jason, and Creon's daughter, her rival.

out of the country: Olympias had Cleopatra, whom Philip had just married, killed; her infant son was killed as well. According to Justin (9. 7. 12) the son was killed in her arms, and she was forced to hang herself; Pausanias (8. 7. 7) reports that they were both drawn over hot coals.

321 *by all his enemies*: we have no other evidence for Macedonian desires for appeasement, which may simply be imagined by Plutarch, who also ignores Alexander's quick expedition to Corinth in 336 to be confirmed as commander of the Greek league established by Philip.

major engagement: the Triballi were in the Danube basin, modern Bulgaria. Plutarch is compressing the events of 335, and omits Alexander's quick attack across the Danube, expedition against the Illyrians to the west of Macedon, and his rapid march back to Greece.

died in the battle: the destruction of Thebes, one of the major cities of Greece for hundreds of years, and with a tradition going back to legendary times, was meant to be an object lesson to the Greeks against further opposition. It exemplifies the ruthless violence of which Alexander was capable, against which Plutarch sets the respect he shows in the next chapter to Timocleia. Pindar is the famous fifth-century Theban poet.

322 *have their freedom and leave*: this story, taken from Aristobulus, is told in a slightly different version in Plutarch's *Virtues in Women*, 259d–260d.

abandoned it: on these Mysteries, see *Alc.* 19 and note.

Dionysus: Plutarch refers ahead to cc. 50–1 (Clitus) and 58 (the hesitation of the troops to attack Nysa). Dionysus though a god was the son of a Theban woman, Semele. As god of wine he was responsible for Alexander's drunken murder of Clitus. He had also founded Nysa, and would have been displeased by Alexander's conquest of the city.

put in charge: this conference (and the meeting with Diogenes, the Cynic philosopher, if it in fact took place) was in the previous year, 336.

323 *I would be Diogenes*: the meeting with Diogenes, conquering king meeting philosopher content to live in an abandoned storage jar (rather like living in a cardboard box), was a much-loved anecdote.

in debt as well: the figures reported for Alexander's army varied considerably, partially depending on whether they included the force already in Asia Minor and various auxiliary forces. After he crossed the Hellespont, the total of Alexander's Macedonian infantry was 15,000. Plutarch may be making an implicit comparison with Roman campaigns in his own day.

324 *for his expedition*: this story of distribution of the king's land is obviously exaggerated, but there is no reason to doubt that Alexander bestowed generous gifts at this time. The Companions (*hetairoi*), never precisely defined in our sources, can usefully be considered as two overlapping groups: (1) close friends honoured at court (like Nearchus and Harpalus, above, c. 10), all but a few of whom were Macedonians, and (2) the Macedonian cavalry, collectively called 'the Companions', which at the Hellespont were 1,800 strong, divided into eight squadrons, one of which, the royal squadron, defended the king in battle. On the army of Alexander, see A. B. Bosworth, *Conquest and Empire: The Reign of Alexander the Great* (Cambridge: Cambridge University Press, 1988), 259–77.

crossed the Hellespont: spring 334.

after his death: the herald of Achilles is Homer. The sacrifice at the tomb honours his putative ancestor and recalls the legendary expedition of the Greeks against Troy, the model for all future invasions of Asia by Europe, and of heroic military achievement.

brave men: in the *Iliad*, the Trojan Paris is regularly called Alexander, and portrayed as a coward. Achilles when sitting out the battle sang of brave men (*Il.* 9. 189).

river Granicus: this river, the modern Can Deresi, on its way to the Sea of Marmora cuts a channel between steep banks, now 3–4 m. high. The battle took place near the modern town of Dimetoka. Since there are difficulties and contradictions in all the accounts of the battle, it has been reconstructed variously.

as a second Artemision: Daesius and Artemision are Macedonian months, roughly equivalent to April and May: Alexander suggests that a second

Artemision be inserted before Daesius. Such intercalation of months was a usual practice to regularize the lunar calendar. We cannot control the accuracy of the story. Plutarch shows Alexander's men fearful, the king confident.

325 *Alexander's sword*: this hand-to-hand combat is variously reported. This Clitus, the commander of the royal squadron of Companion cavalry (called 'the Black' to distinguish him from the fairer Clitus the White), was later killed by Alexander: cf. 50–1. Caesar risked a similar chance of death from one of his own fleeing soldiers at Pharsalus, *Caesar* 39.

326 *Lysippus sculpted*: this famous group of the twenty-five Companions (it did not include the nine infantrymen) was erected at Dium in Macedonia, and taken by the Romans to Rome after they defeated the Macedonians in 148.

the natives of Asia: the ambition lies in speaking not of a particular group, but of all the inhabitants of Asia. Alexander involves the Greeks since his expedition was seen as a retaliation for the Persian invasion of Greece in 480.

to face Darius: Plutarch passes rapidly over the business of subjugating and occupying the conquered territory.

327 *open up for me*: this play of Menander is lost.

Aristotle and philosophy: Theodectes was an orator and tragic poet active at Athens in the 360s and 350s. Apparently Aristotle had discussed his works with Alexander.

Phrygia: Alexander went along the south coast of Asia Minor as far as Side, then in spring 333 turned inland via Aspendus to Phrygia and its chief cities, Celenae and Gordium (near modern Ankara).

Paphlagonia and Cappadocia: Alexander did not actually conquer these lands north and west of Phrygia, but received their surrender at Ankyra (Ankara), then rushed to Tarsus in Cilicia.

towards the interior: Memnon died in summer 333, after threatening Alexander's position by taking Chios and besieging Mytilene.

600,000 men under him: this figure is incredibly large: the real size of the force is unknown.

328 *strength for the war*: Philip had been a friend and doctor of Alexander's since boyhood (cf. Curtius 3. 6. 1): Plutarch reports the story at length to demonstrate Alexander's trust in his friends and their devotion to him.

329 *on his way already*: this Amyntas was a mercenary commander for Darius at the battle of Issus.

for an encampment: apparently Darius had gone north along the east side of Mt. Amanus while Alexander went south along the coast on its west side. Plutarch implies that they were close, but their routes, though only about thirty miles apart, were separated by a mountain range 2,000 m. high. Darius had succeeded in cutting Alexander off from the north, but at the cost of meeting him in a tight space north of the Pillar of Jonah which was favourable to Alexander. See the detailed map in Bosworth, *Conquest and Empire*, 56.

330 *result of the wound*: the major battle of Issus (November 333) is described in a sentence. Plutarch is pleased to be able to contradict the testimony of a contemporary, Chares, with a letter of Alexander's. Chares followed the epic tradition of presenting the two commanders in single combat: he may also have been thinking of Cyrus the Younger's attack on Artaxerxes in Xen. *Anab.* 1. 8.

331 *match her beauty*: Barsine later gave birth to a son, Heracles, who after Alexander's death was briefly a pawn in the fight for power among the Successors.

torment to the eyes: the quote makes a strong ending to Plutarch's account of Alexander's restraint, since it recalls a famous passage in Herodotus, 5. 18, when Persian ambassadors who had just received the submission of the Macedonian king Amyntas could not keep their hands off the Macedonian women, whom they termed 'a torment to the eyes'. The indignant Macedonians killed the Persians.

332 *flaw in our nature*: Plutarch found this comment significant, and refers to it also at *Friends and Flatterers* 65f and *Table Talk* 717f.

queen of Caria: Ada was sister and successor to Pixodarus (cf. 10).

extravagance in there: for Leonidas' severity as Alexander's tutor, see c. 5.

birds for fun: Plutarch cites the Royal Diary at length in 76. The hunting referred to probably occurred when Alexander was in Babylon in 324.

333 *were to spend*: compare the table of the Roman Lucullus, who might spend 50,000 drachmas for a dinner for three (*Luc.* 41). Roman imperial banquets could be still more extravagant.

children, and wives: the narrative resumes after the digression of 21–3.

seven-month siege of Tyre: c. January–July 332.

334 *spoke his name*: the Greeks identified the Tyrian city god Melqart with Heracles. Alexander was reported to have asked to enter the city to sacrifice to him, and the Tyrians refused.

Tyre will be yours: the word 'satyr' (*satyros*) was divided into *sa Tyros*, 'Tyre yours'.

older than Phoenix: cf. *Alex.* 5. Phoenix accompanied Achilles to Troy.

335 *but the twenty-eighth instead*: another example of supplementing the regular lunar calendar (cf. 16). Inserting the extra day showed that Alexander had decided to take the city that month, and would keep inserting days as long as necessary. The determined assault wilted the Tyrians' resistance.

largest city in Syria: September and October 332.

stint the gods any more: Alexander sent approximately fifteen tons of incense and three of myrrh, presumably from the Persian royal stores.

there for safe keeping: presumably Aristotle's recension: cf. c. 8.

336 *name men give it*: the passage, *Odyssey* 4. 354–5, describes the island Pharos, near which Alexander founded Alexandria (winter 332/1).

shrine of Ammon: the sanctuary of Amon-Ra (identified by the Greeks with Zeus) at the oasis of Siwah, in the desert some 500 km. west of Cairo.

337 *and killed them*: in the sixth century BC. Cf. Hdt. 3. 26.

party in its journey: this story is taken as evidence of Callisthenes' desire to flatter Alexander. Other historians report other marvels on the trip: the two crows were in Aristobulus, but Ptolemy said the army was led instead by two talking snakes.

338 *Zeus, pai Dios*: it was normal to take a slip of the tongue or involuntary utterance as an indication of the divine will: cf. the Pythia's words in 14. In what follows Plutarch offers anecdotes on Alexander's attitude towards his alleged relation to Zeus. Plutarch does not note that the ruler of Egypt was considered son of Ammon. He, like other Greek imperial writers, disapproved of deification of living rulers, influenced by the situation of the emperors in his own day (good emperors received some cultic honours while living, and expected the title *divus* (divine) after their death). The position of Alexander himself has been a point of contention from his lifetime to the present. In later years the Greek cities certainly thought that Alexander would be pleased by divine honours: see most recently Bosworth, *Conquest and Empire*, 278–90, 'The Divinity of Alexander', and the bibliography cited there.

blessed gods: Homer, *Il.* 5. 340. The story, which concerns the siege of Massaga in 327, was in Aristobulus, cf. Athenaeus 251a.

Anaxarchus the sophist: Anaxarchus was a rationalist philosopher, said to be follower of Democritus and teacher of Pyrrho, the founder of Scepticism, who accompanied Alexander's expedition. Cf. c. 52.

pleasure or satisfaction: the story of the satraps' heads was reported by Satyrus, according to Athenaeus 6. 250f.

339 *to Phoenicia from Egypt*: Plutarch resumes the narrative—it is spring 331.

alliance with him: Arrian (*Anab.* 2. 25) places this delegation in the previous year, when Alexander was in Tyre; other sources report embassies at various times and with various offers. Plutarch may have held back mention of the embassy until this point so that it could be used to preface the story of Darius' reaction to Alexander's treatment of his wife and the invasion of central provinces of the empire. It ties the narrative to the victory over Darius at Issus and the digression in 21–3.

if I were Parmenio: the anecdote is often taken as hostile to Parmenio: rather it illustrates Alexander's greatness.

died in childbirth: presuming that the queen, Stateira, who had been captured after Issus (cf. 21) was pregnant by Darius, she would have died sometime in 332, during the siege of Tyre, confirming that the delegation from Darius took place in that year. The story that follows, with its dialogue, oaths, and stage directions, must be taken (and perhaps elaborated) from an inventive historian, perhaps Callisthenes. It is found in different form in Curtius 4. 10. 25–34 and Arrian 4. 20.

341   *a million men*: a wildly exaggerated figure: modern estimates agree that Darius had a large numerical advantage over Alexander, but the numbers cannot be established. Cf. Bosworth, *Conquest and Empire*, 78.

Gaugamela: Gaugamela was a village, Arbela the nearest large city: both were used to name the battle, which took place on the plain of Gaugamela, some 30 km. north-east of modern Mosul, *c.* 1 October 331.

home of the camel: more precisely, 'pasture of the camel'. The king was Darius I, according to the geographer Strabo (16. 1. 3).

Mysteries at Athens: this eclipse can be dated to 20 September 331.

344   *wear into battle*: this set description of Alexander's armour, placed prior to his entry into battle, recalls, though in different language, the formulaic arming scenes in Homer, e.g. *Il.* 11. 15–46.

where Darius was: the scene which follows is extraordinarily impressionistic and visual, focused on Alexander and Darius to the exclusion of the rest of the battle.

345   *his part in the battle*: Alexander wished to portray himself as the avenger of the Persian invasion of 480–479. Plutarch mentions two actions specifically recalling the Persian War: the battle of Plataea in 479 and Phayllus' participation in the battle of Salamis, 480 (cf. Hdt. 8. 47). Plataea had been destroyed in 426 and again in 373.

chasm of fire in Adiabene: our manuscripts read Ecbatana, the Persian summer capital in the Iranian plateau (modern Hamadan) which Alexander only reached in the following year, as he was pursuing Darius. The mistake may be due either to Plutarch or a copyist. The name Plutarch meant is uncertain, but Adiabene, on the road from Gaugamela to Babylon, is a region often identified as the site of this spring of naphtha. However, Plutarch may be thinking of any place in Babylonia.

346   *in the tragedy*: Euripides' *Medea*.

347   *go on for too long*: this digression makes an important point about the brilliance and danger of Alexander's dry and fiery nature, at a time when he is triumphing over Darius. On the physics of this passage, and its relation to Alexander, see the article by Sansone cited in Alexander: Introduction. Plutarch chooses to discuss naphtha rather than Alexander's triumphant entrance into Babylon, one of the capitals of the Persian empire, or the administrative arrangements Alexander made during the month he stopped there.

took control of Susa: December 331. Susa, the chief capital of the empire, had surrendered soon after Gaugamela.

for 190 years: Hermione is a Greek coastal city in the Peloponnese, facing the island of Hydra. The purple clothes would have been obtained at the time of Darius I's accession in 521. Since as a weight the talent was about 26 kg., this would be (if true!) 130 metric tons of dyed cloth.

347 *taken refuge there*: Plutarch refers to Persis, the original land of the Persians, in the mountainous region now the Iranian province of Fars, the capital of which, Shiraz, is not far from the two royal cities of Persepolis and Pasargadae.

against the Persians: Plutarch passes quickly over an invasion which required several brilliant tactical moves by Alexander. Cf. Bosworth, *Conquest and Empire*, 88–92. In addition, most editors postulate that an account of the fall of Persepolis has dropped out of our text, but this is not necessary. Plutarch wishes to move directly to Alexander's letter.

to be slaughtered: unlike Babylon and Susa, the Persian heartland had resisted Alexander, and he wished to make an example of it.

348 *four months in Persepolis*: c. February–May 330.

who later became king: Ptolemy became king of Egypt after the death of Alexander, founding the dynasty which was to end with Cleopatra.

destroyed Athens by fire: in 480 BC, cf. Hdt. 8. 53.

349 *as his affairs prospered*: the burning of the palace at Persepolis, an act, whether thoughtless or calculated, which marked the total defeat of the Persians, immediately precedes a series of anecdotes on Alexander's generosity, thoughtfulness, and loyalty towards his friends (39–42). Note the frequent references to Alexander's letters.

one full of wine: the Paeonians, a light cavalry regiment, had seen hard fighting in the three major battles and on many other occasions.

rejected his gifts: Phocion was an Athenian politician noted for his honesty and simple life, and is the subject of a biography by Plutarch. For his relation with Alexander, cf. *Phoc.* 18.

350 *clothing*: the house was given fully furnished, including the enormous supply of clothes left by its former owner.

gently and reasonably: the focus of the anecdotes shifts to the extravagance of Alexander's friends and his own simplicity. If we can trust Plutarch, the nets were 18 km. long.

351 *coming to help*: the dedicatory inscription of this work has been found at Delphi, where Plutarch might have seen it. Craterus was one of Alexander's closest associates, especially after Parmenio's death in 430 (cf. 41, 47, 48, 55). After Alexander's death he played a major role until his death in 321. Lysippus and Leochares were both famous sculptors.

malign him: Plutarch prepares the reader for Macedonian hostility to Alexander which will erupt later in his narrative, but explains it as a weakness of theirs, not of Alexander's.

352 *belonging to Seleucus*: the future king and founder of the Seleucid dynasty.

arrested by Bessus: the dates are uncertain, but Alexander probably left Persepolis at the end of May, about the time Darius abandoned Ecbatana to head east. Darius was deposed on the journey by a coup led by Bessus, the satrap of Bactria.

352 *shortage of water*: estimates vary on the time required and the distance covered to reach Darius (3,300 stades is nearly 600 km. (365 miles)). By any calculation, it was an extremely rapid and arduous chase over water-less terrain. Plutarch stresses Alexander's self-sacrificing endurance. The chase ended near Hecatompylus, west of modern Teheran between Semnan and Damghan.

353 *ranks of his Companions*: Bessus assumed the title of king, with the royal name Artaxerxes, but was arrested and handed over to Alexander in 329, and finally mutilated and killed (there are different stories on the form this took: Plutarch's is the most terrible) in 328.

354 *the Caspian Sea*: he was on the shore of the Caspian Sea. The Euxine Sea is the Black Sea, Lake Maeotis the Sea of Azov, and the supposed four gulfs of the surrounding ocean are the Caspian (imagined as open at the north), the Persian Gulf, the Red Sea, and the Mediterranean Sea. Although Herodotus (1. 202–3) had rightly thought that the Caspian was an enclosed sea, the geography of the area was disputed throughout antiquity.

ransom-money: in other accounts, Alexander immediately followed his threats with action. Plutarch's Alexander is more patient and generous.

marched into Parthian territory: from Zadracarta in Hyrcania east to the satrapy of Parthyaea, in north-west Iran. Plutarch is not clear on Alexander's movements, since in c. 47 he seems once more in Hyrcania. There are also contradictions in our sources.

than the former: Alexander presumably wished to assert his position as successor to Darius as king of Persia, especially after Bessus claimed the throne. Baggy trousers and the *kandys*, a wide-sleeved over-garment, were standard Persian dress; the *tiara*, or conical headdress, was worn on solemn occasions.

355 *suffering from dysentery*: in defending Alexander from softness, Plutarch refers ahead to an incident in summer 329, when Alexander received the two wounds and crossed the Orexartes (or Iaxartes, the modern Syr Darya, which drains into the Aral Sea) to fight the nomads to the north. The Tanaïs, the modern Don, was thought to rise in the east, and so was confused with the Orexartes.

if we believe it: a further digression, prompted by the mention of Scythia. Curtius (6. 5. 24–32) and Diodorus (17. 77. 1–3) report that Thalestris, queen of the Amazons, came to Alexander from the shores of the Black Sea to have a child by him. He honoured her request, and they stayed together thirteen days. Both place the incident in Hyrcania, before Alexander entered Parthia. Plutarch refers to an extraordinary number of sources on this occasion, perhaps because the story made him curious, though he clearly didn't believe it. Lysimachus assumed the title of king in Thrace in 305.

into Hyrcania: Plutarch is confused here: no one else mentions a return to Hyrcania. However, the paragraph has several difficulties and gaps in the text. The gist is clear: Alexander releases many of the Macedonians, and keeps a select army of 20,000 infantry and 3,000 cavalry. Other authors place this action earlier, after the death of Darius, as Alexander was about to enter Hyrcania. This passage, then, might be a flashback to the beginning of c. 44, to lead into the Macedonian problem.

356 *oversee this project*: this decision was probably made in 327; the young men arrived at Susa to join the army in 324 (see 71).

policy he was pursuing: another forward reference: Alexander captured Rhoxane, the daughter of the Bactrian baron, Oxyartes, in 328, and married her in spring 327.

Greeks and Macedonians: for Craterus, see c. 40 note. Hephaestion was a boyhood friend, who after the death of Philotas in 330 shared the cavalry command. He died in 324, and was extravagantly mourned by Alexander (72).

towards his companions: Philotas was commander of the Companion Cavalry until his death.

357 *property in Damascus*: that is, in 333, after the battle of Issus.

358 *the third of these sons*: the execution of Philotas took place in Phrada, the capital of Drangiane, in 330, although Plutarch does not tie it to any time or event. Parmenio, who was now well over 60, had been left behind in Ecbatana. This double execution of two of Alexander's most prominent generals attracted stories from the beginning; our versions present a spectrum of interpretations. Modern scholars think the plot of Dimnus was real, but the role of Philotas is hotly disputed. There was a trial before an assembly of Macedonians, and he was judged guilty. Once Philotas had been executed, it was expedient to kill his father as well.

not . . . by . . . Oeniadae, but by him: Antipater had been left as regent in Macedonia. Oeniadae is a town in Acarnania, near the border with Aetolia.

the business with Clitus too: in autumn 328, in Maracanda (Samarkand). This is Clitus the Black, who saved Alexander at the Granicus (16). After Philotas' death he had been appointed joint commander of the Companion Cavalry with Hephaestion, and recently had been appointed satrap of Bactria and Sogdiana.

359 *Clitus' spirit*: each person could be said to have a supernatural power (*daimon*) associated with him, which led him to his destiny, whatever it might be. Cf. *Them.* 29, *Caesar* 69, *Marius* 46, *Pompey* 74, 76, *Antony* 33, and for the guardian spirit of a whole people, *Alex.* 30.

sacrificed to the Dioscuri: only Plutarch mentions the warnings of danger to Clitus and the planned expiatory sacrifices. The sacrifice to the Dioscuri (Castor and Pollux) in some accounts displaces a sacrifice to Dionysus, furnishing a reason for the evil effects of the drinking at the party. It was common to invite guests to a dinner to eat the sacrificial animal, only a small part of which was actually burnt for the god.

359 *non-Greeks and enemies*: i.e. Persians who had been admitted into Alexander's court.

360 *rule in Greece . . .* : Euripides, *Andromache* 693, the beginning of a speech lamenting that the honour won by the effort of many soldiers is awarded to only one man, the general.

361 *Anaxarchus of Abdera*: Callisthenes of Olynthus was a philosopher and wrote a history of Alexander and a history of Greece, both used by Plutarch. For Anaxarchus, cf. 28 note.

on top of you: a philosopher, particularly one of Anaxarchus' school, was expected to dress in the simplest thin cloak, like Socrates. The anecdote appears only in Plutarch, highlighting Callisthenes' cutting wit.

country of his birth: i.e. he had only come to have citizens of Olynthus restored to their city, which Philip had destroyed, not to win riches.

362 *apply his intelligence to himself*: a quote from a lost tragedy of Euripides.

good material for one's speech: Euripides, *Bacchae* 267.

criminals become respectable: Plutarch cites this hexameter verse from an unknown author also at *Nic.* 11 and elsewhere. The practice of giving a speech on either side of a subject was a common rhetorical exercise: Callisthenes was too good at it.

braver man than you: Homer, *Il.* 21. 107. Bad enough, but worse if Alexander remembered the context: Achilles says this to a man he is about to kill. The unusual reference to the biographer Hermippus perhaps validates the information reported.

act of prostration: this act of homage before the king (in Greek, *proskunēsis*) could run from a slight bow and blowing of a kiss to complete prostration, depending on rank and occasion. The Greeks however, thought it was a cult act and should be reserved only for the gods. Alexander's request that his court follow the Persian custom thus is closely tied with the debate on his desire for divine honours.

363 *associates came to light*: the so-called Pages' Conspiracy: in Bactra (modern Balkh) in 327 a conspiracy to kill Alexander was found (or suspected) among the young nobles attendant upon Alexander, led by Hermolaus. They were discovered, tried, and executed by stoning.

364 *louse-ridden man*: Plutarch probably is thinking of the wound at the Malli town in 325. The congress mentioned was that of the Corinthian League, of which Alexander was still the head (cf. 11).

had missed a rare treat: a repetition of the anecdote found in 37, after Alexander took Persepolis. Here the story ends a sequence of unfavourable anecdotes with one which points to the positive achievement of Alexander, and adds an example of Alexander's generous treatment of those whom he liked—and who praised him. The date of Demaratus' death is not known. On the sequence of stories in 47–56, see Stadter, 'Anecdotes . . .', cited in Alexander: Introduction.

364 *set fire to his men's takings*: this incident is placed by Curtius much earlier, in 329. Alexander crossed the Hindu Kush and invaded India in late spring 327.

365 *relief of their weariness*: the discovery of the spring of oil has a larger significance for Plutarch as well as for the diviners.

Sisimithres' stronghold: also called the rock of Chorienes, taken in winter 328/7. The incidents of this chapter all indicate Alexander's determination, and are not arranged chronologically.

another rock: Aornus, the mountain Pir-Sar north-east of Peshawar on the Indus River, taken in winter 327/6.

Nysa: an Indian city considered sacred to Dionysus, taken in 327.

366 *arable farming*: Taxiles was the official title of the ruler of Taxila, a major urban centre which controlled the land between the Indus and the Hydaspes (modern Jhelum) rivers. The remains of the city, about twenty miles (32 km.) north-west of Islamabad, have been excavated and published (J. Marshall, *Taxila* (Cambridge, 1951), cf. M. Wheeler, *Flames over Persepolis* (New York, 1968), 102–20). Alexander crossed the Indus and arrived there in spring 326.

367 *as a king should*: the incident occurred at the siege of Massaga in modern Swat, in 327.

many of them too: these were the Brahmans, who encouraged the revolts of Musicanus and Sabbas (both in the lower Indus valley), in 325 (cf. 64).

in his letters: Porus, king of the rich country between the Hydaspes (Jhelum) and the Acesines (Chenab), opposed Alexander's crossing of the Hydaspes. By brilliant manoeuvres Alexander got his army across the river and defeated Porus in a pitched battle (summer 326). Plutarch, trusting in the authenticity of Alexander's letter, gives an unusually full account.

your good opinion: Plutarch includes this quote with the idea that Alexander was most likely thinking of the Athenian orators and historians who would ensure his glory.

368 *Potamon of Lesbos*: a rhetorician and historical writer active in the last half of the first century BC, here cited by a writer of miscellanies, Sotion.

369 *600,000 men*: Alexander's men mutinied, in part because of the monsoon rains, when he asked them to cross the Hyphasis (modern Beas), the last river of Punjab, in summer 326. Alexander knew of the Ganges, some 250 miles (400 km.) east, but it is uncertain whether Plutarch confuses the Ganges and the Hyphasis, or simply points toward Alexander's further objective beyond the Hyphasis, as do Diodorus and Curtius. Sandrocottus is Chandragupta, the founder of the Mauryan dynasty, who conquered the Indian satrapies after Alexander's death.

the outer sea: Alexander returned to the Indus, set out down the river in November 326, and reached the Indian Ocean in July 325. The wound he received at the Malli town very nearly killed him, and panicked the army.

370 *great deal of harm*: Plutarch has already mentioned the Brahmans at 59, but he does not distinguish between Brahmans and the ascetics (gymnosophists or naked philosophers) described in 65. The dialogue in this chapter is of a type popular in antiquity, the wise man facing the ruler. Answers six to nine address particularly Alexander's situation.

372 *he turned back*: the emperor Trajan also wished to reach the Ocean on his invasion of Parthia, and arrived at the Persian Gulf in AD 115. Ocean was the general word given to the water which surrounded Europe, Asia, and Africa, though the Greeks had little idea of how large these land masses actually were. One reason Alexander had wished to push east to the Ganges (c. 62) was that he thought he would arrive at the Ocean quickly in that direction.

chief helmsman: this voyage is decribed in the second part of Arrian's *Indica*, based on Nearchus' own account of the journey. Nearchus sailed to the Persian Gulf, and rejoined Alexander at Susa.

satraps and kings: this trip (late in 325) across the desert country of southern Pakistan was immensely difficult and exacted an incredible toll on the army. Alexander's motives for taking this route are obscure: he may have underestimated its difficulty, or wished to challenge earlier rulers, like Cyrus the Great, who had not been able to cross it.

373 *palace of Gedrosia*: this is a slip for Carmania, by Plutarch or a copyist.

came up to see him: leaving his fleet on the coast, Nearchus made a five-day journey inland to report to Alexander, then returned.

374 *turmoil and instability*: Alexander crushed generals and satraps he considered disloyal or thieving: E. Badian describes in detail the period, which he calls 'a reign of terror' (*Journal of Hellenic Studies*, 81 (1961), 16–43).

ruled by a woman: Plutarch schematizes drastically: Olympias had returned to Epirus to assume control in 331, when her brother the king died. Cleopatra, her daughter and the king's widow, returned to Macedonia.

profoundly moved Alexander: this simple tomb still dominates the landscape at the ruins of Pasargadae: see D. Stronach, *Pasargadae* (Oxford, 1978), 24–43.

375 *Tomb of the Indian*: the Indian was an ambassador to Augustus in 20 BC, when the emperor was in Greece. Strabo (15. 686) records the inscription on the tomb, which Plutarch probably had seen: 'Zarmanochegas, an Indian from Bargosa, lies here, having immortalized himself according to the ancestral customs of the Indians.'

upon their drinking: the Greeks normally drank their wine diluted, and four choes is about 13 litres (2.8 gals.). In ancient physiology, wine was a strong coolant, which quenched the heat of the body. Cf. Plutarch's discussion of the question at *Table Talk* 651f ff.

376 *trained and educated*: cf. c. 47.

376 *stipendiary orphans*: this mutiny and reconciliation occurred at Opis in 324. The causes of the soldiers' dissatisfaction are variously reported, but with the mutiny at the Hyphasis it is one of the few occasions where Alexander briefly lost control of his troops. Plutarch is silent on the arrest and execution of the ringleaders described by Arrian (*Anab*. 7. 8–12), and only shows the leaders coming to Alexander unarmed, as submissive citizens, not soldiers.

At Ecbatana in Media: autumn 324.

377 *set out for Babylon*: early in 323.

378 *Antipater and his sons*: Antipater, who had been regent of Macedonia, was relieved of his office and asked to bring new Macedonian recruits to Alexander. After Alexander's death he held on to Macedonia until his own death in 319.

379 *time for him to recover*: Cassander held Macedon after his father's death, opposing any effort to reunite the empire. He had Olympias, Rhoxane, and her son by Alexander all killed. He assumed the title of king in 305, and died in 297.

lowest level and . . . : Plutarch found superstition at least as dangerous as atheism. Cf. *Per*. 6, and his work *On Superstition*. Though a priest at Delphi, he was generally cautious about supposed divine manifestations, cf. *Camillus* 6.

thirtieth of Daesius: our ancient accounts do not agree precisely (just below the Royal Diary gives 28 Daesius), but a Babylonian astronomical tablet published in 1955 establishes the date as 10 June 323.

the Royal Diary: a record of the last days in Babylon, cited at 23 and also by Arrian 7. 25–6. See Alexander: Introduction.

380 *administered the poison*: Cassander avenged his brother in 316 by having Olympias murdered and her body left unburied.

381 *through everything else*: something very cold is seen as needed to destroy Alexander's fiery constitution. Herodotus (6. 67) says that the water of the Styx was thought to drip from a rock at Nonacris in Arcadia.

quarrelling among themselves: there was no agreement on the succession or the means of administering the empire. Eventually the generals reached a compromise that the throne would be shared by Rhoxane's as yet unborn child, if it were a boy, and Alexander's half-brother Arrhidaeus. This was a stop-gap: the wars of Alexander's generals continued for a generation. Only with the battle of Ipsus in 301 was it established that the empire would be divided into a number of separate kingdoms.

poisoned by Olympias: Arrhidaeus, Philip's son by Philinna, would have been about 30. There is no other evidence for Olympias' guilt, and this is probably Cassander's propaganda. It is possible that part of the ending of the Life is missing, as is the beginning of *Caesar*. It might have contained the fate of Rhoxane and her son, killed in 310 by Cassander. However, Plutarch throughout presumes the reader's knowledge of events, and he may have chosen to end with the stories of the alleged poisoning and the uncertain succession.

TEXTUAL NOTES

LYCURGUS

1.8: It looks as though the very beginning of this paragraph has been lost.

6.2: The text of this last sentence is corrupt; I have translated Sintenis' conjecture: δάμῳ δὲ τὰν κυρίαν ἦμεν καὶ κράτος.

6.4: The name has not survived.

10.4: Reading ὄντα <ὄντως>.

19.9: It is likely that some text has dropped out, since all these anecdotes should contain Lycurgan apophthegms. The same anecdote occurs in Plutarch's *spartan sayings*, Lycurgus 23, with the addition: 'When someone asked him why, he said, "So that none of them acquires the habit of giving up when the going is tough."' Apparently a raised hand signalled acceptance of defeat.

27.5: Reading πάντας, Reiske.

SOLON

8.6: There seems no unassailable reason to assume a lacuna in the text at this point, as the Teubner does.

9.3: Euboea is an unlikely place for Plutarch to say the breakwater points towards, because plenty of mainland intervenes between Salamis and Euboea, but the original text is now irrecoverable.

9.6: Reading <τοὺς> ἐκ γῆς προσαγόμενος.

14.9: Reading ἤθελε with the MSS.

THEMISTOCLES

1.1: The beginning of the Life has been lost.

2.3: Reading ὑπερορῶν with the MSS.

9.3: Reading <τοιαύτης> νικῆς.

10.7: The Teubner's ὡς must be a misprint for ὧν.

10.9: Reading πολλοί with the MSS.

12.1: Retaining ἄνωθεν with the MSS.

14.4: Reading Πειραιεύς with Sintenis.

CIMON

1.8: Retaining ἀνῳκοδόμησαν with the MSS.

1.9: Moving the dash to after αἰολίζοντες with several editors.

18.5: Unfortunately, the Greek text is hopelessly corrupt at this point, and there is no chance of determining Cimon's destination. It was presumably somewhere in Cyprus.

PERICLES

3.6: Taking ποτὲ δέ out of the quotation, with Stadter.

7.8: Retaining ἀλλὰ δάκνειν with the MSS.

8.6: Retaining αὐτός with the MSS.

8.6: Retaining μηδέ with the MSS.

9.2: Omitting Ziegler's addition.

10.4: Reading κατελθών with Sintenis.

10.6: Reading πράσσειν with Vulcobius.

11.1: Reading τινα <δυνα>τὸν πρὸς αὐτόν with Sansone.

13.15: Reading εἰς τὰ ἔργα with the MSS.

15.3: The text here is difficult. I suspect there may be a lacuna, to be filled with something along the lines suggested.

24.10: There is no good reason not to retain the MSS reading.

26.4: Reading ποντοπορεῖν with the MSS.

31.4: Omitting τοῦ Περικλέους with Sansone.

32.5: Reading φοβηθεὶς ἐξέπεμψεν [καὶ προύπεμψεν] with Flacelière.

34.2: Retaining the MSS ὅμως.

34.5: Reading χωριτικοῦ with some MSS.

37.4: Reading ἐπράθησαν with the MSS.

NICIAS

1.5: Reading ἀποκαλυπτομένην with the corrector of MS U.

2.6: Reading παρεῖχε with Coraes.

2.6: Reading ὑπερορῶντας instead of θαρροῦντας with MS M.

18.11: Reading καθ' ὥραν with Kraner.

27.5: Reading φόνος with Ziegler.

ALCIBIADES

11.3: Following Page in reading ἄγαμαι (Lindskog), ὃ μῆτις, τρίτα<τα> (Bergk), and Διός (Hermann).

34.7: There seems no overwhelming reason to postulate a lacuna in the text.

38.5: Reading κεὐκόλως with Kronenberg.

AGESILAUS

11.9: Reading δεῖ with Stephanus.

21.2: The lacuna in our text may plausibly be filled by reference to Xenophon, *Hellenica* 4. 4. 19.

29.5: Reading γήθους with some MSS.

ALEXANDER

4.3: Reading τὸν κεραυνοφόρον with the MSS and recent editors, without Coraes's emendation.

7.2: Reading κατάρτυσιν with Hamilton.

7.9: Retaining μετά with the MSS.

10.3: A lacuna in the text should presumably be filled with something like this, and τὸν Ἀλέξανδρον changed to τοῦ Ἀλεξάνδρου.

15.8: Punctuating with a comma after στήλην, with Hamilton.

16.1: Reading τῆς εἰσόδου τῆς ἀρχῆς with Ziegler.

16.11: Reading <πρὸς> ἑτέραν δέ with Hamilton.

17.6: Reading προσεχεῖς ... πάτους with an anonymous editor and Ziegler.

20.13: Reading <καὶ> ἠσκημένα with Sintenis.

21.9: Reading κατὰ τὸ κάλλος with Stephanus, and keeping the words in their original place in the text.

26.6: Reading ἀνήπται with Powell.

26.14: Retaining the MSS text without a lacuna.

32.1: Reading ἐπελθόντας with the Aldine edition.

33.8: Reading ἀποπτυρόμενοι with Held.

34.3: Retaining τι μεθέξων with the MSS.

35.1: Reading Ἀδιαβηνοῖς with Kramer.

35.13: The word 'naphtha' and at least one theory have dropped out of the transmitted text.

37.2: There seems no compelling reason to assume a lacuna in the text, as van Herwerden did.

39.7: Retaining ἐνδόξως ἄγε with the MSS.

42.6: Retaining ἀνυδρίαν with the MSS.

47.1: Reading προσέλαβε, and omitting <πεῖραν>, with an anonymous editor.

47.1: Reading ἐνώπιον with Ziegler.

47.2: Reading ἀφιέναι γε τοὺς βουλομένους ἐφῆκε μαρτυράμενος, without, therefore, a lacuna in the next line, with Coraes.

49.3: Reading Δίμνος here and below with Ziegler, following Curtius and Diodorus.

51.4: Omitting Ziegler's added ἐάν.

51.8: There is no need to posit a lacuna here.

58.6: Hamilton points out that there is no need to read a lacuna here, as the Teubner text does.

60.1: Reading ἀντιπώρους with one MS and recent editors.

60.15: Retaining τοὺς αὐτονόμους with the MSS.

62.4: Reading Σανδρόκοττος with Ziegler, here and below.

68.6: Reading πόλεων, with Reiske.

75.2: There is a short lacuna in the text.

77.4: The text is corrupt, but the sense is secure.

INDEX OF LITERARY AND HISTORICAL SOURCES CITED BY PLUTARCH

(* identifies authors whose works are preserved; the rest are known only through fragments, such as those cited in Plutarch. Most have a fuller entry in *Oxford Classical Dictionary*, third edition, 1996. L = *Lycurgus*, S = *Solon*, T = *Themistocles*, C = *Cimon*, P = *Pericles*, N = *Nicias*, Alc = *Alcibiades*, Ag = *Agesilaus*, A = *Alexander*, and the reference is to chapter number.)

Acestodorus, third-century (?) writer on cities: T13
*Aeschines, fourth-century Athenian orator: S11
Aeschines of Sphettus, student of Socrates and author of Socratic dialogues, including an *Aspasia*: P24
*Aeschylus, Athenian tragedian: T14
Alcman, Spartan lyric poet, seventh cent.: L21
Alexander the Great's letters: A17, 22 (bis), 27, 28, 29, 34, 37, 39 (tris), 41 (quater), 42, 46, 47, 55 (bis), 57, 60 (bis), 71
*Andocides, fifth-century Athenian orator: T32
Androtion, fourth-century Athenian historian: S15
anonymous comic poet(s): P7, 8, 13, 16, 24
anonymous epigrams: T1, C7 (tris)
anonymous song: L21
anonymous tragedians: S20, Alc23, A53
Anticlides, third-century Alexander-historian: A46
Antigenes, Alexander-historian: A46
*Antiphon, fifth-century orator: Alc3
Antisthenes, student of Socrates and founder of the Cynic school, author of Socratic dialogues, including an *Aspasia*: L30, Alc1
Apollodorus, second-century chronographer: L1
Apollothemis, an unknown antiquarian: L31
Archelaus, fifth-century poet: C4 (bis) (via Panaetius?)
Archilochus of Paros, seventh-century iambic and elegiac poet: P28
Archippus, fifth-century comic poet: Alc1
Aristobulus, fourth-century Alexander-historian, accompanied Alexander: A15, 16, 18, 21, 46, 75
Aristocrates of Sparta, first-century BC or AD author on Sparta: L4, 31
Ariston of Ceos, third-century Peripatetic philosopher: T3
*Aristophanes, fifth-century Athenian comic poet: T19, C16, P8, 26, 30, N4, 8, Alc1, 16
*Aristotle, the famous fourth-century philosopher, author (or motivator) of *Constitutions* of Greek cities, including Athens (= *Athpol.*), Sparta, and Samos: L1, 5, 6, 14, 28, 31, S11, 25, 32, T10, C10, P4, 9, 10, 26, 28 (bis), N2.
*Aristoxenus, fourth-century author of lives of philosophers and books on laws and music: L31, A4

Autocleides, author of *Commentaries* which interpreted traditional religious practice, probably in the third century BC: N23

Callisthenes, a late fourth-century historian of Greece and of Alexander the
Great, whom he accompanied: C12, 13, Ag34, A27, 33 (bis)

Chares, court official of Alexander and Alexander-historian: A20, 24, 46, 54,
55, 70

Charon of Lampsacus, fifth-century historian: T27

Cleanthes, third-century Stoic philosopher: Alc6

Cleidemus, fourth-century Athenian historian: T10

Cleitarchus, popular Alexander-historian: T27, A46

Craterus of Macedon (not the general of Alexander), author of a collection of
Athenian decrees: C13 (perhaps used in T, P, N, Alc for decrees)

Cratinus, Athenian comic poet, contemporary of Pericles: S25, C10, P3, 13 (bis),
24

Critias, an uncle of Plato and leader of the Thirty Tyrants, the junta which
briefly ruled Athens after its defeat in the Peloponnesian War, 404–403 BC,
wrote poetry and philosophical works: L9, C10, 16, Alc33

Critolaus, second-century Peripatetic philosopher: P7

Delphic records: S11

Demades, fourth-century Attic orator: S17

Demetrius of Phalerum, fourth-century Peripatetic philosopher and tyrant of
Athens: L23, S23

*Demosthenes, Athenian orator: Alc10

Dicaearchus, fourth-century Peripatetic philosopher, author of *On the Laws at
Sparta* and a kind of Greek history, *Life of Greece*: Ag19

Didymus, prolific first-century scholar: S1

Dieutychidas, unknown, perhaps Dieuchidas, fourth-century author on Megarian
history: L1

Dinon, fourth-century historian of Persia: T27, A36

Diodorus the topographer (or periegete), author of works of popular geography and guidebooks under the Roman empire: T32, C16

Dioscorides, first century BC or AD, author of a *Constitution of Sparta*: L11,
Ag35

Diphilus, fourth-century comic poet: N1

Duris of Samos, fourth-century historian, wrote in a particularly vivid and imaginative style: P28, Alc32, Ag3, A15, 46

Ephorus, fourth-century historian, author of a universal history from the Trojan
War to 341 BC: T27, C12 (bis), P28, Alc32

Eratosthenes, third-century scholar, poet, geographer, and chronographer:
L1, T27, A3, 31

Euanthes of Samos, unknown author, but perhaps the same as Euanthes of
Miletus, who wrote on the Seven Sages: S11 (through Hermippus)

Eupolis, fifth-century Athenian comic poet: C15, P3, 24, N4, Alc13

*Euripides, fifth-century Athenian tragic poet: S1, 22, C4, N5, 9, 17, Alc11,
23, Ag15, A10, 35, 51, 53 (bis)

Gorgias of Leontini, fifth-century orator and sophist: C10

Hecataeus of Eretria, unknown author who mentioned Amazons: A46

Hegesias of Magnesia, third-century historian: A3

Hellanicus of Lesbos, fifth-century historian: Alc21

Heraclides of Pontus, fourth-century Platonist and author: S1, 22, 31, 32, T27, P35, A26

Hereas of Megara, Megarian historian: S10

Hermippus of Athens, fifth-century comic poet: P33

Hermippus, third-century philosopher, wrote on the Seven Sages and on lawgivers: L5, 23, S2, 6, 11, A54

*Herodotus, fifth-century historian of the Persian Wars: T7, 17, 21

*Hesiod, seventh-century didactic poet: S2

Hieronymus of Rhodes, third-century Peripatetic philosopher: Ag13

Hippias, fifth-century sophist: L23

*Homer, epic poet: S10, 25, N9, Ag5, 15, A26, 28, 54

Idomeneus of Lampsacus, third century, wrote on demagogues: P10, 35

Ion of Chios, fifth-century poet, and writer of memoirs: C5, 9, 16, P5

Ister, third-century historian: A46

Laconian records: Ag19

Melanthius, fifth-century poet: C4 (tris)

*Menander, fourth-century comic poet: A17

Nausicrates, unknown orator: C19

Neanthes, third-century historian: T1, 29

Onesicritus, Alexander-historian, accompanied Alexander, was helmsman of Indus fleet: A8, 15, 46 (bis), 60, 61, 65

Panaetius, second-century Stoic philosopher and historian: C4

Pasiphon of Eretria, author of Socratic dialogues: N4

Pataecus, unknown author, perhaps writer of fables: S6 (through Hermippus)

Phaeax, Athenian politician and orator (= pseudo-Andocides): Alc13

Phanias (or Phaenias) of Eresus on Lesbos, fourth-century Peripatetic philosopher, author of two works on tyrants: S14, 32, T1, 7, 13, 27, 29

Phanodemus, fourth-century Athenian historian: T13, C12, 19

Philip of Chalcis, unknown author who mentioned Amazons: A46

Philip of Theangela, unknown author who mentioned Amazons: A46

Philistus of Syracuse, fourth-century historian of Sicily: N1, 19, 28

Philon of Thebes, unknown author who mentioned Amazons: A46

Philochorus, fourth-century Athenian historian, also wrote on religious practice: N23

Philocles, wrote on Solon's laws: S1 (through Didymus)

Philostephanus, third-century scholar: L23

Phrynicus, fifth-century comic poet: N4, Alc4?, 20

Phrynicus, fifth-century tragic poet: Alc4?

Phylarchus, third-century historian: T32

*Pindar, famous fifth-century Theban poet: L21, T8, N1

*Plato, famous fourth-century philosopher: L5, 7, 15, 16, 28, 29, S26, 31, T2, 4, P7, 8, 13, 15, 24, Alc1, 4

Plato, fifth-century Athenian comic poet: T32, P4, N11, Alc13

Polyclitus of Larissa, Alexander-historian: A46

Polyzelus of Rhodes, an obscure historian: S15

Potamon of Lesbos, first-century rhetorician and historian: A61 (through Sotion)

Ptolemy, companion of Alexander, king of Egypt, and Alexander-historian: A46

Simonides of Ceos, lyric and elegiac poet, first part of fifth century: L1, T1, 8, 15, Ag1

Solon, sixth-century poet and lawgiver: S2 (bis), 3 (ter), 8, 14 (bis), 15 (quater), 16 (bis), 18, 25, 26 (bis), 30 (bis), 31 (bis)

*Sophocles, fifth-century Athenian tragic poet: S1, A7

Sosibius, Spartan antiquarian: L25

Sotion, a first-century AD author of miscellanies: A61

Sphaerus, third-century Stoic and reformer, wrote on Spartan constitution: L5

Stesimbrotus, fifth-century sophist and author of a booklet called *Themistocles, Thucydides, and Pericles*: T2, 4, 24, C4, 14, 16 (bis), P8, 13, 26, 36

Teleclides, fifth-century Athenian comic poet: P3, 16, N4

Terpander of Lesbos, seventh-century lyric poet: L21

*Theophrastus of Eresus, student of Aristotle and head of the Peripatetic school, author of many works. Lost works include *Ethics* and *Politics for the Critical Moment*: L10, S4, 31, T25, P23, 35, 38, N10, 11, Alc10, Ag2, 36, A4

Theopompus of Chios, fourth-century historian, author of a Greek history continuing Thucydides and a *Philippica* which included a section on Athenian demagogues: T19, 25, 31, Alc32, Ag10, 31, 32

*Thucydides, fifth-century Athenian historian of the Peloponnesian War: L27, 28, T25, 27, P9, 15, 16, 28 (bis), 33, N1, 4, 19, 20, 28, Alc6, 11, 13, 20, Ag33

Timaeus, third-century historian of Sicily and south Italy, author of a list of Olympic victors: L1, 31, N1, 19, 28 (bis)

Timocreon of Rhodes, fifth-century poet: T21 (tris)

Timon of Phleious, third-century Sceptic philosopher and satiric poet: P4

Timotheus of Miletus, fifth/fourth-century dithyrambic poet: Ag14

Tyrtaeus, seventh-century Spartan elegiac poet: L6

*Xenophon, fourth-century Athenian historian and philosopher, author of, among other works, a Greek history from 411 to 362 BC (*Hellenica*), an encomium of Agesilaus (*Agesilaus*), and a *Constitution of the Lacedaemonians*: L1, Alc32, Ag4, 18, 19, 29, 34

INDEX OF PROPER NAMES

(Authors are collected and more fully identified in the Index of Sources. Names which are simply patronymics have been omitted. L = *Lycurgus*, S = *Solon*, T = *Themistocles*, C = *Cimon*, P = *Pericles*, N = *Nicias*, Alc = *Alcibiades*, Ag = *Agesilaus*, A = *Alexander*.)

Aboulites, Persian satrap: A68

Abydos, city in NE Asia Minor: Alc27, 29, 36

Academeia, sacred grove in Athens: S1, C13

Acamantis, Athenian tribe: P3

Acarnan/ia, ians, region of NW Greece: P17, 19, Ag22, A5, 19

Acestodorus, author: T13

Achaeans, people of Peloponnese: P19

Acharnae, deme of Attica: T24, P33

Achilles, hero of Trojan War: Ag5, A5, 15

Acouphis, Indian: A58

Ada, queen of Caria: A22

Adeimantus, Athenian archon: T5

Adeimantus, Athenian general: Alc36

Adiabene, Persian province: A35

Admetus, king of Molossians: T24

Adonis, Anatolian god: N13, Alc18

Aeacidae, heroes of Salamis: T15

Aeacus, ancient hero: A2

Aegae, city of Macedonia: A41

Aegae, city of NW Asia Minor: T26

Aegean Sea: T21, 25, C8, 18 P17, Alc26

Aegeus, father of Theseus: C8

Aegin/a, -etans, island in Saronic Gulf: T4, 15, 17, P8, 29, 34, 38, N6

Aegospotami, place in Thracian Chersonese: Alc36

Aeol/is, -ians, region in NW Asia Minor: T26

Aepeia, city on Cyprus: S26

Aeschines, Athenian orator: S11

Aeschylus, Athenian tragic poet: A8, T14, C8

Aesop, fabulist: S6, 28

Aetolians, people of NW Greece: N6, A49

Agamemnon, Homeric hero: P28, N5, Ag5, 6, 9

Agariste, mother of Pericles: P3

Agatharchus, painter: P13, Alc16

Agesilaus, king of Sparta: C19, Ag *passim*

Agesipolis, son of Pausanias: Ag24

Agis II of Sparta: Alc23, 24, 25, 34, 38, Ag1, 3, 4,

Agis III of Sparta: Ag5

Agis IV of Sparta: Ag40

Agraulus, wife of Cecrops: Alc15

Agryle, deme of Attica: T23, Alc22

Ahriman, Persian god: T28

Ajax, Homeric hero: S10, Alc1

Alcander, Spartan: L11

Alcetas, Macedonian: A55

Alcibiades, Athenian politician: P20, 37, N9, 10, 11, 12, 13, 14, 15, Alc *passim*

Alcimus, place in Piraeus: T32

Alcmaeon, father of Megacles: S11, 29

Alcmaeonidae, Athenian family: S30, Alc1

Alcman, poet: L28

Alexander I of Macedonia: C14

Alexander III, the Great: Ag15, A *passim*

Alexander of Troy (Paris): A15

Alexander, a Macedonian: A58

Alexandria, city of Egypt: A26

Alexandropolis, city in Thrace: A9

Alexippus, doctor: A41

Alopece, deme of Attica: T32, P11

Amazons, tribe of women: A46

Ambracia, city of NW Greece: P17

Ameinias, fighter at Salamis: T14

Ammon, Egyptian god: C18, N13, A3, 26, 27, 47, 50, 72, 75

Ammonius, philosopher: T30

Amompharetus, Spartan: S10

Amphictyonic League: S11, T20, C8

Amphipolis, city in Thrace: C8, N9, 10

Amycla, nurse of Alcibiades: Alc1

Amyntas, Macedonian: A20

Anacharsis, Scythian sage: S5

Anacreon, poet: P2

Anaphlystus, deme of Attica: C17

Anaxagoras, philosopher: T2, P4, 5, 6, 8, 16, 32, N23
Anaxarchus, philosopher: A8, 28, 52
Anaxilaus, of Byzantium: Alc31
Andocides, orator: T32, N13, Alc21
Androcles, orator: Alc19
Andros, Aegean island: P11, Alc35
Androtion, historian: S15
Antalcidas, Spartan: Ag23, 26, 31, 32
Anthemocritus, Athenian: P30
Anticlides, author: A46
Anticrates, Spartan: Ag35
Antigenes, historian: A46
Antigenes, the one-eyed: A70
Antigone, mistress of Philotas: A48, 49
Antigonus the One-eyed: A77
Antiochus, Athenian: Alc 10, 35
Antiorus, Spartan: L35
Antipater, Macedonian general: A11, 20, 39, 46, 47, 55, 57, 68, 71, 74, 77
Antiphates, beloved of Themistocles: T18
Antiphon, orator: N6, Alc3
Antisthenes, philosopher: P1, Alc1
Anytus, Athenian: Alc4
Apelles, painter: A4
Aphetae, promontory opposite Artemisium: T7
Apollo, Greek god: L5, 6, 13, 29, S4, 9, T15, C19, N3, Alc2, Ag19, A3, 14, 24
Apollodorus, historian: L1
Apollodorus, Babylonian general: A73
Apollophanes of Cyzicus: Ag12
Apollothemis, historian: L31
Apsephion, archon at Athens: C8
Arab/ia, -ians: A24, 68
Arbela, city of Assyria: A31
Arcad/ia, -ians, region of Peloponnese: T6, P29, Ag15, 22, 30, 32, 33
Arcesilas, Spartan: C10
Archelaus, philosopher/poet: C4
Archelaus, Spartan king: L5
Archeptolis, daughter of Themistocles: T32
Archestratus, Athenian commander: Alc16
Archias, Theban: Ag23, 24
Archidamidas, Spartan: L20
Archidamus II of Sparta: C16, P8, 29, 33, Ag1, 2
Archidamus III of Sparta: Ag 25, 33, 34, 40

Archilochus, poet: P2, 28
Archippe, wife of Themistocles: T32
Archippus, comic poet: C1
Architeles, Athenian: T7
Areopagus, Athenian court: S19, 22, 31, T10, C10, 15, P7, 9
Ares, Greek god of war: L20, C7, Ag14
Arethusa, city of Macedonia: L31
Argileonis, mother of Brasidas: L25
Arginusae, islands off coast of Asia Minor: P37
Argos, Argives, region in Peloponnese: L7, T23, P2, N10, Alc12, 15, 19, 23
Ariamenes, brother of Xerxes: T14
Ariomandes, Persian: C12
Ariphron, brother of Pericles: Alc1, 3
Aristander, seer: A2, 14, 25, 31, 33, 50
Aristides, Athenian politician: L1, T3, 5, 7, 11, 12, 16, 20, C6, 10, N11
Aristobulus, epithet of Artemis: T22
Aristocrates, historian: L4, 31
Aristocritus, agent of Pixodarus: A10
Aristodamus, Spartan king: L1, Ag19
Aristodicus, of Tanagra: P10
Ariston, of Athens: S30
Ariston, of Ceos, philosopher: T3
Ariston, of Corinth: N20, 25
Aristophanes, comic poet: T19, C16, P8, 26, 30, N4, 8, Alc1, 16
Aristophanes, Macedonian guard: A51
Aristophon, painter: Alc16
Aristotle, philosopher: L1, 5, 6, 14, 28, 31, S11, 32, T10, C10, P4, 9, 10, 26, 28, N1, 2, A7, 8, 17, 52, 54, 55, 74, 77
Aristoxenus, author: L31, A4
Armenians: C3
Arnaces, Persian: T16
Arrhidaeus, Philip, half-brother of Alexander: A10, 77
Artabanus, Persian: T27
Artabazus, father of Barsine: A21
Artaxerxes I, king of Persia: T26, 27, 28, 29, 31
Artaxerxes II, king of Persia: Alc10, 37, Ag6, 10, 12, 23
Artaxerxes III Ochus, king of Persia: A5, 69
Artayctes, Persian: T13
Artemis, Greek goddess: L18, T8, 22, 31, Ag6, 32, A3
Artemisia, queen of Caria: T14

Artemisium, cape on Euboea: T7, 8, 9

Artemius, of Colophon: A51

Artemon, of Clazomenae: P27

Arthmiadas, Spartan: L5

Arthmius of Zeleia: T6

Arybbas, brother of Olympias: A2

Asia, continent: T16, 24, 25, 31, C12, 19, P17, Ag *passim*, A *passim*

Asia, daughter of Themistocles: T32

Asinaria, festival at Syracuse: N28

Asinarus, river near Syracuse: N27, 28

Asopia, valley of the river Asopus in Boeotia: S9

Aspasia, mistress of Pericles: P24, 25, 30, 32

Aspasia of Phocaea: P24

Aspendus, city in S. Asia Minor: Alc26

Asteria, woman of Salamis: C4

Astyochus, Spartan naval commander: Alc25

Astyphilus, seer: C18

Athena, Greek goddess: L5, 6, 11, S12, T10, 19, P13, 31, N13, Alc2, 34, Ag19, A15

Athenodorus, actor: A29

Athenophanes, Athenian: A35

Athens, Athenians: *passim*

Athos, mountain of N. Greece: A72

Atlantis, mythical island: S26, 31, 32

Attalus, Macedonian noble: A9, 10, 55

Attica, the land of Athens: S10, 13, 15, 22, T9, 12, 13, C4, 19, P10, 22, 30, 33, Alc15, 23

Aulis, city of Boeotia: Ag6

Autocleides, religious expert: N23

Axiochus, father of Aspasia: P24

Babyca, bridge in Sparta: L6

Babylon/ -ians, city of Asia: A37

Bactrians, people of central Asia: A32

Bagaeus, Persian: Alc39

Bagoas, rich Persian: A39

Bagoas, young Persian: A67

Barsine, concubine of Alexander: A21

Bathycles, sculptor: S4

Bel, Babylonian god: A18

Bessus, Persian pretender: A42, 43

Bias of Priene, one of Seven Sages: S4

Bisaltae, people of Thrace: P11

Bithyn/ia, -ians, region of NW Asia Minor: Alc29, A29, 37

Biton of Argos: S27

Blaste, nymph: S12

Boeot/ia, -ians, region of central Greece: L13, T7, 9, C1, P17, 18, 33, N10, 21, Alc1, 14, 24, 31, Ag6, 8, 17, 19, 22, 23, 24, 26, 28

Boges, Persian: C7

Brasidas, Spartan general: L25, 30, N9

Brauron, place in Attica: S10

Bucephalas, horse of Alexander: A6, 16, 32, 44, 61

Bucephalia, city in India: A61

Byzantium, city on Bosporus: C6, 9, P17, N22, Alc31, A9

Cadmeia, citadel of Thebes: Ag23, A11

Caesar, Augustus: P1, A69

Caesar, Julius: A1

Calanus, Indian philosopher: A8, 65, 69

Callaeschrus, Athenian: Alc33

Calliades, Athenian general: N6

Callias, Athenian: N6

Callicrates of Athens, architect: P13

Callicrates of Sparta: Ag35

Callicrates of Syracuse: N18

Callicratidas, Spartan naval commander: L30

Callippides, actor: Alc32, Ag21

Callippus of Syracuse: N14

Callisthenes, historian: C12, 13, Ag34, A27, 33

Cambyses, king of Persia: A26

Canobic mouth of the Nile: S26, A26

Cappadocia, region of Asia Minor: A18

Caranus, descendant of Heracles: A2

Cardia, city on Thracian Chersonese: A51

Caria, region of SW Asia Minor: T1, Alc25, Ag9, 10, A10, 22

Carmania, region in central Asia: A67

Carthag/e, -inians, city of Africa: P20, Alc17

Caspian Sea: A44

Cassander, son of Antipater: A74

Castor, Spartan god: L22

Catana, city in Sicily: N15, 16, Alc20

Caunians, in SW Asia Minor: N29

Cebalinus, Macedonian: A49

Cecrops, legendary Athenian hero: S4

Celts, N. European tribe: S2

Ceos, Aegean island: T3, 5, N2

Cephisus, river of Boeotia: A9

Cerberus, guardian dog in underworld: N1

Chabrias, Athenian naval commander: Ag37

Chaeron of Megalopolis: A3

Chaeronea, city of Boeotia: C1, Ag17, A12

Chalaestra, city of Macedonia: A49

Chalcedon, city in NW Asia Minor: Alc29, 30, 31

Chalcidice, region of N. Greece: L30, N6

Chalc/is, -idians, city of Euboea: P23, A46

Chaldeans, priests of Babylon: A73

Chares, historian: A20, 24, 46, 54, 55, 70

Charicles, Athenian: N4

Charilaus, king of Sparta: L3, 5, 20

Charinus, Athenian: P30

Charon of Lampsacus, historian: T27

Cheileos of Arcadia: T6

Chelidonian Islands, in Gulf of Antalya, S. of Asia Minor: C12, 13

Chersonese, Thracian peninsula adjoining the Dardanelles: C14, P11, 19

Ch/ios, -ians, Aegean island: T32, C12, Alc12, 24, 35

Chiron, centaur: P4

Cholargus, deme of Attica: P3, 13, N11

Chrysogonus, flute-player: Alc32

Cilicia, region of SE Asia Minor: T31, A17, 19, 20, 42, 48

Cimon, Athenian commander: T5, 20, 24, 31, C *passim*, P5, 7, 9, 10, 11, 16, 28, 29, Alc19, 22

Cimoneia, tombs of Cimon's family: C19

Cirrha/ -eans, city near Delphi: L31, S11

Cissus, Macedonian: A41

Citium, city of Cyprus: C19, A32

Clarius, river on Cyprus: S26

Clazomenae, city of W. Asia Minor: P4, N13, Alc28

Cleandridas, Spartan: P22, N28

Cleanthes, Stoic philosopher: Alc 6

Cleidemus, historian: T10

Cleinias, father of Alcibiades: Alc1, 11

Cleinias, friend of Solon: S15

Cleisthenes, Athenian reformer: C15, P3,

Cleitarchus, historian: T27, A46

Cleitor/ -ians, city of Arcadia: C16

Cleobis of Argos: S27

Cleombrotus I, king of Sparta: Ag24, 26, 28

Cleomenes, Laconian diviner: A50

Cleomenes of Sparta: S10

Cleon, Athenian politician: P33, 35, N2, 3, 4, 7, 8, 9

Cleonae, village in territory of Argos: C17

Cleonice, woman of Byzantium: C6

Cleonymus, Spartan: Ag25, 28

Cleopatra, a wife of Philip of Macedon: A9, 10

Cleophantus, son of Themistocles: T32

Cleora, wife of Agesilaus: Ag19

Clitus the Black, companion of Alexander: A13, 16, 50–2

Cnacium, river in Laconia: L6

Cnidos, city in SW Asia Minor: C12, Alc27, Ag17

Codrus, legendary Athenian king: S1

Coenus, companion of Alexander: A60

Colias, cape in Attica: S8

Colophon, city in W. Asia Minor: A51

Comias, Athenian archon: S32

Conon, Athenian naval commander: Alc37, Ag17, 23

Conon, friend of Solon: S15

Corcyra/ -ns, island in Ionian Sea: T24, P29,

Core (Persephone), Greek goddess: N1

Corinth/ -ians, city of central Greece: L13, S1, T5, 24, C17, P29, N6, 10, 19, 20, 25, Alc14, 18, 39, Ag15, 16, 17, 21, 22, A9, 10, 14, 37, 56

Coroebus, Athenian architect: P13

Coronea, city in Boeotia: P18, Alc1, Ag15, 18, 19

Cos, Aegean island: S4, Alc27

Cossaeans, tribe in Asia: A72

Cotys, king of Paphlagonia: Ag11

Coures, name of Epimenides: S12

Craneium, area of Corinth: A14

Crassus, P. Licinius, Roman magnate: N1

Craterus, general of Alexander: A40, 41, 42, 47, 48, 55

Craterus, historian: C13

Cratinus, comic poet: S25, C10, P3, 13, 24

Creophylus, relative of Homer: L4
Crete, Mediterranean island: L4, 31, S12
Critias, Athenian author, one of the Thirty Tyrants: L9, C10, 16, Alc33, 38
Critolaïdas, Spartan: S10
Critolaus of Phaselis, philosopher: P7
Crobylus, Corinthian: A22
Croesus, king of Lydia: S4, 27, 28
Cronus, Greek god: S3, C10, P3, 24
Croton, city of S. Italy: A34
Ctesium, city on Scyros: C8
Cyanean Islands, at the Bosporus: C13
Cybisthus, adopted son of Thales: S7
Cychreus, legendary hero of Salamis: S9
Cydnus, river in SE Asia Minor: A19
Cylon, Athenian: S12, 13
Cyme, city of W. Asia Minor: T26
Cynisca, sister of Agesilaus: Ag20
Cynosarges, gymnasium at Athens: T1
Cypris (Aphrodite), Greek goddess: S26, 31
Cyprus, Mediterranean island: S26, T31, C12, 18, P10, 26, A24, 29
Cyrus the Great, king of Persia: S28, A30, 69
Cyrus the younger, Persian prince: P24, Alc35
Cythera, Aegean island: N6, Ag32,
Cyzicus, city of NW Asia Minor: T29, Alc28, 24, Ag12

Damascus, city of Syria: A20, 21, 24, 48
Damon, friend of Pericles: P4, N6
Damon of Chaeronea: C12
Damon of Macedonia: A24
Damonides of Athens: P9
Dandamis, Indian sage: A8, 65
Danube, river of Europe: A11, 36
Darius I, king of Persia: T4
Darius III, king of Persia: A15–21, 29–30, 31–4, 37–9, 42, 43, 48, 56, 70
Decelea, deme of Attica: T14, C8, Alc23, 34
Deianeira, wife of Heracles: P24
Deinomache, mother of Alcibiades: Alc1
Deirades, deme of Attica: Alc25
Delium, town in Boeotia: N6, Alc7
Delos, Aegean island: N3, P12

Delphi, sanctuary of Apollo: L5, 6, 29, S25, P21, N11, 13, 54, Ag19, A3, 14, 40, 74
Demades, Athenian politician: S17
Demaratus of Corinth: Ag15, A9, 37, 56
Demaratus, king of Sparta: L29, T29
Demeter, Greek goddess: L27, S8, Alc22
Demetrius of Phalerum, philosopher: L23, S23
Demetrius Phidon: A54
Democrates, Athenian: Alc3
Demophon of Cyprus: S26
Demopolis, putative son of Themistocles: T32
Demosthenes, Athenian general: N6–8, 20–1, 22, 27–8, Alc1
Demosthenes, Athenian orator: Alc10, A11
Demostratus, Athenian demagogue: N12, Alc18
Dercyllidas, Spartan commander: L15
Dicaearchus, historian: Ag19
Didymus, scholar: S1
Dieutychidas, historian: L1
Dimnus, Macedonian: A49
Dindymene (Rhea), Greek goddess: T30
Dinon, historian: T27, A36
Diocleides, Athenian: Alc20
Diocles, son of Themistocles: T32
Diodorus, geographer: T32, C16
Diogenes, of Sinope, philosopher: L31, A14, 65
Diomedes, Athenian: Alc12
Dion of Syracuse: N23
Dionassa, mother of Lycurgus: L1
Dionysius of Messene: A73–4
Dionysius of Syracuse: S20
Dionysius 'the Bronze': N5
Dionysus, Greek god: S31, T13, C2, 3, 18, N3, Alc2, A13, 67
Diopithes of Athens: P32
Diopithes of Sparta: Ag3
Dioscorides, author: L11, Ag35
Dioscuri, twin gods (Castor and Pollux): A50
Diphilides, horse breeder: T5
Diphilus, comic poet: N1
Diphridas, Spartan: Ag17
Dodona, sanctuary of NW Greece: T28
Dolopians, inhabitants of Scyros: C8

Dorians, Greek ethnic category: L11, P17, Ag31

Doris, region of central Greece: T9

Draco, Athenian lawgiver: S17, 19, 25

Dracontides, Athenian: P32

Duris of Samos, historian: P28, Alc32, Ag3, A15, 46

Ecbatana, capital of Media: Ag15, A72

Egypt: S2, 26, C18, P20, 37, N9, Ag36, A26, 27, 40, 59

Eïon, city in Thrace: C7, 8

Elatus, Spartan ephor: L7

Eleius, son of Cimon: C16, P29

Eleusis, city of Attica: T15, P13, Alc22, 34, Ag24

Elis, Eleans, city in Peloponnese: L31, 20, 30, N10, Alc15

Elpinice, sister of Cimon: C4, 14, 15, P10, 28

Enyalius, Greek war god: S9

Epaminondas, Theban general: Ag19, 27, 28, 30, 31, 32, 34, 35

Ephesus, city of W. Asia Minor: Alc8, 29, 35, Ag7, 9, A3

Ephialtes of Athens: C10, 13, 15, 16

Ephialtes of Macedonia: A41

Ephorus, historian: T27, C12, P27

Epicles, cithara-player: T5

Epicrates, Athenian: T24

Epicydes, Athenian: T6

Epicydidas, Spartan: Ag15

Epidaurus, city of Peloponnese: P35

Epimenides of Crete, a sage: S12

Epipolae, area of Syracuse: N17, 21

Epirus, region of NW Greece: T24, A9, 68

Epitimius of Pharsalus: P36

Epixyes, Persian: T30

Erasistratus, Athenian: Ag15

Eratosthenes, historian/scientist: L1, T27, A3, 31

Eresus, city of Lesbos: S32

Eretria, city of Euboea: T11, 27

Ergoteles, hunter of Themistocles: T26

Erigyius, Macedonian: A10

Eros, Greek god of love: S1, Alc16

Ethiopians, people of Africa: C3

Etymocles, Spartan: Ag25

Euangelus, bailiff of Pericles: P16

Euanthes of Samos, historian: S11

Euboe/a, -ans, Aegean island: T8, 59, P22, 23

Eumolpidae, Athenian priestly family: Alc22, 33, 34

Eunomus, Spartan: L1, 2

Euphrantides, seer: T13

Euphrates, river: A29, 31, 68, 73

Eupolia, daughter of Agesilaus: Ag19

Eupolia, wife of Archidamus II: Ag1

Eupolis, comic poet: C15, P3, 24, N4, Alc13

Euripides, tragic poet: L31, S22, C4, N5, 9, 17, 29, Alc1, 11, 23, Ag15, A8, 10, 35, 51, 53

Europe, continent: T16, P7, A9

Eurotas, Sparta's river: L12, 15, 16, Ag19, 31, 32, 34

Eurybiades, Spartan commander: T7, 11

Eurycles, Syracusan: N28

Eurylochus, Macedonian: A41

Eurymedon, Athenian commander: N20, 24

Eurymedon, river of S. Asia Minor: C12, 13

Eurypon, Spartan king: L1, 2

Eurypontidae, descendants of Eurypon: L2, 24, 30

Euryptolemus, cousin of Pericles: P7, Alc32

Euryptolemus, father of Isodice: C4, 16

Eurysaces, son of Ajax: S10, Alc1

Euterpe, wife of Themistocles: T1

Euthippus, Athenian: C17

Euthydemus, Athenian general: N20

Euthynus, of Thespiae: Ag34

Euxine (Black) Sea: P20, A44

Exathres, Persian: A43

Execestides, father of Solon: S1, 2

Fabius Maximus, Roman general: P2

Galatians, Celtic tribe: C1

Gandaritae, Indian people: A62

Ganges, Indian river: A62

Gaugamela, town of Assyria: A31–4

Gaza, city of Palestine: A25

Gedrosia, region of Asia: A66–7

Gela, city of Sicily: C8

Geradas, Spartan: L15

Geraestus, promontory of Euboea: Ag6

Glaucon, Athenian: P31

Glaucus, doctor: A72
Gongylus, Corinthian general: N19
Gordium, city of central Asia Minor: A18
Gordyaean mountains, in Asia: A31
Gorgias of Leontini, sophist: C10
Gorgo, wife of Leonidas: L14
Granicus, river of NW Asia Minor: A16–17
Gylippus, Spartan commander: L30, P22, N18–28, Alc23

Habrotonon, mother of Themistocles: T1–2
Hades, Greek god of underworld: P3
Haemus, Thracian mountain: A2
Hagnon of Athens: P32
Hagnon of Teus: A22, 40, 52
Hagnothemis, agent of Antigonus: A77
Halimous, deme of Attica: C4
Hannibal, Carthaginian general: P2
Harpalus, friend of Alexander: A10, 35, 41
Hecataeus of Eretria, historian: A46
Hecataeus, sophist: L20
Hegesias of Magnesia: A3
Hegesipyle, mother of Cimon: C4
Hegestratus, Athenian: S32
Helen of Troy: S4
Helicon, mountain: Ag18
Helicon, weaver: A32
Heliopolis, city of Egypt: S26
Hellanicus of Lesbos, historian: Alc21
Hellespont (strait between Europe and Asia): T16, P17, Alc26, 27, 28, 30, Ag8, 16, A15, 16
Hephaestion, friend of Alexander: A28, 39, 41, 47, 49, 54, 55, 72
Hera, Greek goddess: S27, P2, 24, Ag22, A3
Hera, mother of Callisthenes: A56
Heraclea, city of NW Asia Minor: C6
Heraclidae, descendants of Heracles: L1
Heraclides of Cyme, historian: T27
Heraclides of Pontus, philosopher: S1, 22, 31, 32, P27, 35
Heraclides of Syracuse: N24
Heracles, Greek hero: L30, T1, 13, C3, 4, N1, 24, 25, Ag3, A2, 24, 75
Hereas of Megara, historian: S10
Herippidas, Spartan commander: Ag11

Hermes, Greek god: A20
Hermione, city of Peloponnese: T5, A36
Hermippus, comic poet: P32, 33
Hermippus, historian: L5, 23, Alc6, 11, 52, 54
Hermocrates, Syracusan commander: N1, 16, 26, 28
Hermolaus, page of Alexander: A55
Hermon of Athens: Alc25
Herodotus, historian: T7, 17, 21
Herophylus of Samos: C9
Hesiod, didactic poet: S2
Hestiae/a, -ans, city of Euboea: T8, P23
Hidrieus of Caria: Ag13
Hiero of Athens: N5
Hipparete, wife of Alcibiades: Alc8
Hippias of Elis, sophist: L23
Hippocrates, Athenian general: N6
Hippocrates, mathematician: S2
Hippocrates of Sparta: Alc29–30
Hippolyta, daughter of Agesilaus: Ag19
Hipponicus, father of Callias: P24, Alc8
Hipponicus, friend of Solon: S15
Homer, epic poet: L1, 4, S10, 25, 30, C7, P39, N9, Alc7, Ag5, 9, 15, A8, 26, 28, 54
Hybla, town of Sicily: N15
Hyccara, city of Sicily: N15, Alc39
Hydaspes, Indian river: A60, 61
Hydrus, unknown location: C13
Hyperbolus, Athenian demagogue: N11, Alc13
Hypsichidas, Spartan: S10
Hyrcania/ -ns, region of Asia: A44, 47
Hyrcanian (Caspian) Sea: A44

Iacchus, Greek god: T15, Alc34
Ialysus, city of Rhodes: T21
Iberia, region of Asia near Caucasus Mts.: L4
Ictinus, architect: P13
Idaeus, Agesilaus' scribe: Ag13
Idomeneus of Lampsacus, author: P10, 35
Illyri/a, -ans, region east of Adriatic Sea: A9, 11
India/ -ns, region of Asia: L4, A13, 47, 55, 57, 59, 62, 63, 66, 69
Iolas, son of Antipater: A77
Ion, ancestor of Ionians: S23
Ion of Chios, poet and author: C5, P5, 28

Ioni/a, -ans, coastal region of W. Asia
    Minor: L4, T9, 26, C12, 14, P17, 24,
    28, Alc23, 24, 26, 31, 35, 36
Iphicrates, Athenian commander: Ag22
Iphitus, king of Elis: L1, 23
Isadas, Spartan: Ag34
Ismenias of Thebes: P1
Isocrates, orator: Alc12
Isodice, wife of Cimon: C4, 16
Issorion, town of Laconia: Ag32
Issus, city of SE Asia Minor: A20, 24, 32
Isthmus of Corinth: T9, 11, 21, A14
Istrus, historian: A46
Italia, daughter of Themistocles: T32
Italy: P11, N5, 18, Alc17, 20, Ag15, A34
Ithome, mountain of Messenia: C17

Jason, legendary hero: C3

Lacedaemon/ -ians (= Sparta, Spartans):
    passim
Lacedaemonius, son of Cimon: C16, P29
Lachartus, Corinthian: C17
Laciadae, deme of Attica: C4, 10, Alc22
Laconia, territory of Sparta: L8, 9, 28,
    N6, Ag23, 28, 31, 32, 34, A50
Laïs, courtesan: N15, Alc39
Lamachus, Athenian general: P20, N12,
    14, 15, 18, Alc1, 18, 20, 21
Lampido, mother of Agis: Ag1
Lampon, Athenian diviner: P6
Lampsacus, city of NW Asia Minor:
    T27, 29, Alc36
Laodice, daughter of Priam: C4
Laomedon of Athens: C9
Laomedon of Troy: N1
Larissa, city of Thessaly: Ag16
Laurium, mining region of Attica: T4,
    N4
Leibethra, city of Macedonia: A14
Lemnos, Aegean island: P25
Leobotes, Athenian: T23
Leochares, sculptor: A40
Leocrates, Athenian general: P16
Leon of Byzantium, orator: N22
Leonidas, king of Sparta: L14, 20, T9
Leonidas, tutor of Alexander: A5, 22, 25
Leonidas, Spartan: L3
Leonnatus, Companion of Alexander:
    A21, 40
Leontiadas of Thebes: Ag23, 24

Lesb/os, -ians, Aegean island: P17, N6,
    A61
Leto, Greek goddess: T21
Leucas, island of Ionian Sea: T24
Leuctra, city of Boeotia: Ag15, 28, 29, 40
Libya (= Africa): L4, N12, Alc17, Ag40,
    A68
Lichas, Spartan: C10
Limnaeus, officer of Alexander: A63
Lionhead, village of Asia Minor: T30
Locrians, people of central Greece: P17
Lucullus, Lucius, Roman commander:
    C1, 2, 3
Lycia, region of S. Asia Minor: A17
Lycomedes, Athenian trierarch: T15
Lycomedes, king of Scyros: C8
Lycomidae, Athenian family: T1
Lycon, actor: A29
Lycophron, Corinthian general: N6
Lycurgus, Athenian: S29
Lycurgus of Byzantium: Alc31
Lycurgus, Spartan lawgiver: L *passim*,
    S16, 22, Ag4, 20, 26, 33
Lydia, region of W. Asia Minor: S27,
    T31, C9, Ag10
Lysander, Athenian: T32
Lysander, Spartan: L30, P22, N28,
    Alc35–9, Ag2, 3, 6, 7, 8, 20
Lysicles, Athenian: P24
Lysimachus, bodyguard of Alexander:
    A46, 55
Lysimachus, tutor of Alexander: A5, 24,
    55
Lysippus, sculptor: A4, 16, 40

Macedon/ia, -ians, state in N. Greece:
    L31, C2, 14, Ag15, 16, A *passim*
Maedians, tribe of Thrace: A9
Maeotis, Lake (Sea of Azov): A44
Magi, Persian priestly caste: T29, A3,
    18
Magnesia, city of W. Asia Minor:
    T29–32
Maliac Gulf, north of Boeotia: P17
Mall/ia, -ians, city of India: A63, 68
Mantinea, city of Peloponnese: Alc15,
    19, Ag33, 35
Marathon, deme of Attica: T3, C5
Massalia (Marseilles in France): S2
Mazaeus, Persian: A32, 39
Medea, legendary heroine: A10, 35

Media, Medes, region of Persian empire: T6 7, 20, 21, C1, 3, 5, 6, 7, 18, P28, Ag23, A45, 49, 51, 72

Medius, Macedonian: A75, 76

Megabates, Persian: Ag11

Megacles, Athenian archon: S12

Megacles, grandfather of Alcibiades: Alc1

Megacles, son of Alcmaeon: S29, 30

Megar/a, -ians, city of central Greece: S8, 9, 10, T13, C17, P19, 22, 29, 30, 34, N6, Alc31, Ag27

Melissus of Samos, philosopher: T2, P26–7

Melite, deme of Attica: S10, T22

Melon, Theban: Ag24

Mel/os, -ian, Aegean island: Alc16

Memnon, Persian commander: A18, 21

Menander, comic poet: A17

Menander, friend of Alexander: A57

Menander of Athens: N20, Alc36

Mendes, city of Egypt: Ag38

Menecrates, Spartan doctor: Ag21

Menelaus, Homeric hero: Ag40

Menestheus, legendary Athenian: C7

Menippus, friend of Pericles: P13

Meno, colleague of Phidias: P31

Messana, city of Sicily: Alc22

Messen/ia, -ians, region of Peloponnese: L7, 28, C16, 17, Ag34, 35, A73

Metagenes, architect: P13

Meton, Athenian astronomer: N13, Alc17

Metrobius, comic character: C10

Midas, king of Phrygia: A18

Mieza, city of Macedonia: A7

Miletus, Milesians, city of W. Asia Minor: S4, 6, 12, P24, 28, Alc23, A17

Miltiades, Athenian general: T3, 4, C4, 8

Milto, concubine of Cyrus the younger: P24

Mindarus, Spartan naval commander: Alc27–8

Minoa, island off Megara: N6

Mithras, Persian god: A30

Mithropaustes, Persian: T29

Mitylene, city of Lesbos: S14

Mnesicles, architect: P13

Mnesiphilus, philosopher: T2

Mnesiptolema, daughter of Themistocles: T30, 32

Mnestra, mistress of Cimon: C4

Moloss/is, -ians, region of NW Greece: T24

Munychia, a harbour of Athens: S12

Myous, city of W. Asia Minor: T29

Mycale, promontory opposite Samos: P3

Myron of Athens: S12

Myronides, Athenian general: P16, 24

Narthacium, mountain in Thessaly: Ag16

Nausicrates of Erythrae: C19

Naxos, Aegean island: P11

Naxos, city of Sicily: N16

Neanthes of Cyzicus, historian: T1, 29

Nearchus, friend and admiral of Alexander: A10, 66, 68, 73, 75, 76

Nectanebis, king of Egypt: Ag37–40

Nemea, city in Peloponnese: P19, A16

Neocles, father of Themistocles: T32

Neocles, son of Themistocles: T32

Neoptolemus, son of Achilles: A2

Nicagoras of Troezen: T10

Nicias, Athenian politician: N *passim*, Alc1, 13, 17, 18, 20, 21

Nicias, friend of Agesilaus: Ag13

Nicocreon, king of Salamis on Cyprus: A29

Nicodemus, son-in-law of Themistocles: T32

Nicogenes, Macedonian: T26, 28

Nicomache, daughter of Themistocles: T32

Nicomachus, soldier of Alexander: A49

Nicon, slave: A42

Nile, river of Egypt: S26, A26, 36

Niphates, mountain of Armenia: A31

Nisaea, port of Megara: S12, N6

Nonacris, city of Arcadia: A77

Nysa, city of India: A58

Oa, deme of Attica: P9

Ocean (the water around the known world): A66

Ochus: see Artaxerxes III: A69

Odeum, theatre at Athens: P13

Odysseus, Homeric hero: Ag5

Oeneis, tribe at Athens: C17

Oeniadae, city of NW Greece: P19, A49

Oenous, river in Laconia: L6

Oetaeans, people of central Greece: P17

Olbius, a pedagogue: T26
Olizon, place opposite Artemesium: T8
Olorus, father of Thucydides: C4
Olorus, Thracian king: C4
Olympia, sanctuary of Peloponnese: L23, T5, Alc11, 12, Ag20, A3, 4
Olympias, mother of Alexander: A2, 3, 5, 9, 10, 16, 22, 25, 27, 39, 68, 77
Omphale, legendary queen of Lydia: P24
Onesicritus, historian: A8, 15, 46, 60, 61, 65, 66
Opheltas, king of Boeotians: C1
Orchomen/us, -ians, city of Boeotia: C2, Ag18
Oreitae, people of Asia: A66
Orexartes, river of Asia: A45
Oromazes, Persian god: A30
Orpheus, mythical poet: A14
Orsodates, Persian: A57
Oxus, river of Asia: A57
Oxyartes, father of Rhoxane: A58
Oxyartes, son of Aboulites: A68

Paches, Athenian general: N6
Paeonia, region of Thrace: A39
Pagasae, port of Thessaly: T20
Painted Stoa, in Athens: C4
Palaescepsis, city of W. Asia Minor: T29
Palladium, statue of Athena: N3, 13
Pamphylia, region of S. Asia Minor: C12, A17
Panactum, fortress of Attica: N10, Alc14
Panaetius of Rhodes, philosopher: C4
Panaetius of Tenos: T12
Panthoedes of Chios: T32
Paphlagon/ia, -ians, region of Asia Minor: Ag11, A18
Paralus, son of Pericles: P24, 36
Parmenides, philosopher: P4
Parmenio, general of Alexander: A3, 10, 16, 19, 21, 22, 29, 31, 32, 33, 39, 48, 49, 50
Parthia, region of Asia: A45
Pasicrates, king of Soli on Cyprus: A29
Pasiphon, author: N4
Pataecus, fabulist: S6
Patrae, city of Peloponnese: Alc15
Patroclus, friend of Achilles: A54
Pausanias, doctor: A41
Pausanias, Spartan regent: T21, 23, C6
Pedaritus, Spartan: L25

Pegae, port of Megarian territory: P19
Pelagon of Euboea: T7
Peleus, father of Achilles: A5
Pella, city of Macedonia: A69
Pelopidas, Theban general: Ag24
Peloponnese, the south of Greece: *passim*
Percote, city in W. Asia Minor: T29
Perdiccas, general of Alexander: A15, 41, 77
Pergamia, region of Crete: L31
Periander, tyrant of Corinth: S4, 12
Periclidas, Spartan: C16
Pericles, Athenian statesman: L16, T2, 10, C13–17, P *passim*, N2, 3, 6, 9, 23, Alc1, 3, 6, 7, 14, 17
Perinthus, city of NW Asia Minor: A70
Periphemus, a hero: S9
Peripoltas, ancient seer: C1
Peritas, dog of Alexander: A61
Perithoedae, deme of Attica: N11, Alc13
Persepolis, city of Persia: A37, 38
Perseus, legendary hero: C3
Pers/ia, -ians, region of Asia, and empire: L25, S28, T4, 12, 16, 26–31, C7, 9, 13, 14, P17, 24, Alc23, 37, 45, Ag6, 8, 13, 23, A *passim*
Peucestas, companion of Alexander: A41, 42, 63
Phaeax, Athenian: Alc13, N11
Phaestus, city of Crete: S12
Phaleric Gulf, west of Attica: T12
Phanias of Lesbos, historian: S14, S32, T1, 7, 13, 27, 29
Phanodemus, historian: T13, C12, 19
Pharnabazus, Persian satrap: Alc24, 27–31, 37, 39, Ag8, 11–13, 17, 23
Pharsal/us, -ians, city of Thessaly: P36, Ag16
Pharus, island at Alexandria: A26
Phaselis, city of S. Asia Minor: C12, A17
Phayllus of Croton: A34
Pheaea, deme of Attica: Alc22
Pherendates, Persian general: C12
Phidias, sculptor: P2, 13, 31, 32
Philaeus, son of hero Ajax: S10
Philaïdae, deme of Attica: S10
Philemon, comic poet: P2
Philinna, mother of Philip Arrhidaeus: A77
Philip, a Macedonian: A60

Philip II, father of Alexander: P1, A2, 3, 6, 7, 9–12, 16, 27, 28, 37, 45, 49, 50, 53, 70

Philip of Chalcis, historian: A46

Philip of Theangela, historian: A46

Philistus of Syracuse, historian: N1, 19, 28, A8

Philochorus of Athens, historian: N23

Philocles, author: S1

Philoctetes, hero of Trojan war: T8

Philocyprus, king of Cyprus: S26

Philombrotus, Athenian: S14

Philon of Thebes, historian: A46

Philonicus of Thessaly: A6

Philostephanus, historian: L23

Philotas, general of Alexander: A10, 11, 31, 40, 48–50

Philoxenus, Macedonian: A22

Philoxenus, poet: A8

Phleiasians, people of Peloponnese: Ag24

Phlya, deme of Attica: T1, 15

Phocaea, city of W. Asia Minor: P24

Phocion, Athenian statesman: A39

Phoc/is, -ians, region in central Greece: T9, C1, 17, P17, 21, Ag17, 28, A11

Phocus, Athenian: S14

Phoebidas, Spartan general: Ag23–4, 34

Phoebus (Apollo), Greek god: L6

Phoenici/e, -ans, coastal region of E. Mediterranean: P28, Ag37, A17, 24, 29

Phoenix, mentor of Achilles: A5, 24

Phoenix of Thebes: A11

Phormio, Athenian general: Alc1

Phrasicles, nephew of Themistocles: T32

Phrearrhii, deme of Attica: T1, 2, 5

Phrixus, Spartan: Ag32

Phrygia, region of Asia Minor: T30, C9, Alc37, 39, Ag9–11, A18

Phrynichus, comic poet: N4, Alc4, 20

Phrynichus, tragic poet: T5, Alc4

Phrynichus of Athens: Alc25

Phthia, queen of Molossis: T24

Phylarchus, historian: T32

Pierion, poet: A50

Pillars of Heracles (Straits of Gibraltar): N12, A68

Pinarus, river of S. Asia Minor: A20

Pindar, poet: L21, T8, N1, A1l

Piraeus, port city of Athens: T10, 19, 32, P8, Alc26, Ag24

Pisanactean Stoa: see Painted Stoa

Pisander of Athens: Alc26

Pisander of Sparta: Ag10, 17

Pisistratidae, tyrants at Athens: P3, 16

Pisistratus, tyrant at Athens: S1, 8, 10, 29–32, P7

Pisa, city of Peloponnese: P2

Pisidians, people of Asia Minor: T30, A18

Pissouthnes, Persian satrap at Sardis: P25

Pittacus, tyrant of Mytilene: S14

Pixodarus, satrap of Caria: A10

Platae/a, -ans, city of Boeotia: T16, C13, A11, 34

Plato, comic poet: T32, P4, N11, Alc13

Plato, philosopher: L5, 7, 15, 16, 28, 29, S26, 31, T2, 4, P7, 8, 13, 15, 24, Alc1, 4

Pleistonax, king of Sparta: L20, P22

Plemmyrium, promontory near Syracuse: N20

Pnyx, assembly place at Athens: T19

Pollichus of Syracuse: N24

Polyalces, Spartan: P30

Polyarchus of Aegina: T19

Polyclitus, historian: A46

Polyclitus, sculptor: P2

Polycrates, tyrant of Samos: P26

Polydectes, half-brother of Lycurgus: L1–3

Polydorus, king of Sparta: L6, 8

Polyeuctus, son of Themistocles: T32

Polygnotus of Thasos, painter: C4

Polystratus, soldier of Alexander: A43

Polyzelus of Rhodes, historian: S15

Polyzelus of Syracuse: N27

Pontus, region of N. Asia Minor: L12

Porus, Indian king: A60–2

Poseidon, Greek god: T19, Ag3, 21

Posidonia, city of S. Italy: C18

Potamon of Lesbos, historian: A61

Potidaea, city of N. Greece: P29, Alc7, A3

Poulytion, Athenian: Alc19, 22

Poulomachus, Macedonian: A69

Praesians, people of India: A62

Pranichus, poet: A50

Praxiergidae, Athenian priestly family: Alc34

Priene, city of W. Asia Minor: S4, P25

Procles, ancestor of Lycurgus: L1
Proconnesus, island in Sea of Marmora: Alc28
Promachus, companion of Alexander: A70
Protagoras, sophist: P36, N23
Proteas, friend of Alexander: A39
Prothoüs, Spartan: Ag28
Prothytes of Thebes: A11
Protis, founder of Massilia: S2
Proxenus, Macedonian: A57
Prytanis, father (?) of Lycurgus: L1
Psammon, Egyptian philosopher: A27
Psenopis, Egyptian priest: S26
Psiltoucis, island in Indian Ocean: A66
Ptolemy I, king of Egypt, historian: A10, 38, 46
Pydna, city of Macedonia: T25, A48
Pylos, city of Peloponnese: N7, 9, 10, Alc14
Pyrilampes, Athenian: P13
Pyronides, Athenian: P24
Pythagoras, philosopher: A65
Pythagoras, diviner: A73
Pythia, priestess of Apollo at Delphi: L5, S4, 10, A14, 37
Pytho (= Delphi): L6, S14
Pythoclides, musical theorist: P4
Pythodorus, hunter of Themistocles: T26
Python, companion of Alexander: A76

Rhamnus, deme of Attica: N6
Rhegium, city of S. Italy: Alc20
Rheneia, Aegean island: N3
Rhodes, island of Mediterranean: P17, A32
Rhoesaces of Persia: C10
Rhoesaces, another Persian: A16
Rhône, river (in France): S2
Rhoxane, wife of Alexander: A47, 77
Rhoxanes, Persian: T29
Rome/Romans: C1–3, P1

Sabbas, Indian king: A64
Saïs, city of Nile delta: S26, 31
Salamis, city of Cyprus: A29
Salamis, island near Athens: S8–10, 12, 32, T10–16, C4–5, A34
Sam/os, -ians, Aegean island: S11, T2, C9, P24–8, Alc25, 26, 27, 32, 35, 46, A28

Samothrace, Aegean island: A2
Sandace, sister of Xerxes: T13
Sandrocottus, Indian king: A62
Sarapis, Egyptian god: A73, 76
Sardis, city of W. Asia Minor, capital of Lydia: S27–8, T29, 31, Alc27, Ag10, 11, A17
Scambonidae, deme of Attica: Alc22
Scapte Hyle, place in Thrace: C4
Scarphe, town in central Greece: A29
Sciathos, Aegean island: T7
Scilloustis, island in Indian Ocean: A66
Siradium, promontory on Salamis: S9
Scopadae, Thessalian dynasty: C10
Syros, Aegean island: C8
Scythes, messenger of Agesilaus: Ag16
Scythians, people of Asian steppes: A45, 46
Segest/a, -ans, city of Sicily: N1, 12, 14
Seleucus, companion of Alexander, later king: A62, 76
Selinous, city of Sicily: L20
Selymbr/ia, -ians, city of Thrace: Alc30
Serapion, friend of Alexander: A39
Seriphus, Aegean island: T18
Sestus, city of Thracian Chersonese: C9, Alc37
Sibyrtius, palaestra of, at Athens: Alc3
Sicels, natives of Sicily: N16
Sicinnus, Persian: T12
Sicyonians, people of Peloponnese: P19
Simaetha, courtesan: P30
Simmias, Athenian: P35
Simonides of Ceos, poet: L1, T1, 5, 8, 15, Ag1
Sinope, city of N. Asia Minor: P20, A14
Sisimithres, Persian: A58
Socles, Athenian: T14
Socrates, philosopher: P13, 24, N13, 23, Alc1, 4, 6, 7, A65
Soli, city of Cyprus: S26, A29
Solon, Athenian lawgiver: S *passim*, T2
Sonchis, Egyptian priest: S26
Sophanes, Athenian: C8
Sophocles, tragic poet: S1, C8, P8, N15, A7, 8
Sotion, author: A61
Soüs, Spartan king: L1, 2
Spart/a, -ans, -iates, leading city of Peloponnese: *passim*
Sparto, Boeotian commander: Ag19

Spendon, Laconian poet: L28
Sphaerus of Borysthenes, philosopher: L5
Sphacteria, island to W. of Peloponnese: N7–8, Alc14
Sphodrias, Spartan commander: Ag24–6, 28
Sphines: see Calanus
Spithridates, Persian: Ag8, 11
Spithridates, Persian commander: A16, 50
Stagira, city of N. Greece: A7
Stasicrates, architect: A72
Stateira, daughter of Darius III: A21, 30, 70, 77
Stateira, wife of Darius III: A21, 22, 30, 43
Steiris, deme of Attica: Alc26
Stephanus, slave of Alexander: A35
Stesilaus of Cos: T3
Stesimbrotus of Thasos, author: T2, 4, 24, C4, 14, 16, P8, 13, 26, 36
Stilbides, seer: N23
Stratonicus, cithara-player: L30
Stroebus, friend of Aristotle: A54
Strymon, river of N. Greece: C7
Susa, a capital of Persian Empire: Ag15, A18, 36, 37, 70
Susamithras, Persian: Alc39
Sybaris, city of S. Italy: P11
Sybaris, daughter of Themistocles: T32
Syracus/e, -ans, city of Sicily: N1, 13, 14, 16–20, 21, 22, 24–8, 29, Alc17, 18, 22, 23
Syria: A20, 25
Syrmus, king of Triballians: A11

Tachos, king of Egypt: Ag36, 38
Tanagra, city of Boeotia: C17, P10
Tanaïs, river of Asia: A45
Tarentum, city of S. Italy: A22
Taureas of Athens: Alc16
Taxiles, Indian king: A59, 65
Taygetus, mountain of Peloponnese: L15, 16, C16
Tegea, city of Peloponnese: Ag34
Tegyra, city of Peloponnese: Ag27
Teleclides, comic poet: P3, 16, N4
Teles, Athenian: P33
Telesippa, courtesan: A41
Tellus, Athenian: S27

Telestes, poet: A8
Teleutias, brother of Agesilaus: Ag21
Telmessus, city of Lycia: A2
Tempe, valley of Thessaly: T7
Terpander, poet: L21, 28
Teucer of Athens: Alc20
Thaïs, courtesan: A38
Thales of Crete, poet/lawgiver: L4
Thales of Miletus, philosopher: S2–7, 12
Thapsacus, city of Syria: A68
Thapsus, place near Syracuse: N17
Thargelia, courtesan: P24
Thasos, Aegean island: T25, C4, 14, P13
Theagenes, Theban: A12
Theangela, city of SW Asia Minor: A46
Theano, Athenian priestess: Alc22
Theb/es, -ans, city of Boeotia: L9, 13, 28, 30, S4, T20, Alc2, Ag6, 10, 15, 18, 22–4, 26–9, 31–2, 34, A9, 11–13, 46
Themistocles of Athens: T *passim*, C5, 8–10, 12, 16, 18, P7, Alc37
Themistocles, descendant of the above: T32
Theodectes of Phaselis, poet: A17
Theodorus, friend of Alcibiades: Alc19, 22
Theodorus, priest at Eleusis: Alc33
Theodorus, slave-dealer: A22
Theophilus, armour-maker: A32
Theophrastus of Eresus, philosopher: L10, S4, 31, P23, 38, T25, N10, 11, Alc10, Ag2, 36, A4
Theopompus of Chios, historian: T19, 25, 31, Alc32, Ag10, 31–3
Theopompus, Spartan king: L6, 7, 20, 30
Theorus, Athenian: Alc1
Theramenes, Athenian politician: N2, Alc1, 31
Thermopylae, defile in central Greece: T9, Ag17, A11
Thersippus, Athenian: S31
Theseus, legendary king of Athens: C8
Thespiae, city of Boeotia: Ag24, 34
Thespis, tragic poet: S29
Thessalus, actor: A10, 29
Thessalus, son of Cimon: C16, P29, Alc19, 22
Thessal/y, -ians, region of N. Greece: T7, 20, C1, 14, Ag16–17, A11, 33, 42

Thrac/e, -ians, region of N. Greece: T1, C4, 7, 14, P11, 17, 19, N6, Alc23, 30, 36-7, Ag16-17, A12, 72

Thrasybulus of Steiris: Alc1, 26

Thrasybulus, son of Thraso: Alc36

Thrasyllus, Athenian general: Alc29

Thriasian Plain, in Attica: T15, Ag24

Thucydides, son of Melesias, Athenian politician: P6, 8, 11, 14, 16, N2, 11

Thucydides, son of Olorus, historian: L27, 28, T25, 27, C4, P9, 15, 16, 28, 33, N1, 4, 19, 20, 28, Alc6, 11, 13, 20, Ag33

Thurii, city of S. Italy: P11, N5, Alc22, 23

Thyrea, city of Peloponnese: N6

Timaea, wife of king Agis: Alc23, Ag3

Timaeus, Athenian: Alc21

Timandra, courtesan: Alc39

Timesilaus, tyrant of Sinope: P20

Timocleia of Thebes: A12

Timocreon of Rhodes, poet: T21

Timon of Athens: Alc16

Timon of Phleious: P4

Timotheus of Macedonia: A22

Timotheus of Miletus, poet: Ag14

Tireos, Persian eunuch: A30

Tiribazus, Persian: Ag23

Tisias, Athenian: Alc12

Tissaphernes, Persian satrap: Alc23-8, Ag9-10

Tithraustes, Persian admiral: C10

Tithraustes, Persian satrap: Ag10

Tolmides, Athenian general: P16, 18-19

Tragiae, Aegean island: P25

Triballians, people near Danube: A11

Triopium, cape in SW Asia Minor: C12

Trochalians, Thracian tribe: Ag16

Troezen/ -ians: T10

Troy, city in NW Asia Minor: S4, C4, 7, N1

Tydeus, Athenian general: Alc36, 37

Tynnondas, tyrant of Euboea: S14

Tyre, city of Phoenice: A24, 25

Tyrrhenia (= Etruria), region in Italy: P20

Tyrtaeus, Spartan poet: L6

Xanthippus, father of Pericles: T10, 21, P3, Alc1

Xanthippus, son of Pericles: P13, 24, 36

Xanthus, city of S. Asia Minor: A17

Xenarchus, mime writer: N1

Xenocles of Athens, architect: P13

Xenocles of Sparta: Ag16

Xenocrates, philosopher: A8

Xenodochus of Cardia: A51

Xenophon, Athenian general: N6

Xenophon, historian/philosopher: L1, Alc32

Xerxes, king of Persia: T4, 6, 7, 9, 12-14, 16, 20, 27, C6, 7, 10, 12, Ag4, 9, 16, 18-20, 29, 34, A37-8

Xypate, deme of Attica: P13

Zacynthos, island of Ionian Sea: N23

Zelea, city of NW Asia Minor: T6

Zeno of Elea, philosopher: P4, 5

Zeno of Citium, founder of Stoicism: L31

Zeus, Greek god: L6, S3, 32, T28, 29, P2, 13, N14, 16, Ag5, 21, A27, 28, 33, 65

Zeuxis, painter: P13

Zopyrus, pedagogue of Alcibiades: L16, Alc1

A SELECTION OF   **OXFORD WORLD'S CLASSICS**

	Classical Literary Criticism
	The First Philosophers: The Presocratics and the Sophists
	Greek Lyric Poetry
	Myths from Mesopotamia
APOLLODORUS	**The Library of Greek Mythology**
APOLLONIUS OF RHODES	**Jason and the Golden Fleece**
APULEIUS	**The Golden Ass**
ARISTOPHANES	**Birds and Other Plays**
ARISTOTLE	**The Nicomachean Ethics**
	Physics
	Politics
BOETHIUS	**The Consolation of Philosophy**
CAESAR	**The Civil War**
	The Gallic War
CATULLUS	**The Poems of Catullus**
CICERO	**Defence Speeches**
	The Nature of the Gods
	On Obligations
	The Republic and The Laws
EURIPIDES	**Bacchae and Other Plays**
	Medea and Other Plays
	Orestes and Other Plays
	The Trojan Women and Other Plays
GALEN	**Selected Works**
HERODOTUS	**The Histories**
HOMER	**The Iliad**
	The Odyssey

A SELECTION OF   **OXFORD WORLD'S CLASSICS**

HORACE   **The Complete Odes and Epodes**

JUVENAL   **The Satires**

LIVY   **The Dawn of the Roman Empire**
   The Rise of Rome

MARCUS AURELIUS   **The Meditations**

OVID   **The Love Poems**
   Metamorphoses
   Sorrows of an Exile

PETRONIUS   **The Satyricon**

PLATO   **Defence of Socrates, Euthyphro, and Crito**
   Gorgias
   Phaedo
   Republic
   Symposium

PLAUTUS   **Four Comedies**

PLUTARCH   **Greek Lives**
   Roman Lives
   Selected Essays and Dialogues

PROPERTIUS   **The Poems**

SOPHOCLES   **Antigone, Oedipus the King, and Electra**

STATIUS   **Thebaid**

SUETONIUS   **Lives of the Ceasars**

TACITUS   **Agricola and Germany**
   The Histories

VIRGIL   **The Aeneid**
   The Eclogues and Georgics

A SELECTION OF   **OXFORD WORLD'S CLASSICS**

THOMAS AQUINAS   **Selected Philosophical Writings**

FRANCIS BACON   **The Essays**

WALTER BAGEHOT   **The English Constitution**

GEORGE BERKELEY   **Principles of Human Knowledge** and
                        Three Dialogues

EDMUND BURKE   **A Philosophical Enquiry into the Origin of
                 Our Ideas of the Sublime and Beautiful
    Reflections on the Revolution in France**

CONFUCIUS   **The Analects**

ÉMILE DURKHEIM   **The Elementary Forms of Religious Life**

FRIEDRICH ENGELS   **The Condition of the Working Class in
           England**

JAMES GEORGE FRAZER   **The Golden Bough**

SIGMUND FREUD   **The Interpretation of Dreams**

THOMAS HOBBES   **Human Nature** and **De Corpore Politico
    Leviathan**

JOHN HUME   **Selected Essays**

NICCOLO MACHIAVELLI   **The Prince**

THOMAS MALTHUS   **An Essay on the Principle of Population**

KARL MARX   **Capital
The Communist Manifesto**

J. S. MILL   **On Liberty and Other Essays
Principles of Political Economy** and
                Chapters on Socialism

FRIEDRICH NIETZSCHE   **Beyond Good and Evil
The Birth of Tragedy
On the Genealogy of Morals
Twilight of the Idols**

A SELECTION OF   **OXFORD WORLD'S CLASSICS**

THOMAS PAINE   **Rights of Man, Common Sense, and Other Political Writings**

JEAN-JACQUES ROUSSEAU   **The Social Contract**
Discourse on the Origin of Inequality

ADAM SMITH   **An Inquiry into the Nature and Causes of the Wealth of Nations**

MARY WOLLSTONECRAFT   **A Vindication of the Rights of Woman**

A SELECTION OF   **OXFORD WORLD'S CLASSICS**

Bhagavad Gita

The Bible Authorized King James Version
   With Apocrypha

Dhammapada

Dharmasūtras

The Koran

The Pañcatantra

**The Sauptikaparvan (from the
   Mahabharata)**

**The Tale of Sinuhe and Other Ancient
   Egyptian Poems**

Upaniṣads

ANSELM OF CANTERBURY   **The Major Works**

THOMAS AQUINAS   **Selected Philosophical Writings**

AUGUSTINE   **The Confessions
On Christian Teaching**

BEDE   **The Ecclesiastical History**

HEMACANDRA   **The Lives of the Jain Elders**

KĀLIDĀSA   **The Recognition of Śakuntalā**

MANJHAN   **Madhumalati**

ŚĀNTIDEVA   **The Bodhicaryàvatàra**

*The
Oxford
World's
Classics
Website*

www.worldsclassics.co.uk

- Information about new titles
- Explore the full range of Oxford World's Classics
- Links to other literary sites and the main OUP webpage
- Imaginative competitions, with bookish prizes
- Peruse the Oxford World's Classics Magazine
- Articles by editors
- Extracts from Introductions
- A forum for discussion and feedback on the series
- Special information for teachers and lecturers

www.worldsclassics.co.uk

American Literature

British and Irish Literature

Children's Literature

Classics and Ancient Literature

Colonial Literature

Eastern Literature

European Literature

History

Medieval Literature

Oxford English Drama

Poetry

Philosophy

Politics

Religion

The Oxford Shakespeare

A complete list of Oxford Paperbacks, including Oxford World's Classics, Oxford Shakespeare, Oxford Drama, and Oxford Paperback Reference, is available in the UK from the Academic Division Publicity Department, Oxford University Press, Great Clarendon Street, Oxford OX2 6DP.

In the USA, complete lists are available from the Paperbacks Marketing Manager, Oxford University Press, 198 Madison Avenue, New York, NY 10016.

Oxford Paperbacks are available from all good bookshops. In case of difficulty, customers in the UK can order direct from Oxford University Press Bookshop, Freepost, 116 High Street, Oxford OX1 4BR, enclosing full payment. Please add 10 per cent of published price for postage and packing.